Performance Engineering
of Software Systems

 **Software Engineering Institute**

The SEI Series in Software Engineering

Performance Engineering of Software Systems

Connie U. Smith
L & S Computer Technology, Inc.

ADDISON-WESLEY PUBLISHING COMPANY

Reading, Massachusetts ■ Menlo Park, California ■ New York
Don Mills, Ontario ■ Wokingham, England ■ Amsterdam ■ Bonn
Sydney ■ Singapore ■ Tokyo ■ Madrid ■ San Juan

Software Engineering Institute

The SEI Series in Software Engineering

Many of the designations used by manufacturers and sellers to distinguish their products are claimed as trademarks. Where those designations appear in this book and Addison-Wesley was aware of a trademark claim, the designations have been printed in initial capital or all capital letters.

Library of Congress Cataloging-in-Publication Data

Smith, Connie U.
    Performance engineering of software systems / by Connie U. Smith.
        p.   cm. — (The SEI series in software engineering)
    Includes bibliographical references.
    ISBN 0-201-53769-9
    1. Computer software—Evaluation.   I. Title.   II. Series.
QA76.76.E93S65   1990
005—dc20   89-17633
                                                               CIP

A B C D E F G H I J–MA–943210

PREFACE

This book originates from the conviction that *responsiveness* is a critical property of software systems. Meeting performance requirements (such as responsiveness or throughput) is as vital as meeting requirements of functionality, reliability, and maintainability, yet previous software engineering research has largely ignored performance issues. Human work procedures increasingly rely on computer-system processing, a system that unnecessarily wastes human time, increases costs, and squanders the principal resources of an organization. Similarly, real-time, process-control systems require responsiveness to function correctly. Neither distributed systems nor parallel processing nor any other hardware advance has eliminated performance problems. It is economically prudent to evaluate hardware and software cost alternatives for achieving system requirements and to select the most cost-effective alternative before constructing new systems. It is feasible and relatively easy to use quantitative tools and methods to predict performance implications of alternatives. Thus, engineering software to meet performance requirements is sensible, and furthermore it works.

This books presents and illustrates software performance engineering (SPE) tools and methods. SPE provides the capability to construct software and systems to meet performance objectives. It begins early in the lifecycle and uses quantitative methods to assess requirements, design, and hardware alternatives while the widest range of options exists, and continues throughout the lifecycle to implement systems that meet their performance objectives. SPE methods prescribe the lifecycle steps and pragmatic techniques for their effective use. The methods work for large and small systems, adapt to different hardware and software environments, and apply to all types of software, including business applications, real-time embedded computer systems, operating system software, and so on. SPE has evolved through years of practical experience building performance into systems throughout their lifecycle.

The book's intended audience includes both computer professionals and students of computer science and computer engineering. It is organized to provide some readers an overview of SPE, other readers additional pragmatic advice on executing SPE, and still other readers additional technical details of software performance models. For example, project managers may review the introduction to SPE and the adoption, organization, and other performance management issues; while systems analysts, designers, programmers, and other software engineers will find specific techniques for building performance into new systems. Performance analysts and capacity planners will find systematic methods and pragmatic techniques for conducting SPE studies. Students in software engineering, computer engineering, performance modeling and analysis, and other related areas will find quantitative methods for predicting performance, as well as fertile areas for research and development. Students interested in creating quality software for applications in artificial intelligence, computer-aided design, database management, imaging and visualization, medical applications, and other areas will find practical methods for building responsive software. While many of the pragmatic techniques for resolving real-world problems facing large system developers are not directly applicable to students, the glimpse of reality should be both surprising and enlightening.

The material is self-contained; it does not assume familiarity with graph theory, statistics, queueing network models, or specific software development methodologies. SPE is sophisticated in that it integrates diverse fields of knowledge, but it is elementary in that its application does not require deep, specialized knowledge. SPE combines system design and performance analysis techniques to establish a powerful tool for understanding and controlling the execution behavior of large systems. The approach and presentation are example-driven. Designing for performance is essentially a laboratory subject. Experience is necessary to develop proficiency.

The first chapter contains background information on SPE. It answers the following questions:

- □ Why is performance analysis of software systems important during design?
- □ How does SPE compare to earlier techniques?
- □ What can be accomplished with SPE?
- □ What steps constitute the SPE methods?
- □ How does design-oriented performance analysis work?

Chapters 2 through 9 then follow the steps in the SPE methodology.

Chapter 2 describes how to create responsive software systems. It characterizes the expert knowledge used by people who build performance into new systems. To explain the principles, it

□ Describes the fundamental factors affecting computer system performance

□ Defines seven general principles that favorably influence performance

□ Covers five key design issues and shows how the principles apply to each

□ Prescribes effective use of the principles

Many examples illustrate the principles.

Chapter 3 defines the data required to predict performance of software systems. Good specifications are the key to effective SPE, so Chapter 3 presents practical strategies for obtaining data and for verifying and validating both the specifications and the model results.

Chapters 4, 5, 8, and 9 cover the quantitative methods. They progress from simple back-of-the-envelope calculations to advanced computer system models. Modeling tool requirements are covered, and some suitable, commercially available products are mentioned.

Chapter 6 identifies and evaluates system, software, and hardware alternatives. Techniques identify bottlenecks, revise the specification data, and produce quantitative performance data for the alternatives.

Chapter 7 reviews software performance measurement concepts and software instrumentation techniques. It defines SPE information requirements and suggests an SPE database and a measurement data library to facilitate data retrieval and reporting.

Chapter 10 describes how to implement an SPE program and how to integrate it with other software engineering practices. The chapter addresses the management and organization of SPE projects and reviews their critical success factors. Also described are SPE's compatibility with popular software development methods and with recent software engineering research topics. The chapter relays key factors in SPE's adoption and effective technology transfer. Future trends in SPE research and its application are forecast.

Many examples illustrate the concepts of performance engineering. Comprehensive case studies illustrate the application of the techniques to diverse types of software systems, and carry the SPE evaluation through all steps described in the book. High-level application systems, intermediate-level data management systems, and low-level operating systems are all represented.

The chapters provide useful background information on the modeling fundamentals. It is important to understand the fundamentals if you wish to have confidence in the model capabilities and limitations. Software developers who wish an introduction to SPE and its models but want to delegate performance modeling tasks to experts should skip Chapters 8 and 9. Readers interested in only an overview of SPE and its applicability to software development projects should focus on Chapters 1 and 10. University students and researchers will find applications of modeling technology to software systems throughout the book; it offers a different perspective on modeling theory and addresses an issue vital to all modelers: how to obtain data for modeling studies.

SPE is economically important and should be incorporated into all strategic software development projects. It is not a static subject with a fully complete handbook of procedures and computer-aided support systems. It is a research and development area that has produced broadly applicable results, but that is still maturing. We can anticipate that the spectrum and quality of tools for SPE will significantly grow over the next few years. The basic methods presented here can be extremely effective; the models and procedures are essentially complete. Major changes will consist of additions to the computer-aided tools to support the discipline and of analysis techniques that support evaluation of more complex systems.

This book would not exist without the support and early participation of James C. Browne. He was unfortunately not able to devote the tremendous amount of time necessary to follow through the final years of its evolution and culmination. Jerome Rolia scrutinized an early version of the manuscript, offered many insightful comments on technical content, and suggested significant improvements to its organization. James Bouhana, Douglas McBride, David Loendorf, John Shore, Scott Graham, and Satish Tripathi have assisted by reviewing the book. Nancy McMahon, Faith McLellan, Maria Leib, and Colleen Gavin prepared many versions of the text and figures as the book grew and changed. Financial support was provided in part by the National Science Foundation, the National Aeronautics and Space Administration, and Information Research Associates.

I thank my family for their patience and persistent encouragement.

Connie U. Smith
1114 Buckman Road
450 Paseo de la Tierra
Santa Fe, NM 87501

CONTENTS

LIST OF EXAMPLES

Algorithms

1

Overview of Software Performance Engineering

Software performance engineering (SPE) is a method for constructing software systems to meet performance objectives. The process begins early in the software lifecycle and uses quantitative methods to identify satisfactory designs and to eliminate those that are likely to have unacceptable performance, before developers invest significant time in implementation. SPE continues through the detailed design, coding, and testing stages to predict and manage the performance of the evolving software and to monitor and report actual performance against specifications and predictions. SPE methods cover performance data collection, quantitative analysis techniques, prediction strategies, management of uncertainties, data presentation and tracking, model verification and validation, critical success factors, and performance design principles.

Performance refers to the response time or throughput as seen by the users. Responsiveness limits the amount of work processed, so it determines a system's effectiveness and the productivity of its users. Many users subconsciously base their perception of (computer) service more on system responsiveness than on functionality. Negative perceptions, based on poor responsiveness of new systems, seldom change after correction of performance problems.

The "performance balance" in Figure 1.1 depicts a system that fails to meet performance objectives because resource requirements exceed computer capacity. With SPE, analysts detect these problems early in development and use quantitative methods to support cost-benefit analysis of hardware solutions versus software requirements or design solutions, versus a combination of the two. Developers implement software solutions before problems are manifested in code; organizations implement hardware solutions before testing begins.

1

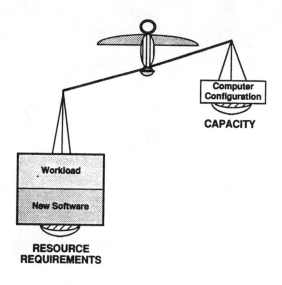

CAPACITY

RESOURCE
REQUIREMENTS

FIGURE 1.1
The Performance Balance. The resource requirements outweigh the computer configuration capacity, thus causing performance degradation. Solutions either increase capacity or decrease demand.

Is SPE necessary? Isn't hardware fast enough and cheap enough to resolve performance problems? Surprisingly, the use of state-of-the-art hardware and software technology dramatically *increases* the risk of performance failures. This seems counter-intuitive—one would expect increased performance—but the newness of the products combined with developers' inexperience with the new environment leads to problems. Example 1.1 is typical of many new development experiences.

EXAMPLE 1.1: Performance Failure

One project created a large network to connect over 200 clusters, each with four workstations, together with two mainframes and their 10–20GB central database. All four workstations served users; in addition, one of the four was the local file server, and one was the external network interface. The software system was to shelter users from communication details.

(continued)

EXAMPLE 1.1 (*Continued*)

The hardware selection was made early: Each of the workstations had 2MB of main memory, Ethernet, and one had a 20-MB hard disk. Twenty-six developers (experienced with large systems) spent 18 months working on the local cluster subsystem (the communication with the external LAN, with the clusters' Ethernet, the file service, and so forth). It was written in C using Berkeley 4.2 Unix and consisted of 110K lines of code. The total "load module" size was 55MB (for a 2MB-workstation!), the resident kernel was 600K.

There were many problems, but the most significant were the extensive use of (overpowered) graphics and windowing tools and the extensive use of Unix forks. A simple task spawned 38 processes, each requiring 1MB of virtual memory to execute (on the 1.4MB available to users and this system software). The response for a trivial request was 15 min. rather than the 400 ms. performance goal. Tuning efforts failed to correct the problem. The forks were too deeply embedded in the design, so design correction was impossible.

A "SWAT team" was called in to save the project. In 8 months, seven system gurus handcrafted a stopgap replacement. It was 46K lines of code, had only five processes, and a total load module size of 1.2MB; thus it ran in real memory, leaving 800K for user software. It had acceptable performance, but could not meet the 400 ms. goal. (The goal was based on advertised raw network bandwidth with no allowance for software overhead.) They determined that it was technically impossible to meet the goal with the hardware configuration selected.

Even though the SWAT team saved the overall project, they did not regard the effort as a success. Their code was virtually unmaintainable because of the extremes necessary to achieve reasonable responsiveness. They felt that the configuration limits should have been found at the requirements phase. If they had used SPE early, they could have changed the hardware and software configuration and would have had the full two years to produce a maintainable and responsive system.   □

Similar examples abound. Are you exempt from performance problems if you stick to tried—and proven—technology? The following example contains a potpourri of "war stories" that demonstrate that similar problems are pervasive in traditional software.

EXAMPLE 1.2: Performance War Stories

Costly error

Developers of a large online system ignored performance predictions during design because problem corrections would take 3 weeks and they were behind schedule. Upon integration testing, problems were so severe that further development was halted while the staff sought tuning improvements. Many performance problems were due to fundamental design choices that were impossible to correct without major rewrites. Six months of tuning efforts failed to remedy performance flaws. After over $20 million had been spent, the project was canceled.

(continued)

EXAMPLE 1.2 (*Continued*)

Batch windows

Many batch systems also have problems, especially since batch windows are shrinking. One such system had to run nightly within a 10-hour window. The system was developed without SPE. During system testing, it was discovered that the elapsed time was over 13 days! Three months of redesign and tuning were required to reduce the elapsed time to 5 to 6 hours.

Unfortunately, performance crises like this may not be viewed as failures because of the 13-day elapsed time, but rather as successes because of the dramatic reduction to less than 6 hours. If problems are detected earlier, performance improvements can be as much as an order of magnitude better than 6 hours, and they require far less effort than tuning improvements—it is 20:1 more costly to modify code versus modifying designs.

Redevelopment may not resolve problems

Another company sought to implement a customer accounting system. The original development time estimate was 2 years. After 7 years, there had been three (re-) implementations, none of which met performance goals. The most recent attempt used 60 times the CPU power of the original "prototype" version.

□

The most serious consequence of performance failures such as these is the possibility of a business failure. The inability to operate on a peak business day, to respond to customer inquiries, to generate bills or process payments can have serious financial consequences. Similarly, excessive operational costs lower profit margins. These performance failures not only cost money to fix; they detract from development resources that could be used on other beneficial projects.

Disastrous performance failures are a relatively recent phenomenon. What causes them? How can you prevent these problems? In this chapter we explore the origin and cause of performance problems, and then the SPE solution is described in overview, with a brief review of the goals and requirements that led to its formation. The final section of the chapter introduces the case studies that will be used throughout the book to demonstrate SPE.

1.1 History of Performance-oriented Software Design

Addressing performance throughout software development is not a revolutionary proposition; developers routinely sought performance in the early years of computing. The space and time required by programs had to be carefully managed so that those programs would fit on small machines. The hardware grew, but rather than eliminating performance problems, it made larger, more complex software feasible, and programs became systems of programs. Performance modeling and assessment of these early systems was labor-intensive and thus expensive. Analysts used hand-crafted simulation models; consequently, creating and solving models was time-consuming, and keeping models up to date with the current state of evolving software systems was also problematic. Thus, modeling and evaluation were cost-effective for only those systems, such as flight-control systems and other mission-critical embedded systems, that had strict performance requirements.

Systems without critical performance requirements adopted the **"fix-it-later"** method. It advocates concentrating on software correctness, defers performance considerations to the integration-testing phase, and (if performance problems are detected then) corrects problems with additional hardware, with system and software "tuning," or both. The results have been acceptable until recently. Fix-it-later was a viable approach in the 1970s, but today the original premises no longer hold, and fix-it-later is archaic and dangerous. The original premises were:

□ Performance problems are rare.

□ Hardware is fast and inexpensive.

□ It's too expensive to build responsive software.

□ You can tune software later, if necessary.

□ Efficiency implies "tricky code."

Each of these premises is reviewed in the following paragraphs.

Performance problems are rare? When fix-it-later was advocated in the early 1970s, the recent introduction of multiprogramming operating systems, virtual memory management, and much larger real memory made the power of the underlying computer technology far greater than the demands of the software systems. Response time was seldom a problem with batch systems. When online systems were first introduced, they had modest resource demands, and there were fewer users and other systems to compete for resources. Since then, the number of users and online systems have grown substantially, and systems now have far more ambitious functions, rely on large databases, use fourth-generation languages, and so forth; thus, resource demand has increased significantly. As Figure 1.2 shows, an increase in demand on the right end of the demand–response-time curve causes an increase in response time much higher than that caused by increased demand on the left.

Increased demand is not the only reason that performance problems are now highly likely. Many software developers in the 1960s and 1970s were experts at performance-oriented design. Their performance intuition led them to create systems with acceptable performance even though they were told not to worry about performance. Today's software developers "grew up" with the fix-it-later method and never acquired their predecessors' intuition. Most are unaware of the performance implications of design decisions. They were trained not to worry

FIGURE 1.2
The Demand–Response-Time Curve. In the past, demand for computer resources
was lower than it is today, so systems that unexpectedly use twice the expected
resources had less effect on responsiveness than they do today. (The formulas that
lead to this graph are in Chapter 5.)

about performance, so resulting performance problems are like a self-fulfilling
prophecy.

Hardware is fast and inexpensive? Increased hardware capacity is the
traditional remedy for performance problems. The performance balance in Figure
1.1 advocates evaluating hardware and software tradeoffs and selecting the economical solution. Hardware may be the most cost-effective remedy; if so, it should
be explicitly chosen early in the lifecycle to make resources available when
needed, not as a last resort chosen after problems occur. Many examples in this
book involve software designs that require excessive hardware resources—orders
of magnitude greater than alternatives that are comparably easy to implement and
maintain. Success stories cited in Section 1.2 found potential business failures that
no amount of hardware would correct.

It's too expensive to build responsive software? The primary motivation
for fix-it-later was to improve development and maintenance productivity. The
newer SPE methods, models, and tools actually increase productivity over fix-it-
later by preventing problems that delay delivery and by preventing tricky-code
maintenance problems.

You can tune software later? Tuning can always improve performance, but
not as much as appropriate design can, as can be seen by drawing an analogy
between a typical software system developed without SPE and a house constructed
before 1970 without energy-efficiency goals. Practically any modification of an
energy-inefficient house yields improvement. The degree of improvement generally correlates with the scope and expense of the undertaking. Modifications can
range from minor ones such as adding weather stripping through intermediate
steps such as installing more efficient heating and cooling systems to major re-

modeling projects such as tearing out ceilings, walls, and floors to add insulation. The older house after all feasible modifications are made, however, is still not as energy-efficient as if it had been constructed with efficiency as a design goal. The original design could have incorporated many passive solar features that cannot be added later. For example, it is not feasible to change the direction the house faces years after it is built. Software systems are similar to houses; it is possible to tune an existing system to improve performance, but the gains are usually modest. Dramatic improvements generally require major modifications to the software. They are expensive and require considerable implementation time. Basic design and implementation choices may preclude desirable performance enhancements.

Efficiency implies "tricky" code? Responsive software is more important than efficiency. The energy-efficiency analogy demonstrates that designed-in performance is preferable to tuned-in performance. Fix-it-later's late tuning may introduce "tricky" code to resolve problems that could be prevented.

The most serious flaw in the fix-it-later approach is that developers detect performance problems late in the software lifecycle. As Figure 1.3 shows, performance problems become apparent in the system integration or maintenance stages. Performance problems that surface during integration can significantly delay software delivery. If software is delivered prematurely (with poor performance), users develop a negative impression that lasts long after problems have been corrected. Poor performance during integration testing decreases the productivity of the software development staff who are forced to wait for test completions. The tuning or optimization process, used to bring the performance of a newly implemented software system to an adequate level, is a time-consuming activity that often results in substantial, ad hoc revisions to the system. These revisions then require changes to program code and retesting. Substantial redesign means that many lifecycle steps must be repeated. Ad hoc tuning modifications frequently lead to increased entropy and complexity and thus to increased cost for maintenance and further enhancements to the software. They also negate many of the benefits of standard software engineering practices, such as structured top-down design and implementation. Performance improvement at this stage is a destructive process, the net effect of which is to shorten the useful life of the software system.

Table 1.1 summarizes the premises that led to fix-it-later, the current reality, and the consequences of late detection of performance problems. The rationale of fix-it-later was to save development time, expense, and maintenance costs. The savings will not be realized, however, if initial performance is unsatisfactory because the additional time and expense for correcting problems are far greater than the cost of built-in performance. **Fix-it-later was once a viable approach, but it is now inappropriate and dangerous.**

Today's alternative is a more moderate development approach, between the extremes of performance-driven development and ostrich-like, performance-neglected development. Performance is vital to most new systems. Software systems that perform customer-service functions, such as reservation systems and

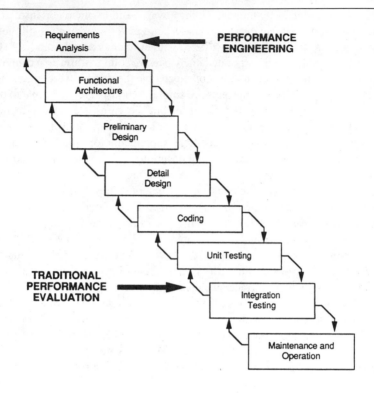

FIGURE 1.3
A Software Development Process Model Based on the Waterfall Lifecycle Model. With "fix-it-later," problems are detected late, so performance focus was on the late lifecycle steps. SPE begins when requirements are proposed and continues throughout the lifecycle. SPE builds performance into new systems rather than adding it (or attempting to) later.

merchandise-checkout systems, must provide rapid response if they are to be acceptable to the customers. Customers are not willing to wait in lines caused by slow computers. If delays happen repeatedly, customers may choose other merchants. Real-time systems, such as flight-control systems, must meet critical response-time requirements (in addition to reliability and correctness requirements) to prevent disasters. If an automated flight-control system does not provide a rapid (and correct) response, the airplane depending on it may crash. Employee support systems, such as management information systems, inventory control systems, and computer-aided design systems, determine the productivity of an entire organization. Timely response from these systems is necessary to make effective use of a company's most important and costly resource: its personnel.

TABLE 1.1
FIX-IT-LATER APPROACH?

Premises	Reality	Consequences (of unacceptable performance)
Performance problems are rare.	The number of online software systems, their size, and their complexity have dramatically increased; many large systems cannot be used initially due to performance problems. Today's software developers seldom have the performance expertise of their predecessors.	Remedies require tuning and/or hardware; neither is immediate. Poor performing software leaves lasting negative impressions.
Hardware is fast and inexpensive.	No installations have unlimited hardware budgets. Procurements require advanced planning and justification. Software demands may exceed all hardware capabilities.	One may lose control of equipment purchase and maintenance budgets and plans.
It's too expensive to build responsive software.	Data on time and cost of building in performance is out of date; methodologies and tools have dramatically reduced time and effort.	Testing is slower, so implementation cost is higher; maintenance costs (for "tuned" code) are higher.
Tuning can be done later.	Problems are usually caused by fundamental architecture or design problems rather than inefficient coding.	Code tuning yields modest improvements; large gains require major revisions. It is very expensive (often infeasible) to change fundamental design choices.
Efficiency implies "tricky" code.	Responsiveness is not the same as efficiency. Acceptable performance is required; it can be designed in early.	"Tricky" code may be the only option for achieving goals late in lifecycle.

There are also many management and cost-control reasons for including SPE as a part of the development process in major software projects. It is important to control the development costs, such as those for the computer system, development personnel, and support staff. Performance problems that surface during development can also threaten the successful and timely completion of software.

The "performance balance" suggests that hardware capacity requirements should be predicted early. If the new software is to run on an existing system, will the workload introduce processing bottlenecks that jeopardize service-level commitments to other users? How many terminals can the hardware and software support without significant response-time degradation? If the software is intended for a new computer system that has not yet been purchased, what is the most appropriate hardware and operating system configuration? These questions must be answered early to enable orderly acquisition of any additional hardware deemed necessary before system integration testing.

Performance, management, and cost factors, then, provide the motivation for abandoning fix-it-later. The alternative—SPE—views performance as an integral part of software development, along with functionality, correctness, usability, maintainability, and other quality factors. Next, we look at the SPE approach for accomplishing these goals.

1.2 Software Performance Engineering Approach

SPE, the alternative to fix-it-later, adopts quantitative methods successfully used in engineering and other fields. An analogy to wine creation explains the quantitative approach for building-in quality (performance).

EXAMPLE 1.3: Wine Creation Analogy

In wine making, the first and primary emphasis is on the grapes. The key steps in creating premium wines include:

- ☐ Choosing vines and root-stock to capitalize on the micro-climate and soil characteristics of the vineyard

- ☐ Cloning vines of various families at the proper time to balance grape quality, yield, and family traits

- ☐ Determining the proper time to pick the grapes to optimize the sugar-acid ratio and the weather conditions

- ☐ Controlling the fermentation temperature

- ☐ Determining the fermentation completion time when the new wine has sufficient color, tannin, and fragrance

- ☐ Additional tasks of analyzing and blending vats, sealing casks at the proper time, separating wine from particles that settle in the casks, determining when to bottle, and so forth

Expert vintners oversee the entire process. They conduct extensive research on vine clones, soil, and weather conditions, and so forth. They supplement their expertise with measurements, analysis, and control of the entire process. During the wine production, they measure sugar content, acidity, temperature, color, yeast content, CO_2 , and so on.

(continued)

EXAMPLE 1.3 (*Continued*)

The analogy to software is to match the expertise of the chief architect to the criticality of the system. Supplement expert skills with quantitative methods to control performance throughout the process. As with wines, if you select the wrong design (grapes), you cannot fix it later; you must start over.

□

Note that neither wine creation nor SPE relies solely on "smart people"; even smart people benefit from quantitative data to support their design decisions. Thus, SPE is similar to practices used successfully in other disciplines, particularly in engineering, to develop high-quality products. Engineering design is an iterative process of refinement. As illustrated in Figure 1.4, at each refinement step engineers *understand* the problem, *create* a hypothetical solution, describe or *represent* the proposed product of the creation step, and then *evaluate* that product's appropriateness. The evaluation assesses a design's *correctness* (adherence to specifications), its *feasibility* (cost, time, and technology to implement), and the *preferability* of one solution over another (simplicity, maintainability, and so on).[1]

SPE begins in the requirements analysis phase, as shown in Figure 1.3.[2] When SPE is included in development, requirements are initially proposed without regard to performance constraints, but the analysis step confirms that with current technology they are feasible and desirable. Then SPE studies and identifies suitable designs. The following are among the benefits of SPE's early lifecycle steps:

- □ *Increased productivity* when developers' time is not invested in an implementation that must later be discarded and when implementation and testing focus on critical parts of the software

- □ *Improved quality and usefulness of the resulting software product* by selecting suitable design and implementation alternatives, thus avoiding widespread tuning modifications

- □ *Controlled costs of the supporting hardware and software* by identifying what equipment is needed and allowing sufficient time for competitive procurement

- □ *Enhanced productivity during the implementation, testing, and early operational stages* by ensuring that sufficient computing power is available

---

[1]Note that we deliberately leave unspecified the specific evaluations to assess correctness, feasibility, and preferability since they vary from one project to the next. For example, on a project where reliability is life-critical, assessing the correctness involves determining whether or not a specified reliability goal is met. On a different project where reliability is not life-critical, the reliability may still be evaluated, but as a facet of preferability. The same is true for performance and other similar factors.

[2]SPE is depicted in the waterfall model of the software lifecycle, but it also blends with other approaches, such as the spiral model, incremental build, rapid prototyping, and object-oriented design. This compatibility is described in Chapters 8 and 10.

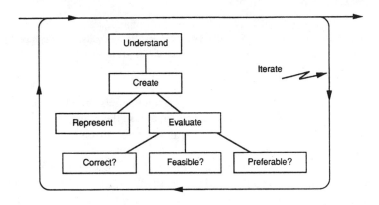

FIGURE 1.4
The engineering design process shows the following steps: Understand the problem, create the solution alternatives, represent each solution (initially with general ideas, later with formal specifications), and evaluate the correctness, feasibility, and preferability of each alternative. It is an iterative process; each iteration refines the design.

In later lifecycle stages, SPE studies algorithms, monitors progress, and assesses the influence of design and implementation changes. It also applies to post-deployment maintenance. Studies report that maintenance accounts for 60 percent of the cost of the software [BOE76]. Maintenance includes software redesign to incorporate additional functions; thus, the revised system is subject to the same performance pitfalls as was the original design. Maintenance also includes tuning to improve performance, so SPE's use throughout the lifecycle reduces maintenance costs.

The preceding are a few of the benefits of SPE. Chapter 10 covers the cost, benefits, and risks of SPE in more detail. In sum, *the best reasons for using SPE are: It is sensible, and it works,* as the following example dramatically illustrates.

EXAMPLE 1.4: SPE Successes

☐ An SPE study was conducted early in the requirements analysis phase of a new real-time system. Initial requirements called for events to be posted to an online, relational database within 3 minutes of event occurrence. The analyst estimated the size of the hardware to support the requirement (assuming a streamlined software system) to be 20 IBM 3090-600s, the largest IBM machine available at the time! Three minutes appeared to be a reasonable goal, but the tremendous data volume had dramatic

(continued)

EXAMPLE 1.4 (*Continued*)

consequences on hardware capacity. The SPE analysis enabled a quantitative assessment and optimal balance of the costs and benefits of the new system.

☐ Dr. Douglas Neuse, vice-president of Scientific and Engineering Software, cites a distributed command and control system design. Analysts modeled the software with the GPSM/PAWS product and found that adaptive fault recovery was essential to performance and availability. A different recovery strategy had been planned— without the models, the software would have failed in crisis-mode operation, and it is unlikely that testing would have found the problems because of the conditions that triggered the failure.

☐ Dr. Robert Goldberg, MIT Sloan School faculty (formerly a vice-president of BGS Systems, Inc.), provides examples of software systems that saved millions of dollars by addressing performance early. One example is a bank developing software for an electronic funds transfer system. Models developed with BGS's Crystal product showed that rather than the desired throughput of $100 billion, the system as designed could only process $50 billion a night—which would have cost the bank interest charges on $50 billion each night. In another case, Crystal models of a collection system identified potential performance failures for some geographical regions and showed the impact of alternative database organizations. Corrections were made in time for scheduled software delivery. Late delivery would have cost $30 million per month.

☐ Allan Levy described a model of a retail merchandise application [LEV87]. Early in development, he discovered that the planned hardware configuration could not handle peak loads. Without the models, the system would have been deployed just before the peak season began, and performance problems would have gone undetected until the peak orders arrived. No hardware upgrade would have resolved the problem! The system would not support the business requirements; product movement and associated revenue would be bottlenecked with no possibility of recovery! Fortunately, they detected the problems early and redesigned the software to correct them.

☐ Another situation involved an 18-month SPE effort to manage performance of an online, high-volume, transaction-oriented application. The performance benchmarks and tests resulted in greater than 400% improvement in transaction rate while meeting response-time goals.

☐

As the above illustrations show, built-in performance is both desirable and feasible. So why doesn't everyone assess performance early in development when the design is malleable and improvements can have the greatest effect? The primary reason is that, until recently, there has been no established discipline for assessing the performance characteristics of a design quickly and easily. Many other factors contribute to the problem: Insufficient time is budgeted for integrating performance analysis into the design process; pressing deadlines then preclude its consideration. Emphasis is placed on implementing a system quickly and improving it later. In most organizations, responsibility for host-system performance is distinct from that for software development. Performance analysts lack the necessary data on new software designs, and systems analysts lack the expertise to analyze performance in a complex host environment. Systems analysts have previously received little feedback regarding the performance or resource usage of software systems they have developed, and therefore have been unable to provide precise performance data on new systems. As a result, they overestimate the quantity of information necessary for prediction, and the time and work required to make reasonable estimates. They also lack confidence in the results of studies based on their "imprecise" estimates. Other reasons are general technology transfer problems (these are covered in Chapter 10).

To improve the situation, SPE calls for project management changes. First, management must strive for timely completion of a *good* product, where performance is one aspect of "good." Timely completion and high quality could be conflicting goals because building good software can take time. To eliminate the conflict, schedules must incorporate SPE tasks. Scheduling is analogous to dining in a fine restaurant. Customers are informed ahead of time that some dishes require a little longer to prepare (but are worth the wait). Restaurants do not serve partially prepared food then return it to the kitchen to "fix it later." Similarly, good software products may take longer to build [BRO75], but not substantially longer. In fact, the time is negligible if assessments reveal no major performance bottlenecks. If there are severe bottlenecks, the total development time would increase anyway if redesign and reimplementation were required.[3]

The next section gives an overview of the SPE's systematic process for addressing performance throughout the lifecycle. As will be seen, it is both practical and easy to use.

1.3 The Software Performance Engineering Process

SPE augments other software engineering methodologies; it does not replace them. With SPE, the standard engineering design steps—understanding, creating, representing, and evaluating—are conducted as usual; then a performance assessment step confirms that performance is satisfactory before proceeding. This process is summarized by the following algorithm:

```
while SOFTWARE DEVELOPS loop
DEV_PHASE_STUDY:
    loop
        DEVELOP DESIGN CONCEPT;   --understand, create
        MODEL;
```

---

[3]Alternatively, projects may reduce the scope of the original development effort to meet the original delivery schedule. This option also has negative consequences.

```
    EVALUATE MODEL SOLUTION;
  exit DEV_PHASE_STUDY when
      predicted performance is satisfactory;
  end loop;
    PROCEED WITH SOFTWARE CREATION;
 end loop;
```

The algorithm presents the general idea; SPE is more specific about the required steps and how to accomplish them. It encompasses principles for creating responsive software, specifications necessary for evaluation, procedures for obtaining performance specifications, and guidelines for the types of evaluations to be conducted at each developmental stage. It incorporates models for representing and predicting software system performance and a set of analysis methods. A more detailed view of the SPE methodology is in Figure 1.5.[4] The following subsection describes the steps in the figure and points to their detailed coverage in the book.

1.3.1 SPE Activities for Each Assessment

The first SPE activity is to **define the SPE assessments for the current lifecycle phase.** Assessments are made to determine whether planned software meets its *performance objectives*, such as acceptable response time or throughput thresholds, or constraints on resource requirements. This is a vital step because one must have a specific, quantitative objective to determine concretely whether or not that objective can be met.

The performance objectives are specified in terms of *responsiveness* as seen by the system users. Both the response time for an interactive task and the number of work units processed in a time interval (throughput) are measures of responsiveness. Responsiveness does not necessarily imply efficient computer resource usage. Efficiency is addressed only if critical computer resource constraints must be satisfied.

Responsiveness is determined in part by the typical user requests and the amount of processing they require. A database query, for example, will be slow if it causes many complex record qualifications and I/O operations, but fast if it consists of a few accesses to already filled system buffers. If the small, fast request is typical, the average responsiveness as seen by the users will be good. Responsiveness is also determined by the computer system resources available. If a few

---

[4]The figure uses SPE's software execution graph notation. Some software engineers dislike the flowchart-like notation, considering it a regression to archaic methods. Execution graphs are not flowcharts (the differences are explained in Chapter 4); the graph is a procedural representation that shows the order of steps, repetitions, and other execution characteristics. Flowcharts and, thus, procedural representations were abandoned when fix-it-later made them unnecessary. SPE resurrects and improves procedural notations.

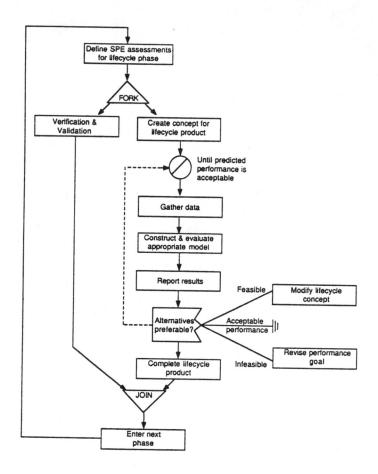

FIGURE 1.5
The SPE Methodology.

users share a large facility, responsiveness is likely to be better than for many users sharing a small facility. It should be evident that there are many external factors such as these that influence software performance. Figure 1.6 shows that usage scenarios, software requirements and design, computer system configuration, and other competing work together determine the resulting performance. It is essential to define performance objectives and expected usage patterns in order to determine

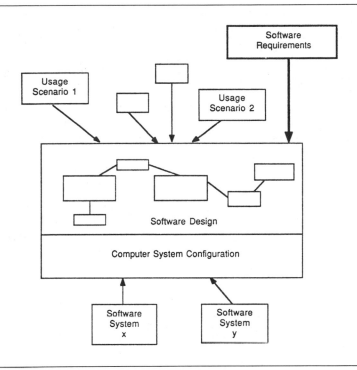

FIGURE 1.6
In a complex computing environment, all the elements shown affect the performance of the new software: the requirements, design, workload (or usage) scenarios, the computer system configuration upon which it executes, and other software systems that compete for resources.

the most appropriate means of achieving them and to avoid devoting time to unintentionally overachieving them. Performance objectives are covered in Chapter 3.

After defining the goals, designers **create the "concept" for the lifecycle product.** For early phases the "concept" is the functional architecture—the software requirements and the high-level plans for satisfying them. In subsequent phases the "concept" is a more detailed design, the algorithms and data structures, the code, and so forth. Chapter 2 presents general principles for creating responsive functional architectures and designs.

Once the lifecycle concept is formulated, we **gather data** sufficient for estimating the performance of the proposal. First we need the projected system workload: how it will *typically* be used. Then we need an explanation of the current design concept. Early in development we use the general system architecture; later we add the proposed decomposition into modules; still later, we incorporate the proposed algorithms and data structures. We also need estimates of the resource usage of the design entities. SPE methods in Chapter 3 provide more details on data requirements and techniques for gathering specifications.

Because the precision of the model results depends on the precision of the resource estimates, and because these are difficult to estimate very early in software development, a **best- and worst-case analysis strategy** is integral to the methodology. We use estimates of the lower and upper bound when there is high uncertainty about resource requirements. Using them, the analysis produces an estimate of both the best- and worst-case performance. If the best-case performance is unsatisfactory, we seek feasible alternatives. If the worst-case performance is satisfactory, we proceed with development. If the results are somewhere in between, we identify critical components whose resource estimates have the greatest effect and focus attention on obtaining more precise data for them. A variety of techniques provides more precision, such as further refining the design concept and constructing more detailed models, or constructing performance benchmarks and measuring resource requirements for key elements. These techniques are also described in Chapter 3.

An overview of the **performance model construction and evaluation** follows in Section 1.3.3. If the model results indicate that the performance is likely to be satisfactory, developers proceed. If not, we **report quantitative results** on the predicted performance of the original design concept. If alternative strategies would improve performance, we report the **alternatives** and their expected (quantitative) improvements. Developers review the findings to determine the cost-effectiveness of the alternatives. If a feasible and cost-effective alternative exists, developers **modify the concept** before the lifecycle product is complete. If none is feasible—as, for example, when the modifications would cause an unacceptable delivery delay—we explicitly **revise the performance goal** to reflect the expected degraded performance. Chapters 4 and 5 cover the basic models; advanced models are covered in Chapters 8 and 9. Techniques for identifying and evaluating alternatives are discussed in Chapter 6.

A vital and ongoing activity of the SPE process is to **verify** that the models represent the software execution behavior and to **validate** model predictions against performance measurements. Compare the model specifications for the workload, software structure, execution structure, and resource requirements to actual usage and software characteristics. Calibrate the model to represent the system behavior. Examine discrepancies to update the performance predictions and to identify the reasons for differences—to prevent similar problems occurring in the future. Similarly, compare system execution model results (response times, throughput, device utilization, and so forth) to measurements. Study discrepancies, identify error sources, and calibrate the model as necessary. One should begin model verification and validation early and continue throughout the lifecycle. In early stages, focus on key performance factors; use prototypes or benchmarks to obtain more precise specifications and measurements as needed.

The evolving software becomes the source of the model verification and validation (V&V) data. V&V are described in Chapter 3; measurements that support V&V are covered in Chapter 7.

The above discussion outlines the steps for one design-evaluation "pass." The steps are repeated throughout the lifecycle. The goals and the evaluation of the objectives change somewhat for each pass. The next subsection discusses the lifecycle stages and the questions to be considered.

1.3.2 Assessments Throughout the Lifecycle

Table 1.2 contains a synopsis of the SPE considerations in each lifecycle stage. The first evaluation occurs during the requirements definition and the initial formulation of the software design; we assess the feasibility and desirability of the

TABLE 1.2
SYNOPSIS OF THE PERFORMANCE ENGINEERING CONSIDERATIONS

Lifecycle stage	Performance considerations
Requirements Analysis; Functional Architecture	What are typical uses?
	How will the software be used?
	What are the performance goals for these scenarios?
	Can the requirements be achieved with acceptable performance?
	Approximately how much computer power is required to support it?
Preliminary Design	Does the expected performance of this design meet specifications?
	Is the proposed configuration adequate? Excessive?
Detailed Design	Have changes occurred that affect earlier predictions?
	What is a more realistic estimate of the projected performance?
Implementation; Integration Testing	How do the performance metrics of the implementation alternatives compare?
	Have any unforeseen problems arisen?
	What are the resource requirements of the critical components?
	Are the performance requirements met?
Maintenance & Operation	What is the effect of the proposed modifications?
	What are the long-range configuration requirements to support future use?

functional architecture to detect infeasible plans. The requirements are usually prescribed before development begins, and many developers perceive them to be nonnegotiable. It is nevertheless prudent to verify that the requirements can be met with reasonable cost and performance. Often simple requirements have serious performance consequences (like the 3-minute update in Example 1.4). When problems are detected early, it is usually possible to negotiate for more cost-effective options.

The next evaluation determines the computer configuration required to support the new product—that is, the power of the supporting hardware and operating system software. These are not independent issues; the design depends on the requirements, and the configuration will vary with the design. Therefore, we evaluate several combinations of requirements, designs, and configurations to determine the best combination.

The design-stage performance analysis and the types of results we can expect are illustrated by the following example (taken from one of the systems that drove the development of the SPE methodology).

EXAMPLE 1.5: Sample Results of a Design Evaluation

This example illustrates results for two system-usage scenarios; an actual SPE study represents the expected system workload with additional scenarios to examine the effect of improvements on multiple system functions. Following the prescribed SPE steps, developers formulated requirements and conceived a preliminary design plan. Then our analysts gathered performance specifications, created a software execution model, and analyzed the best-case performance. The desired performance goal was a maximum 5-second response time with up to 50 users. Case 1 of Table 1.3 shows the predicted response time for a single

TABLE 1.3
RESULTS OF A DESIGN-BASED SOFTWARE EVALUATION

Alternative cases	Estimated response time (sec)	
	Scenario 1	Scenario 2
1. Original proposal	3326	49
2. Requirements change	595	37
3. Design change	694	48
4. Combination 2 & 3	562	36
5. Scenario algorithm change	109	NA
6. Faster CPU (twice as fast)	57	18
7. Largest configuration	26	7

(continued)

EXAMPLE 1.5 (*Continued*)

user using the best-case performance specifications for the original proposal. Clearly, it cannot meet the performance goal, so we evaluated alternatives.

The first alternative (Case 2 in the table) examines a change to the software requirements: adding a new user function and imposing a requirement for retaining intermediate results. We modified the model to reflect the changes, producing the results shown. The performance for both of the scenarios in the table (and the others) improves, but not enough.

Next, Case 3 examines a design alternative that maintains the desired order of a frequently accessed data structure rather than arranging it upon request.[5] There is a tradeoff in this case: Retrieval requests are quicker because it is unnecessary to first arrange the data, but maintaining the order incurs extra time for changes to the data structure. Compare the results for Case 3 to Case 1 in Table 1.3: There is a big improvement for Scenario 1, and only a small gain for Scenario 2. The performance for all other scenarios is also better, so Case 3 also improves the system. It is conceivable that the interaction between the Case 2 and 3 changes could offset the gains for either case alone, so we evaluated the combination in Case 4. Case 5 optimizes the algorithm design for Scenario 1. The algorithm modification changes the pattern of requests for software functions.

Many other improvements to the requirements and design are possible in this example. In fact, it is easy to achieve the performance goal by altering only the requirements and design. These cases suffice to demonstrate the possibilities.

The models also produce data that quantifies the improvement of hardware configuration upgrades. Case 6 shows the improvements with a CPU twice as fast, and Case 7 upgrades both the CPU and I/O devices to the fastest available. (Details of the analysis procedure used for this example and some similar case studies of scenarios and designs are covered throughout the book.)

□

The data in Table 1.3 demonstrates only a few of the types of analyses that are feasible during early lifecycle stages and the leverage of doing so. Scenario 1 achieves a performance gain of *two orders of magnitude*, and, if detected early, there is *no* modification and retesting of code! The result in Example 1.5 was that the system, as originally proposed, failed (by a significant amount of time) to meet responsiveness objectives. With a few relatively minor adjustments early in the lifecycle, it was possible to meet those objectives.[6] The changes are minor if detected early; the changes for Case 2 and Case 3 are virtually impossible *after*

---

[5]The original proposal included the ordering function as a "requirement." It is actually an artificial requirement that overprescribes the implementation. It is not uncommon to find artificial requirements. Identify them early and negotiate the removal of any that degrade performance.

[6]Only a few of the many alternatives are reported in Table 1.3. The study and recommendations were made early enough to enable corrections. For many reasons, developers elected to proceed with the original proposal and fix-it-later if necessary. It was; they tried and failed; and ultimately the project was canceled. This experience demonstrated that early lifecycle performance models can detect serious performance problems. It also demonstrated the need for this methodology to define the systematic, SPE lifecycle procedures and identified some critical success factors for effective SPE (see Chapter 10).

code is written, because of the scope of their effect. They quickly become funda-mental parts of the design.

After establishing a feasible set of requirements, the functional architecture of the software, and the supporting configuration requirements, the focus of SPE changes. We identify components that are critical with respect to meeting perfor-mance goals and implement them first focusing on the predicted performance for their detailed design. This identification of critical components maximizes the impact of the performance efforts and yields early measurement data of actual resource requirements to produce more precise predictions.

In the middle stages of the lifecycle, SPE incorporates additional design details as they evolve and design changes as they occur. Continued analysis helps to detect problems as soon as possible. At this stage, SPE studies provide data for developers to select appropriate data structures, algorithms, and system decom-position strategies. We incorporate operating system overhead for memory man-agement, data management, resource management, and communication into the models. As implementation proceeds, we add implementation details, refine the resource requirements estimates, and use more detailed models to produce more precise predictions.

During the maintenance stage, SPE evaluates both major and minor revisions that correct defects or add functions. Minor changes use mid-lifecycle techniques to incorporate changes into the models and assess their performance impact. Major revisions use early lifecycle techniques to assess the feasibility and desirability of the revised requirements and functional architecture. Then we follow the major revision project with standard SPE steps. Maintenance evaluations require much less effort than original studies when the SPE models are current and complete and can be used as the basis for the analysis.

1.3.3 The Models for Performance Assessment

In order to predict software performance, we construct a model of the software execution that can be solved for the indicative performance metrics. The models are similar to those used for conventional performance evaluation studies. In conventional studies (of existing systems), we model systems to predict the effect of workload or configuration changes. The conventional modeling procedure de-picted in Figure 1.7 is as follows: Study the computer system; construct a model (either a queueing network or a simulation model); measure current execution patterns; characterize workloads; develop model input parameters; validate the model by solving it and by comparing the model results to observed and measured data for the computer system; calibrate the model until its results match the measurement data. Then we use the model to evaluate changes to the computer system by modifying the corresponding workload parameters, the computer sys-tem resource parameters, or both. After each change, we compare the model results to the performance goal. We repeat the change–evaluate process until we

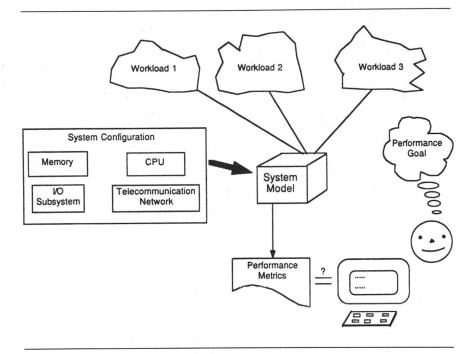

FIGURE 1.7
Conventional models predict the effect on performance metrics of changes to existing computer systems.

identify the desired performance solution. Practitioners rely on these models for computer capacity planning. The model precision is sufficient to predict future configuration requirements. The computer system models are widely used, and they work; so we use them as the basis for SPE. SPE performance modeling is similar; however, because the software does not yet exist, it is not possible to develop the workload parameters from measurement data. We first model the workload explicitly.

Two models satisfy the modeling requirements: **the software execution model** and the **system execution model.** The software execution model represents key facets of software execution behavior; its solution yields workload parameters for the system execution model, which closely resembles the conventional models. Software execution models require five types of data: (1) workload scenarios, (2) performance goals, (3) software design concept, (4) execution environment, and (5) resource usage estimates. The following paragraphs introduce each data requirement. Chapter 3 defines the data requirements and how to get them; Chapter 4 defines the software execution models.

First, we collect specifications for typical workload scenarios. For conventional models, analysts apply statistical methods to characterize existing (representative) workloads to develop performance model specifications. SPE relies on a *specification* of intended behavior. The specifications must be representative of the envisioned uses of the system if the model results are to be representative of the system's performance. We derive the **workload scenario specifications** from the **requirements specification** of all functions to be performed by the system, then define a typical application that will use the functions. The workload specification consists of the specific functions the typical request uses, the order of function requests, and their frequency.

Next, we clarify **performance goals** for the workload scenarios. As stated earlier, it is vital to SPE's success to have precise, quantitative performance goals. A response-time goal is most common. When the response times for the workload scenarios may have significant variance, we specify response-time goals for each scenario.

Next, we specify the proposed **software design.** It is not necessary to have detailed design specifications. We use preliminary, high-level plans for the initial evaluations.

The workload specifications define what the system is to do. The software structure specifications provide a high-level view of how the system is to do it— that is, the organization of the software and the partitioning of software functions into components.[7] The next step combines the two to construct the execution view of the software—that is, when each component executes. For example, when a user initiates a workload scenario, we need to know which software components will be invoked and in what order. This defines the typical execution paths through the software (or those of interest to the performance evaluation) and "prunes" those that are unlikely to be executed. The **software execution model** represents the execution view. Figure 1.8 illustrates this phase of the model construction.

Next, we provide parameters for the software execution model. We need specifications for the probability or number of times each component executes, and estimates for the resource usage for each software component. In order to estimate **resource usage,** we need specifications for the **execution environment:** the hardware and support system software. Software will clearly behave quite differently when executed on an IBM 3090 under MVS than when executed on a PC under MS-DOS, for example. It may be that the hardware configuration or choice of operating systems is not yet fixed. In this case, we specify parameters for each possible environment, and compare the resulting performance metrics.

Figure 1.9 illustrates the software-execution-model-parameter phase of the model construction. We solve this model for the workload parameters for the **system execution model.** The system execution model, defined in Chapter 5, is the same type of model used for conventional performance evaluation studies. By

---

[7]A **component** is a conceptual entity of the software. Later in development the concept becomes one or more logical entities, and still later components become physical modules, procedures, or executable statements in the software.

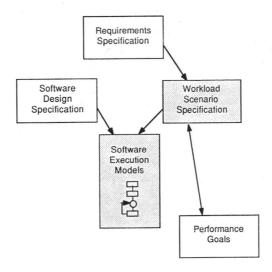

FIGURE 1.8
The first phase in the construction of software execution models produces the software execution model structure. The shaded boxes are created in this phase.

comparing the modeling summary in Figure 1.10 to Figure 1.7, you can see the differences between conventional performance models and the SPE models.

Constructing and evaluating SPE models is not labor-intensive. The models can be created and solved manually, or with one of several commercially available modeling packages. (The performance-modeling tool options are described in Chapters 4 and 5.) With these packages it is possible to solve the performance models interactively in a few seconds. This means that with SPE-modeling techniques, you can evaluate design alternatives in seconds or minutes (once the model is defined) instead of the weeks or months necessary to program and debug large-scale, special-purpose simulators (like those previously used for performance-critical software).

1.4 SPE Goals and Requirements

The primary goal of SPE is to provide a method for the evaluation of the performance of software from its initial conception through its entire lifecycle. This encompasses more than the performance prediction techniques, since they must be

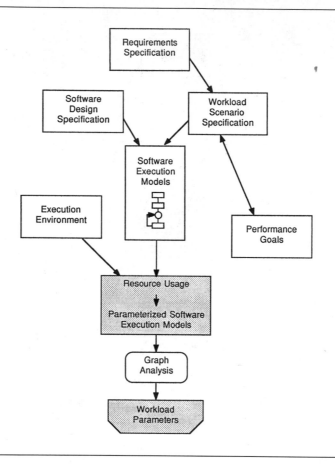

FIGURE 1.9
The second software execution model construction phase uses resource requirements to create model parameters. Graph analysis algorithms then produce workload parameters for the system execution model. The shaded boxes show the
products of this modeling phase.

used if they are to be effective. Therefore, the following goals drove the formation
of the SPE methods:

- □ *Supplement existing methods:* We wish to interface with current software
  development processes rather than replace them—to maximize SPE's adoption potential.

- □ *Ease of use:* SPE must be easier than fix-it-later; it must not require extensive,
  specialized knowledge.

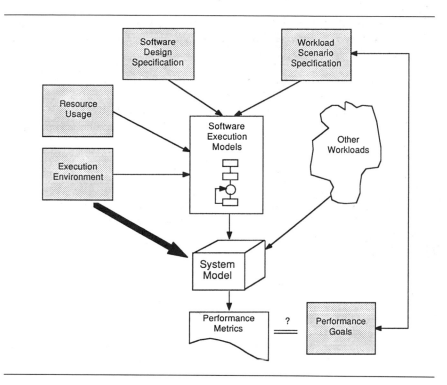

FIGURE 1.10
The software execution models provide the system execution model parameters for software under development.

□ *Rapid assessments:* We wish to produce performance assessments in sufficient time to influence development decisions.

□ *Sufficient precision:* Although precise performance prediction is infeasible,[8] we need sufficient precision to distinguish acceptable design concepts from potentially disastrous ones and to identify software components whose performance is critical. Precision must improve as the software evolves.

□ *Lifecycle usefulness:* We wish to support requirements analysis, design analysis, detailed design and implementation studies, post-deployment revisions, and the inevitable changes throughout the process. We wish to build on early data and models rather than totally replace them.

□ *Wide applicability:* We wish to apply SPE to user-application software, system software, real-time systems, critical-deadline batch, and so on.

[8]Nor is it prudent to devote time to increasing the precision until it is deemed necessary for evaluating design alternatives or for assessing the performance impact of key components.

□ *Adaptability:* We want methods and tools that adapt to changing needs—today's software and the software and hardware technology challenges of the future.

To meet these practicality goals, we applied SPE to systems under development and created methods to solve problems.

These goals impose requirements on the representation of the design and the models for performance assessment. Requirements specifications, design specifications, and programming language statements are all representations of software at different levels of abstraction. The software engineering literature is full of formal languages, graphical techniques, and other strategies for representing software across levels of abstraction. Whatever technique designers select for development purposes, it must explicitly specify the desired *behavior* of the software (what it must do) and the *structure* of the proposed system that will realize that behavior (the decomposition of the system into components and the function of each component). In order to assess performance (and other dynamic characteristics, such as reliability), we require *procedural* information (when, in what order, and other interrelationships of components that execute).

The needed procedural information includes: typical usage scenarios, characteristics of software execution, and dynamics of the execution environment. This information generates a model of the software execution. The software execution model must represent:

□ *Usage scenarios:* To be informative, models must represent the actual system execution behavior. Usage scenarios define the frequently executed or dominant functions of the workload that determine performance and define the applicable boundary conditions, such as peak hour, batch windows, intensity of other competing work, and so forth.

□ *Execution structures:* Sequential, loops, conditional, and recursive execution structures drive the software resource requirements.

□ *Hierarchical resolution of design details:* The models must grow with the software. Expanding the processing details of components also enables specification of resource usage estimates.

□ *Contention for resources:* The resources may be either physical resources, such as processors and disks, or logical resources, such as database records and system tables. Contention delays degrade responsiveness; the intensity of the contention quantifies the effect.

□ *Concurrent processing—communication between and synchronization of software processes:* Concurrent processing within a processor increases resource contention; concurrent processing on distinct processors may add communication overhead or synchronization delays.

It will become evident in Chapters 4, 5, and 8 how the SPE models satisfy these requirements.

SPE matches the modeling effort to the knowledge about the software. Early studies only have "ballpark" specifications, so we use simple, optimistic models to distinguish between feasible and disastrous approaches. Later, as the software becomes better defined, we add additional details to the models so they more realistically represent the ultimate performance.

Now that SPE has been introduced—its motivation, methods, models, goals, and requirements—we are ready to proceed with its definition. It will be explained through the use of comprehensive examples carried through all the SPE steps. These case study examples are introduced next.

1.5 Introduction of Case Studies

SPE and its modeling techniques apply to high-level (or user-level) software systems; intermediate-level systems, such as database management systems; and low-level systems, such as operating systems. The analysis procedures for each type of system will be illustrated by following case studies through the various evaluations.

A simple, automated teller machine (ATM) example will be used throughout the text to introduce the concepts. It is one example of user-level software. A comprehensive case study of a user-level software system demonstrates a more realistic and complex application. It is an interactive system to support a computer-aided engineering design activity: An engineer constructs a model of a proposed aerospace vehicle using computer graphics, stores the model in a relational database, and interactively assesses the design for correctness, feasibility, and quality. (Note the similarity to SPE.) We study one particular usage scenario, DRAWMOD.

The second case study illustrates the evaluation of a proposed engineering database management system (EDMS) to be developed to effectively support the specific data management needs of the engineer. As mentioned earlier, a large software system of this type is usually complex, and the performance of a single component of the system is highly dependent on the performance of the other components. We study two of the important data manipulation commands, FIND and RETRIEVE.

The third case study illustrates the evaluation of "basic" operating system software. We study a representative function of a distributed system: network interprocess communication.

The case studies are presented in the form one would initially encounter them in an actual SPE study. The original inefficiencies are included for illustration. Throughout the text, these case studies will show how SPE progresses with the software, with details added at later stages in the analysis as appropriate.

ATM systems are familiar to most people. Little background information is needed, so they conveniently illustrate SPE concepts. Note that the ATM examples are hypothetical, and *correspond to no actual system.*[9] The other comprehensive case studies illustrate the spectrum of software to which SPE applies and how the models differ for each type. They have been simplified somewhat, but still include some of the hardest problems in software performance prediction. If you understand the techniques used for them, you should be able to apply SPE to most systems you encounter. The interrelationships of the case study systems are explicitly modeled to demonstrate complex software evaluations. Few SPE studies have such a large scope—measurement data is available to simplify the modeling and analysis. Again, understanding harder problems better prepares us to solve easier ones.

1.6 Summary

This chapter introduced the SPE methodology, its relationship to the design process used in other engineering disciplines, and the motivation for applying it to software systems. Then it reviewed the SPE methods, how the evaluation activities differ as the software evolves, and the models used for the performance assessment. It compared the SPE models to conventional models commonly used for computer capacity planning and for system performance tuning. Then it presented some goals and requirements used in the formation of the SPE methodology to ensure practicality and effectiveness.

SPE is gaining widespread acceptance and use. It has been demonstrated to be effective in predicting the performance of software systems early in the design stages and throughout implementation [SMI82b, SMI88a]. The bibliography cites many other references to recent papers that report successful SPE projects. The discipline is not only practical, but also economically important. It is applicable to all software systems; and it can be extremely effective when applied to large development efforts. We anticipate that the spectrum and quality of tools and techniques to support SPE will be broadly expanded over the next few years.

Beginning with the next chapter, we shall review each of the SPE activities in more depth. Chapters 2 through 6 present the information in the order in which Figure 1.5 shows the activities. Chapter 7 covers performance measurements that support the SPE activities. Chapters 8 and 9 present more advanced models for performance assessment, and Chapter 10 focuses on how to establish SPE in your environment.

---

[9]For factual information, about an actual system, see [GIF85].

Exercises

Review

1.1. Summarize SPE: What are the steps in the process? In modeling? What information is needed that is seldom readily available?

1.2. Select a case study documented in the literature or with which you have first-hand experience. Give an overview of its purpose and its performance expectations. (Exercises in later chapters refer to this case study and carry the examination further.)

Further Study

1.3. Select and review one of the historical papers cited in the bibliography (labeled HIST). Identify at least two similarities and two differences between the approach used in the paper and SPE. Explain why the former did not achieve widespread use.

1.4. Select two or more popular software requirements or design methods. Describe them briefly, and then characterize the extent to which they address software performance. Does the method advocate ignoring performance? Is performance specifically addressed? Is there no conflict, but is performance not specifically acknowledged? How difficult would it be to integrate SPE into the method?

1.5. Repeat Exercise 1.4, using two or more popular software-development Computer aided Software Engineering (CASE) tools as your examples.

1.6. Find an article about an important system that suffered major performance problems (or study an actual system if you have access to one). Briefly describe the system and its problems. Which problems could have been anticipated (and thus avoided)? Why do you think they were not anticipated? If possible, quantify the design and programming or the cost of the hardware needed to correct the problem. (*Hint:* You may find an article that describes [subsequent] tuning improvements rather than one that documents problems.)

2

Principles for Creating Responsive Software

Have you ever studied a software system and discovered performance problems as easy to spot as a search light on a pitch-black night? Why do some software developers create systems with such "obvious" performance problems? Why didn't anyone notice (and correct) the problems earlier?

Some software engineers attribute such problems to differences in aptitude and suggest strategies for adapting the software development process to compensate for the differences. For example, Boehm, in his COCOMO software cost-estimation model, adjusts software completion time and cost based on analyst and programmer aptitude [BOE81]. Brooks cites early experimental data on aptitude differences, such as a 10:1 difference in productivity and a 5:1 difference in efficiency, among experienced programmers and suggests team organizations to compensate [BRO75]. Rather than adapt the software development process to compensate for low aptitudes, software psychologists seek *remedies* to aptitude differences. They systematically study the differences among expert and novice, programmers [ADE84] and software designers [SOL84]. They believe that if you understand the differences between the principles that novices and experts use, you can teach expert principles to people with less experience, thereby increasing their aptitude.

Interestingly, performance aptitude used to be widespread (even though it was not documented with formal principles). It began to disappear with the advent of the fix-it-later approach (as discussed in Chapter 1). Developers were told not to worry about performance, so they didn't. Newcomers (and some old timers) never

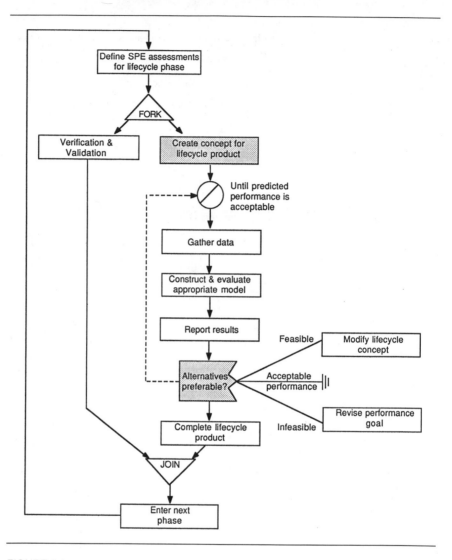

FIGURE 2.1
The SPE Methodology with the Focus of This Chapter Highlighted.

learned the performance skills. It is worthwhile to save this eagle-like knowledge from extinction by formalizing the expert performance principles.[1]

Figure 2.1 highlights this chapter's role in the SPE methodology. The princi-

---

[1]"Expert performance knowledge" conjures up images of artificial intelligence (AI) applications. The principles in this chapter are the type of "expert knowledge" that AI expert systems need, but this chapter does not specifically address the AI implications.

ples defined here are those that experts use to design responsive systems. Many of you will find the concepts familiar (even though you probably do not use this terminology). The goal is to formalize and transfer this expert knowledge to software developers with less experience in building responsive systems.

The principles are necessary, but not sufficient. Consider the following design decision:

EXAMPLE 2.1: Design Decision: Identifying and Filling Optional Fields

In a hypothetical system, one of the most frequently displayed screens contains fields applicable to only a few customers—thus, the fields are usually blank. Displayed values come from the customer's row in a special database table; however, if the customer has no row in the table, the field should be blank. We consider two strategies for determining field contents:

1. Execute the database retrieval command (such as SELECT). If no rows are found, make the corresponding fields blank; otherwise, use data from fields in the row.

2. Maintain a flag in the account header table that specifies which customers require (the extra) database retrievals.

Strategy 1 is easy to implement, but it is expensive to execute unnecessary database retrievals—each one will likely execute over 100K instructions to determine that there is no corresponding data in the table! Strategy 2 avoids this wheel-spinning processing but requires extra code to keep the flags consistent with the database contents, and the flags require more disk space.

□

Which design is better for this hypothetical example? One facet of the decision is performance, but there may be many other facets. We consider the performance of the two strategies in Section 2.2.1. First, however, let's consider another facet: ease of implementation. I once worked for an expert designer who mandated: "Use flags only as a last resort."[2] I quickly learned how much simpler it is to write software without extra code to ensure that database contents always match flag settings. (Debugging is also easier when you do not need constant vigilance over current flag settings.) The "no-flag" principle suggests Strategy 1 in Example 2.1, but what is its performance impact? Does its ease of implementation justify its performance cost? To answer these questions you need to quantify the implementation time and the performance of the two alternatives. This book advocates

---

[2]The designer's theory was that there is always another (usually simpler) way to get the same information provided by flag settings. For example, rather than setting an end-of-file flag, put a trailer record on sequential files with values that automatically trigger end-of-file action. Thus, for a match-merge application, high values in the key of the trailer record automatically cause lower-key records in the other file to be merged. Of course, it makes assumptions about truth conditions that must be preserved during maintenance (you must preserve high-value trailer records). No flags is somewhat difficult to learn, but it tends to simplify initial code.

quantifying the performance of alternatives and using the results to make design decisions. You also need quantitative data for other costs and benefits, but their calculation is beyond the scope of this book.

This chapter provides guidance, based on expert knowledge, for making *performance* decisions. If you incorporate these performance principles into the engineering design process, you can avert perilous problems. The process was introduced in Chapter 1 (refer to Figure 1.4 on page 12 for diagram). Without SPE, the performance evaluation of alternatives is so difficult that many designers are overwhelmed. They use other reasons (like "no flags") to pick alternatives; thus "search-light" performance problems may occur inadvertently.

The principles, unfortunately, do not provide all the answers; you must *use them with the other performance engineering steps* (in Figure 2.1). The following stock-market maxim illustrates that principles alone are insufficient:

> If you want to make a million dollars in the stock market, use this general principle: Buy low and sell high.

Obviously an investor needs more guidance than this. The principles in this chapter are more helpful than this stock-market maxim, but often you need quantitative analyses to determine their performance gains. Back-of-the-envelope calculations are enough for some principles, but others need the models (defined in subsequent chapters) for quantitative data to evaluate cost-benefit tradeoffs (such as the performance cost of the "no-flag" principle).

The seven general principles for creating responsive systems, presented in Section 2.2, are based on both theory (the fundamental performance-determining factors in computer systems) and practice (experience in improving the performance of large systems). The principles apply to creating system requirements (that is, *what* the system is to do), creating system designs (*how* it is to be done), and creating detailed designs (*which* algorithms and data structures are to be used). Note that the principles address software requirements even though these are often prescribed, or "set in concrete." In practice, however, even set-in-concrete requirements may be negotiable, particularly when there are good performance reasons for negotiating (which can be quantified). The principles apply to large or small software systems executing on a spectrum of computer systems: microcomputers, large mainframe computers, distributed systems, and MIMD computers.[3]

These principles address large systems of programs but also apply to individual programs. Although initial creation is their primary focus, they also guide later selection of alternatives (the "create, represent, evaluate" iterations), and, even later, they guide performance-tuning improvements during system maintenance. The magnitude of the performance improvements achievable with these principles

---

[3]The principles apply to systems with conventional von Neuman architectures. This excludes pipelined processors, systolic arrays, and other special-purpose architectures. Such computer systems may have additional performance-determining factors not addressed here.

was demonstrated in Table 1.3 of Chapter 1 and its related example. Further data is provided in Chapter 6.

The remainder of this chapter is devoted to the principles. Section 2.1 describes the basis and rationale for the set of seven principles, and Section 2.2 defines the principles. Section 2.3 presents a different viewpoint: It describes software system design issues and illustrates how to apply the principles to resolve many common design tradeoffs. Section 2.4 advocates system simplicity; Section 2.5 proposes strategies for effective optimization; and Section 2.6 discusses the comprehensive case studies.

As you read this chapter, relate the principles and their applications to systems with which you have experience. The more examples in current systems you can think of, the more useful the principles will be when you design future systems. If you already have experience in performance-oriented design, the examples will help you to transfer expert knowledge to other designers.

2.1 Basis for the Principles

These principles were developed through practical experience with large software systems. On one particular project, severe performance problems were detected during system integration. A thorough performance-tuning study was conducted, and numerous proposals for improvements were formulated. (Many improvements were deemed infeasible due to the magnitude of the change so late in the development stage; others were implemented as proposed.) Each of the proposed improvements was catalogued and classified on the basis of the relationship between the changes and their effect on the parameters of performance models. This relationship is explained in the following paragraphs.

The computer system on which the software executes can be viewed as a simple model, as shown in Figure 2.2. Its **performance depends on the following model characteristics** [LAZ84a, SAU81]:

- □ The *arrival rate* of each *type of job*
- □ The computer-system *resource requirements* of each type of job
- □ The contention delays that result from the *interaction with other jobs* in the system
- □ The *scheduling policies* used to determine which waiting job next obtains the needed system resource

Each of the principles in this section improves performance by favorably affecting the corresponding model characteristic.

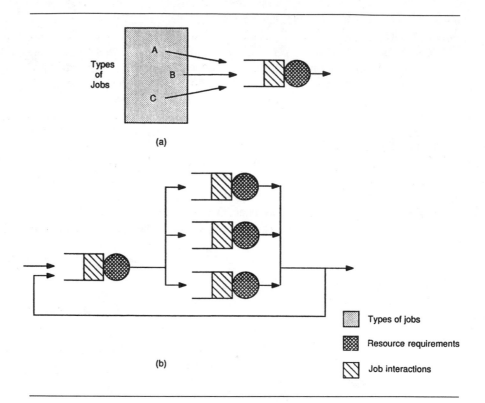

FIGURE 2.2
The simple model in (a) shows several types of jobs (A, B, C, . . .) arriving for service, possibly waiting in a queue for their turn for service, then leaving upon completion. The circle represents a server; jobs wait in its queue if it is busy when they arrive. The arrows show the flow of jobs through the system. The expanded model in (b) identifies more of the computer system resources that each of the jobs may use while being served.

Table 2.1 shows the principles, the corresponding model characteristics, and the type of principle. The **seven performance principles** are as follows:

1. *Fixing-point principle:* concentrates on when and how often processing occurs

2. *Locality-design principle:* pertains to how closely the logical tasks match the characteristics of the physical resources

3. *Processing versus frequency tradeoff principle:* affects the number of requests for resources and the amount of service requested

4. *Shared-resource principle:* influences the number of jobs able to use a resource in a time interval

TABLE 2.1
CORRESPONDENCE BETWEEN PRINCIPLES
AND MODEL CHARACTERISTICS

Performance principle	System parameter correspondence	Type
Fixing-point	Resource requirements	Independent
Locality-design	Resource requirements	Independent
Proc. vs. freq.	Resource requirements	Independent
Locality-design	Job interactions	Synergistic
Shared-resources	Job interactions	Synergistic
Parallel processing	Job interactions	Synergistic
Centering	Types of jobs	Independent
——	Scheduling	——
Instrumenting	——	Control

5. *Parallel processing principle:* determines the extent of parallelism based on the overhead and the competition for resources among the parallel tasks

6. *Centering principle:* focuses on the jobs that are key to the responsiveness of the system

7. *Instrumenting principle:* controls the other factors (rather than directly improving them)

These principles are geared to early lifecycle decisions. Typically, scheduling decisions occur after implementation, when job priorities are manipulated; therefore, this chapter has no scheduling principle. Chapter 8 provides more information for readers who wish to evaluate the performance of scheduling alternatives.

There are **three types of principles** shown in Table 2.1: independent, synergistic, and control. **Independent principles** improve the responsiveness of a "job" by improving the job's own performance parameters (for example, by reducing its resource requirements). Thus, the improvement is *independent* of the characteristics of other types of jobs. The **synergistic principles,** on the other hand, improve the overall system responsiveness through *cooperation.* They can reduce the average waiting time for resources if competing jobs abide by the recommended principle. The locality-design principle is both independent and synergistic because it can improve a job's own responsiveness as well as benefiting competing jobs. As mentioned, the instrumenting principle is used for **control;** it has no direct performance improvement, but it is vital to managing performance.

Most of the principles require a tradeoff decision. Thus, it may be difficult to identify the best-performing alternative, particularly with the synergistic principles, because performance has many complex interrelationships. In practice, the performance engineering models resolve the ambiguities. The general principles are defined in the following sections. After the performance engineering models are defined, in Chapters 3 through 5, the principles are used in Chapter 6 to analyze the quantitative improvements realized with each of the principles.

2.2 General Principles

The following subsections present the seven general principles for creating responsive software systems: fixing-point, locality-design, processing versus frequency tradeoff, shared resource, parallel processing, centering, and instrumenting. Each principle is defined and explained with simple examples, and with the hypothetical automated teller machine (ATM) case study. Examples show how the principles apply to system requirements (what the system is to do) and to system design (how it is to be done).

2.2.1 Fixing-Point Principle

Fixing connects the desired action or function to the instructions that accomplish the action. Fixing also connects the desired result to the data used to produce it. The fixing "point" is a point in time. The latest fixing point is during execution immediately before the instructions or data are required. Fixing could establish connections at several earlier points: earlier in the execution, at program initiation time, at compilation time, or outside the software system. For example, the design decision posed in Example 2.1 deals with fixing results (field contents) to data (database row contents, flags, or "not-found" conditions). For blank fields, flags provide an earlier fixing point than "not-found" conditions. The principle is as follows:

> *Fixing-Point Principle:* **For responsiveness, fixing should establish connections at the earliest feasible point in time, such that retaining the connection is cost-effective.**

First, consider some examples of fixing-point choices. Figure 2.3 illustrates two fixing points for an ATM action, "get checking account balance." Table 2.2 summarizes six additional fixing-point choices.

Item 1 of the table shows alternatives for database queries: ad hoc and managed. General, ad hoc queries use late fixing because the query is parsed and satisfied at run time. Alternatively, managed queries fix earlier, at compilation time; they predefine results that are frequently requested and build a menu or screen with only those result choices. The data is retrieved at run time, but the code to retrieve data is fixed at compilation time. Note that this query example decides what information is to be accessible, not necessarily where it is located. Fixing of "what" and "where" are independent considerations. Examples of both are in Section 2.3.

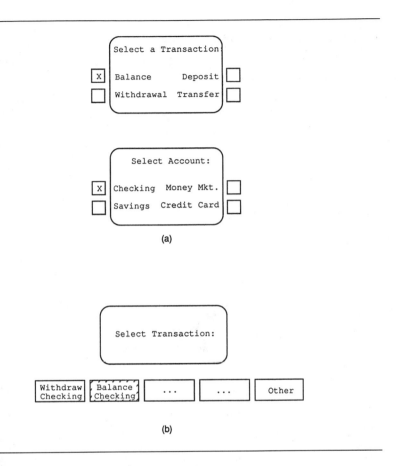

(a)

(b)

FIGURE 2.3
Two Fixing-Point Choices. With the strategy in (a) the user must respond to two screens to request the checking-account-balance transaction. The small buttons on each side of the screen are "soft keys"; their meaning for each screen changes as defined by the software. The buttons at the bottom of the screen in (b) are fixed; their meaning does not change (the figure only shows five of the buttons). Strategy (b) fixes the checking-account-balance transaction earlier, with one screen.

Item 2 determines when data in files or internal tables is ordered. Files or tables kept in the desired order, with all additions preserving the order, are fixed early. Late fixing sorts them at the time the ordered results are requested.[4]

[4]Note that "binding" is a subset of fixing. Item 2 illustrates fixing that is not binding. Some performance experts call Item 2 *extended binding*. Because many subconsciously view binding in a limited context, we use the term *fixing* to encourage broader interpretation.

TABLE 2.2
EXAMPLES OF FIXING-POINT CHOICES

Item	Connection type	Fixing point Early .... Late		Lifecycle stage
1. Database queries	Data	Managed queries	Ad hoc queries	Requirements
2. Data ordering	Data	Preserve order	Sort	Design
3. Data location	Data	Compilation time	Run time	Implementation
4. Fourth generation languages	Instructions	Compiled instructions	Interpret	Requirements
5. User interfaces	Instructions	External button Menu selection	Free-form language	Requirements
6. Table-driven screen formats	Instructions	Generate code	Always use table	Design

Item 3 determines the location of data items within records; compilation time is early, and run time is late fixing. **Item 4** shows compile-time versus run-time alternatives for fixing executable instructions to fourth generation language (4GL) statements.

Item 5 shows user interface choices for fixing user selections to the corresponding instructions. Free-format commands have late fixing when the software parses and interprets the commands, to identify the required processing, at run time. Menu-selection screens, for which the software easily identifies the screen selection, fix at compilation time. The earliest fixing point uses a special key on an input device, generates an interrupt when pressed, and immediately transfers to the instructions that accomplish the desired function.

Item 6 connects instructions that produce screens to table-driven screen specifications. Late fixing examines the table specifications for every field on every screen that is displayed. Earlier fixing uses the table once, to generate code to display the screens.

Of the many fixing alternatives, which are better? The principle says that early fixing leads to better responsiveness *when it is cost-effective to retain the fixing connections*. It is cost-effective to retain the connection when the savings realized with it offset the retention cost.

EXAMPLE 2.2: Performance Comparison of Design Alternatives

For the design-decision example, the operational costs are:

   □ Strategy 1, no flag: no retention costs

(continued)

EXAMPLE 2.2 (*Continued*)

□ Strategy 2, flag: 1 Mbyte disk storage (1 byte of disk storage for each customer)
+ 2,000 instructions per day to update the flag
(20 instructions each × 100 customer changes).

The performance savings is the operational-cost difference between Strategy 1's late fixing and strategy 2's earlier fixing:

□ Strategy 1 costs 5 billion instructions per day:
(100K instructions each × 50K transactions per day)

□ Strategy 2 costs 50.25 million instructions per day:
(5 instructions to check flag
+   (100K instructions to SELECT × 0.01 probability that customer needs optional fields))
×   50K transactions per day

Thus, the performance savings is approximately 4.95 billion instructions per day.   □

You can carry these operational-cost calculations further by computing monetary costs for disk storage, processor execution, and so forth. In this example, retaining the flag for earlier fixing obviously has lower operational costs because the flags are easy to update (20 instructions), updates are infrequent (100 per day), most transactions use the flag to avoid database calls (99 percent), and the "no-flag" strategy is costly (approximately 99,995 more instructions). Do not overgeneralize. In other situations, flags can be detrimental to operational, development, and maintenance costs. This example's flag updates are simple: Only two conditions, during batch processing, cause flag settings to change, and the flag-containing table is already being updated. Imagine the complexity if dozens of different online transactions could cause flag settings to change.

Such back-of-the-envelope calculations, then, determine when early fixing is good for responsiveness. However, the design-decision example reveals other concerns, such as implementation ease. The fixing-point and other principles identify appropriate choices for *responsiveness*, and let you quantify responsiveness costs and benefits. Couple this data with other (quantified) costs and benefits to make the best overall choice.

Cost effectiveness is not the only ingredient in fixing-point choices; the other primary ingredient is **flexibility.** Fixing can be a resource-usage-versus-flexibility tradeoff. Early fixing leads to far more responsive systems, while later fixing may be more flexible and general. Late fixing provides flexibility in two ways: by automatically linking actions to the most recent version of the corresponding instructions (or automatically linking results to the latest data), and by imposing fewer constraints on which actions (or results) can be executed (or accessed). Late fixing is less responsive because more code (to establish connections) is executed for each request, whether or not it is necessary. Late fixing is unnecessary when no changes have occurred since the last use and when common, predictable actions and results are requested. The "no-flag" strategy of the design-decision example executes extra fixing code (SELECTs) unnecessarily for blank fields. "No flag" offers no particular flexibility advantage because flags can automatically link information as effectively as "not-found" conditions.

Ad hoc versus managed queries is another flexibility tradeoff. The former is more flexible because users can ask for any data; nevertheless, the latter is better for responsiveness. How do you quantify the costs and benefits of flexibility? It is difficult, if not impossible, and beyond the scope of this book. Irrespective of its cost, many requirements specifications mandate flexibility. Does this mean you must sacrifice responsiveness?

First, recognize that mandated flexibility (such as, "you must provide ad hoc queries") does not imply that every function must provide the same flexibility. You can allow ad hoc queries and also provide managed queries for high-frequency, predictable requests. A performance engineer offers the following order-taking example of a potential flexibility compromise.

EXAMPLE 2.3: Flexibility Compromise

The requirements for a system rewrite mandated, "Order-taking is to be simplified. Any company employee must be able to take an order." The result was a question-answer dialog that prompted order-takers for everything required. This met the requirements, but overlooked the impact on the high-volume, order-taking clerks. The new process was so cumbersome that they could no longer take orders at their previous high rate and could not keep up with incoming calls, and thus the company lost business.

□

The flexibility-versus-responsiveness tradeoff is best resolved by compromise. Create customized transactions with early fixing for common, predictable actions and results. If you need flexibility, create special screens or menus for uncommon actions and results.

Software is often more general than is necessary. If users (or designers) are uncertain of the use of the system, they build it to be general (usually with late fixing). However, it is better to consider early how generality affects performance, to invest the time to study how systems will likely be used, and to include generality only where it is really needed. As a compromise, use early fixing for the most frequently requested functions, and make only the less frequent ones general.

2.2.2 Locality-Design Principle

Locality refers to the closeness of desired actions, functions, and results to physical resources (such as instructions, files, databases, processors, and storage devices). For example, if a desired screen result is identical to the physical database

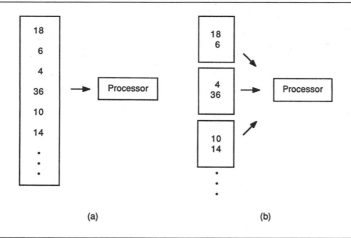

FIGURE 2.4
Temporal Locality Choices. The numbers enclosed in each box are transferred to the processor at the same time. Strategy (a) sends all at once; Strategy (b) transfers two at a time.

row that produces it, we say the locality is good. According to Webster, close means "being near in *time, space, effect* (that is, purpose or intent), or *degree* (that is, intensity or extent)."

The dictionary definition of *close* leads to four types of locality design for performance engineering. These are illustrated with the following example. Con-

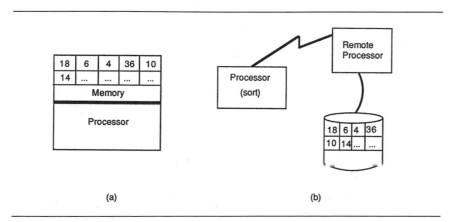

FIGURE 2.5
Spatial Locality Choices. The numbers in Strategy (a) are in the processor's local memory; in (b) they are on a remote disk.

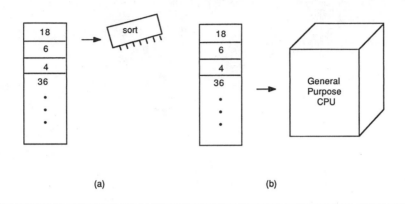

(a)   (b)

FIGURE 2.6
Effectual Locality Choices: The processor in (a) is a special-purpose sort processor, whereas (b)'s processor is a general-purpose CPU.

sider the action to sort a list of numbers. As shown in Figure 2.4, *temporal locality* is better if the numbers are transferred to the physical "sort" processor all at once, rather than a few at a time (with a long time between transfers). Similarly, *spatial locality* is better if the data is near the physical resource that conducts the sort, such as in the processor's local memory, rather than on a disk drive attached to a different machine (see Figure 2.5). The action can execute on different types of physical processors; Figure 2.6 shows the choice of a general-purpose CPU or a

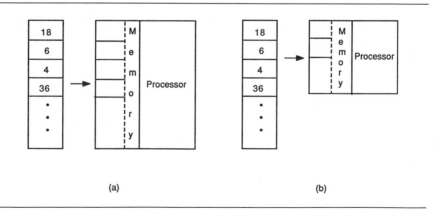

(a)   (b)

FIGURE 2.7
Degree Locality Choices. The processor in (a) is capable of sorting all numbers at once, whereas (b)'s must make multiple passes.

special-purpose chip designed specifically to sort lists of numbers. *Effectual locality* is better for the special-purpose processor, because its purpose is better matched to the action than the general-purpose CPU is. *Degree locality* refers to the extent of the action, as in matching the length of the list of numbers to the capability of the processors, as shown in Figure 2.7.

> *Locality-Design Principle:* **Create actions, functions, and results that are "close" to physical computer resources.**

Table 2.3 summarizes some locality choices. **Item 1** shows alternatives for structuring account data for ATM users. Locality is stronger when account data is

TABLE 2.3
EXAMPLES OF LOCALITY CHOICES

Item	Locality type	Locality		
		Strong		*Weak*
1. Account data to ATM	Spatial	Aggregate likely users		Likely users scattered, unlikely users mixed
2. Menu contents	Spatial	Cluster related actions		Related actions scattered, dissimilar choices mixed
3. Menu hierarchy	Temporal	Present frequent choices immediately, defer unlikely choices		Frequent choices must navigate through multiple menu levels
4. Data organization	Temporal	Assemble data items according to habitual use		Frequent results need multiple records
5. Processor type	Effectual	Special-purpose—geared to desired action		General-purpose—desired action is process-intensive
6. Resource exploitation	Effectual	Adapt algorithms to match processor features	Rely on compilers or special interface routines	Mismatch between actions and processor characteristics
7. Processor size	Degree	Speed and capacity match user requirements		Too small or too large

geographically near the ATM that is most likely to be used, and when account data for highly unlikely users is excluded.

Item 2 shows alternatives for designing menu contents. Locality is stronger when you group related functions together and change menus when users begin a different processing stage. For example, ATMs have different menus for account transfers and balance inquiries. Spatial locality seeks to minimize the number of times you must change menus.

Item 3 shows that temporal locality is better when the most frequent choices appear on the first menu seen by the user and infrequent actions are deferred to later menus. Most ATMs offer a checking-withdrawal choice on the first menu (after sign on). Some ATMs have the most frequent choices on the first menu; to reach low-frequency transactions one selects "other" to see the next-level choices.

Item 4 organizes data such that items frequently used together are stored together despite logical relationships. Concrete examples are in Section 2.3.3.

Item 5 selects the type of processor to match the applications. ATMs use a special-purpose machine customized to the ATM application, rather than a general-purpose terminal console. Similarly, **Item 6** shows alternatives for adapting applications to exploit features of computer system resources. For example, if your processor has special instructions for vector processing, locality is best if you select algorithms geared to those instructions. Locality is poor if your application must continually interrupt vector processing with conditional branches, compose vectors from data scattered throughout memory, and so forth. Moderate locality relies on compilers and other special routines to generate code to adapt algorithms to architectural features.

Item 7 matches the size of the task and its responsiveness requirements to the machine. A microcomputer is sufficient for ATM applications—supercomputers are unnecessary.

In operating systems, the term *locality* usually refers to memory-reference patterns. You can apply the locality-design principle to effective memory use. The two primary **memory locality** considerations are spatial locality and temporal locality. *Spatial memory locality* advocates clustering an action's code and data in a small amount of memory and moving unrelated code and data elsewhere. *Temporal memory locality* advocates clustering frequently requested actions and moving infrequent ones elsewhere. If you improve memory locality, you reduce the software's memory requirements; thus, you can allow more concurrent users. The software also executes faster because it spends less time loading code and data from external storage.

Some examples that achieve spatial and temporal memory locality are:

☐ Arrange code for case statement alternatives according to expected frequency of occurrence.

☐ Group items used together into rows or records.

□ Group global variables such that items used together are defined and stored adjacent to one another.

□ Physically group together procedures that reference one another and do not mix those that are unrelated.

□ Create large blocks of file records when sequential access is frequent.

The other two aspects of general locality design also apply, but for memory locality they need little discussion. *Effectual memory locality*, for example, suggests that data that is accessed randomly should be mapped to a direct-access device rather than to a sequential device. *Degree memory locality* calls for a close match between the virtual memory necessary for execution (during all phases of execution; that is, to hold the working set) and the physical memory available.

Locality design has neither cost-effectiveness nor flexibility tradeoffs. The only tradeoff occurs when ideal data structure locality differs among processes that use the same data. As usual, quantitative analysis identifies the best choice. These locality conflicts are covered in the application section (2.3.2).

2.2.3 Processing Versus Frequency Tradeoff Principle

This principle addresses the amount of work done per processing request and its impact on the number of requests made. The "tradeoff" looks for opportunities to reduce requests by doing more work per request, and vice versa. The principle is as follows:

> *Processing Versus Frequency Tradeoff Principle:* **Minimize the processing times frequency product.**

This says to consider both the number of times software processing executes and the amount of processing per execution and minimize the product. Table 2.4 shows examples of the tradeoffs. Each item identifies the processing and the frequency that must be quantified to evaluate the tradeoff. For example, **Item 1** evaluates the tradeoffs in allowing multiple transactions per session. The comparison is shown in the following example.

EXAMPLE 2.4: Processing vs. Frequency Performance Comparison

Compare the following two strategies:

1. Prompt for session continuation

2. Terminate session after one transaction

The prompt to continue a session requires additional processing time, but with Strategy 2 the total number of sessions may increase, and thus the processing to start and end sessions would increase accordingly.

(continued)

EXAMPLE 2.4 (*Continued*)

To evaluate Strategy 1, quantify the processing with the prompt—say 20 sec, for example. Multiply by the number of sessions when multiple transactions are allowed—say 1,000. To evaluate Strategy 2, quantify the processing without the prompt—say 18 sec. Include additional session overhead by multiplying by the total number of transactions—say 1,200. Thus, for these hypothetical numbers, Strategy 1's product, 20,000 sec, is less than Strategy 2's product, 21,600 sec. Thus, the processing versus frequency tradeoff principle recommends Strategy 1.

Note that some ATMs have more clever strategies, such as automatically terminating sessions after certain transaction types (maximum withdrawals).

□

Item 2 explores alternatives for displaying results of a database query when multiple data items satisfy the query. The choices are to display all results (with a GETALL), or to display only the first result and display each additional one when the user requests a GETNEXT. If users frequently wish to display all results, you need the GETALL. Even though it may be infrequent, users may want the GET-ALL feature (especially after you imply it is feasible). Then you can apply this principle to design alternatives (**Item 3**). You can implement a custom-coded GETALL or just intercept the user's GETALL request, and issue multiple calls to the database (GETFIRST and multiple GETNEXTs), accumulate the results, and transmit all back to the user at once. This is a database-design tradeoff. Similar data processing tradeoffs occur when there may be multiple line items per purchase order, multiple purchases per bill, and the like.

There are three special cases of this principle that commonly occur in large software systems. These special cases relate more directly to software-development decisions, and should provide a better understanding of the general principle. The first two special cases described increase processing and reduce frequency; the third decreases processing.

The first special case is the **"family plan."** The analogy is: Provide service for the first family member for full fee, and for all additional family members—at the same time—for a negligible additional fee. Consider an "access list" strategy that maintains a list of resources that each user has permission to access, and the type of access allowed for each (**Item 4**). For example, it might record permission for me to: read--my-taxes-owed, change--my-taxes-owed, and read--your-salary. A "security guard" within an operating system can obtain all my access rights for all resources for a negligible additional cost over obtaining the access rights for one resource. The family plan applies when I am likely to make many requests for resources within a short period of time.

The second case is the **"maximum use of overhead costs."** With it, software groups service requests into "batches" to fulfill multiple requests for each overhead penalty. Envision a hypothetical distributed-computing environment in which many users share a local machine for editing, compiling, and executing minor tests (**Item 5**). Users submit major tests to a remote machine. Submission requires

TABLE 2.4
EXAMPLES OF PROCESSING VERSUS FREQUENCY TRADEOFFS

Item	Processing choices	Frequency	Lifecycle stage
1. Multiple ATM transactions per session?	Include processing to ask *versus* Exclude asking, but add session over-head	# sessions (when multiple transactions allowed) *versus* Total # transactions	Requirements
2. Display all results of DB query?	GETALL *versus* Display first + GET-NEXT	# GETALL requests, # results each *versus* Total # results needed	Requirements
3. How to fulfill GET-ALL request	Custom GETALL code *versus* Internal call to GET-FIRST + GETNEXT	# GETALL requests, # results each *versus* Total # results needed	Design
4. Family plan: re-trieve all access permissions?	All access permissions *versus* Satisfy only this re-quest	# users making requests *versus* # requests	Design
5. Maximum use of overhead: major test submission	Accumulate tests and submit batches *versus* Submit one at a time	# batches *versus* # tests	Design
6. Expensive pro-cessing reduction: reservation infor-mation display	Display typical info and special info by request *versus* Display all at once	# calls and # spe-cial requests *versus* # calls	Requirements

"overhead" software to establish the communication link, to transmit the major test, and to receive the reply. Maximum use of overhead costs implies that soft-ware should collect (delay) major-test requests and periodically transmit them to the remote machine. It applies when the batching delay is small compared to the duration of the major test and when it is likely that multiple major tests will be submitted during the delay period.

The third special case (**Item 6**) is the **"expensive processing reduction."** With it, expensive processing is done only when it is necessary. Consider a reservation system application: When a customer calls to check previously made airline or car-rental reservations, systems usually present a short record that contains frequently accessed information. Processing takes longer for less frequent requests, such as reserving a special meal.

2.2.4 Shared-Resource Principle

Computer system resources are limited; thus, processes compete for their use. Some resources may be *shared:* Multiple processes can use the resource at the same time. Other resources require *exclusive use:* Processes take turns—each process has exclusive use of the resource, one at a time (that is, the resource is multiplexed). For example, an ATM authorization-code file may be shared, thus allowing any program to read it as needed. An ATM account file requires exclusive use to guarantee that a program does not read or update the file while another program is changing the account balance. **Exclusive use affects performance in two ways:** the additional processing overhead to schedule the resource and the possible contention delay to gain access to the resource. The contention delay depends on how many processes request exclusive use and the length of time they hold it. Remember from Table 2.1 that the shared-resource principle is of the *synergistic type:* It improves overall performance, through cooperation, by reducing contention delays, rather than by reducing individual processing like the *independent-type* principles. The principle is as follows:

> *Shared-Resource Principle:* **Share resources when possible. When exclusive access is required, minimize the sum of the holding time and the scheduling time.**

Resource sharing minimizes both the overhead for scheduling and the wait to gain access (there may be a wait if another process already has exclusive access even though the requestor is willing to share).

Decreasing the sum of the holding time and the scheduling time of multiplexed resources decreases the overall average wait time to gain access to the resource. There are **four ways to minimize holding time:**

1. Minimize the processing time (using the other principles).
2. Hold only while needed.
3. Request smaller resource units.
4. Fragment the resource requests.

The first method decreases the holding time by doing less work while the resource is held. The second says to request a multiplexed resource just before it is used, and release it immediately afterward. The third, requesting smaller resource units, suggests holding less of the resource. For example, the resource unit sizes for a database range from the entire database, one file within the database, a single record within a file within a database, and so forth. The fourth option, fragmenting requests, means to partition one request that requires a long holding time into multiple requests, each of which has a shorter holding time.

Minimizing holding time may increase scheduling time. Smaller resource units require more scheduling overhead, and request-fragments make more scheduling requests. *There is a net improvement only when the additional schedule processing is less than the expected wait time for the larger units or longer requests.* Wait time is difficult to quantify with back-of-the-envelope calculations. To evaluate this tradeoff, you need the performance models described in later chapters.

Table 2.5 shows some ATM examples of the holding-time choices and their impact on scheduling. **Item 1** explores the extent of processing carried out while the resource is held. The streamlined alternative removes processing from the locked phase that does not require exclusive use of the resource. This has no effect on scheduling overhead because the number of requests does not change.

Item 2 looks at the granularity of locks. "Smaller resource units" suggests locking on accounts rather than locking the entire database. Locking the entire database requires only one lock, while locking individual accounts requires many; on the other hand, the scheduling time to search through a list of locked accounts is greater than the time to check one flag for the entire database. Of course, the space requirements for multiple account locks are greater as well. The intermediate

TABLE 2.5
EXAMPLES OF SHARING CHOICES

Item	Type	Holding time	Scheduling overhead
1. Extent of processing	Hold while needed	General processing intermingled *versus* Streamlined update	None
2. Lock granularity	Smaller resource units	Entire account database *versus* Lock account-containing record *versus* Lock account	1 lock *versus* 1 lock per record *versus* 1 lock per account
3. How many updates?	Request fragments	First-need to end-of-session *versus* Duration of each update	≤1 lock per session *versus* 1 lock per change

strategy is used in many database systems—they lock on physical blocks or pages, thus locking everything else within the page.

Item 3 explores request fragments. The software could lock for the first request that requires a change to the database and hold it until the customer completes the ATM session. Alternatively, it could lock and free the database immediately before and after any change. The number of schedule requests increases if the customer's transactions make multiple changes to the account.

Remember, the principle says to minimize the sum of the holding time and scheduling time, and *in database systems lock scheduling overhead is very high.* Chapter 8 has some checkpoint evaluations that tell whether lock contention delay is a potential performance problem. For database locks, choose alternatives that minimize scheduling overhead, and use the checkpoint evaluations to examine the effect on lock wait time.

Note that these principles apply to many other resources too. For example, the entire central computer system is a resource that is shared among all the ATM sites. ATMs may "use it only when needed" by preprocessing transactions on the ATM microcomputer to prompt the customer, collect the responses, format the transaction request, and then ship the entire packet of information to the central site for processing. A similar example uses microcomputers for data entry to preprocess transactions, screen for simple errors, and send filtered transactions to mainframes.

The communication line connecting ATMs to the central computer is another resource. If the communication line multiplexes many ATM sites, then the customer may incur additional delays waiting for the line to be available. The *average* wait time may be reduced if the communication line holding time is reduced by fragmenting the messages into several smaller packets. The additional scheduling time (the time to fragment and compose packets, protocols, and so forth) determines the net effect. An alternative approach minimizes scheduling overhead for communication lines by consolidating data into larger packets for transmission. As before, SPE models provide quantitative data for performance tradeoffs, to be combined with other cost-benefit data, to identify the best choice.

2.2.5 Parallel Processing Principle

Processing time can sometimes be reduced by partitioning a process into multiple concurrent processes. The concurrency can either be real concurrency, in which the processes execute at the same time on different processors, or it can be apparent concurrency, in which the processes are multiplexed on a single processor. For real concurrency, the processing time is reduced by an amount proportional to the number of processors. Apparent concurrency is more complicated: Although some of the processing may be overlapped, if the processes compete for resources (the CPU, memory, files, etcetera), each process may experience additional wait time.

Both real and apparent concurrency require processing overhead to manage the communication and coordination between concurrent processes. The principle is as follows:

> *Parallel Processing Principle:* **Execute processing in parallel (only) when the processing speedup offsets communication overhead and resource contention delays.**

In general, the benefits derived through apparent concurrency are not significant compared to those achievable using other principles. It has the further disadvantage of adding complexity to the software system. Real concurrency will be effective if the processing-time reduction is much greater than the additional overhead for communication and coordination of the concurrent processes. The performance improvement must also be weighed against the cost of the additional processing power and the cost of more complex software, to determine whether it will be effective.

In the ATM example, the microcomputer at the ATM site allows parallel processing. The following is one parallel processing strategy:

1. The ATM microcomputer requests the account information and authorization code and sends them to the central computer.

2. While the central computer is verifying the account number and authorization code, the ATM microcomputer obtains the transaction selection and the information required.

3. The ATM formats and sends the transaction information to the central computer. While the transaction is being processed at the central site, the ATM begins printing the receipt for the customer.

4. While waiting for the response, the ATM micro asks if another transaction is desired, and if so, begins processing it.

This processing strategy is complex because many special cases must be handled. For example, the customer might first request the account balance; while that transaction is being processed by the central computer, the customer requests a withdrawal. When the account balance arrives from the central computer, the balance is insufficient to cover the withdrawal. Thus, the ATM software increases in complexity; you must quantify its responsiveness to see if the complexity is warranted.

ATM processing concurrency is a software design issue. A requirements issue is whether to let the customer "type ahead" on requests. Experienced customers are familiar with ATM prompts; so a type-ahead feature for them would accept a sequence of responses without intervening prompts (similar to typing ahead on timesharing systems).

Data processing installations sometimes use parallel processing to reduce batch processing time. They partition large files and run each partition through batch programs concurrently. This works well when the logical processing of one file partition is totally independent of the others (for example, when the updates for Smith in one partition have no effect on Jones in another). There is an optimum number of partitions before performance degrades due to contention delays. SPE models can identify the value of parallel processing: when batch processes must be partitioned to fit within batch windows and when points of diminishing returns are reached due to excessive contention delays.

The parallel processing principle is another synergistic principle. To assess speedup, contention delays, and communication delays, you need the SPE models defined later. Chapter 8 presents some checkpoint evaluations for detecting potential concurrency problems.

2.2.6 Centering Principle

The five previous principles provide guidance for creating software requirements and designs. Their application improves the performance of the part of the system to which they are applied. Centering is different in that it leverages performance by focusing attention on the parts of large software systems that have the greatest impact on responsiveness.

Centering is based on the folkloric "80–20 rule" for the execution of code within programs (which claims that ≤ 20 percent of a program's code accounts for ≥ 80 percent of its computer resource usage). The principle uses this generalized version: A subset (≤ 20 percent) of the *system functions* that are provided will be requested by the system users most (≥ 80 percent) of the time. Think about your use of text editors, spreadsheets, and other systems—does the rule hold? We call these frequently requested functions the **dominant workload functions.** (They also cause a subset (≤ 20 percent) of the programs or modules in the software system to be executed most (≥ 80 percent) of the time, and the code within modules, and so forth). Performance enhancements made to these key areas of the software system thus greatly affect the overall responsiveness of the system. For example, suppose 150,000 transactions per day have a 2-second average response. With centering, you could complete 95 percent of them in 0.5 sec and 5 percent in 2.5 sec.

$$(0.95 \times 0.5) + (0.05 \times 2.5) = 0.6 \text{ sec average}$$

So, the overall *average* response drops from 2 sec to 0.6 sec! The principle is as follows:

> *Centering Principle:* **Identify the dominant workload functions and minimize their processing.**

That is, create special, streamlined execution paths for the dominant workload functions that are customized and trimmed to include only processing that *must* be done while the user waits. Construct separate paths for more general processing. Use the principles in Sections 2.2.1 through 2.2.5 to minimize processing of the special paths. Table 2.6 shows two examples of centering.

Item 1 in Table 2.6 examines the most frequent ATM transaction: withdrawals. Most ATMs provide a "quick withdrawal" transaction that is quickly selected by pressing one button. Quick withdrawal streamlines processing by eliminating prompts and processing for: account selection, amount, and additional transactions. It dramatically improves performance when the dominant workload is: a single transaction per customer, to withdraw the default amount, from a fat checking account. It seems that the dominant workload has changed since ATMs first introduced this speedup. Now frequent uses would be more streamlined if customers could define the characteristics of their preferred transaction when they sign up for ATM use. For example, mine is to withdraw the maximum amount and get my receipt lightening fast; others may wish to check balances, then withdraw. The "give-me-the-usual" transaction would replace the "quick withdrawal"; it would increase the number of customers able to use the fast path and streamline the processing. Thus, it could dramatically improve responsiveness.

Item 2 shows two different ways of viewing the purpose of high-frequency transactions. The design decision in Example 2.1 looked for ways to fix optional-field contents early. Item 2's streamlined processing *removes* seldom-needed, optional fields from high-frequency screens. This makes processing faster for the vast majority of the customer inquiries (99 percent), but occasionally takes longer when users call up another screen to view the optional fields. The other, more general view tries to maximize the number of customer inquiries satisfied with one screen, by packing it with potentially applicable fields. The latter seems logical to many users, but if you quantify the average time to satisfy customer inquiries, the streamlined processing alternative has far better responsiveness. (A chapter exercise quantifies the differences.) So question the purpose of high-frequency transactions: Is it to minimize the time required to satisfy customer inquiries, or to minimize the number of screens presented to customer-service representatives? They are not necessarily the same.

TABLE 2.6
EXAMPLES OF CENTERING CHOICES

Item	Streamlined processing	General processing
1. Withdrawals	*One* interaction: *default* amount, account, session continuation	*Three* interactions: *select* amount, account, session continuation
2. Optional fields	Remove fields with limited applicability from high-frequency screens	Maximize the number of customer inquiries satisfied with one screen

Focus of the Centering Principle   The centering principle focuses on frequent requests. This implies that it is generally not profitable to worry about the responsiveness of low-frequency functions; modifications to them may lead to negligible improvements, or even to degradations. However, you must engineer performance of *vital* functions (even though they may be infrequent) and functions that have large processing times (the "major consumers" described in the next subsection).

The centering principle applies to all systems, but what one centers on may depend on the performance goal or the type of system. Thus far, the discussion has implicitly addressed application software systems that support online interactive users where the performance goal is responsiveness to the users. When system throughput (number of responses per unit time) is a performance goal, or general-purpose software systems do not have a dominant workload, centering applies to those components with the largest cumulative space × time product across the specified usage scenarios. Note that most general-purpose systems (database systems, operating systems, and other commercial products) have dominant workloads. As developers, you may not know what they are, but (with effort) you can identify them, and it is imperative to do so. For example, one dominant workload in an operating system is the sequential I/O path; it is important to center on it and minimize the path length. If you instead focus on the components with a large cumulative space × time product, you can make improvements by reducing their time, but you may not find other opportunities to shorten the path length by eliminating unnecessary processing steps. It is true that you must meet requirements of all your customers, but *you must also do frequent tasks well* if you wish to satisfy customers.

Lifecycle Differences   Early in the lifecycle, centering focuses on the functions frequently requested by users. The objective is to reduce the time that the user must wait for most of the transactions. Later, during implementation, the centering principle also addresses software components with large resource demands, the **major consumers,** even though they may not be executed frequently. The rationale for including these additional components comes from the shared-resource principle. That is, the time that a job holds a resource affects the time that other users wait to use it. So even though the major consumers may execute infrequently, they can delay the dominant workload functions and thus adversely affect their response time.

There is an additional difference in the early and late lifecycle centering considerations: the effect of the improvements. Early lifecycle centering focuses on the functions frequently requested by the users, the dominant workload functions. It is assumed that reducing the processing time for these requests does not affect the number of times they are requested. Later in the lifecycle we also address the major consumers of resources. When their processing time is reduced, the components that fall in the set of major consumers may change. This is the so-called "tall-pole syndrome"—if you have many poles of varying heights, sawing off the tallest may make another pole the tallest; sawing it off moves the problem elsewhere, and so on. Thus, reducing the resource requirements of the major consumers could be an endless process, because there will always be major consumers of each resource. It is *not* endless because we focus on achieving the performance goal, not on minimizing resource usage.

2.2.7 Instrumenting Principle

Instrumenting software means inserting code at key probe points to enable measurement of pertinent execution characteristics. The principle is:

> *Instrumenting Principle:* **Instrument systems as you build them to enable measurement and analysis of workload scenarios, resource requirements, and performance goal achievement.**

This principle does not in itself improve performance, but it is essential to *controlling* performance. It has its foundations in engineering, particularly process control engineering. Their rule of thumb is: "If you can't measure it, you can't control it."[5]

Insert probes to collect the number of times workload scenarios execute, how often software components execute, and their resource requirements. SPE also calls for measuring how frequently system functions and results are requested. System functions are fixed to code, and results are fixed to data that is accessed. Operating system routines may measure code execution frequency and data access rates, but software systems also need instrumentation to identify and measure the relationships. For example, it is usually easy to measure the number of times an "account-update" procedure executes, but difficult to determine the typical withdrawal amount, unless you code your own counters to tally transaction characteristics.

For the ATM example, you need instrumentation to enable collection of:

- Number of times each ATM site is used, its customer arrival rates, and the peak load characteristics
- Number of times each ATM function is selected, and the number of times errors are made

---

[5]I have always believed that instrumenting software is vital to performance. Nevertheless, I omitted instrumenting in my original set of principles because it does not directly improve performance. Kopetz presented a paper on principles for designing fault-tolerant real-time process control systems, and included an instrumenting principle [KOP86]. He persuaded me that it is vital and should be adopted, even though it does not directly improve performance.

□ Number of times each software component executes

□ For each component: the amount of CPU time, number of I/Os, memory, procedure calls, and so forth

□ The withdrawal amounts, the accounts accessed, the number of transactions local to the bank versus those that access a national network, and the number of transactions in a session

□ The total time for: the user to respond to requests for information, the completion of a transaction, the completion of a session

The above is a partial list of the data of interest. You need to consider this data collection as the system requirements and design are conceived; it is much more difficult to add it after implementation. This is because of limitations in instrumenting technology—most tools collect system-level data, such as program execution time, rather than functional data such as end-to-end response time (for ATM transaction or session time). To collect functional data, programmers must insert code to call system timing routines, and write key events and pertinent data to files for later analysis. **Define these probe points when you define the functions.**

Chapter 7 elaborates on the performance measurement and instrumentation concepts and discusses how to implement the instrumenting functions. It suggests storing data in a performance engineering database for ease of access and analysis. For further reading on instrumentation, refer to the Kopetz paper on principles for creating fault-tolerant, real-time systems [KOP86], and to Bouhana's paper for a general discussion of instrumentation versus measurement versus analysis [BOU85]. This discussion focuses on instrumentation for SPE; you also need to collect data to control other aspects of software quality.

2.2.8 Late Lifecycle Principles

As stated earlier, initial software creation is the primary focus of the general principles, but they also apply later in the lifecycle. You can supplement them with other authors' techniques specifically oriented to the software implementation stages, such as:

□ Techniques for selecting efficient algorithms and data structures [BEN82, KNU68]

□ Techniques for efficient coding [JAL77, McN80, VAN78]

□ Techniques for tuning programs to improve efficiency [BEN82, FER78, FER83a, FER83b, KNU71]

Efficient algorithms and data structures are key implementation issues. There are many books and articles, other than those cited above, that propose implementation algorithms and data structures. Most algorithm specialists use traditional best- and worst-case analysis to select appropriate algorithms and data structures. Alternatively, SPE's principles select algorithms that optimize the performance of the *typical case*.[6] For example, when choosing an algorithm for sorting addresses in a database, the algorithm must correctly handle any combination of addresses. However, if you know that most of the time only a few of the addresses are out of order, SPE selects an algorithm for the nearly sorted, typical case. The algorithm must handle the completely-random-address case, but you care less about its performance because it is unlikely to occur.

2.3 Applying the Principles

Since the performance principles closely correspond to the computer performance factors they affect, they are intuitive to an experienced performance specialist, but they may be less familiar to software system designers. This section illustrates applying the performance principles to software system requirements and design. It illustrates that performance-oriented design does not preclude the use of good software engineering practices.

2.3.1 User-Interface Design

User-interface design defines the structure and strategy for acquiring and viewing results. Thus, for an interactive computer system, we focus on the screen layouts and the interaction scenarios; for batch systems the focus is the report formats and the input-media formats. Batch systems are not specifically addressed here, but the general principles apply to them as well.

SPE advocates applying the performance principles to user-interface design to define **screen contents** and **interaction strategy** during the requirements definition stage and applying them again later, during design and implementation, to define their **physical organization.** This strategy is compatible with software development methods that advocate defining the functional architecture of the system, prototyping, and writing the user manual (including the screen definitions and interactions) in the requirements stage [BRO75, RUB84].

The user-interface design determines both the **amount of data transferred** and the **number of interactions** between the computer system and the user's

---

[6]Note that the typical case is not the same as the average case because the average factors in performance of the other workload functions.

terminal (or device). The time required for these interactions can dominate the total transaction time; careful design of the interface can substantially reduce this time. A summary of the applications to be discussed next is in Table 2.7. User interfaces of the future will rely more on graphics capabilities, so several applications describe graphical user-interface tradeoffs. With graphics, cumbersome interfaces tend to be more prominent, and changes more difficult. Therefore the principles play an even greater role for graphics interfaces than they do in traditional user interfaces.

First apply the fixing-point principle to determine the type of user interface. Section 2.2 pointed out that a user interface with menu selection screens and data-entry panels fixes earlier than one with free-format commands and keywords (which must be parsed and interpreted at run time). Earlier fixing selects frequent activities with function keys on a terminal, buttons (on a device such as an ATM), or direct manipulation with a mouse.

Item 1 in Table 2.7 applies the fixing-point principle to menu design. One menu hierarchy is shown in Figure 2.8(a). This was the first prototype of the "QED" graphical queueing network modeling research project. QED was a state-of-the-art tool in 1983; even so, it taught developers the value of applying the principles to avoid cumbersome interfaces. The newer version of the tool, "GQUE" is shown in Figure 2.8 (b) and is described throughout this section.[7] Item 1 addresses the following QED problem. Suppose a user wants to start the QED tool and then describe a model. The user first sees the level-1 menu, makes a selection (Edit model), and next sees the corresponding level-2-Edit menu, and so on. The user must navigate through three menus before the desired action (add a node) is fixed to the instructions that accomplish the action. In the GQUE alternative in Figure 2.8 (b), the most frequent actions from the leaves of the QED menu tree (such as adding queues and arcs) are in dedicated areas on the screen. Because they are selected directly with a pointing device (a mouse), GQUE fixes instructions to desired actions earlier. On devices with more limited screen area, fix frequent actions early with small icons, and fix less frequent actions later by grouping them into pop-up menus. If your system has no pointing device (such as mouse, track ball, or light pen), apply the same concepts to fix function keys to frequent actions.

With GQUE (Figure 2.8[b]), users can select any of the symbols shown under the "Add" command box in the menu area (on the top-right side of the screen). The selected symbol can be placed anywhere on the grid on the left side of the screen. **Item 2** considers two fixing alternatives, as detailed in the following example.

---

[7]QED was developed in 1983 by graduate students at Duke University: Douglas Elliott, David Harger, Vijay Naik, and Roger Smith. GQUE was developed in 1985 by another Duke graduate student, Thad Jennings.

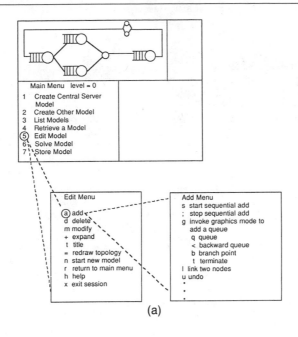

Main Menu   level = 0

1   Create Central Server
    Model
2   Create Other Model
3   List Models
4   Retrieve a Model
⑤   Edit Model
6   Solve Model
7   Store Model

Edit Menu

ⓐ add
d   delete
m   modify
+   expand
t   title
=   redraw topology
n   start new model
r   return to main menu
h   help
x   exit session

Add Menu

s   start sequential add
;   stop sequential add
g   invoke graphics mode to
    add a queue
q   queue
<   backward queue
b   branch point
t   terminate
l   link two nodes
u   undo
    •
    •
    •

(a)

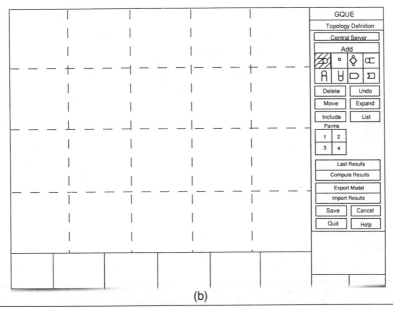

(b)

FIGURE 2.8

Two Menu-Design Strategies. In (a) the user must navigate through three menus in the hierarchy to add a node. The strategy in (b) has only two menus. All drawing commands appear on the first screen; all model evaluation commands appear on a second menu. Users infrequently switch between the two menus. Fixing of the frequent add-node action is much earlier with Strategy (b).

TABLE 2.7
USER-INTERFACE DESIGN

Item	Principle	Maxim
1. Menu design for frequent actions	Fixing-point	Use direct selection (icons + mouse, function keys, etc.) to fix frequent actions to special buttons or function keys rather than layers of menus.
2. Fix frequent actions and symbols early	Fixing-point	Assign most frequent actions and symbols to mouse buttons (Example 2.5), to function keys, or to first-level menus.
3. Fix cursor location to selected actions and symbols	Fixing-point	Predefine centers of gravity for quickly matching screen regions to single symbols or actions (Example 2.6).
4. Reference information	Fixing-point Locality-design	Display and retain information that is likely to be referenced later. Do not cover results that are likely to be needed again with transient information (Example 2.7).
5. Fix frequently used sequences of actions	Fixing-point	For frequently used sequences of actions, automatically execute the next action in sequence, and provide an exit to handle unlikely actions. Avoid asking questions.
6. Fixing screens to programs	Fixing-point Proc. vs. freq.	Minimize the number of screens to accomplish user actions, and group screens and programs to minimize overhead (Example 2.8).
7. Defining screen contents	Temporal and spatial locality-design	Cluster data that is needed within a short period of time in the same screen region; omit other data that is unlikely to be needed at the same time, and structure it hierarchically by likely frequency of use.
8. Match device capabilities to software uses	Effectual locality-design	Use device intelligence, high resolution, color, and windowing to decrease the number of user interactions and maximize perception of results.
9. Match amount of data needed to the amount displayed or entered	Degree locality-design	Use default values to minimize user interactions.

(continued)

TABLE 2.7
(Continued)

Item	Principle	Maxim
10. Hierarchical results	Proc. vs. freq.	Limit processing to most likely needed results; provide more by request.
11. Display reminders or expect the user to remember?	Proc. vs. freq.	Compute the processing to produce reminders, the frequency they are needed, and the number of erroneous responses (without reminders) to determine the best strategy.
12. Placement of data requiring exclusive use	Shared-resources	Segregate shared data from exclusive-use data on screens when shared data alone is useful and exclusive use encounters long delays.
13. Use interactive device intelligence?	Parallel processing	Use asynchronous processing on interactive devices when the response time speedup offsets the overhead (communication and synchronization) processing.
14. Focus on frequent user functions	Centering	Minimize the number of screens and interactions and the processing required to accomplish frequent end-to-end user tasks.
15. Evaluate user interfaces	Instrumenting	Collect the number of times each function is selected, the response time for functions, and the time to complete end-to-end user actions; identify sequences of functions.

EXAMPLE 2.5: Fix Frequent Actions and Picture Symbols

There are at least two alternatives for fixing the desired symbols:

1. *Late fixing.* The user selects the symbol to be added everytime it is placed.

```
Draw-topology;
--Late fixing

while not finished loop
    Select-symbol;
    Select-location;
end loop;
```

(continued)

EXAMPLE 2.5 (*Continued*)

2. *Use mouse buttons for earlier fixing:* Dedicate one mouse button to the frequent function "change the current symbol to the next in sequence." The next in sequence is left to right and top to bottom, and the symbols are placed according to frequency of use—the most likely to be needed are first. The user can thus select a symbol with a mouse button without going back to the menu area.

```
Draw-topology
--Earlier fixing

while not finished loop
Select-symbol;
      while same-symbol loop
      Select-location
      end loop;
end loop;
```

In GQUE, the top-left symbol is typically used more than 90 percent of the time, so GQUE automatically makes it the current picture symbol after every placement (another example of early fixing). Thus, 90 percent of the time only the inner loop (select-location) in Strategy 2 executes.

Note that Strategy 2 is not only convenient for users; it also saves "pits of quicksand processing" that unnecessarily pulls system performance down—everytime you move a mouse from one side of a screen to the other, software must track the mouse movement and draw the cursor at the corresponding screen location. Everytime you select a picture symbol, by pointing to it and pressing a button, many lines of code execute to identify your choice.

□

The next example, **Item 3,** illustrates the processing necessary to fix your selection to the corresponding program instructions.

EXAMPLE 2.6: Fix Cursor Location to Instructions

When you push a mouse button, the system generates an interrupt and passes the x-y coordinates of the cursor's current screen location. Note that any of the hundreds of x-y coordinates that fall within the "Delete" box boundary (shown in Figure 2.8[b]) must be fixed to the instructions that do the deletion.

1. Late fixing checks the coordinates of the cursor location against the coordinates of the box boundaries after the button is pushed as follows:

```
Interpret-request (x, y);
--Late fixing
:
if     (x ≥ left-side-del)
and    (x ≤ right-side-del)
```

(continued)

EXAMPLE 2.6 (*Continued*)

```
and     (y ≤ top-del)
and     (y ≥ bottom-del)
   then call-delete-rtn;
--comparisons for other menu choices
```

2. Earlier fixing uses a "gravity" feature. You predefine centers of gravity, such as grid intersection points or the center of a command box. When the mouse moves, the software computes the nearest center of gravity in the direction of the cursor movement. Note that the software controls the cursor echoed on the screen: It may or may not "jump" to the nearest center of gravity, depending on whether you want smooth movements or whether you need to know the actual cursor interpretations. With gravity, the button-push sends the coordinates of the nearest center of gravity, so the comparison of coordinates (to fix the action to the instructions) is much faster:

```
Interpret-request (grav-x, grav-y);
--Earlier fixing


   :
if      (grav-x = x-center-del)
and     (grav-y = y-center-del)
   then call-delete-rtn;
```

(where grav-x and grav-y are set by the cursor tracking routine)

3. In GQUE, fixing can be even earlier because of the regular shape and placement of command boxes. The following pseudocode checks the x coordinate first to see if the selected command is in the left or right column:

```
Interpret-request (grav-x, grav-y);
--Even earlier fixing
   :
if (x = x-center-of-left-boxes)
     then
           case y is
           when
                y = y-center-del =⟩ call-delete-rtn;
                y = y-center-move =⟩ call-move-rtn;
           end case;
              :
        oloo
     :
end if;
```

Note that **earlier fixing will not always be cost-effective** because of the cost of retaining the connection. GQUE runs on a workstation with an extra graphics processor, which tracks the cursor and computes centers of gravity while the workstation's central processor does other work. Gravity for early fixing is appropriate because GQUE must frequently fix a region on the screen to an action or a symbol, and the cost of retaining the fixing connection is low. Early fixing would not be cost-effective if the cursor tracking and gravity calculation ran on a busy mainframe shared by many users, because the gravity calculation is similar to the command-identification statement in Strategy 1 and it executes more often.

The fixing-point principle also provides guidance for where to place results on the screen and how long to retain them. Consider a hypothetical scenario for viewing information for a large multiple-line-item purchase order (**Item 4**), illustrated in Example 2.7.

EXAMPLE 2.7: Retain Reference Information

The purchase order consists of the header information (such as the purchaser's name, address, dates, a contact person, telephone number, the salesperson responsible, and so forth), and 50–100 line items. In a hypothetical (dominant workload) usage scenario it is highly likely that some line items will need clarification. So design the screens to keep likely-to-be-needed header information on the screen (such as names and telephone numbers of people to contact for clarification) as you scroll through line items. This makes the system easier to use and saves the quicksand processing for repeating the retrieval and retransmitting the header information.   □

Try to segregate high-use data from data that is *occasionally* needed, and then only for a short time, such as line-item descriptions, suppliers' names, or "help" information. For example, if you have an intelligent display device, use a pop-up window to display transient data, and keep the (high-use) covered data in a device buffer. Then you can redisplay the covered data without reprocessing or retransmission. Alternatively, design your screens with a dedicated area for displaying occasional data, so that it does not displace high-use data that would later have to be regenerated. For example, GQUE uses a message-area rectangle in the lower-right portion of the screen (Figure 2.8[b]) for occasional messages.

Strive for early fixing for frequently used sequences of actions (**Item 5**). Envision a frequently used data-entry scenario with the following five steps:

1. The user selects the data-entry transaction from the transaction-selection screen.
2. The data-entry panel is displayed; the user types the requested data and transmits it.
3. The system processes the information and returns the status of the transaction.
4. The user acknowledges the status response.
5. The system displays the transaction-selection screen, and the user begins Step 1 again.

When the users have many transactions to enter and they must return to the selection screen between transactions, fixing is later than necessary. Earlier fixing automatically returns to the data entry panel when an entry is complete; you can provide a special exit (such as a function key or escape key) to allow the user to return to the transaction-selection screen as needed. This fixes the completion of one action to the beginning of the next one, which is desirable when there are many data-entry transactions. **Avoid asking questions:** Do not make Step 6 the question, "Another data entry?" It makes fixing later than the example shown and is annoying to frequent data-entry users.

In some systems, fixing the screens and panels seen by the users, to the corresponding programs, is a search-light performance problem (**Item 6**). Consider the following bizarre example:[8]

EXAMPLE 2.8: Purchase Order Program and Screen Fixing

In this example, the following sequence of events occurs:

1. The user selects the "enter purchase order" transaction.
2. Program 1 receives the request and displays the "enter authorization" screen.
3. The user enters the authorization data.
4. Program 2 receives the data, verifies its accuracy, and displays the "PO Header" screen, and so on.

Figure 2.9(a) shows a separate program for each screen seen by the user. In this example, fixing the programs to the actions is expensive. The following processing occurs each time the user enters information:

1. The program number is matched against a table of all known programs.
2. The program code is located; it may require loading from secondary memory (a page fault or file I/O).
3. Status tables are updated with the program's location and execution state.
4. Memory is allocated to hold local data, etcetera.

Analogous program termination overhead executes after each screen is displayed. An alternative implementation is in Figure 2.9(b): Only one program initiates when the "enter purchase order" transaction is selected, and it terminates after the last line item is entered. This saves a substantial amount of program-fixing overhead.

□

---

[8]If you are a performance expert, this example may seem unreal. Yet I have encountered several large systems with this phenomenon. The tools they use make it is easier for programmers to write separate programs than to write one program that interacts with the screen. The programmers thought that they had used good structured programming techniques. Remember that programmers and analysts may not be aware of the ramifications of such implementation decisions.

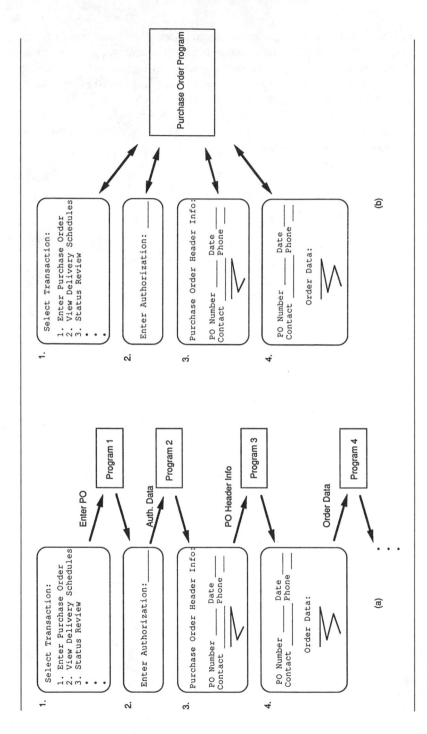

FIGURE 2.9
Fixing Screens to Programs. Strategy (a) fixes a separate program for each screen; (b) fixes one program to several screens. Note that locality would be better if screens were combined.

In one system like that in Example 2.8, the individual programs executed an average of 20 instructions, but each triggered over 10,000 instructions for program initiation and termination. The total system consisted of about 2,000 transactions. With the original strategy in Figure 2.9(a), each transaction executed an average of 20 programs. Compute the total program processing compared to the overhead.

Item 7, locality design for user interfaces suggests that data needed within a short period of time should be closely located on the screen and data not needed at the same time should not be mixed. Screen 4 in Figure 2.9's hypothetical purchase order combines the header with line items, because users often need both within a short period of time. When the amount of data to be viewed is much greater than

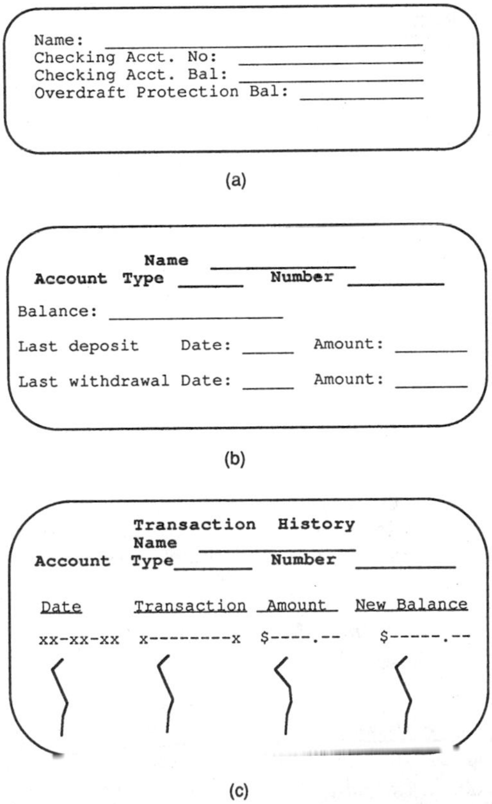

(a)

(b)

(c)

FIGURE 2.10
Screens Designed for Temporal Locality Segregate Data Based on Frequency of use. High-frequency data is on (a), medium-frequency data is on (b), and infrequent data is on (c).

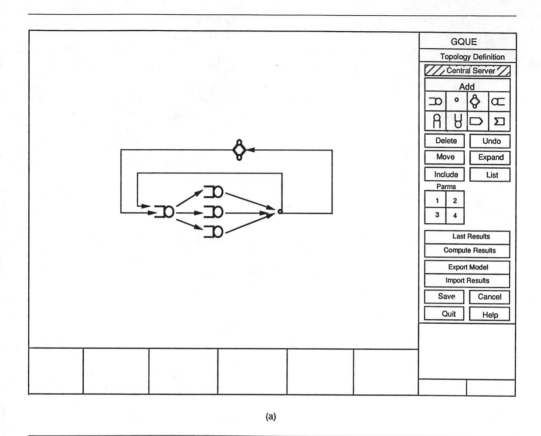

(a)

FIGURE 2.11
Default Pictures Improve Degree Locality. The user creates the picture in (a) by selecting the central-server menu option. One additional menu selection in (b) modifies the picture. Appropriate defaults minimize user interactions.

the screen capacity, and it is likely that all the data is needed, improve locality by transmitting all the purchase order data to an intelligent device, and execute all the viewing manipulation commands (such as paging through data, locating specific information, printing hard copies) on it without intervention from the central processor. This applies when most data is needed. If it is more likely that only a small amount is needed, structure screens hierarchically, based on frequency of data use. Transmit only the information likely to be needed. Figure 2.10 illustrates a hierarchical display for bank account information. The information needed most frequently is on the first screen (a), information needed occasionally is on the next screen (b), and infrequently needed information is on the third (c). Even though it would fit on one screen, the data is not mixed, and each screen is transmitted to the user only when it is requested.

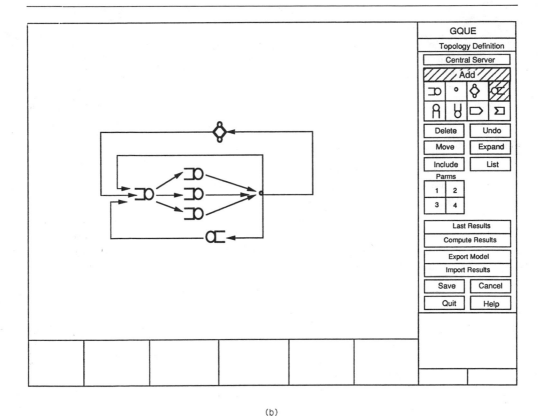

(b)

FIGURE 2.11 (*Continued*)

Effectual locality, **Item 8,** matches display-device capabilities to the software requirements and design. Device capabilities include:

□ *Bit-mapped graphics,* so that only changed data need be transmitted

□ *Device intelligence,* for buffering data and manipulating it without intervention from the central processor

□ *Windowing capabilities,* for viewing and manipulating information concurrently

□ *High-resolution screens,* for matching the size of the information displayed its value at that stage in the processing (the primary information being viewed or manipulated should be large, such as the specifications for the "current module" of interest; other useful information can be smaller, such as a miniature replica of a data-flow diagram showing all modules that interface with the "current module")

    □ *Color displays,* for providing perceptual feedback to the user that may aid in problem solving

Thus, effectual locality design calls for using device intelligence, high resolution, color, and windowing to minimize the number of interactions with the users.

    Degree locality matches the amount of data needed to the amount displayed or entered (**Item 9**). Degree locality is better when you can liberally use default values and only process the exceptions. The ATM quick-withdrawal scenario uses default values for the withdrawal amount, the account (checking), and for session continuation. Figure 2.11(a) shows GQUE's default picture for a queueing network model that one menu selection creates. It is frequently created and then modified with a few screen interactions (as in [b]), thus substantially reducing the total processing to create a new picture.

    The processing versus frequency tradeoff principle also applies to user interfaces. Item 2 in Table 2.4 applied the principle to evaluate the direct GETALL command for getting all matching items. **Item 10** decreases processing with a hierarchical "help" command: You reduce processing if you (only) remind the user of the most-likely-forgotten facts (list a command's required parameters). Frequency may increase, because occasionally users may also request the longer help to get additional facts.

    Figure 2.12 reduces the number of inputs by increasing processing with an "Include" command (to incorporate a predefined model). "Include" can either remind the user of the model names, as in (a), or assume that she or he remembers the name, as in (b). Automatically displaying the list may reduce the number of user inputs (due to errors and to separately selecting the "list" *and* the "include" commands); for frequent, expert users the list is unnecessary. **Item 11** suggests: Compute the processing and the expected frequency to determine the best choice for your application. Do not ask whether you should display the names. If you want to provide both options, respond with (b), and display the list if the user enters a "?".

    The shared-resource principle designs screens that segregate data that is derived from shared files from data that requires exclusive access (**Item 12**). It is appropriate when the shared data alone is useful, especially when there may be a long delay to obtain the non-shared data. The amount of data requiring exclusive access is a data storage issue and is discussed in the next section.

    Several of the earlier examples and **Item 13** suggest asynchronous parallel processing on the mainframe and interactive device (paging through large amounts of data, collecting transactions at the ATM, and transmitting batches of information). Future systems will likely also need to evaluate communication and synchronization overhead of multiple processes that communicate with a single interactive device.

    As usual, the centering principle focuses attention on frequent user functions (**Item 14**). They must meet their performance goals if the overall system is to be

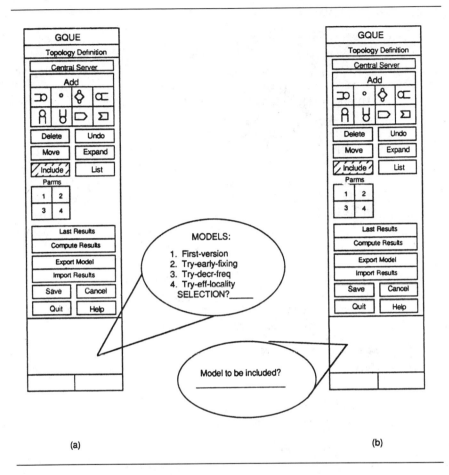

(a)   (b)

FIGURE 2.12
Two Processing Versus Frequency Tradeoffs. The strategy in (a) increases processing by fetching and displaying model names. The strategy in (b) executes less
processing when the user knows the names.

acceptable. Thus, one of the most significant SPE steps is: **Minimize the number
of screens and interactions and the amount of processing needed to accomplish the frequent end-to-end user tasks.**

The instrumenting principle calls for collecting data on the number of times
each user function (such as menu choice) is selected. Also needed are the time for
users to respond to each screen and, if multiple screens are required, the time to
complete the end-to-end user function (**Item 15**).

These are only a few of the ways that the general principles can be applied to
user interfaces. With experience you will likely discover many more.

2.3.2 Data Organization

Data organization determines the number of I/O operations to acquire, display, store, retrieve, and update data. The following analogy demonstrates the magnitude of the effect of I/O: Consider a computer system capable of executing one instruction in 1 microsecond and one I/O operation in 30 milliseconds. If you scale these times to proportional units that humans can perceive, if the instruction took 1 second, the I/O operation would require over 8 hours![9] Thus, each I/O operation requires a substantial amount of time relative to instruction execution time. Furthermore, the mapping of I/O operations coded in a program (logical I/O) to the number of (physical) I/O operations required to accomplish the action is not always 1:1. One logical I/O may require zero physical I/Os if the data is organized sequentially, it is blocked, and the block containing the requested data is already in a buffer in primary memory at the time the request is made. At the other extreme, if the logical I/O is a random retrieval from a DBMS with a complex index structure, run-time binding, and a complex mapping between the physical data and the logical data, many physical I/Os (perhaps 20 or more) may be required for each logical I/O (because database tables must be accessed to locate the data). **For responsiveness, select a data organization that minimizes the number of physical I/Os required.**

There are three primary considerations for data organization:

1. *The structure of the information:* its aggregation into files, records, and data items, and the relationship between aggregates such as ordering and hierarchy

2. *The information content:* its representation and its format

3. *The location of the data:* the physical location of the files, the records within files, and the data items within the records

Thus, data organization decisions concern *what* the structure and contents should be, and *where* data should be located. Table 2.8 summarizes the principles applied to these data organization decisions.

The fixing-point principle applies to when and how often the decisions are made. **Item 1** addresses database management systems; fixing the requested results to the data format and location at run time is more expensive than fixing at compilation time. The disadvantage of compilation-time fixing (binding) is that when the structure of the database changes, the programs that access it must be recompiled, which is impractical if the structure frequently changes. Thus, to

---

[9]Many medium-sized computers have similar ratios of instruction execution speed to I/O completion time (1:30,000). Check the ratio for your computer and scale it to proportional seconds and hours. Some large computers have a ratio of 1:200,000. This ratio is the motivation for multiprocessing systems: While one process waits for I/O, another process uses the CPU. Multiprocessing improves system throughput and resource utilization, but the time that each process spends waiting for the I/O completion still affects its response time.

TABLE 2.8
DATA ORGANIZATION

Item	Principle	Maxim
1. Binding data format and location	Fixing-point	Structure data to make compilation-time fixing practical for high-frequency functions.
2. Temporary data creation and retention a. ATM geographic analysis b. Random database additions	Fixing-point	Pre- or post-process data, using data structures tailored to the processing, to minimize physical I/Os.
3. Streamlined database structures: personnel database	Temporal locality	Cluster together data items that are used together.
4. Distributed data location	Spatial locality	Place data where it is most likely to be needed.
5. Closeness of logical to physical data organizations: a. Database structure b. Binary search—table > real memory	Effectual locality	Evaluate the total time to locate and retrieve the desired data.
6. Data structure and storage medium size	Degree locality	Use buffering, blocking, and cached storage devices to reduce I/Os due to size mismatches.
7. Cluster data items according to exclusive use	Shared-resources	Segregate data—lock only the fields that require exclusive use.
8. Distributed data organizations	Parallel processing	Cluster data to minimize communication and synchronization.
9. Conflicting data organizations for various workloads	Centering	Minimize physical I/O for dominant workload functions. Include sort processing to compute the total resource requirements.
10. Evaluating data organizations	Instrumenting	Instrument software to measure data access patterns and the use of results.

make compilation-time fixing practical, strive for a database structure that makes data items used by dominant workload functions stable (not affected by other database changes).

Item 2 applies the fixing-point principle to "temporary data." Consider the hypothetical geographic analysis of ATM usage in Example 2.9. The principle suggests using similar transformations to map complex database structures into temporary, simpler files for faster processing. For example, it is expensive to make additions to random locations in a database. It is often quicker to temporarily create a "flat file" to hold many additions until all are collected, to sort them into the proper order, then to insert the ordered items into the database.

EXAMPLE 2.9: Temporarily Fix Geographic Data

A bank analyst desires a matrix, such as the following, that shows each ATM region and the fraction of its transactions that use accounts in each of the other regions.

FRACTION OF TRANSACTIONS FOR EACH COMBINATION

Customer Region \ ATM Region	1	2	3	4
1	.70	.20	.07	.03
2	.19	.80	.01	.00
3	.01	.09	.60	.30
4	.02	.03	.05	.90

This means that each account must be fixed to a region. The earliest fixing includes the region in every account record. Alternatively, a mapping file could correlate account addresses (perhaps by zip codes) to regions. Similarly, ATM locations must be fixed to regions.

Suppose we elect to use a mapping file because the interval between uses for the mapping information does not justify retaining it with every account record. The process for building the matrix is: For each ATM transaction, the matrix program reads the account data, then uses the zip code to read the mapping data, and increments the total for the corresponding region. The latest fixing point stores mapping data in an external file that must be accessed for each transaction:

```
--Latest fixing point
while more-transactions loop
        Get-transaction;
        Get-account-data;
        Get-region-from-map-file (transaction-zip);
        Add-to-total;
end loop;
```

(continued)

EXAMPLE 2.9 (*Continued*)

The earlier fixing below "preprocesses" the mapping data in the first phase of the program to create a region table in virtual memory:

```
--Earlier fixing
Load-map-file-to-table;
while more-transactions loop
        Get-transaction;
        Get-account-data;
        Look-up-region-in-table (transaction-zip);
        Add-to-total;
end loop;
```

It is created (and fixed) temporarily and retained only while the program executes. As before, make sure the cost of retaining the fixing information (additional memory) leads to a net gain.   □

Item 3 specifies that data items used together (temporal locality) should be clustered together (have good spatial locality). Instead, designers often use logical relationships to determine external file structures (rather than temporal references).

EXAMPLE 2.10: Temporal Locality Versus Logical Relationships for Structuring Files

The principle can be applied illustratively to personnel data. Traditional personnel systems stored all employee information in the same record. All the information was seldom needed at one time. When printing payroll checks, for example, the name, social security number, net pay, and pertinent data explaining the calculation are needed; but other information about the employee (such as years in current job, or previous job title) is not needed. Database management systems replaced earlier flat files and separated the data into multiple related entities (files, relations, segments, etcetera). A hypothetical personnel data base structure is shown in Figure 2.13. The logical breakdown appears to be reasonable: Personal data, job history, payment history, time-log data, and payroll data are conceptually distinct and are clustered accordingly. The locality is better than the one-big-record structure. For printing checks, though, multiple clusters must be accessed (personal data, time-log data, and payroll data). So temporal locality is not good. Actually, with Figure 2.13's structure, there are few scenarios that access only one cluster. One of the chapter exercises studies temporal alternatives.   □

Data management systems are supposed to separate the conceptual view of data from its physical structure. Use this capability effectively—explore temporal locality of data items (as well as logical relationships) when designing the physical data structure.

Item 4 uses spatial locality to locate data in a distributed database: Data is placed in the location where it is most likely to be needed. If distributed data must

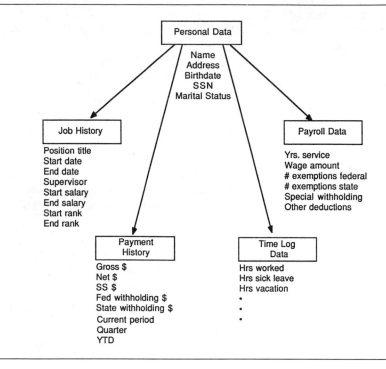

FIGURE 2.13
A Hypothetical Database Organization with Fields Clustered According to Logical Relationships. SPE recommends clustering to improve temporal locality—fields frequently used together should be clustered together.

reside in a remote location, the fixing-point principle determines when it should be accessed. Late fixing gets data from the remote location when it is referenced. Earlier fixing transports data earlier, at run-initiation time or even the beginning of the day.

Note that several fixing-point examples earlier in this section can also be viewed as locality design examples (by focusing on *what* is done rather than *when*). For the geographic analysis scenario, the spatial locality of the data for mapping addresses to regions is better when it is in primary memory than when it is in an external file or database.

Effectual locality design, in **Item 5,** addresses the closeness of the logical to the physical database design. It also applies to the design of internal data structures. For example, a binary search into an ordered data structure is usually best for random retrievals from a large table. However, if the table does not fit entirely in real memory, the binary search probes into the table may result in page faults, making the average access time per probe greater. Thus, effectual locality deals with the total time to locate and retrieve the desired data item: the number of probes into the table and the time per probe (the instructions to make the probe plus page-fault delays)—SPE models help to quantify total time.

Degree locality matches the size of the data structures and the storage medium (**Item 6**). While programs usually need small amounts of data, storage devices process larger amounts more efficiently. For example, a program may only need four words of data, but many disk devices transfer a minimum of one sector. Buffering, blocking, and direct-access storage devices with cache memories improve the closeness.

The shared-resource principle advocates data organizations that maximize sharing (**Item 7**). The granularity of the data organization should match the granularity of the locking that may be required. When possible, segregate data so that only fields that require exclusive use are locked, and allow simultaneous sharing of other fields.

The parallel processing principle (**Item 8**) applies primarily to distributed computing systems. A properly distributed data organization reduces the overhead required for communication and synchronization of processes executing on separate processors, thus making parallel processing viable. Improper organization increases this overhead to the point where parallel processing is no longer effective.

Centering, in **Item 9,** calls for selecting a data organization that minimizes the physical I/O operations for frequent requests (dominant workload functions). For external files and databases there may be conflicting workloads; random access may dominate during the day, for example, while sequential access may dominate for overnight workloads. Similarly, data locality may differ when one batch run needs only a debit table, another needs only a credit table, and prime-time processing always needs both. This situation requires a compromise. You could either optimize the data organization for the most important workload (generally the prime-time workload), or you might need to map the data organization used during the day to a temporary data organization that expedites the nightly processing and, when the nightly processing is complete, create a new daily file. Use the SPE models to determine the best overall organization. Do not use old (batch-oriented) structures out of habit, as happens all too often. For example, measurement tools produce workload profile reports with the total number of times each program executes per day (and its resource usage). On commercial computer installations running production work (as opposed to editing, compiling, and testing), you commonly find that around *30 percent of all the program executions are file sorts!* The sorts use about 30 percent of the total CPU time consumed by programs and do a large proportion of the I/Os. Check the measurements for your installation and see how much "shuffling" you do. A substantial amount of time and resources are spent just reorganizing data. Thus, when you examine alternative data organizations, be sure to include all the sort processing in your calculations.

Item 10 suggests that to evaluate data organizations, you need to instrument the software to collect the frequency of accesses to files, records, and data items. You also need measurements that tell how often the physical data organization differs from the format required by programs and users.

2.3.3 Information Hiding

Information hiding is the principle of hiding implementation details to minimize the dependence of each module on the internal structure of other modules. [PAR72, PAR79]. It hides both data organizations and the implementation of operations on the data. For example, consider the operation FIND ⟨data item⟩. The software *hides* the internal format of ⟨data item⟩; it could be binary, decimal, packed, etcetera. Likewise, it hides the format of the structure that contains ⟨data item⟩, as well as the method of accessing the data structure (sequential search, binary search, direct access, etcetera).

Parnas recommends using the information-hiding principle to "design systems for change." With his method, aspects of systems that are likely to change become "secrets" that are hidden from the rest of the system. Aspects of systems that are unlikely to change can be operations available to, or known by, the rest of the system. When you hide secrets, you localize the effect of changes to them. Thus, the internal format of ⟨data item⟩, its data structure, and the search techniques are secrets that may change without affecting other parts of the system. Software Cost Reduction (SCR) is the formal software development method that embodies Parnas's earlier design-for-change ideas [CLE85, HEN80].

Two *methods of implementing the information-hiding principle* are object-oriented programming and abstract data types (ADTs) [BOO83, LIN76, MEY88]. They may be used with SCR or independently. **Objects** and **ADTs** encapsulate their data definitions and the allowable operations on their data and hide the implementation details from their users. Objects and ADTs generally correspond directly to entities in the user's domain, such as a document, a desk top, an altimeter, or a bank account. For a bank account, both the internal representation and the location of the account number and the associated information are hidden. Examples of operations on the account information are: add an account, get account information, change account information, or valid? (is this a valid account number?).

With information hiding, software is less dependent on the format, location, and current allowable operations than might otherwise be the case. Furthermore, since the objects generally occur in the user's domain, changes tend to affect the way objects are stored or processed, not their existence. For example, the only way a program can access *any* of the account object's data is to call the operation that gets and returns the requested data. Therefore, it is easy to add security checking or encryption to the account. You need to modify only the account object's code; you do not need to change all the programs that use the account. A disadvantage of object-oriented programming is that, without careful implementation, response times may be unacceptable. For example, everytime you need account data, you call a corresponding procedure. Thus, the overhead for procedure calls for the operations may be excessive, the granularity of the data items may be too small (if each individual data item is stored separately), or the locality may be suboptimal. The potential inefficiencies are not inherent defects of information hiding, but without SPE they often occur.

SPE advocates paying close attention to the key operations. Information hiding makes the fundamental assumption that operations are unlikely to change. They may be used throughout the rest of the system, so changes to the operations (such as adding a data item to an operation) can propagate extensively because the change affects *all* references to the operation. Other changes, such as using a different search strategy, are secrets and do not propagate. Therefore, early in the lifecycle, SPE focuses on the operations, evaluates their performance, and resolves problems before they propagate. The internal data representation is easier to

TABLE 2.9
INFORMATION HIDING

Item	Principle	Maxim
1. Key operations	Centering	Look for frequently used operations and minimize their processing. Look for combinations of data items frequently needed together and create special operations for them.
2. I/O for each data item?	Fixing-point	Retrieve all data items for user when multiple requests are likely.
3. Retain data for multiple users?	Fixing-point	Retain data for multiple users when more requests are likely within a short period of time.
4. Fix code to desired operation	Fixing-point	Preprocess and insert code inline for high-frequency operations.
5. Object data and operation choices	Locality-design	Create objects (data items and operations) for frequently used user objects and functions.
6. Sequential retrieval of logical records composed from multiple physical records	Locality-design Proc. vs. freq.	Use hierarchical objects to reduce the overhead processing per logical block.
7. Locking within objects	Shared-resources	Define operations to control request fragments and duration of the lock. Make lock granularity a secret so changes do not propagate.
8. Assigning objects to processors	Parallel processing	Model the communication overhead for operations to determine the optimal assignment of objects to processors.
9. Evaluating object effectiveness	Instrumenting	Record the number of times each operation is called, request patterns, operations' resource requirements, and response times.

change later, so it is not a key consideration, but it is just as easy to do it right the first time.

Sections 2.3.2 and 2.3.4 address internal data representation issues; the remainder of this section addresses the **operations on objects.** The important issues are identifying the operations that are key to responsiveness, fixing early the data needed for the operations, properly retaining the fixing connection, and appropriately decomposing information into objects. Table 2.9 summarizes the following applications.

The centering principle (**Item 1**) calls for identifying the operations most frequently requested and minimizing their processing. Moreover, centering may find new operations that are needed. For example, an account object may have the following data and a separate operation to fetch each item: name, address, social security number, and balance. If a customer wishes to open another account, and the software is to use the information from the first account, it must make three procedure calls to the operations get-name, get-address, and get-social-security-number. This function is not likely to be a dominant workload function; however, if it were, you would need an additional operation for "get all account information" or even "create new account." Look for combinations of data items that are frequently needed together, and create special operations for them.

The fixing-point principle determines when the operations are fixed and how long connections are retained (**Item 2**). Consider Example 2.11.

EXAMPLE 2.11: Fixing Data for Objects

An account object has operations for get-name, get-address, and so forth. The code for each operation performs an I/O to retrieve the desired data element as depicted in Figure 2.14(a). This is fine if the dominant workload functions contain random requests for data elements. But, if they are likely to request multiple data items for the same account, fixing is earlier if all data items are retrieved when the first is requested and are retained for later use.[10] Each operation checks to see if the desired data item is in memory, or if an I/O is needed, as in Figure 2.14(b).

If the object is reentrant and multiple, concurrent processes interface with it, explore the cost of retaining the fixing connection versus expected performance gains (**Item 3**). Late fixing uses the same operation as in (a), and lets the I/O routine check to see if the desired data is in one of its buffers before it starts the physical I/O operation, as in Figure 2.14 (c). Earlier fixing retrieves and retains multiple accounts in its own data structure, one for each user; each operation then checks to see if it has the desired account, or if an I/O is needed, as in (d). Note that (b) only keeps the most recent account, whereas (d) keeps the most recent account for each user.

□

---

[10]Fixing is also earlier if the account data elements are stored together—if not, the locality principle applies, as described later.

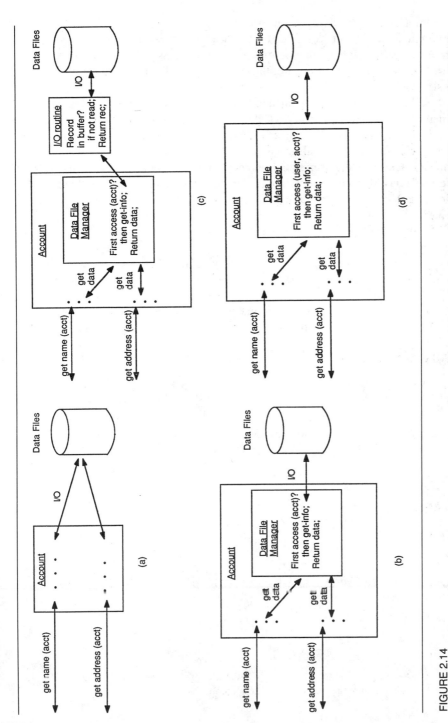

FIGURE 2.14

Choices for Fixing Data Within Objects. In (a) each operation performs an I/O, so fixing is late (even though I/O routines may find data in buffers). Fixing is earlier in (b)—the data file manager keeps all data items for the last account referenced. When multiple users may share the object, (c)'s data file manager retains only the most recent account and relies on the I/O routines to recover accounts for earlier users, while (d) uses earlier fixing to retain the most recent account for each user.

Item 4 applies the fixing-point principle to fix the object's code. If every operation requires a procedure call, the overhead will likely be excessive. However, you fix earlier (at compilation time) if you preprocess and insert the object's code inline. Preprocessing eliminates the procedure calls for high-frequency operations.

Locality design applies to both data representation and operations, as in **Item 5.** There are two aspects of closeness: the closeness of the object to the physical processor (as before), and the object's closeness to the external (user) domain. Effectual locality calls for both to be close. Thus, you need an object for each significant element in the user's environment, such as accounts, statements, and tax forms. You also need an operation for frequent user requests, such as "display replica of last statement," rather than a separate operation to get each field on a statement.

Ideally, the object should also be close to the physical resources—for example, by clustering account data items needed together into the same physical record. Frequent scenarios sometimes lead to suboptimal data structures for other less frequent, but important scenarios. The following example studies how a DBMS applies the processing versus frequency tradeoff principle to reduce overhead when the physical records do not match the logical references (**Item 6**).

EXAMPLE 2.12: Logical Records Composed from Multiple Physical Records

A hypothetical database scenario retrieves multiple logical records, each composed from two physical records:

```
DECLARE   logical-rec CURSOR FOR
SELECT    T1.debit-amt, T1.debit-date
          T2.credit-amt, T2.credit-date

FROM      DEBIT T1, CREDIT T2

WHERE     T1.key = cust
AND       T2.key = cust
END

OPEN logical-rec
while not EOF loop
      FETCH logical-rec;
end loop;
      .

      .

      .
```

Figure 2.15(a) shows a design: For every FETCH the object's operation determines the logical-to-physical mapping, reads the physical records, and translates from physical to

(continued)

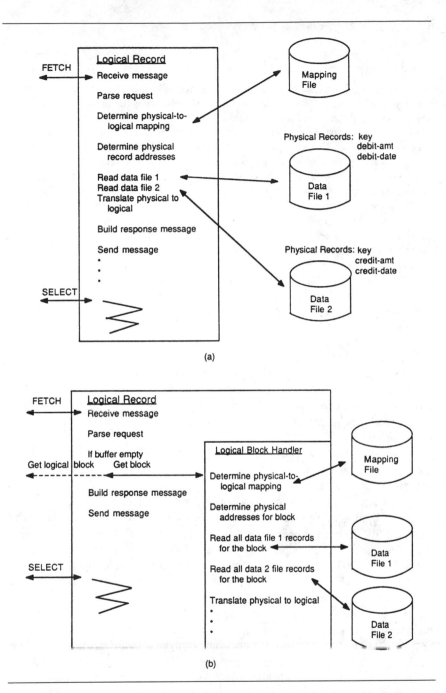

FIGURE 2.15
In (a) logical records are composed from distinct physical records for each FETCH.
The improvement in (b) composes a block of logical records to improve the locality
for subsequent FETCHes.

EXAMPLE 2.12 (*Continued*)

logical. Figure 2.15(b) shows a hierarchical object with a logical-block object nested within the logical-record object. The logical-block object determines the mapping for the block once, reads all the physical records necessary to compose the block, then performs the translation for all. The logical-to-physical mapping information is read and processed only once per logical block rather than once per record. The logical-block object does more processing per call, but it is called less frequently than the logical-record object in (a). The performance is even better if the object establishes the mapping once when logical processing begins. In the worst case, the number of physical data file I/Os is the same as (a), but it may be possible to reduce the number of physical I/Os (depending on the data organization) by reading in larger physical blocks of data. This example focuses on the logical-to-physical mapping overhead, but the locality improvement also reduces other types of DBMS overhead (determining physical record addresses, error checking, buffer management, and the like).

Note that (b)'s operation sequentially retrieves logical records; random retrievals would use the strategy in (a). If a DBMS's dominant workload functions need sequential retrievals, this customized operation *substantially* reduces processing time. If you do not include this operation in the initial design, it may be nearly impossible to later add a streamlined sequential retrieval.

□

In Figure 2.15b, you can also improve locality between the user domain and the object if you give users a "get-logical-block" operation, as shown with the dashed line. "Get logical block" only incurs the DBMS overhead for message passing and request parsing once per block instead of once per record, so responsiveness improves.

Degree locality matches the amount of data needed in the user domain, its granularity within the object, and the amount stored continuously on the storage medium.

You can also improve memory locality with hierarchical objects. You can segregate the high-frequency from the low-frequency operations with hierarchy. Then the low-frequency operations can be loaded only when needed.

The shared-resources principle applies when objects are shared by multiple users (**Item 7**). "Hold while needed" can be enforced through the operations. ATM code for the "update balance" operation can lock and free as part of its processing. Then a transaction cannot hold the lock longer than the duration of the update operation. Similarly, you can control request fragmentation by defining the number of data items handled with one operation (change [address, phone number]). If you have separate operations for data items (change [address], change [phone number]), they will make more lock requests. If you group data items into one operation, you can still hide the locking strategy and change request size as appropriate. Object locks are "secrets," so you can vary the granularity of the locks from the entire database to an account as appropriate, without propagating the change throughout the system.

If the objects may be assigned to different processors, the parallel processing principle applies (**Item 8**). The locality-design principle suggests that one object should not be divided between processors, unless you improve effectual locality by assigning an operation to a special-purpose processor. Objects are well suited to parallel processing because the operations are explicit and the processing is encapsulated; it is easy to model the communication overhead and the processing time of each operation to evaluate the cost effectiveness of various parallel processing strategies.

Instrumenting calls for collecting the number of times each operation is called, request patterns, operation resource requirements, and response times (**Item 9**).

This section applies the principles to design objects: their data structures and operations. A related paper by Booth and Wiecek describes "performance abstract data types" [BOO80]. They advocate extending abstract data type definitions to include performance specifications that facilitate the performance assessment.

2.3.4 Data Availability

Data availability addresses *when* data is available—when it is created, stored, retrieved, or converted. Choices are **upon demand** (when it is needed) or **anticipatory** (before it is needed). Data availability concepts are similar to the data organization and information-hiding concepts discussed in the previous two sections. This section looks at the interaction of organization and access strategy, using the principles, to **ensure that items used most frequently have minimal access delays.** The following applications are summarized in Table 2.10.

The centering principle (**Item 1**) identifies and focuses on the data items that are used most frequently. Early fixing anticipates data access and retrieves data before it is needed. For example, if account information is encrypted (**Item 2**) and most ATM requests require the account balance, then the software could decrypt the balance before it is needed (after session initiation, before the transaction request is received). If the name and address are infrequently needed, postpone their decryption.

The logical-block handler in Figure 2.15(b) and in **Item 3** anticipates that many logical records will be requested and composes (fixes) an entire logical block, from the physical records, before they are requested. In Section 2.3.3 this improvement reduced DBMS overhead; it also improves data availability because it reduces the average time to access a logical record. The logical-block handler in Example 2.12 accomplishes both, but that may not always be the case.

Data availability addresses *when* information is fixed as well as *how long* it is retained. The expected interval between requests to data items determines the best strategy for retaining fixing connections (**Item 4**). For example, a data item may be

TABLE 2.10
DATA AVAILABILITY

Item	Principle	Maxim
1. Key data elements	Centering	Identify frequently accessed data elements and minimize their access delay.
2. Encrypted data items	Fixing-point Proc. vs. freq.	Anticipate upcoming data accesses and decrypt them before needed.
3. Logical-block handler	Fixing-point Proc. vs. freq.	Anticipate logical-record requests and compose them before needed.
4. Bursts of requests: ATM account balance	Fixing-point	During periods of high activity retain data items in locations with minimum access delays.
5. a. High-use indices and other data elements. b. Integrate vs. interface strategies for CAD databases	Locality-design	Identify frequently used subsets of data and maintain in close locations.
6. Effect of lock overhead on access delay	Shared-resources	Use SPE models to weigh reduced lock overhead of one lock-free per session vs. expected wait time for one lock-free per update.
7. Evaluating access delays	Instrumenting	Record the accesses to data elements and their average access delay.

referenced relatively infrequently—less than 100 times per day. However, if the request pattern is "bursty," with long periods of inactivity interspersed with occasional periods of high activity (500 requests within a 5-minute interval, twice per day), then retain the data item in a location that has minimal access delay during the periods of high activity. The ATM example uses the balance for any particular account infrequently. However, within one ATM session it may be repeatedly accessed, perhaps a dozen times. You minimize access delay if you keep the account balance in a local memory variable for the duration of the ATM session, rather than performing a disk I/O for each access. Of course, you must handle security and reliability—the balance must be locked, and you must recover the balance if the system fails.

Locality design also minimizes the access delay for frequently used data items (**Item 5**). For example, the index to the account file is used in all the ATM scenarios (except perhaps those with errors), so it should have minimal access delay. Spatial locality design calls for retaining the master index in memory (as well as on disk—updated on disk when changed). Degree locality design uses a data organization with minimum access delay for the subset of accounts likely to be accessed by ATMs, as in Item 1, Table 2.3.

Another locality-design example occurs in computer-aided design (CAD) systems (**Item 5[b]**). There are two common strategies for organizing data for CAD:

1. *Integrate* the database and the analysis programs by reading data directly from the database at the time it is needed and by inserting results directly into the database as they are produced.

2. *Interface* them by first extracting all the data, feeding it into the analysis program, generating a temporary file of results, and inserting them into the database in bulk.

Strategy 2 is typical, because most of the analysis programs were written before the CAD databases were created. Many CAD experts advocate Strategy 1 due to its flexibility and the overhead involved for the data extraction (preprocessor) and insertion (postprocessor).

Apply locality design to determine which of the two strategies is best for responsiveness. Effectual locality is best if the data organization is close to the needs of the analysis program. The physical data organization within the database may not correspond closely. Even if it does, it does not have the best temporal and spatial locality because the analysis program must interface through the data management routines. If the database is used by many other CAD tools and designers, there is likely to be much more data than any single program needs, so the degree locality may not be good.

Thus, data availability is best for the interface Strategy 2 when existing drafting and analysis programs are adapted to new databases. In the future, unified CAD systems that match database structures to drafting and analysis programs will likely use Strategy 1's integration.

Access delays are minimized if processes share resources. If exclusive access is needed, there is a conflict (**Item 6**). The delay for each access is lower if the data is locked once and held until the data is no longer needed, because the code for locking and unlocking is executed fewer times. This strategy, however, may increase the time that competing jobs must wait to access the item. Performance models described later (Chapters 5 and 8) are necessary to resolve the conflict.

In **Item 7,** instrumenting for data availability calls for tabulating what data is accessed, when, and the average access delay.

2.3.5 Communication in Software Systems

SPE addresses two types of communication: internal and external. **Internal communication** sends and receives information *within a process*, such as passing parameters with procedure calls. **External communication** sends and receives information *between processes*. The processes may be executing on the same processor or on different processors (multiprocessors, distributed systems, or MIMD machines). Communication also refers to "system calls" for operating system services, such as calls to I/O service routines.

Many developers ignore communication early in the lifecycle; their rationale seems to be: it is "transparent" (the operating system handles everything as if by magic); the communication is not part of the "real work," but merely a support activity; and communication lines can transmit millions of bits per second. So why should communication be a problem? It cannot be ignored because *communication overhead is substantial*. Contemplate the work required for one of the fastest mechanisms, procedure-call parameters: An address must be passed for each parameter, the state of the calling routine must be saved, temporary storage may be needed for local variables, and the called procedure may require loading into primary memory. If the procedure only executes a few instructions, you can easily spend more time communicating than processing.

External communication over shared communication lines between processors is far more expensive than internal communication. The following is a partial list of steps required:

1. Overhead processing to allocate memory, package the message, identify the destination process and processor, and pass the message to the communication handler

2. Overhead processing to control the dialog between the sending and receiving processors (the dialog may be either data messages exchanged between processors, or data from one and multiple protocol messages exchanged between them to ensure accurate receipt):

   a. Initiating and terminating the dialog

   b. Transferring "frames" containing data and control information

   c. Coordinating the dialog so that sends occur when both processors are ready, the receiver expects the message, and it responds in finite time

   d. Detecting possible dialog errors due to problems with the communication channel or the protocol, and recovering when necessary

   e. Controlling the partitioning of messages into frames, their proper sequencing, and the receiver's reassembly

3. Processing overhead for managing shared communication lines:

   a. Controlling the routing of frames

   b. Balancing the load on routes to minimize congestion

   c. Scheduling the transmission of frames and detecting and correcting access conflicts

    d. Recognizing and extracting one's own message from all messages on the channel

4. Possible delay for access to the communication channel

5. Processing overhead for the data transmission:

    a. Synchronizing the sending and receiving of bits/characters

    b. Distinguishing between message data and control information

    c. Encoding and decoding messages

    d. Error detection and correction

6. Message transmission time

7. The overhead for the receiving processor to allocate memory to hold the message and to route it to the appropriate process

As you can see, even though the communication may be transparent and communication lines may have very high bandwidths, the processing overhead, and thus the communication time, are substantial. **Communication is often the primary performance bottleneck in large software systems,** even those that execute on a single processor. Communication is a primary SPE target early in the design process. Table 2.11 summarizes the following communication design issues.

The parallel processing principle directly addresses external communication (**Item 1**); it specifies that you should execute processes in parallel only when the processing speedup exceeds the communication overhead (and resource competition). The SPE models provide performance metrics for greater and lesser degrees of parallelism. The other principles seek to minimize the communication overhead, which may make parallel processing viable. They are discussed in the remainder of this section.

For external communication between processors, the sending and receiving processors must be fixed (**Item 2**). A dedicated communication line connecting the two processors is the earliest fixing. The latest fixing is a shared communication line with processors examining each message to determine if it is theirs.

Consider applying the fixing-point principle to communication software design as illustrated in Figure 2.16 (and in **Item 3**). For external communication the sending and receiving processes must be fixed. With the late fixing in (a), messages go to a central "mailbox," and receiving processes periodically check to see if any waiting messages are theirs. Early fixing sends messages directly to the receiving process; for example, via remote procedure calls or system calls (see Figure 2.16[b]). Intermediate fixing sends messages to the private mailbox of the receiving process, as in (c). Two alternatives for fixing (the location of) messages in a private mailbox to the receiving process are shown in (c): Late fixing (bottom right) requires the receiver to call a system routine to get the message (from a

TABLE 2.11
COMMUNICATION

Item	Principle	Maxim
1. Extent of parallelism	Parallel processing	Execute processes in parallel only when the speedup exceeds the communication overhead (and re-source competition).
2. Communication con-figuration require-ments: shared or dedicated lines	Fixing-point	Dedicated communication lines fix sending and receiving processors earlier, but at a greater configura-tion cost. Quantify the perfor-mance benefit with models to evaluate cost-effectiveness.
3. Routing mail between processes	Fixing-point Temporal locality	Route messages directly to re-ceiving processes, and provide re-trieval routines that directly read messages, to expedite message receipt.
4. Routing messages within processes	Fixing-point	Expedite routing by anticipating incoming messages.
5. Strategy for communi-cating new information	Fixing-point	Minimize retransmission (and re-processing) by communicating only when changes occur and by retaining unchanged data for re-use.
6. Nearness of communi-cating processes	Spatial locality-design	Improve locality by allocating pro-cesses to processors based on their frequency of communication and by giving them ready access to messages.
7. Interprocess commu-nication choices	Effectual locality-design	Match communication strategy to the hardware and software sup-port environment.

(continued)

location hidden to the receiver);[11] earlier fixing (top right) allows the receiver to read the message directly, perhaps via shared memory. Note that temporal locality also improves when you minimize the time between message origination and receipt.

The fixing-point principle can also determine which procedure or section of code within a program receives the message (**Item 4**), as illustrated in the follow-ing example.

---

[11]This refers to a generic mailbox: Some unspecified location (such as primary memory or disk) serves as a holding area for messages that have been sent but not yet examined by the receiver.

TABLE 2.11
(*Continued*)

Item	Principle	Maxim
8. Amount of data transmitted	Degree locality-design	Match the amount of data sent, the amount essential to the receiving process, and the communication channel capabilities.
9. Combine messages into fewer, longer messages?	Proc. vs. freq.	Include communication costs in the tradeoff calculations.
10. Competition for shared communication channels	Shared-resources	Evaluate combinations of communication overhead (scheduling time) and message size and transmission frequency (holding time) to determine the total communication costs (processing + wait + transmission).
11. Frequent workload functions and high-volume communication tasks	Centering	Minimize the amount of communication and the overhead for dominant workload functions.
12. Evaluate communication	Instrumenting	Collect message traffic data such as number of data interchanges per transaction, number of messages between origins and destinations, and message-processing times (overhead + wait + transmissions). Also collect exception data such as transmission errors, communication channel conflicts, and lack of buffer space.

EXAMPLE 2.13: Fixing Messages Within Processes

The latest fixing of messages is a central switch routine that examines each incoming message and invokes the appropriate routine:

```
--Late fixing: examine each message destination
Input-routine;
  :
Get-input (msg);
Examine-destination;
case
    when destination is
    To-A =>  call-A (msg);
```

(*continued*)

EXAMPLE 2.13 (*Continued*)

```
        To-B =>  call-B (msg);
        To-C =>  call-C (msg);
      :
    end case;
```

Earlier fixing sets a "switch" that routes subsequent messages directly to routines that expect a series of input messages. Many text editors have an "input mode" that automatically inserts subsequent characters (until input-mode termination), rather than checking to see if subsequent input is a different command. The voucher-dialog example in Figure 2.9, and the GQUE command identification (Example 2.6) are other examples of message-routing choices.[12] In the pseudocode below, process B has set a "switch" and will receive all subsequent input messages until the "switch" is turned off:

```
    --Earlier fixing: route several messages
    Input-routine;
      :
    while switch-to-B loop
          Get-more-input (msg);
          call-B (msg);        --B turns off switch when it
                                 expects no more input
    end loop;
    Get-input (msg);
    Examine-destination;
    case destination is
       when
       To-A =>  call-A (msg);
       To-B =>  call-B (msg);
       To-C =>  call-C (msg);
         :
    end case;
```

☐

Items 1 through 4 are requirements and early design issues. The principles also apply to communication implementation. **Item 5** pertains to communicating changes in pictures on graphics display devices. If part of the picture changes, send only the changed data to the graphics device, and reuse the unchanged sections. Telecommunication packages do similar processing for online edit-updates. The users request data, view it, change portions of it as required, and "enter" the re-

---

[12]Note that several of these examples are similar to the user-interface items in Section 2.3.1. This is because screen layouts and interaction scenarios are considered user-interface requirements and design issues, while I/Os to and from the interactive devices *communicate* with the device. Whether you view the topic as a communication or a user-interface problem, the principles lead you to the preferable performance alternative. It is because of the commonality in the applications that the set of seven principles is a better formulation of the design-creation concepts.

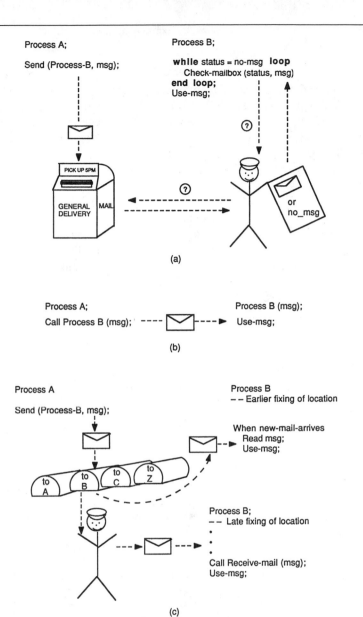

FIGURE 2.16

Fixing-point Choices for Connecting Sender and Receiver. Strategy (a) shows late fixing—messages go to a central mailbox, and processes expecting a message must repeatedly poll to see if mail has arrived; (b) shows early fixing—the sender A calls the receiver B and passes the message as a parameter; (c) shows two intermediate choices—in the strategy on the bottom right, the receiver calls a system routine, Receive-mail, while the earlier fixing shown at the top right lets the user read the mail directly.

vised data. Telecommunication support software (and hardware) checks the revised screen and only transmits (communicates) the changed fields.

Spatial locality applies to the nearness of the communicating processes (**Item 6**). The locality is better when processes are on the same processor than when they are on geographically separated processors. If you also view spatial locality as the access time to the message, then messages in shared memory have better spatial locality than messages in a mailbox that resides on a disk.

Effectual locality matches the communication strategy chosen to the software and hardware environment (**Item 7**). For example, some computer architectures support rapid context switching. On these systems, communication via procedure calls has better effectual locality than communication via message passing. Some operating systems are message-based, so the effectual locality of message passing on them is better than for other mechanisms. A more sophisticated example of communication effectual locality is the Finite Element Machine (FEM) developed at NASA Langley Research Center [LOE83, SMI82]:

EXAMPLE 2.14: Locality Design for the Finite Element Machine (FEM)

FEM's purpose was to solve finite element analysis problems such as the following. Figure 2.17(a) shows an idealized structure. The lines represent beam elements for the structure; the points where beam elements meet represent nodes. Each element has associated material properties. Forces of a specified magnitude (1000 lb. in [a]) are applied to nodes in the structure, and the finite element model solution shows the resulting displacement of the other nodes.

The FEM architecture in (b) is an MIMD computer that solves for node displacements in parallel using displacements of neighboring nodes in the problem. The finite element problem is solved on FEM by assigning each node to a processor, then repeating the following steps: Each node calculates its displacement in parallel (based on the most recent displacements of neighbors and the element and material properties of the connections); sends its displacements to neighboring nodes; receives updated displacements from neighboring nodes; and repeats these steps until the displacements converge.

FEM has good effectual communication locality because there is a direct local-neighbor hardware communication line for each connecting element in the finite element model. Thus there is a one-to-one correspondence between the problem to be solved and the computer architecture that solves it (as long as there are enough processors).

Actually, Figure 2.17(c) shows better spatial locality: It assigns multiple nodes in the finite element problem to the same physical processor. This reduces the amount of parallelism, but actually improves performance [ADA82], a somewhat surprising result. Even though FEM has special high-speed local-neighbor communication lines, the software overhead for sending and receiving messages is relatively high (far less than the earlier list, but high relative to the displacement computation). This is a good example of the parallel processing principle: The communication cost for assigning one node to each processor exceeds the processing speedup of the algorithm.

□

In **Item 8,** degree locality calls for closeness among the amount of data sent, the amount essential to the receiving process, and the bandwidth of the communication channel. In a packet-switching network, for example, degree locality is best if the amount of information transmitted (and needed) is equal to the packet size. For large-volume communication, asynchronous transmission with start and stop bits for each character has less degree locality than bisynchronous transmission with start and stop bits for each block.

Item 9 advises: Include communication time in the processing versus frequency tradeoff calculations. The communication time is an overhead cost, so "maximum use of overhead costs" suggests combining messages into fewer, longer messages rather than transmitting many shorter ones. In the ATM example, this implies that communication overhead is lower if we collect all the ATM transaction data and send it in one message to the mainframe, than if we send a separate message for each user response.[13] Processing versus frequency tradeoff also suggests that responsiveness is better if you minimize the number of parameters passed to subroutines. This does not mean that you must pass less data; you can, for example, group parameters into one "batch" and pass its name to the subroutine. A "batch" is a group item in COBOL or a record in Pascal. Item 5, "communicate only changed information to graphics displays," is also an example of the "expensive processing reduction" version of this principle.

The previous items illustrate the independent aspects of the communication problem: reducing communication overhead to improve one's own performance. In **Item 10,** the shared-resource principle addresses the synergistic aspects of communication. For shared communication channels, the potential wait time (to gain access) and the scheduling time (the communication overhead) determine the best holding time (the message size and the transmission frequency). You need the SPE performance models to determine the net effect of communication alternatives for shared channels, especially when external communication is prevalent in the new software.

Centering calls for minimizing the communication overhead for the dominant workload functions (**Item 11**). For software systems with extensive communication requirements, centering also focuses on workload elements that are major consumers of communication resources, because they affect the responsiveness of the overall system.

In **Item 12,** the instrumenting principle calls for collecting data on message traffic. Some examples are the number of data interchanges per transaction (internal and external), the number of messages sent between each set of origins and

---

[13]This example is not quite so simple. The communication overhead is reduced with this strategy; however, the contention for communication lines must be considered as well as the effective bandwidth of the communication channel to determine the net effect on response time. Therefore, the shared-resource principle also applies.

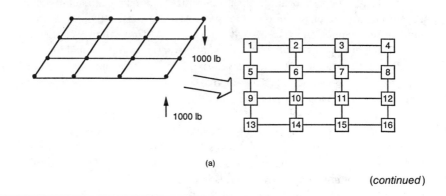

(a)

(continued)

FIGURE 2.17
Finite Element Machine (FEM) Locality: Part (a) shows a finite element structure
with 16 nodes and 24 elements (on the left) and the FEM processors with their local
communication connections (on the right). Displacement equations for each node
can be calculated in parallel. The FEM architecture is in (b). It is an array of processors. Each executes aschronously, has its own local memory, floating point
processor (FP), local-neighbor communications, and global bus interface. Spatial
locality in (c) improves by using only 4 of the 16 processors—each processor
calculates displacement equations for four finite element nodes.

destinations, and the transmission time. It is also valuable to have data on un-
desired events such as the number of transmission errors, the number of communication channel conflicts, and the number of delays due to insufficient
(message) buffer space.

2.4 Simplicity

Section 2.3 addressed software requirements and design issues and looked at their
performance tradeoffs. Developers must weigh performance gains against consequences, such as loss of implementation ease, flexibility, and so on. Developers
seek software simplicity to improve overall system quality—usability, maintainability, implementation ease, flexibility, and other factors. The issues in Section 2.3 are part of Figures 1.4's problem that requires understanding and concept
creation; whereas simplicity, the topic here, is an aspect of preferability. Fortunately, simplicity benefits both performance and quality rather than forcing a
choice between them.

Large software systems naturally tend to be complex. They are complicated
to use; there are many different functions, each with multiple options; processing

FIGURE 2.17 (*Continued*)

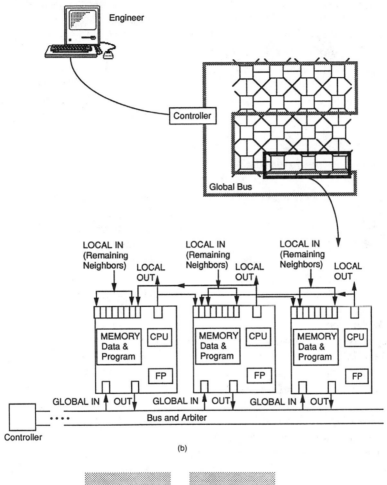

(b)

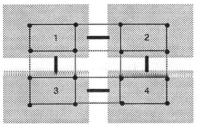

FEM Processor

(c)

is intricate and involved; and (because the world is complex) there are many interdependent combinations of actions. Internally, there are many variables, many flags or switches, many subroutines, and many cases or conditions leading to confusing data and control flow. Complex software is not only difficult to understand and use; it is also difficult to debug and maintain, it is difficult to change and enhance, and it *often has performance problems*. Thus, complexity creeps into systems and causes many problems. The following sections examine two primary conditions that lead to complexity in large software systems—a lack of conceptual integrity and an abundance of unnecessary "features"—and their consequences.

2.4.1 Conceptual Integrity

Conceptual integrity is the key to simplicity. **Conceptual integrity** means that all parts of a system form a unified whole, and there is a consistent architecture throughout the system. Brooks contrasts the Reims Cathedral against other European cathedrals built in the same era to illustrate conceptual integrity [BRO75]. The construction of a cathedral at that time spanned several generations of builders, and most builders adapted designs to use the latest technology to "improve" their creation. The builders of the Reims Cathedral, however, were faithful to the original architecture and created a unified structure.

At the other extreme, the Winchester House in San Jose, California, lacks conceptual integrity. It was built over a period of 38 years, one room at a time. Individual rooms have beautiful details—an imported Venetian wash basin, beautiful Tiffany stained-glass windows, and many more. The house, however, is obviously a collection of individual rooms rather than a unified whole. Among other oddities, stairways lead nowhere; "outdoor" windows look into the next room; a chimney from the ground floor goes up through four floors but stops inches short of the roof so its four fireplaces are useless; interior doors open to solid walls; and the entrance to the back 30 rooms is through a closet.

Lack of conceptual integrity often leads to performance problems when "the pieces do not fit together." In one particular system, individual subroutines were designed well; classic algorithms and data structures were used and coded well. The subroutines had acceptable performance when individually tested, but, when they were combined during integration testing, the overall performance was unacceptable because individual pieces of the system were incompatible. The system had a central memory-allocation routine whose author assumed that it would be called infrequently to allocate large amounts of memory. Developers of other subroutines assumed "allocate" could minimize wasted space, so they called it frequently to allocate a few bytes of memory at a time. "Allocate" was called a dozen times by one of the highest-frequency tasks—the message processor. Each time "allocate" executed over 100K instructions and, often, file I/O as well. Thus, overall performance was unacceptable. Furthermore, corrections called for major changes to the functional architecture.[14]

Conceptual integrity calls for a unified rather than haphazard approach to memory management, as well as to other considerations. Conceptual integrity does not alone guarantee acceptable performance, but, when combined with SPE methods, it improves the likelihood of meeting performance objectives.

2.4.2 Reject Unnecessary Features

Developers who are unsure of exactly which options a user desires or whether functions are needed tend to include extra functions by default, especially when adding them is easy. Designers and programmers believe they improve the system by embellishing it with extra features, but the "features" are often liabilities. Software engineers are not the only people who suffer this habit; consider the following analogy: When daylight savings time last changed to standard time, we had to change over 25 clocks at home! We certainly do not need so many clocks (I remember when two were sufficient), but designers of high-tech gadgets now add clocks to devices because it is so easy to do so. Many would be better off omitted (you should at least be able to turn them off—you cannot just leave a clock showing the wrong time). The analogy to software systems is "just because it is easy does not mean it should be added." The extra processing unnecessarily degrades performance, overly complicates user interfaces, and seriously increases the testing and maintenance burden. Next time you face a decision to add a "feature," make sure that it isn't one of the unnecessary clocks!

Another cause of unnecessary internal complexity is that programmers anticipate future enhancements and put in "hooks" to make it easy for subsequent programmers to insert changes. Often the anticipated enhancements are like the clocks; they are never needed. Furthermore, Hamlet studied these "hooks" and found them to be actually detrimental to maintenance, even when the enhancements are eventually needed [HAM82]. They are detrimental primarily because the person who laid the "trout lines" is usually long gone, and maintainers tend to avoid trout-line code because it has no apparent purpose and they worry about unknown side effects.

Thus, complexity in software systems often leads to inferior quality in many respects; poor responsiveness is only one of them. Software is simplified by including only features and processing that must be done. For performance, the centering principle calls for focusing on the dominant workload functions and simplifying them to do only what is necessary. The following three questions can

---

[14]Lampson cited a similar document-processing example in his paper on "Hints for Computer System Design" [LAM84]. Readers who are unfamiliar with conceptual integrity should refer to Chapter 4 in the *Mythical Man Month* [BRO75].

be asked to determine whether features should be included or processing must be done:

1. How many times will the feature be requested or events occur that call for processing?

2. What is the benefit of including the additional feature or processing to handle the event?

3. What are the consequences of not including it?

The features or processing are needed when the consequences are unacceptable, the benefits are highly valuable, or they are frequently requested.

The space-management problem for a data management system shown in Figure 2.18 illustrates a questionable feature. Data records are stored in "buckets." The records can be variable-length, but the buckets are fixed-length. A diligent space-management component of a database system keeps track of the free space within each bucket. When items are deleted from the bucket, their space is reclaimed; when new items are added to the bucket, free space is used. Knuth has proposed many specific algorithms for tracking and allocating free space, which are fairly easy to implement [KNU68]. However, every addition and deletion (and perhaps every retrieval, depending on the data structure) would execute extra code for free-space management.

Before focusing on the space-management algorithm, first question its necessity. How many times will data records be deleted and (later) added to the same bucket? How often will the added record need to reclaim the space that the deleted

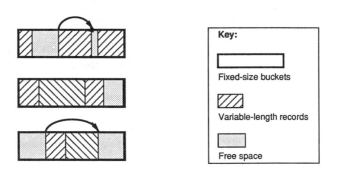

FIGURE 2.18
Proposed Free-Space-Management Feature. Fixed-size buckets contain variable-length records and free space. The proposed feature tracks and uses free space within buckets whenever possible.

record used? How much space will be saved by doing this, and how much processing time will be added? The answers to these questions depend on the characteristics of the database and application. For some circumstances, the best solution is to omit the free-space management. To reclaim unused space, you can rebuild the file with an overnight batch program. This simplifies the online system and reduces the processing overhead for normal additions and deletions. The amount of "wasted" space can be a small price to pay for simplicity and improved efficiency for the typical cases.

2.5 Strategy for Effective Use of the Principles

The general principles are necessary for building performance into new systems, but they are not sufficient—they must also be used *effectively*. Four strategies that determine their effectiveness are:

1. Apply the principles to *appropriate software components*.
2. Make *necessary* improvements.
3. Seek *global improvements*.
4. Make *cost-effective* improvements.

The following paragraphs explain their relationship to the principles.

First, **apply the principles to the software components that are critical to performance.** Identifying these components at design time can be difficult, and intuition can be misleading. Some designers mistake the components that are most difficult to design and implement for the critical components, whereas the components critical to responsiveness are those most frequently executed.

For example, security management software in a distributed network is difficult. The security routines are difficult to design because of the many complex situations they must correctly handle. Security routines may require a fair amount of execution time; however, other network software components, such as the communication protocol routines or I/O paths, probably have a greater effect on performance. Similarly, implementing the binding mechanisms in a database management system is difficult. Binding also requires a considerable amount of execution time; however, the relative frequency of binding-code execution should be low (when application software applies the fixing-point principle). Binding *may* be critical to performance, but do not assume it is critical; use SPE models to decide.

Second, **apply the optimization efforts to software components only when**

necessary. When performance goals are properly stated, you seldom need to overachieve them. Therefore, if a performance goal can be easily attained, do not devote valuable development time to extensive performance enhancements.[15] Similarly, spend little, if any, effort optimizing components of the software system that have little impact on the overall performance.

Another aspect of necessary optimizations is to **distinguish software requirements that are necessary** from those that are both unnecessary and adversely affect responsiveness. Sometimes these artificial requirements slip in during design with the good intention of improving performance. Envision a component that produces a list of items, and the questionable "requirement" that the list be in sorted order. The good intention for the requirement is to reduce subsequent search time. Question the need for the sort: If it is to reduce search time, compare the times for the sort and the search for typical scenarios to see if the sort leads to a net improvement. Use SPE models to quantify times for the two alternatives (keep the list in order, or return unordered results) to determine the preferable choice. Unless there are clear reasons to do otherwise, use the simplest alternative. In this example, if the list is short and if ordered lists are infrequently needed, omit the sort. This straightforward approach may not degrade responsiveness and will result in less code to be maintained.

The third effectiveness strategy is to **apply optimization techniques when they produce global improvements** to the software performance. This is vital during the detailed design and coding stages, when many people are involved in development. Optimizations made in one part of the software system must be consistent with those made in other areas.

As an example, review the following strategy for allocating file buffers.

EXAMPLE 2.15: Buffer Allocation Strategy

The following proposal seeks to minimize I/Os:

1. Allocate file buffer space from a free-space pool.

2. If there is no free space available in the pool, select a "ready" output buffer and write the contents of the buffer to disk.

3. When a process fills an output buffer and "writes," set the "ready" indicator, but wait until the space is needed (in Step 2) before writing it to disk.

The strategy's motive is to (potentially) reduce the number of reads, by finding the requested data already in one of the memory buffers. This goal appears reasonable, but investigate some specific scenarios. What happens when a software file-creator calls this

(continued)

---

[15]If performance goals may differ over the life of the software, include future expectations in the performance goal statement. The explicit expectations clarify which improvements are necessary for long-term versus short-term goals.

EXAMPLE 2.15 (*Continued*)

buffer manager to allocate buffers for the new file? The file-creator repeatedly executes the following sequence of operations: allocate a buffer, fill with information, and "write" the buffer contents. The buffer manager merely records the write requests, but does not write until buffer space is needed. If the new file is colossal, the file-creator will fill all memory buffers before any are written. Then all subsequent buffer allocation requests must wait while the buffer manager writes a buffer, then allocates it. This delay will be experienced by *all concurrent processes* desiring buffer space, not just the file-creator. If file-creators run concurrently with online inquiry transactions, the buffer replacement "optimization" is local, not global.

A better global optimization uses different strategies, depending on the characteristics of buffer use (online, batch, create, view, update, and so forth). So when file-creators use buffers, their writes are processed immediately. Note that writes can be asynchronous, so the file-creator need not wait for writes to complete to continue its creation.   □

The last of the four effectiveness strategies is to **make cost-effective performance improvements.** Weigh the expected savings against the time to implement the optimizations. It may be extremely difficult and time-consuming to achieve the specified performance goals. Quantify the cost of achieving a performance goal and either confirm that it is justified, or negotiate more reasonable performance goals before expending excessive efforts on achieving unrealistic ones.

This chapter focuses on improvements to *software systems* to achieve performance goals. There are other factors that also affect the overall performance of a system. They include:

□ *Workload:* the number of concurrent users, the frequency of requests, and the request patterns

□ *Hardware configuration:* the number and speed of various devices

□ *Operating system* and *other support software*

Optimizations made in these areas also lead to more responsive software systems. For example, job-accounting policies can improve workload characteristics—if you make computing cheaper in the early morning hours, you may shift some of the work to these off-peak hours, thereby improving overall performance. Hardware configuration management and capacity planning improve performance by improving the operating environment. Tuning operating system routines to fit the application and the workload may be another viable means of achieving performance objectives. Many of the operating system routines are dominant workload functions or major resource consumers of the overall system. By improving the performance of these routines, you improve the performance of the overall system. Techniques for tuning the software system environment and for computer configuration management are not included here. They may be found in several reference sources [FER78, FER83b, SAU81, LAZ84a].

2.6 Case Studies

This chapter uses the ATM example (and others) to illustrate general principles for requirements and design tradeoffs. The principles will be applied to more comprehensive case studies to be introduced in Chapter 3. There are some requirements and design inefficiencies in the initial version of the case studies. To reinforce the general principles, as you read the case study descriptions, use the principles to identify potential inefficiencies and various alternatives. Keep a list of those you find. Chapter 6 evaluates the case study models, showing how the general principles identify improvement alternatives and how models give quantitative data for the alternatives. Compare your list of alternatives to those covered in Chapter 6—you may find additional performance improvements!

2.7 Summary and Conclusions

Seven principles for creating responsive software systems were presented and their application to software system requirements and design tradeoffs discussed.

Section 2.3 has several examples in which multiple principles lead to the same improvement. The principles correspond directly to the system performance parameter that they affect (Section 2.1 and Table 2.1). When one design improvement favorably affects multiple system performance parameters, several principles may apply. Since the goal is to create responsive systems, it does not matter which of the principles leads the designer to the desired product. Because more than one may apply, the probability of creating a responsive system increases. There would be a problem if the principles were contradictory, but they are not because they explicitly address the tradeoffs, and the SPE models identify the best alternative. So do not worry if you think of software improvements but cannot decide which of the principles they reflect. The goal is to make performance improvements to the software while it is still in the creation stages, not to classify the improvements.

Note that the principles improve responsiveness, without the adverse effects on maintainability that "fix-it-later" has. Improvements made early in the lifecycle alter only the requirements or the design; they do not change code. In contrast, in fix-it-later, performance tuning usually makes substantial changes to program code and often introduces errors so the code must be retested, and the resulting "tricky" code is more difficult to maintain. Many improvements that are easy early in the lifecycle are infeasible later (like the memory allocation example described in 2.4.1).

The correlation between the response time of a system and its responsiveness in the more general sense is fascinating. For example, the special ATM function for "quick withdrawals" not only produces a much better average response time; it is also easier for the many customers who use it. The GQUE user-interface im-improvements in Section 2.3.1 improved both performance and usability. Thus, the principles improve system responsiveness without adversely affecting quality. They are compatible with good software engineering practices.

Most of the principles require tradeoff decisions. While many are either intuitive or easily evaluated with back-of-the-envelope calculations, others (particularly shared resources and parallel processing) require more sophisticated performance models. The SPE methodology explicitly integrates the model evaluations with design decisions. Subsequent chapters describe the models and show how to use them to quantify requirements and design tradeoffs. The performance principles, combined with the SPE methods, significantly decrease the probability of "search-light" performance problems.

Exercises

Review

2.1. List the principles. Write an informal description for each principle that you would use to explain them to a colleague unfamiliar with the concepts.

2.2. Review the case study you identified in Chapter 1, Exercise 1.2. Create a table (like Tables 2.7–2.11) of potential performance improvements for your case study and identify the principles associated with each. Try to find an example of each principle.

2.3. Use the following data to quantify the performance cost of Example 2.3's flexibility:

Suppose each order requires an average of 15 entries. The question-answer dialog asks 15 questions; the previous order-taking system had one screen with 15 fields. Suppose each question-answer takes 5 sec to transmit the question to the screen, type the answer, and return the answer to the system; the previous system took an average of 30 sec per screen. Suppose each question-answer requires an average of 42 ms processing; the previous system required an average of 600 ms per screen.

  a. Compute the average response time for the two alternatives (ignore contention delays).

  b. Suppose the previous system had a throughput of 3,000 orders per hour. Suppose the target throughput of the new system increases to 3,030 per hour (because more employees can take orders). Compute the average response time if the high-volume, order-taking clerks continue to use the previous system (and process the same transaction volume as before), and the question-answer dialog is used only for the new work.

2.4. Effectual locality design calls for matching processing characteristics to processor features (Table 2.3, Items 5 and 6). Give an example of effectual locality other than those in this chapter. When is maximizing closeness vital? List specific ways to. improve closeness. What are the disadvantages of maximizing effectual locality?

What policy would you advise to maximize performance benefits while minimizing disadvantages?

2.5. Review the database design example in Figure 2.13. Define screen contents for two (hypothetical) high-frequency, online transactions that would view or update such a personnel database. Alternatively, if you have access to a personnel-payroll system, identify and define the screen contents for the two most frequently used screens. Define the database structure that improves temporal and spatial locality for your two screens. Can you apply the user-interface concepts in Section 2.3.1 to improve screen contents? Explain your answer.

2.6. Use the following data to quantify the performance of the two centering alternatives in Table 2.6, Item 2:

Suppose the general processing requires 16 database SELECTs to pack the screen. The streamlined processing can fulfill 95 percent of the requests with one screen that requires 3 SELECTs; 5 percent of the requests require an additional screen that requires 13 SELECTs. Each SELECT requires from 10 to 100 ms CPU time and 1 to 3 I/Os (best-worst, respectively), and each I/O takes an average of 20 ms. Ignore all other processing overhead. Compute the best, worst, and average response times for the general and streamlined processing. List two pros and two cons for the general and streamlined strategies *from the user's perspective*.

Further Study

2.7. Do you believe the 5 and 30 sec times in Exercise 2.3 are realistic? Conduct a simple study to determine how long it would take to respond to one question and to fill in 15 fields on a (familiar) screen. Repeat the calculations in Exercise 2.3 using your data.

2.8. Review Kopetz's principles for fault-tolerant, real-time systems [KOP86]. Are they compatible with principles for creating responsive systems? Explain how they might be used together.

2.9. Review Bouhana's paper on instrumentation versus measurement versus analysis [BOU85]. Define at least five measurements that are desirable for your Chapter 1 case study exercise, which currently could only be measured if probes are manually inserted. Can you define a tool that would make the instrumentation, measurement, and analysis easier?

2.10. Review Lampson's hints for computer system design [LAM84]. What principles does he use in his performance improvement examples?

2.11. Review the improvement formulas for the centering, fixing-point, and processing versus frequency tradeoff principles in [SMI86a]. Pick one of the applications of each principle from the tables in Section 2.2 or Section 2.3, derive some hypothetical data (like in Exercises 2.3 and 2.6), and use the paper's formulas to quantify alternatives.

2.12. Find a reference that describes the communication processing that occurs when an electronic message is routed through a wide area network (such as Arpanet or CS net). Compare the processing to the list in Section 2.3.5, and update the list accordingly. Quantify the performance cost of as many processing steps as possible.

3

SPE Data Gathering

What is the expected performance of your new software system? This question stumps many software designers—let's consider an analogy that shows why software-performance prediction is so difficult, and why the SPE methods resolve the difficulties. Take a few minutes to answer the following question: What is the best, worst, and average time to drive home from work? If you cannot compute specific numbers, jot down the steps you would take to get them.

Now let's consider some of the reasons that the commute-time question (and the software-performance question) is difficult to answer. The first obstacle is that the question is too vague; many factors influence commute time, such as geographic location, time of day, route, speed, type of vehicle, and so forth. To resolve the multi-influence problem, we need to clarify the question. Why do we need the answer—is it to decide among relocation alternatives, to rank cities, to compare cities to suburban and rural locations, to cost-justify mass transit? Let's clarify thusly: Suppose we wish to compare commute times for two relocation alternatives in Austin, Texas. If we first quantify commute times, then factor in the value of our time, housing price differences, and other factors, we can select the optimal alternative. This resolves the geographic location factor and suggests specific commute scenarios, such as 5 to 6 PM Mondays; two specific routes, one freeway, one backroads, traveling by limousine, and so on. Next, we could define steps in each commute scenario, such as: reach limo, exit parking lot, reach freeway, enter freeway, reach exit, and so forth. Then we can estimate best, worst, and average times for each step. For estimates that depend on traffic and environmental conditions, such as freeway onramps with blinking lights to permit entry, define the dependent parameter. For example, the time for metered onramps depends on the rate of permission blinks and the number of cars ahead of you in line.

A difficult commute-time prediction problem is thus resolved one step at a time. We define the goals of the study, specify the boundary conditions with scenarios, identify the processing steps in the scenario, identify environmental factors, and estimate the time requirements for each step. Then we have the *data* we need to compute best, worst, and average times.

SPE uses a similar approach to resolve software-performance prediction difficulties. Many factors influence response times and throughput: time of day,

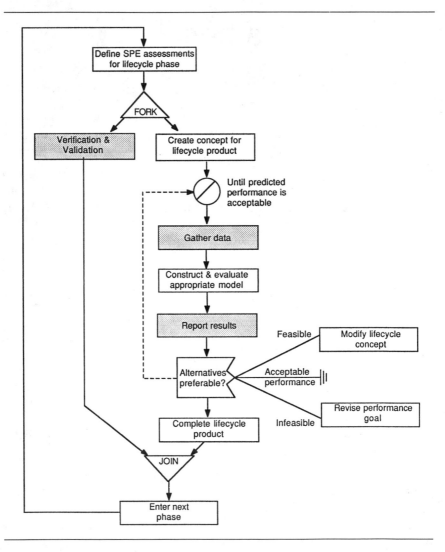

FIGURE 3.1
The SPE Methodology with the Focus of This Chapter Highlighted.

types of transactions, number of users, processing requirements, and more. So we first define the goals of the study, and then specify boundary conditions by defining workload scenarios. Next we use the software plans to define the processing steps in the scenario; we identify the computer hardware and software environment; and finally we estimate the resource requirements for each step.

This chapter focuses on the *data* required to answer the software-performance question. We propose an early lifecycle technique for gathering data: *the performance walkthrough*. Walkthroughs produce data and report results, and we must verify that the data and the results are valid. These three steps in the SPE methodology—gathering data, reporting results, and verification and validation—are highlighted in Figure 3.1 and are the focus of this chapter.

3.1 Model Specifications

The data required for constructing, parameterizing, and evaluating software models is:

- □ Performance goals
- □ Workload specifications
- □ Software execution structure
- □ Execution environment
- □ Resource usage

The following sections describe these in more detail—what is needed, the sources of the information, and why it is important.

3.1.1 Performance Goals

A *performance goal* is the criteria for evaluating the software system plans and the performance of the completed software. Some examples of performance goals are:

- □ Response time of 2 seconds (or less) for trivial transactions[1]
- □ Throughput of 5,000 trivial transactions per hour
- □ Maximum of 100 ms CPU time for a database SELECT

Response time goals may be for individual transactions, or they may be end-to-end times to complete user tasks (which may require multiple transactions).

---

[1]You must also precisely define a "trivial" transaction. In this discussion, *trivial* means transactions that require an insignificant amount of processing: ≤ 10 milliseconds of CPU time and ≤ one I/O operation.

Systems traditionally focused on individual transaction times (because they are easier to measure). If you instead focus on end-to-end times, you can improve *system effectiveness* as well as responsiveness.

The choice of *response time* versus *throughput goals* depends on whether you are more interested in the service you provide (response time), or the efficiency of providing it (throughput). For customer inquiries, you may wish to respond to a question within a specified time (response time) or handle a specified number of calls per hour (throughput). Note that the goals are not the same—design choices that improve responsiveness are not necessarily efficient. You may wish to balance responsiveness *and* efficiency—for example, handle 40 transactions per second with a response time under 1 second.

Evolutionary system-software development may call for *performance constraints*. A new operating system—that is an evolutionary improvement over a previous one—may set performance constraints on key paths, such as "locking must be 20 percent faster." The constraints may be on resource usage rather than time, such as "the path length for SELECT must be less than 250,000 instructions."[2]

Batch-system goals are driven by the "batch window," the time period when online systems are shut down. Nightly batch programs have maximum run-time goals if they must complete before online systems arise.

Regardless of the type of goal you select, it must be *specific* and *measurable*. Vague statements such as "the system must be efficient" or "rapid response is required" are not goals. Brooks recommends "sharp milestones" for the software development process [BRO75]; his rationale also applies to "performance milestones." He claims that fuzzy milestones (such as "coding 90 percent complete") are problematic because our optimistic tendencies delude us into thinking we have achieved them. If you cannot measure and precisely determine whether or not a milestone is met, it is easy to rationalize that no problems exist. A performance goal of "90 percent of the transactions must complete in under 1 second" is fuzzy. Is it 90 percent of transactions defined or transactions executed? During what time period—all day or peak hour? Could a transaction whose expected response time is 5 seconds be accepted as one of the 10 percent? So, when you state goals, use your chisel—define how you will measure goal achievement, define all the influential factors, and sharpen the goals to be specific and measurable.

You can use performance goals to specify values for influential factors. For example, response time and throughput depend on the number of users competing for computer resources; so define conditional performance goals, such as "1 second or less with up to 500 users, and 2 seconds or less with up to 2,000 users." Performance also depends on workload mix. For example, trivial transactions x and y may have average response times of 1 and 30 seconds, respectively. If transaction x is invoked thousands of times each day while transaction y is invoked

---

[2]Seetha Lakshmi illustrates the process of determining performance bounds for general-purpose software in her excellent paper [LAK87] cited in the bibliography.

ten times, the overall performance of the system is good. If the converse is true, the performance would likely be unacceptable. So assign different performance goals to each workload scenario, based on its expected frequency of use. Resolve as many influential factors as possible with goal definitions. A later part of this section presents a technique for resolving other influential factors with scenario definitions or data-dependent resource usage specifications.

Verify that the performance goals are realistic and cost-effective. Make sure that the complexity and ambition of the processing match the goals. Make sure it is cost-effective to achieve them. Tight goals may be too expensive; you may need to compromise on either performance or function. The SPE models quantify performance and configuration requirements to assess cost-effectiveness early in a project's lifecycle.

Be aware that user expectations may change once software is implemented. Users may find it difficult to envision their operational use of a new system. Their past frame of reference and mode of operation will be changing, and it is impossible to anticipate the full impact of a new environment. For example, users might specify a 30-second performance goal for a new interactive transaction that replaces an older batch function. However, after implemention they will realize that 30 seconds is too long to sit at a terminal with nothing else to do, and they will quickly forget the one-week batch-turnaround time. To verify that the performance goal is realistic, compare user expectations to other similar systems, or build a prototype to give users hands-on experience.

Specification of performance targets for this analysis of software systems is not only necessary but also generally desirable. Quantifiable performance targets provide the basis for selecting appropriate design alternatives. The overall goals make sure that individual design choices are globally compatible and consistent with the goals. The performance goal improves development effectiveness by focusing attention on the portions of the software that have significant performance impact and by avoiding excessive work on those whose impact is negligible. The performance goal enables you to decide well in advance the host configuration necessary to meet the overall goals and provides early warning when fixed host configurations are inadequate.

3.1.2 Workload Specification

The workload specification consists of:

□ System uses or requests for system functions

□ The rate at which each is requested

□ Any special patterns of requests

For example, one workload for an ATM system is a deposit to a checking account; the request rate is 100 requests per ATM per day. Another ATM workload may specify the request pattern with a request for checking-account balance followed by an optional request for a checking-account withdrawal. The request rate is 1,000 requests per ATM per day, 850 of which also request the withdrawal.

Each workload specification is called a **scenario.** There is no prescribed scenario size or number of scenarios; the choices depend on the size of the system, the variety of uses, the critical functions of the system, and other considerations. The most important attributes of the SPE scenarios are their representativeness and relevance.

Develop scenarios for **representative workloads.** Consider an analogy to buying supplies for an exploration and camping trip. Functional requirements for some of the trip supplies can be met by a Swiss army knife. There are many different varieties of the Swiss army knife, each supporting different functionality. One type contains two blades, a corkscrew, can opener, toothpick, tweezers, scissors, a wood saw, a metal saw, a rasp, a hole puncher, and two types of screwdrivers. For efficient performance, however, if the traveler plans to do a great deal of sawing (the representative workload), it would be best to take a regular saw and a smaller knife without saw blades. The analogy to software is that all functional requirements must be met. However, those that are requested frequently drive the performance of the entire system. You must *represent* them with workload scenarios to find opportunities for streamlining their processing and to make accurate performance predictions.

Include all **relevant functions** in the workload scenarios. For example, in a distributed software system with many reliability and fault-tolerance mechanisms, a recovery from an error condition is relevant to the scenario only if you expect the error to occur frequently or if the recovery *must* be accomplished in a specified period of time (a critical performance goal). If error recovery is infrequent and other workloads dominate the processing (such as the exchange of electronic mail on a fully operational system), then the error recovery scenario is unnecessary for SPE. You may want it for other purposes, such as testing.

So far, the spotlight has been on workloads initiated by end-users. To evaluate a support system, such as a DBMS, specify the typical data manipulation commands issued, the rate at which each is requested, and any relevant request patterns. To evaluate a DBMS's interactive query language, you need to know typical user queries. To evaluate a DBMS's program interface, you need the database calls issued by typical application programs (and their rate and request patterns), such as the following:

EXAMPLE 3.1: Sample DBMS Workload Specification

DB Command	Requests/sec
FIND	1.00
RETRIEVE	10.00
OPEN	0.05
CLOSE	0.05

(continued)

EXAMPLE 3.1 (*Continued*)

Request patterns

OPEN followed by FIND	95% of time
FIND followed by RETRIEVE	90% of time
FIND followed by OPEN	≤ 1% of time

□

If possible, measure the database workload. If not, specify the user transactions, construct their software models, and then calculate the database requests from the models. The same is true of evaluations of operating system software. If possible, measure the workload (requests for operating system services). If not, derive it from the user-level workload specifications and their models.

3.1.3 Software Execution Structure

The execution structure defines the execution path through the software for each workload scenario:

□ The software components that execute

□ The order of execution

□ Component repetition and conditional execution

Each of the steps in the execution structure corresponds to a **software component** —a conceptual entity of the software system. A simple execution structure for an ATM deposit scenario might be as follows:

EXAMPLE 3.2: ATM Deposit Scenario Execution Structure

1. Initiate_session;
2. Get_request;   −−response is deposit to checking
3. Get_deposit_amount;
4. Update_account_file_and_activity_log;
5. Print_receipt;
6. Terminate_session;

Each of the six steps is a software component. They execute in the order shown.

□

You derive the execution structure from the workload specification and the system structure as follows. The workload scenario specifies the subset of *system functions* of interest for SPE. Figure 3.2 shows some of the available ATM functions. Assume that "get balance" is the most frequent transaction: Define it with a workload scenario. The system design contains components to support all the functional requirements. Design specifications for the complete system include

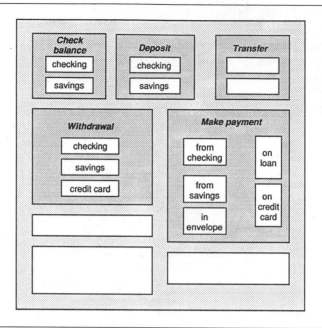

FIGURE 3.2
A Subset of the Available ATM Functions.

the components, their hierarchical organization, possible component-call structures, the data passed between them, and so forth. Figure 3.3 partially illustrates the system structure for the ATM example. It is a Leighton diagram—one method for depicting software structure [PET81, SCO78]. The ATM Leighton diagram shows that the component "get request" can call components "deposit," "get balance," and "withdrawal." "Deposit" can call "get amount," "account file interface," and "error handling." A complete system structure contains all components and defines all possible calling sequences, including error handling routines and others (whether or not they are executed in the typical workload).

Using the scenario specification as a guide, find the software components that execute in the scenario. The execution structure for the "get balance" scenario is:

EXAMPLE 3.3: Get Balance Execution Structure

The following structure shows a high-level system decomposition.

1. Initiate_session;
2. Get_request;   ––response is ⟨get balance⟩, ⟨checking account⟩
3. Get_balance;

(continued)

EXAMPLE 3.3 (*Continued*)

    4. Print_receipt;
    5. Terminate_session;

The execution structure expands to include more detail as design details are resolved. The following shows an expanded execution structure for the "get balance" scenario.

    1. Initiate_session;
        a. Read identification number from machine
        b. Get authorization code from machine
        c. Verify authorization code against code file

    2. Get_request;
        a. Get function selection from machine   --⟨get balance⟩
        b. Get account type from machine   --⟨checking⟩

    3. Get_balance;
        a. Build account key
        b. Read account record
        c. Extract balance

    4. Print_receipt;
        a. Write data to machine printer

    5. Terminate_session;
        a. Send return-card signal to machine

                                                                         □

Typical execution structures also contain loops and conditional execution. Loops are specified with a **loop** construct that lists the components to repeat. For branching, either an **if** or a **case** construct represents the conditional execution of components. Examples of each follow:

EXAMPLE 3.4: Repetition and Conditional Execution

```
Initiate_session;
loop            --⟨2 times⟩
    get_request;
    interpret_request;
    case request is
        when deposit_to_checking =⟩ . . .    --⟨.7⟩
        when deposit_to_savings  =⟩ . . .    --⟨.3⟩
    end case;
end loop;
Terminate_session;
```

                                                                          □

Note that specifications are required for the expected number of times that loops repeat (the loop repetition factor) and the probability that a conditional path executes (the execution probability). These specifications are discussed in more detail in the next chapter.

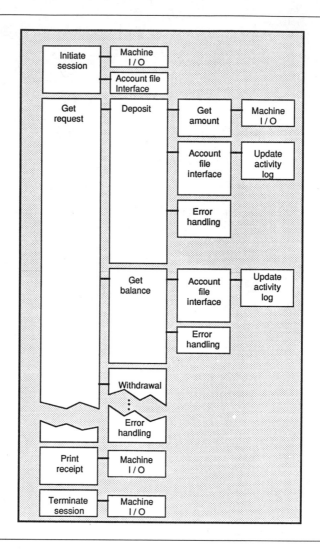

FIGURE 3.3
A Subset of the Components of the ATM System and Their Hierarchical Relationship. Boxes represent components; the larger boxes on the left can call components to their right. The execution order is top to bottom, and left to right.

The deposit scenario is a user-level scenario. The only difference for DBMS or operating system software is in the level of detail. For example, the ATM scenario executes on an abstract machine that provides an interface to the ATM hardware device. The abstract machine provides functions such as "read machine input" and "display message on screen." A scenario for modeling and evaluating the abstract machine interface is:

Get_from_ATM (information);

where (information) could be authorization code, deposit amount, etcetera.

One possible execution structure for Get_from_ATM (information) follows:

1. Prepare_ prompt_message;
2. Display_message_on_screen;
3. Unlock_keyboard;
4. Read_machine_input (information);
5. Lock_keyboard;

To add more processing details, expand the machine I/O operation to include polling or other protocol processing.

Notice that neither the deposit scenario nor the abstract machine interface scenario includes error handling. Presumably the typical workload consists of correct transactions, and both the scenario specification and the execution structure reflect that assumption. Error conditions should be modeled if they are relevant to the performance of the system. Occasionally, error handling constitutes the typical workload of the software!

We need the execution structure for the same reason that we need workload scenarios: to identify those components of the software to be executed most frequently. Most systems have many possible execution paths that are seldom executed. These paths, which are crucial for functionality and reliability, are of little interest for performance assessment. (One such execution path in the ATM example is for a customer who initiates a session by inserting the ATM card and then cannot correctly enter the authorization code.) The total number of execution paths through a large software system is extremely large. Performance analysis of all paths is impossible; however, by focusing on the typical execution paths as identified by the representative workload scenarios, the performance analysis is manageable.

3.1.4 Execution Environment

The execution environment is:

- The **hardware configuration** upon which the system will execute
- The **abstract machine:** the operating system and other support software routines that interface between the new software and the hardware

Workload scenario performance clearly depends on the execution environment. For example, the response times for ATM scenarios depend on the speed of the

CPU, the speed of the I/O devices, the number of ATMs in use simultaneously, and the amount of other work that executes on the computer system (such as printing bank statements and updating personnel files).

Initial performance studies start with the environmental factors that have the greatest effect on software's own performance, such as:

- The speed of the CPU (processing rate for machine instructions and for higher-level-language instructions)

- The speed of the I/O devices

- The resource requirements for the abstract machine functions

- The operating system overhead for control flow mechanisms (such as procedure calls)

You may also need application-dependent information such as the size and structure of a database. Samples for the ATM environment follow:

EXAMPLE 3.5: Sample ATM Environment Specifications

- CPU speed—2 MIPS (million machine instructions per second)
- I/O devices—50 ms per request
- Procedure call overhead—0.5 ms per call/return
- Ratio high-level to machine instructions[3]—1:20
- Abstract machine functions:

Function	Instructions	Machine I/O time (ms)
Read machine input	1,500	100
Display message on screen	1,500	500
Lock/unlock keyboard	250	50
Return card	250	50

□

Later analyses use the system execution model to factor in additional configuration parameters, support system overhead, and external workload specifications. The additional **configuration parameters** required are:

- The total number of terminals
- The amount of memory

---

[3]The language is a very high-level, ATM-application–specific language. The overhead for ATM and file I/O is factored into the 1:20 ratio.

□ The configuration of the I/O subsystem

□ All other physical hardware resources used by the software

For the **support system overhead,** quantify:

□ The overhead to manage each hardware resource, such as the operating system overhead to set up an I/O operation, and memory management overhead

□ The queueing discipline for each resource—that is, the policy for selecting the next job to use a resource when multiple jobs are waiting

The **external workload** characterizes other jobs that share the computer system and thus compete for computer system resources. If an external workload exists, use traditional workload characterization methods [FER83b] to measure the system, to perform statistical analyses, and to identify workload intensity and resource use. If the external workload is also under construction, use SPE techniques to define and analyze its workload scenarios. External workload specifications and configuration parameters for the later analyses are covered in more detail in Chapter 5, after the system execution model is defined.

3.1.5 Resource Usage

For SPE, you need resource usage estimates for each component in the software execution structure. Resource usage estimates include:

□ The number of instructions to be executed

□ The number of I/O operations for each device

□ The number and types of abstract machine service routines used

□ The amount of memory for code and for data

Examples of resource usage specification for the ATM examples are in Table 3.1.

TABLE 3.1
SAMPLE RESOURCE USAGE SPECIFICATIONS

Component	# high-level instructions executed	# I/Os	Memory (Kbytes)	Abstract machine function
Read identification number	100		.5	Read machine input
Verify authorization code	100	2	4.5	
Build account key	25		.2	
Read account record	50	2	4.3	
Extract balance	10		.1	

Resource usage estimates are for *the specified scenario*. You want the estimated number of instructions *to be executed*, not necessarily the total number in the component. There are two differences in these numbers: First, do not include exception-handling code unless it is likely to be executed; and, second, *within a component* when instructions within loops will be executed many times, calculate the total number to be executed for all loop repetitions. For the memory, you need the amount of memory to be actively used.[4] For virtual, paged memory systems, estimate the working set size for each component; for nonvirtual memory systems, estimate the total size of each component. Memory estimates (and evaluations) are discussed more in Chapter 9. First check to see if performance goals can be met with the optimistic assumption that there is no memory management overhead. After you confirm that the big picture looks good, then focus on memory and other details.

There are many **difficulties in estimating resource usage;** yet estimates of resource usage are crucial to the precision of SPE predictions. Previously, software engineers seldom attempted to characterize the resource requirements for four reasons:

1. *It is too difficult unless you have a frame of reference for estimating resource usage*. For example, if you know the resource requirements for similar activities, it is easy to extrapolate to new software.

2. *Resource requirements may depend on many factors external to the software itself,* such as workload characteristics and thus execution paths, application-dependent factors such as database size and structure, and external workloads contending for computer resources.

3. *There is seldom one person with the breadth of knowledge and background for making precise estimates*. System size, complexity, and the many external, influential factors culminate in a division of responsibility and thus fragmented system knowledge.

4. *There was previously no incentive to derive good estimates of resource usage*.

The benefits provided by SPE are the incentive for estimating. SPE methodology uses three techniques to compensate for the other resource-specification problems. The first is to **gather bounded estimates** of resource usage—that is, specify both an upper and a lower bound (worst and best cases) for resource usage for components with high uncertainty. Then conduct the software performance analyses (discussed in the next chapter) using each of the bounds. If performance is satisfactory for the worst-case analysis, then the performance goals will likely be met. If, however, the performance is unacceptable for the best-case analysis, then

---

[4]Most evaluations need the amount of memory actively used. For some evaluations, such as predicting the long-term—(disk)—storage requirements, you need the total memory requirements.

problem solutions must be found. In practice, systems tend to either run or crawl; occasionally they limp, and it is unclear whether or they not they will pass the performance-goal finish line. To find out, use the bounded analysis to identify the components whose performance is critical with respect to meeting the goals. Then implement the critical components first, or construct prototypes and measure their resource usage. Use the measurement data along with the bounded estimates to make more precise performance predictions (and to analyze the performance impact on other components).

Some performance analysts suggest using three estimates: best, worst, and expected values. Our experience shows that software engineers are optimists, so expected values are almost always best cases. For some projects three values may be helpful, but for most the value of the third estimate does not justify the extra analysis work. Thus, the terms *expected value* and *best-case estimate* are used interchangeably throughout this book.

It is not surprising that the bounded-estimates technique works well, considering the software engineering practices currently in use. Software is typically decomposed into units of similar sizes. The CPU execution times of the units are also similar. This makes the performance engineering process viable. Due to the limited frame of reference in Reason 1, the most difficult specification is the CPU requirement; a performance-benchmark study of typical programs produces a reasonable (default) bounded estimate for CPU usage. In most online systems today, the number of I/Os executed is the primary performance-determining factor, and I/Os are fairly easy to estimate.

The second SPE technique tackles **data dependency.** Resource requirements and thus response times of software systems may vary substantially among executions against different sets of data. When this happens, specifications for the expected value and upper bound are insufficient for performance assessment. An example is a database retrieval module: It retains data in buffers and can sometimes satisfy retrievals with data in buffers, thereby eliminating I/O operations and thus substantially reducing resource requirements. You could define a workload scenario that specifies how many times data is found in buffers; however, you could not extend the results to other workloads with unknown buffer-hit characteristics.

SPE identifies the factor(s) causing variability, uses a *data-dependent parameter* to represent each factor, and specifies execution characteristics and resource usage in terms of the data-dependent parameter. For example, a database transaction component's execution frequency may depend on the number of rows qualified in a SELECT. Use a parameter, N, to represent the number of rows qualified. Then possible execution frequencies may be N or $2N$ or $0.3N$, and so on. Similarly, the number of instructions executed within a component could be $500N$. Later, the models study sensitivity to the parameter values. These techniques for handling data dependency are detailed in Chapter 4.

The third technique for resource usage estimation compensates for one person seldom knowing enough to completely specify execution behavior. The *performance walkthrough* technique is described in part of the next section.

3.2 Techniques for Information Capture

It is seldom possible to obtain *precise* information for all the important specifications early in the software's lifecycle. Do not wait to model the system until the information is available (at the detailed design stage or later). Gather guesses, approximations, and bounded estimates to begin, and augment the models as information becomes available. For example, during the requirements analysis phase you can identify some key database tables but may not know their contents. You can get a very general description of high-use screens but may not know all the fields they will ultimately contain. Start with the approximations; if performance is a problem at this stage, it must be corrected early, before more tables and other processing are added. This approach has the added advantage of focusing attention on key workload elements to minimize their processing (as prescribed by the centering principle). Otherwise, designers tend to postpone these important performance drivers in favor of designing more complex but less frequently executed parts of the software.

It is virtually impossible to find a design document that contains sufficient SPE data. Moreover, SPE calls for early studies—long before design specifications are written. Execution structures are qualitatively different from design specifications; they combine workloads, software plans, and environment information to define the dynamic interaction of software components. They are analogous to integration tests of system modules that check the interaction among system modules and their input and output consistency. Both integration tests and execution structures require knowledge of the dynamic interactions of the system and of its behavior when driven by the operational workload. Actually, the process of defining the execution structure is a symbolic integration test early in the lifecycle, so the process has the added benefit of finding integration problems before they make their way into code.

Because one person seldom knows all the information required for the software performance models, we propose *performance walkthroughs* to bring together the people who possess the information necessary to integrate the workload, the software design, and the execution environment. Performance walkthroughs are closely modeled after design and code walkthroughs, but they have a broader scope of participation and an extended concept of specifications. In the following extended discussion of walkthroughs, this section uses descriptions of job functions such as "performance analyst," "designer," and "user." We refer to *roles* or tasks, not necessarily to people. For instance, a software engineer may fill both the designer and performance analyst roles.

3.2.1 Performance Walkthrough

A performance walkthrough coordinates the input of designers, implementers, and users of the system to define the software execution model. The performance walkthrough begins in the requirements analysis phase as soon as a general idea of system functions is available. We wish to obtain the data before requirements or design documents are created in order to detect problems while they can still be changed, so we want the information directly from the creators. Walkthroughs initially address major system functions; later we use these major functions as the high-level framework and elaborate their execution details. Even this high level can reveal problems such as the number of database tables accessed by a high-frequency transaction.

The agenda in Table 3.2 suggests the walkthrough steps and their prescribed order. The walkthrough begins with a discussion of the purpose of the walkthrough and the performance questions to be resolved. Steps 2 through 6, 8, and 9 corre-

TABLE 3.2
PERFORMANCE WALKTHROUGH AGENDA

Activity	Persons
1. Purpose of the walkthrough	All
2. Discuss performance goals	User representatives
3. Overview of systems requirements and representative uses	User representatives
4. Present scenarios; refine performance goal	User representatives
5. Overview of software system structure	Software representatives
6. Execution structure for scenarios	Software representatives; Performance analyst
7. Confirm understanding of execution structure	Performance analyst
8. Proposed configuration	Capacity planner; Project representative
9. Estimate resource requirements	Software representative; Performance analyst
10. Explore alternatives (optional)	Performance analyst
11. Summary of action items	Meeting manager
12. (later) Presentation of results	Performance analyst

spond directly to the model specifications we need (as defined in Section 3.1). In Step 7, the performance analyst summarizes his or her understanding of the execution structure. Step 10 (exploring alternatives) is appropriate when there is strong evidence that the performance goal may not be met. Experienced performance analysts usually have the intuition to quickly identify performance problems and feasible alternatives. When this happens, it is helpful to review potential alternatives, rule out those that are clearly impractical, and identify possibilities for further analysis. The walkthrough concludes with a review of the activities, the action items, persons responsible, and completion dates. Once the performance is analyzed, the group reconvenes to learn the results, set appropriate directions, and schedule the next walkthrough.

To illustrate what transpires during a walkthrough, consider the ATM example. The users of the system are represented by a bank officer knowledgeable of the functions to be provided and the characteristics of the clients' use of the ATM. The designers and implementers are the software specialists who will develop the application programs. They first discuss the SPE purpose: to determine whether the users' response time will be competitive with other banks. Some discussion follows to quantify the current and future response times of the competition and to determine whether the target is the session response time or the user-interaction response time. The bank officer then describes the system requirements, ATM typical use, and specific usage scenarios. The performance analyst asks questions, such as how many customers will use the ATM, the frequency of use, and so forth. Together they identify several key scenarios and their desired response time.

Next, the designers and implementers describe the software plans. Together they identify the components to be executed (the execution structure) for the specified workload scenarios. The performance analyst interprets the information presented and responds by describing an execution graph of the derived execution structure. (Execution graphs are defined in Chapter 4.)

The execution environment is already known (although a system specialist may be consulted to resolve configuration questions that arise during the walkthrough). Therefore, once the execution structures are derived, the walkthrough participants estimate the resource usage, taking into consideration the bank officer's knowledge about the workload, the software specialist's knowledge of the processing, and the performance analyst's knowledge of the environment. There are no obvious performance problems, so alternatives are not discussed. The meeting concludes with a summary of the findings and a schedule for the results presentation and next walkthrough.

Resource requirements are the most difficult specifications to obtain. Use your intuition to identify the resource likely to dominate the performance. For example, a database SELECT command is likely to be dominated by disk accesses rather than by the application program's CPU time required to set up the database call. Focus on the dominant resource usage for the initial SPE studies. Some installations initially ignore application CPU usage because I/O activity dominates their systems performance and it is easier to estimate. Others use rough estimates of the number of instructions to be executed. Model libraries can provide estimates of DBMS CPU and I/O overhead.

You can evaluate the system more precisely as it evolves. Once parts of the system are implemented or prototyped, you can measure the resource usage of key components. Some portions of the system may be fully operational and can be measured, while other parts may still be in early or middle stages of design. Mix measurements of implemented components with walkthroughs of others to develop model specifications.

Critical components may not be completely defined until detailed design and implementation culminate. So continue the performance walkthroughs well into implementation in order to fully resolve the execution structures. This helps to avert the local-but-not-global optimization problems. Users should continue to participate to provide workload information that drives resource requirements, such as data characteristics, cardinality, and percentage of customers affected. Once the system reaches detailed design, much of the walkthrough data can be tabulated in machine-readable form for subsequent use. This is crucial to the performance studies in late lifecycle stages, because large systems have so much data that manual performance analysis quickly becomes intractable. (Automated data collection and SPE data management concepts are discussed in Chapter 7.) Understanding the concept of the performance walkthrough is the beginning; we next turn to pragmatic techniques for making it successful.

3.2.2 Successful Design and Code Walkthroughs

Many organizations conduct regular design and code walkthroughs during development. Mixed success with them is reported. Because performance walkthroughs are patterned after design and code walkthroughs, an examination of their similarities, some success factors common to both, and some differences should be illuminating.

The first similarity is that design and code walkthroughs both rely on **managed meetings** for their success. To manage meetings:

- □ *Appoint a strong leader* to maintain the focus and to maximize the information exchanged in a minimum amount of time.
- □ *Schedule meetings in sufficient time* for key people to participate.
- □ *Plan activities* so all participants understand what is expected, are familiar with pertinent background information, and are prepared to contribute their information.

Effective meeting management is vital to many activities in an organization. Some organizations employ "professional" meeting management staff to run meetings for a variety of purposes; others hire consultants to be meeting facilitators.

The second similarity is the **purpose of the walkthroughs:** to convey specific information and to raise everyone's awareness of the overall system design and the interaction of system components. Usually the walkthrough process implicitly improves the product. The person explaining the system often becomes aware of deficiencies when communicating its parts to others. Listeners may anticipate situations that others overlooked. The more attention is focused on a system, the more likely it is to be improved.

There are also differences between performance and traditional walkthroughs. The first is that the performance walkthrough relies on **user representative involvement** to identify frequent activities, clarify system usage details, and contribute pertinent data characteristics. (The involvement of user representatives should be a feature of regular design walkthroughs, also.) Walking through a typical usage scenario is an early symbolic execution of the system against operational data. Experience shows that many errors found after system delivery are due to operational data characteristics not anticipated by developers or testers. User representative participation increases the chances of locating these problems earlier, as some organizations are beginning to recognize to their benefit.

Because user representation increases the number of participants, all of whom are busy professionals, we want to minimize wasted time. One strategy is to free participants when discussions are not relevant to them, keeping them "on call" and readily available to answer questions when they arise.

Adding user representatives to design walkthroughs leaves only one difference in performance walkthroughs: the discussions of execution behavior and resource usage. These discussions could be integrated with design and code walkthrough activities, with "on call" participation reserved for those not actively involved in these discussions. Two advantages of this approach are: (1) it more closely couples development and performance considerations, so performance is likely to be improved and less likely to be viewed as "nice, but not part of the design," and (2) much of the requirements and software information is already in design walkthroughs, so it need not be repeated. (Some designers resent having to repeat fundamental explanations of software and usage characteristics and "get too busy" to participate in performance walkthroughs.) The disadvantage is that execution behavior and resource estimation lengthen the design walkthrough. There is no best solution; it is organization-dependent. With experience, you will find the best solution for your particular environment.

Note that *walkthroughs are not reviews.* A review critically examines a system and looks for errors, omissions, or other faults. The distinction is important: Reviews require judgments, whereas judgments are inappropriate in walkthroughs. Critical remarks inhibit information exchange and hinder cooperation. Even when problems are found, participants should refrain from making critical remarks. Performance problems are addressed in the results presentation (methods are suggested in Section 3.2.5); other problems are resolved after the walkthrough.

3.2.3 Agenda Activity Rationale

Understanding the purpose of each of the steps in Table 3.2's agenda and the suggested order increases their effectiveness and enables you to better adapt them to your environment. If they are integrated with regular design and code walkthroughs, be sure that all the steps are covered.

The importance of the first step—discussing the purpose of the walkthrough—ranges from a formality for well-defined SPE studies to a vital component for ill-defined studies. Examples of the latter situation are:

☐ When developers are directed to produce a system with "good" performance, but no specific definition of "good" exists

☐ When the user's environment is not well understood or typical uses are not known

☐ When SPE is introduced after development is underway and problems have been found

☐ When SPE is imposed by someone other than the project leader

In these and other situations, we must first understand and clearly state the problems or situations to be addressed to ensure that subsequent discussions provide the necessary data for evaluating them.

Next we clarify the performance goals. We define the metrics (response time, throughput, resource budgets, average, maximum, 90th percentile, and so on), the events to be measured (such as transactions, user interactions, sessions, or user functions), and the measurement environment (peak load, daily average, number of concurrent users, or other factors).

Next we review background information about system requirements and system purpose. By examining *how* the system will be used and *what* it is to do, we confirm that the usage scenarios to be modeled represent the frequent and important activities.

The detailed description of scenario-processing steps provides the basis for the software execution structures. We refine the performance goal to be proportional to the required processing, clearly defining the events to be measured against that goal.

The software structure overview helps you to understand the design approach and confirms that the important components are represented in the software execution models. The execution structures are the basis for the software execution models. Confirm that they are correct before you exert the effort to derive resource specifications and create the models. Software execution graphs (defined in Chapter 4) are an effective means of confirmation. Their chief advantage is that they visually represent the system using a different "language." People tend to see and hear what they expect rather than what is described. Visual description increases the likelihood that misunderstandings and omissions will be noticed and clarified. They are visual aids that focus discussions and hold attention.

The computer configuration may already be known; if so, it can be omitted from the performance walkthrough. However, capacity planners should periodically participate in discussions to confirm that future capacity plans and new system developments are compatible. Sometimes computer configuration is an important variable in the requirements definition stage. Developers of OEM systems wish to minimize initial equipment costs and allow upgrade potential, while delivering systems with competitive performance. In such cases we identify configuration alternatives to be modeled.

Discussion of resource usage comes late in the agenda and is distinct from the execution structure. In practice decoupling the two topics results in better success. Otherwise, when combined, uncertainties are compounded and designers often find them overwhelming. They give up, decide it is impossible to model performance so early, and become skeptical of the model results. Resource usage is the hardest performance specification to obtain. Because it is so important and so difficult for inexperienced practitioners, Section 3.2.4 presents some tactics for obtaining data and coping with uncertainties.

Consider alternatives only when there is strong evidence that performance goals cannot be met. In that case, identify feasible alternatives for later performance analysis. It is presumptuous, when there is no evidence that performance is a problem, to suggest "better ways" of doing things to designers who have spent many hours studying all aspects of the system.

Meeting closure calls for a summary of what has transpired, a review of the action items, who is responsible, when the items will be resolved, a date and time to consider the results, and a schedule for the next walkthrough. Keep the number of action items as small as possible and resolve them as quickly as possible. The rationale for this approach is in the next subsection.

Finally, confer on the results of the performance evaluation. Effectively communicating these results is another difficulty of performance walkthroughs. Section 3.2.5 has strategies for improving the communication process and achieving favorable SPE results.

3.2.4 Specifying Resource Usage

As previously mentioned, resource usage specifications tend to be the hardest to obtain, especially in initial SPE studies. Section 3.1.5 suggests using bounded estimates, best- and worst-case analyses, and data-dependent variables to compensate for uncertainties. Resource usage specification will probably only be a temporary problem. Once designers become familiar with SPE, they should have no trouble providing the data. Nevertheless, you still need at least one successful SPE study to achieve this objective. In the meantime, the following tactics help to obtain enough data to proceed.

It helps if performance analysts begin by explaining that: we understand the difficulty in specifying resource usage for systems that do not exist; we are initially looking for ballpark numbers rather than precise data; approximations suffice to identify critical areas for which precision is vital, and we can follow up on those. The process is very similar to developing budgets and schedules, which are based on general knowledge about the constituent parts, and which are expected to be reasonably accurate but seldom exact.

Next, *focus on one component and one resource at a time*. Since I/Os are easier to estimate, begin by posing a question like, "Approximately how many I/Os will be done in this component?" The worst response you can expect is, "I don't know," "It's too early to tell," "It's not designed yet." When this happens, start a dialog that leads to some preliminary data, asking what data it needs to access, or suggesting some reasonable numbers and phrasing questions that obtain either yes/no or multiple-choice answers. Some examples are: "Does two I/Os seem reasonable?" or "Would it be between three and five?" Again, if the answer is no, ask why it is wrong or what we need to know in order to estimate, or suggest more numbers, perhaps a larger range, until you negotiate an estimate or reasonable bounds. Similar tactics work for the other resources and for the next components.

Another typical response is, "I'm not sure—I'll check into it and get back to you." *Avoid postponing estimates*. Once put off, they tend to be delivered *much later,* sometimes after code is written, or never produced at all. When specifications are developed long after the walkthrough, it is difficult to relate the data to the execution structure—it has very likely changed. Use the sample dialog above to extract a guess, "Just to see how the model looks—we can refine it later." You might add that perhaps you can save the data collection effort if the model results are insensitive to that particular specification. The 80–20 rule says that refined estimates are needed only 20 percent of the time.

Another typical response is "I don't know—it depends." Start a dialog to *understand the dependencies*. Sometimes the scenario definition resolves the dependency. In the ATM execution structure, the resource requirements to process a request depend on what the request is. The "get balance" scenario exemplified earlier specifies the request, so it eliminates the dependency. Even if the scenario definition leaves dependencies, it is sufficient to specify resource requirements for the most frequent functions, if the variability occurs in infrequent ones. If these solutions are inappropriate, focus on isolating the causes of the variability. They become the data-dependent variables; then estimate values or ranges for the variables, and the resource requirements per unit.

3.2.5 Communicating Results

The key factors in communicating results are a **quick response, basis for the results, quantitative results,** and **decision support.** Ideally the results should be presented the next day, or at least within a week. If delayed a month, they are unlikely to be useful. Relate the results to the assumptions about the software and the model. Provide quantitative performance metrics for alternatives, and decision-support data (such as time to fix and maintenance effect), so decision makers can analyze costs and benefits of alternatives. More information about these key factors is in the following paragraphs.

Begin the presentation of results with a brief review of the scenario and status of the software used for the study. Then list the assumptions. Next show the predicted performance metrics for each scenario and for each model case under consideration. The cases include the best case and, depending on results, possibly the worst case, the average for the system as described in the walkthrough, and appropriate alternatives. The presentation may include an interpretation of the results and a recommendation. Some managers prefer recommendations; others prefer to use data to draw their own conclusions and make decisions accordingly. If you do not know which is preferred, prepare a recommendation, but don't present it unless asked.

The cases to be modeled depend on the results. If performance goals are met, a sensitivity analysis identifies key factors to be monitored. If goals are not met, a best-case analysis is key. This strategy has been mentioned several times, and its importance cannot be overemphasized. When results are bad, developers usually question the model assumptions. If they continually find that performance is not better in the cases they envision, but much worse, eventually their attention shifts from the model assumptions to possible solutions. When they find model assumptions that might be invalid and might lead to improvements, designers may continue to hope that performance goals can be met without changes and defer corrective actions (occasionally until it is too late).

When results are inconclusive, as when the best case is fine but the worst case is unacceptable, examine the sensitivity of the results to the model specifications. Isolate the key specifications that drive performance, and use supplemental approaches to derive more precise data. Because this takes longer, present preliminary results so everyone understands the problem areas, and solicit input that may narrow the scope of the supplemental studies.

You may encounter some problems communicating results and influencing the adoption of improvements. Problems occur when performance studies show that changes are required if goals are to be met, but no action is taken. Some symptoms and strategies for overcoming the problems are examined in the following paragraphs.

One problem is the "It won't work—do it this way" presentation. The performance analyst relies on intuition and experience to conclude that his or her recommendations are "obvious" and that it is a waste of time and effort to model something that won't work. Actually, experienced performance analysts are usually right, but when they present "results" in this manner, their recommendations are rarely accepted. One reason is that the results are not obvious to those without such well-developed intuition, and because people have a natural resistance to change, particularly when it is not obvious how much improvement the change will yield.

This phenomenon occurs all too often. Designers have said that after they have spent many long hours considering all facets of a design problem, they are skeptical and even resentful of hastily developed approaches advocating radically different designs presented in such an inconsiderate manner. Antagonism mounts, and cooperation and the chance of a near-term, rational solution are virtually nil. Thus, it is *not a waste of time and effort to model systems that won't work—it is a vital aspect of SPE*. Relate the SPE results to the general principles in Chapter 2 to convey the performance intuition to designers and lead to improved future designs.

Another problem is the "What if . . . " response. Designers think of new cases and want model data for their performance impact, and it is easier to ask "what if" questions indefinitely than it is to proceed with solutions. Try to antici-pate as many "what ifs" as possible, and include them in the initial analyses. This means not just modeling solutions with high-performance improvements (as expe-rienced performance engineers are prone to do), but also including cases with moderate-performance improvements and low impact on the software.

It is impossible to anticipate every case, so another strategy is to negoti-ate conditional decisions prior to analyzing "what ifs." One example is, "Select solution x if the model results show y; otherwise select solution z." If good modeling-support tools are available, you may be able to solve "what if" questions interactively, during the meeting, as they arise.

A related problem is the "What would it take to do that?" decision deferral. This problem occurs when performance results are convincing but decision-support data (such as time to fix, and number of modules affected) is insufficient to select the most appropriate solution. The danger here is that decisions deferred too long become infeasible. It is a Catch–22: If changes are essential, the results must be made available quickly, but it takes longer to gather the decision-support data needed for a spontaneous decision.

The most difficult to resolve is the "You're probably right, but . . . " prob-lem. The response indicates that despite predictions, no corrective action will be taken. There may be valid reasons for the reluctance to act, but if the performance problems are critical, it is important to pursue the reasons. Two causes of reluc-tance that can be resolved are lack of confidence and fear of schedule adjustments.

Managers or designers may be skeptical of results. They may doubt that the modeled workload scenario truly represents the future workload. They may lack confidence in the resource usage estimates. When SPE is new, they may not trust the performance models. These problems can be corrected by first identifying the low-confidence details and compiling evidence that they are accurate, or by study-ing more cases to examine sensitivities and provide more data.

Managers and designers may also be reluctant to act when the time required for corrective action prolongs the delivery schedule. The tendency is to (try to) deliver on time, then "fix it later." If performance problems are severe, it is unlikely that even an inferior product can be delivered on time, because testing takes longer than originally scheduled as well. Poor initial performance causes users to have negative impressions of the software, even when performance problems are corrected later. The solution is to compile data that supports corrective action and appropriate schedule adjustments early, when there are more options to compensate for the additional time. Compile quantitative data that compares the time to correct problems early versus later, the expected performance gains early versus later, total time until initial delivery (adjusting the testing time) and later delivery of a satisfactory product, the expected maintenance effort required for each alternative, personnel costs, hardware capacity, and other factors. Report and *document the results*. If you persist, someone will eventually listen.

You may feel that these tactics are beyond the scope of SPE, but they are another vital component. *The goal of SPE is not just to solve performance models and present results—it is to build performance into systems*. Often this requires negotiation and communications skills in addition to technical performance-modeling skills.

3.2.6 Adaptive Data Collection

Thus far we have considered SPE in an ideal environment: User representatives understand future system usage, software designers have a general system architecture, the computer configuration is known, and resource usage specifications are possible. Actual SPE environments may differ significantly.

Workload predictions have traditionally been unavailable. User representatives help provide useful information when they are knowledgeable of the working environment and its many variations. It is still difficult to project how a system will be used when it offers functions not previously available.

It is beneficial to establish the relationship between business activity and software early. Business planning departments project business activity in *natural forecasting units (NFUs)*. Capacity planners have long recognized the benefits of using NFU forecasts for capacity planning, but they found it virtually impossible to connect business activity to resource usage. SPE models relate NFUs to system functions, usage scenarios, and data-dependent parameters, so it is much easier to establish connections between NFUs and resource usage. NFUs then support verification of workload volumes, and SPE models can project capacity requirements from NFU forecasts.

Software is often an evolutionary version of previous products, and measurements of existing systems can be used to extrapolate future usage. Many new database applications replace earlier systems. When software is developed incrementally, when reusable software libraries are available, or when evolutionary systems reuse components of the previous system, resource usage and path execution specifications can be leveraged with measurement data. Performance benchmarks provide model specifications. When actual data can be easily obtained, it is better to use it than to rely on guesses.

Workload measurements of previous products are also valuable for vendors developing new commercial products. Trace tapes collected at various "friendly installations" provide data on how systems are used in a variety of environments. Analysis of the tapes identifies the frequent usage scenarios across all environments. For example, an operating system may be used on both medium and large systems and may support users in banks, oil companies, insurance companies, and manufacturing firms. Although little commonality is obvious, a key operating system workload scenario is likely to be sequential I/O.

Though somewhat labor-intensive, performance walkthroughs are currently the most effective means of gathering pertinent data, particularly when SPE is new. They have the additional advantage of raising system awareness, which implicitly improves both performance and system quality. As SPE becomes better established, and when developers have experience providing SPE specifications, it may be possible to create questionnaires or automated tools to facilitate data collection.

Eventually automated modeling tools integrated with system development environments will provide sufficient support for developers to do their own performance modeling. Will performance walkthroughs then become extinct? When performance specification matures to the point at which specification by questionnaire is feasible, it will also be possible to quickly cover the specifications in walkthroughs. While many designers will evaluate their own models, others will prefer to delegate this task to an experienced performance analyst. External review, by someone not on the project team, will always play an important role in verification and validation. On the other hand, as SPE matures and its use spreads and is accepted by developers, pragmatic tactics for overcoming reluctance, deferral, and other problems will no longer be necessary.

Thus, performance walkthroughs are important in the near term for gathering pertinent data and developing designers' performance intuition. They may occur less frequently in future environments, but they will continue to support project reviews.

3.2.7 Verification and Validation

Another vital part of SPE is continual verification of the model specifications and validation of model predictions (V&V). It begins early, particularly when model results suggest that major changes are needed. The V&V effort matches the impact of the results and the importance of performance to the project. When performance is critical or when major software changes are indicated, identify the critical components, implement or prototype them, and measure. Verify resource usage and path execution specifications and validate model results against the measurements.

Early V&V is important even when predicted performance is good. Performance analysts drive the resource usage specifications, and analysts tend to be optimistic about how functions will be implemented and about their resource requirements. *Resource usage of the actual system often differs significantly from the optimistic specifications* ([FOX89]). The number of database tables accessed is often optimistic, and the characteristics of the database calls often change. For example, early data may specify a simple SELECT; later an ORDER BY clause may be added that potentially causes a dramatic increase in resource requirements.

Interview users, designers, and programmers to confirm that usage will be as expected and that designed and coded algorithms agree with model assumptions. Make adjustments when appropriate, revise predictions, and give regular status reports.

Perform sensitivity analyses of model parameters and determine thresholds that yield acceptable performance. Then, as the software evolves and code is produced, measure resource usage and path executions and compare them against these thresholds to obtain early warning of potential problems. As software increments are deployed, measure the workload characteristics and compare specified scenario usage to actual to find inaccuracies or omissions. Compare model predictions against measured behavior to confirm that the models represent system behavior. Calibrate models and evaluate the effect of model changes on earlier results.

3.3 Specifications for the Case Studies

Now that we know what data we need to build a software model, we will practice the concepts with the comprehensive case studies. The information is presented as if it were from a performance walkthrough from which we will derive the model specifications. The three case studies are:

- □ Computer-aided design user software
- □ Engineering data management system
- □ Network operating system interprocess communication

3.3.1 Computer-Aided Design User Software: DRAWMOD

This case study examines an interactive system to support an engineering computer-aided design (CAD) activity. Engineers plan to use computer graphics to construct a model of a proposed aerospace vehicle, store the model in a database, and interactively assess the design's correctness, feasibility, and preferability. DRAWMOD is one usage scenario.

The users give an overview of the functions of the CAD software and identify those expected to be most frequently used by the design engineers. Only one of these functions, DRAWMOD, is illustrated; one is sufficient to demonstrate the concepts. An actual SPE study analyzes more scenarios to ensure that improvements made to one function do not adversely affect other important functions. Samples of walkthrough discussions about DRAWMOD are given in Example 3.6.

EXAMPLE 3.6: DRAWMOD Walkthrough

a. User's description of the DRAWMOD requirements

This scenario is a request from an engineer at a graphics terminal to draw an aircraft model previously stored in the database. It is used to view the model data for correctness and completeness.

An example of the drawing to be displayed is in Figure 3.4. A typical model consists of 2,050 beams. Several versions of the aircraft model may exist in the database. The engineer enters the following command at the terminal:

DRAWMOD ⟨specified_mod⟩

to execute the DRAWMOD program and to specify the identification number of the model to be displayed.

b. Software engineer's description of DRAWMOD's top-level design

The model information is stored in a relational database. Two database tables are used in this program: the beam definition and the node location. The attributes of each table are shown below:

BEAM DEFINITION

Beam #	Model ID #	Node-1	Node-2	Other data	

64 bytes/row

NODE LOCATION

Node #	Model ID #	x-coord	y-coord	z-coord	Other data

24 bytes/row

(continued)

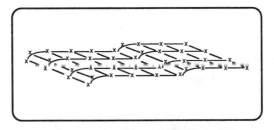

FIGURE 3.4
A Typical Graphics Display to Be Seen by DRAWMOD Users. The Xs represent nodes in the model; the lines represent beams.

EXAMPLE 3.6 (*Continued*)

The engineer's request is received from the terminal and the DRAWMOD program is initiated. The beam definition and node location tables are OPENed. The database FIND locates all beam rows for the "specified_mod" number. The database DBSORT sorts qualifying records into ascending sequence on beam number.

For each beam:

☐ The database RETRIEVE gets the beam data.

☐ The two node numbers in the beam data are extracted.

☐ The database FIND locates the node rows where the model_id number matches the engineer's input *and* the node numbers match those from the beam row.

☐ For each node, a database RETRIEVE gets the node coordinates.

☐ The *x, y,* and *z* coordinates of each node are extracted and used to DRAW the graphic output.

☐ Upon completion, the beam definition and node location tables are CLOSEd.

c. Performance analyst questions

The performance analyst participates in discussions with users and software engineers and asks pertinent questions to clarify information and obtain the necessary performance specifications. Examples of questions and responses (in italics) are:

☐ How often will the engineers execute the DRAWMOD program? {*In any given period of activity, an average of once every five minutes*}

☐ How many engineers will use it concurrently? {*From one to ten*}

☐ How big is the database? What is the average number of beams and nodes per model? {*Beams: 2,050; nodes: 1,500*} How many model versions are typically stored in the database? {*From 4 to 40*} In what order is the data stored in the database? {*Random*}

☐ Are the beams and nodes numbered sequentially? {*Yes; beams are numbered in increasing order from left to right and top to bottom; similarly for nodes. This is by convention, not a model requirement.*}

☐ What is the physical organization of the database (record and block sizes)? {*One row per record; block size is approximately 4K bytes.*}

☐ How much information (number of bytes/screen) is transmitted from and to the terminal? {*20 bytes from; 40 bytes per beam to the terminal*}

☐ How long does it take to DRAW a beam? Or, alternatively, what are its resource requirements? How many lines of code execute? {*50*} How many I/O operations? {*No file I/O; one screen communication*}

☐

We need to turn the example walkthrough description into the model specifications. First, define the performance goals. DRAWMOD is an interactive transaction that is to support the analysis of aircraft designs. Since highly paid design engineers will use the programs, the response should be as rapid as possible to minimize their idle time. However, DRAWMOD must retrieve a large amount of data and produce a large graphical display, so it is infeasible to seek the subsecond response times often sought for management information systems. The client engineer states that a 5- to 10-minute average response time is acceptable, since this would be a great improvement over the one week generally required for previous batch methods. The software engineers suspect that a maximum of 10 seconds should be targeted. After deliberation, participants decide that response times should be minimized, but not at the expense of extensive implementation efforts; tradeoff decisions should favor ease of implementation as long as **average response times are less than 20 seconds for up to 10 active users.**

Next, derive the execution structure for the specified workload scenario. Walkthrough discussions lead to the processing steps in Example 3.7

EXAMPLE 3.7: Execution Structure: DRAWMOD

The scenario has a DRAWMOD driver that issues the following database calls:

```
——DRAWMOD driver calls:
DBOPEN;
FIND beam_row WHERE model_id# = specified_mod;
DBSORT beam_row;
loop                                      ——2600 times
  RETRIEVE (NEXT) beam_row;
  FIND node_row WHERE
    (model_id# = specified_mod)
    AND ((node# = node_1)
    OR (node# = node_2));
    loop                                  ——2 times
        RETRIEVE (NEXT) node_row;
    end loop;
    DRAW;
end loop;
DBCLOSE;
```

Recall that the execution structure represents the typical execution paths rather than all possible paths. Therefore, it excludes infrequent activities such as exception condition processing.   □

Next estimate the resource requirements for each of the functional components in the execution structure. At this point we notice that the DRAWMOD driver code is trivial. It consists almost entirely of database calls; its only processing is in manipulating parameters, and at this stage in design we estimate that CPU and I/O processing for the application program code (to set up the database calls) is minimal: 1,000 instructions and 3 file I/Os, a get-memory and a free-memory.

We need to know the resource requirements for the database commands (DBOPEN, FIND, DBSORT, RETRIEVE, and DBCLOSE) and for the DRAW graphics routine. These lower-level support software systems, such as the DBMS and operating system, usually already exist, so their performance specifications are either available in a library or they can be obtained from measurement studies. Assume that the graphics routines exist and that the resource requirements for the DRAW routine are as shown in Table 3.3. FIND and RETRIEVE are part of the EDMS case study—we will develop models for them and calculate their resource requirements. To limit the scope of this example, we will skip the analysis of DBOPEN, DBSORT, and DBCLOSE and use the results shown in Table 3.3.

3.3.2 Engineering Data Management System: FIND and RETRIEVE

The second case study illustrates the evaluation of a proposed engineering database management system (EDMS). As mentioned earlier, a large software system of this type is usually complex, and the performance of a single component of the system is highly dependent on the performance of other components. We focus on two primary data manipulation commands, FIND and RETRIEVE. Samples of walkthrough discussions about them are in Example 3.8.

TABLE 3.3
DRAWMOD RESOURCE REQUIREMENTS

Component	Instructions executed	I/Os	System routines	
			Name	Number
DRAWMOD	1,000	3	Get/free memory	2
			Screen communication	2
DRAW	50	0	Screen communication	1
EDMS Functions:				
DBOPEN	2,300	6	Get/free memory	1
DBSORT	$1,570 + 15N\log_2 N$	#addr blocks+ #data blocks	Get/free memory	2
DBCLOSE	1,500	2	Get/free memory	1

EXAMPLE 3.8: EDMS Walkthrough Descriptions

a. User's view

FIND command: The syntax of the FIND command is as follows:

FIND ⟨table name⟩ WHERE ⟨condition clause⟩;

The FIND determines the location (address) of all rows in ⟨table name⟩ that satisfy the associated condition clause and builds a scratch file that contains all qualifying addresses. Subsequent RETRIEVE commands obtain the record locations from this scratch file, thus improving their efficiency. No data is retrieved as a result of the FIND command; however, the number of qualifying rows is stored in the variable NUM_QUAL.

RETRIEVE command: The syntax is as follows:

```
                 NEXT
RETRIEVE    (   FIRST      )   ⟨table name⟩;
                 LAST
                 PREVIOUS
```

The RETRIEVE is issued following a FIND command to obtain the attribute values from one of the qualified rows. The optional parameters specify which address on the scratch file is to be used. The "current" address is remembered to facilitate sequential retrievals.

b. Software engineer's proposal for EDMS processing (top-level design)

The request is received by the EDMS Message Processor and routed to the Database Control (DBC) component. The command is parsed, access rights checked, and the appropriate command processor is called (FIND or RETRIEVE in this example). Results are returned to the Database Control component, then to the Message Processor, and finally sent to the requestor.

The FIND processing first calls the btree processor—it searches a btree to find the key referenced and a pointer to a list of addresses where all rows containing that key are located. The list is then sorted with a recursive call to DBSORT, and a scratch file containing this information is created. The number of addresses found is returned.

The RETRIEVE processing consists of calling the scratch file manager to get the address of the desired data, calling the buffer checker to determine if the desired information is already in memory (and, if it is not, a READ ⟨data⟩ operation is initiated); finally, the specified attribute values are extracted from the buffer and returned.

The Message Processor consists of two parts. The DB_MP initiation processing allocates memory, RECEIVEs the request from SYS_EXEC, interprets the request, and for this scenario, transfers control to the DBC. It also routes requests to the query language processor and the database utilities. The DB_MP termination processing formats the reply message, SENDs it to SYS_EXEC for routing, and frees the memory allocated during initiation.

(continued)

EXAMPLE 3.8 (*Continued*)

c. Performance analyst questions

□ What is the size of the scratch file? {*Ten bytes per qualified record, 2K bytes per block*}

□ Why are the scratch file addresses sorted? {*To improve the efficiency of subsequent RETRIEVEs by minimizing disk head movements*}

□ What processing is required to handle complex boolean combinations in WHERE clauses, such as

((key1 < 5) AND (key3 = 100) OR (key7 > 300))

{*The processing details have not yet been resolved.*}

□ What is the difference between the DBSORT referenced in DRAWMOD and DBSORT called by FIND? {*The DBSORT called by DRAWMOD goes through the address list created by FIND; RETRIEVEs each record; extracts the value of the sort key; then creates a new address list with the order of the addresses corresponding to their key values. DBSORT called by FIND bypasses the retrieval of the data record keys and sorts the addresses into ascending sequence.*}

□

To turn this walkthrough description into the model specifications, start with the performance goal. The EDMS performance goal will arbitrarily remain at the application program level: The database commands must be sufficiently fast for the application program to meet the 20-second response time goal. Alternatively, you could place a response time goal on each command, or impose throughput requirements on EDMS. For example, we might impose a response time goal of a maximum of 250 milliseconds for a FIND that qualifies up to 100 objects, or set an average throughput goal of 50 database commands per second.

The database workload is explicitly specified by the DRAWMOD application program. To make a realistic assessment of overall system performance, study additional *representative* application programs. This ensures that optimizations are global improvements rather than local. You do not want local optimizations that improve one application program but adversely affect a significant portion of the workload. The workload characteristics for other scenarios are obtained from software models or by measuring (existing) application programs.

The remaining EDMS commands (such as DBOPEN, DBCLOSE, and LIST RELATIONS) would also be included in a comprehensive evaluation, but their description is omitted here since they give us little additional information. If you are unfamiliar with database processing, btrees, or the terminology used in this discussion, the btree inset offers some background information.

Background: Btrees and Data Retrieval Terminology

A btree is a data structure often used as an index to locate information corresponding to desired key values [COM79]. As illustrated below, a btree has multiple *levels*. At each level are *nodes* containing key values and pointers. To find a specific value, one begins at the top level, with the *root node,* and searches for the pointer to the next-level node that contains the range of values desired. At the lowest level are *leaf nodes* that contain the value and a pointer to a *list of addresses* of data records that contain that key value. Multiple records may contain the key value.

In the diagram, the btree has three levels. The left-most pointer in the root node points to the next-level node containing key values ≤ 12. The level below it is a leaf node. Three address lists are illustrated. The leaves show only one record address for key value 3, several records for 7, and two blocks of addresses to records with key value 12.

Specific rules for additions and deletions in the btree preserve the order of values within index nodes and ensure that all "branches" of the tree have the same number of levels. Varieties of btrees differ in the fullness of each node; whether key values occur once in the tree or carry through to the leaves, as above; and in other ways.

There is one btree per *key* per table (or file). In the EDMS case study, each WHERE *condition clause* triggers a btree search. For complex combinations of condition clauses, an intermediate address list may be created for each condition; then in a final pass, intersections or unions of intermediate lists create the final address list.

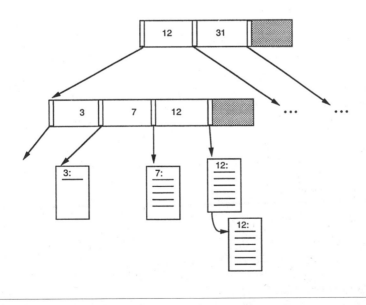

EXAMPLE 3.9: FIND and RETRIEVE Execution Structures

The execution structure for the top-level processing of the FIND and RETRIEVE commands is:

a. Database control processing
⟨⟨DBC⟩⟩ Database Control, a driver process activated by DB_MP initiation:
--DBC driver calls:
Parse_command;
Check_access_rights;
case request **is**
when FIND =⟩–a driver process calls:
      Btree_processor (address_list);
      DBSORT (address_list);
      Create (final_address_list);
when RETRIEVE =⟩– a driver process calls:
      Scratch_file_manager;
      --Buffer_checker:
      if not_in_memory **then**
          Read (data);
      end if;
when other =⟩ appropriate_processing;
end case;

Upon completion, control returns to DB_MP Termination.

b. DB_MP processing
--DB_MP Initiation:
Allocate_memory;
RECEIVE (request);
Interpret (request);

--DB_MP Termination:
Format_reply;
SEND (reply);
Free_memory;

□

Next estimate resource usage for the components. Table 3.4 shows the lower-bound estimates for instructions executed, number of I/Os, and system routines requested. Other specifications will be introduced later. Note that some of these estimates are dependent on characteristics of the database, such as the number of addresses in an address list, the size of an address, the size of a record, and the

TABLE 3.4
EDMS LOWER-BOUND RESOURCE ESTIMATES

Component	Instructions executed	I/Os	System routines Name	Number
DBC	25	0		
Parse_command	100	0	Get/free memory	2
Check_access_ rights	75	4		
Request?	10	0		
Allocate memory	0	0	Get/free memory	1
Interpret request	10	0		
Format reply	25	0		
Free memory	0	0	Get/free memory	1
FIND driver	50	0		
Get_addresses_ from_btree	50 + 150/condition + 100/block	1/block	Get/free memory	1/key
DBSORT	$1,570 + 15N\log_2 N$	# blocks	Get/free memory	2
Create_final_ address_list	100	1/block	Get/free memory	2
RETRIEVE driver	25	0		
Scratch_file_ manager	50	0	Get/free memory	1
Buffer_checker	150	.005		
Read (data)	100/block	1/block		

number of records in a block. These dependencies are discussed in more detail in the next chapter.

3.3.3 Network Operating System Interprocess Communication: SYS_EXEC

The third case study illustrates the evaluation of basic operating system software. We evaluate a representative function of a distributed system: network inter-process communication. Samples of walkthrough discussions about interprocess communication are in Example 3.10.

EXAMPLE 3.10: Interprocess Communication Walkthrough Description: SYS_EXEC

a. User's description of the communication functions

flag: = ESTABLISH (channel_type, length, name_list, calling_process_name);

This function establishes a potential data path for the process executing the ESTABLISH function. The type of data object that can be sent through a channel and its length in bytes are specified. "Name list" specifies all processes that may use the channel. Flag is an integer whose value determines the validity of function execution. If the ESTABLISH is success-ful, the flag is the integer channel ID.

channel: = REQUEST (process_name, channel_type, length);

This function, if successful, returns an integer identifier of a channel of the specified type and length to the process name given in a call. It "opens" the channel for use by the process.

flag: = SEND (channel, mode, process_name, data_address);

This function sends along the named channel a data object of the type defined by the established channel definition. The mode is either synchronous or asynchronous. The sending process and the location of the data object are specified. The flag value returned by SEND is undefined until the SEND is completed or aborted.

flag: = RECEIVE (channel, mode, process_name, data_address);

This function receives from the named channel a data object of the type defined by the established channel definition. RECEIVE is either synchronous or asynchronous, depend-ing on the mode parameter. The receiving process name and the location where the data object is to be placed are specified. The value of the flag is undefined until the RECEIVE is completed or aborted.

flag: = DELETE (channel, process_name);

This function deletes a channel previously established by "process name" from those available for REQUESTs.

flag: = RELEASE (channel, process_name);

This function detaches the named process from those currently sending or receiving using the specified channel. It "closes" the channel to the process. The flag value indicates the completion status.

b. Software engineer's description of a possible implementation

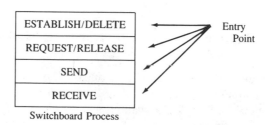

Switchboard Process

(continued)

EXAMPLE 3.10 (*Continued*)

The interprocess communication primitives will be implemented by a Switchboard process with four entry points, each representing one of the primitives. The Switchboard process will build tables defining channels and move data between processes by copying data to its internal buffers, and then from its internal buffers to the address space of the receiving process. It will store messages for blocked processes for a time-out period, buffering to external storage if necessary. The algorithms and data structures to be determined include table structures for storage of channel definitions and buffer space allocation for objects in transit. The Switchboard process will negotiate with the process scheduler to activate processes to clean out channel traffic. A deadlock detection algorithm will be integral to the Switchboard process.

c. Performance analyst questions

☐ What is the maximum message size? {*64 bytes*}

☐ How large is the Switchboard's buffer? {*8K bytes*}

☐ What is the buffer overflow algorithm? {*It is not yet resolved—LRU is our current strategy.*}

☐ Are there interactions with resource scheduling—Effect of activations to receive messages? Amount of resources idled by waits for messages? {*The designers are unsure; the answers are to be derived from the analysis of the other software.*}

☐ What are the characteristics of channel traffic—Distribution of message sizes including variance? Arrival rate for messages of each size? Fraction of traffic that must be held due to blocked processes? {*The answers to these questions will be derived from the analysis of the proposed CAD application and DBMS software.*}

☐ What communication processing is required when an application program requests EDMS processing? {*The application program's request is packaged into a message or messages; it is sent to SYS_EXEC for routing; the application program then does a RECEIVE and awaits the response.*}

☐

The execution structures for the DRAWMOD scenario and EDMS processing were fairly easy to derive from the walkthrough descriptions. The processing for communication is not as clear. This uncomfortable feeling from sketchy descriptions is common in initial SPE studies. Don't give up, and don't feel stupid because you don't understand—the system hasn't been completely explained. Clarify the description by posing a scenario such as passing a message from DRAWMOD to EDMS, and ask what processing steps would execute. The discussions for the case study are not presented; we skip to their findings. The designers draw a figure like Figure 3.5 to show the communication flow in the network operating system. The difference between the SEND referenced in Figure 3.5's Step 1 and the SYS_EXEC Switchboard (Send) is not obvious. The software engineers offer the following explanation. There are two components of the communication processing: Step 1 SEND moves the message to a staging area and adds the EDMS request to the SYS_EXEC pending queue; Step 3 is the low-level

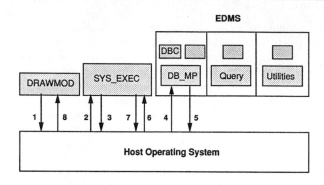

FIGURE 3.5
Processing Flow for Interprocess Communication. Each EDMS call in the DRAW-MOD scenario formats the EDMS request and SENDs a message to SYS_EXEC requesting database service (arrows 1 and 2); then DRAWMOD does a RECEIVE and waits for EDMS completion. SYS_EXEC periodically activates, processes all pending requests, and deactivates when no more are pending (arrows 3 and 4 represent DRAWMOD's request to EDMS). DB_MP allocates memory for the request, RECEIVEs the request for service, interprets the request, and transfers control to the component that executes it. Upon completion, DB_MP formats the reply, SENDs the resulting data to (DRAWMOD via) SYS_EXEC (arrows 5 and 6 to SYS_EXEC, arrows 7 and 8 back to DRAWMOD), and frees the memory requested earlier.

flag : = SEND described in Example 3.10. There is a similar distinction between RECEIVE and Switchboard (Receive). Eventually we derive the execution structure in Example 3.11.

TABLE 3.5
COMMUNICATION RESOURCE ESTIMATES

Component	Instructions executed	File I/O	System routines Name	Number
Format EDMS request	10	0		
SEND to SYS_EXEC (per message)	50	.001	SYS_EXEC	1
RECEIVE reply (per message)	50	0		
Request pending?	3	0		
Sleep	2	0		
Switchboard (Receive)	50	0		
Determine destination & package	16	0		
Adjust task schedule	10	0		
Switchboard (Send)	50	.001		

EXAMPLE 3.11: Interprocess Communication Execution Structure

When DRAWMOD makes an EDMS request, the following executes:

--EDMS call processing:
Format-EDMS-request;
SEND (EDMS-request);
RECEIVE (EDMS-reply);

SYS_EXEC has two parts: a loop that checks to see if requests are pending, and the processing to route messages for pending requests. The loop is as follows:

--SYS_EXEC loop:
loop   --forever
   Delay-until-activation;
   case message **is**
    when EDMS_request => SYS_EXEC_ processing;
    when nil   => SLEEP;
   end case;
end loop;

The message-routing is as follows:

--SYS_EXEC processing:
flag:=RECEIVE (fm_chan_name, async, receive_proc,
            rec_data_arca);
--ck flag
Determine_dest_and_pkg;
Adjust_task_schedule;
flag:= SEND (to_chan_name, async, send_proc,
         send_data_area);
--ck flag

The DB_MP processing, which receives EDMS requests, routes them within EDMS, and sends replies, is already described in the EDMS execution structure.

                                                      □

The implementation details of Switchboard and its internal routines have not yet been resolved. Their current resource usage estimates are in Table 3.5. Note that the low-level send-receive processing is factored into the DRAWMOD and EDMS overhead by specifying one call to the system routine SYS_EXEC for each high-level SEND. Alternatively, we could associate the communication processing with RECEIVE or prorate it between SEND and RECEIVE. This model suffices for the initial analysis.

In this example, the typical execution path is modeled; that is, the communication path has already been ESTABLISHed and REQUESTed, and the most frequent function is SENDs and RECEIVEs of messages between processes.[5]

3.3.4 Execution Environment for the Case Studies

All the case studies execute in the same environment. A sample walkthrough discussion of the proposed configuration follows.

EXAMPLE 3.12: Execution Environment Walkthrough Description

The software will execute in a distributed environment consisting of a network of engineering workstations. EDMS is to execute on the workstations. Copies of EDMS and data should be movable, with no impact on the application program software. Requests should be dynamically routed to EDMS on an appropriate host to satisfy the request. Each workstation in the network can have up to 10 local users.

Each workstation has a CPU that processes 5 million instructions per second (MIPS), and up to 8 hard disks with an average service time of 30 milliseconds per I/O.

□

From this description and from some additional information from discussions and measurements, we derive the execution environment specifications shown in Table 3.6. Additional configuration specifications will be introduced later when required for the system model of execution.

3.3.5 Case Study Relationship

Note that the case studies are interrelated. The CAD user software calls the EDMS, and EDMS uses the network operating system's interprocess communication facilities to exchange information with the system executive (SYS_EXEC), which communicates with the application programs, other EDMS processes, and processes on other hosts. All systems have a similar hierarchy of workloads: Users generate the work for application programs, which generate work for system software, and so on. Figure 3.6 illustrates some possible execution paths through a system. When an execution path crosses a software boundary, we need a workload specification for the model. For example, for the teleprocessing software and the execution path highlighted in Figure 3.6 you need a workload specification for

---

[5]In your studies, model scenarios that include important, infrequent functions such as ESTABLISH and REQUEST. If this is overlooked during the development of a text editor, for example, functions such as searches and changes may be rapid, but if it takes too long to open a file, the editor may be unusable.

TABLE 3.6
EXECUTION ENVIRONMENT SPECIFICATION:
OPERATING SYSTEM OVERHEAD

Factor	# instructions*	I/O time (sec)
Procedure call/return	5	0
Transfer control	2	0
I/O Processing		
Supervisor	100	
I/O device		0.03
Screen Communication:		
Supervisor	50	
Communication line		0.01
Get/free memory	10	0

*These instructions are "high-level" instructions. The average expansion of high-level instructions to machine instructions is 1:3.

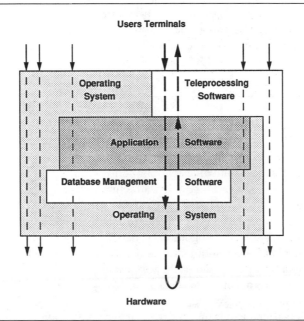

FIGURE 3.6
User requests may call for service from various system components to enable execution on the underlying hardware. The dashed lines show some of the possible execution paths.

the inbound work from the terminal and for the outbound work coming from the transaction (application) programs. If an older version of the system exists, measure the characteristics of the workload, and use the measurement data for the teleprocessing software models. If no similar software exists, then develop models of the interrelated software. These case studies illustrate a "worst case": Models of each interrelated subsystem define the workload for the other software. In most SPE studies, you will be able to measure the workload from the "surrounding" subsystems. These measurements are covered in more detail in Chapter 7.

The environment specifications for the subsystems are similarly interrelated. For example, if you can measure the execution characteristics of FIND and RE-TRIEVE, you can use the measurement data to derive their resource requirements for the application software's system routine calls. In these case studies we also model support subsystems, and calculate their (estimated) resource requirements.

Notice also that all the case study information in the walkthrough discussions was not pertinent to the execution structure for this analysis. For example, Switchboard's deadlock detection algorithm is not represented in the first-pass execution structure. It will be factored in later, after details are resolved, if it is executed in the message-routing scenario.

This completes the initial specifications for the performance goals, the workload specifications, the software execution structures, the execution environment, and the resource usage for each of the case studies. The next step is the creation and analysis of the software models, as described in the next chapter.

3.4 Summary

This chapter addressed data gathering for SPE. It described five types of specifications necessary for the quantitative analysis: performance goals, workload specifications (scenarios), software execution structure, execution environment, and resource usage.

This specification data clarifies the performance questions and sets the stage for further analysis just as analogous data enabled the commute-time evaluation. After a discussion of *what* information is necessary, we considered some of the problems in obtaining it. We studied the *performance walkthrough*, recommended as a viable technique for getting the data during early lifecycle stages. We covered pragmatic techniques for getting the needed data, communicating results, and confirming the specifications and the performance predictions. We then applied the concepts to derive data for the comprehensive case studies. The next SPE step uses this data to construct the software execution models.

This chapter focused on the early lifecycle model definition. Later, Chapter 7 supplements these data gathering and V&V activities with performance measurements.

Exercises

Review

3.1. List and briefly describe in your own words the five types of data needed for SPE. Give examples of each type.

3.2. Performance walkthroughs and SPE studies are more successful when all participants understand the performance prediction process, what data is needed, and the role that each data element plays in the SPE process. Prepare a presentation that explains these to an experienced software engineer who is unfamiliar with SPE. Use your own analogies and simple case studies to illustrate.

3.3. Define the SPE data for the case study you selected in Exercise 1.2. If you selected a case study from the literature or cannot meet with user representatives, software developers, or system gurus, be creative—find someone willing to play the roles and improvise, or (if all else fails) invent the missing data. Note that later studies will be more interesting if the initial specification has a few performance traps.

Further Study

3.4. Find a small software system under development—either in a production environment or a software engineering course team project. Conduct a performance walkthrough to gather the pertinent SPE data. (If performance analysis is new to you, review Chapter 4 first to become familiar with software analysis, before you conduct the trial walkthrough.)

3.5. Select a popular software development method or CASE tool. Compare the software specifications it collects to the SPE data required. What is covered? What is missing? How could you integrate the SPE data into the method/tool?

3.6. Sit in on a design walkthrough, and compare the information covered to the SPE data required. Do performance questions arise? How are they resolved? What SPE data is covered? What is missing? Could you factor in the additional topics, or would you need a separate walkthrough? (If you cannot view a walkthrough, work from literature that gives a detailed description of what transpires.)

4

Software Execution Models

Remember the tragic skywalk collapse at a hotel in Kansas City in 1981? Obviously, it is better to detect and correct structural problems early in development than to have skywalks fail during a party. Skywalk designers can use models to predict the effect of loading conditions on structures. Early in design, the skywalk is a concept: Designers start with target dimensions and materials but have not determined specific material properties. A simple model (depicted in Figure 4.1[a]) assesses whether the concept is sound and identifies critical areas (in the region of the load and the end supports). Later, as designers refine the specifications for the structure, they augment the model using a finer mesh in the critical areas and more precise data on materials (Figure 4.1[b]).[1]

Early in development, when requirements are formulated and preliminary designs considered, there is insufficient data for precise modeling of a system's ultimate performance. So, like successful skywalk designers, we construct simple models that capture essential software performance behavior. The models are easily solved, often interactively, and provide initial feedback on whether or not planned software is likely to meet performance goals. Later we refine the software execution model in the critical areas and produce parameters for the system execution model (described in Chapter 5) to more precisely model additional performance-determining factors, such as multiple users of a system and queueing delays caused by resource contention.

Figure 4.2 highlights the subject of this chapter: constructing and evaluating

---

[1] Despite the availability of these methods, the skywalk failed. Some possible reasons and methods to prevent such failures are mentioned later.

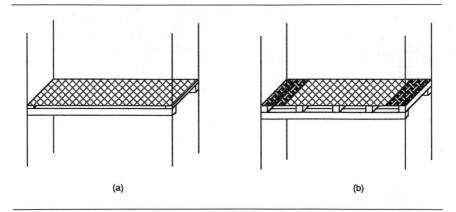

FIGURE 4.1
Models to Assess Design Concepts. The simple model in (a) provides initial feedback and identifies critical areas. The model in (b) depicts more of the design details
and refines the model in the critical areas.

the simple high-level performance model. The chapter focuses on one type of
software execution model: the execution graph. The graph has the advantage of
being a visual representation of software that helps to communicate execution
behavior. It also provides a formal, graph-theoretical basis for the analysis algorithms that evaluate the model's performance.

4.1 Execution Graph Model Definition

Execution graph models are based on elementary graph theory [BER58]. We
create an execution graph from the execution structure *for each workload scenario*. Each component of a system is a node in the graph. A **component** is a
collection of program statements, procedures, and abstract machine calls that
perform a logical function in the software design. **Control paths** connecting the
components are represented by arcs. Traversal of an arc represents a switch to the
next execution step in the execution structure. It may also imply a context switch,
such as a procedure call or an operating system call, if the execution steps are not
contained within the same program or procedure.

4.1.1 Graph Notation

This section defines the execution graph nodes and arcs and shows how to represent execution structures with them. **Basic nodes** represent components at the

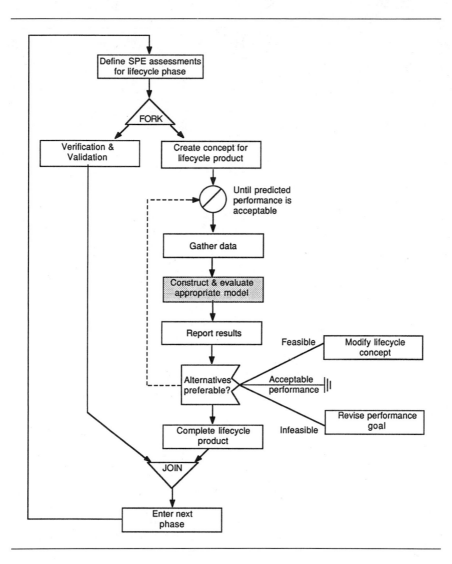

FIGURE 4.2
The SPE Methodology with the Focus of This Chapter Highlighted.

lowest level of detail appropriate for the current design or implementation stage. Resource requirements are specified for each basic node. **Standard arcs** represent a transfer of control; that is, when processing in one component is complete, its execution terminates and execution begins in the next component in the execution structure.

For example, early in design we can construct the execution graph in Figure 4.3 for the ATM deposit scenario from Example 3.2. The figure specifies that

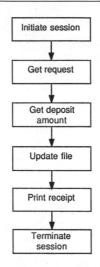

FIGURE 4.3
A Simple Execution Graph of the ATM Deposit Scenario.

processing begins in the "initiate session" component. When it completes, the "get request" component executes, and so on until the "terminate session" component completes. Each node in this graph is a basic node. The nodes are connected by standard arcs.

Further resolution of the design allows further resolution of the execution graph. The "initiate session" node is expanded in Figure 4.4: Processing begins with the "get customer ID" component to get the identification number from the machine, then switches to "get auth. code" for the authorization code, and then switches to "verify code" to compare the authorization code against the file. Each node in the subgraph is a basic node, and the nodes are connected by standard arcs. We replace the "initiate session" basic node from Figure 4.3 with the expanded node in Figure 4.4. We use the convention that processing details of **expanded nodes** are defined by a subgraph at the next level of detail. We continue adding expanded nodes to subgraphs as designers resolve additional levels of detail. There is no limit to the number of levels. In the ATM example, each of the basic nodes in Figure 4.3 eventually becomes an expanded node, and subgraphs depict their additional processing details.

Represent looping with a **repetition node** that shows which components are repeated (Figure 4.5); the *repetition factor* in the node specifies the number of times the components repeat. A special arc connects the last component repeated with the repetition node. Figure 4.5 shows that the sequence "get request" followed by "process request" repeats two times; then "terminate session" executes.

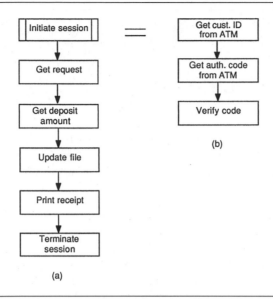

(a)

(b)

FIGURE 4.4
The simple execution graph in (a) is extended to show additional processing details of the "initiate session" component in its subgraph (b).

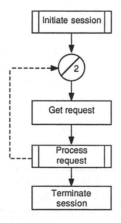

FIGURE 4.5
A repetition node specifies that the sequence of components "get request" followed by "process request" is repeated two times.

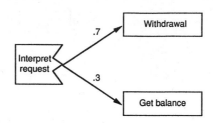

FIGURE 4.6
A case node specifies the probability that attached components execute.

The special (dashed) arc connects the last component in the loop, "process request," to the repetition node.[2]

Case nodes represent conditional execution of components. The graph in Figure 4.6 shows a subgraph for the "process request" node in the previous example. In it the component "interpret request" executes first. With probability 0.7 the request is "withdrawal"; with probability 0.3 "get balance" executes instead. The probabilities and repetition factors must be specified. They can be data-dependent variables (data dependency is covered in Section 4.3.3).

Branching is not restricted to two paths as in this example; you can have one or more conditionally executed paths. Neither is it necessary for probabilities to sum to 1, but the sum cannot be greater than 1. Figure 4.7 shows a "check buffers" case node: With probability 0.7, further processing executes to "fetch info" before proceeding to "process info."

Typical software systems have more complex control structures than the transfer of control represented by standard arcs. **Call-return arcs** represent control that eventually returns to the origin node, as in a procedure call. A **series of call-return arcs** represents nested procedure calls. To illustrate, envision a different expansion of the "process request" node of Figure 4.5. The nested procedure calls in Figure 4.8 could execute for withdrawal requests: The component "interpret request" calls "process withdrawal," which calls "update account balance." When "update account balance" completes, control returns to "process withdrawal." When it completes, control returns to "interpret request."

Another control structure represents "driver" components that call many other components and regains control between each of the calls. A **driver arc** shows the components called, their execution order, and the caller. In Figure 4.9 the component "process transfer" is a driver that first calls "process withdrawal."

---

[2]We use a dashed line for this arc because high-level models do not associate resource requirements with repetition arcs. Use standard arcs and associate resource requirements for repetition arcs in your models when appropriate.

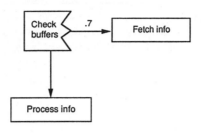

FIGURE 4.7
Case nodes may have one or more conditionally executed components. "Fetch info" executes before "process info" 70 percent of the time.

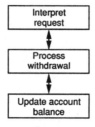

FIGURE 4.8
Double-headed arcs represent procedure call-returns. A series of call-return arcs shows nested procedure calls. Calls are made top to bottom; returns are bottom to top.

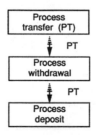

FIGURE 4.9
Driver arcs represent procedure calls made by one component to many other components and show the order of the calls. The dashed arrowhead on the arc signifies that the caller is the component identified by the arc's label. The called component executes after the component above, but there is no direct connection between them.

Upon "process withdrawal" completion, control returns to "process transfer," which then calls "process deposit." Upon its completion, control returns to "process transfer." The "PT" is a *driver identifier* that shows the caller is "process transfer." Note that "process withdrawal" executes before "process deposit," but there is *no direct connection between them.* The driver arc is a shorthand notation for representing the order of the procedure calls to each of the components. Drivers generally call many other components. We could explicitly connect the driver to each component it calls; however, the graphs quickly become unintelligible when dozens of arcs emanate from one component, and you cannot tell their order of execution. The compensating driver arcs may seem awkward, but you get used to them quickly.

Let's look next at more complex combinations of nodes and arcs that may be found in software systems. The graph in Figure 4.10 shows that driver module A calls component B three times and then calls component C. Note that the arc representing the procedure call to B is inside the loop because the call executes three times. A **dummy arc** connects A to the repetition node when there is no procedure call processing that takes place at that point. A dummy arc shows precedence between nodes; no processing is associated with it.

We represent concurrent processing and synchronization within a software system with **fork** and **join** and **split nodes.** Figure 4.11 depicts a hypothetical software system with internal concurrency and synchronization: A terminal user requests remote data; asynchronous, concurrent processing fetches the data while the user continues other processing; later the user requests the reply from the asynchronous process. Both of the concurrent chains must complete before the remote data can be used. The fork node shows where concurrent processing

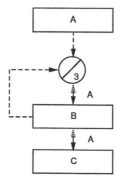

FIGURE 4.10

Combinations of Nodes and Arcs. Component A is a driver that calls component B three times before calling C. The dashed arc out of A is a dummy arc; the procedure call to B executes three times, so its arc is inside the loop.

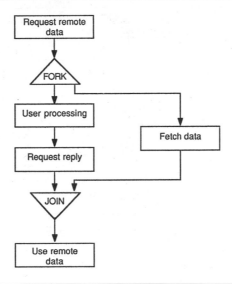

FIGURE 4.11
FORK nodes show where concurrent processing begins. JOIN nodes show where they must synchronize. "Fetch data" executes concurrently with "user processing" and "request reply." Both must complete before processing continues.

begins; the join shows where they must synchronize before proceeding. You can have any arbitrary number of concurrent chains. Split nodes initiate concurrent chains that need not join later. An example is in Chapter 8.

Execution graphs can also depict mutual exclusion. This occurs when database keys and pointers are held in exclusion to be updated. **Lock** and **free nodes** delineate processing that must occur in a locked, or mutually exclusive, state. The execution graph in Figure 4.12 shows locking for an account balance update. Execution begins with the component "validate request." Next the update scenario requests exclusive access to the account file. If it is free (not held by another job), update obtains the lock and continues processing. If another job has the account file locked, the job desiring the lock must wait until it has been freed. "Update balance" executes when it gets the lock. When it completes, it frees the lock, and then normal processing resumes in the component "finish processing."

We use **share nodes** when:

- □ Only one job is allowed exclusive access to a particular resource
- □ Any number of jobs can share the resource on a nonexclusive basis
- □ Jobs desiring exclusive access to a resource must wait until no other jobs have the lock, and no other job is sharing the resource
- □ Jobs desiring shared access must wait until no locks are held

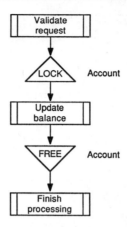

FIGURE 4.12
LOCK and FREE nodes delineate the scope of processing that requires exclusive use of the "Account" resource.

For example, several database transactions update information and require exclusive access to do so, while others retrieve information but cannot do so if it is being changed. The graph in Figure 4.13 illustrates share nodes.

The fork, join, split, lock, free, and share nodes are special **phase identification nodes** that reflect changes in the processing state. There are two other types of phase identification nodes: **send** and **receive** represent communication between

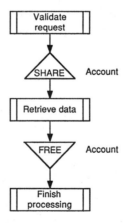

FIGURE 4.13
SHARE and FREE nodes delineate the scope of processing that requires shared use of the "Account" resource.

processes; **acquire** and **release,** a more general form of lock and free, indicate when a resource, such as a communication channel, must be acquired-released during execution. Acquire may have to wait if the resource is not available. Processing phases and their analysis are discussed in more detail in Chapter 8.

Figure 4.14 summarizes the graph notation. Basic nodes represent compo-

Name	Symbol	Represents
Basic node		Functional component at current level of refinement.
Expanded node		The function has been refined; details are in a subgraph.
Repetition node	 n	Subsequent nodes repeat n times; the last node in the loop has an arc to this node.
Case node		Identifies nodes that are conditionally executed and their execution probabilities.
State identification nodes	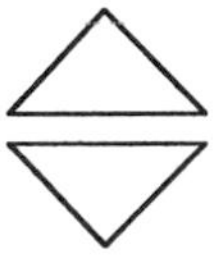	Show lock-free, fork-join, send-receive, and acquire-release processing events.
Split node	 SPLIT	Shows the initiation of concurrent processes that need not join.
Arc		Flow passes from the origin to the destination.
Call-return arc		Flow passes to the destination and returns to the origin node upon completion.
Driver arc	 X	Same as above, except that control returns to the driver, X.
Dummy arc		No processing time is associated with the arc; they may be bi-directional.

FIGURE 4.14
Execution Graph Notation Summary.

nents at their current lowest level of resolution. Expanded nodes show further resolution; a subgraph shows the next level of detail. Repetition nodes identify components that are repeatedly executed, and case nodes identify components conditionally executed. Phase identification nodes show lock-share-free and acquire-release of resources, fork-join-split of concurrent processes, and send-receive of messages. Arc types show transfer of control, procedure call-returns, and "driver" call-returns. Dummy arcs show flow with no processing overhead.

4.1.2 Graph Restrictions

An **initial node** is the first component executed in the graph. Initial nodes can only be the origin of arcs, not the destination. For the analysis algorithms in Section 4.3.1 to apply, *graphs and subgraphs can have only one initial node*. This is a minor restriction, because you can first use a case node and show each component that could be executed.[3] Figure 4.15 shows equivalent graphs. The graph in (a) is illegal; (b) is equivalent and legal.

Loops are also restricted. *All loops in the graph must be repetition loops*. This does not reduce modeling power, because you can find equivalent representations that contain only repetition loops. Figure 4.16(a) shows an execution graph that violates the loop restriction. The arc from "process request" to "get request" introduces a loop that is not a repetition loop. The revised graph in (b) represents the same processing with a repetition loop.

4.1.3 Modeling with Execution Graphs

Execution graphs are similar to program flowcharts but are not the same. The graphs show the frequency of path execution and model only paths that are key to performance. Some of the execution graph symbols are based on the "PAD" graphical notation [FUT81]. PAD is successfully used in development organizations, and it is better to use successful techniques than to invent a replacement. Actually, it is not necessary to use these, or any, symbols in software execution models. You can substitute pseudocode or another language-based model.

Just as it is possible to construct very different programs that perform identical functions, it is also possible to construct different execution graph models that represent the same software. There is no single "right way." Graphs may differ in their representation of software hierarchy and in the details they abstract. The selection of the details to model is the "art" of performance modeling.

An important lesson learned in modeling evolving systems may help you with the abstraction. It is best illustrated by example. Many seminar attendees have

[3]Specify zero resource requirements if there is no processing for the decision.

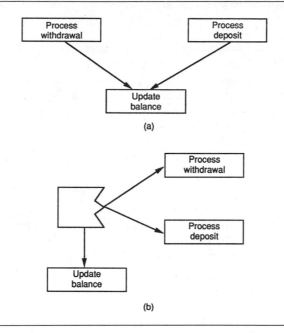

(a)

(b)

FIGURE 4.15
Initial Node Restriction. The graph in (a) is illegal because it has two initial nodes; the graph in (b) is equivalent and legal.

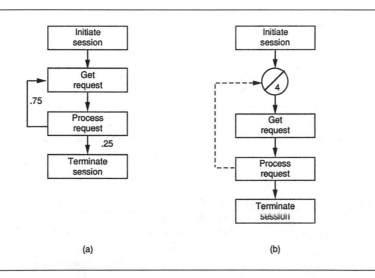

(a)

(b)

FIGURE 4.16
Loop Restriction. The graph in (a) has an illegal loop from "process request" to "get request"; the graph in (b) is equivalent and legal.

questioned the need to carefully model the control flow with the various types of arcs early in design. Their argument is that the control-flow resource requirement is usually small compared to the large entities represented by each early-design node. While this is true, there are systems in which the number of procedure calls is quite large and thus procedure-call overhead is a major performance bottleneck. The number of procedure calls grows as a system evolves. Unless they are captured from the beginning, it is difficult, if not impossible, to detect when procedure-call overhead becomes a problem and incorporate it into the model at that point. You may have to wait until you can measure control flow—too late to prevent problems. Similarly, control flow can represent the program-initiation overhead in online transactions to detect the separate-program-per-screen problem (in Example 2.8). The control flow specifications are also necessary for the memory models (in Chapter 9). You can skip these details early in design for the initial best-case analyses with little loss of precision. But you must be able to later recover the evolving data and incorporate it into the models if you hope to catch the performance problems that crop up during implementation.

For the same reason, it is important to continue the SPE modeling throughout development. Do not become complacent when preliminary results indicate that performance is satisfactory. Early models are more abstract and model ideal environments. The evolving software may be quite different.

4.2 Case Study Execution Graphs

We use execution graphs in walkthroughs to confirm our understanding of the processing steps. The case study execution graphs in this section are described as they would be in a walkthrough session. Occasional parenthetical comments clarify the execution graph choices. We take up where we left off, gathering the case study information. Before you proceed, review Section 3.3 pages 138 to 152, and construct your own execution graph models for the three case studies. Then compare your results to the models in this section.

Figure 4.17 depicts the DRAWMOD scenario. The DRAWMOD driver is the first node. It calls EDMS routines to retrieve the data for drawing the requested model. DRAWMOD first calls DBOPEN to open the database tables. (DBOPEN's processing details are not part of the case study, so it is a basic node.) Next DRAWMOD calls FIND to locate all the beams for the specified model. (FIND and RETRIEVE are expanded nodes because their processing details are in the EDMS subgraphs.) Next DBSORT puts the beams into ascending sequence. Then the steps in the outer repetition loop execute once per beam, or approximately 2,050 times. (Note that the driver arc is inside the loop, and a dummy arc precedes the loop. This models the processing overhead for the 2,050 driver calls. If the

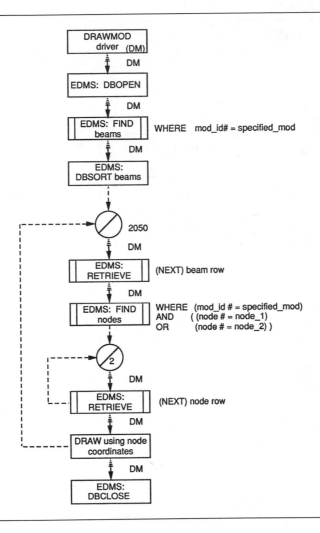

FIGURE 4.17
The Execution Graph Model of the DRAWMOD Scenario.

driver arc were outside the loop, it would only account for the processing overhead for one of the calls.) The remainder of the execution graph corresponds directly to the walkthrough description in Example 3.6, and its execution structure in Example 3.7.

Figure 4.18 shows the EDMS execution graphs. The top-level graph in (a) shows the general database control (DBC) processing. "DB_MP initiation" receives the request and routes it to the database control. The DBC driver calls "parse

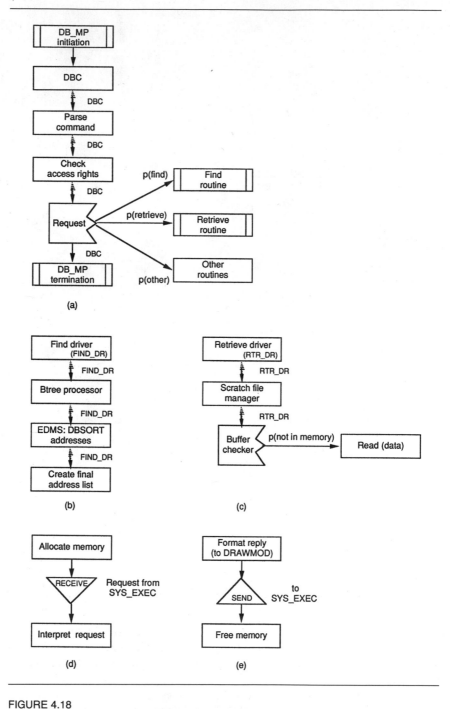

FIGURE 4.18
The Execution Graph Models of the EDMS. DBC processing is in (a), the Find routine is in (b), the Retrieve routine is in (c), DB_MP Initiation is in (d), and DB_MP Termination is in (e).

command," then calls "check access rights," then calls the appropriate routine to process the request. The case node shows the request processing currently defined. The Find and Retrieve routines are represented by expanded nodes; their subgraphs are in 4.18(b) and (c), respectively. The execution probabilities are data-dependent variables; values will be assigned to the variables in the graph analysis step. (The data dependency is described in Section 4.3 and illustrated in the case study analysis in Section 4.4.) Upon completion, DBC transfers control to "DB_MP termination."

The Find and Retrieve subgraphs match the description of the execution structure based on Example 3.9. Note the case node for the "buffer checker" in (c). When the desired data is not found in a buffer, the "Read (data)" component executes. "Read (data)" also has a data-dependent execution probability.

Parts (d) and (e) of Figure 4.18 show that "DB_MP initiation" gets requests for EDMS functions, allocates memory for the process, RECEIVEs, and interprets the request. In this scenario, the request is for DBC processing (DB_MP also receives requests for the query language and the utility functions—see Figure 3.5). When the EDMS function completes, "DB_MP termination" formats the reply, SENDs it to DRAWMOD via SYS_EXEC, and frees memory.

Figure 4.19 shows the communication execution graphs; it also shows how the previous graphs relate to one another. When DRAWMOD requests an EDMS function, the process depicted in 4.19(a) executes. When DRAWMOD is coded, it will contain instructions that format the request, SEND the request to SYS_EXEC, and RECEIVE to wait for the reply. Figure 4.19(b) shows the SYS_EXEC loop. When activated, it checks to see if requests are pending. When none are pending, it deactivates (sleeps) for a predetermined period of time. As long as requests are pending, it processes them before deactivating.

Figure 4.19(c) shows that Switchboard (Receive) gets the EDMS message, packages and prepares it for routing (in this case to DB_MP), updates the task schedule to activate DB_MP, and Switchboard (Send) forwards the message to DB_MP. Similarly, SYS_EXEC is invoked when EDMS processing completes. SYS_EXEC receives the completion message, determines the destination (DRAWMOD), packages it, adjusts the schedule (to reactivate DRAWMOD), and Switchboard (Send) forwards the message.

Note that a significant amount of communication overhead executes when application programs call EDMS functions. If we were modeling only the user-level software and using measured resource requirements for EDMS functions, the communication overhead would be included in the measurements. Because we explicitly model all the software levels, we must account for the communication processing in the DRAWMOD scenario. We do so by computing the communication time for the DRAWMOD driver arcs that call EDMS functions (in the execution graph in Figure 4.17). This will show the effect on user response time of SYS_EXEC communication design alternatives.

These are the processing details resolved so far. As more information be-

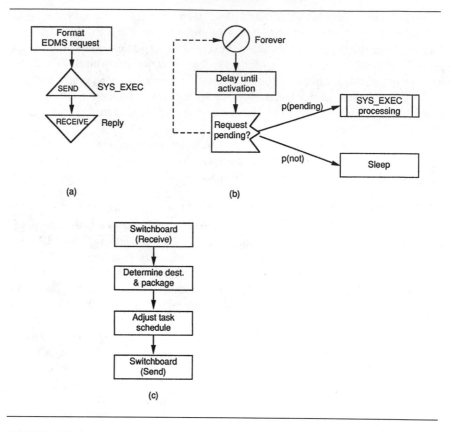

FIGURE 4.19
The Execution Graph Models of the SYS_EXEC Communication Processing. The EDMS call processing is in (a), the SYS_EXEC loop is in (b), and the SYS_EXEC processing is expanded in (c).

comes available for EDMS and communication processing, we would replace basic nodes with expanded nodes and add subgraphs. The next step is to analyze these graphs.

4.3 Software Model Analysis

As you remember, the primary purpose of the software model analysis is to derive the parameters for the system execution model. We also use them for a quick check of the best-case response time.

Using graphs to represent software execution is not new. Other researchers have proposed analyzing graphs to evaluate software performance. The bibliography cites the early work that led to the graph analysis algorithms in this section. Notable among them are papers by Graham, Clancey, and DeVaney [GRA73], Beizer [BEI78, BEI84], Sholl and Booth [BOO79a, BOO79b, SHO75], Kelly [KEL74], Sanguinetti [SAN78, SAN79], and Smith and Browne [SMI79a, SMI79b, SMI80a, SMI80b]. Because all the work is based on graph theory, the algorithms are essentially the same, though they differ in terminology and in problems and applications addressed.

It is interesting to note that these references date back to the early 1970s, but saw little practical use until recently. There are several reasons for the change. First, the algorithms were proposed for calculating execution times—they did not include queueing delays for computer system resources. Adapting them to calculate system model parameters makes them viable. The second major reason why they did not see extensive use initially was because of the difficulty in obtaining model parameters. These problems are resolved with the techniques in Chapter 3. These graph analysis algorithms are now an important step in SPE.

Note that the algorithms are formulated for evaluating execution graphs. The graphs are the formal basis for the algorithms. Once understood, you can apply the algorithms to other types of software models. Thus, it is not necessary to draw a case node to compute its execution time; you can use the algorithms to analyze a textual description of the execution structure as long as you can identify its conditional execution. Section 4.5 delves into other software-modeling options.

4.3.1 Graph Analysis Algorithms

The analysis algorithms are intuitively easy to understand: You essentially examine the graphs and identify a basic structure, compute the "time" for the structure, and reduce the structure to a "computed node," continuing to reduce the structures until the graph reduces to a single computed node, its "time" the result of the analysis. The basic structures are: sequences, loops, and cases. When the structure is a **sequence,** as in Figure 4.20(a), the computed node "time" is the sum of the "times" of the nodes in sequence. For **loop** structures, multiply the node "time" by the loop repetition factor as in (b). The computation for **case** nodes differs for shortest-path, longest-path, and average analyses. For the shortest path, it is the minimum of the nodes conditionally executed; for the longest path, it is the maximum; and for the average, in (c), multiply each node's "time" by its execution probability.

In this section, *"time"* is generic. The algorithms apply irrespective of the interpretation of "time." Section 4.3.2 has procedures for using elapsed-time estimates, resource requirements, and other values for "time" in these algorithms for various performance analyses. Similarly, the "time" for control flow is not explicitly included in the graph algorithms. Instead, the control flow is included in the computation of node times in Section 4.3.2.

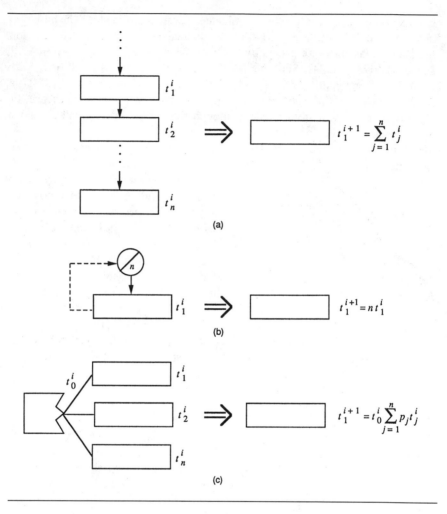

FIGURE 4.20
Basic Graph Reduction Rules for Average Time Computation. Sequential-path reduction is in (a); repetition-path reduction is in (b); and conditional-path reduction is
in (c).

The formal mathematical statement of the graph algorithms follows. It is
adapted from Kelly's original analysis; a complete discussion and proof of the
formulas can be found in [KEL74]. Let t_j be the "time" for node j. Iteratively apply
reduction rules to transform a graph into an equivalent one with fewer nodes and
arcs; continue until you reduce the graph to a single node. Then the average "time"
for the original execution graph is the resulting time for the reduced graph. The
basic reduction rules are:

ALGORITHM 4.1: Basic Graph Reduction Rules

Part 1: Average time computation

Begin with the iteration number, i, initially equal to 1.

The sequential-path reduction rule says that the time for the computed node for the $(i + 1)^{st}$ iteration is the sum of the times of the nodes in sequence in the ith iteration (see Figure 4.20[a]):

Sequential-Path Reduction Rule: $$t_1^{i+1} = \sum_{j=1}^{n} t_j^i$$

The repetition-path reduction rule multiplies the node time in the ith iteration by the loop repetition factor (see Figure 4.20[b]):

Repetition-Path Reduction Rule: $t_1^{i+1} = n t_1^i$

The conditional-path reduction rule multiplies each node time in the ith iteration by its execution probability, and adds the sum to t_0, the time for determining which condition holds (see Figure 4.20[c]):

Conditional-Path Reduction Rule: $$t_1^{i+1} = t_0^i + \sum_{j=1}^{n} p_j t_j^i$$

The copying rule updates iteration numbers. For example, if you need a reduction to produce Node 2 in Figure 4.20(a) before you can apply the sequential-path reduction rule, you also apply the copying rule to Node 1 and Nodes 3 through n to update their superscripts appropriately:

Copying Rule: $t_1^{i+1} = t_1^i$

For expanded nodes, compute the time for their subgraph using the reduction rules, and use the computed time for the expanded node:

Expanded Node Assignment Rule: $t_j^i = t_1^k$

where the single computed node t_1 is produced by the kth reduction of the subgraph corresponding to t_j.

Part 2: Shortest- and Longest-Time Computation

The shortest- and longest-path algorithms are similar. The only rule to change is the conditional-path rule.

The shortest path uses the minimum of the case alternatives.

Shortest-Path Conditional Reduction Rule: $t_1^{i+1} = t_0^i + \min_j (t_j^i)$

The longest path uses the maximum of the case alternatives.

Longest-Path Conditional Reduction Rule: $t_1^{i+1} = t_0^i + \max_j (t_j^i)$

□

The variance computation is more complicated. Moreover, variance must be specified when a node's "time" may vary significantly. The variance computation is detailed in Algorithm 4.2.

ALGORITHM 4.2: Variance Computation

Let v_j be the specified variance for node j, and $v_d = 0$ for all nodes d (for "default") for which variance is not specified.

Variance Sequential-Path Reduction Rule: $\quad v_1^{i+1} = \sum_{j=1}^{n} v_j^i$

Variance Repetition-Path Reduction Rule: $\quad v_1^{i+1} = n v_1^i + t_1^2 n_v$

where n is the loop repetition factor and n_v is its variance.

Variance Conditional-Path Reduction Rule:

$\quad$ for $c = 1$, $v_1^{i+1} = v_0^i + v_1^i$

$\quad$ for $c \geq 2$, $v_1^{i+1} = v_0^i + \sum_{i=1}^{n} p_i v_i \sum_{i,j\in I} p_i p_j (t_i - t_j)^2$

Where c is the number of conditional paths, and I is an index set consisting of all combinations of the set $\{1,2,3, \ldots ,c\}$ taken two at a time. There are $\binom{c}{2}$ such combinations.

Copying Rule: $\qquad\qquad\qquad\qquad\qquad v_1^{i+1} = v_1^i$

Expanded Node Assignment Rule: $\qquad\qquad v_j^i = v_1^k$

$\square$

As you can see, the variance computation is more complex than the others, and requires that variances be specified. Moreover, the resulting variance does not account for variance due to processes competing for resources.

There are also formulas for computing distribution functions [KEL74, SMI80a]. They require a specification for distribution functions for each node whose time varies; computation is more complex than for variance, and the resulting distribution function ignores competitive effects. The algorithms are not included here because few SPE studies have sufficiently precise data early enough in development to justify the additional analyses. There are, however, some situations in which you may need this type of analysis. Further information about the formulas can be found in the references just cited; distribution approximation techniques are in [SMI80a], and methods and tools for deriving distribution functions for a more general set of graphs are in [SAH85a, SAH85b]. Note that some system execution model analysis tools produce response time distributions that account for competitive effects. System execution modeling tools are mentioned in Chapter 5.

TABLE 4.1
NODE TIMES FOR ATM CALCULATION

Node	Time	Variance
Get customer ID#	10	0
Get authorization code	10	0
Verify authorization code	50	10
Get request	20	20
Interpret request	10	0
Withdrawal	200	50
Get balance	50	0
Terminate session	100	100

EXAMPLE 4.1: Best, Worst, and Average "Times" for ATM Scenario

To illustrate the basic path reductions, consider the ATM scenario in Figure 4.5, the subgraph for "process request" in Figure 4.6, and the subgraph for "initiate session" in Figure 4.4(b). Assume the node "times" and variances in Table 4.1.

First reduce the subgraph for "initiate session" using the sequential-path reduction rules.

Initiate session:	$10 + 10 + 50$	=	70
Variance:	$0 + 0 + 10$	=	10

The shortest, longest, and average paths are the same because the subgraph has no conditional execution.

Next use the conditional-path reduction rule to compute the time for "process request" in Figure 4.6. The shortest path is "interpret request" + "get balance." The longest path is "interpret request" + "withdrawal."

Process request:

Shortest path:	$10 + 50$	=	60
Longest path:	$10 + 200$	=	210
Average:	$10 + .7(200) + .3(50)$	=	165
Variance:	$0 + ((.7)(50) + 0) + ((.7)(.3)(200 - 50)^2)$	=	4760

Next use these calculations to evaluate the session scenario graph in Figure 4.5. Combine repetition-path reduction and sequential-path reduction to get:

Session:

Shortest path:	$70 + 2(20 + 60) + 100$	=	330
Longest path:	$0 + 2(20 + 210) + 100$	=	630
Average path:	$70 + 2(20 + 165) + 100$	=	540

Assume that the variance of the loop repetition factor is 1. Then the session variance is:

Variance:	$10 + ((2)(20 + 4760) + (20 + 165)^2(1)) + 100 = 43{,}895$

□

So far the discussions have been simplified because we focus on basic structures. We have not yet considered state identification nodes. The analysis of state
identification nodes differ depending on the analysis and type of node. This section
analyzes graphs for an initial comparison to performance goals. The slightly more
complex analysis to derive system model parameters for state identification nodes
is described in Chapter 8. First, consider the fork and join nodes.

ALGORITHM 4.3: Fork-Join Shortest- and Longest-Time Computation

The shortest-path analysis assumes that the concurrent processes do not interfere with one
another and that the processes join when the last one completes (that is, there is no additional
synchronization delay). The time interval between the fork and join is thus the time of the
longest of the concurrent paths in Figure 4.21:

Fork-Join Shortest Path: $t_1^{i+1} = t_0^i + (\max_{j=1,n} t_j^i) + t_{n+1}^i$

The longest-path analysis assumes that the concurrent processes serialize and that there is
no processing overlap.

Fork-Join Longest Path: $t_1^{i+1} = \sum_{j=0}^{n+1} t_j^i$

Note that these formulas ignore the effects of resource competition between concurrent
processes. Chapter 8 factors in the potential resource contention delays.   □

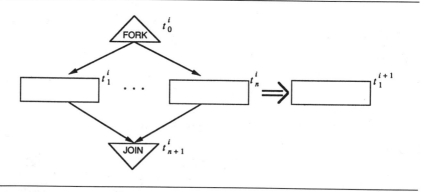

FIGURE 4.21
The Fork and Join Graph Reduction. The shortest path uses the longest of the
concurrent paths; the longest path uses the sum of the concurrent paths.

The lock-free nodes are a special case of acquire-release nodes. Both use the following algorithm.

ALGORITHM 4.4: Lock-Free and Acquire-Release Shortest- and Longest-Time Computation

The shortest path assumes that resources are immediately available and that there is no delay. It includes processing time for the acquire (state identification node), but no additional wait time. So the lock-free and acquire-release shortest path uses the basic reduction rules (average-, shortest-, and longest-path computations) and treats the lock-free and acquire-release nodes like basic nodes.

The longest path assumes the longest delay. For the lock scenario in Figure 4.22, assume that the longest wait is for all other users (of the same scenario) to complete their processing. Let N be the number of concurrent users of the scenario.

Lock-Free and Acquire-Release Longest Path: $t_1^{i+1} = t_0^i + Nt_1^i + t_2^i$

It is also possible for different scenarios to have exclusive or shared access to the same resource. To include this item, let N_k represent the number of concurrent users and t_k^{i+1} the time in the locked state for scenario k. The formula becomes:

Lock-Free and Acquire-Release (in Different Scenarios) Longest Path:

$$t_1^{i+1} = t_0^i + Nt_1^i + t_2^i + \overset{\textit{total scenarios}}{\underset{k=1}{\sum}} N_k t_k^{i+1}$$

Again, this ignores competition for other resources. For a more precise analysis, use the system execution model.

□

For the send-receive computation there are many complex situations. We consider only the simple case in Figure 4.23, in which one process writes messages and another reads them.

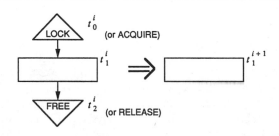

FIGURE 4.22
The Lock-Free and Acquire-Release Graph Reduction.

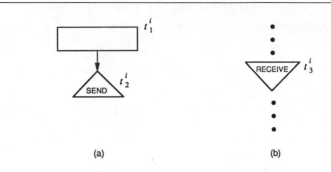

FIGURE 4.23
The Simple-Case Send-Receive Graph Reduction.

ALGORITHM 4.5: Simple Send-Receive Shortest- and Longest-Time Computation

The shortest-path analysis for send and receive assumes that communication lines, messages, and other resources are immediately available when needed. We include specified time for the send and receive nodes, but no additional delay, so the send-receive shortest path treats send-receive like basic nodes and uses the basic reduction rules.

For the send-receive longest path, assume that receive must wait for both t_1 and t_2 to complete before receive can begin. The total time for receive is:

$$t_j^{i+1} = t_1^i + t_2^i + t_3^i$$

$\square$

We could compute the time as in Algorithm 4.5 for "send" when we must wait for other concurrent processes to free the communication resources. Rather than examine more special cases and derive formulas to estimate the time, let us defer the analysis to the system execution model in Chapter 8.

4.3.2 Analysis Procedures

After you gather performance specifications and create the software models from the execution structures, you evaluate the proposed system. Recall the two crucial analysis strategies: (1) Use both expected-value and upper-bound resource requirements, and (2) begin with a simplistic analysis of the best case, introducing more sophisticated analyses of realistic cases as more detailed information becomes available.

Section 4.3.1 defined the formulas for software model analysis using a generic "time." This section substitutes different data values for "time" to calculate the metrics of interest. For example, if a scenario consists of one sequential path (like Figure 4.3), and you use the lower bound for CPU time for each node in the sequential-path reduction rule, the result is the lower bound for the CPU time for the scenario. Alternatively, if you estimate the lower-bound elapsed time for each node and use it in the same formula, the result is the lower-bound elapsed time for the scenario. The next few paragraphs state these concepts formally.

Each basic node has specified software resource requirements a_j, representing the service units desired from each software resource j, $1 \leq j \leq m$. Consider the hypothetical expansion of an ATM "Withdrawal" shown on the left side of Figure 4.24. It consists of three components, "Get account and amount," "Verify amount OK," and "Update balance," which are sequentially executed. The chart in Figure 4.24 shows the *specified* software resources, a_j, required for each component. For example, the software resources are: control flow, CPU instructions, ATM interaction, I/Os, and event recording. Component "Verify" requires 1 control flow, 108 CPU instructions, no (0) ATM interactions, 1 I/O, and no (0) event recording ($a_1 = 1$, $a_2 = 108$, $a_3 = 0$, $a_4 = 1$, $a_5 = 0$).

Table 4.2 shows the computer resource requirements w_{ij} for each of the a_j requests for software resource j. For example, the *column* for I/O ($j = 4$) specifies that each component I/O requires 5 CPU instructions and 1 "visit" to the I/O device DEV1 (and no visits to the ATM device). Control flow (column $j = 1$) requires 2 CPU instructions and no ATM or I/O requirements. The numbers in the table are hypothetical (and probably unrealistically low). Your SPE models will use w_{ij} derived from measurement data for your computer environment or from specifications for path lengths. (This shows more specifically what data you need for environment specifications.)

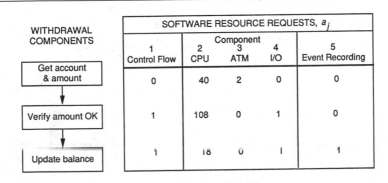

WITHDRAWAL COMPONENTS	SOFTWARE RESOURCE REQUESTS, a_j				
	1 Control Flow	2 CPU	Component 3 ATM	4 I/O	5 Event Recording
Get account & amount	0	40	2	0	0
Verify amount OK	1	108	0	1	0
Update balance	1	18	0	1	1

FIGURE 4.24
Software Resource Requirements, a_j: Each row in the chart specifies the corresponding components' software resource requirements, a_j, for each of the j software resources. The chart has one column for each software resource.

TABLE 4.2
COMPUTER RESOURCES PER SOFTWARE REQUEST (Each table entry, w_{ij}, specifies the amount of computer resource i required for each of the a_j requests for software resource j.)

Computer resources, i		Software resources, j				
		1	Component			5
		Control	2	3	4	Event
i	Name	Flow	CPU	ATM	I/O	Recording
1	CPU	2	1	5	5	5
2	ATM	0	0	1	0	0
3	DEV1	0	0	0	1	1

With these specifications, the first analysis step is to calculate the **total computer resources required per software resource, r_{ij}.** Figure 4.25 shows the requirements for the "Update balance" component. Multiply the "Update balance" software resource request row in Figure 4.24 *by each row* in the w_{ij} matrix, to get the r_{ij} totals in the chart in Figure 4.25. That is,

Computer resources per software resource:

$$r_{ij} = a_j w_{ij} \qquad \text{for all } i \text{ and } j, i = 1, \ldots, k \text{ and } j = 1, \ldots, m$$

The r_{ij} chart says that for event recording, "Update balance" requires 5 CPU instructions and 1 I/O to DEV1. Similarly, the a_j specifications for "Update balance" software resource requests call for 1 I/O, so the $j = 4$ column in Figure

Update balance	=	COMPUTER RESOURCES, i		COMPUTER RESOURCES PER SOFTWARE RESOURCE, r_{ij}					TOTAL COMPUTER RESOURCES, r_i
				1	Component			5	
				Control	2	3	4	Event	
		i	Name	Flow	CPU	ATM	I/O	Recording	
		1	CPU	2	18	0	5	5	30
		2	ATM	0	0	0	0	0	0
		3	DEV1	0	0	0	1	1	2

FIGURE 4.25
Total Computer Resource Requirements per Component, r_j. Each element in the r_{ij} columns in the chart is the result of multiplying the corresponding a_j by its w_{ij}; each element in the r_i column is the sum of the r_{ij} in the corresponding row.

4.25 is $(1 \times 5, 1 \times 0, 1 \times 1) = (5, 0, 1)$. If a_j had called for 6 I/Os, the $j = 4$ column in Figure 4.25 would have been $(6 \times 5, 6 \times 0, 6 \times 1) = (30, 0, 6)$. Check your understanding by computing r_{ij} for "Verify amount."

Step 2 computes the **total computer resource requirements, r_i.** The chart in Figure 4.25 shows the total for each row:

$$r_i = \sum_{j=1}^{m} r_{ij}$$

So "Update balance" requires 30 CPU instructions:

2	Control Flow
18	Component CPU
0	Component ATM
5	Component I/O
5	Event Recording
30	CPU instructions

Compute the r_i totals for each computer resource for "Verify Amount."

The following algorithm summarizes the steps for computing resource requirements.

ALGORITHM 4.6: Total Requirements for Each Computer Resource i for a Node: r_i

Start with specifications for:

a_j	$j = 1, \ldots, m$	Number of requests for software resource j
w_{ij}	$i = 1, \ldots, k$ $j = 1, \ldots, m$	The computer resources i required for each software resource request a_j

and compute:

r_{ij}	$i = 1, \ldots, k$ and $j = 1, \ldots, m$	The total requirements for computer resource i for each software resource j
r_i	$i = 1, \ldots, k$	The total requirements for computer resource i for a node

Step 1: $r_{ij} = a_j w_{ij}$ for all $i = 1, \ldots, k$ and $j = 1, \ldots, m$

Step 2: $r_i = \displaystyle\sum_{j=1}^{m} r_{ij}$ for all $i = 1, \ldots, k$

□

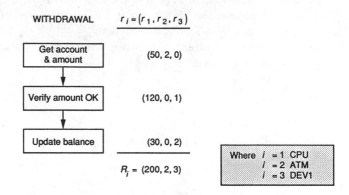

FIGURE 4.26
Total Computer Resource Requirements for the Scenario R_j. The graph reduction rules in Section 4.3.1 provide the graph total.

Next use the computer resource requirements in Section 4.3.1's basic reduction rules to **calculate the total computer resource requirements for the subgraph.** Figure 4.26 shows the r_i for each component. Note the (30, 0, 2) for "Update balance" that we just computed. Your total for "Verify amount" should

INITIATE SESSION	SOFTWARE RESOURCES, a_j					COMPUTER RESOURCES, r_i		
			Component					
	1 Control Flow	2 CPU	3 ATM	4 I/O	5 Event Recording	1 CPU	2 ATM	3 DEV1
Get customer ID from ATM	0	20	1	0	0	25	1	0
Get auth. code from ATM	1	20	1	0	0	27	1	0
Verify code	1	11	0	1	0	18	0	1

$$R_i = (70, 2, 1)$$

FIGURE 4.27
Condensed Computer Resource Requirement Chart. The chart shows the a_j specifications and the r_i and R_i results without the intermediate steps.

match the figure. Sequential-path reduction adds the r_i to get the R_i for the graph (substitute a resource requirement, r_i, for "time," t_j, in the earlier formula). So the total for "Withdrawal" is 200 CPU instructions, 2 ATM interactions, and 3 I/Os, or R_i = (200, 2, 3). R_i **represents the total units of service needed from computer resource i for the scenario** (or graph), where $R_i \geq 0$, $i = 1, \ldots, k$.

This discussion illustrates the computer resource computation r_i with two separate figures and one table. Subsequent examples condense the calculation into one figure as shown in Figure 4.27 (the "Initiate session" subgraph). It shows the software resource requirements, a_j, for each component in the left chart, and the result of the r_i computation on the right. You should be able to derive the same results using the w_{ij} specified in Table 4.2. Try it.

These computations used only the sequential-path reduction rule. The other graph analysis rules are illustrated next. The discussion assumes that you understand the computer resource computation r_i, and it shows how to use r_i in the graph analysis algorithms.

EXAMPLE 4.2: Computation of R_i for the General ATM Scenario

Figure 4.28 has a tuple next to each node in the graph with the results of the r_i calculation (as in Figure 4.27). The tuple (r_1, r_2, r_3) contains: CPU requirement r_1, the total ATM interactions r_2, and the total I/Os r_3 for each node.

Step 1. Reduce the case structure:

Interpret request	(10, 1, 0)
+2/3 (Withdrawal)	+(400/3, 4/3, 2)
+1/3 (Get balance)	+(50/3, 1/3, 1/3)
	(160, 8/3, 7/3)

Step 2. Combine that result with "Get request" to get the total for each loop repetition:

Get request	(20, 1, 0)
+ Step 1	+(160, 8/3, 7/3)
	(180, 11/3, 7/3)

Step 3. Multiply the Step 2 result by the number of loop repetitions:

3 × Step 2	3(180, 11/3, 7/3)
	(540, 11, 7)

Step 4. Add that result to the remaining nodes to give:

Initiate session	(70, 2, 1)
+ Step 3	(540, 11, 7)
+ Terminate	(100, 1, 1)
R_i =	(710, 14, 9)

□

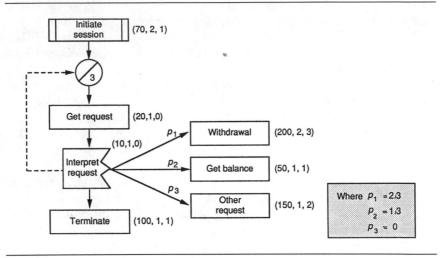

FIGURE 4.28
The General ATM Scenario with the Results of the r_i (Computer Resource Requirements) Calculation.

Use the total R_i requirements for the key computer system resources for an initial performance evaluation. For example, for online transactions against a large database, the number of I/O operations is a key performance indicator. So use the above procedure to compute the total I/Os. Then compare the execution graph I/O results to an I/O threshold for your environment for early problem detection. Chapter 5 shows how to use models to determine your threshold for the maximum number of I/Os that can be processed without degrading response time; Chapter 7 gives an empirical performance-benchmark method.

You can also compute an optimistic estimate of the elapsed time for a scenario from the software execution models. Let w_i represent the average time to process a service request for computer resource i. Using Example 3.5's environment specifications, the CPU processes 2 million machine instructions per second, so the average time to execute one instruction is 0.000005 sec (the reciprocal). There are 20 machine instructions per high-level instruction, so the time to execute one high-level instruction is w_1 = .00001. Assume ATM interactions take 1 sec, w_2 = 1, and w_3 = 0.05 sec per I/O (from Example 3.5). Then the (optimistic) elapsed time for Example 4.2's scenario is:

$$(710 \times .00001) + (14 \times 1) + (9 \times .05) = 14.46 \text{ sec}$$

The time is optimistic because it excludes queueing delays. (We will use the system execution model in Chapter 5 to analyze delays.) This optimistic estimate is the *total processing units* for the scenario; it represents the total units of processing (in our example, the total seconds) required from all the computer system resources. So **T is the total processing units of a scenario**:

Total processing units: $$T = \sum_{i=1}^{k} R_i w_i$$

The scenario algorithm is summarized below.

ALGORITHM 4.7: Scenario Totals: R_i and T

Start with the calculated r_i: the total requirements for computer resource i for each node.

Part 1: Compute:

R_i for all $i = 1, \ldots, k$ The total units of service for each computer resource i for the scenario

Substitute r_i for "time," t_j, in the basic graph reduction Algorithm 4.1 (and in Algorithms 4.3–4.5 if you have state identification nodes).

Part 2: Start with the R_i calculated in Part 1 and a specification for:

w_i for all $i = 1, \ldots, k$ The average time to process a service request for computer resource i

and compute the total processing units for the scenario, T:

$$T = \sum_{i=1}^{k} R_i w_i$$

□

In summary, this section calculated the total resource requirements for each computer system resource and used the algorithms in Section 4.3.1 to compute the total processing units for a scenario. Recall that some nodes may have both upper-bound and expected resource requirements. Use the upper-bound resource require-ments in the longest-path graph analysis to derive pessimistic results for resource requirements. Similarly, the lower-bound estimates in the shortest-path analysis give optimistic results. So, combine various values for resource requirements with the algorithms to examine the sensitivity of the results to the parameters and to derive optimistic and pessimistic results. Next we consider data-dependent specifi cations.

4.3.3 Data Dependency

The dependency of resource requirements on characteristics of data makes estima-ting resource requirements difficult. The solution is to identify the data objects upon which performance depends and to provide specifications in terms of these objects. This section gives more specific information and several examples of the analysis of scenarios with data-dependent execution. This should clarify both the analysis of software models with data dependency and the model specifications needed.

This section describes four analysis techniques: best-case, worst-case, scenario definition, and data-dependent variables. In a large software system there are many areas in which execution behavior can be tied to data characteristics. Many have a negligible effect on overall performance, but a few of them are key. The **best- and worst-case** analyses already described evaluate the sensitivity of performance to the data-dependent variable. If there is little difference in the best and worst cases, you can safely ignore the data-dependent variable.

When you find vital dependencies, the **scenario definition** technique promotes the dependency to high visibility. For example, for an ATM session, the execution characteristics depend on the type of transaction a user selects (the workload). If you define separate scenarios for the most important transactions—a withdrawal scenario, a get balance scenario, and a general scenario—the type of transaction is no longer a dependency in two of the three scenarios. For important but less critical dependencies, the fourth technique uses **variables** in the analysis to quantify the performance impact of the key data objects.

When data objects cause large changes in execution characteristics, it is usually because they control the execution paths: the number of loop repetitions or

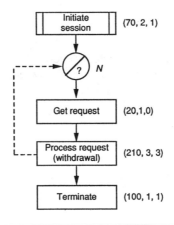

FIGURE 4.29
A Scenario with a Data-Dependent Variable, N, Specifying the Loop Repetition Factor.

the conditional execution probabilities. Figure 4.29 shows **loop repetition dependency:** It models variability in the number of transactions in a session. The example comes from Figure 4.5; in addition to varying the number of repetitions, we simplify the example by assuming that the request is a withdrawal and show results of the computer resource calculation r_i for each node. The following example calculates the processing time function:

EXAMPLE 4.3: Processing Time Function for Variable Loop Repetitions

1. Apply the sequential-path reduction rule to the loop body:

   $(20, 1, 0) + (210, 3, 3) = (230, 4, 3)$

2. Multiply the loop body by the loop repetition factor, N, and apply the sequential-path reduction rules to the scenario:

   $R_i = (70, 2, 1) + N(230, 4, 3) + (100, 1, 1)$

3. Simplify the equation:

   $R_i = (170, 3, 2) + N(230, 4, 3)$

4. Assume that $w_i = (0.001, 1, 0.1)$ sec.[4] Then calculate the total processing units T as a function of N:

   $T = (0.170 + 3.0 + 0.2) + (0.230 + 4.0 + 0.3)N$ sec $= (3.37 + 4.53N)$ sec

   ☐

After deriving the processing time function, there are **three strategies for assigning values to the data-dependent variables and evaluating the effect.** The first is to *substitute ranges of values:* the best, worst, and typical values. For Example 4.3, the best case is $N = 1$, the worst is the maximum allowable transactions (ask the bank officer), and a typical value is 2. The second strategy augments the first: *conditional performance goals.* In this case, we may have separate performance goals for representative values of N:

for $N = 1$ response time ≤ 5 sec
for $N = 2$ response time ≤ 10 sec
for $N \leq 5$ response time ≤ 20 sec

We would then evaluate each of the cases separately, using both the software models, and later the system models. Conditional performance goals are appropriate for complex situations and will be applied again later. The third strategy is *deferred parameter assignment;* its description is postponed until we cover a more complex example.

---

[4]These are not the w_i values used earlier—this merely illustrates the calculation.

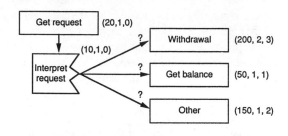

FIGURE 4.30
A Scenario with Data-Dependent Variables Specifying Execution Path Probabilities.

Example 4.3 shows variable loop repetitions. Next consider the other prevalent effect of data dependency: variable execution probabilities.

EXAMPLE 4.4: Processing Time Calculation for Variable Execution Probabilities

Figure 4.30 shows a hypothetical scenario with the results of the computer resource calculation. First use variables for the execution probabilities in the basic reduction rules to get:

$$R_i = (30, 2, 0) + p_1(200, 2, 3) + p_2(50, 1, 1) + p_3(150, 1, 2)$$

when $w_i = (0.001, 1, 0.1)$ sec

$$T = (2.03 + 2.5p_1 + 1.15p_2 + 1.35p_3) \text{ sec}$$

Then substitute ranges of values and calculate the average T for each:

	Probability ranges			
Cases	p_1	p_2	p_3	**Average T**
Best case	0	1	0	3.18
Worst case	1	0	0	4.53
Range 1	.8	.1	.1	4.28
Range 2	.7	.2	.1	4.15
Range 3	.7	.1	.2	4.17

□

You can also define conditional performance goals for cases of interest and compare them to analysis results (throughout development). Next consider the combination of the previous two examples.

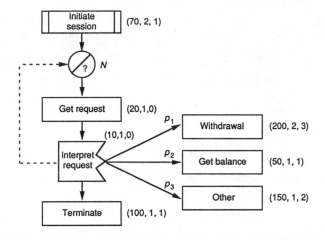

FIGURE 4.31
A Scenario with Data-Dependent Variables for Both Loop Repetitions and Execution Path Probabilities.

EXAMPLE 4.5: Processing Time Calculation for Combined Loop and Probability Variation

The combined scenario is in Figure 4.31. Check your understanding of the calculations:

1. Apply basic reduction rules to produce R_i
2. Assume that $w_i = (0.001, 1, 0.1)$ sec
3. Calculate T

You should get:

$$T = 3.37 + N(2.03 + 2.5p_1 + 1.15p_2 + 1.35p_3)$$

You can next specify values for each of the data-dependent variables: N, p_1, p_2, p_3. Alternatively, you can replace these variables with new ones that represent the expected number of each type of transaction in a session:

N_w = number of "Withdrawals" in a session (Np_1)
N_b = number of "Get balances" in a session (Np_2)
N_o = number of "Others" in a session (Np_3)

Transform the processing time equation by calculating the resource requirements for each new variable as follows. The inner loop for each "withdrawal" corresponds to $p_1 = 1, p_2 = p_3 = 0$:

$$2.03 + 2.5(1) + 1.15(0) + 1.35(0) = 4.53 \text{ sec}$$

(continued)

EXAMPLE 4.5 (*Continued*)

Similarly, the inner loop for "Get balance" takes 3.18 sec; and for "Other" it is 3.38 sec. So, the revised processing time function, with the session initiation and termination, is:

$$T = (3.37 + 4.53N_w + 3.18N_b + 3.38N_o) \text{ sec}$$

The new variables simplify the value assignment. For example, evaluating a session with one "Get balance" and two "Withdrawals" is conceptually easier than evaluating $N = 3, p_1 = 2/3, p_2 = 1/3$, and $p_3 = 0$, even though the calculations are the same.   □

The next example shows another combination of loop and execution probability variability; it illustrates the third strategy for assigning values to data-dependent variables: **deferred parameter assignment.**

EXAMPLE 4.6: Processing Time Calculation for General-Purpose Software

The execution graph in Figure 4.32 shows a hypothetical "Request record" component. When a record is requested, "Check buffers" first checks to see if the record is already in one of its buffers. If so, it is used; otherwise, "Fetch info" allocates a new buffer, reads the record into it, and returns to "check buffer." $R_i = (30, 0) + p_{not} (110, 1)$. Assume that:

$$w_i = (0.0001, 0.03) \text{ sec}$$

(These w_i values reflect execution on a different computer system than the earlier ATM scenarios. Chapter 5 describes the derivation of w_i values.)
    Then the processing time function is:

$$T = 0.003 + p_{not} (0.041) \text{ sec}$$

In the best case, the record is always found and $p_{not} = 0; T = 0.003$ sec. In the worst case, the record is never found and $p_{not} = 1; T = 0.044$ sec. For more realistic evaluations, you need scenarios that specify how "Request record" is used.   □

The probability that the requested record is not found in the buffer, p_{not}, depends on its use in the scenario: It depends on the number of buffers, the record

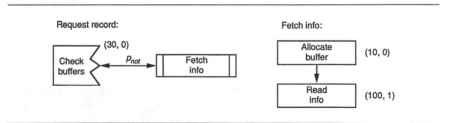

FIGURE 4.32
General-Purpose Software with Data-Dependent Execution Probability.

and block size, frequency of access, and the access method. For example, if "Request record" is a database routine called by such diverse applications as ATM, computer-aided engineering, and business data processing scenarios, we would expect the value of p_{not} to vary greatly among them.

As before, you can calculate the best and worst cases for p_{not}, and use conditional performance goals for several representative values of N. Example 4.6 deferred assigning a value to p_{not} because the "Request record" routine is a general-purpose routine used for many different file types, sizes, and access methods. Instead, it calculated the resource units and processing time requirements as a function of the probability that the record is found in a buffer. The following example defines a user scenario that provides enough information to assign a value to the deferred parameter.

EXAMPLE 4.7: Processing Time Calculation with Scenario Definition and Deferred Parameter Assignment

The hypothetical scenario in Figure 4.33 examines an event-log file and retrieves the requested events. It calls the "Request record" component in Figure 4.32 to read the events. The computer resource requirements for the scenario are:

$$R_i = (250, 2) + N[(60, 0) + p_{not} (110, 1)]$$
$$\text{for } w_i = (0.0001, 0.03) \text{ sec}$$
$$T = 0.085 + N[0.006 + p_{not} (0.041)] \text{ sec}$$

(continued)

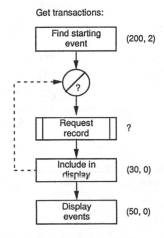

Get transactions:

Find starting event   (200, 2)

?

Request record   ?

Include in display   (30, 0)

Display events   (50, 0)

FIGURE 4.33
A Specific Scenario That Calls the General-Purpose Software Scenario in Figure 4.32.

EXAMPLE 4.7 (*Continued*)

Thus, the scenario has two data-dependent variables: the number of events requested, N, and p_{not}, the probability that "Request record" executes an I/O because the event is not in a buffer.

Suppose we define the scenario in Figure 4.33 to be "examine the log file and retrieve all events that occurred after 5 PM." Then we check with a user representative to get some typical values for the number of events, and learn that the range is between 100 and 500. This gives two bounds for T:

Lower bound, $N = 100$: $T = (.685 + p_{not} (4.1))$ sec
Upper bound, $N = 500$: $T = (3.085 + p_{not} (20.5))$ sec

To use scenario-level assignment for p_{not} we ask the software designers to specify the proposed file structure; we learn that the event-log records are stored sequentially and there are 10 records per block. So, "Request record" reads a block of 10 records with 1 I/O, and the next 9 requests are found in the buffer. Thus, $p_{not} = 1/10$—1 out of 10 records requires the I/O. Substituting in the above equations yields:

$N = 100$, $p_{not} = 0.1$ $T = 1.095$ sec
$N = 500$, $p_{not} = 0.1$ $T = 5.135$ sec

□

Thus far we have considered execution path variability where the data dependency specifies which paths are taken and how often. Most instances of data variability influence the execution paths, as illustrated by the next example.

EXAMPLE 4.8: Processing Time Calculation for Variable Execution Times

Consider the following hypothetical scenario to locate information in an airport database.

```
FIND airports WHERE altitude > 5000 ft;
loop                    --until complete
     RETRIEVE (NEXT) airport_row;
     DISPLAY_DATA;
end loop;
```

The response time for the query clearly depends on database characteristics (and the design and implementation of the database routines). Suppose the database routines are like those in the EDMS case study. Then the Find routine is as shown in Figure 4.34(a). The execution time for each component other than the Find driver depends on the data.

The "Create final address list" component shows how to compute the variable execution time. Its resource requirements depend on the number of addresses in the list. If its processing details are expanded as in Figure 4.34(b), the variable execution time is caused by a loop repetition factor. Thus, you use the analysis technique in Examples 4.3–4.5 to compute the variable execution time.

Sometimes you can characterize data-dependent processing time by using *algorithm analysis techniques*. (See [KNU68] for algorithm analysis background.) For example, the

(*continued*)

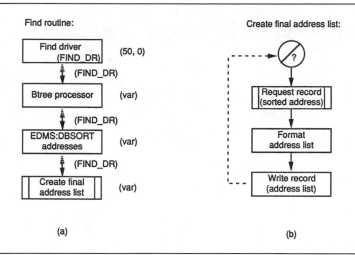

Find routine: Create final address list:

(a)   (b)

FIGURE 4.34
The scenario in (a) has variable execution times for components. The subgraph for the "create final address component" in (b) shows that the variable execution time can be associated with a data-dependent loop repetition factor.

EXAMPLE 4.8 *(Continued)*

"EDMS: DBSORT addresses" component resource requirements also depend on the number of addresses. Algorithm analysis of sort routines yields that computer resource usage for the best case is proportional to $n\log_2 n$. Suppose 1 I/O executes for every 100 addresses; then $r_2 = 0.01 n \log_2 n$. The 0.01 is a constant factor in the data-dependent expression. You calculate the constant factor (such as number of instructions) for each computer resource, r. Once you derive the data-dependent expressions for each node, the analysis proceeds as previously described.

□

It is also possible to express the execution variability of components with random variables and specify their distribution of values. The analysis is more complex, and its additional precision is seldom necessary for data processing applications. It is a viable technique for evaluating reliability of software, especially general-purpose system software, such as compilers. Refer to Sahner [SAH85a, SAH85b], Kelly [KEL71], and Smith [SMI80a] for further information.

The evaluation of variability for models with state identification nodes, such as lock-free or send-receive, has not been discussed. The techniques in this section can be extended for use with them; however, the primary tool for analyzing their performance is the system execution model. Therefore, further discussion of state identification nodes is postponed until after the system model is described.

4.4 Software Model Analyses for Case Studies

So far, we have defined the case studies' performance goals, workloads, software execution structures, environments, and resource usages (in Chapter 3). Then Section 4.2 defined execution graphs for the three case studies. Refer to Section 3.3 (pages 138 to 152) and Section 4.2 (pages 170 to 174) if you need to review our progress. The three case studies are interrelated; DRAWMOD calls the EDMS routines, and both use the network operating system to communicate. In most SPE studies, the scenario components are either part of the engineered software or part of the computer system environment. For the former we specify resource usage, and for the latter we use environment specifications as we did for DBOPEN and DBCLOSE in Table 3.3.

The interrelationship of the three case studies introduces three problems that postpone analysis of DRAWMOD. We need to know: (1) the resource requirements for FIND and RETRIEVE, (2) the "EDMS call processing" requirements (for the arcs in DRAWMOD), and (3) the processing requirements for SEND and RECEIVE (for DB_MP). Therefore, the following analyses evaluate the communication case study first, then EDMS, and conclude with DRAWMOD. The best-case analysis is first.

4.4.1 SYS_EXEC Analysis

We proceed with the analysis of SYS_EXEC using the algorithms in Section 4.3 and the specified resource requirements. Figure 4.35 shows the analysis of the "SYS_EXEC processing" graph from Figure 4.19(c). In each resource chart, the subscripts i and j have the following definitions:

Software Resources	Computer Resources
$j = 1$ control flow	$i = 1$ CPU
$j = 2$ component CPU	$i = 2$ I/O subsystem
$j = 3$ component I/O	$i = 3$ terminal I/O
$j = 4$ get/free memory	
$j = 5$ screen communication	
$j = 6$ SYS_EXEC	

Columns that are zero are usually omitted, as in Figure 4.35. The values in the j columns are the number of requests a_j for the jth software resource. The environment specifications in Table 3.6 tell us the computer resource requirements w_{ij} for each; Table 4.3 summarizes the case study w_{ij}. Note that we must calculate the SYS_EXEC and EDMS call columns.

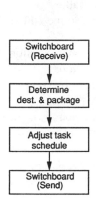

	SOFTWARE RESOURCES, a_j			COMPUTER RESOURCES, i	
	1 Control Flow	Component 2 CPU	3 I/O	1 CPU	2 I/O
Switchboard (Receive)	0	50	0	50	0
Determine dest. & package	1	16	0	18	0
Adjust task schedule	1	10	0	12	0
Switchboard (Send)	1	50	.001	52	.001

Best case: R_i = (132, .001, 0)

FIGURE 4.35
SYS_EXEC Processing: Computer Resource Requirements for Each Component and for the Subgraph. The results are the computer resource requirements for each SYS_EXEC software resource request (for column 6 of Table 4.3).

TABLE 4.3
CASE STUDY w_{ij}: COMPUTER RESOURCE i FOR EACH OF THE a_j REQUESTS FOR SOFTWARE RESOURCE j

	Software resources, j							
	1			2	3	4	5	6
Computer resources, i	Control flow			Component		Get/free	Screen	SYS_
i Name	Transfer	Proc call	EDMS call	CPU	I/O	memory	commun.	EXEC
1 CPU	2	5	*	1	100	100	50	†
2 I/O	0	0	*	0	1	0	0	†
3 Terminal I/O	0	0	*	0	0	0	1	†

*To be calculated from EDMS call processing model
† To be calculated from SYS_EXEC loop model

The software resource requirements, a_j, in Figure 4.35 come from the resource usage specifications in Table 3.5. The control flow in column $j = 1$ is for the component's incoming arc. For this graph, the arcs represent transfer of control, and from Table 4.3, each requires 2 instructions. Table 4.3 also specifies that each I/O operation requires 100 (CPU) instructions. So the CPU computer resource requirement, r_1, for Switchboard (Send) is $(1 \times 2) + (50 \times 1) + (.001 \times 100) = 52.1$. In this analysis, though, we (arbitrarily) ignore instructions for I/O that are nonintegers, so we use 52 rather than 52.1. Confirm your understanding of the calculation of computer resource requirements for nodes by computing the r_i for "Adjust task schedule," and compare to the results in the chart.

Next apply the sequential-path reduction rule to the graph. This yields $R_i = (132, 0.001, 0)$. Note that column $i = 3$ Terminal I/O is omitted from the chart because all $r_3 = 0$.

Figure 4.36 uses this calculated time for the "SYS_EXEC processing" ex-

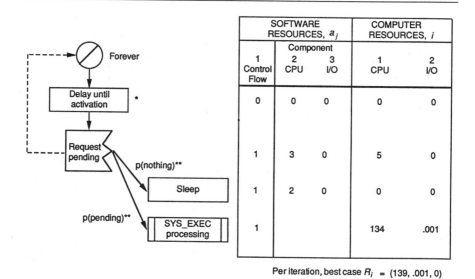

Per iteration, best case $R_i = (139, .001, 0)$

FIGURE 4.36
SYS_EXEC Loop Analysis. The SYS_EXEC processing results from Figure 4.35 plus the control flow give the computer resources on the last row in the chart. The best case assumes no delay until activation (the *), excludes overhead to check for pending requests when nothing is found (**p(nothing) = 0 and p(pending) = 1), and assumes no wait for other requests to complete SYS_EXEC processing. The SYS_EXEC loop analysis result is the time for the control flow for each EDMS call (for column 1 in Table 4.3).

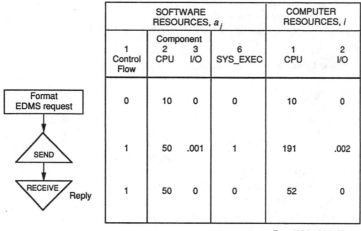

		SOFTWARE RESOURCES, a_j			COMPUTER RESOURCES, i	
	1 Control Flow	Component 2 CPU	3 I/O	6 SYS_EXEC	1 CPU	2 I/O
Format EDMS request	0	10	0	0	10	0
SEND	1	50	.001	1	191	.002
RECEIVE Reply	1	50	0	0	52	0

$$R_i = (253, .002, 0)$$

FIGURE 4.37
EDMS call processing uses the results calculated from the communication models for SYS_EXEC overhead.

panded node. For the best-case analysis, assume there are no other pending requests and no delays until activation. Thus, resource requirements for "Delay until activation" are 0, p(nothing) $= 0$, and p(pending) $= 1$. The CPU requirement shown for the component "SYS_EXEC processing" uses the R_i calculated in Figure 4.35 and the additional two instructions for control flow (transfer of control). The best-case resource requirement for one loop iteration is thus $R_i = (139, 0.001, 0)$. **These are the results we need for column 6 in Table 4.3.**

Figure 4.37 shows the "EDMS call processing": the result we need for Table 4.3's EDMS-call control flow (used for arcs in the DRAWMOD scenario that call EDMS routines). The computer resource requirements for the "SEND to SYS_EXEC" node are calculated as in Example 4.9.

EXAMPLE 4.9: "SEND to SYS_EXEC" Computer Resource Calculation

Table 3.5's communication resource estimates show that for each message, "SEND to SYS_EXEC" executes 50 instructions ($j = 2$), requests 0.001 file I/Os ($j = 3$), and makes 1 call to the SYS_EXEC routine ($j = 6$). The software model also shows 1 transfer of control

(continued)

EXAMPLE 4.9 (*Continued*)

($j = 1$). Assume a best-case—that the SEND requires only 1 message. Multiply each of these a_j requests by the corresponding w_{ij} from Table 4.3 and compute the total r_i as follows:

j	Number, a_j	Computer resource req. for each (CPU, I/O)		Total for j (CPU, I/O)
1	1	$\times$	(2, 0)	=	(2, 0)
2	50	$\times$	(1, 0)	=	(50, 0)
3	0.001	$\times$	(100, 1)	=	(0, 0.001)
6	1	$\times$	(139, 0.001)	=	(139, 0.001)
		SEND to SYS_EXEC:		r_i =	(191, 0.002)

We will use this format for subsequent calculations in this section. The first column corresponds to the software resources j. The second is the number of requests for each a_j; the third is computer resource requirements per each request w_{ij}, and the last column is the product of columns 2 and 3. Note the SYS_EXEC routine results calculated in Figure 4.36 are on the row for $j = 6$. Summing the last column gives the total resource requirements for the SEND component.

□

Compute the computer resource requirements for the other components. Then apply the sequential-path reduction rule to the computer resources chart in Figure 4.37. Compare your total to the total resource requirements shown in the figure: $R_i = (253, 0.002, 0)$. **These are the values for the EDMS call processing in Table 4.3.**

If we had performance goals for the communication routines, we could compare them either to the total resource requirements or to the total processing units. If $w_i = (0.001, 0.03, 0.1)$ sec, the total processing units for EDMS calls is $T \cong 0.253$ sec, and for SYS_EXEC, $T \cong 0.139$ sec. Note that these are not the actual w_i values; they merely illustrate the calculation.

4.4.2 EDMS Analysis

Next we use these results to analyze EDMS. Figure 4.38(a) shows the analysis of the "DB_MP termination" subgraph introduced in Figure 4.18(e). The specifications for the first and last nodes are from Table 3.4; SEND comes from Table 3.5. The calculation yields $R_i = (318, 0.002, 0)$. Figure 4.38(b) shows the analogous calculation for "DB_MP initiation," which yields $R_i = (164, 0, 0)$.

Figure 4.39 shows the Retrieve routine analysis. The execution graph was introduced in Figure 4.18(c), and the resource specifications in Table 3.4. The RTR_DR driver arcs in this graph are procedure calls. From Table 4.3 each requires $(5, 0)$. The arc between "Buffer checker" and "Read (data)," however, is a transfer of control requiring $(2, 0)$. The data-dependent variable p_{not} is retained in the calculations for deferred assignment, as described in Section 4.3.3. The other

	SOFTWARE RESOURCES, a_j					COMPUTER RESOURCES, i	
	Component						
	1 Control Flow	2 CPU	3 I/O	4 Get/free memory	6 SYS_EXEC	1 CPU	2 I/O
Format reply (to DRAWMOD)	0	25	0	0	0	25	0
SEND	1	50	.001	0	1	191	.002
Free memory	1	0	0	1	0	102	0

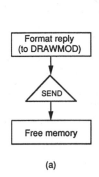

(a)

$R_i = (318, .002, 0)$

	SOFTWARE RESOURCES, a_j					COMPUTER RESOURCES, i	
	Component						
	1 Control Flow	2 CPU	3 I/O	4 Get/free memory	6 SYS_EXEC	1 CPU	2 I/O
Allocate memory	0	0	0	1	0	100	0
RECEIVE	1	50	0	0	0	52	0
Interpret request	1	10	0	0	0	12	0

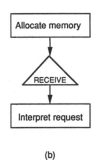

(b)

$R_i = (164, 0, 0)$

FIGURE 4.38
DB_MP termination analysis is in (a); DB_MP initiation analysis is in (b). The results are used for EDMS_DBC processing analysis.

calculations are the same as before. Confirm your understanding by calculating the computer resource requirements for "Read (data)" and the total R_i for the graph.

The Find routine from Figure 4.18(b) is analyzed in Figure 4.40. The specifications are also from Table 3.4. The data-dependent variable B represents the number of address blocks, C is the number of condition clauses in the FIND, and N

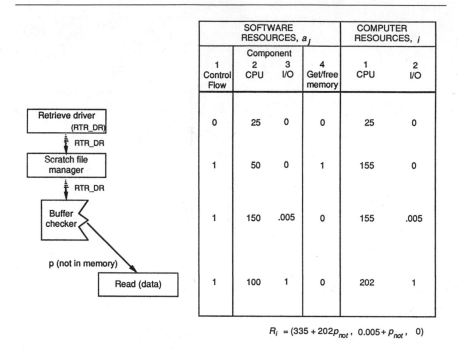

	SOFTWARE RESOURCES, a_j				COMPUTER RESOURCES, i	
		Component				
	1 Control Flow	2 CPU	3 I/O	4 Get/free memory	1 CPU	2 I/O
Retrieve driver (RTR_DR)	0	25	0	0	25	0
Scratch file manager	1	50	0	1	155	0
Buffer checker	1	150	.005	0	155	.005
Read (data)	1	100	1	0	202	1

$$R_i = (335 + 202p_{not}, \ 0.005 + p_{not}, \ 0)$$

FIGURE 4.39
The Retrieve Routine Analysis. The results are used for EDMS_DBC processing analysis.

is the number of addresses expected to satisfy all FIND conditions. The following example calculates r_i for component "Btree processor."

EXAMPLE 4.10: "Btree Processor" Computer Resource Calculation

j	Number, a_j	Computer resource req. for each (CPU, I/O)		Total for j (CPU, I/O)
1	1	×	(5, 0) =	(5, 0)
2	$50 + 150C + 100B$	×	(1, 0) =	$(50 + 150C + 100B, 0)$
3	$1B$	×	(100, 1) =	$(100B, 1B)$
4	$1C$	×	(100, 0) =	$(100C, 0)$
		Btree processor:	$r_i =$	$\overline{(55 + 250C + 200B, 1B)}$

□

Next we calculate resource requirements for "EDMS: DBSORT addresses." As specified in Chapter 3, this is a recursive call to the EDMS routines to sort the qualifying addresses into ascending sequence. Because it is an internal call it bypasses "EDMS call processing" and "SYS_EXEC"; thus, the control flow is a

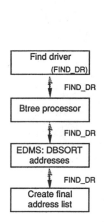

	SOFTWARE RESOURCES, a_j				COMPUTER RESOURCES, i	
		Component				
	1 Control Flow	2 CPU	3 I/O	4 Get/free memory	1 CPU	2 I/O
Find driver (FIND_DR)	0	50	0	0	50	0
Btree processor	1	$50+150C+100B$	$1B$	1	$55+250C+200B$	$1B$
EDMS: DBSORT addresses	1	$1570+15N\log_2N$	B	2	$1775+100B+15N\log_2N$	B
Create final address list	1	100	$1B$	2	$305+100B$	$1B$

$$R_i = (2185 + 250C + 400B + 15N\log_2N, \; 3B, \; 0)$$

Where N = Total number of qualifying addresses
B = Number of address blocks
C = Number of condition clauses

FIGURE 4.40
The Find Routine Analysis. The results are used for EDMS_DBC processing analysis.

procedure call. The component specifications come from Table 3.4. N and B represent the same data-dependent variables as before.

EXAMPLE 4.11: "EDMS: DBSORT Addresses" Computer Resource Calculation

j	Number, a_j	Computer resource req. for each (CPU, I/O)		Total for j (CPU, I/O)
1	1	× (5, 0)	=	(5, 0)
2	$1{,}570 + 15N\log_2N$	× (1, 0)	=	$(1570 + 15N\log_2N, 0)$
3	B	× (100, 1)	=	$(100B, B)$
4	2	× (100, 0)	=	(200, 0)
		DBSORT addresses:	$r_i =$	$(1775 + 15N\log_2N + 100B, B)$

□

Verify the requirements for "Create final address list."

With the sequential-path reduction rule, the total for the Find routine graph is:

$$R_i = (2185 + 250C + 400B + 15N\log_2 N, 3B, 0)$$

We can **assign a value to the data-dependent variable** B if we know the number of addresses to be stored in a block. The designers specify that they plan to store

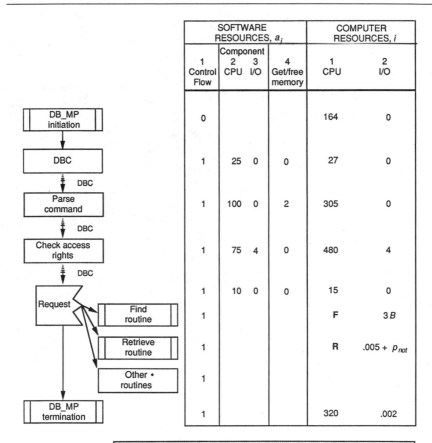

	SOFTWARE RESOURCES, a_j				COMPUTER RESOURCES, i	
	1 Control Flow	Component 2 CPU	3 I/O	4 Get/free memory	1 CPU	2 I/O
DB_MP initiation	0				164	0
DBC	1	25	0	0	27	0
DBC Parse command	1	100	0	2	305	0
DBC Check access rights	1	75	4	0	480	4
DBC	1	10	0	0	15	0
Request Find routine	1				F	3B
Retrieve routine	1				R	.005 + p_{not}
Other routines	1					
DB_MP termination	1				320	.002

Where $F = 2190 + 250C + 400B + 15N\log_2 N$, and $R = 340 + 202\,p_{not}$

EDMS:FIND: $R_i = (3501 + 250C + 400B + 15N\log_2 N,\ 4.002 + 3B,\ 0)$

EDMS:RETRIEVE: $R_i = (1651 + 202p_{not},\ 4.007 + p_{not},\ 0)$

FIGURE 4.41
The EDMS_DBC processing analysis incorporates the previous subgraph results (The "Other routines" are excluded from the case study analysis.)

200 per block. Thus, $B = N/200$, and substituting in the previous expression for the Find routine's R_i gives:

Find routine, $R_i = (2185 + 250C + 2N + 15N\log_2 N, 0.015N, 0)$

Next we use the results for the Find and Retrieve routines and DB_MP initiation and termination for analysis of "EDMS_DBC processing." Figure 4.41 shows the execution structure from Figure 4.18(a), the specified resource usages from Table 3.4, and the calculated requirements for the expanded nodes. We omit the "other routines" (such as DBOPEN, DBCLOSE, and DBSORT) from the EDMS case study analysis; DRAWMOD specifies their resource requirements in Table 3.3. Scenario level assignment, described in Section 4.3.3, resolves the data-dependent variables $p(find)$ and $p(retrieve)$. Recall that you first assume $p(find) = 1$ and analyze the graph to derive resource requirements for FIND, then do the same for $p(retrieve) = 1$. This yields:

EDMS:FIND, $R_i = (3501 + 250C + 2N + 15N\log_2 N, 4.002 + 0.015N, 0)$
EDMS:RETRIEVE, $R_i = (1651 + 202p_{not}, 4.007 + p_{not}, 0)$

If we had performance goals for the EDMS routines, we could compare them either to the total resource requirements for CPU or I/O, or to the total processing units. The calculation is not as straightforward as in the communication analysis because of the data-dependent variables. The following example uses several values for each of the variables.

EXAMPLE 4.12: Preliminary Evaluation of EDMS Processing

Part 1: FIND

Use the expressions derived in Figure 4.41:

CPU: $3501 + 250C + 2N + 15N\log_2 N$
I/O: $4.002 + 0.015N$

and substitute representative values for the data-dependent variables:

C: the number of condition clauses
N: number of addresses expected to satisfy FIND conditions

Designers and user representatives provide the following representative values.

Case	CPU	I/O (rounded)
Best:		
$C = 1, N = 0$	3,751	4
Upper bound:		
$C = 5, N = 2^{20}$	$4751 + (302 \times 2^{20})$	15,733
FIND beams:		
$C = 1, N = 2050 (\cong 2^{11})$	346,101	35
FIND nodes		
$C = 3, N = 2 (= 2^1)$	4,285	4

(continued)

EXAMPLE 4.12 (*Continued*)

Part 2: RETRIEVE

The expressions from Figure 4.41 are:

CPU: $1651 + 202p_{not}$
I/O: $4.007 + p_{not}$

The data-dependent variable p_{not} is the probability the requested record requires a physical I/O.

Case	CPU	I/O (rounded)
Best, $p_{not} = 0$	1651	4
Worst, $p_{not} = 1$	1853	5

□

Experienced system software developers will recognize the potential performance problems from these results. Actual SPE studies would consider other design alternatives at this point. For each alternative, modify the software model, revise the resource requirements accordingly, and repeat the analysis steps to quantify the effect on performance. In this example, we would first examine DBSORT since it has the largest resource consumption. Some alternatives are to use a custom sort routine or to eliminate the sort by preserving the order of the addresses when additions and deletions are made. The analysis of alternatives is covered in greater detail in Chapter 6.

4.4.3 DRAWMOD Analysis

We continue with the evaluation of the DRAWMOD scenario using the calculated resource requirements for EDMS FIND and RETRIEVE from Figure 4.41. Figure 4.42 shows the software model, the calculated resource usage, and specified requirements for the remaining components. Recall that the control flow in this model is the "EDMS call processing" calculated in Figure 4.37 (except for the procedure call to "DRAW" as noted in the figure). The following chart demonstrates the computation of the resource requirements for the "EDMS: DBOPEN" component.

j	Number, a_j	Computer resource req. for each (CPU, I/O)		Total for j (CPU, I/O)
1	1	×	(253, .002, 0)	=	(253, .002, 0)
2	2300	×	(1, 0, 0)	=	(2300, 0, 0)
3	6	×	(100, 1, 0)	=	(600, 6, 0)
4	1	×	(100, 0, 0)	=	(100, 0, 0)
		EDMS:DBOPEN,		$r_j =$	(3253, 6.002, 0)

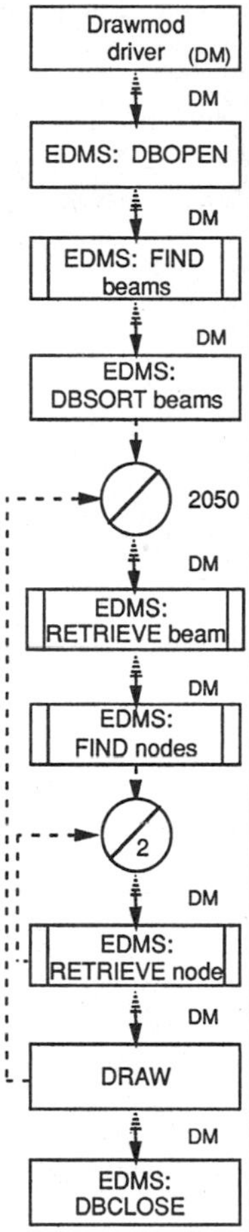

	SOFTWARE RESOURCES, a_j						COMPUTER RESOURCES, i		
	1 EDMS	Component 2 CPU	3 I/O	4 Get/free memory	5 Screen Commun.	6 SYS_ EXEC	1 CPU	2 I/O	3 Term. I/O
Drawmod driver (DM)	0	1000	3	2	2	0	1600	3	2
↓ DM									
EDMS: DBOPEN	1	2300	6	1	0	0	3253	6.002	0
↓ DM									
EDMS: FIND beams	1						F	$(4.004 + .3\,B)$	0
↓ DM									
EDMS: DBSORT beams	1	$1570+15\log_2 N$	$B+D$	2	0	0	S	$(.002 + B + D)$	0
⊘ 2050									
↓ DM									
EDMS: RETRIEVE beam	1						R	$(4.009 + p_{not})$	0
↓ DM									
EDMS: FIND nodes	1						F	$(4.004+.3B)$	0
⊘ 2									
↓ DM									
EDMS: RETRIEVE node	1						R	$(4.009 + p_{not})$	0
↓ DM									
DRAW	1*	50	0	0	1	0	60	0	1
↓ DM									
EDMS: DBCLOSE	1	1500	2	1	0	0	2103	2.002	0

Where: N, B, and p_{not} represent the same data dependent parameters;
D is the number of data blocks.
$F = (3754 + 250C + 400B + 15N\log_2 N)$
$S = (2023 + 15N\log_2 N + 100B + 100D)$
$R = (1904 + 202 p_{not})$

FIGURE 4.42
Computer Resource Calculation for Each Component in the DRAWMOD Scenario.
The calculations use the results of the SYS_EXEC analysis to quantify the overhead
of EDMS calls, and the results of the EDMS analysis for FINDs and RETRIEVEs.
Note that the control flow for the DRAW component is a standard procedure call
rather than an EDMS call, so its w_{ij} differs.

The DRAWMOD driver component calls the screen communication routine. From Table 4.3, its requirements are (50, 0, 1). Using this, the DRAWMOD driver component requirement can be calculated as shown in the following chart.

j	Number, a_j	Computer resource req. for each (CPU, I/O)		Total for j (CPU, I/O)
1	0			
2	1000	×	(1, 0, 0) =	(1000, 0, 0)
3	3	×	(100, 1, 0) =	(300, 3, 0)
4	2	×	(100, 0, 0) =	(200, 0, 0)
5	2	×	(50, 0, 1) =	(100, 0, 2)
		DRAWMOD driver component,	$r_i =$	(1600, 3, 2)

Confirm your understanding by calculating the requirements for EDMS: FIND beams and for DBCLOSE.

Next, assign values to as many of the data-dependent parameters as possible. We (arbitrarily) assign values before computing R_i to simplify the calculation.

EXAMPLE 4.13: DRAWMOD Data-Dependent Variable Assignments

a. EDMS: FIND beams

Figure 4.42 gives the following expressions for r_i:

CPU: $(3754 + 250C + 400B + 15N\log_2N)$
I/O: $(4.004 + 0.3B)$

N has the value specified for the loop repetition factor, 2,050; $C = 1$ because we are looking for the "specified_mod"; and $B = N/200$ as before. So EDMS: FIND beams takes

CPU: 346,354
I/O: 34.754

Before, we rounded the I/Os, but for this analysis we arbitrarily keep the fractional I/Os.

b. EDMS: DBSORT beams

Figure 4.42 gives the following expressions for r_i:

CPU: $(2023 + 15N\log_2N + 100B + 100D)$
I/O: $(0.002 + B + D)$

We sort 2050 beams, so $N = 2050$. The number of address blocks to get them is $2050/200 = 10.25$, but you cannot read a partial block, so $B = 11$. The number of data blocks, D, is N divided by the blocking factor. The walkthrough in Example 3.6 specifies that blocks contain 4,096 bytes, and rows contain 64 bytes, so there are 64 beam rows per block. Thus $D = 2050/64 \cong 33$. So EDMS: DBSORT beams takes

CPU: 344,673
I/O: 44.002

(continued)

EXAMPLE 4.13 (*Continued*)

c. EDMS: RETRIEVE beams

The r_i are:

> CPU: $1904 + 202\,p_{not}$
> I/O: $4.009 + p_{not}$

One beam block contains 64 rows (from [b] above). The best case assumes that records are retrieved sequentially, so 1/64 of them requires an I/O; the rest do not. Thus $p_{not} = 1/64 = 0.015625$. EDMS: RETRIEVE beams takes:

> CPU: 1907
> I/O: 4.025

d. EDMS: FIND nodes

The r_i are the same expressions as in (a) above. $N = 2$: the number of nodes per beam, and $C = 3$ for the "specified_mod," "node_1," and "node_2." EDMS: FIND nodes takes:

> CPU: 4538
> I/O: 4.034

e. EDMS: RETRIEVE nodes

The r_i are the same as (c) above. Node rows have 24 bytes, so each block contains 4,096/24 = 170 rows. With the best-case sequential-retrieval assumption, p_{not} is 1/170 = 0.0058823. EDMS: RETRIEVE nodes takes:

> CPU: 1905
> I/O: 4.015

□

Figure 4.43 shows the DRAWMOD scenario analysis. The results of the data-dependent variable assignments are shown by their nodes. First apply the loop-reduction rule to the innermost loop, giving (3810, 8.03, 0). Then apply the sequential-path reduction rule to the beam loop body, giving (10,315, 16.089, 1). The loop-reduction rule then gives (21,145,750, 32,982, 2050). The sequential-path reduction rule gives the scenario result:

> $R_i = (21{,}843{,}733,\ 33{,}072,\ 2{,}052)$

Clearly the 20-second performance goal will not be met. Using $w_i = (0.0000006, 0.03, 0.01)$ sec (from Example 3.12 and Table 3.6), $T = 1026$ sec, or 17 minutes! Furthermore, this analysis uses many best-case resource usage estimates and does not consider multiple users competing for resources. It will be a challenge to reduce this time to achieve the performance goal, but in Chapter 6 we will see how it can be done. Obviously, when the performance is this far over the goal, it would be virtually impossible to implement the system and then try to tune it. Note that we carried through the analysis even though we suspected much earlier that the software would have performance problems.

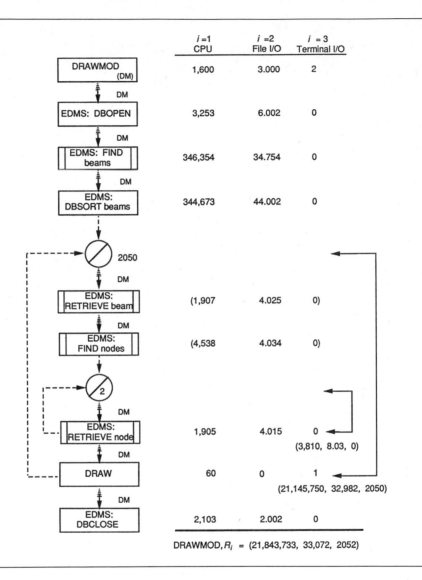

	$i = 1$ CPU	$i = 2$ File I/O	$i = 3$ Terminal I/O
DRAWMOD (DM)	1,600	3.000	2
EDMS: DBOPEN	3,253	6.002	0
EDMS: FIND beams	346,354	34.754	0
EDMS: DBSORT beams	344,673	44.002	0
2050			
EDMS: RETRIEVE beam	(1,907	4.025	0)
EDMS: FIND nodes	(4,538	4.034	0)
2			
EDMS: RETRIEVE node	1,905	4.015	0
			(3,810, 8.03, 0)
DRAW	60	0	1
			(21,145,750, 32,982, 2050)
EDMS: DBCLOSE	2,103	2.002	0

DRAWMOD, R_i = (21,843,733, 33,072, 2052)

FIGURE 4.43
The basic path reduction rules produce the total computer resource requirements for the DRAWMOD scenario.

You should be able to identify many improvements. Take some time now to list those you would consider, using the general principles from Chapter 2. You should be able to apply the software model analysis algorithms to quantify the effect of each. We will review some alternatives in Chapter 6. If you pursue your evaluation now, you will see why the topics addressed in the next section are important. It examines the role of execution graphs in software model evaluation, and describes some tools for automating the analysis.

4.5 Software Execution Model Options

Thus far the terms "software execution models" and "execution graph models" have been used interchangeably. Now let us distinguish between them and examine the viability of execution graph models.

Software execution models do not have to be execution graph models. The advantage of execution graphs is their visual representation, which aids in communication, helps verify understanding of processing steps and their order, and may help to highlight problem areas and their solutions. Graph theory is the basis for the analysis algorithms, but once you understand the algorithms, you can apply them to other forms of software execution models; it is not necessary to draw these symbols. The next section distinguishes software execution models from their predecessors. Then Sections 4.5.2 and 4.5.3 review some tools that support software execution model evaluation.

4.5.1 Software Execution Models Versus Historical Methods

Some historical software prediction techniques (annotation [HIST] in the bibliography) proposed models based on flowcharts. Subsequently, both software performance prediction and flowcharts were abandoned. Now SPE suggests execution graph models of software. Are the wheels of progress grinding to a halt? Should we resurrect flowcharts from old software development ghost towns? No, but we should reopen performance mines and modernize their equipment to make mining viable. The following paragraphs explain the equipment-modernization thesis.

First, flowcharts disappeared partly because "fix-it-later" focused on a system's data flow and hierarchical structure and ignored execution behavior. Specification techniques other than flowcharts better represent data flow and hierarchical composition. *In order to predict software performance, though, you must specify its execution structure.* The specification need not be graphical. The following example shows the evaluation of a language-based software execution model.

EXAMPLE 4.14: Analysis of Language-Based Software Execution Model

The following is an Ada psuedocode representation of the ATM scenario in Figure 4.28. Note the different loop repetition value and different branching probabilities.

(continued)

EXAMPLE 4.14 (*Continued*)

Statements		Resource requirements
Initiate-session;		(70, 2, 1)
loop	--2 times	
Get-request;		(20, 1, 0)
Interpret-request;		(10, 1, 0)
case request **is**		
when Withdrawal $\Rightarrow$ . . .	--.8	(200, 2, 3)
when Get-balance $\Rightarrow$ . . .	--.1	(50, 1, 1)
when Other-request $\Rightarrow$ . . .	--.1	(150, 1, 2)
when other $\Rightarrow$ . . .	--0	(150, 1, 2)
end case;		
end loop;		
Terminate-session;		(100, 1, 1)

Each statement specifies its resource requirements, $r_i =$ (CPU, ATM, File I/O). The four "graph" reduction steps are:

1. Apply the conditional-path reduction rule to the **case** statement:

   (180, 1.8, 2.7)

2. Apply the sequential-path reduction rule to the **loop** body:

   (210, 4.8, 2.7)

3. Apply the loop-reduction rule to the result of Step 2:

   (420, 9.6, 5.4)

4. Apply the sequential-path reduction rule to the scenario:

   $R_i =$ (590, 12.6, 7.4)

   □

Thus, any graphical, language, or other representation is suitable for SPE if it represents the following **three essential requirements for a software execution model:**

- □ *Sequential execution, looping,* and *conditional execution*
- □ *State identification* constructs (such as lock-free and fork-join)
- □ *Restricted structures,* defined in Section 4.1.2 (loop restriction and one initial node)

You can thus adapt to SPE other types of graphs (such as data-flow graphs and petri nets), other design-description languages (Ada, PSL/PSA, Warnicr_Orr, APL) and even special-purpose descriptions (in databases, spreadsheets, and so forth).

Note that *execution graphs are not the same as flowcharts:* Execution graphs are streamlined to represent only key execution paths and to prune most of a flowchart's complexity, and they use structured constructs to remove spider web complexity. Historical flowchart-based prediction methods were abandoned, not because of the flowcharts, but rather because of a lack of methods for lifecycle data collection, adaptive modeling, tools to expedite modeling and analysis, and so on.

So, the software execution models, graphs or others, are not a step back— they are an improved technique vital to the performance-mine reopening.

Next, we contrast the analysis algorithms and procedures in Sections 4.3.1 and 4.3.2 against another traditional software analysis method, algorithm analysis (as described in [KNU68] and in many other references). The primary difference between them is that algorithm analysis seeks proportional resource usage by focusing on what we consider "data-dependent parameters," and by abstracting "constant factors" that represent resource usage, whereas SPE techniques include the resource usage constant factors. You need resource usage to quantify performance. A second major difference is that with algorithm analysis, the *end result* is the expression of the relative impact of data-dependent parameters, whereas our analysis seeks resource usage data as an *interim result* to be input to the system execution model. The methods are otherwise the same, so we can combine them when appropriate. Example 4.8 incorporated algorithm analysis into the software model evaluation. Similarly, the EDMS specification for DBSORT's CPU resource requirements (in Table 3.3) gave an expression of resources proportional to the number of items sorted. The expression was derived from an algorithm analysis of a proposed sort.

4.5.2 Software Execution Modeling Tools

The analysis algorithms are not complex. The calculations can be done with pencil and paper or a calculator. There are several disadvantages to manual methods, though: If you pursued the suggestions at the end of Section 4.4, you probably discovered that it is easy to make mistakes and that minor changes to the models often cause extensive recalculation. Because the software systems are large and have many evolutionary changes, automated analysis tools are essential. Three approaches are described here: (1) using general-purpose tools, (2) developing special-purpose programs, and (3) using commercial software analysis products. Note that vendors mentioned in this section are mentioned in a separate vendor reference section. Citations for them are distinguished from literature references—they appear in italics with no year.

You can quickly "program" **general-purpose tools,** such as spreadsheets and statistical analysis packages, to perform the calculations in Section 4.3. The SAS statistical analysis package has an integrated database that you can use to store software design information (see Section 7.6). You can integrate these general-purpose tools with data presentation packages to produce graphs, histograms, or resource usage pie charts.

Alternatively, you could use a database management package that provides calculation functions. RTI/RIM is a product that allows you to specify vectors (of resource requirements), and mathematical expressions for evaluating graph totals [*RTIa*]. The advantages of the database approach are that the products are reasonably priced, they can be "programmed" quickly, they improve the accuracy of the results (over "manual" calculations), and you can easily substitute data values in several algorithms to analyze lower bounds; upper bounds; typical values; shortest, longest, and average paths; and so on. The primary disadvantage is that it may be tedious to create and update the software models with standard DBMS query functions.

The second approach is to create your own **special-purpose programs** that minimize the labor needed to create and change the software models. It is fairly easy to code the analysis algorithms—the time-consuming parts are designing and building the user interface with which to create and change the models, designing and building routines to view and interpret results, and maintaining the software. Several tools for software execution model analysis have been built; some knowledge gained on early projects is documented in [SMI85b]. Two of the successful tools, DESIGN and PERFORM, are described later in more detail.

The third approach is to purchase a **commercial software analysis product.** Currently available tools automatically combine the software models with system execution models. They calculate the model parameters and solve the system model. The three representative products described here are not the only products, nor necessarily best for your needs, but they illustrate the types of products available.

The first commercially available product of this type was Crystal [*BGS*]. It uses a language-based description of software execution. Its specifications directly correspond to the categories of specifications described in Chapter 3: It has environment, workload, processing steps, and resource requirements specifications. Users define data-dependent parameters in a global parameter section and specify expressions of these variables when appropriate. Because the software analysis results are automatically used for the system execution model, it does not compute response time functions. Instead, one must assign values to the parameters and solve for the resulting performance metrics. This widely used product is effective for SPE studies.

The second commercial software analysis product is SES Workbench [*SES*]. It is also a combination of software and system models. It has both a language-based description language and a graphics model builder. The current version of this tool is closer to a system modeling tool, but supports software modeling.

The third commercial product is SCERT II [*PSI*]. Its conceptual model uses a pseudocode description of future processing and provides default resource usage specifications for standard verbs. It calculates workload characteristics and automatically uses them for the "simulation-ready models of today's hardware and support software systems," for system execution model evaluation.

There are some differences in these tools that are not mentioned here. Should you choose to buy an automated analysis package, you should examine all available products and compare their features to your needs. You will also want to examine the system execution modeling products reviewed in the next chapter.

4.5.3 Research Tools for Software Execution Models

This section describes some research tools that investigated concepts and requirements for automated tools to support SPE. As a result they incorporate some interesting features. The reason for including their description, even though they are not currently commercially available, is to point out the interesting features and describe their user interface, model description format, and the design data organization. These features may shorten your development time and enhance your tools if you elect to build your own.

Because the models are used early in the software development lifecycle, all support tools should meet the following requirements:

- □ The modeling overhead must be low.

- □ The models must accommodate incremental refinement. Initially the definitions are incomplete; information is added incrementally.

- □ Initial performance specifications will be imprecise, but they will improve during development. It must be easy to revise specifications.

- □ Because many structural changes occur during development, the model topology must be easy to revise.

- □ Tools should facilitate the evaluation of alternatives; sensitivity to specifications; best, worst, and typical cases; and data-dependent specifications.

These requirements drove the design of the following tools.

DESIGN DESIGN is a language-based software execution model evaluation tool.[5] It is written in C and runs under UNIX using standard CRT terminals. It was developed specifically to provide a user-friendly system for both specifying and analyzing software designs.

The user interface to the tool is menu-driven. There is a menu selection for each task that the user must perform. DESIGN recognizes and supports five *"phases of use"* for software execution modeling: (1) Specify the software structure, (2) specify the execution scenario (the order of execution for each of the previously defined software components), (3) specify execution paths and resource requirements, (4) evaluate the performance, and (5) view the current status of the software information. "Phase of use" means, for example, that the user first

---

[5]DESIGN was developed by Kin L. Wong, formerly a graduate student at Duke University, and it is described in more detail in [WON83].

specifies the execution structure, then *later* specifies resource requirements; the tool segregates the two steps and provides separate menu choices for each. In order to specify the scenario information, the software structure, or the resource requirements, the user fills in blanks on screen panels (rather than entering a free-format declarative language). DESIGN accepts data-dependent variables in specifications; during the analysis, the user can either assign values to them or solve for processing-time functions.

A number of features make the tool easy to use. The specifications are hierarchical. Thus the user can choose to view only the current level in the hierarchy, include a specified number of lower levels or zoom in on lower-level details of a selected component. The printed specifications use a C-like language. It is possible to interrupt any of the specification or evaluation phases to view other related design information. When viewing the design information, the user can choose to view only component names, to zoom in on component details, or include details where components are referenced. DESIGN also includes a "telephone call feature" to help the user recover from interruptions. Examples of these features are in [WON83].

The data representation is customized to the access patterns. Hierarchical UNIX files hold the user's "active" design information, and DESIGN maintains a table of frequently referenced components in main memory to minimize physical I/Os. DESIGN envisioned that a user would create the files of "local" design information by extracting the desired "active" information from an integrated design database (IDB) containing more general design information. Upon completion of the evaluation, the information would then be archived into the IDB. This combines the performance benefits of the customized data representation with the general features of a DBMS.

DESIGN succeeded in providing a user interface that was much easier to use than previous versions of research tools. Its creators learned that the *direct support of the phases of use* is key to the tool's usability. The features for hierarchical display with the option of either incorporating details into one information display, or allowing the user to zoom in on selected details, also make viewing convenient. A user evaluating design alternatives often wants to see one component immediately, as opposed to browsing through voluminous design specifications to find the desired information. The many features that were added to make the tool usable were effective; however, *user interfaces can always be improved*. If you choose to develop special-purpose programs, you will quickly see how many iterations it takes to create a truly "friendly" package.

PERFORM   PERFORM is an execution-graph-based software evaluation tool.[6] It reuses much of the design and software in the system modeling tool, GQUE, described in Chapter 5. PERFORM is written in C and runs under UNIX currently

---

[6]PERFORM was developed by Dorlisa King and Peter Flur, as an undergraduate honors thesis at Duke University.

on Masscomp and SUN workstations. Its purpose was to support the graph-based software models, to experiment with visual perception of results, to display more of the scenario hierarchy on the screen concurrently, and to simplify the menu structure of DESIGN while providing the same functions.

The user interface is primarily direct manipulation; the user points to the function desired. It also supports the usage phases identified in DESIGN. Figure 4.44 shows the first-phase (the topology definition) functions on the right side of the screen. To create an execution graph, the user selects the type of node to be placed and points to its desired location on the screen. Many features minimize the number of user interactions required to construct an execution graph.

The model hierarchy is displayed in the small "navigation" tiles on the left side of the screen; each contains a miniature replica of an execution graph (see Figure 4.44). The correspondence between an expanded node and its subgraph is shown with color. When a node is expanded, its color becomes the same as its corresponding subgraph. The user may zoom in on a component's details by pointing to its subgraph; it then appears in the large window in the middle.

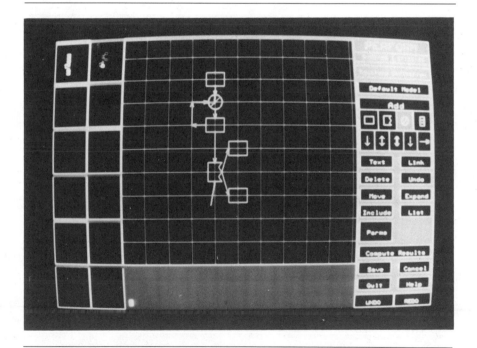

FIGURE 4.44
PERFORM uses color to show model hierarchy. The top-level model is in the upper-left small tile. It contains a purple node that is expanded; the expansion is in the small upper-right tile. The yellow node in it is expanded; its details are in the large work area.

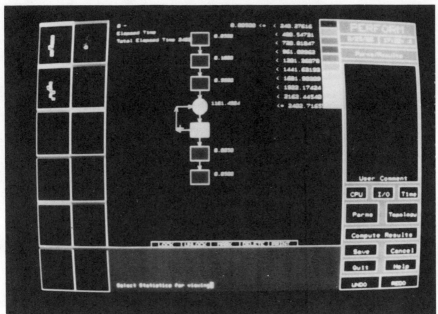

(a)

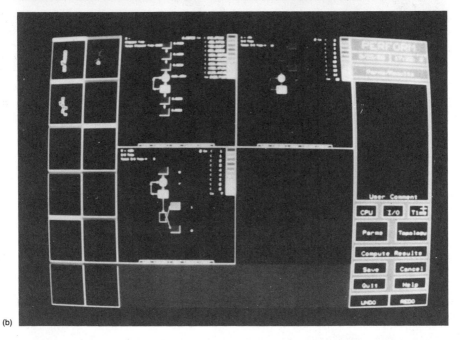

(b)

FIGURE 4.45
PERFORM uses color to show model results. The total processing units for the top-level model is in (a). PERFORM also displays multiple sets of results concurrently in (b); (a)'s results are in the top-left quadrant; the I/O time for the second-level model is in the top-right quadrant; and the I/O time for the lowest-level model is in the bottom-left quadrant.

Some interesting features are used to view results. Currently three results are calculated: CPU and I/O resource requirements and total processing units. The user sees both their numeric values and the corresponding color on a modified heated object scale.[7] Thus, the user can easily perceive the "hot spots" and zoom in on them. Figure 4.45(a) demonstrates. The user can view up to four result displays in any desired combination, as illustrated in Figure 4.45(b). It is also possible to change a graph and concurrently view results produced before and after the change. PERFORM automatically does a "least recently used" replacement of displays and lets the user identify quadrants that should not be removed. The file structure is from the earlier software, GQUE. Its internal data structure is an object-oriented linked list. It has "import" and "export" functions for transferring data between tools and an integrated design database.

PERFORM's user interface is a great success. It is extremely easy to create and evaluate execution graph models. The visual results and concurrent view of both hierarchy and results greatly enhance model evaluation. The use of color to show hierarchy is effective, but less so than in GQUE.[8] An important success was its reuse of the GQUE infrastructure. The graphics user interface, screen area manager, and basic topology, and viewing functions are well designed and should easily transfer to many other similar tools.

4.6 Summary

In this chapter we covered the first type of model used for SPE studies, the software execution model. One specific type of model was defined: the execution graph model. We used it to model the comprehensive case studies and as the basis for the analysis algorithms. The evaluation of software execution models was described and then illustrated with the case studies. Finally, we examined several options for software execution models and some tools that automate their solutions.

These are the tools to prevent skywalk-like performance disasters. If skywalk designers had models and tools like these, why did the hotel skywalk collapse? Did designers use models? Were the models correct? Were predictions of maximum load accurate? Was the skywalk constructed as designed? Did the materials match specifications? Were they properly installed? There were many such allegations during the skywalk investigation; I do not know the final verdict. All the factors have the potential for causing a catastrophe. The solution is continual verification of specifications and model validation (V&V).

---

[7]The modification provides maximum color distinction within the constraints of the hardware device.

[8]Because more nodes are expanded in PERFORM, there is less base color in the graph to establish the visual image.

This vividly points out that models and predictions are not the end result of SPE; the goal is to develop systems that meet performance objectives. The models, accurate SPE data, and V&V are key to achieving the goal. One SPE practitioner recommends using an SPE policy similar to that used in the construction industry: Conduct modeling studies early to find a design that meets performance objectives, then *build the system to match the model*. The alternative is to continually monitor the design and implementation and keep the models up to date with the software. The changing-model strategy is obviously infeasible for skywalks—which policy should you use for SPE?

Exercises

Review

4.1. Calculate the computer resources, r_i, for the "Parse command" component of the EDMS: DBC processing graph. Do the same for the "DRAW" component of the DRAWMOD graph. Compare your results to Figures 4.41 and 4.42.

4.2. (a) Revise the EDMS: DBC processing graph as follows: The first time "Check access rights" executes, it reads in all access rights for a user. This takes 150 instructions, 4 I/Os, and 1 get/free memory. For the duration of the user scenario, "Check access rights" takes 75 instructions, 0 I/Os, and 0 get/free memory.

(b) Compute the best, worst, and average time for EDMS: FIND and EDMS: RETRIEVE.

4.3. Use the following specifications for nodes in the fork-join scenario in Figure 4.11.

Node	Software resources, a_j (CPU, I/O)
Request remote data	(5, 0)
FORK	(2, 2)
User processing	(100, 5)
Request reply	(5, 0)
Fetch data	(250, 3)
JOIN	(25, 1)
Use remote data	(50, 3)

Use the following w_{ij}:

Computer resources	Software resources Component CPU	Component I/O
CPU	1	100
I/O	0	1

Ignore other software resources. Calculate the best and worst resource requirements for the scenario. Use $w_i = (1, 0.03)$. Compute the best and worst total processing units.

4.4. (a) Review the btree and data retrieval terminology in Chapter 3's inset (page 145). Construct an execution graph for the following btree processor. The btree processor builds a list of addresses that satisfy a where clause associated with a database query. An example is:

```
SELECT   Name, Phone# FROM  Registrations
WHERE    License = 'FUNLVN'  AND  State = 'NM';
```

For this example, the btree processor returns the list of addresses of all rows in the Registrations table that contain both of the specified key values.

The **btree processor usage scenario** is as follows. *Btree-CTL* is a driver that calls (expanded) component *Get-list* once for each condition in the where clause in order to build an intermediate list of addresses satisfying that condition. Control returns to *Btree-CTL*, which then calls either *AND-processing* or *OR-processing*, if necessary, to create a new intermediate list of addresses satisfying the logical combination. After all logical (and, or) operations are completed, *Btree-CTL* then returns the address of the resulting list. Component *Get-list* is composed of *Read-root-node*, followed by a loop (executed once for each level in the btree) consisting of a transfer to *Search-level* (to find the address corresponding to the key) followed by *Get-rec* to read the record at the address found above. Next, control passes to *Sort-list* followed by *Return-list-pointer*.

(b) The following are some resource estimates for the components in the btree execution graph. Compute the average resource requirements for the graph for the sample query modeled in (a). (Make reasonable assumptions for unspecified details and document them.)

BTREE RESOURCE ESTIMATES

Component	CPU	I/O
Btree-CTL	1	0
AND-processing	5	0
OR-processing	5	0
Read-root-node	1	1
Search-level	0.5	0
Get-rec	0.5	1
Sort-list	5	0
Return-list-pointer	0.5	0

4.5. Create an execution graph for your continuing case study. Use the data you gathered in Chapter 3, gather more if you need it, plug in the resource usage for each component, and compute total resource requirements R_i and total processing units T for the scenario.

4.6. Make a list of the performance improvements you found for the comprehensive case studies and the general principles associated with each.

Further Study

4.7. Construct the execution graph model for the software system you studied in walk-through Exercise 3.4. Use the data you gathered and solve the software execution model.

4.8. Find a primary natural forecasting unit (NFU) in your environment. Find an online transaction or a batch program whose execution time is likely to depend on the NFU. Construct a software execution model of it, specify resource usage in terms of the NFU, and solve the model.

5

Elementary System Execution Models

Have you ever had an office that was too cold in the morning and too warm in the afternoon, even though the thermostat setting is not changed? After a building is constructed, heating and airconditioning system mistakes are obvious, but predicting their performance in advance is complicated. Static analyses are relatively easy—a diagram with duct sizes and locations and thermostat locations can confirm basic capacity requirements. But it cannot show dynamic effects on temperature, such as the effects of sun reflection and absorption. Imagine a dynamic, visual model that shows your building on a color graphics screen and animates (simulates) the sun's daily movements. It could show how the sun hits the building at various times of day and its effect on the temperature in various inside locations. Geographic coordinates could be specified, and it could animate seasonal variations. You could start with simple sun-only scenarios, then add additional complexities later, such as wind conditions, cloud movements, the effect of adjacent buildings, and so forth, to conduct detailed analyses of the heating and airconditioning system design.

As with heating and airconditioning systems, models are essential to examine software system complexities and the many alternatives. We start with the (static) software execution models to confirm the basic system concept. Then we use (dynamic) system execution models to examine external influences on performance.

Figure 5.1 highlights the subject of this chapter: constructing and evaluating an appropriate performance model. This is the same SPE methodology box highlighted in Chapter 4, the definition of "appropriate" changes. The static software execution models assume an ideal, dedicated computer system and provide op-

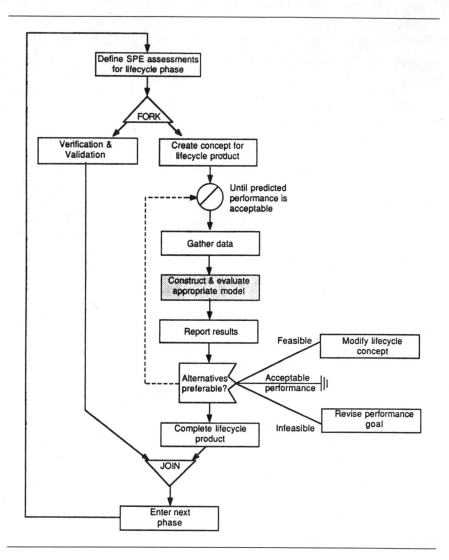

FIGURE 5.1
The SPE Methodology with the Focus of This Chapter Highlighted.

timistic performance metrics for early comparison against performance goals. In reality, most large software systems execute on large mainframe systems and compete with other software for computer system resources. This resource conten-tion introduces delays when software is ready to use a resource, such as the CPU, but it is busy serving another job. On a system with heavy contention, the optimis-tic performance metrics produced by the software execution model may differ greatly from actual performance. So, as the software evolves, we use dynamic

elementary system execution models to represent additional facets of execution behavior.

The system execution model provides the following additional information:

◻ More precise metrics that account for resource contention

◻ Sensitivity of performance metrics to variations in workload composition

◻ Effect of new software on service-level objectives of other systems

◻ Identification of bottleneck resources

◻ Comparative data on performance improvement options to the workload demands, software changes, hardware upgrades, and various combinations of each

This chapter defines the procedures that include the resource contention effects on the execution behavior of software. Fortunately, performance modeling of multiprogrammed computer systems rests on a well-established base of technology and practical application. One type of system execution model, the elementary Information Processing Graph (IPG) is defined here. It is a visual representation of computer system execution that is easily tied to the software execution models. IPGs *represent* the system execution characteristics; analysis tools *solve* for the desired performance metrics. We will consider several analysis tool options later.

This chapter is oriented to the *application* of queueing network models (QNM) rather than QNM *technology*. It assumes that you will use an automated model solution package for system execution model analysis. This chapter's introduction to QNMs is sufficient to demonstrate their modeling power and utility for SPE. It will not make you an expert user of the technology. If you expect to delegate the SPE modeling to an experienced performance analyst, this introduction is sufficient. If you are interested in building your modeling proficiency, consult a textbook oriented to performance modeling technology. Lazowska et al. ([LAZ84a]) and Sauer and Chandy ([SAU81]) are two excellent sources of information. There are also numerous seminars offered on performance modeling.

5.1 System Execution Model Concepts

This section reviews the system execution model concepts. Readers familiar with conventional QNMs may skip to the following section for the definition of elementary IPGs.

Let us examine the sources of contention for resources in a computer system:

◻ There may be **multiple users** of an application or transaction executing at one time. For example, several ATM customers may request a withdrawal at approximately the same time.

- Multiprogrammed systems usually have many **different systems or applications running concurrently.** In a bank, the ATM system may run with mortgage loan amortizations, employee payroll, bank analyst decision support systems, and others.

- Software under consideration may have **separate concurrent processes.** A communication system that may be simultaneously processing input and output streams is an example.

- A system may be **multithreaded** to handle concurrent requests for different external processes. An example is a data management system that executes a FIND for one process concurrent with a RETRIEVE for an unrelated process.

The system execution model can characterize the delays due to each of these sources of contention.

Next, consider the computer system's view of a job's execution behavior. A job enters the system and requires CPU processing to begin execution. If the CPU is busy, the job enters a queue. When its turn arises, it is selected from the queue and receives the required amount of service from the CPU (the system *resource* or *server*). On completion of the processing, the job leaves the server, then leaves the system if its processing is complete, or it requests service from another system resource (such as the I/O subsystem), where the execution pattern repeats.

The performance metrics of interest for each server are:

- **Residence time:** the average time jobs spend at the server, in service and waiting

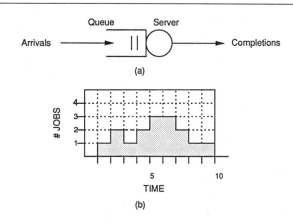

(a)

(b)

FIGURE 5.2
Queue-Server Representation of a Single Computer System Resource (a). A hypothetical profile of its execution is in (b). Each step up represents an arrival, and each step down represents a completion. Simultaneous arrivals and completions are not allowed.

□ **Utilization:** the percentage of the time the server is busy providing service

□ **Throughput:** the average rate at which jobs complete service

□ **Queue length:** the average number of jobs at the server (receiving service and waiting)

These metrics are determined by the number of jobs, the amount of service they need, the rate at which the system resource can process jobs, and the policy used to select the next job from the queue.

Figure 5.2(a) models the execution behavior of *a single computer system resource* (assume it is the CPU). Jobs or requests for service arrive, wait in the queue if necessary, receive service, then leave upon completion. Figure 5.2(b) shows a hypothetical execution profile over time.

Figure 5.2 and Example 5.1 illustrate how to model a resource with a queue server and how to calculate performance metrics for an execution profile. The execution profile comes from observing the resource, counting (measuring) the arrivals, completions, the length of the observation period, and the busy time during the period. The performance metrics (averages) result from a straightforward analysis of the measurement data.

EXAMPLE 5.1: Calculation of Performance Metrics for Execution Profile

The following metrics are easily derived from the execution profile in Figure 5.2(b):

Metric	Value
Length of observation, T	10
# Arrivals, N	4
# Completions, C	4
Busy time, B	9
Utilization, $U = \dfrac{B}{T}$	$\dfrac{9}{10} = .90$
Throughput, $X = \dfrac{C}{T}$	$\dfrac{4}{10} = 0.4$ jobs/time unit
Mean service time, $S = \dfrac{B}{C}$	$\dfrac{9}{4} = 2.25$ time units
Area under graph $A = \sum_{time}$ (# jobs)	$0 + 1 + 2 + 1 + 2 + 3 + 3 + 2 + 1 + 1 = 10$ job-time units
Queue length, $N = \dfrac{A}{T}$	16 job-time units/10 time units = 1.6 jobs
Residence time $RT = \dfrac{A}{C}$	16 job-time units/4 jobs = 4 time units
Time in queue (excluding service) $RT - S$	$4 - 2.25 = 1.75$ time units

(continued)

In the observation period—10 time units—4 requests arrive and 4 complete. The server is busy 9 of the time units, so the utilization is 90%. Four requests complete in 10 time units; thus the throughput is 0.4 jobs per time unit. The server is busy 9 time units for 4 requests, so each job requires an average service time of 2.25 time units. The area under the graph leads to the average queue length and residence time. The area is the sum of the number of jobs present at each time unit, 16 *job-time units*. The average queue length (including the job in service) is the job-time-unit area divided by the time units observed, 1.6 jobs. The average residence time (including the service time) is the job-time-unit area divided by the number of jobs observed, 4 time units. Jobs spent an average 1.75 time units waiting in the queue for service.

□

These computations shown in Example 5.1 are "fundamental operational laws": their formal basis is described in [DEN78]. To emphasize how to calculate performance metrics, we rely on Denning and Buzen's operational analysis results (rather than derive each formula).

For performance predictions, rather than use measurements we use similar computations based on predicted *arrival rates* and *service requirements*. We make the assumption that the system is fast enough to handle the arrivals, and thus the *arrival rate equals the completion rate or throughput*. This property is called **job-flow balance.** Example 5.2 illustrates how a specified arrival rate and average service time lead to the calculated average throughput, utilization, residence time, and queue length. Again, the derivation of these formulas is in [DEN78]. This model addresses the first source of resource contention mentioned in this section, **multiple users of a single scenario;** it will be extended to accommodate the other sources.

EXAMPLE 5.2: Calculate Performance Metrics from Queueing Model

Specify:

Arrival rate, λ	.4 requests per second
Mean service time, S	2 seconds

Calculate:

Throughput, $X = \lambda$	.4 requests per second
Utilization, $U = XS$	$(.4)(2) = .8$
Residence time, $RT = \dfrac{S}{1 - U}$	$\dfrac{2}{1 - .8} = 10$ seconds
Queue length, $N = X \cdot RT$	$(.4)(10) = 4$ requests

□

The formula for queue length is fundamental to the system execution model analysis. It is known as **Little's Law** after its author, J. D. C. Little ([LIT61]). It shows the relationship of queue length, throughput, and residence time. Example 5.2 uses it to calculate queue length, but it is used anytime you know two of the metrics and need the third. We use it for the system execution model, but it also applies to many other types of queueing systems. Apply it next time you wait in line at a ticket office, doctor's office, or for other service. Use the throughput (or arrival rate) and the number of customers ahead of you and compute your expected residence time. If one customer leaves every 2 minutes, and there are 10 ahead of you, how long should you expect to wait? If you apply Little's Law, you will discover an important point in system model analysis. The specifications and the results calculated from the simple, analytic formulas are *average values;* the metrics for a specific job may differ from the average. The difference depends on the *distribution* of arrivals and service requirements.

Next, consider how a job's **service requirement affects the other perfor-mance metrics,** as shown in Figure 5.3. Part (a) shows how the service require-ment affects residence time. The figure holds the arrival rate constant at 0.5 jobs per second. For job-flow balance to hold, the service time must be less than 2 seconds, because one job must complete every 2 seconds to handle the arrival rate (1 job/2 seconds = 0.5 jobs/second). Parts (b) and (c) of Figure 5.3 show how service time affects utilization and queue length. Note the dramatic effect on residence time and queue length as the service time approaches 2. The general principles in Chapter 2 (fixing point, locality design, and processing versus fre-quency tradeoff) reduce service times to improve performance. The graphs in Figure 5.3 show why this is important.

It is easy to calculate the effect of competing work on a job's response time. If we increase the number of jobs (or users), we increase the request arrival rate. Continue the example started in Example 5.2. Suppose one user generates 0.1 service requests per second; then 2 users generate 0.2 requests per second, and 4 users generate 0.4 requests per second. If the service time remains 2 seconds, calculate the performance metrics for 1, 2, and 4 users. To reinforce the concepts, first use the formulas in Example 5.2, and then compare your results to Table 5.1.

Thus far we have computed the effect of increased competition for a single resource. We must extend the model, to a **network of queues,** to adequately characterize computer system resources. Most software requires service from several resources. If we model a system with two queue servers (CPU and I/O

TABLE 5.1
EFFECT OF INCREASED COMPETITION

Performance metrics	# users		
	1	2	4
Arrival rate, λ	.1	.2	.4
Service time, S	2	2	2
Throughput, X	.1	.2	.4
Utilization, U	.2	.4	.8
Residence time, RT	2.5	3.33	10
Queue length, N	.25	.666	4

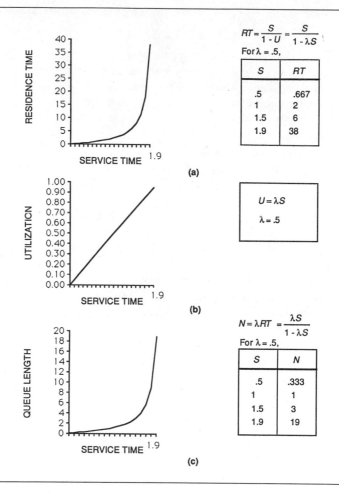

FIGURE 5.3
Effect of Service Time on Performance Metrics. The residence time is in (a), ulitization is in (b), and queue length is in (c).

subsystem) and two users competing for the servers, some of their processing may be concurrent (while one user receives service from the CPU, the other may either receive service from the I/O subsystem or wait for the CPU).

We can describe a multiprogrammed computer system as a set of devices (CPUs, disks, terminals, etcetera). Access to each device is controlled by a queue of requests for its service. The operating system orders or *schedules* the requests for service. This suggests that the devices should be represented by queue servers. Each job requests service from a device and receives service when its turn comes. After it obtains the required quantity of service from the device, it requests service from some other device and is entered on the queue for that device. This suggests that the queue servers should be connected to represent the possible flow patterns between devices.

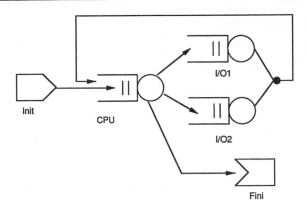

FIGURE 5.4
A Queueing Network Model of a Computer System.

Figure 5.4 shows a simple **queueing network model (QNM)** of a computer system. In it, jobs arrive from the source (Init) and proceed to the CPU. Upon leaving the CPU, they request service from either of the two I/O subsystems, or, if all processing is complete, they leave the system (Fini). Upon I/O completion, jobs always return to the CPU. Note that jobs do not actually "move" in the system; their *locus of execution* moves.

Figure 5.4 shows the QNM **topology.** Next, we specify the **model parameters** based on the execution environment (device service rates) and the workload (arrival rates and service requirements from each device). The resulting model parameters are the *arrival rate*, the *average service time* at each of the devices, and the *number of visits* to each device.

The solution procedure for this model is similar to that in Example 5.2. The solution formulas are shown in Algorithm 5.1 and are applied to sample parameters in Example 5.3.

ALGORITHM 5.1: Open QNM Computation

Specify the following model parameters:

λ System arrival rate
V_i No. of visits to device i
S_i Mean service time at device i

Calculate the performance metrics as follows:

1. The **system throughput** equals the system arrival rate because we assume job-flow balance:

   X_0, System throughput: $X_0 = \lambda$

   (*continued*)

ALGORITHM 5.1 (*Continued*)

2. **Device throughput** is the system throughput times the number of visits to the device:

   X_i, Throughput of device i: $X_i = X_0 V_i$

3. **Device utilization** is device throughput multiplied by its mean service time:

   U_i, Utilization of device i: $U_i = X_i S_i$

4. The **device residence time** is:

   RT_i, Residence time at device i: $\dfrac{RT_i}{1 - U_i}$

5. The device residence time and throughput give the **device mean queue length:**

   N_i, Queue length at device i: $N_i = X_i RT_i$

6. The **average number of jobs** in the entire QNM is the sum of the mean device queue lengths:

   N, System queue length: $N = \displaystyle\sum_{i=1}^{k} N_i$

7. The **system response time** uses Little's Law:

   RT, System response time: $RT = \dfrac{N}{X_0}$

   □

EXAMPLE 5.3: Open QNM Solution

Sample parameters:

System arrival rate, λ	5 jobs/second
# visits, V	
I/O1	3
I/O2	1
Mean service time, S	
CPU	0.01
I/O1	0.03
I/O2	0.02

First, compute the number of visits to each device i, V_i. The sample parameters specify that I/O1 has three visits and I/O2 has one visit. This implies that the CPU has five visits, because we visit the CPU after each I/O and once when processing begins ($1 + 3 + 1 = 5$). The visits to each device are on Line 1 in Table 5.2. Next, use the formulas in Algorithm 5.1 steps 1 and 2 to compute the throughput through each device. The device throughput on

(*continued*)

TABLE 5.2
CALCULATED PERFORMANCE METRICS

Metrics	CPU	I/O1	I/O2
1. V_i # visits	5	3	1
2. X_i throughput	25	15	5
3. S_i mean service time	.01	.03	.02
4. U_i utilization	.25	.45	.10
5. RT_i residence time	.013	.055	.022
6. N_i queue length	.325	.825	.111

System Response Time: $RT = \dfrac{N}{X}$ $N = \sum_i N_i = 1.26$

$$RT = \frac{1.26}{5} = .252$$

EXAMPLE 5.3 (*Continued*)

Line 2 in the table is the system throughput (5) multiplied by the values on Line 1. Line 3, mean service time, has the previous parameter values. Next, compute the utilization of each device; on Line 4, the utilization of the CPU is 25%, I/O1 is 45%, and I/O2 is 10%. Step 4 computes the residence time at each device; the results are on Line 5. The residence time and the throughput for each device give its mean queue length in Line 6. The average number of jobs in the system is the sum of the mean device queue lengths on Line 6. In this example, the average number in the system is 1.26, and the system throughput equals the arrival rate, 5 jobs/second, so the system response time is 0.252 seconds.   □

To reinforce your understanding of the concepts, calculate the effect on the system of doubling the number of users. Assume that the characteristics of each job remain the same (same number of visits to each device and same mean service times). Doubling the number of users increases the system arrival rate from 5 to 10 jobs/second. Perform the computations in Algorithm 5.1; then compare your results to Table 5.3.

Example 5.3 shows how to extend the calculations in Example 5.2 to networks of queues. There are two key factors implicit in this analysis. First, note that the *time units must be consistent*. The job arrival rate was specified in seconds, so the mean service time must also be in seconds. You can use any time unit (minutes, milliseconds, etcetera), as long as you are consistent. Second, there is a restricted class of *queueing disciplines and service distributions* for which this simple analysis applies (a notable exception is priority scheduling). The restrictions and the analysis strategies are discussed later. In general, SPE practitioners rely on automated tools to solve QNMs. These examples give insight into the effects of queueing and the algorithms that solve the models.

TABLE 5.3
PERFORMANCE METRICS WHEN NUMBER
OF USERS DOUBLES

Metrics	CPU	I/O1	I/O2
1. V_i # visits	5	3	1
2. X_i throughput	50	30	10
3. S_i mean service time	.01	.03	.02
4. U_i utilization	.50	.90	.20
5. RT_i residence time	.02	.3	.025
6. N_i queue length	1	9	.25

System Response Time: $N = 10.25$ $RT = \dfrac{10.25}{10} = 1.025$

The model described is appropriate for online systems in which the workload can be characterized by its arrival rate and the arrival rate does not depend on the response time. In queueing network terminology it is an **"open model."** A slightly different representation models batch or interactive systems in which a user continually interacts with the system, submitting a new request each time a reply is received. In QNM terminology, this is a **"closed model."** Figure 5.5 shows such a system. The source and sink are replaced with a delay node. The terminal user enters a request (at the delay node TERM) and transmits it to the system. The job cycles through the devices as before. Upon completion, the response goes to TERM, the user spends time examining the response, enters the next request, and the process repeats. Rather than specify an arrival rate, this model needs the

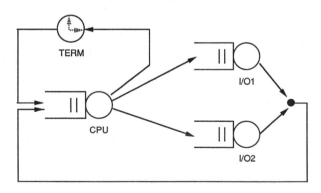

FIGURE 5.5
A "Closed" Queueing Network Model. The TERM node represents user activity. Users continually enter requests, examine results, and submit the next request after the specified delay time.

number of users (or terminals) and the "*think time*": the average delay between the receipt of a response and submission of the next.

The system throughput in this model depends on the system response time, so the solution method is more complex than Algorithm 5.1 (it uses throughput to calculate response time). Typically, tools calculate metrics for closed models with a "mean value analysis algorithm" (MVA) derived from Little's Law. The solution procedure is not presented here as it is beyond the scope of this discussion. Model solutions are discussed later in this chapter.

To handle the second source of contention mentioned in this section—multiple, distinct jobs or applications—define multiple **types of jobs.** Each type of job has its own arrival rate (or number of users) and its own pattern of service requests (number of visits per device and mean service time). The formulas in Algorithm 5.1 adapt to calculate performance metrics for each type of job. If the competing jobs are under development, software execution models provide their model parameters. If they represent existing work on the computer system, measurement data provides model parameters.

QNMs abstract many details of computer system execution that affect the precision of the model solution. Experience shows that model device utilizations are within 10 percent and response times within 30 percent of measurements of the actual system ([LAZ84a]). Note that response times are typically in seconds, so this precision is usually sufficient for SPE studies, particularly since model parameters arc only approximate in early lifecycle studies. Performance problems in early studies tend to have order-of-magnitude effects on performance metrics. QNMs can easily identify these problems and point to remedies.

The other two sources of contention, forking multiple concurrent processes and multithreaded software systems, require a tighter coupling of software and system execution models. The analysis of these facets of contention is described in Chapter 8.

So far, we have discussed what queueing network models can do. It is also important to review what they cannot do, or more specifically, **what QNMs cannot do quickly and easily.** There are limits in the ability of QNMs to represent execution behavior that can be solved with efficient, exact analytic methods. For example, a job was earlier described as moving its locus of execution from one device to another. In computer systems, though, jobs may have simultaneous resource possession. For example, a job may be executing on the CPU, issue a request to prefetch data from disk, then continue its CPU execution while the disk request executes in parallel. Additionally, special measures are needed for *passive resources:* resources required for processing that do not actively provide service. Memory is the classic example. Programs require memory to execute on the CPU, but memory does not process jobs.[1] Other passive resources include locks for exclusive access to data or files, messages passed between processes, and so forth.

---

[1]It is true that memory accesses have a cycle time, but it is already factored into CPU instruction execution speed.

Other computer system characteristics that present problems for QNMs are:

- Routing to queue servers that depends on data characteristics or the state of the computer system

- Job execution (resource request) patterns that vary significantly over the life of the job (called *job phases*)

- Jobs that fork into multiple processes, then later join and continue processing

- Certain combinations of queue-scheduling disciplines and service time distributions

It is not difficult to *represent* these additional facets of execution behavior, but the model solution becomes increasingly complex. The effect on performance metrics can often be approximated using some iterative or approximate solution methods. More precise results require simulation. Some automated analysis tools offer hybrid solution methods: Analytic methods are used for model subsets and combined with simulation of the troublesome characteristics. This makes model solution faster than pure simulation models.

SPE acknowledges these properties of QNMs and adapts models to the software lifecycle phase in which they are applied. Section 5.3.2 suggests some system execution model pragmatics.

5.2 Elementary Information Processing Graphs

You should now intuitively understand how QNMs account for contention delays when they produce response time metrics. The following discussion assumes that you have a tool to solve system execution models (Section 5.5 has some options) and focuses on how to *use* them for SPE. Following Figure 1.4's prescribed engineering design process, we now separate system execution model *representation* from *assessment*. Many automated assessment tools are available; while they all rely on the QNM framework, they differ in features provided and terminology used. So a common representation for system execution models is used here, an **information processing graph (IPG),** which can be solved with the automated analysis tool of your choice. An IPG combines information in software execution models with the resource characterization and connectivity information carried by the system execution model topology. The software model associates resource usage with software-defined logical entities. An IPG represents the mapping of that resource usage onto a graph that explicitly represents computer system resources. Software models represent distinct execution scenarios. Combinations of scenarios that execute concurrently are explicitly represented in IPGs.

IPGs were first introduced by Scientific and Engineering Software (*SES*) as an intermediate representation for QNM to aid in translating a computer network description into SES's solution package [NEU83, *SES*]. (Their product and other solution options are described in Section 5.5.) Because model representation is an important step in the process, a generic representation helps one to *view the concepts independent of the solution technique*. Rather than invent a new representation, we use IPGs. This does cause some problems, particularly with terminology. For example, Section 5.1 is based on operational analysis, which describes a *transaction* as a unit of work characterized in part by its arrival rate, and distinguishes it from a time sharing or closed unit of work that is characterized in part by the number of users and their think time. IPGs, however, use the term **transaction** as a generic unit of work that includes both the preceding definitions. Other conflicts between the operational analysis framework and IPG's inherent stochastic modeling framework also crop up.[2] This discussion retains the IPG terminology, so if you consult IPG references, they will generally be consistent with this definition.[3] Other terminology differences are identified as they are encountered.

IPGs are made up of *model topology* and *model parameters*. The topology includes a schematic that shows *nodes* and *edges* (or arcs) that specify node interconnection. We combine *environment* and *software execution* characteristics to obtain the model parameters. This section presents a subset of IPG features that can be solved analytically. This IPG subset can be called the **elementary IPG** or the **elementary system execution model**. Later, in Chapters 8 and 9, we analyze software systems with passive resource use and other IPG extensions.

Figure 5.6 shows (a subset of) the **types of IPG nodes** and the symbols for representing them. Each node represents a *resource* or a *routing choice*. Each edge or arc represents information flow between nodes in the direction of the arc (there is only one type of arc). Resource nodes include service nodes, delay nodes, and submodel nodes. **Service nodes** represent active resources in the computer system. The CPU node in Figure 5.7(a) is a service node. **Delay nodes** represent resources for which there is no queue. They have a specified service time, but there is no wait to use the resource. For example, user terminals are represented with delay nodes: The service time is the user's average think time; there is no queueing delay. The ATM node in Figure 5.7(a) is a delay node. **Submodel nodes** are analogous to expanded nodes in execution graphs. For each submodel node there is an expanded IPG with the same syntax. Submodels may contain more submodels. The only limit to the expansion is the capability of the chosen analysis tool. The I/O subsystem node in Figure 5.7(a) is a submodel node; its expansion is in (b).

Routing nodes show information flow. A **branch node** shows that multiple paths into the node, out of the node—or both—are possible. Nodes B1 and B2 in Figure 5.7(b) are branch nodes. Also note that the CPU node has multiple paths

---

[2] QNM technology purists may find this mixture disconcerting, but practitioners should find this approach useful (and not too confusing). The mixture is unavoidable because one representation must suffice for the two different solution approaches.

[3] IPGs are relatively new and still evolving. It is conceivable that some of the terms may change over time. Also note that here IPGs specifically represent computer systems, but they also represent more general systems (SES uses grocery stores and auto rental agencies to illustrate concepts).

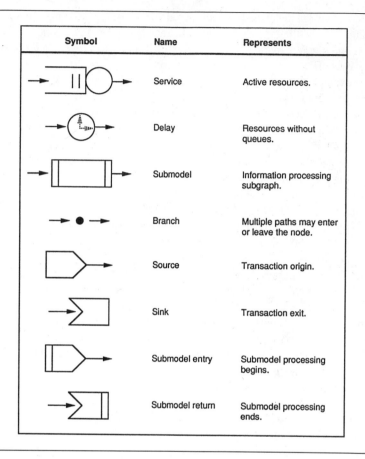

Symbol	Name	Represents
	Service	Active resources.
	Delay	Resources without queues.
	Submodel	Information processing subgraph.
	Branch	Multiple paths may enter or leave the node.
	Source	Transaction origin.
	Sink	Transaction exit.
	Submodel entry	Submodel processing begins.
	Submodel return	Submodel processing ends.

FIGURE 5.6
Elementary Information Processing Graph Summary.

leaving it. Branch nodes are for convenience; it is not necessary to explicitly model multiple paths with them. **Source nodes** show where transactions enter the system, and **sink nodes** show where they leave. In Figure 5.7(a), "Init" shows the origin of ATM transaction requests, and "Fini" shows where they leave. A **submodel entry node** shows where processing begins in a submodel, and a **submodel exit node** shows where it completes. A *unique* submodel entry and exit node are required in each submodel. Source and sink nodes are only required for transactions characterized by arrival rates ("open workloads" or "transaction" workloads in operational analysis terms). All IPG nodes have *unique names*.

Arcs connect the nodes in the IPG to show possible paths through the system. In Figure 5.7(a), a transaction originates at "Init" and visits the ATM, goes to the CPU, then either makes a request of the user at the ATM or goes to the I/O subsystem. It then returns to the CPU, repeats this cycle until processing is com-

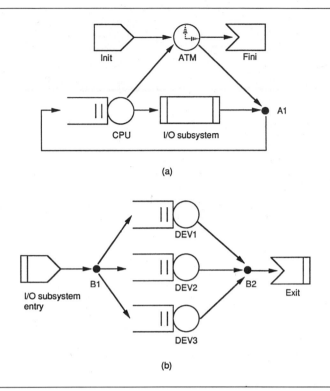

(a)

(b)

FIGURE 5.7
Sample Model Topology. The ATM IPG is in (a); it contains an I/O subsystem "submodel node" that is expanded in (b). Note that there are 50 ATM devices represented by the ATM delay server.

plete, and terminates at "Fini." In the submodel, I/O requests either go to DEV1, DEV2, or DEV3, then exit the submodel. The topology shows possible paths through the nodes, and the model parameters define the frequency of each.

Workloads are defined by **transactions.** Transaction **categories** distinguish workload elements with different execution characteristics. (Transaction categories are called "job types" or "job classes" by other tools and solution methods.) For example, one transaction category may define the execution behavior of ATM transactions, and another may define batch programs that execute concurrently on the computer system. Categories could also distinguish ATM withdrawals from payment transactions. Each category has a unique name.

This completes the model topology definition for the elementary IPG. Next, we combine computer system environment and software execution characteristics to get the elementary IPG model parameters. The **model parameters** we need are the transaction categories, their workload intensity, the IPG service nodes' queue-scheduling discipline, the mean number of service requests, and mean service

TABLE 5.4
ELEMENTARY IPG QUEUE SCHEDULING AND SERVICE TIME COMBINATIONS

QD	Service time conditions
First-come-first-served (FCFS)	Same mean service time for all transaction categories
Processor sharing (PS)	Different mean service times OK
Last-come-first-served preemptive resume (LCFSPR)	Different mean service times OK

TABLE 5.5
IPG MODEL SOLUTION

Arrival rate = 1 session/second

Node	Throughput	Utilization	Residence time	Queue length
ATM	14	.28	1	14
CPU	22	.007	.00033	.007
DEV1	9	.45	.0909	.818
DEV2	0	0	0	0
DEV3	0	0	0	0

System population = 14.83

Average session response time = 14.83/1 = 14.83 seconds

Arrival rate = 1.5 sessions/second

Node	Throughput	Utilization	Residence time	Queue length
ATM	21	.42	1	21
CPU	33	.011	.00033	.011
DEV1	13.5	.675	.154	2.08

System population = 23.1

Average session response time = 15.4 seconds

Arrival rate = 2 sessions/second

Node	Throughput	Utilization	Residence time	Queue length
ATM	28	.56	1	28
CPU	44	.014	.00033	.014
DEV1	18	.90	.5	9

System population = 37

Average session response time = 18.5

time. The computer system environment gives the queue-scheduling disciplines (QD) and the device execution characteristics. For the elementary system execution model, we restrict the QDs and service time combinations to the set that permits (exact) analytic solutions. They are: processor sharing (PS), first-come-first-served (FCFS), and last-come-first-served preemptive resume (LCFSPR). The allowable combinations of QDs and service times are in Table 5.4. Some tools provide good approximation techniques for other QDs, such as priority scheduling, and other model features. You can adapt your models to include model features that you can solve quickly and easily (but you may sacrifice portability to other analysis tools).

The software execution characteristics identify the transaction categories, their execution flow, and their service requests. Each *transaction category* has a *workload intensity:* either an arrival rate (from a source node) or a number of concurrent transactions of that category. Each makes a specified average number of *visits* to each of the IPG nodes, and requests a specified *amount of service* from each. Example 5.4 illustrates the model parameters needed for Figure 5.7

EXAMPLE 5.4: IPG Model Parameters

The QDs for each service node in Figure 5.7 are:

Service node	Queue-scheduling discipline (QD)
CPU	PS
DEV1	FCFS
DEV2	FCFS
DEV3	FCFS

Neither delay nodes nor submodel nodes have QDs.

There is one category: GENERAL with an arrival rate of 1 session/second. The execution profile of each GENERAL transaction is:

Node	# visits	Mean service time (sec)
Init	1	
ATM	14	1
CPU	22	0.000323
A1	22	
Fini	1	
I/O subsystem:	9	
DEV1	9	0.05
DEV2	0	0.05
DEV3	0	0.05
B1	9	
B2	9	

Note that you specify mean service times only for service and delay nodes. Source and sink nodes always have 1 visit. The results for this example are in Table 5.5.

□

In summary, an IPG representation of the elementary system execution model consists of:

1. The model topology:

   a. Resource nodes (service, delay, submodel)

   b. Routing nodes (branch, source, sink, submodel entry and exit)

   c. Edges (show connectivity)

2. Model parameters:

   a. Workload (categories and intensity)

   b. Device parameters (QDs and processing speeds)

   c. Service requests (visits and resource requirements)

After you construct the model, use an automated tool to solve for response time, device throughput, utilization, residence time, and queue length. Having defined the elementary IPGs, we next use them for SPE.

5.3 Using the Elementary System Execution Model for SPE

The first task in using the elementary system execution model for SPE is to create and derive parameters for an elementary IPG. The next tasks examine the IPG solution, assess problems, and evaluate alternatives. The discussion in Section 5.3.1 describes these tasks. Section 5.3.2 gives pragmatic strategies for identifying key computer system execution and environment parameters, representing workloads, and adapting models to the software development status.

5.3.1 Elementary IPG Modeling Procedure

The following steps construct and evaluate the elementary IPG:

1. Create model topology.
2. Use environment specifications to specify device parameters.
3. Derive workload parameters from software execution models.
4. Compute service requests from software execution models.
5. Develop parameters for existing work.
6. Solve the model.

7. Check for reasonable model results.

8. Evaluate model results and identify bottlenecks.

9. Correlate system execution model results with software components.

10. Evaluate component elapsed time.

11. Identify and evaluate alternatives.

12. Verify data and validate model results.

Each step is described in the following paragraphs.

Step 1: Create Model Topology   Represent the key active devices (or computer resources, *r*) whose resource requirements are specified in the software execution models. (Note that you must identify devices that are key to performance to specify the software execution model.) Identifying the devices that are key to performance is the art of performance modeling. Some strategies are given in Section 5.3.2. Your intuition will improve with experience, so practice with case studies to develop intuition. Once you identify the devices, represent their connectivity. (This combines knowledge of the computer system environment and the software execution patterns—obtain this information from a performance specialist during your walkthrough if you need help.)

Next, decide whether the workload is better modeled as an open or closed workload. If it is open, you need a source and a sink node; otherwise use a (terminal) delay server. **Closed workloads** model continual work performed by terminal users for long periods of time. As soon as users receive and examine a response, the users begin to enter the next request. For example, use closed workloads to model data-entry clerks with large quantities of data to be entered. **Open workloads** are characterized by the average number of requests made during the modeled time interval. The number does not depend on the response time of other requests. Some automated analysis tools solve models with open workloads faster than with closed workloads. So you may want to create an initial (approximate) model with them to quickly study many alternatives, then later use closed work when more precise metrics are justified.[4]

Figure 5.7 models the ATM scenario with an open workload, and specifies the average customer arrival rate expected in the time interval modeled. The model includes the ATM device because the scenario models the entire customer session with its multiple interactions with the ATM device. During a particular session, the rate that the customer enters information at the ATM depends on the time required for the software to respond. So by showing all visits to the ATM during a session, we can easily derive average response times for the individual ATM *interactions*, for ATM *transactions*, and for the customer *session*.

[4]The discussion pertains to online software. Engineered software may also be critical-deadline batch. Although batch work is not specifically addressed, all the techniques are applicable. Refer to [LAZ84a] for specific techniques for representing batch work in QNMs.

This completes the topology definition. The result is an elementary IPG topology such as that in Figure 5.8. For variety, the devices from the submodel in Figure 5.7(b) are arbitrarily included in the higher-level model in Figure 5.8. The question of when submodels are appropriate will be discussed in the "pragmatic" section—because submodels do not affect the model solution; they make model-

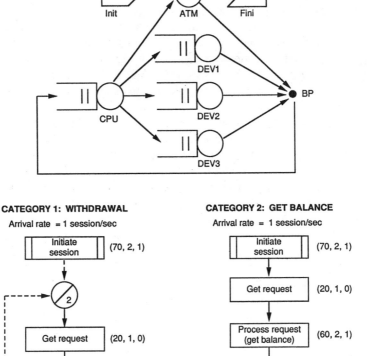

FIGURE 5.8
The ATM IPG and the Dual-Category Software Execution Models That Provide the IPG Model Parameters.

ing more convenient and may speed up solutions when models are solved repeatedly. Next, we combine the environment specifications and software execution models to get the elementary IPG model parameters.

Step 2: Use Environment Specifications to Specify Device Parameters
The environment specifications provide the queue-scheduling disciplines and the device processing speeds. The QD is built into some automated analysis tools and need not be specified. For other tools, select from the set that yields analytic solutions. For the initial IPG, use processor sharing for the CPU, and FCFS for the I/O devices. This leads to fast solutions with reasonable precision. You can add priority scheduling, other scheduling disciplines, or differing service times (for FCFS) to later models if the additional computational effort is justified. For this ATM example, we use the QD specifications from Example 5.4.

We next need the device processing speeds. For the CPU, you need the approximate **instruction execution rate.** The exact rate is controversial—it depends on the instructions executed, the compiler, competing work, and other factors. Examine the model's sensitivity by varying the rate and comparing the results, or with a performance benchmark to confirm that your approximation is sufficient. Relative rates for processors periodically appear in computer trade publications. An interesting method to account for execution speed variability is in [EIN87].

From the ATM environment specifications (Example 3.5), the CPU instruction execution rate is (approximately) 2 million machine instructions per second (MIPS), and there is an average of 20 machine instructions per high-level language instruction. Thus the high-level language (HL) execution rate is 2 million/20 = 100,000 HL instructions per second, and the mean HL instruction execution time is 1/100,000 = 0.00001 sec. This is the w_i that we used in Chapter 4 to estimate the total processing units, T, for the software execution model.

For I/O devices, we need the **average time to complete an I/O.** First note that all of the I/O in this initial IPG is consolidated into one queue server. Expand the I/O later into channels, controllers, and I/O devices (disks, solid state devices, etcetera) if you need more precise results. A "ballpark average" I/O completion time may be reported by your system performance measurements reports. The ballpark average for the ATM example is 50 ms per request (Example 3.5). Without this knowledge, estimate I/O completion time from the:

- *Seek*—average time for a disk head to move in or out to the desired position
- *Rotational delay*—time for the disk to spin to the sector desired
- *Transfer time*—time to move the data between the disk and the memory buffer

Assume the average seek time is 30 ms, rotational delay is 8 ms, and transfer rate is 4 megabytes per second. If the average amount of data transferred is 8,000 bytes (this comes from the software specialist), the average time for the data transfer is 8,000/4,000,000 = .002 sec, and the mean service time for an I/O is 30 + 8 + 2 = 40 ms.

Adapt the calculation to account for device characteristics. For example, fixed-head disks have no seek time. Estimating I/O completion time is nontrivial; multiple channel paths, channel reconnect, cached controllers, and other factors complicate the analysis. A detailed description of all estimation techniques is beyond the scope of this discussion. Some analysis tools represent the I/O sub-system components—they automatically generate the I/O subsystem model and parameters from a configuration description.

Early in SPE, we model a minimal number of devices and use approximate average service times. This is usually adequate in early development stages because processing details and file organizations have not yet been determined. Chapter 8 has some strategies applicable later when more precision is needed. The CPU, terminals, and I/O devices sufficiently represent most execution environments for early SPE studies. When you must represent other devices, compute their mean service time in a manner similar to that for I/O devices.

Step 3: Derive Workload Parameters from Software Execution Models

The software execution models identify the transaction categories, their execution flow, and their service requests. Generally, each software scenario becomes a transaction category. This makes it easy to relate the performance metrics produced by the system execution model to the software scenario. For example, the mean response time for a Withdrawal scenario is easy to get if it is a distinct category in the IPG; if it is combined with other types of ATM requests, it is more difficult to separate the time for Withdrawals. The disadvantage of a separate category for each scenario is that model solution time is proportional to the number of categories (and their population and the size of the model). So, when scenarios have similar execution characteristics, they can be combined in early SPE models.

Example 5.4 modeled the general ATM scenario from Figure 4.28. In this section, we create a model with two categories: one for a Withdrawal scenario, and another for a Get balance scenario. Then you can see how to derive the parameters for multiple categories (and compare the solutions to see the difference). Figure 5.8 shows software execution models for the two categories.

The software workload specifications provide the arrival rate for open workload categories and the population of closed workload categories. The arrival rate for both category 1 (Withdrawal) and category 2 (Get balance) in this example is 1 job per second. It is not necessary for arrival rates or populations for all categories to be the same. Note that this model is not identical to that in Example 5.4. Compare the software execution model in Figure 4.28 to Figure 5.8. Can you see the difference? The earlier model has one session with three requests. With an arrival rate of 1 session per second, there are 2 Withdrawal and 1 Get balance requests arriving each second. Figure 5.4 models a similar situation. It has 1 Get balance and 1 Withdrawal session per second. Since the Withdrawal session scenario has two Withdrawal requests, there are 2 Withdrawal requests arriving each second. So the overall transaction rate is the same; the difference is that Figure 5.8 models more session overhead. This makes the model parameters different and changes the model solution.

Step 4: Compute Service Requests from Software Execution Models   The software execution models provide the tuple of resource requests for each computer resource in the elementary IPG. For category 1 in Figure 5.8, $R_i = (630, 11, 8)$. For the ATM and I/O devices, R_i is the number of service requests (the visits, V_i). Note that the system execution model needs the number of *physical I/Os*. This discussion assumes that the software model specifies physical I/Os. If the specification is for logical I/Os, you must first convert them to (approximate) physical I/Os. Similarly, the system execution model needs the number of I/Os to each device, so the software model needs corresponding R_i for each device. Some automated analysis packages tally the number of I/Os to each file and use environment specifications to translate file I/O to device I/O.

For the CPU, R_{CPU} is not the number of visits; it is the number of instructions executed, and the CPU executes multiple instructions per visit. A three-step algorithm converts the R_i into the visits and mean service times for the CPU and the other devices.

ALGORITHM 5.2: Calculate Visits, V_i, and Mean Service Times, S_i, from Computer Resource Requirements, R_i

1. Use the R_i for each i that directly corresponds to the number of visits.

2. Compute the number of visits for the remaining nodes. The following equation computes the visits to device j:

$$\sum_{i=0}^{k} p_{ij}V_i = V_j \qquad \text{(Eq. 5.1)}$$

   It multiplies the number of visits at device i that feed device j by the probability that a job goes from device i to device j. The sum of visits coming from each possible origin is the total visits for V_j.

3. Compute the mean service time for each node. The formula is:[5]

$$S_i = \frac{R_i w_i}{V_i} \qquad \text{for } V_i > 0$$
$$= w_i \qquad \text{for } V_i = 0 \qquad \text{(Eq. 5.2)}$$

(continued)

---

[5]Technically, S_i is unnecessary when $V_i = 0$; this assignment avoids undefined values for S_i.

ALGORITHM 5.2 (*Continued*)

where:

S_i is the mean service time for computer system device (or node) i
R_i is the total units of service needed from device i for the scenario
w_i is the average time for device i to process a service unit
V_i is the number of visits to device i

R_i comes from the software execution model, the V_i were calculated in Steps 1 and 2, and the w_i for the service nodes were calculated earlier from the environment specifications. For the ATM device, w_i comes from the workload and software specifications: the average time for a customer to respond to requests. Note that for devices such as the ATM and I/O devices, R_i and V_i are equal, so from Equation 5.2, $S_i = w_i$. For the CPU, S_i is the *average* time per visit to the CPU. It assumes that the I/O device and ATM requests are equally spread throughout the processing. This is a reasonable assumption for early SPE models. Techniques are described in Chapter 8 for more precisely modeling variable CPU processing bursts.

□

Let's apply Algorithm 5.2 to the ATM IPG in Figure 5.8 (see Example 5.5).

EXAMPLE 5.5: Compute Visits and Service Times for Withdrawal and Get Balance Categories

Start with   Category 1, Withdrawal $R_i = (630, 11, 8)$
and   Category 2, Get balance $R_i = (250, 6, 3)$

Algorithm 5.2, **Step 1** uses R_2 and R_3, combined with the knowledge that there is always one visit for source and sink nodes, to specify the number of visits for categories 1 and 2 for lines 1 through 6 in Table 5.6.

For **Step 2,** assign the following subscripts to the nodes in Figure 5.8: $i = 0$ is Begin, $i = 1$ is the ATM, $i = 2$ is End, $i = 3$ is DEV1, $i = 4$ is DEV2, $i = 5$ is DEV3, $i = 6$ is A1, and $i = 7$ is the CPU. Step 1 gives the V_i for nodes 0–5 (from their R_i). Next consider $j = 6$ (A1). Only the arcs from $j = 3$ (DEV1) and $j = 1$ (ATM) have non-zero probabilities. Step 2's formula gives:

$$p_{36}V_3 + p_{16}V_1 = V_6 \qquad\qquad \text{(Eq. 5.3)}$$

We already know V_1, V_3, and $p_{36} = 1$. We need p_{16}. The probabilities of outgoing arcs of a node must sum to 1. So $p_{16} = (1 - p_{12})$. Equation 5.1 gives:

$$p_{12}V_1 = V_2$$

so $p_{12} = \dfrac{1}{11}$ and $p_{16} = \left(1 - \dfrac{1}{11}\right) = \dfrac{10}{11}$ for category 1

$\quad\quad p_{12} = \dfrac{1}{6}$ and $p_{16} = \left(1 - \dfrac{1}{6}\right) = \dfrac{5}{6}$ for category 2

(continued)

TABLE 5.6
ATM IPG MODEL PARAMETERS

Nodes	# visits, V_i CAT1	CAT2	Avg. time to process a request, w_i	Mean service time, S_i CAT1	CAT2
1. Init	1	1			
2. ATM	11	6	1	1	1
3. Fini	1	1			
4. DEV1	8	3	0.05	0.05	0.05
5. DEV2	0	0	0.05	0.05	0.05
6. DEV3	0	0	0.05	0.05	0.05
7. A1	18	8			
8. CPU	18	8	0.00001	0.00035	0.000313

EXAMPLE 5.5 (*Continued*)

Substituting into Equation 5.3 gives:

$$(1)(8) + \left(\frac{10}{11} \right)(11) = 18 = V_6 \text{ for category 1}$$

similarly,

$$(1)(3) + \left(\frac{5}{6} \right)(6) = 8 = V_6 \text{ for category 2}$$

The number of visits to the CPU comes from the visits to A1, since it has the only arc leading to the CPU node. This gives lines 7 and 8 in Table 5.6.

Step 3 computes the mean service times in Table 5.6. For the ATM and for DEV1 through DEV3, $S_i = w_i$ in the table. From Equation 5.2, the mean CPU service time for category 1 is:

$$\frac{630 \times 0.00001}{18} = 0.00035 \text{ sec}$$

The CPU service time for category 2 uses the same formula. □

Check your understanding of Algorithm 5.2 by using the software model in Example 4.2 and the w_i in Table 5.6 to compute the model parameters for the single-category model in Figure 5.7. Compare your results to the parameters in Example 5.4.

This completes the IPG specifications for the engineered software. A checkpoint evaluation early in software development assesses the IPG model with only the new work. The new software must have acceptable performance on a system without other competing work—it will not improve with additional competition for resources. Later, we add workloads to the IPGs to represent the competition.

Step 5: Develop Parameters for Existing Work   To derive model parameters for existing work, you need the same parameters, but they come from measurement data. The **first step is to identify the workloads** to be modeled. Since model solution time increases with the number of categories, we want to combine the existing work into a minimum number of categories. Ideally, make one category for "other work." When batch work executes concurrently with online work, you probably need two "other" categories, "other online" and "other batch," because batch and online work have very different resource consumption patterns. If you have existing systems with critical response time requirements, they also need a distinct category so you can assess how the new software affects their performance.

Next, derive the number of visits and mean service times for the existing work for the IPG's devices. System measurement reports supply the data; the translation to model parameters depends on the computer system and its measurement tools. Because of the wide variety, the process is not described here. Levy describes the derivation of specific model parameters for the *BEST/1* modeling tool from IBM's RMF reports in [LEV80]. Lazowska and colleagues also describe parameter derivation from RMF reports, other general strategies, and automated parameter derivation in [LAZ84a]. You can adapt these procedures to your computer systems and measurement reports to derive IPG model parameters.

The **next step is the verification and validation of the model of existing work.** Solve the IPG model without the categories for the new software. Compare the model results to measurement results to confirm that it adequately represents the existing system. If necessary, calibrate the model to adequately represent the existing system. Be sure to compare results to measurements for multiple sets of parameter values. For example, confirm that the model represents peak loads, slack loads, and several different transaction mixes. *Do not assume* that if the model is correct for one set of parameter values, it is correct for all.

The **final step** in the derivation of parameters for existing work is to **project the existing workload parameters for the future environment** with the new software. The best case is that existing work will either decrease or remain the same. This is another possible checkpoint evaluation. If existing work is likely to increase, forecast the future arrival rate for open categories and number of users for closed categories. Then examine the effect on visits and service time. Will future work be essentially the same as present, only more of it? Or will more work be done? Experienced capacity planners will recognize that this is a complex step. On the other hand, capacity planners may already have some reasonable parameters for software modelers to use. If not, use some optimistic values for the early models; then examine the sensitivity of results to reasonable bounds on growth.

Step 6: Solve the Model   Having derived the IPG model parameters, the next step is to use the IPG to create the input specifications, in the syntax required for the chosen solution package, to produce the results. The following example shows sample specifications for two different solution packages.

EXAMPLE 5.6: Sample Specifications for Different Solvers

MAP Workload Specification [*QSP*]

```
CLASS          Get_balance
TYPE           TRANSACTION
ARRIVAL_RATE   1

CLASS          Withdrawal
TYPE           TRANSACTION
ARRIVAL_RATE   1
```

MAP calls categories "classes" and requires their TYPE declaration. For open categories (TYPE TRANSACTION) it infers that there is a source node.

PAWS Workload Specification [*SES*]

```
DECLARE
   NODES         Init, ATM, CPU, . . . .
   CATEGORIES    Get_balance, Withdrawal;

DEFINE
   INIT
   TYPE          SOURCE
   REQUEST       〈Withdrawal〉     EXPO (1);
   REQUEST       〈Get_balance〉    EXPO (1);
```

PAWS infers that the category is open from the presence of the source node. The keyword EXPO specifies that the arrival distribution is exponential; it allows other distributions but does not solve them analytically.

□

As you can see, the translation from IPG to solver is straightforward, but it differs among solvers. Some solvers make default assumptions and do not need all the IPG information. Section 5.5 presents system execution model options and describes the basic translation differences. Having solved the IPG, you can proceed with its assessment.

Step 7: Check for Reasonable Model Results The model solver produces the performance metrics in Table 5.7. Before you evaluate the results and look for improvements, verify that the model is formulated correctly. First, check that no **device utilizations** are over 100 percent. The results in Table 5.7 meet this criterion. Also check that the **response time for a single user** (with no contention) matches the total processing units T computed from the software execution models. To check this for open models, like the ATM example, change the session arrival rate to represent one ATM device. For example, if 50 devices produce 1 session per second, then one device produces 1/50 session per second. For experience, change this parameter and solve the revised model.

Another quick check for open models examines the **total system population.** In this example, there are only 50 ATM devices, so the total system population

TABLE 5.7
ATM IPG MODEL RESULTS

	ATM	CPU	DEV1
Throughput			
Withdrawal	11	18	8
Get balance	6	8	3
Utilization			
Withdrawal	.22	.0063	.4
Get balance	.12	.0025	.15
Total	.34	.0088	.55
Residence Time			
Withdrawal	1	.00035	.1111
Get balance	1	.00032	.1111
Queue Length			
Withdrawal	11	.0064	.8888
Get balance	6	.0025	.3333

System population:	
Withdrawal	11.9
Get balance	6.3
Total	18.2
Session response time:	
Withdrawal	11.9
Get balance	6.3
Average	9.1

must be ≤ 50 (it is). For closed models, the system population is specified, and the solution must match the specification. If the populations do not match, there is an error in the solver (unlikely if it is a commercial product) or in the model parameters (more likely). For open models, check the **arrival rate.** Each ATM's session must complete before the next one begins, so the session arrival rate for each ATM device must be less than the reciprocal of the session response time:

$$\frac{1}{\# \text{ ATMs}} \cdot \lambda < \frac{1}{RT}$$

In this example, the system population is not a problem, but if it were and the arrival rate were correct, the ATM think time (mean service time) could be incorrect.

Finally, examine the **relative device utilizations.** Do they appear reasonable? Is the bottleneck device one that you expected? Are devices with low utilizations lightly used by the software execution model (or much faster than devices with higher utilizations)? These checks do not guarantee that the model is *correct*, but it is easy to confirm that the model is *reasonable*. This is an important step since it is not yet possible to compare model results to actual software performance. With practice, you will develop additional checks for your environment.

Step 8: Evaluate Model Results and Identify Bottlenecks   The primary metrics of interest for SPE are: **system response time** (or throughput), for comparison to performance goals; and **device utilization,** to identify performance bottlenecks.

Table 5.7 shows the average response times for one session with two withdrawals (11.9 seconds), a get balance session (6.3 seconds), and the overall average (9.1 seconds). The performance for this checkpoint evaluation is reasonable. This is a best-case evaluation—the SPE assessment can proceed to evaluate worst case, competing workloads, sensitivity to arrival rates, and so forth. The table also shows the device utilization by scenario and the total for the device. For ATMs, the utilization 0.34 means that on the average, of the 50 ATM devices, 50 × 0.34 = 17 ATM devices are busy. It also means that on the average each ATM device is busy 34 percent of the time.

Next, use the following algorithm to identify the bottleneck resources.

ALGORITHM 5.3: Bottleneck Identification

The system saturates when a device becomes 100 percent busy. At that point, the system throughput, X_0, is at its maximum—work cannot be processed faster. The bottleneck device is the one to first reach 100 percent utilization. The device utilization and device throughput formulas from Algorithm 5.1 give:

$$U_i = X_i S_i \text{ and } X_i = V_i X_0,$$
$$U_i = V_i X_0 S_i \qquad\qquad \text{(Eq. 5.4)}$$

X_0 is constant for all the IPG devices, i, so the bottleneck device, b, is the device i with the max $\{V_i S_i\}$. Note that this is the total $V_i S_i$ for all categories, c, at each device.

Step 1: Identify bottleneck device, b:

$$\text{Bottleneck device,}[6] \ b = max_i\left\{\sum_c V_{ic}S_{ic}\right\} \qquad\qquad \text{(Eq. 5.5)}$$

The bottleneck device limits system throughput, and the maximum system throughput occurs when $U_b = 1$, so Equation 5.4 gives the following:

Step 2: Calculate maximum throughput:

$$max \ X_0 = \frac{1}{V_b S_b} \qquad\qquad \text{(Eq. 5.6)}$$

$\square$

---

[6]When there are multiple servers (the ATM device has $N_i = 50$ servers),

$$b = max_i\left\{\frac{\sum_c V_{ic}S_{ic}}{N_i}\right\}$$

$X_0 = 1$ for each category in Table 5.7, so Equation 5.4 says that $V_i S_i$ equals the utilization. The sum for the two categories in Equation 5.5 is the "Total utilization" for each device in the table. Thus the bottleneck device is DEV1. The maximum system throughput is $1/0.55 = 1.8$ sessions per second. Note the queueing delay for DEV1: The residence time minus the service time $= 0.111 - 0.05 = 0.065$. Requests to DEV1 spend more time in the queue than in service.

Step 9: Correlate System Execution Model Results with Software Components   Next, we associate the system execution model results with the software execution model and examine the effect of contention on each scenario. First, we examine the usage of the bottleneck resource by each component in the software execution model. In the ATM example the bottleneck is DEV1. Table 5.8 shows the bottleneck analysis. Each component's use of the bottleneck device, r_b, is divided by the scenario's use, R_b, to get the percentage shown in the second column in the table.

TABLE 5.8
BOTTLENECK RESOURCE USAGE
BY SOFTWARE COMPONENT

Node r_i	Bottleneck analysis: DEV1	
Withdrawal: $R_3 = 8$ Total = 11	*% of scenario requests* $\dfrac{r_3}{R_3}$	*% of all requests* $\dfrac{X_{0c}r_{3c}}{\text{Total}}$
Initiate session (70, 2, 1)	.125	.09
Get request $2 \cdot (20, 1, 0)$	0	0
Process request $2 \cdot (210, 3, 3)$	.75	.55
Terminate (100, 1, 1)	.125	.09
Get balance: $R_3 = 3$ Total = 11		
Initiate session (70, 2, 1)	.33	.09
Get request (20, 1, 0)	0	0
Process request (60, 2, 1)	.33	.09
Terminate (100, 1, 1)	.33	.09

The third column is the ratio of the component's use of the bottleneck device to the total use for all workloads:

$$\frac{r_{bc}X_{0c}}{\sum_{c} R_{bc}X_{0c}}$$

(Eq. 5.7)

where c is the scenario's category

The formula multiplies the total scenario (category) use of the bottleneck device, R_{bc}, by the throughput of the category and sums for all categories. We weight the component and scenario usage by the throughput (rate of requests) to show the relative usage when scenario arrivals vary. For example, if Withdrawals are requested twice as often as Get balances, their use of the bottleneck resource has a greater effect than when both arrival rates are equal. To see this, compute the percentage of total requests when $X_{01} = 2$, and $X_{02} = 1$. (Note that changing the

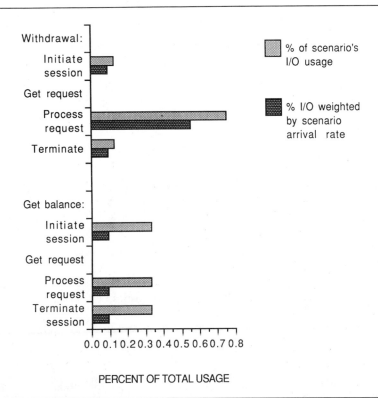

FIGURE 5.9
Bottleneck Resource Usage of Each Software Component in the Withdrawal and Get Balance Scenarios.

arrival rate of the scenarios changes the model residence times, utilizations, queue lengths, and response times, but it does not affect the number of service requests r_i or R_i.) Figure 5.9 shows the bottleneck resource usage graphically. For each scenario it shows the usage of the bottleneck resource by each software component.

Step 10: Evaluate Component Elapsed Time   Next, we examine the average elapsed time of each component. Remember the checkpoint evaluation of total processing units used in Algorithm 4.7 for the software models ($T = R_i w_i$)? It is an optimistic evaluation because the processing time w_i for device i excludes queueing delays. The system execution model produces the residence time RT that includes the average queueing delay. We use RT to compute w_i', the average processing time plus queueing time per visit. Then we use the w_i' to compute the average elapsed time for each component in the software execution model.

ALGORITHM 5.4: Average Elapsed Time for Software Components

1. **Calculate the average elapsed time for each computer resource request, r_i.**

    a. When each computer resource request, r_i, requires one visit to a device, $R_i = V_i$, the elapsed time for each visit (service unit), w_i', is the residence time, RT_i:

    $$w_i' = RT_i$$

    b. For other devices (such as the CPU), one visit processes multiple service unit requests (instructions), so $R_i \neq V_i$. Equation 5.2 computes the mean service time S for each visit to a device:[7]

    $$S_i = \frac{R_i w_i}{V_i} \text{ for } V_i > 0$$

    The same formula relates the elapsed time for each visit V_i to the elapsed time for each computer resource request R_i. By substituting RT_i for S_i and w_i' for w_i, we get:

    $$RT_i = \frac{R_i w_i'}{V_i} \quad \text{so}$$

    $$w_i' = \frac{RT_i V_i}{R_i} \tag{Eq. 5.8}$$

2. **Calculate the average elapsed time of each software component:**

    $$ET = \sum_{i=1}^{k} r_i w_i' \tag{Eq. 5.9}$$

□

For example, for the Get balance scenario, $RT_{CPU} = 0.00032$ comes from the model results for Get balance in Table 5.7; $R_i = 250$ comes from the software execution model in Figure 5.8, and $V_i = 8$ comes from the IPG model parameters

[7]When $V_i = 0$ there is no need to calculate w_i'.

in Table 5.6. So w_i', the average elapsed time for each CPU instruction for the Get balance scenario, is:

$$w_i' = \frac{(0.00032)(8)}{250} = 0.0000102$$

In this example, there is little difference in S_i and RT_i for the CPU because its utilization is low and queueing delays are minimal. The formulas of Algorithm 5.4 are applied as demonstrated in Example 5.7.

EXAMPLE 5.7: **Withdrawal and Get_Balance Elapsed Time Calculation**

First use Algorithm 5.4, Step 1 to compute w_i' for each device and category. The average time for each service unit request for the withdrawal scenario is:

$$w_{CPU}' = .00001$$
$$w_{ATM}' = 1$$
$$w_{DEV1}' = .1111$$

The w_i' for each scenario are shown with each scenario in Table 5.9. Next compute $r_i\,w_i'$ for each component and device. The CPU, ATM, and DEV1 columns in the table show the results. For Withdrawal's initiate session, $r_i = (70, 2, 1)$ so:

$$
\begin{aligned}
r_i w_i' &= 70 \times 0.00001 &&= 0.0007 &&\text{for the CPU} \\
&= 2 \times 1 &&= 2 &&\text{for the ATM} \\
&= 1 \times 0.1111 &&= 0.1111 &&\text{for the DEV1}
\end{aligned}
$$

The Elapsed Time column uses Equation 5.9 for Withdrawal's initiate session, $ET = (0.00007 + 2 + 0.1111) = 2.11$. The last column is the component's percentage of the total response time for the scenario: $ET/Response\ Time$. For Withdrawal's initiate session it is $2.11/11.9 = 0.18$. Note that the results for Get balance's initiate session are slightly different because the w_i' and total RT are different. Figure 5.10 shows these results graphically. For each scenario, it shows each component and its percentage of the elapsed time.

□

Step 11: Identify and Evaluate Alternatives   The next SPE model evaluation step is to look for opportunities for improvements. When there are performance problems, the cause may be excessive total resource usage, contention delays, or both. Improvements may be made by revising the software to make fewer service requests (r_i), changing the pattern of requests (by moving some of the r_3 requests from DEV1 to another device), or by using faster devices (reducing w_i). To evaluate their effect on performance, we adjust the software model or the system model accordingly, and repeat this process. The general principles from Chapter 2 suggest alternatives—some specific improvement alternatives are analyzed in the next chapter.

Step 12: Verify Data and Validate Model Results   First, verify the software model specifications and validate the software execution models as specified in

TABLE 5.9
ELAPSED TIME OF SOFTWARE COMPONENTS

Node r_i	Elapsed time computation				
	CPU $r_1w'_1$	ATM $r_2w'_2$	$DEV1$ $r_3w'_3$	$Elapsed\ Time$ $ET = \sum_i r_iw'_i$	ET / $Total\ RT$
Withdrawal: $w'_1 = .00001$ $w'_2 = 1$ $w'_3 = .1111$ Total $RT = 11.9$					
Initiate session (70, 2, 1)	.0007	2	.111	2.11	.18
Get request 2 · (20, 1, 0)	.0004	2	0	2.00	.17
Process request 2 · (210, 3, 3)	.0042	6	.666	6.67	.56
Terminate (100, 1, 1)	.001	1	.111	1.11	.09
Get balance: $w'_1 = .0000102$ $w'_2 = 1$ $w'_3 = .1111$ Total $RT = 6.3$					
Initiate session (70, 2, 1)	.000714	2	.111	2.11	.33
Get request (20, 1, 0)	.000204	1	0	1.00	.16
Process request (60, 2, 1)	.000612	2	.111	2.11	.33
Terminate (100, 1, 1)	.000102	1	.111	1.11	.18

Chapter 3. After confirming that these accurately represent the new system, next confirm that the system execution model is valid. Start with the quick checks in Step 7. When you include existing work in the model, use Step 5's tactics to confirm that the underlying models are valid. Then conduct early benchmark studies to compare SPE model predictions with measurements (see Chapter 7). Compare multiple sets of parameters, for heavy and light loads, to corresponding measurements. As the software evolves, replace resource estimates with measurements and repeat the verification and validation process.

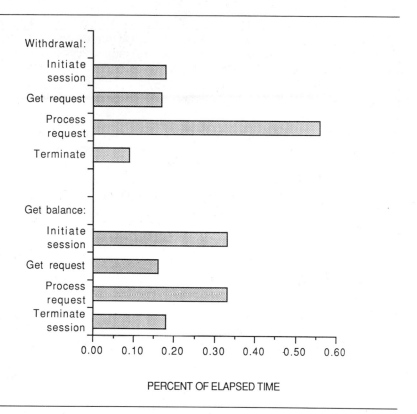

PERCENT OF ELAPSED TIME

FIGURE 5.10
Elapsed Time of Each Component in the Withdrawal and Get Balance Senarios.

This step is crucial to SPE. The model precision depends on how closely the parameters match the software execution characteristics, and how closely your model represents the key performance drivers. It takes constant vigilance to make sure they match.

5.3.2 System Execution Model Pragmatics

The preceding steps for using elementary IPGs for SPE defined *what* is needed; this section offers some pragmatic information on *how* to execute these steps. Formulating a system execution model that accurately represents the system's performance is the art of computer performance modeling. This may change as the technology matures; meanwhile, this section offers advice on how to construct models for SPE. This information is sufficient for you to get started. Your proficiency will improve with experience, and you will hasten the learning process if you solve many models to examine the effect of slight differences in topology and model parameters. The following subsections will introduce you to the topics of workload selection, general strategy for formulating and solving SPE models, representation issues, model parameter selection, and execution characteristics that are best modeled in later lifecycle stages.

Workload Selection   This section first examines the single- and dual-category ATM model formulations and then examines workload choices for SPE. Compare the model results in Tables 5.5 and 5.7. Both models show that the bottleneck resource is DEV1, so both would point to appropriate remedies for performance problems. The response times, though, are different for the two formulations. The total session initiation and termination overhead differs in the two models, noticeably affecting the response times. This illustrates the impact of the workload definition on the performance metrics. **The workload scenario and its execution structure are fundamental to the software model specification.**

Make the choice between the two different workload descriptions—a single session consisting of one Get balance and two Withdrawal requests, versus one session with one Get balance and another session with two Withdrawals—with the user representatives during the walkthrough. Do not try to decide alone! In this ATM example, it is likely that neither of the two models is representative. Another option that appears more reasonable is:

> CAT 1: A session with one Get balance
> CAT 2: A session with two Withdrawals[8]
> CAT 3: A session with one Get balance and one Withdrawal
> CAT 4: A Quick Withdrawal

The bank officer should specify the appropriate combination. When users are uncertain, conduct sensitivity studies to examine the effect of different combinations. Note that the four-category formulation references the same software components in multiple scenarios—with expanded nodes in the software models you can describe them once and reuse them in different scenarios.

Modeling Strategy   Use the fundamental SPE strategy to construct models: Begin with simple, optimistic models of performance, and gradually incorporate more realistic properties as the system evolves. Simple, abstract models of computer systems can be solved quickly (analytically). Although they hide many execution characteristics, they still yield sufficient precision to identify major performance problems and their appropriate solutions. If you find severe performance problems, the simple, optimistic models are easier to explain, and the

---

[8]This models the early ATM systems that limited the withdrawal amount per transaction but allowed two maximum-amount withdrawals per session. More recent ATM systems allow users to withdraw the maximum daily amount with one transaction.

model assumptions are more easily justified. Early in the lifecycle, it is seldom cost-effective to formulate and solve more realistic models. It is better to provide rapid feedback of simpler model results than to spend longer on more realistic models. Also, many aspects of the software design are uncertain and likely to change, so you have to maintain the (more complex) model parameters as the software evolves, and the model results may be volatile.

Open Versus Closed Models   What should be represented in the early SPE models? Models with only open workloads can be solved with a calculator or spreadsheet package. For models with many devices, categories, and large populations, an open model provides a rapid checkpoint evaluation and enables rapid evaluation of many tradeoffs. So use open models when possible to simplify modeling and analysis. Likewise represent the minimum number of categories in early models. Add other workload categories that compete for resource usage later, after meeting the initial checkpoint evaluation.

Device Representation   Section 5.3.1 recommends an early IPG topology with the minimum number of devices that adequately characterize performance. Early models combine I/O subsystems into one queue server and represent the telecommunication network with one queue server (if at all). Some analysts partition response time into a network component and a computer system component and examine only the computer system component to see if the "host time" meets its (part of the) response time goal. Chapter 8 covers techniques for augmenting the early models with more realistic network and I/O subsystem devices.

The queue-scheduling discipline not only affects solution time, but also may affect the model precision. For example, priority scheduling is common for CPU scheduling, yet early models use processor sharing (PS) for rapid solution. The resulting response time (with PS) for the high-priority category is higher than the response time would be with priority scheduling, and the response time for the lower-priority category is lower. If the CPU has low utilization, the queueing delay is insignificant, and the response time difference is unimportant. If the CPU utilization is high, the queue-scheduling discipline is more important. The checkpoint evaluation uses the simpler models; its results indicate whether a more realistic representation is necessary. Chapter 8 covers models with priority scheduling.

Submodels   Submodels simplify model formulation and evaluation. Some model solution packages solve submodels hierarchically, retaining intermediate results and reusing them to avoid recomputing the same values. Recomputation is unnecessary when you replicate submodels in the higher-level model (when there are several identical I/O subsystems), and when you solve a model repeatedly with slightly different parameters that have no effect on submodels (different populations and so forth). Submodels also provide performance metrics for the devices in the submodel as well as summary statistics for the entire submodel. For example, they provide utilization and residence time for each individual device and for the entire submodel. They also simplify model topology by hiding the details of the submodel from the higher-level model. This may make model evaluation quicker by either abstracting unimportant information when the bottleneck is not in the submodel, or by localizing the bottleneck when it is within a submodel. Hierarchy in system execution models improves communication and comprehension, and thus has advantages similar to those of hierarchy in software systems.

Parameter Choices   How do you compensate for uncertainties when you specify early lifecycle IPG model parameters? There are two common IPG uncertainties: device service rates and visits to I/O devices. First consider device service rates. CPU service rates are the most difficult to precisely state; yet, as long as CPUs are much faster than peripheral devices, you do not need precise rates—published MIP rates for processors are usually close enough. (Conduct a sensitivity study or performance benchmark if you don't believe that the published data is sufficiently accurate for your environment.) Many systems have I/O bottlenecks, so the average I/O service rate influences the model's precision more than CPU rates, and, fortunately, I/O is much easier to estimate.

Next, consider visits to devices. The IPG visits to I/O devices must specify physical rather than logical I/Os. Estimate the logical-to-physical I/Os for each software execution model component. To compensate for logical-to-physical uncertainties, use the best and worst cases (and other techniques described in Chapter 4). After estimating physical I/Os, you still need to know which I/O device they visit. File placements are seldom determined early in the lifecycle. Start with an optimistic assumption that I/O visits are equally spread across devices. A worst case assumes that all I/Os visit the same device. (This results in maximum contention delays and thus response times—Section 5.4 shows an example.) Start with these bounds; later use the models to evaluate file placement alternatives.

Defer Complexity   The elementary IPG minimizes the number of categories and the number of devices, uses approximations of device processing rates, and evenly distributes visits across devices. It uses the queue-scheduling conditions and service time distributions that yield efficient, exact, analytic solutions, and assumes that CPU bursts are evenly distributed throughout the processing. It ignores overhead for memory management and delays that may occur when there is a limit on the maximum number of concurrent processes or "threads" allowed. It also ignores contention for other passive resources such as locks, forks and joins of concurrent processes, and sends and receives for messages. Keep the model simple so you can quickly and easily explore many alternatives and explain results without being bogged down in details. Later, once you achieve the performance goal checkpoint with the elementary IPG, incorporate these additional aspects of system execution using the techniques described in Chapters 8 and 9.

5.4 System Execution Model for Case Studies

Now let's apply the 12 system execution modeling steps to the case studies. You may wish to review our progress (in section 3.3 [pages 138 to 152], section 4.2 [170 to 174], and section 4.4 [pages 198 to 212]) before proceeding.

In Chapter 4, the interrelationship of the case studies led us to evaluate SYS_EXEC first, then EDMS, and finally DRAWMOD. Then the DRAWMOD scenario's resource requirements, R_i, included EDMS and SYS_EXEC interprocess communication. So for the system execution model, we formulate the IPG topology to reflect the DRAWMOD execution environment. Then we model one transaction category for the DRAWMOD scenario. Its solution reflects the combined effects of the three case study designs. To examine the effect of changes to one—for example, communication—change its software model accordingly, recompute the effect on EDMS and DRAWMOD resource requirements, R_i, derive new IPG model parameters, and solve the revised system execution model.[9]

The execution environment was described in Example 3.12. It is a distributed network of engineering workstations. EDMS may be assigned to any of them; application program requests (DRAWMOD and others) are routed to the appropriate workstation. Following the "best-case first, realistic later" strategy, assume for the initial model that EDMS is on DRAWMOD's local processor. Model only that processor with no incoming requests from other machines and no outgoing requests to others. This is optimistic because both cause additional delays, so response time is longer. Additionally, while workstations can have one to eight hard disks, we first examine the largest configuration: eight disks.

This elementary IPG model topology is shown in Figure 5.11. It is a closed model because the workload specifies the maximum number of (local) users and their think time, rather than an arrival rate. Each of the 10 USERS makes a DRAWMOD request and enters it. Execution begins at the CPU, then proceeds to an I/O device, and returns to the CPU. DRAWMOD subsequently sends intermediate results to the user's terminal, and processing continues at the CPU and I/O devices until the complete picture has been transmitted to the user. The user then spends an average of 5 minutes examining the result (5-minute think time is specified in Example 3.6), then repeats the process. Note that this model is different from the ATM IPG: It does not model the end-to-end response. DRAWMOD visits the USERS terminal many times before it completes the picture. This changes the way you calculate the model parameters for the USERS node, and the way you interpret results.

Next, we compute the model parameters. As stated, there are up to 10 users

---

[9]Note that other model formulations are possible; this is the simplest. Chapter 8 shows a different formulation that explicitly represents distributed processing and communication and the three distinct categories in the IPG.

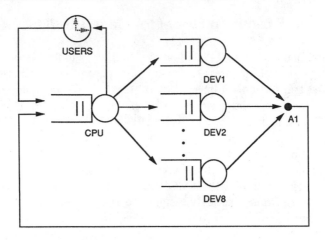

FIGURE 5.11
The Elementary IPG Model Topology for the Case Studies. The initial, optimistic model represents the largest disk configuration.

(we examine the results for each population, 1–10), and the average think time between requests is 5 minutes. To keep the parameter units consistent, we use $5 \times 60 = 300$ seconds think time.

From Chapter 4, the R_i for DRAWMOD is (21,843,733; 33,072; 2052) for CPU instructions, I/O requests, and terminal I/Os, respectively. The IPG parameters are in Table 5.10. The number of visits to the USERS node is 2052 (per user). One of them has $w_i = 300$; the remainder have $w_i = 0.01$, the time to draw a result on the screen. This value comes from Table 3.6's I/O time for screen communication (the 50 instructions are included in the software model). We use the weighted average think time for all visits:

$$w_{\text{USERS}} = \frac{300 + (2051)(.01)}{2052} = .15619$$

Next, we compute the number of visits to each I/O device. We make the optimistic assumption that the requests are equally spread across the eight devices.[10] So the number of visits to each device is $33,072/8 = 4134$. The time to service each is from Table 3.6:

$$w_{\text{DEV}i} = .03$$

The number of visits to A1 is the sum of the visits to the I/O devices, 33072. The number of visits to the CPU is the sum of the visits to A1 plus the number of visits

[10]If the requests are skewed, the response time increases. Confirm this by modifying the model to eight disks with the following visits: 1654, 3307, 4961, 6614, 4134, 4134, 4134, 4134.

TABLE 5.10
CASE STUDY: ELEMENTARY IPG MODEL PARAMETERS

Node	# visits, V_i	Avg. time to process a request, w_i	Mean service time, S_i
USERS	2,052	$\dfrac{300 + (2,051)(.01)}{2,052}$	.15619
DEV1	4,134	.03	.03
DEV2	4,134	.03	.03
DEV3	4,134	.03	.03
DEV4	4,134	.03	.03
DEV5	4,134	.03	.03
DEV6	4,134	.03	.03
DEV7	4,134	.03	.03
DEV8	4,134	.03	.03
A1	33,072		
CPU	35,123	.0000006	.00037

Number of users: Maximum 10
Think time: 5 minutes
DRAWMOD scenario: R_i = (21,843,733; 33,072; 2052)
where i = 1 is the CPU

i = 2 is the I/O subsystem

i = 3 is terminal I/O

to USERS: 33,072 + 2,052 = 35,123. R_{CPU} is the number of high-level instructions executed. Example 3.12 says that the workstation CPU processes 5 million (machine) instructions per second. Table 3.6 shows that there is an average of 3 machine instructions for each high-level instruction. So,

$$w_{CPU} = \frac{1}{5,000,000} \text{ sec/machine instr.} \times 3 \text{ machine/high-level instr.}$$

$$= .0000006 \text{ sec/high-level instr.}$$

The mean service time per visit to the CPU is:

$$S_{CPU} = \frac{R_i w_i}{V_i} = \frac{(21,843,733)(.0000006)}{35,123} = .00037$$

This completes the model parameters for the DRAWMOD elementary IPG. We use an automated solution package to produce the results in Tables 5.11 and 5.12.

Table 5.11 shows the average residence time at each device (for all visits to the device) and the overall average DRAWMOD response time as the population increases from 1 to 10. Note that the residence time of the USERS node is adjusted to exclude the 300 seconds think time, so the residence time shown for USERS includes only the time to draw intermediate results. Note also that the result for

TABLE 5.11
CASE STUDY: IPG MODEL RESULTS
(Residence times for devices and total response time)

Number of users	USERS*	Each I/O visit	Total I/O	Each CPU visit	Total CPU	Response time
1	20.51	0.03000	992.16	0.00038	13.35	1026
2	20.51	0.03281	1084.95	0.00038	13.49	1119
3	20.51	0.03573	1181.82	0.00039	13.61	1216
4	20.51	0.03877	1282.22	0.00039	13.71	1316
5	20.51	0.04190	1385.67	0.00039	13.81	1420
6	20.51	0.04511	1491.73	0.00040	13.89	1526
7	20.51	0.04838	1600.02	0.00040	13.96	1634
8	20.51	0.05171	1710.20	0.00040	14.03	1745
9	20.51	0.05509	1821.99	0.00040	14.08	1857
10	20.51	0.05851	1935.16	0.00040	14.14	1970

*Note that 300 is subtracted from USERS to exclude the think time

population 1 is the same as the total processing units result in Chapter 4. With population 1, there is no queueing delay, so the results should match. Table 5.12 shows the utilization of each device. It shows only one I/O device—since the traffic is equally distributed, the average utilization is the same for all I/O devices. These results are shown graphically in Figure 5.12.

Clearly, the I/O is a bottleneck. Actually, we knew from the software model that the response time goal of 20 seconds would not be achieved with the original design. Ordinarily, the problems would be resolved before proceeding to the system model. Nevertheless, let's continue the software model assessment. For each software component, Figure 5.13 shows the percentage of its I/O service

TABLE 5.12
UTILIZATION

Number of users	USERS	Each I/O device	CPU
1	0.024	0.094	0.010
2	0.045	0.175	0.019
3	0.063	0.245	0.026
4	0.079	0.307	0.033
5	0.093	0.361	0.039
6	0.105	0.407	0.044
7	0.116	0.449	0.048
8	0.125	0.485	0.052
9	0.134	0.518	0.056
10	0.141	0.546	0.059

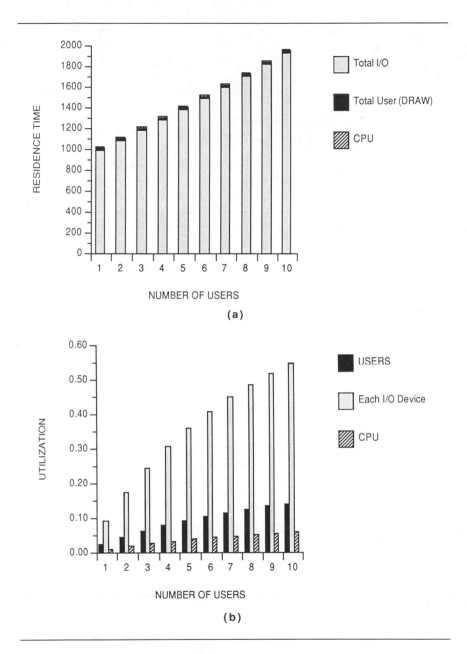

FIGURE 5.12
Graphical Model Results for the Case Study. Part (a) shows DRAWMOD's residence time for each device and overall as the number of users increases from 1 to 10; (b) shows the utilization of each device for the same range.

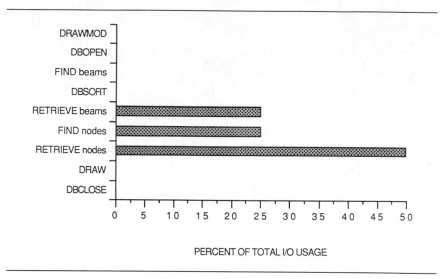

FIGURE 5.13
Case Study Graphical Results: The Percentage of I/Os by DRAWMOD Component.

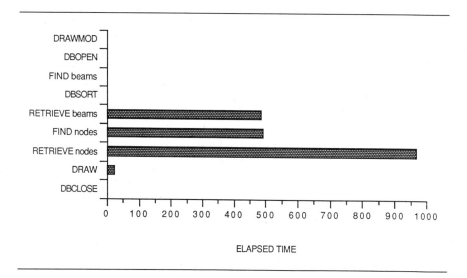

FIGURE 5.14
Case Study Graphical Results: The Percentage of Elapsed Time of Each DRAW-MOD Component.

requests to the total requests for the scenario. You can construct similar graphs for each resource. Since the I/O is the bottleneck, its graph is more informative. Figure 5.14 shows the elapsed time of each component as a percentage of the total. It uses the w_i' computed from the system model using the earlier formula:

$$w_i' = \frac{(RT_i)V_i}{R_i}$$

$$w_{CPU}' = \frac{(.0004024)(35,123)}{21,843,733} = .000000647$$

$$w_{DEVi}' = .05851$$

$$w_{USERS}' = .01 \text{ (excluding think time)}$$

The next step is to identify some performance improvement alternatives and evaluate them. This process is described in Chapter 6.

5.5 System Execution Model Options

Chapter 4 introduced execution graphs and alternative software execution models. This chapter uses IPGs for the system execution model. The elementary IPG represents the fundamental elements of competition for computer system resources. Alternatives to IPGs differ only in terminology and syntax and thus are fundamentally the same. Chapters 8 and 9 introduce extensions to the elementary IPG to represent additional execution behavior. They increase the system execution modeling power but do not change the model. The options, therefore, are not in the system execution model representation, but are instead in the methods and tools for solving the model.

5.5.1 Tool Differences

There are many commercially available tools for solving IPGs. They all employ the same underlying technology; the differences are in the solution methods (analytic, simulation, or hybrid), their analytic approximations, the user interfaces, and the high-level functions they support. The tools were created primarily for performance management of existing systems and capacity management for future growth. Thus, their user interfaces and features are oriented to those uses rather than to SPE uses. Section 5.5.2 describes features desirable for SPE.

There are three key differences in the way IPGs translate to specific model syntax: service requests, arrivals, and routing information. Note that the IPGs provide the model parameters for all; they are merely expressed differently for different solution methods.

In Example 5.4, **service requests** are expressed with mean service *times* (0.05 seconds per DEV2 request). Some solution methods want mean service *rates* (20 requests per second). The conversion is straightforward: Service rates are the reciprocal of service times. That is, 1 request/0.05 second = 20 requests/second. Similarly, the ATM node service rate is 1/1 = 1 request per second, and for the CPU, 1/0.000323 = 1642.

There is a similar difference for **arrivals;** some methods want interarrival times rather than arrival rates. Again it is the reciprocal of the arrival rate. In Example 5.4 the arrival rate for the GENERAL category is 1 session/second, so the interarrival time is 1/1 = 1 second.

The last difference is in **routing information.** Some methods want node visits, while others want execution probabilities for the arcs: p_{ij}, the probability of a completion at node i proceeding to node j. Again the conversion is easy. Consider the arc between the CPU node and the I/O subsystem node in Figure 5.7(a). The CPU node is visited (an average of) 22 times and the I/O subsystem 9 times, so the execution probability for the arc from the CPU to the I/O subsystem is 9/22. The remaining completions at the CPU go to the ATM, so the CPU-ATM arc has execution probability (22 − 9)/22 = 13/22. Nodes such as Begin, A1, and I/O subsystem have only one outgoing arc, so its execution probability is 1. The calculated execution probabilities of each arc in Figure 5.7 are in Table 5.13.

TABLE 5.13
EXECUTION PROBABILITIES
FOR IPG ARCS

Arc	Execution probability
Init-ATM	1
ATM-Fini	1/14
ATM-A1	13/14
A1-CPU	1
CPU-ATM	13/22
CPU-I/O subsystem	9/22
Entry-B1	1
B1-DEV1	9/9 = 1
B1-DEV2	0/9 = 0
B1-DEV3	0/9 = 0
DEV1-B2	1
DEV2-B2	0
DEV3-B2	0
B2-Exit	1

The formal version of the algorithm we just used is:

$$V_0 = 1$$

$$\sum_{i=1}^{k} V_i p_{ij} = V_j \qquad\qquad\qquad\text{(Eq. 5.10)}$$

where $i = 0$ is the source node of an IPG

The first equation says the number of visits of the source node of the graph is 1. The second says to multiply the number of visits for each origin node by the probability of going to the destination node, to sum this quantity for each incoming arc of the destination node, then solve for the unknown p_{ij} (as in Equation 5.1). The formulas yield a system of equations for the IPG that can be solved for a unique set of values for the p_{ij}. For example, for the arc from the CPU node to the ATM node, using the equations, let $i = 0$ be the source node, $i = 1$ be the CPU node, and $i = 2$ be the ATM node. To solve for the CPU-ATM arc, p_{12}:

$$V_0 = 1$$

$$V_0 p_{02} + V_1 p_{12} = V_2$$

Substituting into Equation 5.10:

$$(1)(1) + 22p_{12} = 14$$

$$p_{12} = \frac{(14 - 1)}{22} = \frac{13}{22}$$

Note that we fudged some by substituting $p_{02} = 1$, because we know there is only one arc out of the source node. If we applied the formulas literally, we would have to solve the system of equations.

5.5.2 SPE Tool Requirements

The differences in model terminology and syntax are minor. All the commercial tools listed subsequently provide adequate model solutions, but some may be easier to use for SPE. The following are SPE requirements for model solvers:

- They must be able to solve the elementary IPGs and accommodate extensions for the advanced IPGs without significant changes to the model description.
- The corollary is: They must provide for abstraction—they should not require extremely detailed information for early analysis.
- They must provide rapid solutions, preferably interactive solutions.
- It must be easy to assimilate results—it is undesirable to pore through pages of results to find the key performance indicators.

□ It must be easy to evaluate alternatives in workload characteristics, in software design, in mapping software onto computer system resources, and in the computer configuration.

An ideal tool would automatically extract parameters from the software execution model and automatically create parameters for existing work. The early representation of existing work would be abstract to enable rapid solution and to match the level of detail used for the new software. (When software execution models represent vague ideas, there is no need to represent low-level details of existing work.) The ideal tool would provide reasonable default values, such as the (simple) model topology for existing computer systems, and best-case model parameters such as evenly distributed visits to I/O devices. It would automatically provide best- and worst-case results and use adaptive solution methods as the system execution model evolves: analytic solutions for elementary IPGs, then approximations, then simulations for only those parts that require more detailed analysis. As the software evolves, it would also support analysis of more detailed I/O subsystems, automatic assignments of files to I/O devices, computation of physical I/Os from logical, and so on. These features and more are likely to be supported by tools of the future. The requirements have heretofore not been documented. As the demand for SPE products grows, so will their availability and their features.

5.5.3 Alternatives

While the perfect tool is still on the horizon, there are many viable alternatives. This section examines the possibilities of (1) implementing solution algorithms with general-purpose tools, (2) developing special-purpose programs, and (3) using commercially available products. The first two approaches are similar. The algorithms for solving the elementary IPGs are published. Schwetman in [SCH82] gives a concise explanation that is easily implemented. Lazowska et al. also describe the algorithms and provide Fortran code fragments for some of them ([LAZ84a]). The analysis algorithms are easy to implement; the time-consuming parts of the process are designing and building the user interface, error detection and handling, and ensuring numerical stability when model parameters differ by several orders of magnitude (think times or arrival rates in minutes versus device processing rates in nanoseconds). Once implemented, the tools must be maintained.

General-purpose tools, such as spreadsheets, statistical analysis packages, and database management calculation functions, can easily implement the analysis algorithms. They ease the burden of building the user interface somewhat. With them, the simple analytic solution algorithms from Section 5.1 can be implemented in less than a day.[11] This does not include time for implementing error

---

[11]Note that they will not be as robust as those found in commercial solvers, but they will suffice for simple analyses.

detection and handling features or for numerical accuracy provisions. Using general-purpose tools is a good approach, though, if you have no other model solvers. It is relatively quick and easy and can be used for practice and experience with IPGs to develop performance intuition. If modeling is new in your organization, this is a good way to get started—it is better than buying a commercial product and then discovering that is not well-suited to your needs—but you will want a modeling product for "industrial-strength" SPE studies. The primary disadvantage of this approach is the difficulty of evaluating alternatives. The calculation of the revised model parameters is external to the solver.

A variation of this approach is to use a general-purpose simulation language such as SIMSCRIPT ([KIV69], [RUS76]), SLAM ([PRI79]), SIMULA ([DAH66]), or GPSS ([GOR78], [SCH74]). It is even more labor-intensive and does not automatically provide analytic solutions. It is feasible and may be appropriate for detailed operating system, networks, or hardware design.

The second approach, **developing a special-purpose program,** enables you to customize the user interface for your particular SPE applications. It can minimize the effort needed to create and modify models, and can incorporate other features of the ideal tool. As stated earlier, designing effective user interfaces is an iterative process. A research tool, GQUE, developed to study graphical user interfaces is described later. Perhaps it can save you a few iterations.

The third approach is to **use a commercially-available product.** The first commercial products were introduced in the 1970s. Before 1980 there were only a few products available and less than a hundred active users of them. Since 1980 there has been a dramatic increase in the number of users of such products, and a corresponding increase in the number of products offered to meet this demand. Because the market is changing rapidly and change is likely to continue over the next few years, it is impossible to provide a product review that will remain current and accurate. Instead, some product categories are described, with a list of some of the available products. As before, do not assume that this list is complete or that these are the best products for your needs. Check the vendor offerings at the Computer Measurement Group conferences, the Applied Computer Research product directory, the standard references to computer products (such as Auerbach or Datapro), and the computer trade publications for current product information.

There are several ways that one could distinguish products:

☐ By solution method—analytic, simulation, or hybrid

☐ Whether they are special-purpose tools or general-purpose tools useful for any system that can be represented by networks of queues

☐ Whether they are oriented to software analysis or to computer system performance

☐ Whether they run on mainframes, workstations, or personal computers

☐ Special features they provide, such as graphical input and output, automatic parameter generation, expert system interpretation of results, and so forth

TABLE 5.14
PRODUCTS FOR SOLVING SYSTEM
EXECUTION MODELS

Product	Reference
BEST/1	[*BGS*]
CADS	[*SES*]
COPE	[BEI84]
CRYSTAL	[*BGS*]
GPSM	[*SES*]
CA/ISS three	[*CA*]
MAP	[*QSP*]
MEDOC	[LeM82]
MODEL300	[*BOO*]
PANACEA	[RAM82]
PAW	[MEL85]
PAWS	[*SES*]
PET	[FAR86]
QNAP2	[VER84]
RESQ	[SAU82a, SAU82b]
SCERT II	[*PSI*]
VM PREDICTOR	[BAR78]

Vendor references are in italics.

Any such distinction, however, is unreliable because it is likely to change. There-fore, Table 5.14 simply lists some of the generally available products and cites a published or vendor reference for further information. The number of products is extensive and rapidly growing. With this competition, as users we can expect future products with advances in user interfaces, high-level support features, and automation of many of the SPE tasks.

5.5.4 Research Tools

GQUE is a research tool developed to investigate issues in graphical user inter-faces.[12] The next few paragraphs give an overview of some of its interesting features. For a thorough description, see [JEN87].

GQUE was the predecessor of the PERFORM tool described in Chapter 4. Thus it served as the testbed for many of the visual interface features described in Chapter 4 and in Chapter 2. The requirements that drove its design were:

□ Emphasis on performance assessment and problem solving (rather than model creation)

---

[12]Several graduate students at Duke University contributed to its development: Thad Jen-nings was its chief architect; Jack Briner and Mike Lyons developed screen area manage-ment routines; and Douglas Elliott, David Harger, Vijay Naik, and Roger Smith contributed code from an earlier research tool, QED.

☐ Rapid creation of visual models—this implies making frequent actions easy and providing a useful default topology and realistic default parameters

☐ Abstract, early models (without extremely detailed information)—they must be easily adapted later when details are available and when revisions are necessary

☐ Rapid and easy assimilation of results

☐ Combinations of results that can be tailored to the problem analysis

☐ Minimal effort to "drive" the tool—concentration on the performance results is more important

Many of the features of GQUE are similar to those in PERFORM. GQUE supports phases of use with two screens: one for topology, and the other for parameters and results. It also uses miniature replicas of submodels in navigation tiles to portray the model hierarchy. GQUE needs fewer tiles for submodels and places them across the bottom of the screen, as shown in Figure 5.15. The correspondence between a submodel node and its expansion is shown with color.

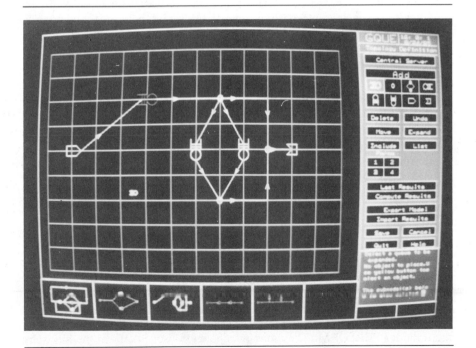

FIGURE 5.15
GQUE Topology Screen. The model hierarchy is depicted with colors. The levels in the hierarchy are in the navigation tiles at the bottom of the screen. To change levels, the user points to the desired tile and clicks the mouse button.

GQUE also uses default model parameters: It assumes an equal distribution of visits to devices when a node has multiple outgoing arcs, and it uses default mean service times. The user may specify the default service time; the standard value is 30 ms, which corresponds to a typical disk server, the most common node in a computer system model. There is also a default topology: a central server model. It is created with one menu selection and is easily modified when necessary.

Because the execution graphs differ from queueing network models, GQUE topology creation differs from that of PERFORM. The topology is created with the Add command. The Add command box is partitioned (see Figure 5.15), so the user can select the Add command and the type of node at the same time. The cursor takes the shape of the node to be added; the cursor (node to be added) is changed by stepping up or down the list of node symbols using "puck buttons." The list is ordered by typical frequency of use—the forward queue is most common. After each placement (with another puck button), the cursor reverts to the forward queue (the default). The user may select and place many nodes and arcs without returning to the menu.

To suit user preferences, GQUE allows considerable flexibility in adding arcs. One option uses a puck button to start an arc at an origin node. A "rubber band line" then follows the cursor as it moves until the destination node is placed. The other option connects arcs to existing nodes—the user just points to the nodes to be connected in succession.

GQUE expedites the frequent actions of placing queues and connecting them. Queues are ordered by frequency of use, and the most frequent one is the default. The entire topology can be constructed with one menu selection, by using the node-select, node-place, and arc-place buttons.

The viewing of results is different than with PERFORM because GQUE's performance metrics differ. GQUE provides both numerical and perceptual results (using the modified heated-object scale). It presents up to four sets of results concurrently. Users can view selected performance metrics by transaction category and by submodel. Users can concurrently view the results produced before and after changes. These results are in virtual screens in quadrants of the main work area. A least-recently-used algorithm replaces virtual screens; the user can control replacement decisions (with "locks" on virtual screens exempt from replacement, and so forth).

Figure 5.16 shows a concurrent results display. It shows the "MVS" model described in [MAC85]. It is a hierarchical model with two transaction categories; category 1 is TSO and category 2 is batch. Figure 5.16 shows utilization results for both categories at both levels in the hierarchy.

GQUE's user interface is a great success. Because it worked so well, it was the basis for PERFORM. The direct-manipulation user interface, the hierarchy and navigation features, the visual results, and the concurrent results display combine to make a tool for easily creating models and focusing on their assessment. Color plays an important role in assimilating results and comprehending model hierarchy. The visual model supports the user's cognitive process.

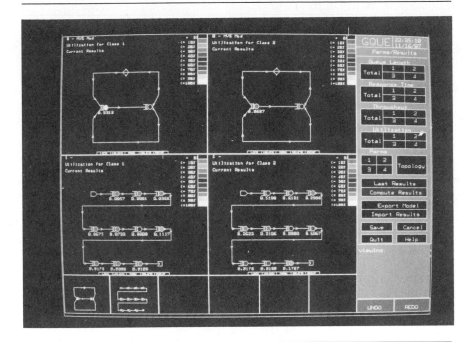

FIGURE 5.16
GQUE Model Results.

The number of model solution tools available is growing, and their sophistication is evolving rapidly. The underlying technology is relatively stable—the changes occur in user interaction and high-level features. GQUE is representative of the next generation of visual tools. It is not necessary, though, to have leading-edge tools to conduct an SPE study. You can implement the solution algorithms with general-purpose tools for early experience and insight into your tool requirements. You need a commercial product for detailed analysis of very large systems, when you need to study many systems, and when you have no time to create and maintain solvers.

5.6 Summary

This chapter covered the elementary system execution model. It examined the performance effects of dynamic execution behavior using a heating and airconditioning analogy. After presenting background information on representing computer system execution with queueing network models, the chapter defined the elementary Information Processing Graph. Next it described how to create elementary IPGs from software execution models and offered pragmatic techniques for early SPE studies.

We then used these techniques to construct an elementary IPG for the comprehensive case studies to quantify the effects of contention on response time and to identify performance bottlenecks. We related the system execution model results to the software execution model to examine bottleneck resource usage by software component and to identify critical components. Finally, we examined the options for automated tools for solving the elementary system execution model. The next chapter uses the model results to identify alternatives and study their performance effect.

Exercises

Review

5.1. Construct IPGs for the models in Figure 5.7 and Figure 5.8, solve the models, and compare your results to Tables 5.5 and 5.7.

5.2. Construct an IPG with the topology in Figure 5.8. Derive the model specifications from the following:

Environment parameters:
Arrival rate: 0.444444 sessions/sec
ATM think time: 1 sec
DEV mean service time: 0.1 sec

Computer resource requirements, r_i

Node	CPU (ms)	DEV1	ATM
Initiate session	20	3	1
Get request	15	0	1
Process request	25	5	2
Terminate session	10	2	1

Loop repetition factor: 3

Conduct the following four studies and build a table containing the following performance metrics for each study: Session response time; utilization for CPU, DEV1, DEV2, DEV3, ATM; residence time for CPU, DEV1, DEV2, DEV3; queue length for CPU, DEV1, DEV2, DEV3.

Studies:
   a. Results for original model above
   b. Change the mean service time for DEV1 to 0.0333 sec. Solve.
   c. Restore DEV1 service time to 0.10 sec. Then revise the routing to equally balance the load across the three DEVs. Solve.
   d. Restore the service time to the original values. Use the loop repetition factor 3. Change the scenario computer resource requirements to those below, and solve.

Node	CPU (ms)	DEV1	DEV2	ATM
Initiate session	15	0	1	1
Get request	10	0	0	1
Process request	15	2	1	2
Terminate session	10	0	0	1

5.3. Construct an IPG like the topology in Figure 5.11, but with only two I/O DEVs. Calculate parameters for the three workload categories below:

Category 1: New Transactions
10 users, 30-sec think time.

Component resource requirements, r_i:

Component	CPU (ms)	DEV1	DEV2
SELECT one row from Worktab	3	2	0
OPEN a cursor & FETCH 10 rows from Accounttab	17	0	11
UPDATE 10 rows in Accounttab	18	0	14
UPDATE 3 rows, then CLOSE cursor	6	0	3
INSERT 1 row into Stats	9	6	0
COMMIT	5	2	2
THREAD overhead	14	1	0
CICS overhead	10	2	0
Transaction program processing	6	0	0

Category 2: Existing Work
10 users, 10-sec think time.
Total computer resource requirements, R_i:
 CPU: 140 ms
DEV1: 4 I/Os

Category 3: New Queries
1 user, 60-sec think time.

Computer resource requirements, r_i:

Component	CPU (ms)	DEV1	DEV2
PREPARE (dynamic bind)	44	8	0
FETCH Tab1 & Tab2 and JOIN	10,977	1,005	11,000
COMMIT (always 1 for QMF queries)	3	0	0
THREAD overhead	9	1	0

Environment parameters:
Mean service time for both DEV1 and DEV2 is 20 ms.

Formulate and solve the model. Create a table of results with the following performance metrics for each category and for all combined: response time; utilization for CPU, DEV1, DEV2; residence time for CPU, DEV1, DEV2; queue length for CPU, DEV1, DEV2.

5.4. Construct an IPG for your Chapter 1 case study. Solve the model.

Further Study

5.5. Implement a spreadsheet algorithm (or a program) that solves an open model with two categories and two nodes.

5.6. Repeat Exercise 5.3 using a different model solver. (If you do not have two solvers, obtain a detailed description of the model input for another solver and create its model specifications.) Describe three specific differences in the two packages. Which do you prefer? Document three specific limitations in their use for SPE. What are some features you would like to have that are not provided?

6

Software Performance Evaluation

Contemplate the vast number of alternatives in the design and implementation of a large system. For example, consider the heating and airconditioning specialist's alternatives for thermostat location. The specialist wants a temperature reading that is *representative* of all offices on each subsystem. But individual temperatures vary with the location of the office, the windows, the time of day, weather, season, proximity to heat-producing equipment, and so on. Early in design, the assignment of offices to subsystems can change as well. The specialist needs quantitative data for alternatives to make appropriate choices from among them.

Both the heating and airconditioning specialist and the performance engineer use similar steps to produce quantitative data and to evaluate alternatives. They define performance objectives, gather data, create and solve models, evaluate results, use design principles to formulate alternatives, revise models, and repeat the analysis. This produces quantitative data to assess performance tradeoffs. As before, we focus on performance, coupling the results with other data on implementation ease, maintainability, and so on to identify the best approach.

Figure 6.1 highlights the subjects in this chapter: reporting results and identifying, evaluating, and reporting alternatives. Once the models produce the performance metrics, reports combine results for multiple scenarios; best, worst, and typical cases; various job mixes; and sensitivity to model assumptions and parameters. When performance goals are not met, we identify alternatives, modify the software and system execution models appropriately, and report the new results. Earlier chapters define the *techniques* needed for this SPE step; this chapter shows *how to use them* to manage software performance.

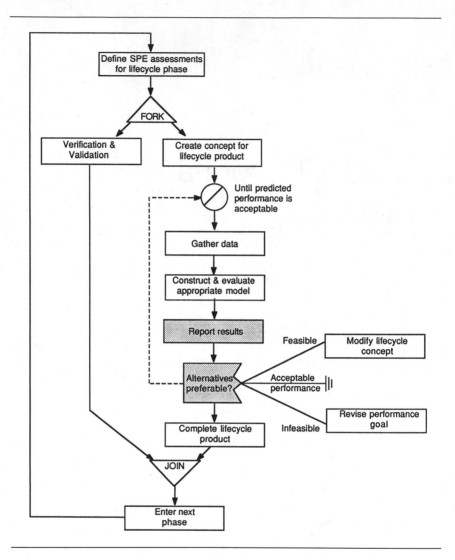

FIGURE 6.1
The SPE Methodology with the Focus of This Chapter Highlighted.

6.1 Report Results

Report results *as soon as possible* after each performance study. Chapter 3 suggested performance walkthroughs with an initial presentation of results within 1 to 5 days—in time for any necessary corrective action—and offered other presentation strategies to enhance communication and to ensure recognition and solution of success-threatening problems. This section elaborates on the results needed, reviews elements of presentations, and suggests how to tailor reports to the findings and to the recipients.

Reports contain the following seven basic elements:

- Best-case predicted performance
- Worst-case predicted performance
- Typical cases
- Sensitivity to assumptions
- Multiple scenarios
- Variations in workload mix
- Verification and validation

Each is described in the following paragraphs.

The **best and worst cases** show bounds on performance. "Best" and "worst" are difficult to define precisely. For example, consider a worst-case ATM scenario: It would occur during a peak load and would reflect behavior that causes maximum resource usage. Would it represent invalid ATM responses and retries? If so, how many? Would it represent session aborts and retries? If so, how do you represent session aborts in the software model (within one or in multiple scenarios)? A pragmatic, operational definition of "best" and "worst" is important. Initially, define the characteristics of "best" and "worst" in the walkthrough and *agree on their definition*. Keep the definition simple—don't try to define *realistic* best and worst cases. For example, the scenario in Figure 4.32 needs the probability of finding a data record in a buffer; in the simplified best case the record is always found, and in the worst case, it is never found. Neither the "always" nor the "never" is realistic, but any other assumption opens the door to debate on its realism and complicates the analysis.

Typical cases reflect characteristics of scenarios that are likely to occur in the delivered software. The best and worst cases show the performance bounds; the typical cases show how close the expected operational conditions are to the extremes.

Sensitivity analysis examines potential changes in key specification values and their effects on performance. For example, what if workload intensity specifications, such as arrival rates, number of users, or think times, are incorrect? Sensitivity results also point out specifications that have little effect on performance.

Multiple workload scenarios show when performance problems occur in isolated cases, and when they affect all software. They show when alternatives favorably affect one workload but are detrimental to others. They also provide results for all candidates when you are uncertain which of them is the dominant workload.

Variations in workload mix examine relative differences in workload intensity between scenarios. For example, with two workload scenarios you can examine the effect of equal arrival rates, and of either rate being much higher than the other.

Verification and validation (V&V) confirms that the critical performance specifications are correct and that the model accurately predicts performance. Sensitivity studies identify the key parameters that need confirmation, such as arrival rates, execution path probabilities and repetitions, and resource requirements. They also identify instrumentation requirements and workload or benchmark studies that may be needed. V&V are ongoing activities. Conduct these sensitivity analyses to identify future V&V studies that will confirm the results of this report, and present the outcome of current studies that seek to confirm earlier model results.

The seven elements define what to present; the method of presenting them is another consideration. Chapter 3 prescribes the following presentation steps:

1. Review the software models.

2. Review the model assumptions.

3. Show summary results (for the basic report elements defined here).

4. Provide model details when necessary.

Before you continue, check your understanding of the basic seven elements of reports. Review the ATM software models in Figure 5.8; then pause and define the characteristics of an ATM example for best, worst, and typical cases; the sensitivity studies; and the workload mixes. Suggest appropriate V&V studies. Then compare your definitions to those in the following example. When you read the cases reported, they may seem obvious. Try to define your own examples first to gain an appreciation of the many possibilities and of the importance of defining the cases *before* you solve the models.

EXAMPLE 6.1 Sample ATM Results Presentation

Software model review:

This ATM example uses the four workload scenarios (software models) shown in Figure 6.2. (These are the "more realistic" workload scenarios suggested in Section 5.3.2.) There are four different sessions corresponding to expected customer requests: one Get balance per session, two Withdrawals per session, one Get balance and one Withdrawal per session, and finally a single Withdrawal per session. An actual presentation explains the execution steps and the rationale for the resource specifications for each. [You should be familiar with these models, so this step is omitted, as is the description of the IPG (it is the model in Figure 5.8).]

(*continued*)

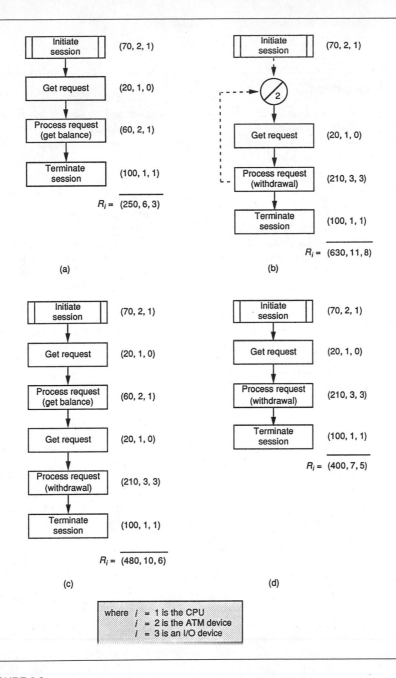

Initiate session	(70, 2, 1)	
Get request	(20, 1, 0)	
Process request (get balance)	(60, 2, 1)	
Terminate session	(100, 1, 1)	

$R_i = \overline{(250, 6, 3)}$

(a)

Initiate session	(70, 2, 1)	
⊘ 2		
Get request	(20, 1, 0)	
Process request (withdrawal)	(210, 3, 3)	
Terminate session	(100, 1, 1)	

$R_i = \overline{(630, 11, 8)}$

(b)

Initiate session	(70, 2, 1)	
Get request	(20, 1, 0)	
Process request (get balance)	(60, 2, 1)	
Get request	(20, 1, 0)	
Process request (withdrawal)	(210, 3, 3)	
Terminate session	(100, 1, 1)	

$R_i = \overline{(480, 10, 6)}$

(c)

Initiate session	(70, 2, 1)	
Get request	(20, 1, 0)	
Process request (withdrawal)	(210, 3, 3)	
Terminate session	(100, 1, 1)	

$R_i = \overline{(400, 7, 5)}$

(d)

where i = 1 is the CPU
       i = 2 is the ATM device
       i = 3 is an I/O device

FIGURE 6.2
ATM Workload Scenarios. Part (a) shows one Get balance per session; (b) shows two Withdrawals per session; (c) depicts one Get balance and one Withdrawal; and (d) models one Withdrawal per session.

EXAMPLE 6.1 (*Continued*)

Assumptions:

All scenarios specify transactions for local bank customers, and we assume that (correct) Withdrawal and Get balance transactions are the dominant workload. The workload definitions reflect these primary assumptions. We explain other assumptions for each case in the following discussion of results.

Results:

Table 6.1 shows a typical results summary. It shows eight cases, each with the average session response time, highest-utilization devices, and the maximum achievable throughput. Because CPU utilization is always less than 1 percent, it is omitted from the bottleneck column. Maximum throughput has two columns. ATM units are tied up throughout the session, so the left throughput column, *customers*, shows for each case the maximum number of customer sessions per second when 50 ATM units are available. Processing throughput within the computer system is limited by the I/O DEVs, so the DEV throughput column shows, for each case, the maximum number of sessions per second with the proposed hardware configuration. The lower of the two limits overall system throughput. For example, consider Case 1's "best-case" results—an average response time of 6.2 seconds. The ATM availability limits throughput to a maximum of 8.33 customers per second. By increasing the number of ATMs, the system could handle 20 best-case sessions per second.

The "worst-case" scenario has more processing, and thus the resource requirements for each component are higher. [The specific data is not in the summary presentation; in an actual presentation, you may walk through the worst-case software model and resource requirements if your audience is unfamiliar with its definition. You should be familiar with software models, so the "worst-case" is not described here.]

Cases 3 and 4 show two different workload mixes. Note that Case 4's performance improves over Case 3 when 90 percent of the requests are Withdrawals, but the improvement is not dramatic. The relatively low improvement is primarily due to low device utilizations; the improvement would be greater in a more heavily loaded system.

Cases 5 through 7 explore parameter sensitivity. Case 5 shows that the system can easily handle increased arrival rates. Notice that the maximum throughput for Case 5 is the same as that for Case 4. [Does this make sense? Explain it to the briefing audience to improve their performance intuition.]

Case 6 shows that the customer throughput is sensitive to think time, but the hardware environment is not. This makes sense—the ATM devices are tied up almost twice as long. An experienced performance engineer expects these results. [It is recommended that you solve models like this and include their results in the presentation, even though you expect the results. People with less performance experience than you have may not have your performance intuition.]

Case 7 shows that performance is not particularly sensitive to I/O subsystem balance for the specified workload, because the I/O subsystem has relatively low I/O device utilizations. If I/O demands increase significantly in other workload mixes, the sensitivity increases.

(continued)

TABLE 6.1
RESULTS SUMMARY

Case	Average session response time (sec)	Utilization		Max. throughput (jobs/sec)	
		ATM	Max. DEV	Customers (50 ATMs)	DEV
1. "Best" case: 1 Get balance per session I/O evenly spread No other customers	6.2	.12	.05	8.33	20.0
2. "Worst" case: 1 Get balance & 2 Withdrawals per session "Worst" case resource req: R_i = (1950, 33, 19) All I/O to DEV1 1 session/sec arrival	52.0	.66	.95	1.52	1.1
3. Scenarios a–d Equally likely 1 session/sec arrival	8.8 (6.2, 11.4, 10.3, 7.3)	.17	.09	5.88	11.1
4. Scenarios a–d 90% are 1 Withdrawal Others equally likely 1 session/sec arrival	7.5 (6.2, 11.4, 10.3, 7.3)	.14	.09	6.95	11.1
5. Sensitivity to arrival rate? Same as #4 with 5 sessions/sec arrival	7.6 (6.3, 11.7, 10.5, 7.4)	.72	.42	6.95	11.1
6. Sensitivity to think time? Same as #4 with 2 sec think time	14.7 (12.2, 22.4, 20.3, 14.3)	.29	.08	3.47	12.5

7. Sensitivity to I/O balance?
Same as #4
with 50% of I/O to DEV1
    33% of I/O to DEV2
    17% of I/O to DEV3
	7.5
	(6.2, 11.5, 10.3, 7.3)
		.14	.13	6.95	7.7

8. Effect of Quick withdrawal?
Same as #5
with modified withdrawal
  Resource requirements:
  R_i = (240, 3, 5)
	4.0
	(6.3, 11.7, 10.5, 3.4)
		.36	.42	13.89	11.1

EXAMPLE 6.1 (*Continued*)

Case 8 shows the effect of replacing the general-purpose withdrawal scenario with a special-purpose Quick withdrawal, with appropriately reduced resource requirements. [It is discussed further in the next section.]

[Have the detailed data available in case participants want more information on the models or their results. For example, if you are asked, show the elementary IPG, its model parameters, and the detailed performance metrics for each IPG node; examples were presented in Tables 5.6 and 5.7, respectively.]

These results suggest three areas for verification and validation:

□ Customer session characteristics, such as the average number and types of transactions typically requested per session

□ Average think times

□ Specifications for the numbers of I/Os and of ATM interactions per software component

[Discuss the possibility of workload studies for the first two, and instrumentation to measure actual data for all three when the software becomes operational.]
□

In Example 6.1 there are no severe performance problems. Your SPE studies may identify problem areas. You need to tailor your results to the situation—for example, worst-case results are probably unnecessary when the best case shows severe problems; show that performance is likely to be degraded significantly with typical cases, and *offer insight into why*. Include bottleneck identification reports, such as that shown in Figure 5.9, to relate the bottleneck resource requirements to the software components and thus show causes. Then explain alternatives with software models and system execution model results. Review the walkthrough strategies in Section 3.2.5 to effectively communicate the results and to elicit corrective action.

6.2   Identify and Evaluate Alternatives

This section first reviews the SPE process, then suggests how to use the SPE methods to identify and assess alternatives.

6.2.1 SPE Process Review

SPE begins early in the lifecycle, just after developers define the system concept. The general principles guide the creation of the proposed functional architecture. You gather data on the workload, performance goal, software execution structure, execution environment, and resource requirements, usually in a performance walkthrough. You model the concept with a software execution model (as in Figure 6.2), and perform an optimistic checkpoint evaluation to identify potential problems. Table 6.1's Case 1 shows the optimistic results for the ATM example. In general, this step rules out potentially disastrous concepts, selects suitable ones, and identifies critical components before proceeding further in the analysis.

Once this first checkpoint is achieved, you construct and evaluate an elementary system execution model to examine the interaction between the new software and its environment. You check to see if resource contention seriously degrades performance of new software, or if new software impedes existing work. The system execution model provides metrics for bottleneck identification and shows the effect of changes in workload intensity, resource requirements, and device service rates. When problems occur, you use the general principles to identify alternatives. Once this checkpoint is passed, you construct more precise software models, augmenting the elementary system execution models to represent more realistic behavior.

6.2.2 Bottleneck Identification

Recall that the bottleneck device is the one that saturates first. Algorithm 5.3 states that it is the device, i, with the maximum visits times mean service time for all classes, c, that visit the device:

$$\text{Bottleneck device,}^1 \; b = max\left\{\sum_i \sum_c V_{ic}S_{ic}\right\}$$

Identify the bottleneck device and study the profile of bottleneck resource use by each software component. Figure 6.3(a) demonstrates: It has the percentage of I/O and ATM use by each software component in the scenarios in Figure 6.2. When one software component appears in multiple scenarios, as in the ATM example, produce a summary report of the total resource use of components for all scenarios. Figure 6.3(b) shows the summary resource usage of ATM software components. This identifies components that have a small effect on individual scenarios but a significant net effect when used by many scenarios.

Also examine the number of times each component is invoked and the overhead of control flow. Small changes in the execution characteristics and control flow of high-frequency components have a widespread effect.

Examine these reports and isolate the major resource usage. Then study how to correct problems.

---

[1] When there are multiple servers (the ATM device has $N_i = 50$ servers), it is

$$\frac{\sum_c V_{ic}S_{ic}}{N_i}$$

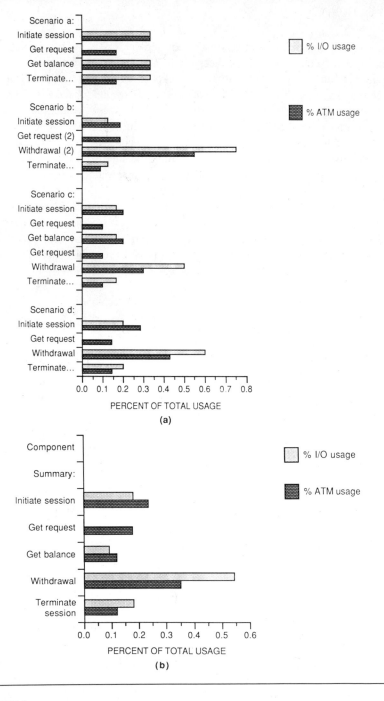

FIGURE 6.3
Graphical ATM Model Results. The percentage of I/O and ATM use by each scenario component is in (a); the total resource usage of ATM software components for all scenarios is in (b).

6.2.3 Alternatives

Traditional system tuning seeks configuration solutions, such as upgrading hardware or allocating files differently to reduce I/O contention. SPE suggests also exploring software solutions such as:

- □ Reducing resource requests by changing software functions and processing characteristics
- □ Reducing resource requests by changing the software design

The general principles identify potential improvements. This section demonstrates applying the centering principle to give ATM alternatives.

The ATM results in Table 6.1 show that in some cases the number of ATMs is a bottleneck; in other cases the I/O subsystem saturates first. Software improvements should reduce either the number of requests, V_i, to the ATM and I/O subsystem, reduce the time to service a request, S_i, or both. The **centering principle** suggests identifying dominant workload functions and minimizing their processing. The user representatives specify that they expect 90 percent of the sessions to be Scenario (d)—1 withdrawal per session. The centering principle suggests reducing ATM visits by determining the characteristics (the account and the amount) of typical withdrawals and creating a Quick withdrawal transaction that uses these defaults rather than asking the customer.

Figure 6.4 shows the revised scenario. The first two components are the same. When the request is Quick withdrawal, there are no further user interactions (ATM visits) and correspondingly fewer instructions executed. By changing the functions provided to users, this proposed alternative reduces the software's resource requirements; it reduces both V_i for the ATM and S_i for the CPU.

Evaluate alternatives by:

- □ Revising the software model to reflect the proposed changes
- □ Repeating the previous analysis steps

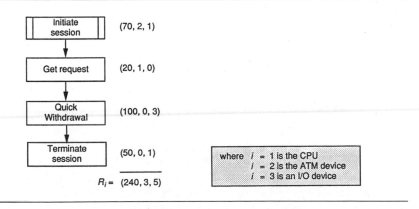

FIGURE 6.4
The ATM Quick Withdrawal Scenario and Its Computer Resource Requirements.

Figure 6.4 shows the revised software model's R_i. The revision produces new parameters for the elementary system execution model: The number of ATM visits decreases, and the CPU service time changes. Other alternatives may also change the IPG topology. Solve the system execution model again to see the new performance metrics.

Table 6.1's Case 8 shows the results for the ATM. Note the dramatic improvement: The quick withdrawal takes only 3.4 seconds on the average, and the *overall* average response time reduces to 4.0 seconds from 7.6 for Case 5. The maximum throughput increases from 6.95 customers per second to 11.1 with the same hardware configuration. The 50 ATMs are no longer the bottleneck. Of course, this assumes that 90 percent of the sessions will use quick withdrawal.

Many ATMs have a default withdrawal amount aimed at matching the needs of most ATM customers. Note that an improved version of Quick withdrawal lets customers define their own "usual session" when they set up their ATM account. One might be "Give me the maximum you allow." A college student might request the minimum amount; others may wish to see their balance first. The result is that users could request their "usual session," which may comprise several transactions, with one ATM interaction. This greatly increases the probability that users select the streamlined option. It dramatically improves system performance and improves customer satisfaction. It is simple to implement if included early in the requirements definition phase.

Table 6.1 shows results of several model solutions. All require *minor* changes to the model between solutions. For example, after defining and solving the model for Case 3 (four scenarios equally likely), the modification for Case 4 (different workload mix) and Case 5 (higher arrival rate) only requires a change to the arrival rate parameters. Case 6 (think time) only requires a change to the service time for one node (ATM). Case 7 (I/O balance) only requires changing the visits to the DEV nodes. Thus, the eight models can easily be created and solved in a half-hour or less (with appropriate modeling tools such as those described in Section 5.5).

6.3 Case Studies

This section presents the case study results and identifies and evaluates alternatives. The explanation of results illustrates the presentation methods prescribed in Section 6.1. (Some details are occasionally omitted for brevity.) Let us review the software models and the model assumptions before considering the results and alternatives. The models were developed in earlier chapters: Section 3.3 (pages 138 to 152) specifies the model data, Section 4.2 (pages 170 to 174) defines the software execution model, Section 4.4 (pages 198 to 212) produces the software execution model results, and Section 5.4 (pages 265 to 271) defines the system execution model.

6.3.1 Review of Software Models

Figure 6.5 shows the DRAWMOD software model developed thus far. The processing it represents is summarized in Example 6.2.

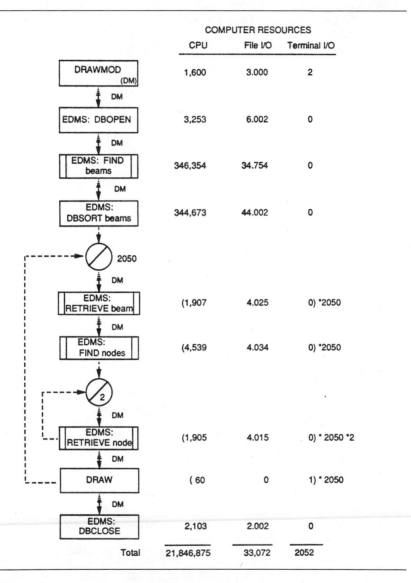

	COMPUTER RESOURCES		
	CPU	File I/O	Terminal I/O
DRAWMOD (DM)	1,600	3.000	2
EDMS: DBOPEN	3,253	6.002	0
EDMS: FIND beams	346,354	34.754	0
EDMS: DBSORT beams	344,673	44.002	0
EDMS: RETRIEVE beam	(1,907	4.025	0) *2050
EDMS: FIND nodes	(4,539	4.034	0) *2050
EDMS: RETRIEVE node	(1,905	4.015	0) * 2050 *2
DRAW	(60	0	1) * 2050
EDMS: DBCLOSE	2,103	2.002	0
Total	21,846,875	33,072	2052

FIGURE 6.5
The DRAWMOD Scenario and Computer Resource Requirements. Note that the total for CPU instructions differs slightly from Chapter 4's results—see footnote 2.

EXAMPLE 6.2: DRAWMOD Processing Review

To view an aircraft model on a graphics screen, the user requests the DRAWMOD transaction and enters the desired model number. The software execution begins with the DRAWMOD driver. It first calls the EDMS routine DBOPEN to open the beam and node tables. Then DRAWMOD calls the EDMS routine FIND to locate all the beam rows for the selected model. Then DRAWMOD calls EDMS's DBSORT to order them in ascending sequence. For each beam (2,050 of them), DRAMOD calls EDMS's RETRIEVE to get the beam row and uses its node numbers to FIND the (two) node rows for the beam. DRAWMOD calls EDMS RETRIEVE (twice) to get the node rows, then uses their coordinates to DRAW the beams on the graphics screen. After all 2,050 beams are drawn, DRAWMOD calls EDMS DBCLOSE to close the tables, and its processing is complete.   □

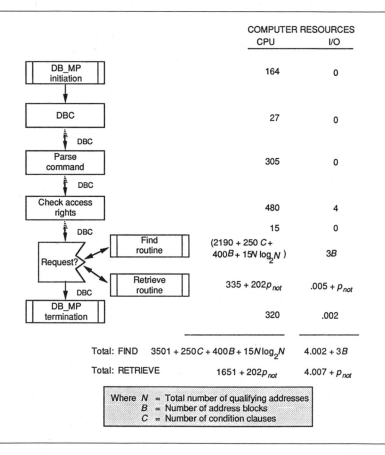

COMPUTER RESOURCES

	CPU	I/O
DB_MP initiation	164	0
DBC	27	0
Parse command	305	0
Check access rights	480	4
	15	0
Find routine	$(2190 + 250C + 400B + 15N \log_2 N)$	$3B$
Retrieve routine	$335 + 202p_{not}$	$.005 + p_{not}$
DB_MP termination	320	.002

Total: FIND $3501 + 250C + 400B + 15N\log_2 N$ $4.002 + 3B$

Total: RETRIEVE $1651 + 202p_{not}$ $4.007 + p_{not}$

Where N = Total number of qualifying addresses
B = Number of address blocks
C = Number of condition clauses

FIGURE 6.6
The EDMS: DBC Processing Scenario.

After a processing review, most SPE presentations next review the performance specifications for the scenario and each software component. Our case study also models EDMS and the Network Operating System, so we review their processing before discussing specifications.

Figure 6.6 shows the Data Base Control (DBC) routine invoked for each of the EDMS calls. Its processing is summarized in Example 6.3.

EXAMPLE 6.3: EDMS: DBC Processing Review

DB_MP is the EDMS message routine that communicates with other processes. DB_MP Initiation receives requests; when they are to be processed by Data Base Control, DB_MP Initiation transfers control to the DBC driver. Then DBC calls Parse Command to decipher the request. DBC then calls Check Access Rights to confirm the user's authority, and upon successful completion calls the appropriate routine to process the request. These models assume either the Find or Retrieve routine is called. (More comprehensive models would also include the other EDMS routines.) After the Find or Retrieve completes, DB_MP Termination communicates the results back to the application software.   □

The software models for the Find and Retrieve routines are shown in Figures 6.7 and 6.8, respectively. Their processing descriptions are omitted. (The steps were introduced in Examples 3.8 and 3.9 if you wish to review.)

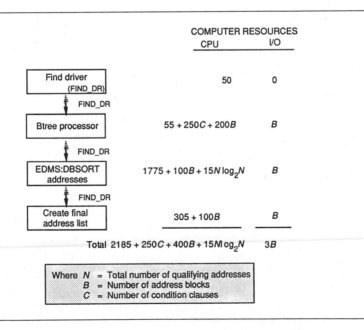

FIGURE 6.7
The Find Routine Software Execution Model.

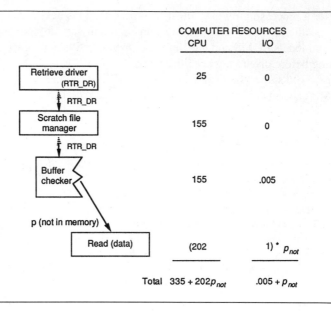

FIGURE 6.8
The Retrieve Routine Software Execution Model.

The Network Operating System provides the interprocess communication between DRAWMOD and EDMS. Figure 6.9 shows the processing required.

EXAMPLE 6.4: EDMS Call Processing Review

Each time DRAWMOD calls EDMS, the processing in Figure 6.9 takes place. First, the call processing code formats the EDMS request message, then SENDs it (through SYS_EXEC), and waits to RECEIVE the reply. Note that EDMS also SENDs its reply through SYS_EXEC (within DBC's DB_MP Terminate component), so the communication processing executes twice for each EDMS call.

□

The processing description for SYS_EXEC is omitted here. It is described in Section 4.2 and depicted in Figure 4.19. Its software models are analyzed in Figures 4.35 and 4.36. Network Operating System processing is also required to Establish, Open, Release, and Delete communication channels. Only SEND and RECEIVE are explicitly modeled here, to reduce the complexity of the case studies.

Next consider the software model results for FIND and RETRIEVE. In your presentation, illustrate how to compute the computer resources from the software

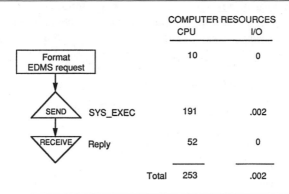

FIGURE 6.9
The EDMS Call Processing Scenario.

resource requirements for a few key components. Then show the calculated resource requirements for each node. The following explanation starts with the calculated resource requirements for FIND and RETRIEVE and uses their results in DRAWMOD.

EXAMPLE 6.5: Explanation of Computer Resource Requirements

Note that the Find routine in Figure 6.7 takes $2185 + 250C + 400B + 15N\log_2 N$ CPU instructions and $3B$ I/Os. We use these totals for the Find's expanded node in Figure 6.6; we add an additional 5 instructions for control flow. We derive the results for the Retrieve routine similarly. The total computer resources for EDMS FIND and its DBC processing are in 6.6: $3501 + 250C + 400B + 15N\log_2 N$ instructions and $4.002 + 3B$ I/Os. The totals for EDMS RETRIEVE are also shown in the figure.

Figure 6.5 shows the computer resource requirements for DRAWMOD components. We specify software resource requirements for the DRAWMOD driver, DBOPEN, DBSORT, DRAW, and DBCLOSE. We calculate computer resource requirements from them (as in Section 4.3.2). The FINDs and RETRIEVEs are calculated from the formulas in Figure 6.6, with appropriate substitutions for the data-dependent variables B, C, N, and p_{not}. For example, FIND beams uses: $B = N/200$, which assumes 200 addresses per block; $C = 1$ for the model number condition clause; and $N = 2050$ for the specified number of beams in the model.

$\square$

The other data-dependent variable assignments are in Example 4.13. Include the data-dependent variable assignments in your presentation. Each component in the DRAWMOD scenario also includes control-flow overhead. Figure 6.9 shows that each EDMS call requires 253 instructions and 0.002 I/Os. In your presentation, you may wish to show how to derive the result for SEND to SYS_EXEC from its software models, and how to include the call processing in the DRAWMOD resource requirements. Then proceed to the results explained in Example 6.6.

EXAMPLE 6.6: Explanation of Results

The total computer resource requirements for DRAWMOD are:

21,846,875	CPU instructions[2]
33,072	I/Os
2,052	Terminal I/Os

If the average time to process each request (w_i) is .0000006 for the CPU, 0.03 per I/O, and 0.01 per Terminal I/O (from Section 5.4), then the best-case response time for one user with no contention delays is:

21,846,875 × .0000006	13
33,072 × .03	992
2,052 × .01	21
	1,026 sec ≈ 17 min.

This best case greatly exceeds the performance goal specification of 20 seconds for up to 10 users.

□

Because the best case greatly exceeds the performance goal, there is little need to model the worst case. You may wish to examine the sensitivity to the number of users and present results such as those in Tables 5.11 and 5.12. They show that with 10 users the response time increases to 1,970 seconds, or approximately 33 minutes *average* to draw the model on the screen. The next step is to examine the problems and seek alternatives.

6.3.2 Identify Problems

Section 5.3.1 described how to create visuals that relate computer resource usage to software component usage. Section 5.4 produced graphs for DRAWMOD that identify the I/O bottleneck and show the software components with the highest I/O usage. These and other charts can be incorporated into your presentation to offer insight into the cause of the problems and their potential solution, as shown in Example 6.7.

---

[2]This total differs slightly from the results in Chapter 4. These results come from a tool that carries more significant digits. So, for example, the total CPU instructions computed for RETRIEVE nodes is 1905.19, and the total computed for RETRIEVE beams is 1907.16. These occur in loops, so the totals differ from earlier computations that used integers. The tool also evaluated the alternatives presented later, so they may not match your hand calculations.

EXAMPLE 6.7: Explanation of Performance Bottleneck

Figure 6.10(a) shows the average DRAWMOD response times as the number of users increases from 1 to 10. It also shows that the I/O residence time accounts for most of the long response. Figure 6.10(b) confirms that the I/O subsystem is the bottleneck, even though we made the optimistic assumption that I/Os are equally distributed across devices. Figure 6.10(c) identifies the three software components that use the most I/O: RETRIEVE beams, FIND nodes, and RETRIEVE nodes. This is primarily because of the large number of times these components are repeated.

□

Note that this model charges all the resources required by EDMS and by SYS_EXEC interprocess communication to the DRAWMOD scenario. First, we look for application scenario improvements; later we examine the other software. Improvements to the lower-level software can have a dramatic effect at higher levels.

6.3.3 Identify and Evaluate Alternatives

We seek ways to reduce the number of physical I/Os. A standard system tuning improvement increases block sizes to reduce I/Os. Increasing block size is an example of the **processing versus frequency tradeoff principle**—do more work for each I/O and thus reduce the number of I/Os. It is relatively easy to evaluate the effect of this alternative, as shown in the following example.

EXAMPLE 6.8: Larger Block Size Alternative

The data-dependent parameters B and p_{not} represent the performance effect of block sizes. The original scenario has 200 addresses per block. We examine the improvement with 1,000 addresses per block.

$$B = \frac{N}{1000}$$

The original scenario assumes 4K data blocks. Increase data blocks to 20K and examine the performance effect of these increases. For beams, 20,480 bytes per block and 64 bytes per record yield 320 records per block, so

Beams: $p_{not} = \frac{1}{320} = .00313$

For nodes, 20,480 bytes per block and 24 bytes per record yield 853 records per block, so

Nodes: $p_{not} = \frac{1}{853} = .00117$

Figure 6.11 shows the computer resources derived with the new data-dependent parameters. The best-case response is 994 seconds. Performance improves with larger block sizes, but not enough to meet the 20-second response time goal.

□

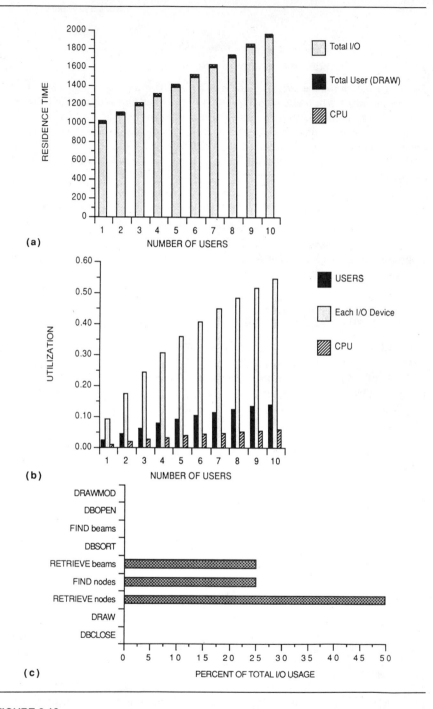

FIGURE 6.10
Case Study Bottleneck Analysis. The DRAWMOD residence time is in (a); the DRAWMOD device utilization is in (b); and the I/Os by DRAWMOD component is in (c).

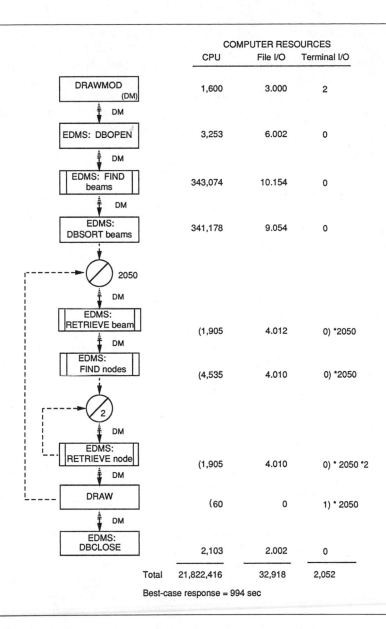

| | COMPUTER RESOURCES | | |
	CPU	File I/O	Terminal I/O
DRAWMOD (DM)	1,600	3.000	2
EDMS: DBOPEN	3,253	6.002	0
EDMS: FIND beams	343,074	10.154	0
EDMS: DBSORT beams	341,178	9.054	0
2050			
EDMS: RETRIEVE beam	(1,905	4.012	0) *2050
EDMS: FIND nodes	(4,535	4.010	0) *2050
2			
EDMS: RETRIEVE node	(1,905	4.010	0) * 2050 *2
DRAW	(60	0	1) * 2050
EDMS: DBCLOSE	2,103	2.002	0
Total	21,822,416	32,918	2,052

Best-case response = 994 sec

FIGURE 6.11
DRAWMOD Scenario Analysis with Larger Block Size for Beam and Node Data.
The best-case response time reduces to 994 seconds.

Note that block size increase may cause memory problems. Nevertheless, our first analysis optimistically ignores memory effects. We wish to see if the best case meets the performance goals. If not, we explore other alternatives; if so, we proceed with sensitivity analyses and with more realistic models (discussed in Chapter 8 and 9) that include memory and other processing details.

Most of the I/Os are for finding and retrieving nodes. The next alternative applies the **fixing-point principle** to reduce the number of FINDs and RETRIEVEs.

EXAMPLE 6.9: Node Retrievals Needed?

Consider the sample portion of the engineer's aircraft model in Figure 6.12(a). Part of the model is exploded to show beam and node numbers. Consider the processing that occurs when we RETRIEVE the data for beam 21. We FIND nodes 42 and 43, RETRIEVE each of them, and draw the beam. Then we RETRIEVE beam 22, FIND nodes 43 and 44, and RETRIEVE each of them. Note that we already have the data for node 43. By recognizing this and fixing its coordinates with the data we have in memory, we need not repeat its FIND or its RETRIEVE. This happens if the beams are numbered so that adjacent beams are processed in order. We check with users and find that adjacent beam numbers are ordered to facilitate this alternative.

The rest of Figure 6.12 shows how to revise the software models to evaluate the performance effect. It models two cases: Part (b) shows the case when we need 2 nodes (for model borders), and (c) shows the model for 1 FIND and RETRIEVE. The DRAWMOD scenario is revised in (d) to show the two cases. We first evaluate with conservative probabilities (provided by users) for the two cases:

- ▢ 90% are interior beams.
- ▢ 10% are on a boundary.

Note that we (arbitrarily) examine the additive improvement of these alternatives, so Figure 6.12 also uses larger block sizes. The results show another improvement, 796 seconds best-case response, but still not enough.

□

Next we apply the **locality-design principle** to further reduce the number of FINDs and RETRIEVEs. Note the relatively large amount of processing required to associate node coordinates with their beams. There are at least two alternatives. One possibility is to store node coordinates within the beam rows, which improves the locality of beam and node data *for this scenario*. This has the advantage of eliminating the FIND and RETRIEVE for nodes. Check your understanding of the model revision and analysis process, and compute the computer resources for this alternative.

Database specialists will notice that this alternative has the disadvantage that the revised database is *not normalized*. For example, the same node coordinates for node 43 would appear in three different beam rows. Not only is more storage required for replicated data, but it complicates updates when multiple rows must remain consistent. In this scenario, updates are not a problem because node coordi-

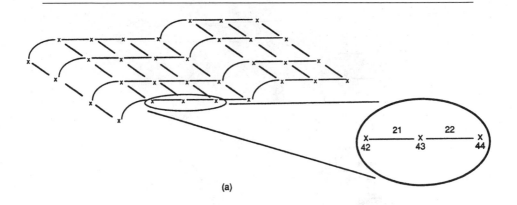

(a)

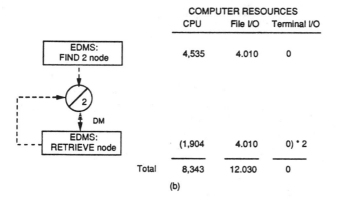

	COMPUTER RESOURCES		
	CPU	File I/O	Terminal I/O
EDMS: FIND 2 node	4,535	4.010	0
EDMS: RETRIEVE node	(1,904	4.010	0) * 2
Total	8,343	12.030	0

(b)

	COMPUTER RESOURCES		
	CPU	File I/O	Terminal I/O
EDMS: FIND 1 nodes	4,004	4.007	0
EDMS: RETRIEVE node	1,904	4.010	0
Total	5,908	8.017	0

(c)

(continued)

FIGURE 6.12
A sample drawing to be displayed by DRAWMOD is in (a). Note that both beam 21 and 22 need the coordinates for node 43. The subgraph in (b) gets both nodes for a beam; the subgraph in (c) gets one node; the modified DRAWMOD scenario in (d) has a case node to decide which subgraph executes.

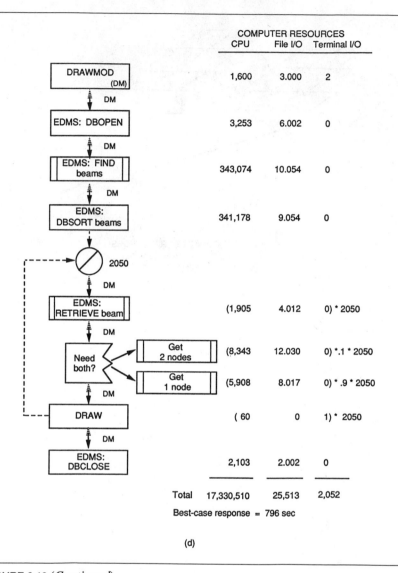

| | COMPUTER RESOURCES | | |
	CPU	File I/O	Terminal I/O
DRAWMOD (DM)	1,600	3.000	2
EDMS: DBOPEN	3,253	6.002	0
EDMS: FIND beams	343,074	10.054	0
EDMS: DBSORT beams	341,178	9.054	0
2050			
EDMS: RETRIEVE beam	(1,905	4.012	0) * 2050
Get 2 nodes	(8,343	12.030	0) *.1 * 2050
Get 1 node	(5,908	8.017	0) * .9 * 2050
DRAW	(60	0	1) * 2050
EDMS: DBCLOSE	2,103	2.002	0
Total	17,330,510	25,513	2,052

Best-case response = 796 sec

(d)

FIGURE 6.12 (*Continued*)

nates seldom change unless an entirely new model is generated. So it may be appropriate to use a non-normalized database. To decide, we would evaluate the effect on other scenarios to see whether beam and node information are frequently needed together or separately, and consider other costs and benefits.

Next, we model another alternative (Example 6.10) for improving the locality of beam and node information, even though they are physically stored in separate relations. Note that this scenario needs all the beams and all the nodes in the aircraft model. Furthermore, node information is used multiple times. **Locality improves** (and the fixing point is earlier) if we extract all the beam and node information once and store it in a table within the DRAWMOD program for later processing.

EXAMPLE 6.10: Retrieve Beams and Nodes Once

Figure 6.13 shows the proposed scenario alternative. After the DBOPEN, FIND beams, and DBSORT beams, we repeat RETRIEVE to get all beams and store them in a table. Then we FIND all nodes for the model and repeat RETRIEVE to get and store them in a table. After the extraction, a loop Matches the beam and node coordinates with a simple table lookup, and DRAWs. Then we DBCLOSE as usual. We could close after the extraction, before the DRAW loop, but it would not change the computer resources for this model.

The performance specifications for each component are the same as before, except for the data-dependent variables for FIND nodes:

N = number of nodes per model = 1500

$\log_2 N \approx 11$

$C = 1$ (all nodes for model)

$B = \dfrac{N}{1000} = 1.5$

The computer resources are again reduced, and the best-case response becomes 454 seconds.

$\square$

Next we apply the **centering principle** and study the advantage of adding a new EDMS function. The dominant EDMS workload function in the last alternative extracts large amounts of data from the database. We evaluate DRAWMOD's performance with a proposed new routine to RETRIEVE logical blocks of data with one call: EDMS: RETRIEVE BLOCK.

EXAMPLE 6.11: Retrieve Logical Blocks

Figure 6.14 replaces the two RETRIEVEs with RETRIEVE BLOCK. Consider the performance specifications. Suppose that RETRIEVE BLOCK can SEND 4K of data through SYS_EXEC at a time.[3] Then RETRIEVE BLOCK is called once for each 4K message, so

$$\frac{2050 \text{ beams}}{64 \text{ per 4K message}} = 33 \text{ calls for beams}$$

$$\frac{1500 \text{ nodes}}{170 \text{ per 4K message}} = 9 \text{ calls for nodes}$$

(continued)

---

[3]The specifications in Chapter 3 call for 64-byte message blocks. Chapter 8 uses 4K blocks. We arbitrarily use 4K for this example. Chapter 6 exercises and Chapter 8 examine the effect of different message sizes.

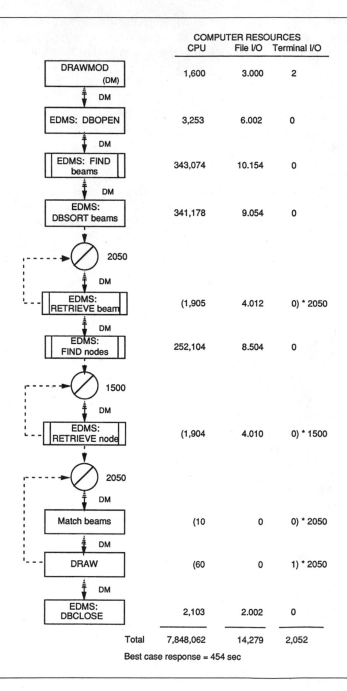

	COMPUTER RESOURCES		
	CPU	File I/O	Terminal I/O
DRAWMOD (DM)	1,600	3.000	2
EDMS: DBOPEN	3,253	6.002	0
EDMS: FIND beams	343,074	10.154	0
EDMS: DBSORT beams	341,178	9.054	0
EDMS: RETRIEVE beam	(1,905	4.012	0) * 2050
EDMS: FIND nodes	252,104	8.504	0
EDMS: RETRIEVE node	(1,904	4.010	0) * 1500
Match beams	(10	0	0) * 2050
DRAW	(60	0	1) * 2050
EDMS: DBCLOSE	2,103	2.002	0
Total	7,848,062	14,279	2,052

Best case response = 454 sec

FIGURE 6.13
DRAWMOD Modifications to Extract All Beam and Node Data Once.

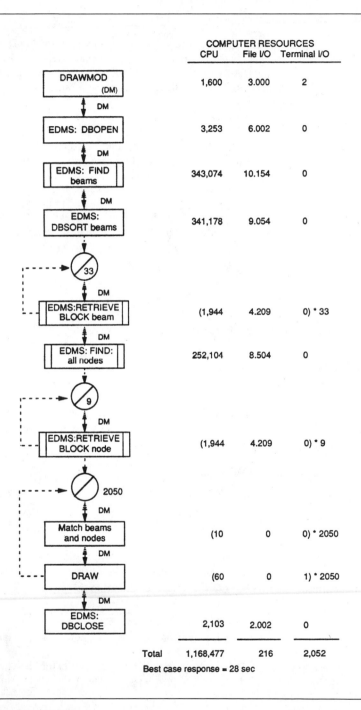

| | COMPUTER RESOURCES | | |
	CPU	File I/O	Terminal I/O
DRAWMOD (DM)	1,600	3.000	2
EDMS: DBOPEN	3,253	6.002	0
EDMS: FIND beams	343,074	10.154	0
EDMS: DBSORT beams	341,178	9.054	0
EDMS:RETRIEVE BLOCK beam	(1,944	4.209	0) * 33
EDMS: FIND: all nodes	252,104	8.504	0
EDMS:RETRIEVE BLOCK node	(1,944	4.209	0) * 9
Match beams and nodes	(10	0	0) * 2050
DRAW	(60	0	1) * 2050
EDMS: DBCLOSE	2,103	2.002	0
Total	1,168,477	216	2,052

Best case response = 28 sec

FIGURE 6.14
DRAWMOD Modifications to Retrieve a Logical Block with One EDMS Call.

EXAMPLE 6.11 (*Continued*)

We make the simplifying assumption that the resource requirements for FIND and RE-
TRIEVE BLOCK are the same as the previous version of FIND and RETRIEVE,[4] except
for the following data-dependent parameter change. If we physically store the beam and
node data in 20K blocks, and RETRIEVE BLOCK gets 4K at a time, then

$$p_{not} = \frac{4K}{20K} = .2 \text{ for beams and nodes}$$

Figure 6.14 shows the results for each component and overall. This alternative dramatically
reduces the computer resource requirements, and the best-case response becomes 28 seconds.

□

The performance goal is 20 seconds with up to 10 users; we have 28 seconds
with 1 user, so we continue to evaluate alternatives. Note that the last alternative
moves the bottleneck to the Terminal I/O—20.52 seconds of the 28 is in DRAW.
The next alternative (Example 6.12) applies the **locality-design principle** to hardware selection.

EXAMPLE 6.12: Hardware Alternatives: Concurrent Graphics

The scenario model assumes that DRAWMOD must wait for graphics commands to complete. If we select a workstation with a separate graphics processor, we can execute graphics
(drawing) commands concurrently with database and other processing.[5] Suppose we can
reduce DRAWMOD's delay for Terminal I/O (to draw) from 0.01 seconds to 0.001
seconds with different hardware. The other computer resource requirements remain the
same:

$$R_i = (1,168,477, \quad 216, \quad 2,052)$$

The average time to process each request, w_i, becomes

$$w_i = (.0000006, .03, .001)$$

So the best-case response time becomes 10 seconds.

□

At this point we can construct the system execution model to examine the
performance as we increase the number of users. We first study additional improvement alternatives within EDMS to further illustrate the process as it applies
to system software.

---

[4]If they differ, revise their software model accordingly, and use new resource requirement
equations for DRAWMOD.

[5]Other hardware solutions are also viable, such as building the model image in a memory
frame buffer and displaying it with one Terminal I/O. The example shown is simple and
suffices to demonstrate the technique.

6.3.4 EDMS Analysis

Figure 6.15 graphs the average CPU and I/O resource usage of the DBC processing scenario components. The average I/O requirements per EDMS call, the
average profile for the Find routine components, and Retrieve routine's average
profile are in Figure 6.15(a). The graph shows that, on the average, most I/O
occurs in the Find routine, and within it, I/O is distributed evenly across three of
the four components. Figure 6.15(b) shows the same breakdown for CPU requirements.

One improvement alternative applies the **fixing-point principle** to reduce
FIND's I/O by eliminating the address sort. To do this, we need to either maintain
the desired order each time we add or delete rows, or relax the requirement that the
address list be ordered. First we examine the performance effect on this scenario of
eliminating the sort. Then, if it appears to be desirable, we study its feasibility by
analyzing the effect on other scenarios—of maintaining order or relaxing the
requirement (and analyze the effect on implementation, maintenance, and other
development concerns). Note that if we elect to maintain the addresses in primary
key sequence (beam sequence), we can also eliminate DRAWMOD's DBSORT
beams. Figure 6.16 applies this alternative to FIND.

EXAMPLE 6.13: Maintain Beam and Node Order

The Find routine model omits DBSORT. The total computer resource requirements are (410
+ 250C + 300B) instructions and 2B I/Os. Substitute these values into the DBC processing
computation, and you get (1726 + 250C + 300B) instructions and (4.002 + 2B) I/Os.
   For FIND beams,

$$B = \frac{2050}{1000}, C = 1$$

So,

   R_i = (2591, 8.102, 0) (plus EDMS call processing)

   For FIND nodes,

$$B = \frac{1500}{1000}, C = 1$$

So,

   R_i = (2426, 7.002, 0) (plus EDMS call processing)

Table 6.2 uses these results to examine the effect on DRAWMOD. The best-case response
time becomes 8.3 seconds. It improves, but since we have greatly reduced the number of
FINDs with other alternatives, the effect is not as dramatic as with earlier options. Note,
however, that if you first consider this improvement to the original scenario, its improvement is much greater.

                                                                              □

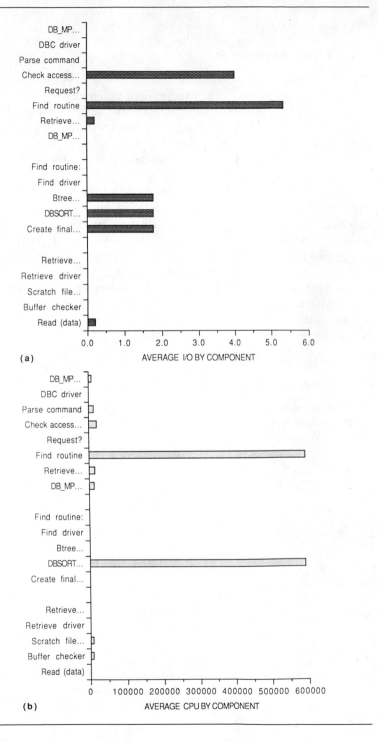

(a)

AVERAGE I/O BY COMPONENT

(b)

AVERAGE CPU BY COMPONENT

FIGURE 6.15
DBC Processing Scenario Component's Resource Usage.

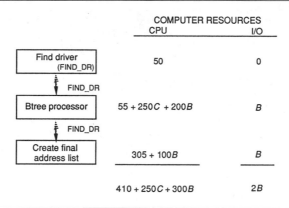

FIGURE 6.16
Find Routine Modifications to Maintain Beam and Node Order.

Next consider the graphs in Figure 6.17, which show the total resource requirements for all EDMS calls in this scenario (2 FINDs + 42 RETRIEVE BLOCKs). These graphs show that most I/Os now occur in the Check access rights component. They occur because designers propose to keep access information, such as access privileges to tables and lock-share status, in an "internal" database relation. So when a user wants to FIND or RETRIEVE, the corresponding DBC routines do an internal Find and Retrieve to get the access rights.

One alternative (Example 6.14) applies the **locality-design principle**. When a user first accesses the database, we will extract the access rights from the internal relation and temporarily maintain it in a file of "active access rights" that can be checked more quickly.

TABLE 6.2
DRAWMOD PROCESSING

Node	CPU	I/O	Terminal I/O
DRAWMOD	1,600	3.000	2
EDMS:DBOPEN	3,253	6.002	0
EDMS:FIND beams	2,844	8.104	0
EDMS:RETRIEVE BLOCK beams	(1,944	4.209	0) * 33
EDMS:FIND all nodes	2,679	7.004	0
EDMS:RETRIEVE BLOCK nodes	(1,944	4.209	0) * 9
Match beams & nodes	(10	0	0) * 2050
DRAW	(60	0	1) * 2050
EDMS:DBCLOSE	2,103	2.002	0
Total	237,644	203	2,052
Best-case response = 8.3 seconds			

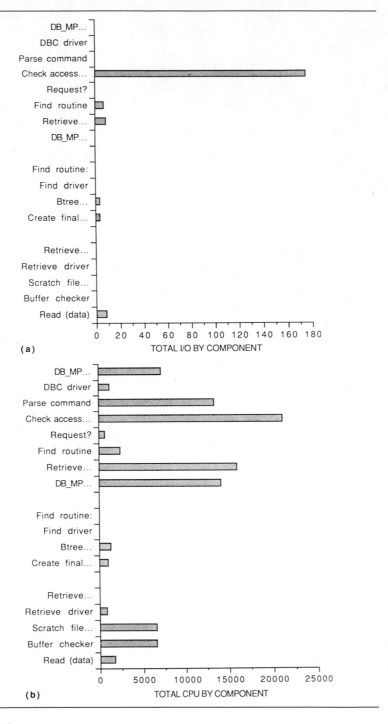

FIGURE 6.17
Resource Requirement Profile for All EDMS Calls with All SPE Improvements.

EXAMPLE 6.14: Access Rights in File

To analyze the effect, reduce the number of I/Os for Check access rights from 4 to 1. This also reduces the number of instructions (100 per I/O). Use a conservative assumption that the number of instructions otherwise remains the same as before. Again, we only evaluate the performance effect on checking access rights (without the initialization processing). If it appears desirable, we then examine the effect on DBOPEN or whichever routine builds and maintains the active access rights.

So the revised computer resource requirements for Check access rights becomes (180, 1, 0). The total computer resource requirements for EDMS: DBC processing becomes:

EDMS: FIND

$$R_i = (1426 + 250C + 300B, 1.002 + 2B, 0)$$

For FIND beams,

$$B = \frac{2050}{1000}, C = 1$$

So,

$$R_i = (2291, 5.102, 0) \text{ (plus EDMS call processing)}$$

For FIND nodes,

$$B = \frac{1500}{1000}, C = 1$$

So

$$R_i = (2126, 4.002, 0) \text{ (plus EDMS call processing)}$$

EDMS: RETRIEVE BLOCK

$$R_i = (1351 + 202p_{not}, 1.007 + p_{not}, 0)$$

From Example 6.11, $p_{not} = 0.2$ for beams and nodes, so

$$R_i = (1391, 1.207, 0) \text{ (plus EDMS call processing)}$$

Table 6.3 uses these results to calculate the effect on DRAWMOD. The best-case response becomes 4.3 seconds.

□

6.3.5 Summary of Software Alternatives

Table 6.4 consolidates and summarizes the results for the original scenario and for each of the alternatives in Examples 6.8 through 6.14. Note the dramatic reduction

TABLE 6.3
ACCESS RIGHTS IN FILE: DRAWMOD PROCESSING

Node	CPU	I/O	Terminal I/O
DRAWMOD	1,600	3.000	2
EDMS:DBOPEN	3,253	6.002	0
EDMS:FIND beams	2,544	5.104	0
EDMS:RETRIEVE BLOCK beams	(1,644	1.209	0) * 33
EDMS:FIND all nodes	2,379	4.004	0
EDMS:RETRIEVE BLOCK nodes	(1,644	1.209	0) * 9
Match beams & nodes	(10	0	0) * 2050
DRAW	(60	0	1) * 2050
EDMS:DBCLOSE	2,103	2.002	1
Total	224,427	70.890	2,052

Best-case response = 4.3 seconds

in the best-case response from 17 minutes to 4 seconds with relatively minor changes. Many are minor only if detected early in design, however. After code is written, changes for some could be so extensive that they would be infeasible. The study is not yet complete. To be thorough we need to factor in details we omitted for viable alternatives, such as line 8's processing to extract access rights and load them into an active file. We may also want to consider different combinations of alternatives, such as all except Case 7.

Table 6.4 shows alternatives for DRAWMOD application software design, EDMS software requirements and design, and hardware alternatives. Even though this book focuses on software performance, one should not rule out hardware solutions to performance problems. Experienced SPE proponents, however, advocate consciously choosing hardware solutions *early* in development, based on quantitative data on alternatives. We did not consider SYS_EXEC alternatives in these examples, though many are possible. Consideration of SYS_EXEC message

TABLE 6.4
SUMMARY SOFTWARE MODEL RESULTS

Case	CPU	I/O	Terminal I/O	Best-case response
1. Original scenario	21,846,875	33,072	2,052	1,026
2. Larger block size	21,822,416	32,918	2,052	994
3. Node retrievals needed?	17,330,510	25,513	2,052	796
4. Retrieve beams & nodes once	7,848,062	14,279	2,052	454
5. Retrieve logical blocks	1,168,477	216	2,052	28
6. Concurrent graphics	1,168,477	216	2,052	10
7. Maintain beam & node order	237,644	203	2,052	8.3
8. Access rights in file	224,427	71	2,052	4.3

buffer size is deferred to Chapter 8's more detailed models of interprocess communication.

6.3.6 System Execution Model

The next analysis step selects viable alternatives and uses them in the system execution models to assess the impact of contention delays on response time, and the sensitivity to various parameters. Figure 6.18 uses Table 6.4, line 8's resource requirements in a system execution model to analyze the effect of increasing the number of users. The Elementary IPG topology is in Figure 6.18, and the model parameters are in Table 6.5. Tables 6.6 and 6.7 show the results. The device residence times and the average response time are in Table 6.6. The results show that the average response time remains under 5 seconds with up to 10 users. Table 6.7 shows device utilizations and explains why response time stays low for more users (device utilizations are very low). The tables show the USERS utilization is high—most of it due to the 5-minute think time. Figure 6.19 graphs the response time and the proportions of CPU, I/O, and Terminal I/O (to draw). It indicates that further response time improvements require reducing one or more of the follow-

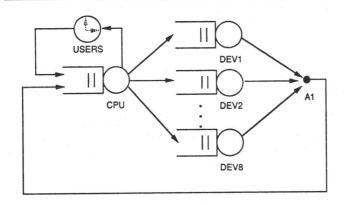

Number of users: Maximum 10

Think time: 5 minutes

DRAWMOD scenario: R_i = (224,427, 71, 2052)

Where i = 1 is CPU
i = 2 is I/O subsystem
i = 3 is Terminal I/O (Users)

FIGURE 6.18
The System Execution Model with the Revised DRAWMOD Computer Resource Requirements.

TABLE 6.5
REVISED SYSTEM EXECUTION MODEL PARAMETERS

Node	# visits, V_i*	Avg. time to process a request, w_i	Mean service time, S_i
USERS	2052	$\dfrac{300 + (2051)(.001)}{2052}$	.14720
DEV1	9	.03	.03
DEV2	9	.03	.03
DEV3	9	.03	.03
DEV4	9	.03	.03
DEV5	9	.03	.03
DEV6	9	.03	.03
DEV7	9	.03	.03
DEV8	9	.03	.03
A1	72		
CPU	2,124	.0000006	.0000633

*The I/Os were arbitrarily increased to 72 because it divides evenly across 8 devices.

ing: the time to draw, the number of I/Os, or the I/O service time. All are feasible and relatively easy, but if designers adopt the alternatives included in Table 6.4's line 8, further reductions are unnecessary because they achieve the specified performance goal.

TABLE 6.6
CASE STUDY: REVISED SYSTEM EXECUTION MODEL RESIDENCE AND RESPONSE TIMES

Number of users	USERS*	Each I/O visit	Each I/O device	Total I/O	Each CPU visit	Total CPU	Response time
1	2.05100	0.03000	0.27	2.16000	0.00006	0.13466	4.346
2	2.05100	0.03003	0.27	2.16192	0.00006	0.13472	4.348
3	2.05100	0.03005	0.27	2.16384	0.00006	0.13478	4.350
4	2.05100	0.03008	0.27	2.16576	0.00006	0.13484	4.352
5	2.05100	0.03011	0.27	2.16769	0.00006	0.13489	4.354
6	2.05100	0.03013	0.27	2.16962	0.00006	0.13495	4.356
7	2.05100	0.03016	0.27	2.17155	0.00006	0.13501	4.358
8	2.05100	0.03019	0.27	2.17348	0.00006	0.13507	4.360
9	2.05100	0.03021	0.27	2.17542	0.00006	0.13513	4.362
10	2.05100	0.03024	0.27	2.17737	0.00006	0.13519	4.364

*Note that the USERS residence time excludes the think time.

TABLE 6.7
CASE STUDY:
REVISED MODEL UTILIZATIONS

Number of users	USERS	Each I/O device	CPU
1	0.09925	0.00089	0.00044
2	0.19849	0.00177	0.00088
3	0.29773	0.00266	0.00133
4	0.39698	0.00355	0.00177
5	0.49622	0.00444	0.00221
6	0.59546	0.00532	0.00265
7	0.69470	0.00621	0.00310
8	0.79393	0.00710	0.00354
9	0.89317	0.00798	0.00398
10	0.99240	0.00887	0.00442

The next analysis step is to conduct sensitivity studies, vary workload mixes, and verify and validate models as in Table 6.1. Chapter exercises confirm your understanding of these additional analyses.

This concludes the comprehensive coverage of the case studies. Chapter 8

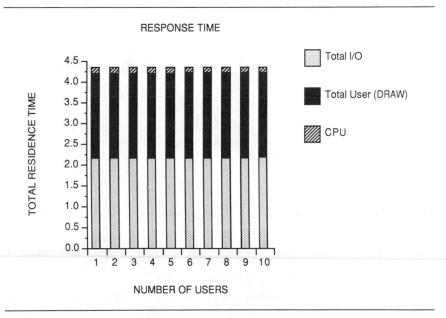

FIGURE 6.19
The New Residence Time Profile for the DRAWMOD Scenario as the Number of Users Increases.

carries the SYS_ EXEC message size analysis further and introduces advanced model analysis techniques that apply to the case studies.

6.4 Summary

This chapter applied the SPE methods we learned in earlier chapters: data gathering, the software execution models, and the system execution models. We used them to predict and evaluate the performance of proposed software systems, then applied the general principles to identify alternatives when we detected problems. Techniques were suggested for presenting the results—we began with basic elements for results reports: best and worst cases, typical cases, sensitivity, multiple scenarios, variations in workload mix, and verification and validation. The case studies were used to illustrate techniques for communicating results and the general principles that improve performance. We use these SPE techniques to manage the evaluation and implementation of the many design alternatives. Next, Chapter 7 ties performance measurements of evolving software into the models for verification and validation and to increase precision.

Exercises

Review

6.1. a. Construct your own software models for the case study in Figures 6.5 through 6.9. Use an automated software modeling tool, a spreadsheet package, or your own analysis program to solve the models. Make the modifications for each of the alternatives in Examples 6.8 through 6.14. Make each change to the original design, rather than the additive changes in the examples. Create a results table like Table 6.4.

b. Construct and solve the IPG for the final version of the case study in Example 6.11. Compare your results to Tables 6.6 and 6.7.

6.2. Revise the software resource requirements for DBOPEN to include the following additional processing for initialization of access rights: 500 additional instructions and 2 additional I/Os. Compute the new best-case response time.

6.3. Compute the best-case response time for the following additional message sizes for RETRIEVE BLOCK (Example 6.11):

a. 64 bytes per message

b. 8K bytes per message

6.4. Compare the list of case study performance improvements that you created in Exercise 4.6 to the alternatives in Table 6.4. Construct models and evaluate the performance of your additional improvements.

6.5. Conduct a sensitivity study for the model for Exercise 5.3. Create a table, like Table 6.1, that reports the results for each case you study.

6.6. Construct and evaluate models of alternatives for your continuing Chapter 1 case study. Conduct sensitivity studies and prepare a presentation of its results.

7

SPE Performance Measurement

Remember the process control engineer's adage: "If you can't measure it, you can't control it"? And the master vintner's need to measure grapes, fermentation temperature, color, tannin, fragrance, and so on? Our SPE models make performance predictions for conceptual designs (grape expectations), but when you reach implementation stages (grape juices begin to ferment), it is time to turn to measurements. Even earlier, we supplement the dreams with reality whenever possible (*measure* grape acidity, sugar levels, and so forth before assigning grapes to vats).

There are at least **five SPE uses for measurement data:**

- □ Incorporating measurement data from *existing systems* into the SPE models
- □ Using measurements of experiments or prototypes to *derive performance specifications*
- □ *Updating performance specifications* (estimates) with measurements of the evolving software to improve model precision
- □ *Verifying and validating* the SPE models
- □ *Evaluating software performance* and identifying areas for improvements

Figure 7.1 shows this chapter's role in the SPE methodology by highlighting the steps that benefit from performance measurements.

Now it is time to face reality. So far, suggestions of supplementing SPE studies with measurements have been issued as if these measurements are easy to make. The implication was that as soon as code exists, you can measure it. This is

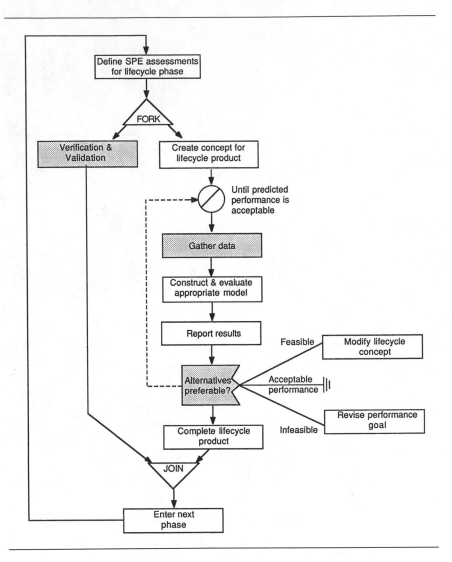

FIGURE 7.1
The SPE Methodology with the Focus of This Chapter Highlighted.

true, but not the whole truth. In today's reality, the performance management concepts are well known, and many measurement tools exist, but they seldom provide exactly the data you need in the form that you need it. We rely on software instrumentation to provide much of the data.

7.1 Measurements Needed

Table 7.1 illustrates the performance metrics pertinent to SPE and the uses for each. The five uses listed in the previous section and in the table are integral to the SPE methodology, and they are referenced throughout the book. The **performance metrics** include *workload data, data characteristics, execution characteristics,* and *computer system usage*. When part of the software exists, it is easier to measure it and use the measurement data in the SPE models. Figure 3.6 illustrated workload hierarchies and the interrelationships of software subsystems. For any subsystem in the figure, we would like to measure the workload requests coming from "above" and the resource usages for the functions provided "below" in the chart. As shown in Table 7.1, the performance metrics we need depend on their SPE use.

The table summarizes the **workload data** you need for SPE models (the detailed definition is in Section 3.1.2). Thus, for existing and evolving workloads, measure the number of requests for each function, the rate at which they are requested, and patterns of requests. For example, for the EDMS case study, if the application programs (DRAWMOD, VIEW, etcetera) already exist (if they currently use a general-purpose DBMS), then measure the number of calls to each data management function (FIND, RETRIEVE, DBOPEN, etcetera), the number of requests per second (or other time units of interest), and the relationship between FINDs and RETRIEVEs (how many RETRIEVEs per FIND and so on).

Similarly, when **data** exists, measure the amount of data and the size of each data item. The frequency of requests to each data item and the locality of references are also enlightening when the database is used for a similar purpose to that of the new software, and when the software that uses the database is to be redesigned. Continuing the EDMS example, measure the characteristics of the engineer's database: the size of each table, the size of each entry, and the relationships between entries (how many beams per model, and so on).

Table 7.1 shows that data characteristics and workload measurements have similar uses. For existing systems, data measurements provide system model parameters. For new software, they help you estimate resource usage and path executions and replace estimates as the software evolves. They also verify that the model parameters agree with measured values.

There are three types of **execution characteristics** to be measured: *resource requirements, support software services,* and *path characteristics*. **Resource requirements** refer to the amount of service required from each of the key computer system resources. The key resources include the CPU, the I/O subsystem (channel, controller, disks and other types of I/O devices), memory, communication lines, and any other resources that are limited and must be shared among the executing processes. Measure how much service each job uses from each of the

TABLE 7.1
PERFORMANCE DATA OF INTEREST FOR SPE

Performance metrics	SPE uses				
	Existing systems	Deriving specs	Updating models	Model V & V	Evaluating software performance
Workload data:					
Requests for each function, request rate, request patterns	yes	some	yes	yes	some
Data characteristics:					
Volume (# entries of each type), size of each, relationships	yes	some	yes	yes	some
Execution characteristics:					
Resource requirements:					
CPU usage, file I/O, memory, communication lines, other shared resources	yes	yes	yes	yes	yes
Support software services:					
Types requested, elapsed execution time, resource requirements	yes			yes	some
Path characteristics:					
Execution probabilities, loop repetitions		yes	yes	yes	some
Computer system usage:					
Response time, throughput, resource service times and wait times, resource utilization and throughput, and queue lengths				yes	yes

key resources to derive existing-work parameters for the system execution model, to validate the software model (when the measured resource requirements for the job match those calculated by the software model), and thus to verify the software model parameters that feed the system model.

In addition to measuring the total resource requirements for a job, measure the resource requirements for each component of the software. Note that the components are of varying levels of detail. For example, the "Get balance" scenario in Example 3.3 has a "Get account file balance" component that consists of three subcomponents. You need specifications for the greatest level of detail, so measure the resource requirements for the three subcomponents to either derive performance specifications or to replace estimates with evolving data. For model V&V and performance evaluation, measure the combined resource usage for the "Get account file balance" component and for the entire "Get balance" scenario.

Use measurements of **support software services** whenever the new software uses them extensively, the support software exists, and the data is not otherwise available. Measure the following for each of the support services requested: the average elapsed execution time, the CPU time required (or the number of instructions executed), and its use of the other key computer system resources (memory, number of I/Os to each file or device, etcetera). The measurements also support verification that estimated model parameters for support software agree with the actual usage. Occasionally you can use the data to evaluate reductions in support software usage (due to tuning support software or calling it fewer times).

For the **path characteristics,** measure the number of times each significant path is executed. From this measurement, compute the loop repetition and the execution probabilities for conditional paths.

We use the **computer system usage** metrics primarily for validating the system execution model, evaluating performance, and identifying bottlenecks in the processing. Measure the following:

- The *scenario response time*—the elapsed time from the scenario request until its completion (the actual service time and the time spent waiting in queues)
- *Scenario throughput*—the number of scenarios processed per time unit
- Key computer system *resource usage* by each workload scenario—the actual service time as well as the wait time
- *Resource utilization*—the percentage of time busy
- *Resource throughput*—the rate at which the resource completes service requests
- *Resource queue lengths*—the average number of jobs waiting for service

Measure these statistics for components of scenarios as well as the complete scenario.

7.2 Performance Measurement Concepts

This section briefly introduces the performance measurement concepts you need for SPE. If you are unfamiliar with them, follow up on the rich set of measurement literature referenced in the bibliography, and consult your local systems performance analysts about tools available in your environment. Some good introductory references are by Bouhana ([BOU85]), Ferrari, Serazzi, and Zeigner ([FER83b]), Nutt ([NUT75]), and Svobodova ([SVO77]). The *Conference Proceedings* and *Transactions* of the Computer Measurement Group are also an excellent source of recent publications on measurement tools, techniques, and concepts.

We are interested in measuring computer system hardware and software states. An *event* in a computer system is any change in the system's state. There are two measurement techniques: *recording events* and observing or *monitoring* states. For event recording, define the events of interest, and everytime one occurs record its occurrence and the appropriate performance data. Monitors are usually *sampling monitors*. They activate at predetermined time intervals and record the current state and the appropriate performance data. Monitors can either be *software monitors,* programs or subroutines that execute independently from the software to be measured, or *hardware monitors,* external devices that are attached to the computer system hardware through external wires or probes. The measurement can be of the overall computer system or of individual programs executing on the system. A *system monitor* observes the state of the overall system, while a *program monitor* observes the state of the program being measured. For *program event recording,* the events are pertinent to the program being measured, such as an I/O completion or a page fault; for *system event recording,* the events for all executing programs are of interest. The performance measurement can be integrated into a program *(internal),* or can execute *external* to it. *Internal measurement* requires code within programs to detect events and record the pertinent performance data. While a compiler option or a preprocessor could insert and invoke the data collection code, these measurements usually require programmers to insert their own code.[1]

All measurement techniques offer a range in level of detail. The **granularity of events** varies from initiation and completion of jobs, programs, subroutines, or actions within subroutines. Similarly, there are three choices for managing the **amount of data collected:** recording details, reducing the data as it is collected, and a compromise that tallies data between events and records it upon event

---

[1]The instrumentation principle currently requires internal measurement as described in Section 7.4. Future advances in external measurement tools may relieve some of the burden from programmers.

occurrence. For example, suppose you want to measure the number of I/Os in a program. You could record each I/O event and later compute the total; count each I/O operation as the program executes and record the total once at the end of the job; count the I/Os within each subroutine and write the total upon each subroutine exit; count the I/Os and write the total once per second, minute, or other time unit $j;$ and so on. Regardless of the data collection technique, you collect and store the performance data, then later run programs to *analyze the data* and *report results*.

There are several differences in the measurement techniques that may affect the usefulness of the data for SPE. First, the measurement process may perturb the system being measured. This usually affects system measurements more than program measurements, and usually when the system already has severe performance bottlenecks. The measurements may make a poor-performing sytem worse. Second, there are differences in the "capture ratios" and the way that resource usage is charged to programs. For example, software sampling monitors work by setting a timer interrupt at specified intervals. At the end of the time interval, however, another higher-priority process (such as an operating system service routine) may be executing, which delays the monitor execution slightly. Can the time delay be captured, and, if so, how should it be reported? Sometimes monitors can determine that there was such a delay, how long, and why. The capture ratio characterizes the percentage of time that the measurement technique accounts for (directly or by inference). Similarly, the monitor may account for the execution time of operating system service routines. Some are clearly chargeable to the program that made the service request (such as a file I/O). Others are not so clear. (What program should be charged for CPU scheduling overhead? How should page faults be charged?—they may be caused by the program that needed the page or caused by another program that holds a large portion of real memory, leaving other programs with too little memory to execute.)

You must control the measurement process if the results are to be meaningful. For example, the granularity of events must match the resolution of the system clock used to time them. The events should not be too short compared to the clock's time units (a subroutine that executes in 10 microseconds but the clock only measures to milliseconds). Similarly, the sampling interval for monitors must be short enough to detect the states of interest, but not too short; otherwise the amount of data collected (thus the measurement overhead) is much greater than necessary.

You may also need to control the measurement environment: the workload, the time of day, and duration of the measurements. Other work that executes on the computer system influences the performance metrics (wait times, support software services, and computer system usage statistics). Therefore, you may need to exclude the other work during measurement periods, particularly if you need *reproducible* results. For example, if you want to study whether allocating more memory to a process improves its performance, measure its execution before and after increasing the memory allocation and compare the results. They are only comparable, though, if you collect the two measurements when the workload, time of day, and duration of measurements are comparable.

Many of the metrics are averages over the measurement period. Averages may not be meaningful if the period is too long. For example, peak loads may be 50 percent or higher than average loads. So an average for an entire day does not capture the performance of a two-hour peak load.

7.3 Measurement Tools

Many computer system vendors offer performance data collection tools with their systems. There are also many commerically available software products that collect and report performance data. It is impossible to completely enumerate the products currently available and to keep the list current in this book. Therefore some representative tools are mentioned here. Please do not assume that these are the only tools, or even the best available. Consult with your systems performance analysts to learn which tools are available to you. There are also several good sources of information on current measurement products. The Computer Measurement Group has a vendor exhibit at their annual conference ([CMG]). Most vendors of performance measurement products participate, so it is a good place to learn what is available and to hear new product announcements. Applied Computer Research publishes an annual review of performance measurement products ([ACR]). The traditional sources of information on software products, Auerbach and Datapro also help. As usual, the vendors mentioned in this section are listed in their own reference section distinct from the literature references.

System monitors observe system level states and thus require detailed information on operating system data structures and algorithms to identify the states and record the pertinent data. Most of the commercially available products are software monitors for IBM operating systems. They include Boole and Babbage's CMF ([BOO]), Candle's Omegamon ([CAN]), and Legent's Performance Management Facilities ([LEG]).[2] Because system monitors rely heavily on the operating systems, some vendors offer software system monitors with their operating systems, such as IBM's RMF, Unisys (Sperry)'s SIP, and Unisys (Burroughs)'s Flame and SMFII.

Program monitors are less dependent on the operating system, but they may

---

[2]Other system monitors report performance to console operators for dynamic, online problem detection and resolution. They are not included in this list because of their limited usefulness for SPE.

be programming-language dependent (if they relate performance metrics to language statements). Programart's Strobe works with several languages and subsystems on IBM MVS systems ([PRO]). Boole and Babbage's PPE runs with several languages and computers ([BOO]). The standard "Profil" tool monitors UNIX programs.

System event recording, if available, is one of the operating system services. Examples are IBM's SMF[3], and Unisys's SIP, Flame, and SMFII (these products have both event recording and system monitoring in one package). Commercial products are also available for storing, analyzing, and reporting the system event data. Some packages primarily view the data as "accounting data," and their reports are oriented to charging for services. Others have a more comprehensive view, such as Merrill Consultants' MXG ([MER]), and Legent's MICS ([LEG]). Generic data analysis products, such as SAS ([SAS]), BMD ([DIX79]), and SPSS ([NIE75]), are also useful for summarizing and reporting system event data.

External program event recorders "trace" program execution by recording sequences of events. Most programming languages offer an option to record each subroutine execution (usually for debugging purposes rather than for performance measurement). Operating systems usually offer a trace option to record system event occurrence. This data is usually too detailed and may not report the performance metrics of interest for SPE. Nevertheless, system event recording is helpful when you must construct models of low-level event handling, as when hardware and basic operating system software are to be redesigned. "Trace data banks," which contain representative system-level traces in several different operating environments, are very useful for system software SPE studies; include traces in your measurement data library (Section 7.6 defines measurement libraries).

Major subsystems, such as database management systems and teleprocessing systems, usually record **internal events.** For example, IBM's database products, IMS and DB2, and teleprocessing product, CICS, each collect and report their own performance statistics. Commercially available database, teleprocessing, and other products offer varying performance metrics. Other internal event recording relies on instrumentation (see Section 7.4).

Table 7.2 illustrates the performance metrics needed for SPE and measurement techniques for collecting each. **Workload** requests and request rates come from system event recorders when the workload functions are the same as the measurement units. For example, the number of database FINDs is likely to be automatically counted by the database management software. On the other hand, system measurement tools are unlikely to record the number of ATM "Get balance" scenarios—unless you can compute scenario characteristics from the number of times a specific program executes, you need an event counter internal to the

---

[3]Refer to Merrill ([MER85]) for a comprehensive description of the data available with SMF.

TABLE 7.2
PERFORMANCE DATA COLLECTION TECHNIQUES

	Data collection technique				
Performance metrics	System monitor	Program monitor	System event recorder	External program event recorder	Internal event recorder
Workload data:					
Requests for each function, request rate,			X		X
request patterns			X		X
					X
Data characteristics:					
Volume (# entries of each type), size of each,					X
access locality					X
					X
Execution characteristics:					
Resource requirements:					
Scenario resource usage	X	X	X		X
Component level resource usage		X			X
Support software services:					
Types requested, resource req.,	X	X			
Elapsed execution time					X
Path characteristics:					
Execution probabilities, loop repetitions		X		X	X
Computer system usage: Response time, throughput, resource service times and wait times, resource utilization and throughput, and queue lengths	X		X		

ATM software to capture scenario characteristics. Currently available commercial products do not measure request patterns or locality; they must be tallied by internal event counters until more support tools are available.

You can collect many of the **data characteristics** with static analysis tools that examine the data and report the statistics. For example, you can compute the size of the database statically—the database transactions do not have to be executing. The access locality, on the other hand, is a dynamic metric. As with workload locality, until additional support tools are available, data access locality must be gathered with internal event recorders.

You can derive **resource requirements** for scenarios from system monitors or system event recorders, if you can identify the scenarios on the reports. If not, program monitors may report the desired level of granularity; otherwise you need an internal event recorder. Similarly, system-level tools seldom report component resource usage, so you need program monitors or internal event recorders.

You can usually find the types of **support software services** and their resource requirements in system-monitor or program-monitor reports. You may need an internal event recorder to collect their elapsed execution times.

You can usually derive **path-execution characteristics** from program monitors or external program-event recorders. It may be more convenient to obtain specific data from internal event recorders, though, because the other tools (such as external event recorders) may mix path data with much other data, making its isolation difficult. For example, to get loop repetitions, you may have to pore through lists of subroutine calls and count the number of calls to each.

Computer resource usage usually comes from system monitors. You may have to hunt for some of the data from the system-event recorders, depending on your tool set.

Do not be misled by Table 7.2. It is seldom as easy as the chart implies to collect data; it is rarely in exactly the granularity, nor does one report contain all the data you need.[4] When you need data from several tools, it is difficult to correlate their results (the data collection intervals or capture ratios may differ). Today, most SPE data items come from internal event recorders.

7.4 Instrumenting Software Systems

In Chapter 2, the instrumenting principle called for "instrumenting systems as you build them to enable measurement and analysis of workload scenarios, resource requirements, and performance goal achievement." Then Section 7.3.3 implied that you can gather performance data with standard performance measurement tools. Do these statements conflict? There are at least **three reasons for using instrumentation** to supplement the standard tools: convenience, data granularity, and control. Although standard measurement tools may report SPE data, there are no known tools that currently generate one report containing precisely the SPE data you need. Thus, it is inconvenient to get the data, at best. Some data,

[4]Sometimes you can run performance benchmarks to manipulate the data on the reports to match the granularity you need (make the component a job and run it many times to get the resource requirements for the "job" printed on the standard reports).

such as the locality of user and data requests, is practically impossible to gather with standard measurement tools—you must analyze detailed traces and derive logical events from them. With instrumentation, you tally user requests within the software where they are easily identified and produce **convenient** reports with exactly the data you need.

The second reason for instrumenting is that the **data granularity** from standard measurement tools seldom matches the SPE requirements. For example, suppose we want the response time for a typical ATM session. Most data collection tools report performance data for online systems by "user interaction"—that is, the starting event is the receipt of data or control information from the user's terminal, and the ending event is the transmission of a response. Using this definition, there are four user interactions in the ATM "Get balance" session in Example 3.3 (insert card, enter authorization code, request "Get balance" transaction, and specify checking account). To use the standard measurement tools, you must gather data for each user interaction, then calculate the session total from the individual times. In this scenario, we know which programs to tally, but often it is more difficult to associate the logical events we wish to measure to their physical execution properties.

Furthermore, you need to associate the computer system usage metrics with the functional components defined in the execution structure specifications and to collect the data for components at varying levels of refinement. The standard measurement tools associate the metrics with programs, and it is virtually impossible to use them for measurements of functional components and subcomponents.

The third reason for instrumenting is to **control the measurement** process. For SPE, we seldom need all of the measurement data all of the time; rather, we periodically need some of the data. Collecting data with standard measurement tools is not just a matter of flipping a switch; measurement requires many execution and data analysis steps. If measurements are infrequent, or if experienced personnel are unavailable, others must recreate the measurement steps.

So supplement your standard performance measurement tools with software instrumentation. Why does the instrumentation principle call for designing probes into the software—why not insert them later when you need the measurements? There are two primary reasons: It is easiest to define probe points when designers define the logical functions, and the data collection and analysis tend to incur less processing overhead if integrated as the design evolves. You control processing overhead by balancing the data collection and dynamic data reduction overhead against the overhead for recording and analyzing measurements (Section 7.4.1 provides more information on processing overhead). The need for designed-in instrumentation is best explained by relating it to another problem observed by software engineers: requirements traceability. That is, software engineers find it difficult to relate a system's functional requirements to the code that implements them (to verify that all have been satisfied, and for maintenance). This is because the implementation of any particular requirement may cross many component, program, or procedure boundaries. In general, there is a direct correspondence between the user functions that we wish to measure and many of the functional requirements of the software system, so instrumentation of user functions has the same difficulties as requirements traceability. It is much easier to establish and maintain the relationship as the design evolves than to try to reconstruct it later.

There are other advantages of the resulting instrumentation. The data is useful for system testing (to assess test coverage, ensure that performance goals are met, and so on), for diagnosing the cause of problems, and possibly for assisting with the traceability of requirements and quantifying the execution cost of each requirement.

7.4.1 Instrumentation Design Considerations

Having discussed why and when we need instrumentation, we next examine some alternatives for designing and implementing it. There are **three primary design considerations:** defining *the events* to be measured, choosing the *granularity* of the measurements, and *dynamically selecting* the data to be recorded. The **events** include the beginning-and-end of logical functions and the beginning-and-end of critical processing steps.

There are at least three choices for the **granularity** of the measurements. The finest granularity is to record *all* events and metrics (such as the process ID, a sequence number, a time stamp, the event, and other processing state definitions), to write them to archival storage, and to analyze the data and compute the desired performance metrics later. This option offers the greatest flexibility, but at the greatest cost, because many events are likely and each event has a significant amount of data.

A coarser granularity is to use the same recording technique but to define event *hierarchies*. Thus, rather than recording every event, we could selectively record the data at varying levels of detail, such as only major components, or major and intermediate level components, or all components.

The coarsest of the event-recording techniques is to define *types or classes of events,* to tally the metrics for each, and then compute the averages, variances, or distributions of the metrics. An ATM example might define an event to be a "Get balance" scenario and sum the number of requests, the CPU and elapsed time for each, and compute and print the average CPU and elapsed time *at the end of the measurement period.*

The third instrumentation design consideration is **dynamically selecting** the data to be recorded. You seldom need all the performance data, and recording and analyzing unnecessary data incurs unnecessary overhead processing, so use instrumentation parameters to vary the metrics collected and their granularity. Define hierarchies of events and data. Then use the instrumentation parameters to trigger the recording of classes of events in the hierarchy and classes of data. For example, you could have two levels of events for the ATM example, scenario or component levels, and two classes of data, resource usage or locality data.

7.4.2 Implementation Alternatives

Among the implementation alternatives, the first integrates instrumentation specifications into the program and data specifications, thus making instrumentation another product of development. For example, the ATM software programmer would have a specification to count the number of times that users request the "Get balance" scenario.

Another alternative is to collect and record data with a custom-created subroutine. This isolates the collection and recording functions and is appropriate for collecting data that requires "expert" knowledge of the environment, such as the operating system tables that contain resource-usage statistics. To collect data, programs (selectively) call the subroutines; a macro expansion could include the subroutine's code inline to minimize procedure call overhead.

The third alternative uses standard system event recording tools. To use them, programs call subroutines to record events and performance data on the standard system event archive file (for example, on IBM's SMF file).

There are a number of more sophisticated approaches. One is to modify the compilers or run-time systems. For example, change the standard "trace" routine or the "debugger" to also collect performance data. Another is to augment the compiler-generated code for procedure calls and returns to recognize and record logical events. For example, require programs to update a logical-state identifier as events occur; then the augmented procedure call return code checks the state, tallies performance data for each logical event, and records the results at appropriate times. Another sophisticated approach is to augment the operating system services with custom-created data collection and recording subroutines. Then, to collect data, programs still call the custom routine; the call triggers an operating system service call. You can devise many other sophisticated techniques for your environment; however, due to the expertise required to implement them and to maintain their consistency with changing operating system environments, they are inappropriate for most user environments and thus are not discussed further here.

You probably want a combination of these techniques. For example, use program instrumentation to measure logical events and locality. Use the other techniques to record system metrics that are inaccessable to application programs.

7.4.3 Data Reporting

When customized, internal, instrumentation code collects data, you need special programs to analyze and report it. Commercially available reporting tools such as fourth-generation languages make reporting easy. You could input data to PC spreadsheet or charting packages, or to statistical analysis packages, such as BMD ([DIX79]), SAS ([*SAS*]), or SPSS ([NIE75]). You could use report generators provided by your database management system to facilitate data presentation. If you integrate data collection into the standard system event recording, you can use its standard reporting capabilities.

Whether you use a commercial reporting tool or write a custom report program, reuse it for other SPE projects. This is best accomplished if you develop and adhere to *data collection standards*. Then use the same conventions for all projects to define and collect the events and metrics. You can then develop and use standard SPE data-reporting tools for all SPE projects.

7.5 Performance Benchmarks

Benchmarks are experiments to produce data (primarily) for:

□ *Hardware or software system evaluations*—for selecting major systems when comparisons require reliable data that is otherwise unavailable

□ *Volume testing*—to analyze the effect of varying the number of users on a system

□ *Performance measurement*—to gather performance metrics for SPE

This discussion focuses on collecting performance metrics from benchmarks conducted for any of these purposes.

There are **two key considerations in designing benchmarks:** They must be *representative*, and they must be *reproducible*. Benchmarks, like experiments, must capture the essential characteristics of the system under study. The goal is to design a benchmark that balances the effort to construct and execute benchmarks against the precision of the resultant data. The effort is reduced if unimportant details are abstracted and essential performance factors are **representative** of the system. The factors that affect performance were identified earlier: workload, software, and computer system environment. Performance benchmarks must accurately represent each factor. The second key consideration, **reproducibility,** gives confidence in the results: You must be able to repeat the experiment and see the same results.

Workload selection is the most difficult aspect of benchmark design. User behavior, the requested functions, and data characteristics must match the actual environment. For some SPE studies, such as measuring CPU time or I/O counts, it is unnecessary to represent multiple concurrent users of the software. For system evaluations, volume testing, and other SPE studies (such as model validity), it is essential to represent multiple users. It is virtually impossible to represent multiple users with actual terminal users—it is too difficult to control the experiment and to reproduce results. Most multiple-user benchmarks rely on **load drivers**—software products that simulate user behavior. Workload profiles are input, and output is a replica of user requests. The workload profile specifies the number of users to simulate, the transaction arrival rate, the frequency of each transaction type, and a distribution of input values to generate. The load driver generates the transactions and measures response times. Once generated, they look like actual user requests, so the software executes normally.

The benchmarked software can be programs, a representative subset of them, or synthetic programs. Synthetic programs mimic the execution characteristics of the actual programs without doing the processing. For example, consider an edit transaction that receives input data, does some processing to verify the input is valid, accesses a file to check consistency, and transmits the reply. A synthetic edit transaction issues the same number of file I/Os and uses the same amount of CPU time between each, but does not actually check data validity.

The benchmark environment must represent the essential elements of the execution environment. The operating system, the computer system resources, and resource competition must be comparable. Often benchmarks must be run in isolation to eliminate the effects of competition and to enhance reproducibility. For other studies, average or peak load environments provide more realistic measurements of expected performance by including the side effects of queuing for resources.

Use the traditional **scientific method to design and conduct benchmarks.** Its step are:

1. Understand the purpose of the benchmark—the questions to answer or the hypothesis to test.

2. Identify the data needed to answer the questions and the data collection tools and techniques.

3. Identify experimental variables and controls.

4. Define the test cases: workload, software, and the environment for each test.

5. Execute the tests and collect the data.

6. Analyze, interpret, and present the results.

All steps in the scientific method apply to SPE benchmarks, but experience shows that the following are especially *vital to success:* careful design of the experimental test cases, identification of necessary data, and the collection and coordination of the measurement results. **Designing the test cases** means selecting the approach for representing the workload, software, and environment, and developing a test plan with priorities for the tests to be run. Identify the necessary **measurements and data-gathering tools before beginning the experiment.** Too much data obscures essential results and may even perturb them because of the data collection overhead. Too little data reduces the experiment's usefulness. If the data comes from multiple sources, **coordinate the measurements:** Match the start and finish of the data collection intervals and the granularity of the measurements. For example, you cannot equate CPU time usage collected during an hour-long test with CPU utilization averaged over an eight-hour period.

Murphy should have specific benchmark-study laws! The potential for problems is astounding: The software, hardware, and workload combinations are incredibly complex, their performance is influenced by many factors, and the amount of data can be overwhelming (if not controlled); the studies are labor-intensive and usually time-constrained; the setup of the workload generator, the software, and measurement tools encounters constant problems; control of the system parameters and environmental factors is problematic; software bugs and hardware failures often stall the experiments; and the number of tests is further constrained when they must run in isolation. It is unlikely that you will have time to run all desired tests; without test plan priorities you are likely to run out of time and then discover that you are missing the most important data.

To illustrate, consider the design of a performance benchmark for the EDMS case study. Within the EDMS FIND execution in Example 3.9 is a processing step to DBSORT (address_list). Suppose we must determine whether DBSORT should call a system subroutine or have its own custom sort routine. The considerations and benchmark design follow.

EXAMPLE 7.1: DBSORT Performance Benchmark Design

Define purpose

The benchmark is to quantify the performance of two alternatives for implementing the EDMS function DBSORT (address_list). Using a system sort routine minimizes implementation and maintenance efforts, but the system sort may not meet performance goals. For a cost-benefit analysis, we need to know the difference in response times for the custom sort and the system sort routines.

Data collection

The EDMS case study performance goal is a 20-second response time for the CAD user scenario in Example 3.7. We will measure the resource requirements for each sort alternative, then use the SPE models to quantify the response times for each alternative. It is sufficient to measure the resource requirements for one user, because the SPE models use service times to derive the response times for multiple users. (Thus, we do not need a load driver.) The resources of interest are CPU time, number of I/Os, and memory requirements. The system event recorder collects this data for programs, but includes benchmark program initiation and termination and test case setup processing in its totals. We can either run some experiments to quantify the overhead (to be backed out), or use internal instrumentation to tally the metric of interest. In either case, we want to measure the procedure call overhead for calling the sort.

(continued)

EXAMPLE 7.1 (*Continued*)

Experimental variables

The sort's performance depends on the number and size of the sort keys, the number of items, item length, the original data order, and the sort algorithm. In this case study, the sort key is the "address"; the designers specify that the key length is one word, and the item length is two words. The users estimate that the number of items will be a minimum of 1, a maximum of 1 million, and a range (for the scenario) of 2 to 2,050. The designers and users agree that it is likely that the lists will already be "almost sorted" because of the expected use of the system and its internal design.

We select a published sort algorithm that is expected to perform best for a problem with these characteristics. This will provide sufficient data for the cost-benefit analysis; further algorithm testing can be done later if deemed appropriate.

We do not want the resource measurements to be perturbed by other work executing on the computer system, but "stand-alone" tests are likewise undesirable. Because system event recorders filter out most external effects, we will run some tests to compare stand-alone measurements to those collected during "normal" processing times. Unless the differences are significant, we will proceed with testing during normal processing.

Test cases

We will construct a driver program that generates test cases and calls both the system and custom routines to sort each test. The tests include:

- ☐ Isolation versus normal processing
- ☐ Overhead for test program
- ☐ List length: 2 items
- ☐ List length: 2,050 items, almost sorted
- ☐ List length: 1,500 items, almost sorted

We can add other experiments as time permits, such as the effect of allocating different amounts of memory for the sort, different list lengths, and random ordering.

Executing the tests

We will run each test multiple times to verify that the results are reproducible.

Results

We will produce a table showing the test cases and the resource requirements for each. Because the measurements are intermediate results, we will also use them to produce and report response times for the CAD user scenario for the two sorts.

Other considerations

This illustrates the steps in benchmark design. Your environment may require other data collection techniques and other test cases.   ☐

Load-driver benchmarks are necessary to simulate user behavior under loading conditions. They must run in isolation and are time-consuming and labor-intensive; therefore it is preferable to use performance models for most SPE tasks. Benchmarks are not cost-effective for design tradeoff studies. They are useful for deriving performance specifications for the models, verifying and validating the models, and for confirming SPE conclusions when they have major consequences.

7.6 SPE Data Storage and Retrieval

SPE data is needed many times throughout the lifecycle. Conserve your efforts for SPE studies by keeping data readily available for quick reference. This section suggests two mechanisms: a measurement data library containing environment data needed for all new software systems and an SPE database for each project.

7.6.1 Measurement Data Library

You almost always need resource estimates for **support software services.** Measuring and storing this data in a library is convenient and time-saving when many SPE studies may need it. Using data for multiple studies justifies spending more time on getting precise measurements and improves consistency across SPE models. If the new software is to provide support services or if its data may be used by other software systems, store the evolving performance data in the library.

Because specifying resource usage of software components is difficult without a past frame of reference, you can help designers by compiling and making available measurements of similar software systems. For example, when adding new functions to ATM software, it is easier to specify workload and resource usage if you can refer to measurements for existing functions.

Many software systems execute in the same hardware and software environment, so store the **other environment specifications** (defined in Section 3.1.4) in the measurement data library for ready reference.

As SPE matures and expands in your organization, build tools to automate data collection tasks. Some examples are automatically collecting software support services data and regularly updating the measurement data library, and automatically accessing the library and incorporating the most recent version of the measurement data into SPE models. The measurement data library contents and uses will grow as you gain more experience with SPE.

Some large corporate environments have a problem with disclosing confidential performance data, even within the corporation. Clever use of a measurement data library offers some help in controlling the accessibility of this sensitive data.

For example, you can build tools that incorporate data and show totals for scenarios without revealing details.

7.6.2 SPE Database

Over the course of an SPE project, mountains of data emerge. To be useful, the data must be organized, easily retrieved, and easily reused for further study, reference, and reporting. Furthermore, you need ready access to the latest SPE data, to earlier versions of it, and to status information that identifies each version. The **reasons for building SPE databases** include SPE tracking and status reporting, verification and validation, document assumptions, clarification, knowledge base for estimates, implementation tradeoff studies, future SPE studies, capacity planning, and leveraged SPE efforts.

Track and report SPE status throughout the project. Provide *SPE milestone reports* at key development milestones, showing current predicted performance versus goals, projected capacity requirements, and acceptance dates for developers, users, analysts, and others. Provide *regular SPE status reports* showing studies conducted, issues considered, problem resolutions, and justifications. Be prepared to provide the *latest performance predictions on demand* showing performance goal achievability, problem severity, response times for key scenarios, critical components, workload projections, computer capacity projections, and so forth. Prepare periodic *verification and validation reports* for workload projections, resource requirements for critical components, measured versus predicted performance, measured versus predicted specifications, and an explanation of variances.

Track evolving resource usage estimates, path execution characteristics, and workload intensity in a form that facilitates (later) comparison against measurements for **verification** of specifications and **validation** of model predictions. Many changes occur during development. Unless you establish a link between early specifications and later changes, you will find it difficult, if not impossible, to relate them after project completion. For example, one component in an early software execution model later disappeared; its function turned out to be trivial, so it was absorbed into two other components. How can you later compare its actual resource usage with early predictions?

Also track the **assumptions** used in making estimates. Measurements are usually higher than the early, optimistic, best-case estimates, but measurements should fall within the upper and lower bounds. Do they? Compare the assumptions to the reality—do assumptions account for differences between measurements and specifications? When assumptions prove to be incorrect, report the discrepancies so future performance engineers can learn from past experience.

Keep everything necessary to **clarify earlier results,** revert back to earlier models, and conduct "what if" studies with them. SPE models look to the future; after completing one study, modelers move on to determine other future directions. As software developers reach the point of implementing earlier choices, they have specific questions about model assumptions and the effects of different conditions. Preserve earlier SPE models and their assumptions, and use them to clarify developers' questions.

Keep your SPE estimates readily available for a **knowledge base** for others to use in specifying their software execution models. Also give your specifiers feedback on how close their estimates matched reality, and give insights into the mismatches. Performance data feedback works like biofeedback to help you improve future specifications.

Capture the mountains of performance data as each molehill emerges to facilitate **implementation tradeoff studies.** You need to pick implementation alternatives that meet global performance objectives. To pick the best global choice you need the latest data for interrelated components. Software develops fast and furiously during implementation, and unless you can collect data as it evolves, you will be unable to respond quickly to crucial implementation decisions.

Maintain the SPE data after project completion to **evaluate software enhancements.** When the bulk of the data is ready, you only need specifications of new features. You can also use up-to-date models for long-range **capacity planning.**

The software models tie resource requirements to the parameters upon which they depend. These parameters usually correspond directly to a meaningful business growth parameter (the "natural forecasting unit" or NFU). For example, if you know that the resource requirements for a query transaction depend on the number of bank customers, and if your models use data-dependent variables to compute the resource requirements from the number of customers, then you can project future resource requirements from future customer projections. NFUs are key business variables and are more readily available than projections of future resource requirements.

Define a standard SPE database for all projects, then you can **leverage** the **development** of customized data collection, analysis, and reporting programs by reusing them for other SPE projects.

The SPE database must grow gracefully along with the software. SPE data (resource requirements, software execution structures, execution environment, etcetera) not only grows in the level of detail, but also changes. Data manipulation requirements include:

□ Revising the design and resource requirements, and adding details as they evolve (and the rippling effects they may cause)

□ Updating workload and environment specifications

□ Changing values of data-dependent parameters

□ Incorporating measurement data

□ Baselining versions of SPE data

Ideally the SPE data would be integrated with other software design information (through CASE tools) so that software changes would trigger SPE updates.

This integration may evolve in the near future. Meanwhile, we will focus on the SPE data we need. The following **data requirements** have been mentioned so far:

- ☐ Performance goals
- ☐ Workload specifications
- ☐ Software execution structure
- ☐ Execution path frequency
- ☐ Environment specifications
- ☐ Resource estimates
- ☐ Data-dependent parameters
- ☐ Software status
- ☐ System model description and assumptions
- ☐ Performance predictions
- ☐ Measured resource requirements
- ☐ Measured performance

Most commercial database management systems provide the capabilities you need for the performance engineering database. You can use database query languages to access the SPE data, and supplement them with customized interface programs to make the access and reporting more convenient. Apply the centering principle: Identify the SPE data frequently needed by your designers and analysts, and then customize programs to produce it. Also use the locality principle: For each frequently used SPE data reporting function, identify the data that should be combined into the report (both the performance data and more general design data) and the data that is irrelevant and should be omitted.

In summary, the SPE database provides a central repository of SPE project data, facilitates data collection and reporting, and leverages SPE tasks for multiple projects. This section points to some general information requirements and capabilities we have learned from previous SPE studies. Start with this description and customize the SPE data collected, its organization, and access for your installation and project needs.[5] Grow the SPE database as you gain experience on SPE projects.

7.7 Ideal Performance Measurement Support

The data collection methods described in this chapter are geared to today's tools and techniques, but they do not provide ideal performance measurement support.

---

[5]A sample SPE database organization is in [SMI80b]. It is a good starting point, but by no means complete. [SMI85b] describes some of the requirements for the SPE database.

There are few real limitations in the state of the art in measurement techniques. Most SPE tasks could be better supported by automated tools, but the SPE data requirements were only recently stated precisely.

Ideally, we could identify states within the software (by updating a logical event name in a specified location), and use an external monitor to observe the state and (selectively) record precisely the data we want for each state, such as the number of times it is observed in the state, the elapsed time, its resource usage, the computer system metrics, and support system services. We could easily and selectively define the granularity of events and of data. The data collection would not only be efficient, but would also have a cost proportional to the results desired. The reports produced would have only the information we need and would be easily understood. Tools would also automatically update the SPE database to support data analysis, such as specifed-versus-actual performance and problem identification. Current measurement technology supports these requirements. Ideally, as SPE matures, the data requirements will be better understood, and when demand is greater, more software measurement tools will become available.

As measurement tools mature, so will the software to be measured. Thus, there are some interesting research topics in SPE measurement. Distributed systems, for example, call for advances in the state of the art in measurement technology. Distributed "system state" spans multiple processors; thus, there may be an exponential increase in the data to be recorded. The processors may have clocks that operate at slightly different speeds; thus, comparing the different time measurements and identifying the order of logical events may be difficult. The number of events of interest also increases dramatically. Each logical function, for example, may have several processing options: local, geographically remote, and intermediate. Locality is also more difficult to measure.

So internal instrumentation is currently the best source of SPE performance data. We need new SPE measurement tools to relieve the duplication of effort; much more support could be provided with today's technology. We also need advances in the state of the art in measurement technology for SPE measurement tools of the future.

7.8 Summary

This chapter reviews performance measurement concepts and tools and shows how to use them in SPE studies. Most of the data comes from software instrumentation, so Section 7.4 focused on instrumentation design, implementation, and reporting. Performance benchmarks are experiments that employ measurement tools to produce performance metrics. Careful design of the experiment increases the likelihood of its successful completion. The measurement data library consolidates environment data for ready reference, and the SPE database organizes SPE project data for tracking, reporting, verification and validation, clarification of earlier results, implementation tradeoff studies, capacity planning, and future studies. These measurement capabilities enable you to monitor, control, and engineer software performance as the software matures, just as master vintners use measurements to create vintage wines.

Exercises

Review

7.1. Identify the measurement tools available in your environment. Find a sample report produced by each of the five types of data collection techniques in Table 7.2.

7.2. List the specific measurements you would need to verify specifications and validate performance predictions for (a) DRAWMOD, (b) EDMS FIND and RETRIEVE, and (c) SYS_EXEC processing.

7.3. Design a benchmark study to compare actual DRAWMOD response times to the SPE model predictions. Create a detailed test plan, specify priorities for experiments, and define the measurements to be collected, the measurement tools to be run, and sample reports for the benchmark results.

7.4. Conduct the DBSORT benchmark study described in Example 7.1, gather measurements, and report the results.

Further Study

7.5. Identify your top 10 batch users of CPU time and I/O time last week. Identify your top 10 CPU and I/O online users for a peak period last week.

7.6. Run a program monitor (or an available tool that provides similar information) against one of your top 10 CPU users. Identify the portion of the code that accounts for ≥ 90 percent of the CPU usage.

7.7. Review the literature on distributed system measurements. Summarize the state of the art and state of the practice. What is the most significant outstanding problem?

7.8. Most database management systems manage their own buffers in an attempt to minimize physical I/Os. For example, IBM's DB2 performs sequential prefetch, asynchronous writes, and other global strategies to minimize I/Os. Because of these optimizations it is extremely difficult to predict the number of physical I/Os caused by SQL statements. Design a benchmark study that will produce reasonable physical I/O default values for an SQL SELECT.

8

Advanced System
Execution Models

So far, we have used very simple SPE models. Perhaps you are skeptical about their usefulness for "real" systems assessment. Experience shows that simple models can detect serious performance problems very early in the development process. The simple models isolate problems and focus attention on their resolution (rather than on assumptions used for more realistic models). After they serve this primary purpose, though, we need to augment them, as the software evolves, to make more realistic performance predictions. This chapter covers the same SPE methodology steps (in Figure 8.1) covered in Chapters 4 and 5: constructing and evaluating an appropriate performance model. It differs from the earlier chapters in the level of detail represented by the models. The advanced system execution models defined in this chapter are usually appropriate when the software reaches the detailed-design lifecycle stage. Even when it is easy to incorporate the additional execution characteristics earlier, it is better to defer them to the advanced system execution model. It is seldom easy, however, and the time to construct and evaluate the advanced models usually does not match the input data precision early in the lifecycle.

The modeling difficulty arises from several sources. First, advances in modeling technology follow the introduction of new hardware and operating system features. So accurate models of new computer system resources are active research topics. For example, I/O subsystems may have channel reconnect, path selection when multiple channel paths are available, disk cache controllers, and other features. Models of these resources are evolving.

The second modeling difficulty is that special software features such as lock-free and acquire-release require **passive resources**—resources that are required

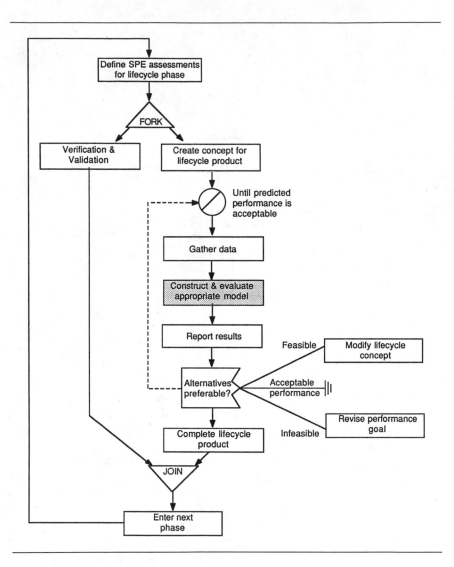

FIGURE 8.1
The SPE Methodology with the Focus of This Chapter Highlighted.

for processing but that do no work themselves. They are held while the software uses one or more active resources; the queueing delays for active resources influence the duration of passive resource usage. For example, if a bank account balance is to be updated, we permit only one job at a time to update, to ensure data integrity. A lock-free mechanism ensures mutually exclusive access to the account balance. If one job locks the account and another desires access to it, the second must wait until the account is available. The impact of these passive resource delays is two-fold. The response of jobs forced to wait on the objects will be slower, but because these waiting jobs do not use active resources while they wait, other jobs may execute at a faster rate due to the decreased contention. Passive resources are difficult to model with analytic queueing network models; quantitative data for queueing delays requires a queue server node, but its service time depends on the time spent in other queue servers.

A third modeling difficulty is that computer system environment characteristics such as distributed processing, parallel processing, concurrent and multithreaded software, and memory management overhead challenge model technology. They either use passive resources, have complex model topologies, or tightly couple the models of software and system execution.

These facets of execution behavior are represented in the advanced system execution model. It augments the elementary IPG model with additional nodes. Then procedures specify how to calculate corresponding model parameters from software models and how to solve the advanced IPGs. SPE methods specify "checkpoint evaluations" to identify those aspects of the execution behavior that require closer examination.

8.1 Advanced Information Processing Graphs

Advanced IPGs augment the elementary IPGs of Chapter 5 with additional nodes, queue-scheduling disciplines, and transaction processing phases. Figure 8.2 shows the additional nodes in the advanced IPG topology. The first node, the **phase-change node,** adjusts transaction processing characteristics. Transactions belong to categories that characterize the work they do. Transaction categories may also have temporary processing phases to identify when processing characteristics (such as service requirements or routing) change during execution. Transactions go to phase-change nodes to change from one phase to another.

Figure 8.3 shows an example. It modifies the earlier ATM scenario (in Figure 4.28) to distinguish Phase 1 (the overhead processing for initiating sessions, getting and interpreting requests, and terminating sessions) from Phase 2 (the actual processing to satisfy the request and update accounts). The execution flow through the IPG in Figure 8.3(b) is as follows. An ATM_SESSION arrives in Phase 1, and while in that phase, its execution moves through the CPU, ATM, and I/O nodes. After identifying a user request (after "Interpret request"), ATM_SESSION goes to the CHG node and changes to Phase 2 before processing the request. While in Phase 2, ATM_SESSION uses the CPU, I/O, and ATM nodes. When the request processing completes (before going back to "Get request"), ATM_SESSION goes to CHG and reenters Phase 1. When users make additional requests,

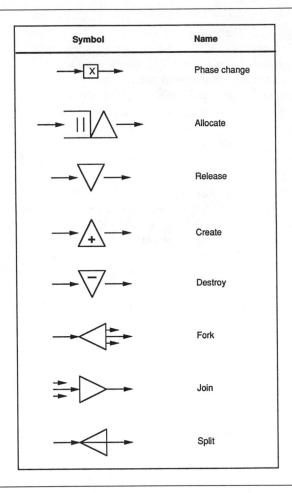

Symbol	Name
	Phase change
	Allocate
	Release
	Create
	Destroy
	Fork
	Join
	Split

FIGURE 8.2
The advanced IPG nodes in the figure supplement the elementary IPG nodes in Figure 5.6.

the phase changes accordingly. Upon completion, the ATM_SESSION leaves the system.

Advanced IPGs specify model parameters for each category and phase. First, specify the initial phase for source node arrivals. For service nodes, specify the number of visits for each category and phase, and the service requirement by category and phase. Table 8.1 shows the visit parameters for the ATM node by phase. In this example, the ATM node's service time remains 1 second for each visit irrespective of the phase. Phase service times need not be the same, as shown

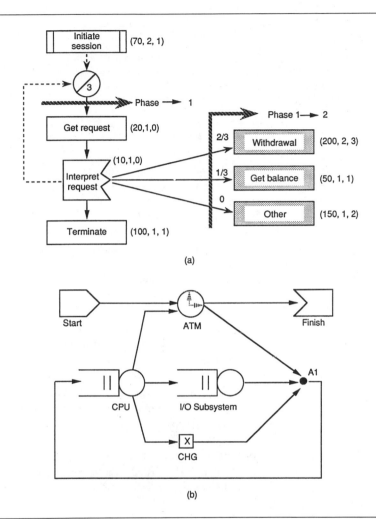

FIGURE 8.3
Phase changes distinguish processing characteristics. In (a) the phase changes distinguish overhead processing from customer-request processing. In (b) transactions visit the phase-change node as specified by model parameters. Service requirements and routing may differ by processing phase.

by the parameters for the CPU node. Parameters for change nodes specify the number of visits for each (old) category phase, the new phase, and the change probability. In Table 8.2, ATM_SESSION Phase 1 visits the CHG node three times (the scenario models three user requests). Each time it changes to Phase 2, so the change probability is 1. Similarly, ATM_SESSION Phase 2 changes back to

TABLE 8.1
MODEL PARAMETERS BY PHASE
(Category: ATM_SESSION—Phase 1: overhead
processing, Phase 2: account processing)

Category, phase	# visits	Mean service time
ATM node:		
ATM_SESSION, 1	9	1
ATM_SESSION, 2	5	1
CPU node:		
ATM_SESSION, 1	13	0.0006846
ATM_SESSION, 2	15	0.0003

Phase 1 three times. Advanced IPGs allow other combinations. To check your understanding, modify the example to distinguish Withdrawal requests-Phase 2 from Get balance requests-Phase 3.

The next four advanced IPGs nodes in Figure 8.2 represent actions on passive resources. **Tokens** represent the passive resources; there is a distinct **token type** for each passive resource modeled. **Allocate nodes** grant tokens to transactions. A transaction arrives at an allocate node and requests a specified number of tokens of various types. If they are not available, the transaction waits in a queue. The transaction leaves the allocate node when the request is granted. It keeps the tokens until it reaches a **release node** (or until it leaves the system). Release nodes take the specified number of tokens of various types from the transaction and give them to the designated allocate node. **Create nodes** create new tokens for designated allocate nodes. **Destroy nodes** remove tokens from designated allocate nodes.

Figure 8.4 shows a simple example. In it, transactions originate at START and proceed to the allocate node named #USERS. It initially has one token for each user allowed concurrently in the system. A transaction requests one of these tokens (which represent permission to execute). When granted, the transaction proceeds through the PROCESS submodel (to simplify this example, its details are not shown). Upon completion, the transaction releases its "permission" token at the COMPLETED node and exits the system. This illustrates allocate and release nodes; an example with create and destroy nodes appears later.

TABLE 8.2
PHASE-CHANGE SPECIFICATIONS

Category, phase	# visits	New phase	# times	Probability
CHG node:				
ATM_SESSION, 1	3	2	3	1
ATM_SESSION, 2	3	1	3	1

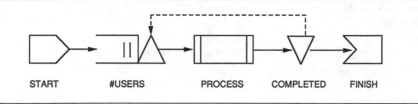

START   #USERS   PROCESS   COMPLETED   FINISH

FIGURE 8.4
An Advanced IPG with Allocate and Release Nodes.

The **parameters for allocate nodes** are:

- □ A declaration of token types and the number of each initially available
- □ Category phase specifications (number of visits and token request specifications)
- □ The queue-scheduling discipline (FCFS or priority are allowed), and a SKIP option grants subsequent requests when possible, even though the head of the queue must wait longer

Table 8.3 shows the parameters for the #USERS allocate node. Three types of tokens are declared, representing permission for a maximum of 50 CIS transac-

TABLE 8.3
ALLOCATE NODE SPECIFICATIONS

#USERS node:
QD: *FCFS SKIP*

Token type	Initial qty.
MAX_CIS	50
MAX_INQ	25
MAX_BATCH	1

Visits:

Cat, phase	Number
CIS	1
INQ	1
BATCH	1

Requests:

Cat, phase	Token	Number
CIS	MAX_CIS	1
INQ	MAX_INQ	1
BATCH	MAX_BATCH	1

tions, 25 INQ transactions, and 1 BATCH transaction to execute concurrently. Each category visits the #USERS node once (no phases are specified). Each category requests one permission token of its corresponding type. Permission is granted first-come-first-served, FCFS, with SKIP. So if the #USERS node has only one CIS token, and both an INQ and a CIS transaction want to execute, with the SKIP option the CIS transaction can proceed even if the INQ transaction arrives first.

Release nodes need parameters for each category phase. As shown in Table 8.4, in addition to the number of visits for each category phase, it needs the number of tokens of each type to be released and the name of the allocate node that is to receive them. In the example, each category releases its (one) permission token to the #USERS node. **Create and destroy nodes** need the number of visits for each category phase, and the request for creation (or destruction) of a specified number of token types to be added to (removed from) designated allocate nodes.

Figure 8.2 also shows three routing nodes for advanced IPGs. **Fork nodes** divide a transaction into child transactions. The children execute in parallel while the parent waits. Each child ceases execution when it reaches a **join node.** When all children reach the join node, the parent resumes execution (at the join node). A **split node** creates new transactions; the original and the new ones proceed in parallel. Upon completion, the split transactions leave the system; they do not join one another.

Figure 8.5 shows a simple example. Transactions arrive at START and receive service at the CPU and I/O nodes. When initial processing is complete, they FORK into child transactions, and each receives service at the CPU and I/O nodes. When concurrent processing is complete, they JOIN, complete the final processing at the CPU and I/O nodes, and leave the system.

TABLE 8.4
RELEASE NODE SPECIFICATIONS

COMPLETED node:
Visits:

Cat, phase	Number
CIS	1
INQ	1
BATCH	1

Requests:

Cat, phase	Token	Number	To node
CIS	MAX_CIS	1	#USERS
INQ	MAX_INQ	1	#USERS
BATCH	MAX_BATCH	1	#USERS

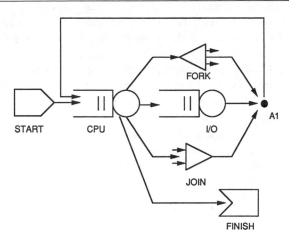

FIGURE 8.5
An Advanced IPG with Fork and Join Nodes.

Fork and split nodes need the number of visits and requests for each category phase that specify the number of children (or siblings) to be created and their category phase. Join nodes need only the number of visits for each category phase. Examples of these parameter specifications appear later.

In addition to the topology nodes, advanced IPGs also add **preemptive-priority scheduling** to the queue-scheduling disciplines for elementary IPG service nodes. With priority scheduling, each service request specifies the priority of each transaction category phase. Transactions are scheduled according to their priority value: The waiting transaction with the *greatest priority value* is granted its request first. *Preemptive priority* means that when a transaction arrives at the queue, if its priority is higher than that of the transaction currently in service, it preempts the transaction and begins execution without waiting. The preempted transaction is rescheduled. For example, a CPU node may specify preemptive-priority scheduling. The following is a hypothetical CPU request specification for each transaction category phase. Category CIS, Phase 1 has the highest priority, and the BATCH category has the lowest for CPU requests.

Category, phase	Priority	Mean service time
CIS, 1	10	50
CIS, 2	8	100
INQ	8	75
BATCH	1	1500

Advanced IPGs use the same modeling procedure as elementary IPGs: Create the model topology, derive the parameters from environment and software specifications, solve the model, and evaluate the results. IPGs can be solved either by simulation methods or by analytic solution techniques. Some tools are described later, in Section 8.7. The translation from IPGs to simulation packages is straightforward. The translation to analytic solvers is more difficult because passive resources and transaction forks, joins, and splits are not explicitly represented in all analytic packages. Few of the advanced IPG features permit efficient, exact analytic solutions; most require **approximate solution methods.**

Analytic solution tools differ in the features they support. Many have built-in approximate solution techniques. Advanced IPG features that tools may support include:

- □ Maximum number of concurrent users (or domains) for categories
- □ Finite queue sizes
- □ Preemptive-priority scheduling
- □ Phase changes
- □ Processing details within I/O subsystems

Model solutions are easy if your solution tool directly supports advanced IPG features. Approximate solution techniques are evolving rapidly, and if you use a tool that incorporates new techniques as they evolve, you will minimize your SPE modeling efforts. If your solver lacks the automatic approximation features, use the approximation techniques in this chapter for checkpoint evaluations to determine if further analysis is warranted.

As usual, a common approximation technique uses bounded analysis such as best- and worst-case solutions. The definition of best- and worst-case parameter values and successive refinements to them are given for each of the examples in Sections 8.3 and 8.4.

8.2 Advanced IPG Modeling Techniques

Advanced IPGs add features to elementary IPGs to increase their modeling power and allow more realistic models. As a result of the additional features, though, some advanced IPG features violate the conditions that enable efficient, exact analytic solutions. These conditions include:

- □ Passive resource usage
- □ Priority scheduling
- □ Transactions that spawn other concurrent processes (forks, splits, and joins)

While advanced IPGs with these features are easily solved with simulation tools, SPE suggests that you quickly assess the magnitude of the feature's effect on the performance metrics to see if the additional modeling effort and solution time are warranted. For example, if locks have an insignificant impact on performance, you can use simpler models without locks and focus on other dominant effects. Thus the SPE simple-to-realistic modeling strategy drives the use of advanced IPGs. We start with simple advanced IPGs and add additional features as they become significant.

8.2.1 Processing Phases

First consider the ability to change processing **phases** with advanced IPGs. Phase changes distinguish processing characteristics that differ over the life of the job; they also differentiate the resulting performance metrics. For example, the model in Figure 8.3 distinguishes the ATM request processing from the session over-head. The results show the estimated elapsed time and the device utilization by processing phase.

In simulation models, **phases control a job's flow** through the model topology. The following example illustrates this key difference between analytic and simulation solutions. Consider modeling a hypothetical system such as Figure 8.6(a) in which transactions arrive and flow through the CPU and I/OSS (twice each). After the third visit to the CPU, the transaction requests a lock before the I/O. Upon receiving it, the transaction executes the I/O, releases the lock, and returns to the CPU. It completes its CPU and I/OSS processing, then leaves the system.

The model in Figure 8.6(a) reflects the average behavior of this transaction. It correctly specifies the total visits to each device, and, if you estimate the average delay for a transaction to obtain the lock (at ReqLock), you can compute the transaction's elapsed time and other performance metrics. (Techniques for estima-ting the delay to obtain a passive resource are described in Section 8.3.) Notice the model's routing specifications: Transactions visit the CPU five times; when a transaction leaves the CPU, on the average 1 of 5 goes to Finish, 1 of 5 goes to ReqLock, and 3 of 5 go to I/OSS. Similarly, transactions visit I/OSS four times; upon completion, 1 of 4 goes to RelLock, and 3 of 4 return to the CPU. Analytic solutions compute statistics from these average values, but simulation solutions compute statistics by mimicking the processing steps for simulated transactions.

In a simulation model, when a transaction leaves I/OSS, the simulator makes a probabilistic decision to determine where it goes next. With the model specifica-tion in Figure 8.6(a), transactions next visit RelLock 1 of 4 times on the average, but each decision is an independent event and may differ from the average. It is like flipping a coin—50 percent of the time the coin will be heads, but it is possible to see four or more consecutive tails. So the probabilistic decisions could generate the

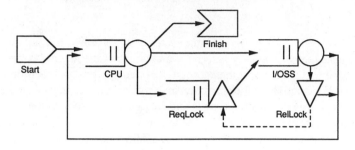

NODES	# VISITS
CPU	5
I/OSS	4
ReqLock	1
RelLock	1

(a)

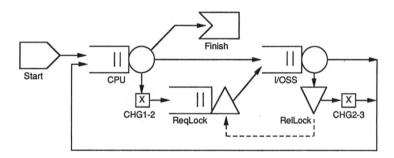

NODES	CATEGORY, PHASE	# VISITS
Start	Job, 1	1
CPU	Job, 1	3
	Job, 2	0
	Job, 3	2
I/OSS	Job, 1	2
	Job, 2	1
	Job, 3	1
Finish	Job, 3	1
CHG1-2	Job, 1	1
ReqLock	Job, 2	1
RelLock	Job, 2	1
CHG2-3	Job, 2	1

(b)

FIGURE 8.6
The advanced IPG in (a) specifies that, on the average, jobs make one visit to
ReqLock and RelLock. The model in (b) controls the routing with phase changes
to make sure that the visits occur in the desired sequence.

following sequence of visits for a transaction: . . . CPU, ReqLock, I/OSS, CPU, Finish. If there is only one lock token, this sequence causes the system to deadlock—a transaction leaves the system with the token, which is destroyed, and no one else can get it. For a simulation solution, the model parameters must ensure that the routing be ReqLock, I/OSS, RelLock.

The model in Figure 8.6(b) correctly controls the routing with phase changes. Before visiting ReqLock, transactions visit CHG1-2 where they change from Phase 1 to Phase 2. After completing the I/OSS visit, they must visit RelLock (Phase 2 makes no visits to the CPU), then visit CHG2-3 where they change to Phase 3 for the final processing. This model guarantees that transactions that visit ReqLock also visit RelLock. To check your understanding, review the model specifications and determine whether it is possible for a transaction to Finish without requesting the lock. How would you modify the specifications to allow, on the average, 2 I/Os and 1 visit to the CPU while the lock is held, and still ensure that the lock is freed before the Finish?

An ideal solver would take care of these deadlock-avoidance details for you. Check your solution tool's features to see how it controls routing. Note that some tools support phases by providing job-associated variables. The analyst sets the variables to record the job's execution phase (or state) and changes phases by changing the value of the variable. Solvers may not report results by phase; you may have to compute phase results from summary statistics based on the proportional resource use of each phase.

The previous example illustrates the routing problem with allocate and release nodes, but similar routing problems may occur in other advanced IPGs. For example, to solve the FORK and JOIN model in Figure 8.5 with a simulator, you need phase specifications to control routing. Sections 8.3 and 8.4 have other models with similar routing requirements. In these examples the model specifications for simulations are more complex than their analytic approximation. The checkpoint evaluations in Sections 8.3 and 8.4 seek to identify the situations that warrant this additional effort and the additional solution time.

The checkpoint evaluations use analytic approximation techniques. Some **general approximation methods** reviewed here are surrogate delays, flow equivalent servers, and shadow servers. The following sections introduce the methods; more detailed information is in [AGR83a] and [AGR83b].

8.2.2 Surrogate Delay Servers

Surrogate delay servers replace nodes, such as allocate nodes, whose residence times are difficult to calculate analytically. The surrogate nodes are delay nodes— they have no queueing. You estimate the service time for the surrogate delay server and solve the model iteratively: Estimate the service time, solve the model, and, if necessary, adjust the service time and repeat. Approximation techniques (described in Sections 8.3 and 8.4) supply procedures for service time estimates. With good approximations, you only need two to three iterations.

For example, you can use surrogate delays to limit the maximum number of users in Figure 8.4. Replace the #USERS allocate node with a delay server (and replace the COMPLETED release node with a branch point, because it has no service requirement). The best-case model has no delay, so solve it first to see if a delay is needed. If the number of transactions in each category in the PROCESS submodel is less than the maximum, the best-case model is sufficient. If any categories exceed the maximum, adjust their delay time and re-solve. Repeat until the delay appropriately limits the number of users. This is the general method. Specific approximation techniques (for maximum number of users and other problems) prescribe the service time calculations, how to determine the accuracy of the estimate, and how to adjust the service time if necessary.

8.2.3 Flow-Equivalent Servers

Flow-equivalent servers replace submodel details; flow-equivalent residence time and throughput represent the more detailed model without the computational expense. Use them in large models when you can calculate performance data for the submodel once and reuse it for other analyses. For example, you could calculate I/O subsystem performance and use the results for an I/OSS flow-equivalent server to study software design alternatives that vary the number of I/O requests (but do not vary the time to satisfy a request). You can also use flow-equivalent servers to mix the solution techniques: You can derive the submodel performance specifications for residence time or throughput from measurements, simulations, or analysis. The submodel residence time is the total elapsed time between an arrival and its departure from the subsystem. The submodel throughput is the rate of departures from the subsystem. Both depend on the workload intensity in the submodel, so you need a matrix with the range of submodel populations and the corresponding residence time or throughput. (Use this approach for submodels with small populations; it is easier to solve the original model for large submodel populations.)

Tools that analytically solve models containing a flow-equivalent server use a service rate that depends on the queue length. Tools may call flow-equivalent servers **load-dependent servers,** and they may automatically produce and retain the matrix of population and residence time (or throughput) for submodels. Details of the solution algorithms are beyond the scope of this concept discussion. For more information about them, see [LAZ84a] or [SCH82].

8.2.4 Shadow Servers

Shadow servers replace one service node that violates conditions required for efficient, exact analytic solution with two or more servers that enable efficient

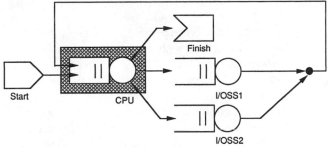

Parameters :

NODES	CATEGORY	# VISITS	SERVICE TIME
CPU	cust	18	.025
	ovhd	8	.055
I/OSS1	cust	11	.05
	ovhd	2	.05
I/OSS2	cust	6	.05
	ovhd	5	.05
Arrival rates: cust 1/sec			
ovhd 1/sec			

(a)

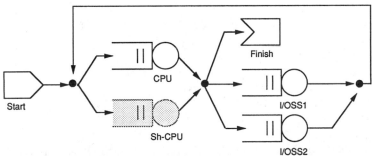

Revised Parameters: *

NODES	CATEGORY	# VISITS	SERVICE TIME
CPU	cust	18	.025
	ovhd	0	
Sh-CPU	cust	0	
	ovhd	8	.100

* Arrival rates and parameters for other nodes are unchanged.

(b)

FIGURE 8.7
The advanced IPG in (a) has a CPU with preemptive-priority scheduling that prevents efficient, exact analytic solution. The shadow-server model in (b) replaces the CPU with shadow servers that permit quick, approximate analytic solutions.

analytic solution, and whose combined performance represents the original server. A prime example is a CPU server with a priority queue-scheduling discipline. Replace the CPU server with shadow CPU servers and route jobs with different priorities to different servers. Approximation techniques adjust the service times of the shadow servers and iteratively solve the model until transactions experience comparable residence times to the original server with priority scheduling.

Because priority scheduling is important to system performance, let us consider how to derive shadow-server parameters for **preemptive-priority scheduling.** Consider the example in Figure 8.7. The original model in part (a) has a CPU with preemptive-priority scheduling. There are two transaction categories: Cust are transactions that provide customer services, and ovhd are transactions that provide internal services. The cust transactions have priority over ovhd transactions for CPU service. So if both cust and ovhd transactions are in the CPU queue, only the cust transactions can execute. If an ovhd transaction is receiving CPU service when a cust arrives, ovhd is immediately preempted and cust executes. Ovhd resumes when no cust transactions are present. This preemptive-priority queue-scheduling discipline prevents efficient, exact analytic solution (with the methods presented so far).

An easy approximation solves the model with the processor sharing (PS) discipline for the CPU. This approximation shows more contention for cust transactions at the CPU than is experienced in the actual system, so it gives a pessimistic total response time. (If the pessimistic results are well under the response time goal, this approximation is sufficient for SPE.)

The following approximation provides more realistic results. It is the **shadow-server method for preemptive-priority scheduling** proposed by Sevcik and described in [AGR83b], [LAZ84a], and [SEV77].

ALGORITHM 8.1: Sevcik's Shadow-Server Method for Preemptive-Priority Scheduling

For each server that permits preemptive-priority scheduling, add $P - 1$ shadow servers, where P is the number of different priorities. Route jobs to different servers depending on their priority class. The solution to this model would adequately represent the highest-priority jobs, but lower-priority jobs would experience less contention than the actual system. The lower-priority transactions see diminished capacity proportional to the utilization of the server by higher-priority jobs.

Sevcik proposes the following formula for the adjusted service time for shadow servers:

Adjusted service time for category j, $S'_j = \dfrac{S_j}{1 - \sum\limits_{k=1}^{j-1} U_k}$

(continued)

ALGORITHM 8.1 (*Continued*)

That is, set S'_j equal to the original service time for category j (S_j) divided by the capacity available to this category (1 minus the utilization of all the higher-priority categories—1 through $j - 1$).

Note that for closed models, the utilization is a model result—it is not known a priori. Thus closed models require iteration. Initially set the shadow-server time

$$S'_j = S_j$$

Solve the model, use the resulting utilization of the CPU servers in the above formula, and repeat until the throughput of the shadow server is sufficiently close to the previous solution.

For open models, the utilization is easy to calculate. From the formula in Chapter 5, the utilization of category k is equal to the server's throughput for category k times k's service time:

$$U_k = X_k S_k$$

So the adjusted service time formula for open models is:

$$S'_j = \frac{S_j}{1 - \sum_{k=1}^{j-1} X_k S_k}$$

□

The following example applies Sevcik's shadow-server method to the example in Figure 8.7.

EXAMPLE 8.1: Shadow-Server Approximation

The example depicted in Figure 8.7(b) has two categories with different priorities, so it needs one shadow server, called Sh-CPU. The original CPU server remains, but its queue scheduling changes to processor sharing (PS). All transactions with the highest priority (cust) go to the CPU server; all lower-priority transactions (ovhd) go to the shadow server. This removes the interference seen by the cust transactions with the PS approximation, but it also incorrectly removes the interference experienced by ovhd transactions when cust transactions want CPU service. Sevcik's adjusted service time for the ovhd jobs at the Sh-CPU server is:

$$S'_{ovhd} = \frac{S_{ovhd}}{1 - X_{cust} S_{cust}}$$

$$= \frac{.055}{1 - (18)(.025)} = .100 \text{ sec}$$

Figure 8.7(b) shows the shadow-server model parameters that differ from the processor-sharing model.

The model results are in Table 8.5. It shows both analytic and simulation results for comparison. The analytic results for Start, I/OSS1, and I/OSS2 are the same for the

(*continued*)

TABLE 8.5
RESULTS OF SHADOW-SERVER APPROXIMATION
FOR PREEMPTIVE-PRIORITY SCHEDULING

	Throughput		Utilization		Residence time		Total response time	
	cust	ovhd	cust	ovhd	cust	ovhd	cust	ovhd
Start								
analytic	1	1						
simulation	.97	1.10						
I/OSS1								
analytic	11	2	.55	.10	.143	.143		
simulation	10.3	2.2	.52	.11	.121	.159		
I/OSS2								
analytic	6	5	.30	.25	.111	.111		
simulation	5.7	5.1	.29	.25	.100	.128		
CPU:								
analytic-PS	18	8	.45	.44	.227	.500	6.33	4.84
analytic-shadow:							3.06	4.84
CPU	18	——	.45	——	.045	——		
Sh-CPU	——	8	——	.8	——	.500		
simulation	17	8.4	.42	.46	.063	.595	2.83	5.37

EXAMPLE 8.1 (*Continued*)

shadow-server and the processor-sharing approximations. The CPU results and the total response time differ. Note the dramatic difference in the total response time for the processor-sharing and shadow-server approximations. In this example, the response time for high-priority jobs is greatly overestimated with the processor-sharing approximation. The response time difference depends on the demand of lower-priority jobs. Sevcik's shadow-server approximation works well when lower-priority jobs infrequently make large service demands.   ☐

The results in Example 8.1 show another difference between analytic and simulation solutions. The simulation model parameters specify that arrivals have an exponential distribution with a mean of 1 second. The results for the Start node show that the simulated arrival rate (throughput) varies slightly from the mean. This affects the other simulation results—for example, the simulated node throughput of cust transactions is lower than the analytic, and the ovhd is higher for all other nodes. The utilization, residence time, and queue length also differ accordingly. Simulation solutions have another problem that analytic solutions do not: The results differ depending on the length of the simulation run. This example ran for 200 (simulated) seconds; the (transient) results were discarded; then it ran for 500 (simulated) seconds to produce the results shown. If we wish to see average arrival rates closer to 1, the simulation must run longer. It is vital, but nontrivial, to determine the length of time that simulators must run to produce reliable results. Most simulators provide guidance in their documentation. A general discussion of the problem and viable solutions are in [SAU81].

There are many other approximation techniques for preemptive-priority scheduling. Agrawal suggests a variation of Sevcik's method with a different adjusted service time. He also developed a technique that uses a "load-dependent server" for the shadow server [AGR83b]. Several techniques modify the solution equations rather than the model formulation ([BRY83], [CHA83]). The latter cannot be used with commercial solvers because users do not have access to the solution equations; however, most commercial solvers have built-in approximations for priority scheduling. Why include this discussion if commercial products have built-in approximations?—to illustrate the shadow-server method, provide insight into approximation techniques, and to guide those without built-in approximations. The shadow-server method applies to other types of models with servers that prevent efficient, exact, analytic analysis. Another application is discussed in Section 8.3.

8.2.5 Advanced IPG Modeling Strategy

As their development progresses, complex systems require more detailed models than those in Chapter 5 for more precise performance predictions. More complex models are appropriate when the software system design evolves and developers can provide more precise performance specifications. This maintains the balance between the precision of the model's input data and the model complexity.

The advanced system execution models reflect the synergism between the software, the environment, and other workloads. For example, locking delays the new software when the resource is unavailable. Locks also affect the environment because transactions that suspend to await locks temporarily reduce the contention for other shared computer resources, and lock scheduling adds overhead processing. Locks may affect other workloads that access the locked resource. The optimistic analyses of the elementary system execution models ignore locking. Advanced IPGs represent the synergistic effects of locks.

The advanced modeling strategy represents the synergism with advanced IPGs and uses checkpoint evaluations to identify models that warrant further study with more detailed simulation models. The analytic approximations produce performance metrics to assess average behavior. When they indicate that the synergistic effects are significant, you not only need more precise estimates of average behavior—you also need to examine closely the interactions among scenarios. For example, the *average* lock contention delay may lead to acceptable average response times, but under some conditions a log jam may build up waiting for lock possession, and it may take a very long time to clear the log jam. During that time interval, responsiveness may be unacceptable. Similar phenomena occur in parallel and distributed processing systems. The analytic checkpoint evaluations identify situations like this that warrant further study with more detailed models and solution techniques.

The checkpoint evaluations use proven analytic approximation techniques. There are many approximations in the literature; this chapter describes *how to use a proven method* for each checkpoint evaluation—it does not provide derivations of the methods, nor does it cover the spectrum of available methods. The emphasis is on using checkpoint evaluations for SPE. References are provided for those who want more detailed information on approximations.

Complex software systems may have many synergistic effects. The next two sections cover topics vital to the performance of many large software systems in the near future: serialization delays due to exclusive resource use, and parallel and distributed processing (and Chapter 9 covers a third—memory use).

Even with this limited coverage, this chapter is the largest in the book. It is impossible to thoroughly cover all relevant topics, so the detailed discussion is limited to topics for which advanced system execution models are essential for reasonable performance predictions and which have well-established modeling technology. Section 8.5 briefly describes other software design challenges and other computer environment challenges.

8.3 Serialization Delays

During processing, jobs may need exclusive use of a system resource. For example, file or database indices and data records require exclusive use when they are updated to preserve their integrity. If two jobs try to update at the same time, the contents may be garbled. Other resources that require exclusive use include message buffers and operating system–critical sections. *Serialization delay* is the time that a job must wait to gain exclusive use of the resource. It affects performance in three ways:

- ☐ The response time of jobs forced to wait on the objects is lengthened.
- ☐ The waiting jobs do not use other active resources while they wait, so the contention for active resources is reduced and other jobs execute at a faster rate.
- ☐ The time to schedule the resources increases the job service requirements.

If jobs hold resources for a short time and request them infrequently, the performance degradation is negligible. If, on the other hand, the opposite is true, lock contention may lead to a situation with only one process at a time able to execute.

Software acquire-release strategies vary from one extreme, obtaining exclusive data at the beginning of execution and releasing it upon job completion, to the opposite extreme of holding a data object only when ready to actually change the information, and reprocessing the transaction if the information has been changed by an intervening job.

The pertinent performance engineering principle (in Chapter 2) is:

> *Shared resources principle:* **Share resources when possible; when exclusive access is required, minimize the sum of the holding time and the scheduling time.**

Use advanced IPGs to identify the appropriate holding and scheduling combination and quantify the performance effect of each. System software designers can use the same models to select from among designs for their locking mechanisms. The following subsections prescribe models for three SPE evaluations:

1. Jobs that queue for exclusive use of resources

2. Resources that allow either shared or exclusive use

3. Locking mechanism evaluations

For each evaluation, we represent the synergistic behavior with advanced IPGs, then use some checkpoint evaluations to identify when the performance effect warrants more detailed study.

8.3.1 Exclusive Use of Resources

The first evaluation represents and analyzes serialization delays due to queueing for exclusive use of resources. We represent this behavior in the software execution model with lock-free or acquire-release nodes that delineate the scope of the exclusive use. Then we distinguish locked and unlocked processing phases, and compute distinct IPG parameters (visits and service requirements) for each phase.

EXAMPLE 8.2: Acquire and Release in Software and Advanced System Execution Models

The revised ATM session software model in Figure 8.8(a) locks the account file after successfully initiating a session and frees it just before termination. Resource requirements are specified for the lock and free nodes. The corresponding advanced IPG is in Figure 8.8(b). To simplify the discussion, it has only one I/O device; the extension to more detailed topologies is straightforward. An allocate node, REQ, represents the request for the lock on the account file. REQ initially contains one *Acct-lock* token. The corresponding release node, REL, returns the *Acct-lock* token to the REQ node. A phase-change node, CHG,

(continued)

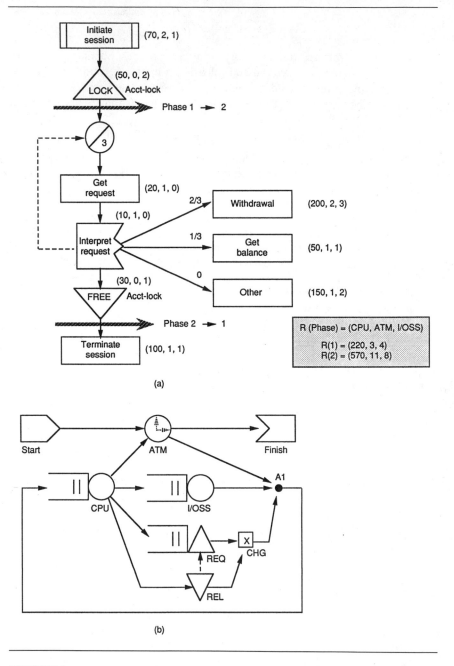

FIGURE 8.8
The software execution model in (a) specifies the proposed strategy to lock and free the account file. Phase changes control the routing and distinguish performance metrics in the advanced IPG. The advanced IPG in (b) uses allocate and release nodes to control the account lock.

EXAMPLE 8.2 (*Continued*)

distinguishes processing (and performance metrics) in the locked state from processing in the unlocked state. The dashed line in the software model shows where phase changes occur. Note that in this model the change from Phase 1 (unlocked) to Phase 2 (locked) takes place after the lock is obtained. In these models of intermediate complexity, it is convenient to attribute all the overhead to obtain locks to one phase or the other, rather than try to obtain a more realistic apportionment. If it is easy for you to divide the lock and free overhead between the locked and unlocked states, your models can be more realistic. Note that a best-case study assumes that lock and free overhead is all Phase 1, while a worst-case study assumes it is all Phase 2.

The next step is to compute the **advanced IPG model parameters.** First compute the total resource requirements, R, separately for each phase. Apply Algorithm 4.1's basic path reduction rules to calculate the total computer resource requirements for each phase. Figure 8.8(a) shows the results for Phases 1 and 2: $R(1) = (220, 3, 4)$ and $R(2) = (570, 11, 8)$. Next compute the visits to each node in the advanced IPG for each phase. Table 8.6 shows the model parameters. The first column shows the nodes in the graph. The second identifies the category-phase combinations that visit each node. For example, only Phase 1 sessions visit

(*continued*)

TABLE 8.6
ADVANCED IPG MODEL PARAMETERS FOR EXCLUSIVE RESOURCE USE

Nodes	Cat, phase	# visits	QD	Request Serv. time	Other
Start	session, 1	1			1 session/sec
ATM	session, 1	3	Delay	1	
	session, 2	11		1	
CPU	session, 1	7	PS	.000314	
	session, 2	20		.000285	
I/OSS	session, 1	4	FCFS	.05	
	session, 2	8		.05	
REQ	session, 1	1	FCFS		# tokens = 1, type = Acct-lock (initial Acct-lock = 1)
REL	session, 2	1			# tokens = 1 type = Acct-lock tonode = REQ
A1	session, 1	7			
	session, 2	20			
CHG	session, 1	1			newphase = 2 # times = 1
	session, 2	1			newphase = 1 # times = 1
Finish	session, 1	1			

EXAMPLE 8.2 (*Continued*)

the Start, Finish, and REQ nodes. Only Phase 2 sessions visit the REL node. The other nodes are visited by sessions in either phase. The third column shows the number of visits for each. From the software model, Phase 1 sessions visit the ATM 3 times and the I/OSS 4 times. Similarly, Phase 2 sessions visit the ATM 11 times and the I/OSS 8 times. Phase 1 sessions make one REQ, and Phase 2 make one REL. From this information, compute the number of visits to A1 by each phase; then use the result to compute the number of visits to the CPU. Check your understanding by computing the number of visits by each phase to A1 and to the CPU and compare your results to the table.

The fourth column shows the queue-scheduling discipline for the resource nodes. The fifth column defines the request made by each category phase at each service node. The mean service time is specified for active servers: The ATM service time is the mean "think time," 1 second, and the I/OSS (disk) is 0.05 seconds. For the CPU, the mean service time formula (3) in Algorithm 5.2 gives the service time for each category phase:

$$S = \frac{Rw}{V}$$

Phase 1: $\dfrac{220 \times .00001}{7} = .000314$

Phase 2: $\dfrac{570 \times .00001}{20} = .000285$

The request for the REQ and REL nodes (in column 6) specifies the number of tokens of each type requested or released for each phase. The nodes are not active servers, so there is no service time. The specification for the CHG node says that Phase 1 jobs always change to Phase 2, and Phase 2 jobs always change to Phase 1. This completes the model specification.

□

Queueing network models with passive resource nodes (such as REQ and REL) cannot (efficiently) be solved exactly with analytic methods. You can use a simulation solver to obtain the performance metrics: response time, throughput, device residence time, utilization, and queue length. The phases distinguish the performance metrics for locked and unlocked processing. The simulation results also report the waiting time for exclusive access and the overall response time. The REQ utilization and queue length indicate the contention for exclusive access. Simulation results appear later in this section.

Analytic checkpoint evaluations identify systems with bottlenecks due to exclusive resource use. The **best-case evaluation** assumes there is no delay to get exclusive use. To solve the best case analytically, replace the REQ and REL nodes with branch nodes. The results for Example 8.2 are in Table 8.7. The best-case scenario has a 15.5-second response time; however, notice that there would be a total of 12 jobs in Phase 2-locked. Since at most one job may be locked, the best-case model indicates that further study is needed.

A **more realistic model** represents the queueing for exclusive resource use. It

TABLE 8.7
ANALYTIC CHECKPOINT EVALUATION: BEST CASE

	ATM	I/OSS	CPU	System
Throughput:				1
Unlocked	3	4	7	
Locked	11	8	20	
Utilization:				
Unlocked	3/50	.20	.0022	
Locked	11/50	.40	.0057	
Residence Time:				
Unlocked	1	.125	.000315	3.5
Locked	11	.125	.000287	12.0
				15.5 Total
Queue Length:				
Unlocked	3	.5	.0022	3.5022
Locked	11	1	.0057	12.0057

is based on the **aggregate-server method** of Agrawal and Buzen [AGR83a]. To use the method, we perform the following steps:

1. Clone each active server visited by locked phases to create "shadow servers" that segregate locked from unlocked processing. Create a surrogate delay server to represent the delay to obtain exclusive use.

2. Compute the visits and mean service times from the software execution model's results for each processing phase.

3. Adjust the service times to approximate the contention between locked and unlocked jobs.

4. Aggregate the "locked" shadow servers and the surrogate delay server into a single server and approximate its mean service time.

5. Solve the model to obtain approximate response times, device throughput, utilization, queue length, and residence times.

The method is explained with the following examples; it is formally defined in the inset.

EXAMPLE 8.3: Approximation of Lock Contention Delay

In Figure 8.9(a), **shadow servers** segregate processing that occurs in locked and unlocked phases. The Lockdel node is a surrogate delay node that approximates the delay to acquire the lock. The job flow is as follows: Transactions arrive, flow from the ATM-1 to the

(*continued*)

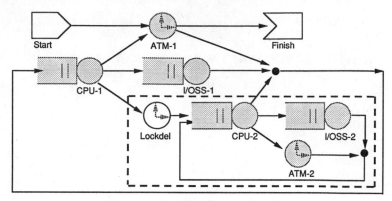

NODE	# VISITS	MEAN SERVICE TIME, s_I	ADJUSTED MEAN SERVICE TIME, s'_I
ATM-1	3	1	1
CPU-1	7	0.000314	0.0003158
I/OSS-1	4	0.05	0.08333
Lockdel	1	?	
CPU-2	20	0.000285	0.0002856
I/OSS-2	8	0.05	0.0625
ATM-2	11	1	1

(a)

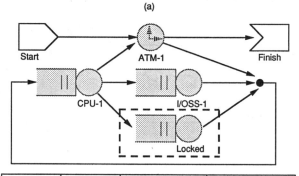

NODE	# VISITS	MEAN SERVICE TIME, s_I	ADJUSTED MEAN SERVICE TIME, s'_I
ATM-1	3	1	1
CPU-1	7	0.000314	0.0003158
I/OSS-1	4	0.05	0.08333
Locked	1	11.4057	11.506

(b)

FIGURE 8.9
Approximation of Lock Contention Delay. The advanced IPG in (a) uses shadow servers to segregate processing in the locked versus unlocked state. The aggregate server model in (b) consolidates the "locked" set of shadow servers into the Locked queue server.

EXAMPLE 8.3 (*Continued*)

CPU-1, and cycle through the CPU-1, ATM-1, and I/OSS-1 nodes until they need the *Acct-lock*. They then go to the Lockdel node, and upon their departure they flow through CPU-2, ATM-2, and I/OSS-2 until they complete all locked processing (through the Free node in the software model). Then they return to CPU-1 and cycle through CPU-1, ATM-1, and I/OSS-1 until the session is complete.

Derive the model parameters as follows. The visits to the "unlocked" servers come from the Phase 1 software evaluation in Figure 8.8(a): $R(1) = (220, 3, 4)$, so there are 3 visits to ATM-1, 4 to I/OSS-1, and 7 to CPU-1 (2 come from ATM-1, 4 from I/OSS-1, and 1 from completion of locked processing, at CPU-2). The visits to the "locked" servers also come from the software evaluation, $R(2) = (570, 11, 8)$. So there are 8 visits to I/OSS-2, 11 to ATM-2, and 20 visits to CPU-2.

The third column in the chart shows the mean service time for each node. The ATM-1 and I/OSS-1 times come from the environment specifications, as usual. For CPU-1 it is:

$$\frac{Rw}{V} = \frac{(220)(.00001)}{7} = .000314$$

and for CPU-2:

$$\frac{(570)(.00001)}{20} = .000285$$

The service time for the Lockdel node is covered later. First, we derive the more realistic model parameters for the other servers. Because all the locked processing is removed from the CPU-1, ATM-1, and I/OSS-1 nodes, and all the unlocked processing is removed from CPU-2, ATM-2, and I/OSS-2, a solution of this model shows less contention for the servers than actually occurs. To compensate, we use an heuristic algorithm for elongating their services times to approximate the actual contention delays due to the "missing" workload: Elongate the service time based on the fraction of the capacity of the server available to jobs of this category phase.

$$\text{Adjusted service time, } S_i' = \frac{S_i}{1 - X_0\, Vsh_i\, Ssh_i}$$

where:
Vsh_i is the number of visits to the sister shadow server, i
Ssh_i is the mean service time of the sister shadow server, i

For example:

$$\text{for I/OSS-1, } S_i' = \frac{.05}{1 - (1)(8)(.05)} = .0833$$

because there are 8 visits to the sister shadow server I/OSS-2 with shadow service time = 0.05. Similarly,

$$\text{for I/OSS-2, } S_i' = \frac{.05}{1 - (1)(4)(.05)} = .0625$$

(*continued*)

EXAMPLE 8.3 (*Continued*)

because there are 4 visits to the sister shadow server I/OSS-1. This elongated service time approximates the contention delays of the actual I/OSS server. When a node's sister shadow server has low utilization, the node's elongated service time is close to the original service time. If the sister has high utilization, the node's elongated service time is correspondingly higher. Check your understanding of the elongated service time formula by computing adjusted service times for CPU-1 and CPU-2. Do not elongate the service time for the delay nodes (such as the ATM) because they have no queue, so you do not need to approximate contention delays.

The next step in the aggregate-server method for approximate lock results is to aggregate the "locked" shadow servers and the Lockdel surrogate-delay server into a single active queue server as shown in Figure 8.9(b). Only one job may be locked; thus the new queue incorporates into its residence time the (possible) delay to acquire the lock. The mean service time for the new Locked node is the combined service from each "locked" shadow server:

$$
\begin{aligned}
\text{CPU-2} &= 20 \text{ visits} \times .0002856 = &.005712 \\
+ \text{ IOSS-2} &= 8 \text{ visits} \times .0625 &= &.5 \\
+ \text{ ATM-2} &= 11 \text{ visits} \times 1.0 &= &\underline{11.0} \\
& & &11.506
\end{aligned}
$$

□

Agrawal and Buzen report good results with the elongated service time heuristic in [AGR83a], and other experience has shown that it yields reasonably close results. Later in this section, you can compare simulation results to analytic approximations that use this heuristic.

If you try to solve the model in Example 8.3 with Algorithm 5.1's open QNM computation, you will find that the Locked node is saturated. From the device throughput formula in Algorithm 5.1, $X_i = X_0 V_i$, the Locked device throughput must be the system throughput X_0, which is 1 session per second, times the number of visits to the node, which is 1. So the Locked throughput, X_i, must be 1 transaction per second. This means that the *maximum* Locked service time is $1/X_i$ or 1 second; otherwise the system saturates. Because the Locked service time in this example is over 11 seconds, the lock strategy has serious problems. Actually, the software should hold the lock much less than 1 second, because when the Locked queue has high utilization, the response time increases greatly (for Locked service time = 0.99 seconds in this example; the system response time is 103.5 seconds!). So, with easy, analytic, checkpoint evaluations, you can identify problems in lock strategies.

Let's continue with the example to see the analytic results when there are no lock problems. The previous analysis shows that the lock holding time must be less than 1 second. Since ATM interactions take 1 second, there can be no interactions while the lock is held. This implies that the software should request the lock after the customer completes the withdrawal request definition, and free the lock before going back to the ATM.

ALGORITHM 8.2: Aggregate-Server Method for Approximating Delays for Exclusive Resource Use in Open Models

1. Clone each active server visited by locked phases to create shadow servers. Create a surrogate delay server to represent the delay to obtain exclusive use.

2. Specify the routing so that unlocked jobs visit one set of shadow servers, and locked jobs visit the sister set of shadow servers. Compute the visits to each server from the software execution model's results for locked and unlocked phases.

3.

a. First compute the mean service time of the active servers i from the environment specifications and the software execution model's results for locked and unlocked phases by adapting Algorithm 5.2 to use R_i results for each phase:

$$S_i = \frac{R\,(phase)_i w_i}{V\,(phase)_i}$$

b. The service time parameters in Step 3a represent less contention for the active resources than actually occurs. To compensate, use the following heuristic algorithm to elongate the service time of the shadow servers to approximate the actual contention delays due to the "missing" workload:

Adjusted service time, $S_i' = \dfrac{S_i}{1 - X_0 Vsh_i Ssh_i}$

where Vsh_i is the number of visits to the sister shadow server, i
Ssh_i is the mean service time of the sister shadow server, i

4. Aggregate the surrogate delay server and all the "locked" shadow servers into a single active queue server. Its mean service time is the total visits $\times$ adjusted service time of each of the shadow servers:

$$S_{locked}' = \sum_{i \in sh_{locked}} V_i S_i'$$

where sh_{locked} is the set of "locked" shadow servers

5. Solve the model.

EXAMPLE 8.4: Revised Locking Strategy

Figure 8.10(a) and (b) revises the software model to reduce lock holding time. All the locked processing is within the withdrawal node expansion in part (a). The advanced IPG topology is like Figure 8.9(a), except that the ATM-2 server is not needed. The aggregate server model is like Figure 8.9(b).

The revised parameters for the best-case model are not shown; their calculation is

(continued)

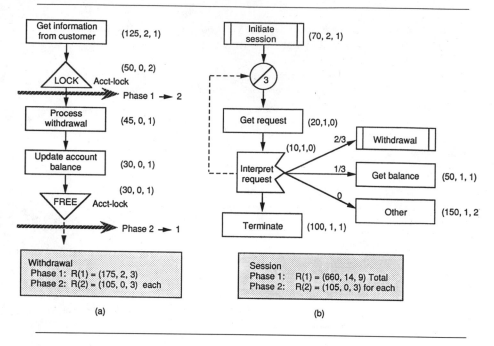

FIGURE 8.10
The revised locking strategy lock's and free's within the withdrawal processing is shown in (a). The revised session processing is in (b).

EXAMPLE 8.4 (*Continued*)

straightforward. The revised parameters for the more realistic model are in Table 8.8. The number of visits in the second column comes from $R(1) = (660, 14, 9)$, and $R(2) = (105, 0, 3)$ for each of 2 locks. So I/OSS-1 has 9 visits and I/OSS-2 has $3 \times 2 = 6$ visits. Compute the mean service times as before; then compute the elongated service times from the heuristic. Check your understanding by computing service and elongated service times. Note that in the aggregate model, there are 2 visits to the Locked node since there are two withdrawals. Each visit's adjusted service time is $((8 \times .000262 + (6 \times .0909))/2 = 0.2738$.

Table 8.9 shows the best-case model results (with no lock delay). The scenario response time is 17.01 seconds, but the queue length of locked jobs is 1.202, so further study is needed. The more realistic results using the parameters in Table 8.8 are also in Table 8.9. The scenario response time is 17.02 seconds. The queue length of locked jobs is 1.21, but it includes the jobs waiting to obtain the lock.

□

These analytic results are only approximate, but they are sufficient to identify problems. In this example, the revised lock strategy yields satisfactory performance. If the lock holding time is closer to the maximum holding time, further

TABLE 8.8
REVISED PARAMETERS
FOR REALISTIC
CHECKPOINT EVALUATION

Node	# visits	Mean service time	Adjusted service time
ATM-1	14	1	1
CPU-1	24	.000257	.0002755
I/OSS-1	9	.05	.0714
CPU-2	8	.0002625	.0002642
I/OSS-2	6	.05	.0909
Locked	2	.151	.2738

study is advised. The heuristic for elongated service time gives reasonably close device residence times. The results are optimistic because the aggregate server time aggregates the elongated service times but does not include contention delays at each of the "locked" shadow servers. These examples illustrate the

TABLE 8.9
REVISED LOCKING STRATEGY RESULTS

Best case	ATM	I/OSS	CPU	Locked	System
Throughput:					1
Unlocked	14	9	22		
Locked	0	6	6		
Utilization:					
Unlocked	14/50	.45	.0068		
Locked	0	.3	.0019		
Residence Time:					
Unlocked	1	.12	.00025		15.81
Locked		.08	.00006		1.20
					17.01 Total
Queue Length:					
Unlocked	14	1.8	.0069		15.807
Locked	0	1.2	.0019		1.202
More Realistic:					
Throughput	14	9	24	2	1
Utilization	14/50	.6426	.0066	.5476	
Residence Time	1	.1998	.00028	.6052	17.02
Queue Length	14	1.798	.0067	1.2104	17.02

procedure for open models; the models for closed systems are slightly different. Details on them can be found in [AGR83a].

Finally, these models produce average values for performance metrics. While locking affects the averages, the influence on the variance and distribution is greater. Until better analytic approximation techniques are developed for quickly and easily getting approximate means and variances, simulation solutions offer the best results. Tables 8.10 and 8.11 show the model parameters and simulation results, respectively, for the revised lock strategy. The averages are reasonably close to the analytic approximation. The analytic results show slightly lower response time and lock contention than the corresponding simulation results. Note the standard deviations. In particular, the session response time was as high as 167 seconds. Although the average number of sessions in the REQ queue is 0.63, the detailed simulation results reported that approximately 15 percent of the time there were more than three waiting. Thus simulation results indicated that the mean response time was acceptable, but the standard deviation was high. So further reductions in the lock holding time should be examined during detailed design. The lock holding time should be carefully tracked during implementation because it is critical to performance.

TABLE 8.10
ADVANCED IPG MODEL PARAMETERS

Nodes	Cat, phase	# visits	QD	Request Serv. time	Other
Start	session, 1	1			1 session/sec
ATM	session, 1	14	Delay	1	
CPU	session, 1	24	PS	.0002749	
	session, 2	8		.0002625	
I/OSS	session, 1	9	FCFS	.05	
	session, 2	6		.05	
REQ	session, 1	1	FCFS		# tokens = 1, type = Acct-lock (initial Acct-lock = 1)
REL	session, 2	1			# tokens = 1 type = Acct-lock tonode = REQ
A1	session, 1	24			
	session, 2	8			
CHG	session, 1	2			newphase = 2 # times = 2
	session, 2	2			newphase = 1 # times = 1
Finish	session, 1	1			

TABLE 8.11
REVISED LOCKING STRATEGY SIMULATION RESULTS

Nodes	Throughput	Utilization	Residence time		Queue length	
			Mean	Std. dev.	Mean	Std. dev.
ATM	14.57		0.99	1.01	14.57	3.61
CPU	33.6	0.0092	0.000287	0.00029	0.01	0.1
I/OSS	15.8	0.78	0.12	0.107	1.89	1.68
REQ	2.17		0.63	0.988	1.37	2.35
Acct-lock		0.596				
System	1.038		17.17	18.25		
Maximum Response Time 167 seconds						

8.3.2 Resource Sharing and Locking

Next, consider modeling systems that allow both sharing and locking of resources. This occurs when:

□ Only one transaction can lock a resource.

□ Any number can share it.

□ Transactions needing exclusive use must wait until no other transaction has the lock and no other transaction is sharing it.

□ Transactions needing shared access must wait until no locks are held.

EXAMPLE 8.5: Lock, Free, and Share in Software and Advanced System Execution Models

Chapter 4 uses lock, free, and share nodes to specify passive resource use in software execution models. Figure 8.11 gives an example. Category 1 is the Withdrawal scenario from Figure 5.8 modified to use the revised strategy for lock and free of *Acct-lock* (as in Figure 8.10[a]). Category 2 is the Get balance scenario from Figure 5.8. The "Process request (Get balance)" expansion shows the request for shared access to *Acct-lock* to ensure that the account balance is not being changed. Resource requirements are specified for the share and free nodes. Phase 2 identifies processing performed while the resource is shared. Phase 1 identifies processing that does not use the resource. The resource requirements for each phase are calculated separately, as before.

The advanced IPG topology for this model is the same as in Figure 8.8(b). The model parameters differ: They include two transaction categories, and the REQ and REL parameters differ for shared and exclusive resource use. The REQ node grants both share and lock requests, but the model parameter requests differ. The parameters are in Table 8.12. The first column contains the IPG node names. The second lists each transaction category and phase that visits each node, and column 3 specifies the number of visits. The phases control

(continued)

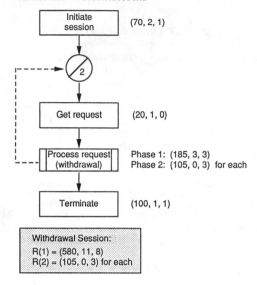

CATEGORY 1: WITHDRAWAL SESSION
Arrival rate = 1 session/second

Initiate session	(70, 2, 1)
2	
Get request	(20, 1, 0)
Process request (withdrawal)	Phase 1: (185, 3, 3) Phase 2: (105, 0, 3) for each
Terminate	(100, 1, 1)

Withdrawal Session:
R(1) = (580, 11, 8)
R(2) = (105, 0, 3) for each

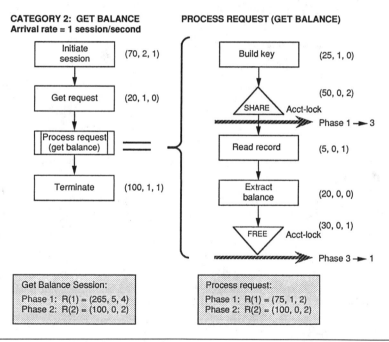

CATEGORY 2: GET BALANCE
Arrival rate = 1 session/second

PROCESS REQUEST (GET BALANCE)

Initiate session	(70, 2, 1)
Get request	(20, 1, 0)
Process request (get balance)	
Terminate	(100, 1, 1)

Build key	(25, 1, 0)
SHARE Acct-lock	(50, 0, 2) Phase 1 → 3
Read record	(5, 0, 1)
Extract balance	(20, 0, 0)
FREE Acct-lock	(30, 0, 1) Phase 3 → 1

Get Balance Session:
Phase 1: R(1) = (265, 5, 4)
Phase 2: R(2) = (100, 0, 2)

Process request:
Phase 1: R(1) = (75, 1, 2)
Phase 2: R(2) = (100, 0, 2)

FIGURE 8.11
Software Execution Models That Represent Both Locked and Shared Resource Usage.

380

EXAMPLE 8.5 (*Continued*)

the transaction routing. The transaction flow is as follows. A Withdrawal session arrives from the source node, Start (in Phase 1), and flows through the ATM, CPU, and I/OSS until it needs exclusive use of the account file. Then it goes to REQ. After receiving exclusive access, it changes to Phase 2 and cycles through the CPU and I/OSS. When it is ready to free the account file, it goes to REL, changes back to Phase 1, and continues to cycle through the CPU, I/OSS and ATM nodes. The session has two withdrawals, so it repeats the lock request, Phase 2 processing, and release before completing the session and leaving the system. The flow is similar for a Get balance transaction. After receiving its Share request, it changes to Phase 2, cycles through the CPU and I/OSS, releases the resource, and

(*continued*)

TABLE 8.12
ADVANCED IPG FOR SHARED AND EXCLUSIVE RESOURCE USE

Nodes	Cat, phase	# visits	QD	Request Service time	Other
Start	wdraw, 1	1			1 session/sec
	gbal, 1	1			1 session/sec
ATM	wdraw, 1	11	Delay	1	
	gbal, 1	5		1	
CPU	wdraw, 1	20	PS	.00029	
	wdraw, 2	8		.0002625	
	gbal, 1	9		.0002944	
	gbal, 2	3		.000333	
I/OSS	wdraw, 1	8	FCFS	.05	
	wdraw, 2	6			
	gbal, 1	4			
	gbal, 2	2			
REQ	wdraw, 1	2	FCFS		(initial Acct-lock = ⟨max⟩) # tokens = ⟨max⟩ type = Acct-lock
	gbal, 1	1			# tokens = 1 type = Acct-lock
REL	wdraw, 2	2			# tokens = ⟨max⟩ tonode = REQ
	gbal, 2	1			# tokens = 1 tonode = REQ
CHG	wdraw, 1	2			newphase = 2, #times = 2
	wdraw, 2	2			newphase = 1, #times = 2
	gbal, 1	1			newphase = 2, #times = 1
	gbal, 2	1			newphase = 1, #times = 1

EXAMPLE 8.5 (*Continued*)

changes back to Phase 1. There is only one Get balance request, so it visits REQ and REL once, and CHG twice—once in Phase 1 and once in Phase 2.

Derive the queue-scheduling discipline, QD, and service time specifications as usual. Note the token request and release specifications. Initially there are enough tokens for the maximum number of sessions in the system at one time. Each session that needs shared access requests one token and releases it when done. Each session needing exclusive use requests all the tokens. If any sessions have shared access at the time, the session needing exclusive access must wait for them to complete because all tokens are not available.

□

As usual, we start with **analytic checkpoint evaluations** to identify situations that warrant further study. The **best-case evaluation** assumes there is no

TABLE 8.13
**BEST-CASE MODEL PARAMETERS FOR SHARED
AND EXCLUSIVE RESOURCE USE**

Nodes	Cat, phase	# visits	QD	Request Service time	Other
Start	wdraw, 1	1			1 session/sec
	gbal, 1	1			1 session/sec
ATM	wdraw, 1	11	Delay	1	
	gbal, 1	5		1	
CPU	wdraw, 1	20	PS	.00029	
	wdraw, 2	8		.0002625	
	gbal, 1	9		.0002944	
	gbal, 2	3		.000333	
I/OSS	wdraw, 1	8	FCFS	.05	
	wdraw, 2	6			
	gbal, 1	4			
	gbal, 2	2			
REQ	wdraw, 1	2			*Replace with branch node
	gbal, 1	1			
REL	wdraw, 2	2			*Replace with branch node
	gbal, 2	1			
CHG	wdraw, 1	2			newphase = 2, #times = 2
	wdraw, 2	2			newphase = 1, #times = 2
	gbal, 1	1			newphase = 2, #times = 1
	gbal, 2	1			newphase = 1, #times = 1

delay to get exclusive or shared use. To check your understanding, compute the model parameters for the best-case model. Next, note the parameters in Table 8.13 for the I/OSS node for the best-case model. The device utilization and device throughput formulas in Algorithm 5.1,

$$U_i = X_i S_i, \text{ where } X_i = X_0 V_i$$

applied to the I/OSS node, show that $X_0 = 1$, and $V_i = 20$ (total visits for all categories and phases), so $X_i = 20$. When $S_i = 0.05$, $U_i = 100\%$. That is, the I/OSS node is saturated. This checkpoint evaluation indicates serious problems with this strategy for locking and sharing, and that further study is needed. This also illustrates that relatively small increases in resource requirements for bottleneck devices can have dramatic consequences for performance. Software solutions to the problem call for reducing the number of I/O operations. System solutions call for spreading the I/Os across multiple devices or getting faster devices.

Let's continue with the best-case evaluation using faster devices to further illustrate the analytic checkpoint evaluations. Table 8.14 shows the best-case

TABLE 8.14
ANALYTIC CHECKPOINT EVALUATION: BEST-CASE RESULTS

	ATM	I/OSS*	CPU	System Wdraw	Gbal
Throughput:				1	1
wdraw, unlocked	11	8	18		
wdraw, locked	0	6	6		
gbal, free	5	4	8		
gbal, shared	0	2	2		
Utilization:					
wdraw, unlocked	11/50	.32	.0059		
wdraw, locked	0	.24	.0020		
gbal, free	5/50	.16	.0030		
gbal, shared	0	.08	.0007		
Residence Time:					
wdraw, unlocked	1	.2	.00059	12.6	
wdraw, locked	——	.2	.00020	1.2	
gbal, free	1	.2	.00030		5.8
gbal, shared	——	.2	.00007		.4
				Total 13.8	6.2
Queue Length:					
wdraw, unlocked	11	1.6	.00059	12.6	
wdraw, locked	0	1.2	.00020	1.2	
gbal, free	5	.8	.00030		5.8
gbal, shared	0	.4	.00007		.4

*I/OSS devices with mean service time = 0.04

model results for an I/OSS mean service time of 0.04 seconds. The Withdrawal scenario has a total response time of 13.8 seconds; the Get balance takes 6.2 seconds. The queue length of locked transactions is 1.2; since it is greater than 1, further study is advised.

A **more realistic assessment** approximates the time jobs wait for shared or exclusive resource use. This approximation method augments Algorithm 8.2's aggregate-server method to include shadow servers for shared processing and additional surrogate delay nodes, and specifies the new model parameter calculation. The method is explained with an example and is defined formally in the inset.

EXAMPLE 8.6: Approximating Lock and Share Contention Delay

Model topology

The model topology in Figure 8.12 replaces the CPU and I/OSS active servers with "shadow servers." The shadow servers segregate processing for the locked state, the shared state, and the unlocked and free states. It is not necessary to add a shadow server for ATM because no visits are made to it by locked or shared transactions. The model has three surrogate delay servers, **Sharedel, Sharewt,** and **Lockwt,** to represent delays for passive resources. The job flow is as follows: Transactions arrive, flow from the ATM to CPU-1, and cycle through the ATM, CPU-1, and I/OSS-1 nodes until they need either shared or exclusive access to the Account file. Share transactions change to Phase 2 at CHG and go to Sharedel, and after obtaining shared use they cycle through the CPU-S and I/OSS-S nodes until they complete the shared use. Then they change back to Phase 1 at CHG and continue to cycle through ATM, CPU-1, and I/OSS-1 until the session is complete. Lock transactions change to Phase 2, then visit Sharewt, which approximates the delay for earlier share jobs to free Acct-lock; then they visit Lockwt, which approximates the delay due to earlier lock jobs. After obtaining the lock, the transaction cycles through CPU-L and I/OSS-L until lock processing completes. Then they change back to Phase 1 and return to CPU-1, I/OSS-1, and ATM, where they complete the session processing.

Model parameters

The model parameters in Table 8.15 are derived from the software model's R_i for each phase. The first column has the node names; the second column shows the transaction category phase that visits each. The third column shows the number of visits. First consider the Withdrawal scenario: From Figure 8.11, $R(unlocked) = (580, 11, 8)$ total, and $R(locked) = (105, 0, 3)$ for each of the two withdrawals. So unlocked withdrawals visit the ATM 11 times, the I/OSS-1 8 times, and CHG once for each lock—2 times. They visit CPU-1 20 times: 10 from ATM + 8 from I/OSS-1 + 2 from CHG. Locked withdrawals (Phase 2) visit Sharewt and Lockwt once for each lock—a total of 2 each, and I/OSS-L 3 times for each lock—a total of 6 visits. They make 8 visits to CPU-L, 6 from I/OSS-L, and 2 from Lockwt. Finally, locked withdrawals make a total of 2 visits to CHG to change back to Phase 1-unlocked. Check your understanding by computing visits for the Get balance scenario.

(continued)

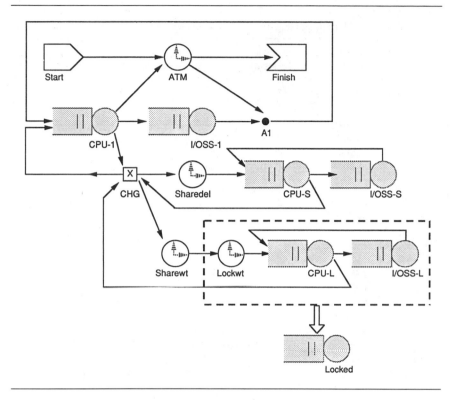

FIGURE 8.12
The Aggregate-Server Method Extensions to Approximate Delays for Shared and Locked Access.

EXAMPLE 8.6 (*Continued*)

The fourth column shows the mean service time for each server. The ATM and I/OSS times come from the environment specifications, as usual. Note that we still assume faster I/O devices. For the CPU servers, the mean service time is Rw/V:

$$\text{CPU-1} = \frac{(580)(.00001)}{20} = .00029$$

$$\text{CPU-L} = \frac{(2 \times 105)(.00001)}{8} = .0002625$$

Check your understanding by computing the service times for Get balance.

This model puts lock and share processing in shadow servers, so a solution using the service times in column 4 shows less device contention than actually occurs. We **elongate**

(*continued*)

TABLE 8.15
REALISTIC ANALYTIC CHECKPOINT EVALUATION: MODEL PARAMETERS

Node	Cat, phase	# visits	Mean service time, S_i	Adjusted service time, S_i'
ATM-1	wdraw, 1	11	1	1
	gbal, 1	5	1	1
CPU-1	wdraw, 1	20	.00029	.0002906
	gbal, 1	9	.0002944	.0002946
I/OSS-1	wdraw, 1	8	.04	.05882
	gbal, 1	4	.04	.05882
Sharedel	gbal, 2	1		.3314
CPU-S	gbal, 2	3	.000333	.0003365
I/OSS-S	gbal, 2	2	.04	.14286
Sharewt	wdraw, 2	2		.1153
CPU-L	wdraw, 2	8	.0002625	.000265
I/OSS-L	wdraw, 2	6	.04	.0909
CHG	wdraw, 1	2	changes to wdraw, 2	
	wdraw, 2	2	changes to wdraw, 1	
	gbal, 1	1	changes to gbal, 2	
	gbal, 2	1	changes to gbal, 1	
Locked	wdraw, 2	2		.2738

EXAMPLE 8.6 (*Continued*)

the service times as before to approximate the delays that actually occur. The adjusted service time formula is:

$$S_i' = \frac{S_i}{1 - X_0 \sum_{\substack{j \in sh \\ i \neq j}} Vsh_j Ssh_j}$$

where the summation in the denominator combines the visits × service time of all sister shadow servers

This gives the remaining server capacity available to shadow server i. This specification is for a model with a single transaction category. Algorithm 8.3 adapts it for multiple categories. First consider the adjusted service time for I/OSS-S. We want the denominator to include all other service at the actual I/OSS server, so we include 8 visits to I/OSS-1 by $\langle wdraw, 1 \rangle$, 4 visits to I/OSS-1 by $\langle gbal, 1 \rangle$, and 6 visits to I/OSS-L by $\langle wdraw, 2 \rangle$:

$$S_{I/OSS\text{-}S}' = \frac{.04}{1 - 1((8 \times .04) + (4 \times .04) + (6 \times .04))} = .14286$$

(*continued*)

EXAMPLE 8.6 (*Continued*)

Similarly,

$$S'_{I/OSS-L} := \frac{.04}{1 - 1((8 \times .04) + (4 \times .04) + (2 \times .04))} = .0909$$

In our simple IPG models, I/OSS-1 has queue-scheduling discipline FCFS, and all categories must have the same mean service time (refer to Table 5.4 and related discussions). This does not affect I/OSS-S or I/OSS-L because the categories visit different servers, but both categories visit I/OSS-1. So its adjusted service time combines visits to shadow servers I/OSS-S (2 visits) and I/OSS-L (6 visits) as follows:

$$S'_{I/OSS-1} = \frac{.04}{1 - 1((2 \times .04) + (6 \times .04))} = .05882$$

The CPU adjusted service time computation differs because it has the processor sharing queue-scheduling discipline. We compute an adjusted service time separately for each transaction category. First consider CPU-S. It only has visits by ⟨gbal,2⟩. We reduce its capacity by the service required by all other categories and shadow servers as before:

$$S'_{CPU-S} = \frac{.000333}{1 - 1((20 \times .00029) + (9 \times .0002944) + (8 \times .0002625))} = .0003365$$

Check your understanding by computing S'_{CPU-L}. Next, consider CPU-1. It has visits by both ⟨wdraw,1⟩ and ⟨gbal,1⟩. We adjust ⟨wdraw,1⟩ to account for the server capacity used by ⟨wdraw,2⟩ and adjust ⟨gbal,1⟩ for the capacity used by ⟨gbal,2⟩. Together all other contention is reflected. So the adjusted service time for CPU-1 is:

$$\text{for } \langle wdraw,1 \rangle = \frac{.00029}{1 - 1(8 \times .0002625)} = .0002906$$

Compute the adjusted time for ⟨gbal,1⟩ and compare your results to Table 8.15.

Finally we need **delay times** for Sharedel, Sharewt, and Lockwt. First consider **transactions that lock.** The shadow servers CPU-L and I/OSS-L represent the processing for the locked state. We aggregate Lockwt, CPU-L, and I/OSS-L into a single queue server, Locked, as in Section 8.3.1. Compute the mean service time for Locked as before.

$$
\begin{array}{llll}
\text{CPU-L:} & 8 \text{ visits} \times .000265 & = & .0021 \\
+ \text{ I/OSS-L:} & 6 \text{ visits} \times .0909 & = & .5454 \\
\text{Total locked (2 visits)} & & = & .5475 \\
& \text{per visit } S'_i & = & .2738
\end{array}
$$

The approximate delay due to earlier locked jobs (Lockwt) is automatically reflected in its residence time. Transactions needing locks may also be delayed by earlier transactions with shared access (at node Sharewt). Approximate this delay with the following technique. Imagine an aggregated server called "Shared" (similar to Locked) that has mean service time computed from the shared shadow servers as before:

$$
\begin{array}{llll}
\text{CPU-S:} & 3 \text{ visits} \times .0003365 & = & .0011 \\
+ \text{ I/OSS-S:} & 2 \text{ visits} \times .14286 & = & .2857 \\
& \text{Shared processing} & = & .2868
\end{array}
$$

(*continued*)

EXAMPLE 8.6 (*Continued*)

We do not actually want a "Shared" node in the model because share transactions need not wait for earlier share transactions to complete. But this imaginary node's residence time gives an average wait time for share jobs to complete. We use this wait time to approximate the delay to locked transactions that must wait for earlier share transactions (at Sharewt). This is a reasonable approximation; you can check the sensitivity of the results by comparing them to an optimistic evaluation with no Sharewt and a pessimistic evaluation with Sharewt = Total Share processing (which assumes that a share transaction begins the instant before the lock transaction reaches the head of the REQ queue).

A node's wait time is the residence time RT_i minus the service time S_i'. Residence time is a model result rather than an input. You can either create the imaginary queue and solve the model to get its residence time, or, since open models use simple equations, you can calculate it as follows:

$$RT_i = \frac{S_i'}{1 - X_0 V_i S_i}$$

$$= \frac{(.2868)}{1 - (1)(1)(.2868)} = .40213$$

Then the average wait time is:

$$RT_i - S_i' = .40213 - .2868 = .1153$$

So the mean service time for Sharewt is 0.1153.

The last model parameter is the **estimated delay for Share transactions,** Sharedel. They need not wait on other share transactions, only on those that lock. Thus Sharedel is the same as Lockwt, which is the average wait time for the aggregate server, Locked. We compute the average wait time from the residence time as before:

$$RT_i = \frac{S_i'}{1 - X_0 V_i S_i}$$

$$= \frac{.2738}{1 - (1)(2)(.2738)} = .6052$$

$$RT_i - S_i' = .6052 - .2738 = .3314$$

So the mean service time for Sharedel is 0.3314.

Example results

The performance results for each device are in Table 8.16, and the scenario summary is in Table 8.17. The response times 13.3 and 6.05 seconds are acceptable, and the queue length of locked jobs, 0.55, is less than 1, so this locking/sharing strategy is reasonable. We did, however, have to assume faster I/O devices to achieve this result. One of the chapter exercises examines another alternative.

□

This approximation technique is sufficient for identifying locking and sharing situations that warrant further investigation. The modeling and analysis to get approximate analytic solutions is nontrivial. Large software systems often have

TABLE 8.16
REALISTIC ANALYSIS FOR COMBINATION LOCK AND SHARE:
NODE RESULTS

Node	Categories	Through-put	Utilization	Residence time	Queue length
ATM	wdraw, unlocked	11	11/50	1	11
	gbal, free	5	5/50	1	5
CPU-1	wdraw, unlocked	20	.0058	.0002922	.0058
	gbal, free	9	.0027	.0002053	.0027
I/OSS-1	wdraw, unlocked	8	.4706	.1111	.8888
	gbal, free	4	.2353	.0769	.3076
Sharedel	gbal, shared	1	.3313	.3313	.3313
CPU-S	gbal, shared	3	.0010	.003368	.0110
I/OSS-S	gbal, shared	2	.2857	.2	.4
Sharewt	wdraw, locked	2	.2306	.1153	.2306
Locked	wdraw, locked	2	.5475	.6050	1.2100

more intricate lock and share situations. There may be many more scenarios, each requesting different combinations of shared or exclusive access to resources. If so, the software models contain several lock and share requests to different resources. Use the analytic best-case checkpoint evaluation to identify situations that require further study. The realistic checkpoint evaluation can also be adapted (see [AGR83b] for extensions). As the complexity of the analytic model increases, however, we require more time and expertise to construct and evaluate analytic models. Until the approximate solution techniques are automated and hidden inside model solvers, simulation solution methods are easier to use.

TABLE 8.17
REALISTIC ANALYSIS FOR COMBINATION LOCK AND SHARE:
SCENARIO SUMMARY

Scenarios	System queue length	System response time
wdraw:		
Unlocked	11.89	11.89
Waiting for lock	.89	.89
Locked	.55	.55
Overall	13.33	13.33 sec
gbal:		
Free	5.31	5.31
Waiting to share	.33	.33
Shared	.41	.41
Overall	6.05	6.05 sec

Note that Queue length = Response time because in this example throughput = 1

ALGORITHM 8.3: Aggregate-Server Adaptation for Approximating Delays for Shared and Exclusive Use in Open Models

1. Clone each active server visited by locked or shared phases to create "shadow servers." Create surrogate delay servers to represent:

   □ Shared phases delay due to locked jobs with exclusive use: Sharedel

   □ Locked phases delay due to shared jobs with resource possession: Sharewt

   □ Locked phases delay due to locked jobs with exclusive use: Lockwt

2. Specify the routing so that jobs with exclusive use visit one set of shadow servers, jobs with shared access visit another set, and jobs not desiring use of the resource visit a third set. Compute the visits to each server from the software execution model's results for lock, share, and free phases.

3.

a. First compute the mean service time of the active servers i from the environment specifications and the software execution model's results for locked and unlocked phases by adapting Algorithm 5.2 to use R_i results for each phase:

$$S_i = \frac{R\ (phase)_i\ w_i}{V\ (phase)_i}$$

b. The service time parameters in Step 3a represent less contention for the active resources than actually occurs. To compensate, use the following heuristic algorithm to elongate the service time of the shadow servers to approximate the actual contention delays due to the "missing" workload:

$$\text{Adjusted service time, } S_i' = \frac{S_i}{1 - X_0 \sum_{j \in sh} Vsh_j\,Ssh_j}$$

where the summation in the denominator combines the visits × service time of all sister shadow servers, sh.

c. Adapt the service time formula to multiple categories, c, as follows. For servers with same mean service time for all categories:

$$S_i' = \frac{S_{ic}}{1 - \sum_{j \in sh} X_{0c} Vsh_{jc}\,Ssh_{jc}}$$

For servers with different mean service time for each category:

$$S_{ic}' = \frac{S_{ic}}{1 - \sum_{j \in sh} X_{0c} Vsh_{jc}\,Ssh_{jc}}$$

(continued)

ALGORITHM 8.3 (*Continued*)

4. Aggregate the Lockwt surrogate delay server and all "locked" shadow servers into a single active queue server, Locked. Its mean service time is the total visits × adjusted service time of each of the shadow servers:

$$S'_{locked} = \sum_{i \in sh_{locked}} V_i S'_i$$

where sh_{locked} is the set of "locked" shadow servers

5. Approximate the Sharewt surrogate delay time as follows:
   a. Compute the service time of an imaginary aggregate "shared" node:

$$S'_{shared} = \sum_{i \in sh_{shared}} V_i S'_i$$

where sh_{shared} is the set of "shared" shadow servers

   b. Compute the residence time of the imaginary aggregate "shared" node:

$$RT_{shared} = \frac{S'_{shared}}{1 - X_0 V_{shared} S'_{shared}}$$

   c. Compute the Sharewt surrogate delay time from the imaginary aggregate "shared" node wait time:

$$S_{Sharewt} = RT_{shared} - S'_{shared}$$

6. Approximate the Sharedel surrogate delay time using the wait time of the "Locked" aggregate server:

$$RT_{locked} = \frac{S'_{locked}}{1 - X_0 V_{locked} S'_{locked}}$$

$$S_{Sharedel} = RT_{locked} - S'_{locked}$$

7. Solve the model.

The simulation solution results for this model (using I/OSS service time 0.04 sec) are in Table 8.18. The simulation results are comparable to the approximate analytic results in Tables 8.16 and 8.17. As in the locking model, the analytic results underestimate the delay to obtain Shared and Locked access (because the share- and lock-delay estimates are based only on elongated service time for shared and locked processing, not on residence times). As before, the mean values for the performance metrics identify design problems and feasible alternatives. Simulation results reflect standard deviations and resulting variations in response time. Table 8.18 shows that the maximum response time for withdrawals is 126 seconds, with 56 seconds for balances.

The following example shows that advanced IPGs are easily extended to represent combinations of resource requests.

TABLE 8.18
SIMULATION RESULTS FOR SHARED AND EXCLUSIVE USE

Nodes	Category	Through-put	Utili-zation	Residence time Mean	Residence time Std. dev.	Queue length Mean	Queue length Std. dev.
ATM	wdraw	11.72		1.00	1.00	11.70	3.26
	gbal	5.01		.99	1.02	4.98	2.33
CPU	wdraw	30.04	.008	.0003	.0003	.009	.10
	gbal	12.10	.004	.0003	.0003	.004	.07
I/OSS	wdraw	15.03	.60	.01	.10	1.64	1.47
	gbal	6.00	.24	.12	.11	.74	1.07
REQ	wdraw	2.17		.86	1.17	1.87	2.76
	gbal	1.05		.80	1.08	.84	1.41
Acct-lock*	wdraw		.54				
	gbal		.004				
System	wdraw	1.06		14.37	14.84		
	gbal	1.00		6.56	6.92		
Max Response Time	wdraw	126.4 sec					
	gbal	55.7 sec					

*Note: Maximum tokens = 50, mean number held: wdraw = 26.8, gbal = 0.2

EXAMPLE 8.7: Combinations of Lock and Share Requests

A transaction may make several requests for different types of tokens at a REQ node. For example, a request for exclusive use of three tables named CREDITS, DEBITS, and HISTORY, and shared use of USERREP is:

> REQUEST   # tokens = MAXNO   type = CREDIT
> # tokens = MAXNO   type = DEBIT
> # tokens = MAXNO   type = HISTORY
> # tokens = 1   type = USERREP;

With this specification, a transaction may not receive a partial request— it either gets all or none. If it is possible to use CREDIT and DEBIT for preliminary processing, then later request HISTORY and USERREP, modify the model to either use two different request nodes, or change the transaction's phase and use a different request specification for each phase.

□

8.3.3 Lock Mechanism Design Evaluation

To evaluate lock-share-free processing overhead in software scenarios, we represent it in the software models with execution graph nodes, specify resource requirements for the lock, share and free processing, then evaluate the software models to derive parameters for the system execution model. If we instead wish to evaluate design alternatives for operating system, lock-mechanism routines, the procedure is similar. For locking, the key steps are linking the lock-mechanism software models to user-level scenarios, and evaluating the combination with advanced IPGs.

First represent the proposed lock-mechanism design with software models that define the processing steps required for lock, share, and free. A simple model in Figure 8.13 illustrates; an actual design is more complex. Next specify resource requirements for each processing step; then evaluate the software model as usual. Best- and worst-case checkpoint evaluations identify potential lock-mechanism problems. The best and worst cases for Figure 8.13 are $R = (40, 2)$ and $R = (45, 2)$, respectively.

Next study the dynamic performance of the lock mechanism: Use walkthroughs or measurements to construct user-level scenarios that specify typical software execution steps and their lock-free-share requests, such as the user-level scenarios in Figures 8.10 and 8.11. In those earlier models, we specified resource requirements for the lock, free, and share nodes. For these models we use the lock mechanism's software model results for the user scenario's lock, share, and free nodes. For Figure 8.13's lock design, we use $R = (40, 2)$ for the lock node in Figure 8.10(a) for an optimistic evaluation, and $R = (45, 2)$ for a pessimistic one. The user-level scenarios then provide advanced IPG parameters for further checkpoint evaluations of different load conditions. To examine alternate lock-

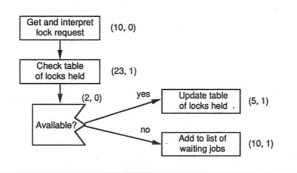

FIGURE 8.13
Lock-Mechanism Software Execution Model.

mechanism designs, modify the lock-mechanism software models accordingly, recompute the resource requirements, and use them in the user-level scenarios to compute new advanced IPG model parameters.

The simple checkpoint evaluations identify feasible lock-mechanism design alternatives. More precise evaluations detect potential concurrency problems. They require simulation IPGs that can vary execution characteristics as load conditions vary. For example, resource requirements for the lock node differ when the lock is available and when it is not. A more detailed lock-mechanism model can represent other variations that depend on system congestion. Simulation IPGs accommodate these analyses; using them, a transaction category may check queue lengths or other system-state indicators to determine processing phase changes. Simulation IPGs also produce data for evaluating the variability of performance metrics in addition to the average values. Petri net models also enable evaluation of execution behavior for unlikely combinations of events. As stated earlier, performance variability can cause log-jam performance bottlenecks that are difficult to detect with models that favor typical or average behavior. An overview of both simulation IPGs and Petri net models that enable more detailed investigation is in Section 8.6.

8.3.4 Further Reading

Analytic approximation techniques for models with passive resources are active research areas. This section proposed one type of checkpoint evaluation for lock and one for share to identify situations that need further study. Other strategies have been proposed. Agrawal and Buzen describe additional details of the "aggregate server method" in [AGR83a] and [AGR83b]. Jacobsen and Lazowska describe a variation in [JAC83]. Balbo, Bruell, and Ghanta use Petri nets to more precisely analyze the effects of blocking in [BAL85a]. Lazowska, Zahorjan, Sevcik, and Graham mention a procedure for analyzing database transactions that abort when unable to obtain locks in [LAZ84a]. Tay, Goodman, and Suri examine several different database locking strategies in [TAY84], and Sevcik compares locking strategies with analytic models in [SEV83]. Thomasian has approximation techniques for serialization delays in [THO83]. Smith and Browne describe another method in [SMI80a].

8.4 Parallel and Distributed Processing

This section models software that executes on multiple processors. It covers the performance issues that arise when components of a scenario may execute at the same time on separate processors. This section distinguishes between **multiple**

servers, such as multiple CPUs that serve a queue of ready processes *within* an operating system, and **multiple processors** that operate autonomously with their own operating system and (usually) their own (local) memory and peripheral devices.

Parallel processing and distributed processing are similar. They both have multiple autonomous processors. We distinguish them primarily by the "distance" between the processors—that is, the resource cost of communication. Parallel processors may have shared memory or special interconnection networks that expedite communication, whereas distributed processors are usually geographically separated. We can also distinguish parallel from distributed processing by the performance-oriented design issues that arise. Software design for parallel processing (usually) means dividing the scenario components into separately executing processes so that the scenario completes faster. Distributed processing design assigns entire scenarios to processors to maximize local processing and minimize communication (to access data that resides on a remote processor). *The distinction between parallel and distributed processing is not rigorous*—the performance concepts are similar enough to combine in this section.

The **distributed processing performance issue** we address here is how to model scenarios with remote data accesses and interprocessor communication. Remote accesses may be due to geographically distributed data, such as in a nationwide ATM network, or due to a "tiered data architecture" in which processors have a hierarchical tree structure with a root containing global data and successive levels containing data local to their section of the tree. An example is the engineering database in the case study—the top tier contains global data about the engineering design, and the second contains an engineer's data about his or her part of the overall design. We need models to assess the cost of remote data accesses and interprocessor communication to quantify the congestion on the network and on the remote system.

The **parallel processing performance issues** we address here are how to divide scenario components into *processes* that can execute in parallel, how to assign processes to the multiple processors, and how to communicate with other processes. Dividing components into separate processes allows more processing overlap, but requires more overhead to pass data between separate processes than to pass data between procedures within the same process. Similarly, assigning processes to separate processors increases the concurrency, but requires even more overhead for interprocessor communication.

The pertinent performance engineering principle (in Chapter 2) is:

Parallel processing should be done in parallel (only) when the processing speedup offsets the communication overhead and the resource contention delays.

Advanced IPGs quantify both the communication cost and the effect on responsiveness due to parallel processing. The rest of this section describes advanced IPG models for remote data accesses, process structure and process allocation, and messages for interprocess communication. We represent each problem with an advanced IPG, and then use analytic checkpoint evaluations to get best- and worst-case performance data. The checkpoint evaluations identify feasible alternatives and indicate when further study is advisable.

8.4.1 Remote Data Accesses

Software models represent data accesses with specifications for the number of I/Os to each device. For parallel and distributed systems, you must also specify the number of accesses to data that resides on remote systems. Remote data accesses differ from local I/Os: They have different resource requirements; and a local I/O makes one visit to a local device, whereas remote data accesses may visit several devices to reach the remote device. There may also be transmission delays and contention delays on the remote system.

The following is an **overview of the remote data access models.** Examples that illustrate the steps follow. To model remote data accesses, extend the software models as follows:

1. Provide distinct specifications for remote versus local I/Os.

2. Augment the w_{ij} to include the computer resources i for each of the a_j requests for remote resource j.

3. Calculate the total computer resources required on both the local and the remote system.

Then create an advanced IPG that represents the remote system with a submodel node and represents incoming requests from remote systems with source and sink nodes. Compute best-case model parameters:

4. Substitute a delay node for the submodel node. Set its service time equal to the lower bound on the network transmission delay and the service times on remote devices.

5. Assume an equal distribution of remote requests across the network. Set the arrival rate of incoming requests to the throughput of the submodel node.

Solve the model. If the best case is problematic, seek remedies before proceeding to the more detailed models described later in this section.

EXAMPLE 8.8: Remote Data Access Software Model

Suppose that one-tenth of the ATM session requests are for accounts at another bank branch or another bank in a nationwide network. Then the ATM session must access remote data.

(continued)

TABLE 8.19
SOFTWARE MODEL FOR REMOTE DATA ACCESS

| Components | Software resources, a_j | | | | | | Computer resources, r_i | | | |
| | 1 Control flow | Component | | | | | 1 CPU | 2 ATM | 3 DEV1 | 4 Remote I/O |
		2 CPU	3 ATM	4 I/O	5 Remote I/O	6 Event recording				
Initiate Session	0	50	2	0.9	0.1	1	74.5	2	0.9	0.1
Get Request *3	1	13	1	0	0	0	20	1	0	0
Interpret Request *3	1	3	1	0	0	0	10	1	0	0
Withdrawal *2	1	168	2	2.7	0.3	1	213.5	2	2.7	0.3
Get Balance *1	1	33	1	0.9	0.1	1	54.5	1	0.9	0.1
Terminate	1	83	1	0.9	0.1	1	104.5	1	0.9	0.1
TOTAL							760.5	14	8.1	0.9

EXAMPLE 8.8 (*Continued*)

The scenario for this example is the same as in Figure 4.28.[1] Note that the execution structure is identical to the previous scenario—all processing executes locally, and each file I/O is routed to the local or remote system when the I/O is issued. An alternate design would collect the transaction information, then route the entire request to a remote system for processing. A chapter exercise examines this alternative.

The resource requirements for each component in the new software model are in Table 8.19; note the added column for remote I/O. The Initiate session component has the same number of software resource requests for control flow, event recording, and component CPU and ATM as in Chapter 4. The Initiate session component I/O changes: It previously had 1 (local) I/O; now 10 percent or 0.1 is remote and 0.9 is local. Prorate the I/Os for the other components with the same ratio to get the specifications in the columns for $j = 4$ and 5.

Next compute the total computer resource requirements, R_i. For this example, use the same w_{ij}, the resource requirements for (local) computer resource i for each of the a_j requests for the software resources j on the local computer, and add 50 CPU instructions for each remote data access. The extended w_{ij} matrix is in Table 8.20. For each component, multiply the number of software resource requests, a_j in the left side of Table 8.19, by the above resource requirements for each a_j to get the (local) computer resource requirements in the right side of Table 8.19. Thus the CPU requirement for the Withdrawal component is (1×2) + (168×1) + (2×5) + (2.7×5) + ($.3 \times 50$) + (1×5) = 213.5 per execution. Derive the total local computer system resource requirements using Algorithm 4.1's basic path reduction rules, as usual. Get request and Interpret request execute three times, Withdrawal executes twice, and the other components execute once, so R_i = (760.5, 14, 8.1, 0.9).

Remote data accesses also require remote computer system resources. For this example, assume that each one requires 50 instructions on the remote CPU and 1 I/O on the remote device. R_i' is the total requirement for resources on the remote system; so R_i' = (50, 0, 1, 0) represents 50 instructions on its CPU and 1 I/O to its disk.

□

The next step creates an advanced IPG to model the system execution behavior. It represents the primary IPG nodes visited by the remote data access with a submodel node. The details within the submodel are simplified for initial best-case studies, or elaborated for more detailed investigation. The advanced IPG for the "Local computer" may also need additional workload categories to represent the data requests it receives from remote systems. The following illustrates the extensions to the IPG for the previous example.

---

[1]The processing steps are the same for the high-level, preliminary design—during detailed design, processing differences for remote accounts are modeled within the expanded nodes for high-level components. Note that this is a hypothetical ATM example to illustrate remote data access models—it does not represent any actual ATM system.

TABLE 8.20
COMPUTER RESOURCE REQUIREMENTS FOR EACH SOFTWARE RESOURCE REQUEST (w_{ij}: Computer resource i required for each of the a_j requests for software resource j)

Computer resources		Software resources, a_j					
			Component				
i	Name	1 Control flow	2 CPU	3 ATM	4 I/O	5 Remote I/O	6 Event recording
1	CPU	2	1	5	5	50	5
2	ATM	0	0	1	0	0	0
3	DEV1	0	0	0	1	0	0
4	Remote I/O	0	0	0	0	1	1

EXAMPLE 8.9: Remote Data Access—Advanced IPG

Model topology

Figure 8.14's advanced IPG uses a Remote I/O submodel node to represent the remote data access processing. Its details depend on the depth of the analysis and are given later. It also has two new entry and exit nodes, Remote-req and Remote-reply. So a remote data access

(continued)

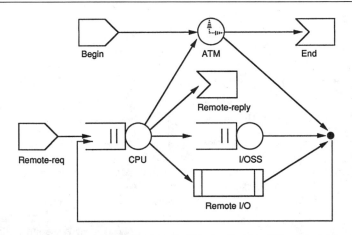

FIGURE 8.14
Advanced IPG for Remote Data Access. The Remote I/O submodel node represents processing to reach the remote system, retrieve the data, and return it to this (Local) computer. The Remote-req and Remote-reply nodes represent incoming requests from other systems for this Local computer's data.

EXAMPLE 8.9 (*Continued*)

from other systems arrives at Remote-req, goes to the CPU, then to the I/OSS, returns to the CPU, then leaves through Remote-reply. In keeping with the simple, optimistic model paradigm, we begin with a simple open model. Later in this section we augment the models to explicitly link the local and remote computer systems.

Best-case model parameters

The model parameters for the best-case model are in Table 8.21. Cat1 represents the ATM sessions that originate on the Local computer system, and Cat2 represents the processing for remote data accesses for accounts on the Local computer that arrive from other computers. The node names are in the first column. The number of visits for each category is computed from R_i as usual. For Category 1:

$$R(1)_i = (760.5, 14, 8.1, .9)$$

So the ATM has 14 visits, I/OSS has 8.1, and Remote I/O has 0.9. The CPU visits come from these numbers: 8.1 come from I/OSS + 0.9 come from Remote I/O + 13 (of the 14) ATM visits go to the CPU = 22 CPU visits. We assume that incoming remote data accesses, Cat2, have the same processing requirements as our remote data accesses to other computers: 50 CPU instructions and 1 I/O to I/OSS, $R(2)_i = (50, 0, 1, 0)$. So the number of visits for Cat2 to the CPU is 1 from the I/OSS + 1 from Remote-req = 2.

Derive the mean service times for the CPU and I/OSS nodes as usual. Remote I/O is different. The best-case model replaces the Remote I/O submodel with a delay server (like the ATM node, it has no queueing). We estimate the delay time as follows. In the best case, our remote data access will not encounter queueing delays on the remote system, so its total processing time is

$$\sum_i R'_i w_i$$

Assuming the w_i is the same on the remote system, $w_i = (0.00001, 1, 0.05)$, then the best-case elapsed time is

$$(50 \times .00001) + (1 \times .05) = .0505 \text{ sec}$$

We also estimate that the best-case transmission delay—the time it takes a request leaving one computer to reach the other—is 1 second. (This is an environment specification obtained from measurements of the network, or from performance walkthroughs.) There are two transmissions, one for the request and one for the reply. The total transmission time for the best case is thus 2 seconds, and total best-case delay for Remote I/O is $2 + 0.0505 = 2.0505$.

The last column in Table 8.21 gives the arrival rates for the two source nodes and shows that the best-case model substitutes a delay server for the Remote I/O submodel. The arrival rate for Remote-req comes from the assumption that the Remote computer has the same software execution model as the Local computer (in Table 8.19). The Remote I/O node's throughput in the local computer then gives the rate at which remote requests are

(*continued*)

TABLE 8.21
REMOTE DATA ACCESS: BEST-CASE MODEL PARAMETERS

Nodes	# visits		Mean service time		Other
	Cat1	Cat2	Cat1	Cat2	
Begin	1	0			1 session/sec
ATM	14	0	1		
End	1	0			
Remote-req	0	1			0.9 req/sec
CPU	22	2	0.000346	0.00025	
I/OSS	8.1	1	0.05	0.05	
Remote I/O	0.9	0	2.0505		(QD = Delay)
Remote-reply	0	1			

EXAMPLE 8.9 (*Continued*)

made by the Remote computer. Recall that in an open model a node's throughput, X_i, is the system throughput, X_0, times the number of visits to the node, V_i.

$$X_i = X_0 V_i = 1 \times .9 = .9 \text{ for Remote I/O}$$

This best-case arrival-rate computation implicitly assumes that remote requests are equally distributed throughout the network. The submodel expansion, described later, illustrates how to vary the distribution of requests.

□

This completes the best-case IPG; however, it is saturated. To satisfy job-flow balance, each node's service rate must be greater than its arrival rate:

$$\frac{1}{S_i} \geq X_i$$

The Remote I/O node has service rate $1/2.0505 = 0.4877$ requests per second, but its arrival rate is 0.9 requests per second. Thus the revised ATM system cannot process 1 session per second and does not meet its performance goal. The job flow of Remote I/O must be balanced by reducing its mean service time or the number of visits to it (thus its arrival rate).

The main component of the remote data access service time is the network transmission delay. One alternative is to make improvements to the network configuration. You can easily compute a bound on the acceptable transmission delay and use it to guide the evaluation of network configuration alternatives. First, set a maximum acceptable utilization for the bottleneck node, Remote I/O. Then use the utilization formula from Algorithm 5.1 to compute the maximum service time for the Remote I/O node. Finally, prorate the maximum service time to the constituent parts of the service time. The following example demonstrates the calculation.

EXAMPLE 8.10: Upper Bound on Network Transmission Delay

In this best-case model network transmission is represented by a delay server, so 100 percent utilization is okay. (In the more realistic model described later, you need to set lower limits on the utilization of the corresponding active servers.) If the number of visits, V_i, remains the same,

$$U_i = V_i S_i =\rangle 1 = (.9) \times (max\ S_i)$$

so,

$$max\ S_i = 1.111$$

The service time includes remote service time and transmission delays

$$S_i = (2 \times \text{transmission delay}) + (\text{remote service})$$
$$(maxS_i) = (2 \times \text{max. transmission}) + (.0505)$$
$$\text{max. transmission} = \frac{1.111 - .0505}{2} = .53$$

So network alternatives must reduce the (one-way) transmission delay from 1 second to less than 0.53 second.

□

Note that queueing delays on the remote system were not included in this analysis. They may further limit the maximum transmission delay. So, if you pursue network solutions to remote data access sluggishness, further study is advised to quantify remote queueing delays. Because software design solutions are usually preferable to hardware changes, we next examine alternatives that reduce the number of visits to Remote I/O by modifying the software model. We also introduce a split node to create an asynchronous process to access remote data while regular processing proceeds.

EXAMPLE 8.11: Revised Remote Data Access with Asynchronous Data Updates

Revised software model

Figure 8.15 changes the scenario structure.[2] When an ATM session for a remote account initiates, it fetches all necessary account information, such as the authorization code, the balance, and the maximum withdrawal amount allowed. With this information, the rest of the session processing executes on the Local computer. At the end of the session, all activity against the account is posted to the Remote computer. It is not necessary for the customer to wait for posting to complete, so we use a *split node* to show that one process completes the session processing and exits while the other posts the account activity, then exits.

We next compute the total resource requirements, R_i, from the revised software

(continued)

---

[2]The alternative described illustrates remote I/O models and transaction splits. It *does not resemble* actual ATM software strategies.

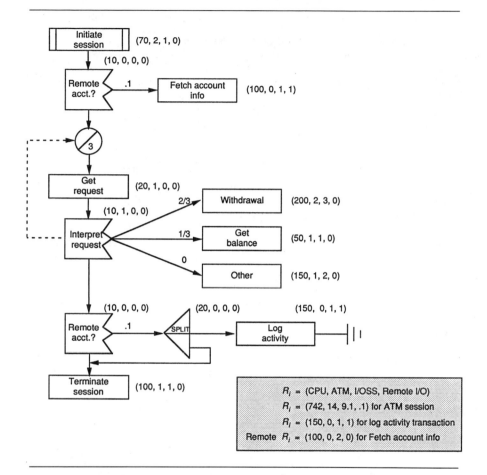

FIGURE 8.15
**The revised software execution model fetches all account information for re-
mote accounts at the beginning of the session and logs the activity to the remote
system at the end of the session.**

EXAMPLE 8.11 *(Continued)*

model. The computation uses the path reduction rules as usual—with the exception of the
path that contains the split node. Check your understanding by computing the total resource
requirements, R_i, for everything except the SPLIT and Log activity. When a transaction
splits into sibling transactions, we specify resource requirements for each sibling separately. The processing required to split is (20, 0, 0, 0) and it occurs 10 percent of the time.
So add $20 \times 0.1 = 2$ instructions to the ATM session transaction for split overhead. The
total for the ATM session becomes (742, 14, 9.1, 0.1). The resource requirements for Log
activity are (150, 0, 1, 1), and they go with the new (split) Log activity transaction.

(continued)

EXAMPLE 8.11 (*Continued*)

The remote data accesses in this example require more processing to get and format the account information and to update a flag that indicates when a remote session is in progress. Therefore, in this example, we assume that each remote data access takes (100, 0, 2, 0) on the Remote computer. Making the resource requirements for all remote data accesses the same (the fetch info and the post updates) simplifies this example. One of the chapter exercises changes the Remote computer resource requirements for posting updates.

Revised topology for the advanced IPG

The revised IPG in Figure 8.16 adds an IPG split node, **ToLog.** The flow through the model is similar to that in Figure 8.14: ATM sessions arrive at the Start node and flow through the ATM, CPU, and I/OSS. When a remote data access is needed, it goes to the Remote I/O node. Just before termination, sessions against remote accounts go to ToLog *where the transaction splits:* One completes the session by cycling through the CPU, I/OSS, and ATM nodes before leaving the system through the Finish node; the other split transaction (Cat3-Log activity) cycles through the CPU, I/OSS, and Remote I/O nodes before leaving the system. Note that the Log activity transaction can leave through any sink node, so, to simplify the topology drawing, we route it to Remote-reply.

The revised model parameters for the best-case model are in Table 8.22. The visits to each node for Cat1-Sessions is computed from the R_i as usual, with the exception of the

(*continued*)

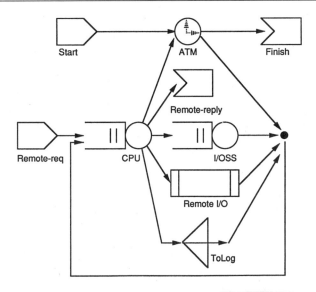

FIGURE 8.16
The revised IPG adds a split node to log the activity for remote accounts with an asychronous process.

TABLE 8.22
REVISED IPG MODEL: BEST-CASE PARAMETERS

| Nodes | # visits | | | |
| | Cat1 | Cat2 | Cat3 | |
	Session	Remote access	Log activity	
Begin	0	0	0	
ATM	14	0	0	
End	1	0	0	
Remote-req	0	1	0	
CPU	22.3	3	3	
I/OSS	9.1	2	1	
Remote I/O	0.1	0	1	
ToLog	0.1	0	(origin)	
Remote-reply	0	1	1	

| Nodes | Mean service time | | | Other |
| | Cat1 | Cat2 | Cat3 | |
	Session	Remote access	Log activity	
Begin				1 session/sec
ATM	1			
End				
Remote-req				0.2 req./sec for Cat2
CPU	.00033	.00033	.0005	
I/OSS	.05	.05	.05	
Remote I/O	2.101		2.101	
ToLog				Cat → 1 Cat1 & 1 Cat3
Remote-reply				

EXAMPLE 8.11 (*Continued*)

number of visits to ToLog, which comes from the probability of the Split in the software model, 0.1. The number of visits to each device for Cat2-Remote accesses is computed as in Table 8.21; the values change to reflect the increased resource requirements for remote data accesses. The visits for Cat3-Log activity come from the software model $R_i = (150, 0, 1, 1)$, as usual. It has 3 visits to the CPU: 1 from I/OSS, 1 from Remote I/O, and 1 from its origination at ToLog.

The mean service time for the Remote I/O node uses the same assumptions as the model in Table 8.21. The values change to reflect the revised processing requirements as follows:

$$
\begin{array}{lll}
100 \text{ instructions} \times .00001 & = .001 & \text{CPU time} \\
+ 2 \times .05 & = .100 & \text{I/O time} \\
+ 2 \times 1 & = 2.000 & \text{Transmission time} \\
\hline
& 2.101 & \text{Total elapsed time (best case)}
\end{array}
$$

The CPU service times are:

$$
\begin{array}{lll}
742 \times .00001/22.3 & = .00033 & \text{for Cat1} \\
100 \times .00001/3 & = .00033 & \text{for Cat2} \\
150 \times .00001/3 & = .0005 & \text{for Cat3}
\end{array}
$$

The arrival rate for ATM sessions remains 1 session per second. The split node, ToLog, converts one Cat1 ATM session into two transactions: the ATM session completion (Cat1) and the Log activity transaction (Cat3). Incoming remote requests arrive at a rate of 0.1 requests per second from Cat1 ATM sessions on remote systems, plus 0.1 per second from Log activity transactions on remote systems for a total of 0.2 requests per second.   □

If your analytic solver does not allow transactions to split, the model requires a slight conversion for analytic solution. First replace the split node with a branch node—this essentially nullifies the split. This does not affect the ATM session or remote access parameters, but it eliminates the arrival of split transactions. Mimic the arrival of split transactions by generating arrivals at a source node at the same rate that they would be generated at the split node. For open models their arrival rate is the same as the throughput of the split node. Note that a slightly different strategy maps closed models with split nodes to analytic solvers.[3]

---

[3]The split node is replaced with a branch point, and a separate category represents the split transactions. A surrogate delay server is used instead of a source node to introduce the split transactions. They flow from the surrogate delay server to the CPU and through the Local computer. Upon completion they return to the surrogate delay server. The mean service time of the surrogate delay is adjusted until its throughput equals that of node ToLog. This may require iterative solutions: Approximate the surrogate delay, solve the model, compare the ToLog throughput to the surrogate delay throughput, and, if necessary, change the delay time and re-solve.

TABLE 8.23
REVISED IPG MODEL: BEST-CASE RESULTS

Node and category	Throughput	Utilization	Residence time
ATM:			
Session	14	14	1
CPU:			
Session	22.3	.0074	.0003
Remote Access	.6	.0002	.0003
Log Activity	.3	.0002	.0005
I/OSS:			
Session	9.1	.455	.092
Remote Access	.4	.020	.051
Log Activity	.1	.005	.050
Remote I/O:			
Session	.1	.210	2.101
Log Activity	.1	.210	2.101
ToLog:			
Session	.1		
Log Activity	.1		

Total Response Time: Session = 15.05 seconds

EXAMPLE 8.12: Analytic Solution of IPGs with Split Nodes

Replace the ToLog split node with a branch node. Compute the arrival rate of Cat3 transactions from the throughput of the ToLog split node:

$$X_i = X_0 V_i = (1 \text{ session/sec})(.1 \text{ visits}) = .1 \text{ per sec}$$

Modify the parameters for Remote-req to generate 0.1 Cat3 transactions per second (in addition to the Cat2 transaction arrivals).

The analytic model solution is in Table 8.23. The best-case performance meets the objectives. Session response time averages 15.05 compared to the average 14.8 when all sessions are local (from Table 5.5). □

Of course, network congestion, contention delays on the remote system, and nonuniform distribution of remote requests make the best-case performance unlikely. Estimates of the upper-bound performance use upper bounds for service requirements of remote data accesses, increase the arrival rate to model a higher percentage of incoming requests for the Local computer, and uses other upper bounds for the software model.

A more **realistic model** represents the network, the computer systems that interact with one another, and the distribution of remote requests. The computer system and network are specified with submodel nodes in a high-level model. Each submodel expansion specifies its computer system topology. Each computer system has its own transaction arrivals. Those that use only local computer system resources remain within the submodel for the duration of their processing. Those that require remote data access flow from the submodel to the network and on to the remote system. Upon completion of the remote data access, they exit the remote system submodel and go to the network and back to the original computer system. The distribution of requests is controlled in the high-level model by specifying the visits to the computer system submodels.

EXAMPLE 8.13: Representing Computer System and Network Interactions

Figure 8.17(a) shows a hypothetical high-level configuration. A request from a system goes to the Network for routing to the desired system; upon completion it returns to the Network to be routed back to the original system. Figure 8.17(b) shows a submodel expansion. In this example, all the computer system submodels have the same topology. The submodel has no Remote I/O node—remote requests instead go to the network (ToNet), and return (FromNet) upon completion.

The flow is as follows: CatL transactions come from the Start node on the Local computer. A CatL session begins in its Initial phase and cycles through the ATM, CPU, and I/OSS nodes. Then it goes to the change node, ToRemote?; 90 percent change to the Local-acct phase, and 10 percent change to the Remote-acct phase. This corresponds to the software model processing for Initiate session and Remote account? Sessions for local accounts continue through the CPU, I/OSS, and ATM nodes until they complete and go to Finish. Sessions for remote accounts change to the outgoing phase, go to the (higher-level model) Network, to the Remote system where they complete the remote access and change to the return phase, go back through the Network, and reenter the submodel as returned requests at FromNet. They cycle through the CPU, I/OSS, and ATM. They visit ToLog to split into (1) a CatL, Log-out phase to notify the remote system and (2) the continuation of the CatL, Remote-acct phase to terminate the session. The Log transaction starts in the outgoing phase, visits the Network, the Remote system (changes to the return phase), goes through the Network, and reenters in the return phase through FromNet. After completing its CPU and I/O processing, it goes to Finish.

Sessions from remote systems enter through FromNet in their outgoing phase, visit the CPU and I/OSS, then go to Return, change to their return phase, go back to the Network, and then to their original computer system.

This describes the flow on the Local computer. Both RemoteA and RemoteB are analogous. CatA comes form A's Start node, and CatB comes from B's Start node.   □

The IPG model parameters specify the arrival rate of each category, the percentage of the transactions for local versus remote accounts, and the distribution of remote-account requests across the network. Initially, use best-case values

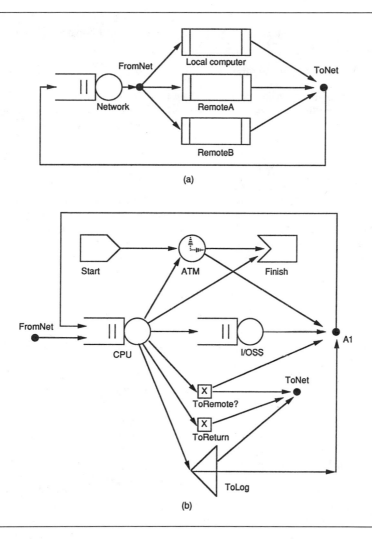

FIGURE 8.17
The high-level IPG in (a) represents each of the interacting computer systems with submodel nodes. The expansion in (b) shows the details of one of the computer systems. FromNet and ToNet are the branch nodes in the top-level configuration.

for network transmission delays. The software models for each local computer system determine the visits and service requirements for the submodel nodes. The remote data access specifications w_{ij} contribute the computer resource requirements for remote resource i for each of the a_j remote accesses.

EXAMPLE 8.14: Parameters for Computer System and Network Interaction Model

High-level model parameters

The workload parameters in Table 8.24 show the distribution of remote requests. For example, the first line of the table shows that 90 percent of the sessions originating on the Local computer are for its local accounts, 4 percent are for accounts on RemoteA, and 6 percent are for accounts on RemoteB. All three computer systems have ATM sessions arriving once per second.

This data translates into the number of visits for nodes in the top-level model, in Table 8.25. The model has three transaction categories corresponding to the computer system where transactions originate. The remote accesses may be either to fetch the account information or to log the transaction. In this example the visits are the same for both. Outgoing requests visit the Network, then go to a Remote system. The table shows that 40 percent of the CatL requests for remote accounts go to RemoteA, and 60 percent go to RemoteB. Upon completion at the Remote system, they become Return requests, and all CatL return to the Local computer.

The number of visits to top-level nodes is per remote access; the number of remote accesses is triggered by the submodel parameters (which come from the corresponding software model). In this example, each session for a remote account goes to the top-level model twice, once to fetch account information and once to Log.

Table 8.25 also specifies parameters for the Network node. The network service time is 200 ms, and it has FCFS scheduling. This is a very simplistic view of the network. A more detailed network model would also include visits for network protocol such as message polling and acknowledgment. This model includes all network overhead in the Network node's mean service time. A realistic model is beyond the scope of this discussion. References to more realistic network models are provided later. The parameters for the other nodes are specified for each submodel expansion.

Submodel parameters

First derive the computer system resource requirements for CatL sessions from the software model in Figure 8.15. Processing for the Initial phase includes Initiate session,

(continued)

TABLE 8.24
DISTRIBUTION OF ACCOUNT REQUESTS

| | Account location: | | |
Origin	Local	RemoteA	RemoteB
Local computer	.90	.04	.06
RemoteA	.067	.90	.033
RemoteB	.08	.02	.90

Session arrival rate for all computers = 1 session/sec

TABLE 8.25
HIGH-LEVEL MODEL PARAMETERS

| | # visits | | | | | |
| | CatL | | CatA | | CatB | |
Nodes	out	return	out	return	out	return
Network	1	1	1	1	1	1
Local computer	0	1	0.67	0	0.8	0
RemoteA	0.4	0	0	1	0.2	0
RemoteB	0.6	0	0.33	0	0	1

Network mean service time = 0.2 sec
Network QD = FCFS

EXAMPLE 8.14 (*Continued*)

Remote-acct? and Fetch account info. The latter is included in the Initial phase for convenience; its processing could be done after the remote data access, or prorated before and after. The Initial phase uses:

$$
\begin{array}{ll}
& (70, 2, 1, 0) \\
+ & (10, 0, 0, 0) \\
+ & .1\ (100, 0, 1, 1) \\
\text{Initial } R_i \quad = & \overline{(90, 2, 1.1, .1)}
\end{array}
$$

The resource requirements for the remainder of the session are calculated as usual to give:

$$
\begin{array}{lll}
\text{Local Account } R_i & = & (652, 12, 8, 0) \\
\text{Remote Account } R_i & = & (652, 12, 8, 0) \\
\text{plus } R_i & = & (150, 0, 1, 1) \quad \text{for Log}
\end{array}
$$

Each remote data access has $R_i = (100, 0, 2, 0)$ on the Remote computer system.

Table 8.26 shows the visits for nodes in the Local computer. The visits for the ATM and I/OSS are derived as usual. The remote data accesses are explicitly represented as follows: The ToRemote? change node makes 90 percent of requests Local-accts and 10 percent Remote-accts (as specified in Table 8.24). The remote data accesses go to ToNet, so it has 1 visit for the Remote-acct (out) phase and 1 visit for the Log (out) phase. They return through FromNet, so it also has 1 visit for Remote-acct (return) and 1 for Log (return). The number of CPU visits is computed from these: For Remote-acct it is 11 from ATM + 8 from I/OSS + 1 from ToLog (to Terminate session) + 1 from FromNet (upon return with account information) = 21. Table 8.27 shows the request specifications for the submodel nodes. The mean service time for the CPU for the Remote-acct phase is $(652 \times .00001)/21 = 0.00031$. The I/OSS service time, 0.05, comes from the environment specification.

The parameters for CatL Log phase also come from the software model: $R_i = (150, 0, 1, 1)$. So for each Log phase, I/OSS has 1 visit, and both ToNet and FromNet have 1 visit for the remote access. Log phase originates at ToLog and completes at Finish. The CPU visits are thus 1 from I/OSS + 1 from FromNet = 2. Its mean service time is $(150 \times .00001)/2 = 0.00075$.

(*continued*)

TABLE 8.26
VISITS TO LOCAL COMPUTER DEVICES*

| Nodes | # visits | | | | CatA all phases |
| | CatL | | | | CatB all phases |
	Initial	Local-acct	Remote-acct	Log	
Start	1	0	0	0	0
ATM	2	12	12	0	0
Finish	0	1	1	1	0
FromNet	0	0	1	1	1
CPU	3.1	20	21	2	3
I/OSS	1.1	8	8	1	2
ToRemote?	1	(origin)	(origin)	0	0
ToReturn	0	0	0	0	1
ToLog	0	0	1	(origin)	0
ToNet	0	0	1	1	1

Arrival rate at node Start = 1 Cat1 session/sec

*Note: Parameters are analogous for RemoteA and RemoteB.

TABLE 8.27
REQUEST SPECIFICATIONS FOR LOCAL COMPUTER DEVICES*

| Nodes | Request specifications—Local computer | |
	Cat, phase	Request
Start	CatL, Initial	1 session/sec
ATM	all, all	1 sec think time
CPU	CatL, Initial	.00029 sec
	CatL, Local-acct	.000326 sec
	CatL, Remote-acct-return	.00031 sec
	CatL, Log-return	.00075 sec
	CatA, all	.00033 sec
	CatB, all	.00033 sec
I/OSS	all, all	.05 sec
ToRemote?	CatL, Initial	Local-acct .9
		Remote-acct-out .1
ToReturn	CatA,out	Return 1.0
	CatB,out	Return 1.0
ToLog	CatL, Remote-acct-return	1CatL, Remote-acct-return
		1 CatL, Log-out

*Note: Parameters are analogous for RemoteA and RemoteB.

EXAMPLE 8.14 (*Continued*)

The Local computer also receives requests from CatA and CatB jobs for access to its account data. From the software model, both account information and logs require $R_i = (100, 0, 2, 0)$. So I/OSS has 2 visits, FromNet has 1 visit to receive the request, ToReturn has 1 to signal that it is to return, and ToNet has 1 to send the reply. The CPU has 3 visits. Its mean service time is $(100 \times .00001)/3 = 0.00033$. Note that the submodel parameters for Cat2 and 3 specify the visits and service time per request. The higher-level model specifies how the requests are distributed.

Note that the parameters for CatL are for sessions originating on the Local computer. The parameters for each computer system submodel are analogous in this example because we assume that each computer system has the same software model (Figure 8.15). If they differ, you construct software models for each computer system and compute the model parameters from them. Compare these model parameters to those in Table 8.22. Note the difference is that this model explicitly represents remote data accesses, so the model results quantify their contention delays. This model also represents routing to Remote computer systems. For each computer system, this model has 90 percent of all sessions for its local accounts. To vary the percentage, vary the probabilities for each ToRemote? change, and modify the probability of executing Fetch account info (which changes its average resource requirements).

Model solution

This completes the model definition. To solve analytically, convert each submodel as before: Replace ToLog with a branch node, and add a source node to originate log transactions at the same rate.

The simulation results are in Table 8.28. All systems have light loads and the network traffic is low, so performance is fine. The number of sessions for remote accounts is low, and the distribution of requests is balanced, so there is little difference in the metrics for the computer system submodels. With this model, it is fairly easy to vary the network service times, the distribution of remote requests, and the percentage of sessions that access remote accounts. You can also expand the Network node to evaluate additional facets of its performance.

□

In summary, we represented remote data accesses in the software execution model with distinct specifications for local versus remote I/Os. Then we created a Remote I/O submodel node in the IPG to represent remote data accesses. The initial best-case checkpoint evaluation substituted a delay node for the submodel with a lower bound for the remote access service time. We examined an improvement alternative that reduced the number of remote data accesses, and used asynchronous processing (split transactions) when it was not necessary to wait for completion. Finally we constructed more realistic models of the distributed computer system and network interactions. The inset summarizes these modeling steps. Next we examine communication in parallel and distributed systems.

TABLE 8.28
MORE REALISTIC REMOTE DATA ACCESS SIMULATION RESULTS

Node	Category	Throughput	Utilization	Residence time
Start	CatL	1.02		
	CatA	.97		
	CatB	1.01		
Network	CatL	.49	.097	.269
	CatA	.38	.070	.260
	CatB	.42	.079	.244
Local Computer:				
L-CPU	CatL	23.57	.008	.00033
	CatA	.40	.000	.00035
	CatB	.49	.000	.00036
L-I/OSS	CatL	9.31	.467	.094
	CatA	.28	.014	.094
	CatB	.32	.015	.091
L-FromNet	CatL	.24		
	CatA	.13		
	CatB	.17		
RemoteA:				
A-CPU	CatL	.26	.000	.00033
	CatA	23.04	.007	.00032
	CatB	.14	.000	.00036
A-I/OSS	CatL	.17	.007	.072
	CatA	9.11	.454	.094
	CatB	.10	.006	.101
A-FromNet	CatL	.09		
	CatA	.19		
	CatB	.04		
RemoteB:				
B-CPU	CatL	.48	.000	.00033
	CatA	.18	.000	.00033
	CatB	23.35	.007	.00032
B-I/OSS	CatL	.33	.017	.100
	CatA	.12	.006	.095
	CatB	9.23	.464	.095
B-FromNet	CatL	.16		
	CatA	.06		
	CatB	.21		

	System Response Time	Remote Data Access Elapsed Time
CatL	14.79	.721
CatA	14.95	.717
CatB	14.87	.675

Summary of Remote Data Access Modeling Techniques

Initial models

1. Extend the software models:

□ Provide distinct specifications for remote versus local I/Os.

□ Augment the w_{ij} to include the computer resources i for each of the a_j requests for remote resource j.

□ Calculate the total computer resources required on both the local and the remote system.

2. Create an advanced IPG that represents the remote system with a submodel node, and represent incoming requests from remote systems with source and sink nodes. Compute best-case model parameters:

□ Substitute a delay node for the submodel node. Set its service time equal to the lower bound on the network transmission delay and the service times on remote devices.

□ Assume an equal distribution of remote requests across the network. Set the arrival rate of incoming requests to the throughput of the submodel node.

3. Solve the model. If the best case is problematic, seek remedies before proceeding to more realistic models.

Asynchronous remote I/O

1. Specify asynchronous process creation in the software model with either FORK-JOIN or SPLIT nodes (depending on whether they must synchronize before termination). Calculate model parameters for each process separately.

2. Add FORK-JOIN or SPLIT nodes to the IPG. Specify model parameters for each process.

3. If your analytic solver does not allow transactions to split, mimic the arrival of split transactions by generating arrivals at a source node at the same rate (throughput of the split node).

Model interacting computing systems

1. Represent the network and the computer systems that interact with one another with submodel nodes in a high-level model. Define a separate workload category for each of the computer systems. Specify visits to other computer systems according to the distribution of their remote data accesses.

2. Calculate computer system submodel parameters for local processing from:

□ The software models for local processing

□ Additional overhead resource requirements to set up remote accesses to other computer systems

3. Calculate computer system submodel parameters for incoming remote data accesses from the w_{ij} computer resource requirements for remote resource i for each of the a_j remote accesses.

8.4.2 Messages for Interprocess Communication

The previous section's remote data access models do not delve to a level low enough to show the operating system routines that move the data between processors. One mechanism for exchanging information is **message passing.** When a process sends a message to another process, it calls a SEND routine, whose syntax is similar to that in the Network Operating System case study in Example 3.10. Similarly, when a process wishes to receive information, it calls a RECEIVE routine. The SEND may be delayed if message buffer space is unavailable; the RECEIVE may be delayed pending the message's arrival. The Network Operating System elementary IPG best-case models ignore these delays. This section shows more realistic models for message SEND and RECEIVE activities.

The following steps create **more realistic software execution models** for message-based interprocess communication:

1. Define the message processing flow.

2. Model each communicating process and each (operating system) message transmittor with a distinct software model.

3. Use SEND and RECEIVE nodes to specify where interprocess communication occurs.

4. Use phase changes to distinguish message types when they determine processing characteristics.

The following example demonstrates these software modeling steps. We first model message passing between processes on the same processor. The models for interprocess communication among multiple processors use similar concepts. They are covered in Section 8.4.3.

EXAMPLE 8.15: Message-Based Interprocess Communication—Software Execution Models

First we create more realistic models of the case studies by representing the message-based interprocess communication that were omitted from the earlier case study models. Figure 8.18 shows the figure from Chapter 3 that specified the message flow. The host operating system sees separate processes for the user scenarios, the SYS_EXEC processing, and the EDMS processing. User scenarios make EDMS calls by SENDing a request to the EDMS. SYS_EXEC, part of a Network Operating System, routes messages between processes (it may route messages to processes on different processors, but that complication is not included in this model). So SYS_EXEC gets the request from the user scenario and routes it to EDMS. The user scenario issues a RECEIVE and waits for the reply. EDMS is likewise a separate process. EDMS issues a RECEIVE and waits for a service request. When one arrives, EDMS processes it and SENDs the reply. SYS_EXEC also routes reply messages from EDMS to the requesting user scenario.

The software models for the three processes are in Figures 8.19–8.21. The first, in 8.19(a), is a modified version of DRAWMOD, called VIEW. It is a user scenario for

(*continued*)

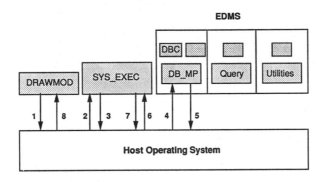

FIGURE 8.18
The Message Flow Between the DRAWMOD, SYS_EXEC, and EDMS Case Studies. The numbers on the arrows show the order of the messages passed.

EXAMPLE 8.15 (*Continued*)

retrieving beam data and viewing it on the screen. The View driver sends requests for EDMS service to DBOPEN the database, FIND the beams, DBSORT them, RETRIEVE each of the 2050 beams, then DBCLOSE the database. As the beam data is received, it is sent to the screen. Figure 8.19(b) shows the same processing from a different perspective: It abstracts the EDMS request but explicitly represents the communication processing (that we previously associated with each of the arcs in the scenario). It begins with VIEW processing (Phase 1). Then it changes to Phase 2, formats the message to request EDMS DBOPEN, and SENDs it to EDMS (via SYS_EXEC). It issues a RECEIVE and waits for the reply. After the reply is received, VIEW changes phases and the format-send-receive cycle repeats: for EDMS FIND beams, Phase 3; for EDMS DBSORT, Phase 4; and for EDMS RETRIEVE beams, Phase 5. When the beam data is received (Phase 5), the phase changes to 6 and Send to screen executes. Processing alternates between Phases 5 and 6 for all 2050 beams; then Phase 7 DBCLOSEs the database, and processing completes.

Figure 8.20 shows the revised software model for the EDMS process. It prepares to receive a message and waits at RECEIVE until it gets a service request. Then it changes to the phase corresponding to the request. For the user scenario specified in Figure 8.19(b), EDMS sees the following ratio of requests:

1/2054 for DBOPEN (Phase 2)
1/2054 for FIND (Phase 3)
1/2054 for DBSORT (Phase 4)
2050/2054 for RETRIEVE (Phase 5)
1/2054 for DBCLOSE (Phase 7)

The resource requirements for each type of request are shown in the figure. When the request processing is complete, the EDMS process formats and SENDs the reply to the VIEW process via SYS_EXEC. VIEW changes to Phase 8, performs cleanup activities, and one processing cycle is complete (Fini).

(*continued*)

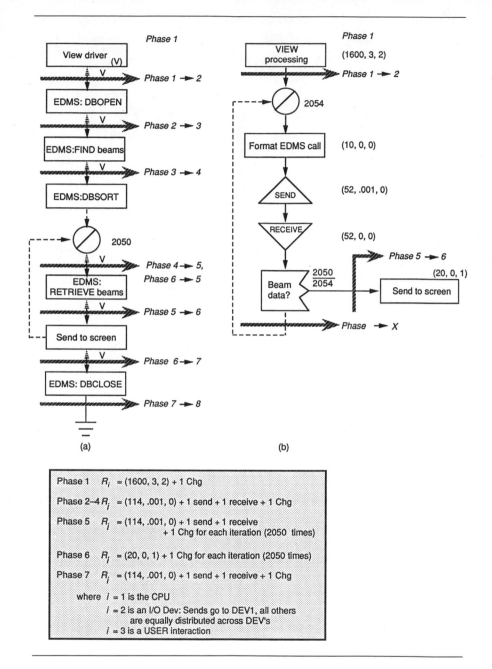

Phase 1	R_i = (1600, 3, 2) + 1 Chg
Phase 2–4	R_i = (114, .001, 0) + 1 send + 1 receive + 1 Chg
Phase 5	R_i = (114, .001, 0) + 1 send + 1 receive + 1 Chg for each iteration (2050 times)
Phase 6	R_i = (20, 0, 1) + 1 Chg for each iteration (2050 times)
Phase 7	R_i = (114, .001, 0) + 1 send + 1 receive + 1 Chg

where i = 1 is the CPU
i = 2 is an I/O Dev: Sends go to DEV1, all others
   are equally distributed across DEV's
i = 3 is a USER interaction

FIGURE 8.19
The VIEW software execution model is in (a). It is a simplified version of the DRAWMOD scenario. The version in (b) is the same processing from a different perspective. It focuses on the communication and consolidates the VIEW processing and the EDMS processing into one node for each. This version models EDMS processing and SYS_EXEC processing independently rather than all in one like the earlier DRAWMOD models.

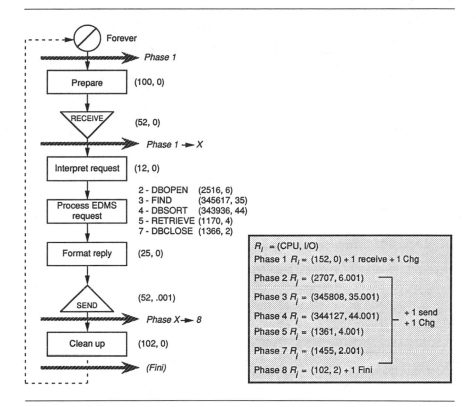

FIGURE 8.20
The independent EDMS processing model explicitly represents the communication to RECEIVE requests for service and SEND the results. Processing phases distinguish the type of EDMS request.

EXAMPLE 8.15 *(Continued)*

Figure 8.21 shows the revised SYS_EXEC process software model. It issues a Switchboard (Receive) and waits for any type of message to arrive. Upon arrival, it changes to Phase 2, determines the message destination, packages the message, adjusts the task schedule, then passes it to the appropriate destination with Switchboard (Send). The cycle completes (Fini). Switchboard Send and Receive are different from VIEW's and EDMS's SEND and RECEIVE. VIEW must first obtain a message buffer before SENDing—if none is available, it must wait. We make a simplifying assumption that the reply uses the same message buffer.[4] After VIEW RECEIVEs the reply, it frees the message buffer. SYS_EXEC does message routing but does not create or remove messages itself.   □

---

[4]The extension to separate buffers leads to a more complex model, but the procedure is straightforward.

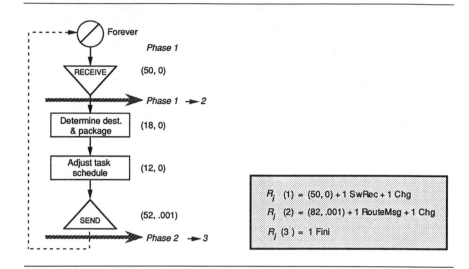

FIGURE 8.21
The independent SYS_EXEC processing model routes messages between VIEW and SYS_EXEC.

The VIEW scenario represents the processing differently than the case study models in Chapters 4 through 6. Rather than include the time for SYS_EXEC and EDMS in the user scenario, this model represents VIEW's delay to receive the EDMS reply. On the average, the time to receive the reply equals the processing time for SYS_EXEC and EDMS plus the communication delays. The SYS_EXEC software model is also slightly different than the version of SYS_EXEC presented earlier, which had a delay until activation. To simplify this model, the delay is not shown here. Later in this section we will discuss the additional model requirements for an activation delay.

To represent the interprocess communication with an advanced IPG:

▢ Represent the communicating processes and operating system transmittors with distinct categories.

▢ Use tokens to represent messages and buffers.

▢ Use allocate and release nodes to request and release message buffers.

▢ Use create nodes to represent message SENDs, and specify the allocate node to RECEIVE the message.

▢ Use allocate nodes to request message RECEIVEs—transaction categories request tokens corresponding to the expected message—and wait if the message has not yet arrived.

The following advanced IPG represents the message flow from the earlier example.

EXAMPLE 8.16: Message-Based Interprocess Communication—Advanced IPG Representation

Figure 8.22 has the advanced IPG for this model. It has three transaction categories: VIEW, EDMS, and SYSEXEC. There may be up to 10 users VIEWing beam data. The average (think) time between VIEWs is 300 seconds. First consider VIEW's flow through the topology in Figure 8.22. Users submit a VIEW request (in Phase 1) after an average think time of 300 seconds. Phase 1 processing cycles through the CPU, the I/O DEVs, and the

(continued)

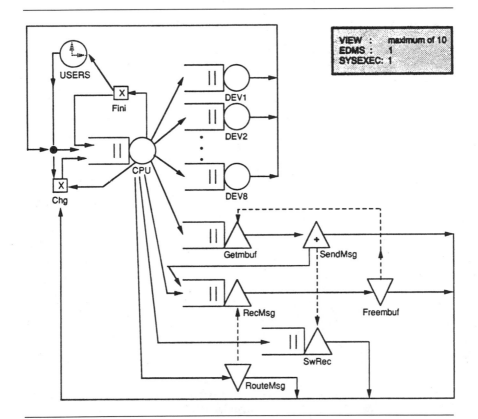

FIGURE 8.22
The Advanced IPG for Routing Messages Between Process. Both VIEW and EDMS jobs visit Getmbuf to get a buffer to transmit messages; then they visit the create node, SendMsg, to generate (SEND) the message. SYSEXEC jobs wait at SwRec until a message arrives, execute the processing in the software execution model, then visit the RouteMsg node to pass the message to the receiving process. Both VIEW and EDMS jobs visit RecMsg to receive incoming messages (and visit Freembuf to free the buffer).

EXAMPLE 8.16 (*Continued*)

USERS node. Then VIEW goes to Chg where it becomes Phase 2. After returning for CPU and occasionally DEV1 processing, it SENDs a message.

This advanced IPG represents the software model's SEND with two nodes—first an allocate node, Getmbuf, which requests a message buffer token, mbuf. The allocate node initially has one mbuf token for each message buffer. In this model, we assume there is a fixed number of message buffers (128 buffers with 64 bytes each), and that the SENDs for all processes require only one message. To model multiple messages, adjust the number of visits to Getmbuf and SendMsg accordingly. The allocation of additional message buffers is addressed later. The second IPG node for SEND, SendMsg, creates a token corresponding to the message type and puts it in the allocate node visited by SYSEXEC, SwRec. When VIEW requests EDMS service, it creates an edms-req token. Then VIEW waits to RECEIVE the reply.

This advanced IPG also represents the software model's RECEIVE with two nodes. The first is an allocate node, RecMsg, which requests a reply token. RecMsg initially has no message tokens. They are created by sending processes at the SendMsg node, and routed through SYSEXEC (SwRec and RouteMsg) to the RecMsg node. The second IPG node for RECEIVE, Freembuf, frees the message buffer by releasing the mbuf token to the Getmbuf allocate node.

When VIEW receives a reply token and frees the message buffer, it goes to Chg where it changes to Phase 3, then repeats the format-send-receive cycle. The processing for each phase is similar, with the exception of Phase 6: It flows through the CPU, USERS, then Chg to change back to Phase 5 (to Retrieve more beam data), and changes to Phase 7 after all beam data has been retrieved. Phase 7 goes through the format-send-receive cycle to DBCLOSE the database, then goes to Fini and the VIEW scenario completes.

Next consider the flow for the EDMS transaction category. It originates at node Fini in Phase 1 and goes to the CPU. It prepares to RECEIVE, then goes to RecMsg where it waits for an edms-req message token. When one arrives, EDMS changes phases to model the type of request according to the ratio given earlier. Each request type has different service time requirements for CPU and I/O resources, so the flow through the CPU and the I/O DEVs differs. Upon completion, EDMS goes to SendMsg and creates a message token, reply, that goes to SYSEXEC's allocate node. EDMS changes to Phase 8, goes back to the CPU, and completes its cycle at Fini. The Fini node has no delay, so EDMS immediately returns to the CPU in Phase 1 to prepare to RECEIVE another service request.

The third transaction category, SYSEXEC, also originates at Fini in Phase 1. It goes to the CPU where it prepares to route a message. It then goes to its allocate node, corresponding to Switchboard (Receive), SwRec. It waits for any type of message token to arrive—either edms-req or reply. When one arrives, SYSEXEC changes to Phase 2, goes to the CPU, and occasionally also visits DEV1. Upon completion of its routing processing, SYSEXEC routes the message by going to the release node, RouteMsg, where it releases the token it got at SwRec to the RecMsg node that represents the VIEW and EDMS processes' RECEIVE. SYSEXEC then changes to Phase 3 and completes its cycle by going to Fini. SYSEXEC also immediately returns to the CPU where it prepares to route another message.

□

Specify advanced IPG model parameters as follows:

1. Represent the number of active threads for each transaction category.
2. Specify the number of message buffers initially available.
3. Calculate model parameters by processing phase as before.

The following example shows the parameters.

EXAMPLE 8.17: Message-Based Interprocess Communication—Advanced IPG Parameters

There is a maximum of 10 concurrent View scenarios. First, we model one EDMS and one SYSEXEC scenario. This corresponds to single-thread execution. We later evaluate multi-thread execution by increasing the population in each transaction category accordingly.

Table 8.29 shows most of the model parameters. By now you should be able to specify CPU, DEV, and USER parameters. The token request specifications for Getmbuf, Send-Msg, SwRec, RouteMsg, RecMsg, and Freembuf correspond directly to the flow described for each scenario. The number of visits needs some explanation. With this model, EDMS responds to one service request per cycle (from Fini through the system and back to Fini). Similarly, SYSEXEC routes one message per cycle. So the number of visits corresponds to the R_i in Figures 8.20 and 8.21 for one pass through the "forever" repetition loop. This means that each EDMS cycle makes one visit to Chg to change from Phase 1 to Phase X where the probability that X is Phase 2 is $1/2054$, and X is 5 with probability $2050/2054$, and so on. Similarly, (EDMS, X) makes one visit to Chg to change to Phase 8. The number of visits for SYSEXEC is also per cycle and is calculated with an analogous procedure.

VIEW is different. It models all requests for the user scenario. Because there is one request each for DBOPEN, FIND, DBSORT, and DBCLOSE, the number of visits for those processing phases (2–4 and 7) is straightforward. Let's examine what happens when Phase 4 changes to Phase 5 to execute the first Retrieve. (VIEW, 5) goes to the CPU, then cycles through the DEVs, CPU, the send path, and the receive path. Then it RECEIVEs the beam data and goes to Chg, where it becomes Phase 6. Phase 6 does its processing and goes back to Chg to return to Phase 5. This happens 2049 times. The last time Phase 6 goes to Chg it becomes Phase 7. Both Phases 5 and 6 make a total of 2050 visits to Chg. Each time a (VIEW, 5) comes from Chg, it makes 1 visit to the send path; since this happens 2050 times, the total number of visits to the send path (both Getmbuf and SendMsg) is 2050. Similarly, there are 2050 visits by (VIEW, 5) to RecMsg and Freembuf. Each time VIEW SENDs, it causes one SwRec and one RouteMsg by SYSEXEC, so each VIEW SEND causes one cycle of SYSEXEC (and the EDMS reply causes another).   □

This completes the model definition. The create, allocate, and release nodes preclude its efficient, exact analytic solution. For an **analytic checkpoint evaluation,** remove the create and release nodes, and replace the allocate nodes with surrogate delay nodes. Estimate the best-case delay time from the software model. The minimum delay time is the best-case elapsed time of the processing that

TABLE 8.29
MODEL PARAMETERS FOR THE ADVANCED IPG
FOR MESSAGES

Node	Cat, phase	# visits	Request
Getmbuf	VIEW, 2–4, 7	1	1 mbuf
	VIEW, 5	2050	1 mbuf
SendMsg	VIEW, 2–4, 7	1	1 edms-req to SwRec
	VIEW, 5	2050	1 edms-req to SwRec
	EDMS, 2–5, 7	1	1 reply to SwRec
SwRec	SYSEXEC, 1	1	1 edms-req OR 1 reply
RouteMsg	SYSEXEC, 2	1	Release all to RecMsg
RecMsg	VIEW, 2–4, 7	1	1 reply
	VIEW, 5	2050	1 reply
	EDMS, 1	1	1 edms-req
Freembuf	VIEW, 2–4, 7	1	1 mbuf to Getmbuf
	VIEW, 5	2050	1 mbuf to Getmbuf
Chg	VIEW, 1	1	VIEW, 2
	VIEW, 2	1	VIEW, 3
	VIEW, 3	1	VIEW, 4
	VIEW, 4	1	VIEW, 5
	VIEW, 5	2050	VIEW, 6
	VIEW, 6	2049	VIEW, 5
	VIEW, 6	1	VIEW, 7
	VIEW, 7	1	VIEW, 8
	EDMS, 1	1	1/2054 to (EDMS, 2)
			1/2054 to (EDMS, 3)
			1/2054 to (EDMS, 4)
			2050/2054 to (EDMS, 5)
			1/2054 to (EDMS, 7)
	EDMS, 2–5, 7	1	(EDMS, 8)
	SYSEXEC, 2	1	(SYSEXEC, 3)
Fini	SYSEXEC, 3	1	(SYSEXEC, 1)
	EDMS, 8	1	(EDMS, 1)
	VIEW, 8	1	(VIEW, 1)

produces the message. Thus the VIEW process waits for one SYSEXEC cycle to forward its request to EDMS, one EDMS cycle, and one SYSEXEC cycle to route the reply. The minimum delay adds no queueing for SYSEXEC or EDMS requests made by other processes. Similarly, EDMS waits for SYSEXEC to route its previous reply, VIEW to prepare the next, and SYSEXEC to route it. Since 10 VIEW processes execute concurrently, on the average EDMS sees only 1/10 of the delay for one process. Similar analysis gives the delay for SYSEXEC.

As you can see, it is nontrivial to correctly estimate the actual delay time.

Furthermore, the minimum delay maximizes device contention, so the model result may not reflect the best case. The actual delays for the three processes depend on one another in a complex manner. Therefore it is much more difficult to develop analytic approximations for models of this type, and even more difficult to generalize the procedure for other patterns of interprocess communication. It may be easier for you to derive delay approximations for your specific applications. If so, you can use an analytic checkpoint evaluation. If not, it may be much easier to rely on simulation results, as in Example 8.18.

EXAMPLE 8.18: Message-Based Interprocess Communication—Results and Alternatives

Table 8.30 shows the simulation results. VIEW's response time is high, and it is not surprising that most of the VIEW transactions are waiting for the EDMS reply. Since the
(continued)

TABLE 8.30
SIMULATION RESULTS

Node	Category	Throughput	Utilization	Queue length	Residence time
USERS	VIEW	8.3		3.176	.41
CPU	VIEW	16.6	.0007	.0006	.0004
	EDMS	57.7	.0098	.010	.00017
	SYSEXEC	33.1	.0013	.001	.00004
DEV1	VIEW	.01	.0003	.0003	.0268
	EDMS	4.12	.1237	.124	.0300
	SYSEXEC	.02	.0005	.0005	.0286
DEV4	VIEW	.01	.0001	.0001	.0286
	EDMS	4.12	.1242	.124	.0301
	SYSEXEC	0	.0000	0	0
Getmbuf	VIEW	8.3		0	0
SendMsg	VIEW	8.3			
	EDMS	8.3			
RecMsg	VIEW	8.3		6.823	.824
	EDMS	8.3		.0002	.00003
SwRec	SYSEXEC	16.6		.998	.060
RouteMsg	SYSEXEC	16.6			

Scenario	Response (sec)
VIEW	690
EDMS	0.121
SYSEXEC	<0.001

EXAMPLE 8.18 (*Continued*)

message buffer use is low, it is feasible to create more EDMS threads (processes). More SYSEXEC threads are unnecessary because SYSEXEC spends most of its time waiting for messages to route.

To evaluate the improvement with 4 threads, change the number of EDMSs from 1 to 4 and re-solve. In this example, additional threads reduce response times by about 250 seconds. Because message buffers are plentiful, another potential improvement reduces EDMS processing with RETRIEVE BLOCKS, as in Chapter 6. To evaluate this alternative, increase the size of the message buffers and reduce the number of buffers accordingly. For example, rather than 128 buffers with 64 bytes each, evaluate 2 buffers with 4K bytes each. With RETRIEVE BLOCKS, 1 Retrieve could return data for 64 beams: 4096 bytes per buffer/64 bytes per beam = 64 beams per buffer. So 2050 beams/64 per bulk retrieve = 33 bulk retrieves. Revise the model by revising the Getmbuf specifications to have 2 *mbufs* initially; decreasing the number of Retrievals to 33 block retrievals; and modifying the EDMS change probabilities to reflect the revised proportions. After these changes, you can evaluate the benefit of 1 EDMS thread versus 4 as before.

□

The inset summarizes the procedure for modeling message-based inter-process communication. You may need to model additional execution characteristics not included here, such as dynamic creation and allocation of message buffers, or the delay before activation of SYS_EXEC. **Dynamic message buffer creation** can be represented with a create node, Makembuf, that adds another block of buffers, say 64, to Getmbuf each time it executes. With an advanced IPG, you estimate the number of visits to Makembuf, or evaluate the performance for a range of visits. If the software frees the message buffers when they are no longer needed, add a destroy node to the advanced IPG and estimate its visits similarly.

A more precise model checks the number of message buffers available and allocates more when they are needed. This is difficult to model with an advanced IPG because of the behavior of allocate nodes. When a process goes to an allocate node, it makes a request and, if the request is unavailable, waits until it is. There is no way to leave the node until the request is granted. *Simulation IPGs* provide the modeling power to represent this behavior more precisely. They can check the state of other nodes and set processing phases accordingly. They are described in Section 8.6.

Models of the **delay before activation** of SYS_EXEC have a similar problem. The SYS_EXEC behavior described in Chapters 3 and 4 has a "forever" loop that periodically activates and checks to see if requests are pending—if not, it sleeps again. If a request arrives while SYS_EXEC is asleep, the request waits until SYS_EXEC awakens. With an advanced IPG, you can estimate a delay before entering an allocate node, but once the process enters, it begins processing the next request as soon as it arrives. This "delay then allocate" approximation is reasonable; a more precise model needs to first check the number of tokens at the

---

Summary of Message-Based
Interprocess Communication Modeling Procedure

1. Create software execution models as follows:

□ Define the message processing flow.

□ Model each communicating process and each (operating system) message transmittor with a distinct software model.

□ Use SEND and RETRIEVE nodes to specify where interprocess communication occurs.

□ Use phase changes to distinguish message types when they determine processing characteristics.

2. To represent the interprocess communication with an advanced IPG:

□ Represent the communicating processes and operating system transmittors with distinct categories.

□ Use tokens to represent messages and buffers.

□ Use allocate and free nodes to request and release message buffers.

□ Use create nodes to represent message SENDs, and specify the allocate node to RECEIVE the message.

□ Use allocate nodes to request message RECEIVEs—transaction categories request tokens corresponding to the expected message and wait if the message has not yet arrived.

3. Specify the advanced IPG model parameters as follows:

□ Represent the number of active threads for each transaction category.

□ Specify the number of message buffers initially available.

□ Calculate model parameters by processing phase as before.

4. For an analytic checkpoint evaluation, remove the create and release nodes, and replace the allocate nodes with surrogate delay nodes. Estimate the best-case delay time from the software model. The minimum delay time is the best-case elapsed time of the processing that produces the message.

5. When the interactions are too complex to permit easy estimation of delays, use simulation solvers.

---

allocate node and, if there are no pending requests, defer the visit to the allocate node. Simulation IPGs provide this feature.

There are **several differences in this model of the case study and earlier models.** This one explicitly models the separate processes, so it is easy to evaluate the effect of multiple threads. With this model formulation, however, it is more difficult to associate resource requirements for EDMS requests with the scenarios that make them. For example, the model results in Tables 5.11 and 5.12 and Figure 5.13 show that there is an I/O bottleneck and that most of the I/O requests are made by Retrieve beams, Find nodes, and Retrieve nodes. This model has the same information, but requires some interpretation of results to arrive at the same conclusion. For example, most of VIEW's elapsed time is at RecMsg. The I/O devices are a system bottleneck, most of the requests are made by EDMS, and most are Phase 5-Retrieve requests; so bottleneck resolutions should either reduce the I/O for Retrieve or reduce the number of Retrieve requests. In this example, it is not difficult to arrive at the same conclusion as the earlier examples, but it is much more difficult when there are many scenarios that have different patterns of EDMS requests.

This model formulation introduces another subtle difference in model results due to the decoupled behavior of VIEW and EDMS. Consider the following example. VIEW makes its first request, DBOPEN, and waits for a reply. Meanwhile, EDMS RECEIVEs a request, sets its phase according to the probability of the various requests, executes the corresponding processing, and SENDs the reply. Even though VIEW requests DBOPEN, it is probable that EDMS changes to Phase 5-Retrieve (2050/2054). This model formulation thus represents "generic behavior"—the *average* wait time for EDMS requests for the entire VIEW scenario is correct, but an individual request may differ significantly from the average. For example, upon VIEW completion, on the average, one of the 2054 EDMS requests has the execution behavior of DBOPEN, but it was not necessarily the first request. So the average behavior is represented with this model, but the actual variance and distribution of response time differ.

A more precise model has tokens corresponding to the request types, so VIEW's DBOPEN makes an *o-request* and waits for an *o-reply*. The model specifications are more complex. A simulation IPG is required to coordinate phase changes with token types. The simulation IPG produces average results that are approximately the same as this model, but produces more precise results for the variance and distribution.

8.4.3 Process Structure and Allocation

This section evaluates alternatives for decomposing scenarios into processes that can execute in parallel on different computers. **Process structure** refers to how software scenario components are assigned to processes, and **process allocation** refers to how the processes are assigned to processors. We seek a process structure and allocation strategy to maximize the performance benefits of concurrency. This section uses a signal-processing scenario to explain the process structure and allocation models and analysis.

EXAMPLE 8.19: Signal-Processing Scenario

Consider the real-time signal-processing scenario in Figure 8.23. The first step gets the image or *frame* to be processed and performs calculations to calibrate it. Next, spatial filter calculations use values of adjacent pixels to remove noise. Then temporal filter calculations use values of pixels in previous frames to remove noise. Threshold calculations remove clutter. Objects of interest are identified; then calculations look for object movement—direction and velocity. Finally, the scenario collects path data for object movements of interest. The performance goal for this scenario is a throughput of 1 frame per second. The proposed environment has eight processors—we need to know if eight is sufficient, and if not, how many we need.

□

From this description, the potential for parallel execution may not be obvious because each step in the scenario requires results from the previous step. We examine two types of parallel execution. The first uses *pipeline processing:* Scenario steps execute in parallel on different frames of data. The second also *parti-*

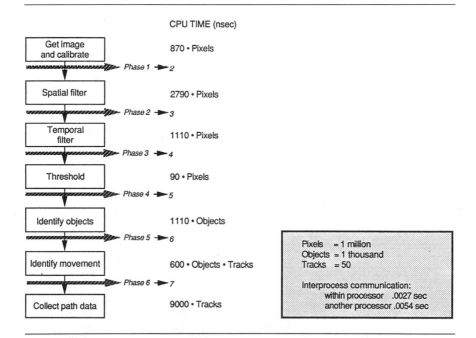

FIGURE 8.23
Signal-Processing Software Execution Model. The phases synchronize the processing steps when they execute on separate processors.

tions the calculations: Several processors execute in parallel on different regions of frames in the same step. To model the pipeline processing, we:

1. Define the synchronization processing.
2. Divide the scenario into processes.
3. Allocate the processes to processors.
4. Use processing phases to identify synchronization points.

First we define the **synchronization** required to pipeline this scenario. We divide the scenario into processes that perform successive operations on frames.

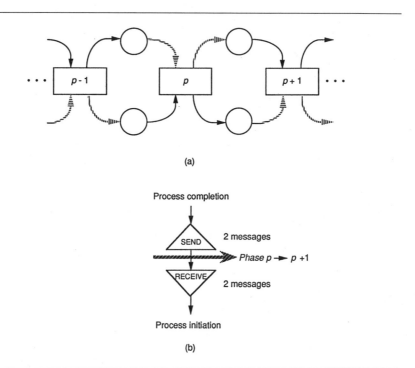

(a)

(b)

FIGURE 8.24
The processes, *p*, in (a) are pipelined. The circles represent buffers for shared data. Each process has two input buffers and two output buffers, and alternates between them. The solid arcs in the figure show the buffers that process *p* is currently using. The software execution model in (b) shows the synchronization required between pipelined processes. When process *p* completes, it sends messages to notify adjacent processes; *p* waits to receive messages from adjacent processes before beginning the next processing phase.

Visualize one of the processes in the middle of the pipeline—call it p—shown in Figure 8.24(a). As frames arrive, process p takes the results of process $p - 1$, performs its calculations, and creates the data for process $p + 1$. Process p needs the results of process $p - 1$ before it can begin, so process $p - 1$ must be finished with the frame. Process p also needs a place to put its results for process $p + 1$, so $p + 1$ must be finished using the previous frame. We want to overlap the processing so that process p works on its frame while $p - 1$ prepares the next, and so on. This means we need (at least) two frame buffers between each process. In Figure 8.24(a), the rectangles represent the processes and the circles represent the buffers. The solid arcs show that p uses the frame from the "lower" buffer on the left as input and puts its results in the "lower" buffer on the right. At the same time, $p - 1$ prepares the next frame and puts it in the "upper" buffer. Similarly, $p + 1$ is currently using the "upper" buffer. Each of the processes switches buffers for the next frame. The processes take different amounts of time, so before a process begins its next frame, it must check that both its predecessor and its successor processes have completed. Each time a process completes, it must notify its two neighbors.

EXAMPLE 8.20: Signal-Processing Scenario—Process Structure and Allocation Software Model

A software model represents the pipeline synchronization with SEND and RECEIVE nodes as shown in Figure 8.24(b). The SEND transmits a "phase p finished with lower input buffer" message to the process performing the $p - 1$ step and an analogous message for $p + 1$. Process p RECEIVEs a similar message from $p - 1$ and $p + 1$ before it begins processing the next frame. This synchronization occurs for every arc in the signal-processing scenario that connects separate processes.

   With this in mind, we next divide the scenario into processes. Figure 8.25 shows the first alternative. The first four components each become separate processes, while the last three components combine into one process. Then we allocate the processes to processors. In this example, each process goes on a different processor; thus the scenario requires only five of the eight processors.

□

This example allocates processes to separate processors, but more general allocations can also be modeled easily. For example, two short processes from different pipeline stages may be allocated to the same processor to fill "slack time"—the time that a processor waits for either predecessors or successors to complete.

   Next we model the dynamic execution behavior of the parallel processing and synchronization with an advanced IPG. The first model formulation creates one transaction category for each scenario, as before (later we contrast an alternative

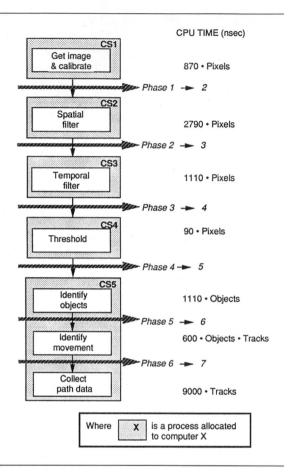

FIGURE 8.25
The software execution model specifies process structure and allocation. Each component in the scenario is assigned to a process; the shaded boxes show how the seven components are allocated to five processors.

formulation with one category per process). To represent the parallel processing and synchronization execution behavior with an IPG:

- □ Use create nodes to generate completion-signal tokens.
- □ Use allocate nodes to synchronize—processes visit the nodes and request appropriate completion-signal tokens and wait, if necessary, for the tokens to arrive.
- □ Use phase changes to control routing and to control sequencing of token creation and allocation.
- □ Represent the parallel processors with submodel nodes.

The following example demonstrates the signal-processing IPG representation.

EXAMPLE 8.21: Signal-Processing Scenario IPG

Figure 8.26 shows the advanced IPG. Transactions, $\langle Fr, 1 \rangle$, arrive at Start. They proceed to the ReqPer[1] allocate node to synchronize. When granted permission, execution proceeds on the appropriate processor, submodel nodes CS1 through CS5. Upon completion, Sig-Compl signals to the appropriate ReqPer nodes that processing is complete, the transaction changes phases, and the request-execute-signal cycle repeats. The transaction leaves the system after the last step.

We represent the SEND and RECEIVE for pipeline synchronization with IPG create and allocate nodes. The SEND creates a token corresponding to the message type, and RECEIVE waits at an allocate node, if necessary, until a desired message token arrives. So, for the signal-processing scenario, when process 2 completes, it creates two tokens at node SigCompl—one token indicates that the input data for process 3 is ready (it sends one *in* token to ReqPer[3]), and one token indicates that an output buffer is available for process 1 (it sends one *out* token to ReqPer[1]). Before process 2 begins, it visits the allocate node, ReqPer[2], and requests one (ready) input buffer (in, 1) and one (free) output buffer (out, 1). Note that it is not necessary to free message tokens—they are destroyed when they reach the sink node, Finish. Initially, all output buffers are available. Also note that process 1 needs only an output buffer to begin, so it will not wait when it first requests (synchronization) permission.

□

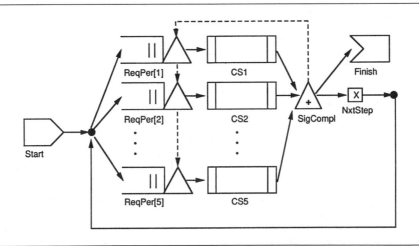

FIGURE 8.26
The Advanced IPG for the Signal-Processing Scenario. Submodel nodes represent each of the five processors. The ReqPer allocate nodes synchronize the processing stages. The SigCompl node creates the completion messages.

The IPG parameters consist of the following:

- Arrival rate for the scenario
- Visits by phase
- Phase changes
- Message-token (permission) requests by phase
- Computer system service time requirements: processing plus synchronization (communication) overhead

The following example demonstrates.

EXAMPLE 8.22: Signal-Processing Scenario IPG Parameters

Table 8.31 shows the IPG model parameters. Frames arrive in Phase 1 at a rate of 1 per second. Each transaction category phase visits its corresponding ReqPer and CS node once, proceeds to the SigCompl (once), then changes to the next phase at NxtStep and repeats the cycle. The message-token creation and requests for the processing described in Example 8.21 are also in the table.

Next calculate the service requirements for the processors. The frame data is in shared memory buffers, so no I/O is needed. Thus each submodel node in this example represents one CPU. The best-case model assumes there is sufficient memory for all frames of data and there are no memory access conflicts. Figure 8.23 specifies the CPU requirement for each node's calculations; we need to add the interprocess communication for the pipeline synchronization. The communication overhead depends on the process structure and allocation: As shown in the figure, each message that stays within a processor takes 0.0027 seconds, and each message between processors takes 0.0054 seconds (for this example). One-half of the time is for SEND and one-half for RECEIVE. In this example, all communication is between processors. So process 2 takes

$$
\begin{array}{l}
.0054 \text{ sec to receive 2 permission messages} \\
+ \ (2790 \text{ nsec} \times 1{,}000{,}000 \text{ pixels}) \text{ for processing} \\
+ \ .0054 \text{ sec to send 2 completion messages} \\
\hline
2.8 \text{ sec TOTAL}
\end{array}
$$

Check your understanding by computing the service time requirements for the other processes. Note that processes 1 and 5 are at the beginning and end of the pipe, respectively, so they do one-half the communication of the other processes. Note that process 5 is composed of three components. The individual components do not require the synchronization because the components are procedures within the process. Thus the procedure return automatically signals completion, and the process calls the next procedure knowing that the buffers are free.

□

This model formulation uses one category, *Fr*. Each arrival represents one frame, and the category changes phases to represent the processes required for a frame. An alternative model formulation represents each process as a separate

TABLE 8.31
SIGNAL-PROCESSING MODEL PARAMETERS

Node	Cat, phase	# visits	Request
Start	Fr, 1	1	1/sec
ReqPer[1]	Fr, 1	1	(out,1)
CS1	Fr, 1	1	.88 sec
ReqPer[2]	Fr, 2	1	(in, 1)(out, 1)
CS2	Fr, 2	1	2.80 sec
ReqPer[3]	Fr, 3	1	(in, 1)(out, 1)
CS3	Fr, 3	1	1.12 sec
ReqPer[4]	Fr, 4	1	(in, 1)(out, 1)
CS4	Fr, 4	1	.91 sec
ReqPer[5]	Fr, 5	1	(in, 1)
CS5	Fr, 5	1	.048 sec*
NxtStep	Fr, j	1	Fr, $j + 1$
Finish	Fr, 7	1	

Cat, phase	SigCompl	
	# visits	Request†
Fr 1	1	(in, 1) to ReqPer[2]
Fr, 2	1	(out, 1) to ReqPer[1] (in, 1) to ReqPer[3]
Fr, 3	1	(out, 1) to ReqPer[2] (in, 1) to ReqPer[4]
Fr, 4	1	(out, 1) to ReqPer[3] (in, 1) to ReqPer[5]
Fr, 5	1	(out, 1) to ReqPer[4]

*CS5 has a phase change node within its submodel for Phases 6 and 7. Details are not included.

†Initially each ReqPer[j] has 2 out tokens.

category. Each executes on its processor, and upon completion signals at Sig-Compl, then goes to its ReqPer node to await another frame (the phase change is unnecessary with multiple categories). Both model formulations work, but with the single category it is easier to derive the total time to process a frame and it is somewhat easier to solve the model analytically. Furthermore, with the single-category formulation the *in* tokens are unnecessary. Consider a Phase 1 process $\langle Fr, 1 \rangle$ completion: It sends an *in* token to ReqPer[2] to indicate the input buffer is filled. Then it changes to $\langle Fr, 2 \rangle$ at NxtStep and goes to ReqPer[2], where it requests an *out* token and the *in* token it just sent. So, with the single-category model we can omit the *in* token requests and creations because there is never a wait for an *in* token—the phase change essentially *represents* the downstream buffer synchronization. The phase change is only in the models, not the software—the SEND and RECEIVE processing executes in the software to synchronize the concurrent processes; so include the synchronization resource requirements in the service requirements even if you omit the downstream tokens from the model.

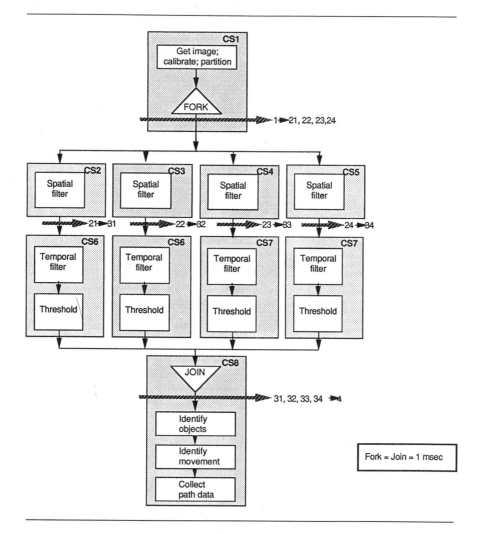

FIGURE 8.27
The Revised Process Structure and Allocation for the Signal-Processing Scenario. The spatial filter component is divided into four processes, one for each quadrant of the data; each process is allocated to a separate processor. Similarly, the temporal filter and threshold components are divided into four processes; two processes are allocated to each of two processors.

This completes the advanced IPG model. Note that the system arrival rate is 1 frame per second, but both processors 2 and 3 have service times greater than 1 second. Thus the system is saturated, and further study is required. The following examples demonstrate a revised process structure and allocation, and the second type of parallel processing: *partitioning the calculations* so several processors execute in parallel on different regions of the same frame.

EXAMPLE 8.23: Signal-Processing Scenario—Revised Process Structure and Allocation Software Model

Figure 8.27 shows an alternate process structure. The software model FORKs the filter and threshold steps into four components, each of which processes one-fourth of a frame. The flow through the software model is as follows. The first process gets the frame and performs calculations to calibrate it. The results are partitioned into four output buffers. Then the first process FORKs into four processes to perform the spatial-filter calculations in parallel on their quadrant of the frame. The next four processes perform the temporal filter and threshold calculations on their fourth of the frame. When all are complete, the processes JOIN, and the last process completes the calculation.

Figure 8.27 also shows the process allocation. Process 1 executes on processor CS1. The four spatial-filter processes, 21 through 24, execute on processors CS2, CS3, CS4, and CS5, respectively. Both processes 31 and 32 execute on CS6, and 33 and 34 on CS7. Process 4 executes on processor CS8.

□

To represent the four partitions, we add FORK and JOIN nodes to the IPG.

EXAMPLE 8.24: Signal-Processing Scenario—Revised IPG

Figure 8.28 shows the revised advanced IPG with FORK and JOIN nodes. It has a single-transaction category as before. A frame transaction, Fr, arrives at Start and goes to ReqPer[1], where it waits, if necessary, for four output buffers (one for each quadrant of the frame). Phase 1 executes on CS1, then proceeds to NxtStep and changes to Phase 4 (it skips SigCompl because (downstream) *in* tokens for Phase 2 are unnecessary). Phase 4 visits the FORK node, where the parent process creates four child processes. The parent remains at the FORK node until all the children arrive at the JOIN node. (Note that other frame transactions, (Fr,1), arrive from Start while earlier frame parents wait.) The child processes cycle through the system as usual. As each process 31, 32, 33, and 34 completes, it goes to the JOIN node, releases its tokens to the parent process (Fr,4) and terminates. After all children finish, the parent process leaves the FORK node and goes immediately to the JOIN node, where it resumes execution. The rest of the processing is the same as in the previous model.

Table 8.32 shows the model parameters. Frames arrive once per second. The service

(continued)

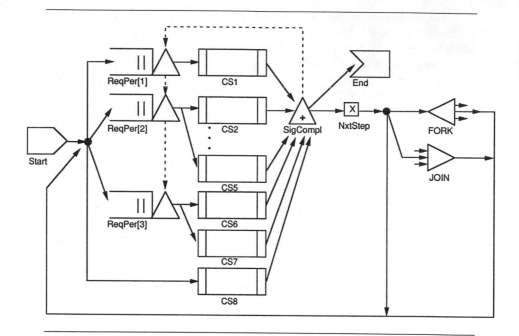

FIGURE 8.28
The revised IPG has a FORK node to create the additional processes and a JOIN node to synchronize their completion. It has ReqPer allocate nodes to synchronize the beginning of Phases 1 through 3—all the Phase 2 jobs (21–24) visit ReqPer[2] then proceed to their designated processor. The processing for Phase 3 is similar. The JOIN node synchronizes the beginning of Phase 4, so it does not need a ReqPer node.

EXAMPLE 8.24 (*Continued*)

time calculation uses the same procedure as before. The resulting values are different because both the communication and the number of calculations are different. For Phase 1,

$$
\begin{array}{ll}
   & 870 \quad\text{nsec} \times 1,000,000 \text{ pixels} \\
+ & .0027 \text{ sec} \times 4 \text{ completion messages} \\
+ & .001 \quad\text{sec for FORK} \\
\hline
  & .8818 \text{ sec TOTAL}
\end{array}
$$

For Phases 21 through 24,

$$
\begin{array}{ll}
   & 2790 \quad\text{nsec} \times 250,000 \text{ pixels} \\
+ & .0027 \text{ sec} \times 2 \text{ permission messages} \\
+ & .0027 \text{ sec} \times 2 \text{ completion messages} \\
\hline
  & .7083 \text{ sec TOTAL}
\end{array}
$$

(*continued*)

TABLE 8.32
REVISED IPG MODEL PARAMETERS

Node	Cat, phase	# visits	Request
Start	Fr 1	1	1/sec
CS1	Fr, 1	1	.8818 sec
CS2	Fr, 21	1	.7083 sec
CS3	Fr, 22	1	.7083 sec
CS4	Fr, 23	1	.7083 sec
CS5	Fr, 24	1	.7083 sec
CS6	Fr, 31	1	.3108 sec
CS6	Fr, 32	1	.3108 sec
CS7	Fr, 33	1	.3108 sec
CS7	Fr, 34	1	.3108 sec
CS8	Fr, 4	1	.0542 sec
ReqPer[1]	Fr, 1	1	(out1, 1)(out2, 1)(out3, 1)(out4, 1)
ReqPer[2]	Fr, 21	1	(out1, 1)
	Fr, 22	1	(out2, 1)
	Fr, 23	1	(out3, 1)
	Fr, 24	1	(out4, 1)
ReqPer[3]	Fr, 31	1	(out1, 1)
	Fr, 32	1	(out2, 1)
	Fr, 33	1	(out3, 1)
	Fr, 34	1	(out4, 1)
NxtStep	Fr, 2j	1	(Fr, 3j)
NxtStep	Fr, 1	1	(Fr, 4)
Fork	Fr, 4	1	(Fr, 4)$\rightarrow$(Fr, 21)(Fr, 22)(Fr, 23)(Fr, 24)
End	Fr, 4	1	

	SigCompl		
Cat, phase	# visits		Request
Fr, 2j	1		(out$j$, 1) to ReqPer[1]
Fr, 3j	1		(out$j$, 1) to ReqPer[2]
Fr, 4	1		(out1, 1)(out2, 1)(out3, 1)(out4, 1) to ReqPer[3]

Where the j in the phase and token specification ranges from 1–4 corresponding to the quadrant. For example, Fr, 23 corresponds to Phase 2 for quadrant 3—it sends one out3 token to ReqPer[1].

EXAMPLE 8.24 (*Continued*)

For Phases 31 through 34,

$$(1110 \quad \text{nsec} + 90 \text{ nsec}) \times 250,000 \text{ pixels}$$
$$+ \quad .0027 \text{ sec} \times 2 \text{ permission messages}$$
$$+ \quad .0027 \text{ sec} \times 2 \text{ completion messages}$$
$$\overline{.3108 \text{ sec TOTAL}}$$

(*continued*)

EXAMPLE 8.24 (*Continued*)

For Phase 4,

$$
\begin{array}{ll}
1110 & \text{nsec} \times 1000 \text{ objects} \\
+\ \ 600 & \text{nsec} \times 1000 \text{ objects} \times 50 \text{ tracks} \\
+\ 9000 & \text{nsec} \times 50 \text{ tracks} \\
+ & .0027 \text{ sec} \times 4 \text{ permission messages} \\
+ & .0027 \text{ sec} \times 4 \text{ completion messages} \\
+ & .001 \ \ \text{sec for JOIN} \\
\hline
& .0542 \text{ sec TOTAL}
\end{array}
$$

At node NxtStep, phase Fr,1 changes to Fr,4 (then waits at the FORK node until its children complete before executing the Phase 4 processing). Each of the four Phase 2 processes changes to the corresponding Phase 3 process. For example, (Fr,22), the Phase 2 process for quadrant 2, changes to (Fr,32), the Phase 3 process for quadrant 2. At node FORK, the parent process Fr,4 creates 1 of each of the Phase 2 processes, (Fr,21), (Fr,22), (Fr,23), and (Fr,24).

The requests for ReqPer and SigCompl are similar to the previous. We omit the specifications for *in* tokens. Since the frame is divided into quadrants in process 1, four tokens are used—one for each quadrant buffer (*out1* is the output buffer for quadrant 1). So process 1 waits for all four *out* tokens before beginning. Remember, the software still SENDs the synchronization messages, but our model does not need to create or wait for the corresponding *in* tokens. Processes 21–24 and 31–34 each request one output (quadrant) buffer to begin, and, upon completion, indicate that the *out* token is available. When process 4 completes, it indicates that four *out* tokens are available for Phase 3 processing.   □

We can solve an analytical approximation for a checkpoint evaluation of the model. The best-case model assumes it is never necessary to wait for a buffer, and replaces ReqPer nodes with branch points. A more realistic approximation replaces the ReqPer nodes with a surrogate delay server. In this example it is easy to estimate the delay for each phase. Since the processing includes only CPU service, we can estimate the processing time from the software model.[5] The modeling procedure for process structure and allocation is summarized in the inset.

Notice that the synchronization causes all processes to execute at the same average rate as the slowest process in the pipe. The faster processes complete earlier but must wait for permission from the slower one. In this example, the slowest is (Fr,1) at 0.8818 seconds. Similarly, the utilization of processor 1 is 0.8818 sec/1 sec = 88.18 percent. Process 1 takes 0.8818 sec; then it waits an average of $1 - 0.8818 = 0.1182$ sec for the next frame to arrive. Similarly,

---

[5]If the software also requires service from other computer systems devices, use the total processing units *T* for the submodel for a first delay approximation. For more realistic delay estimates, apply Little's Law to the submodel *j*:

$$
RT_j = \frac{N_j}{X_j}
$$

Summary of Process Structure and Allocation Pipeline Processing Modeling Procedure

1. Construct software execution models of the scenario as follows:

□ Define the synchronization processing.

□ Divide the scenario into processes.

□ Allocate the processes to processors.

□ Use processing phases to identify synchronization points.

□ Use SEND and RECEIVE to transmit synchronization "signals."

2. Create advanced IPGs to represent the parallel processing and synchronization:

□ Use create nodes to generate completion-signal tokens.

□ Use allocate nodes to synchronize—processes visit the nodes and request appropriate completion-signal tokens and wait, if necessary, for the tokens to arrive.

□ Use phase changes to control routing and to control sequencing of token creation and allocation.

□ Represent the parallel processors with submodel nodes.

3. Specify the following advanced IPG parameters:

□ Arrival rate for the scenario

□ Visits by phase

□ Phase changes

□ Message token (permission) requests by phase

□ Computer system service time requirements: processing plus synchronization (communication) overhead

4. For an analytic checkpoint evaluation, the best-case model assumes it is never necessary to wait on another process, and replaces allocate nodes with branch points. A more realistic approximation replaces allocate nodes with a surrogate delay server. Estimate delay from the software execution model processing time, T.

---

the utilization of processors 2 through 5 is 0.7083 sec/1 sec = 70.83 percent. Processors 6 and 7 execute the calculations for two quadrants, so the utilization of each is (0.3108 sec + 0.3108 sec)/1 sec = 62.16 percent, and processor 8 is 5.42 percent utilized. The throughput is 1 frame per second, but the response time is longer. It is 0.8818 sec for the first step (get image, calibrate, and partition) + 0.7083 sec for parallel execution of the spatial filter + (0.3108 × 2) for the temporal filter and threshold calculations (because two quadrants execute on the same processor, and both must finish before the next stage begins) + 0.0542 sec for the last step = 2.2659 sec total to process a frame. This is an unusual pipe because successive stages take less time than the previous. So for the average case, processes do not wait for a free output buffer, only for the input to be ready. If a slower process were downstream, intermediate processes would have to wait on it, so the response would be slower. We will not consider all the special cases and their analytic solution at this time.

In this example, the checkpoint analysis has sufficient precision, we do not need to simulate the system. This is because the service times for the processes are close to the mean—the same number of calculations is executed for each frame; there is little variance[6] (we expect the service time distribution for CS1–CS8 is hyperexponential with variance less than 1 ms). Similarly, the frame arrival rate has little variance. The simulation results with the hyperexponential distributions correspond to the checkpoint analytic results for this model.

For other models with less regularity, best-case analytic models with unacceptable performance indicate that further study is needed. However, best-case analytic results may be insufficient for complex models. Petri net models are an alternative representation that provide both analytic and simulation results for parallel systems that require frequent synchronization. The simulation solution of the advanced IPG also provides more precise performance metrics.

8.4.4 Summary and Further Reading

This section described three important modeling topics for parallel processing and distributed processing. First, Section 8.4.1 covered models for remote data accesses. The basic model looks at a Local computer, adds incoming traffic that accesses its local data, and estimates delays to receive responses from remote systems. More complex models couple the interacting computer systems to see how traffic distributions affect each of the systems. Then Section 8.4.2 modeled messages for interprocess communication. The advanced IPG examines the performance effect of passing messages that represent service requests between three concurrent workloads. Finally, Section 8.4.3 constructed models that allow the evaluation of alternatives for partitioning software into parallel tasks or processes, and alternative allocations to processors. The concepts were illustrated with three specific examples.

Other related work covers similar concepts for modeling parallel and distributed processing. Yau, Yang, and Shatz describe a software model that represents concurrent execution and an analytic approximation of best- and worst-case

---

[6]Actually, the last processing phase's service time varies because in the actual system the number of tracks varies. Because the processing for the last phase is much shorter than for the others the variance has a negligible effect. It is handled by solving the models separately for different values for "tracks."

performance ([YAU81]). Sanguinetti models and analyzes concurrent execution characteristics of operating system software in [SAN77]. Sholl and Kim use a similar approach to modeling real-time distributed systems in [SHO86]. Bagrodia employs a language that represents concurrent execution characteristics and a companion message-based simulator that produces performance results ([BAG84a, BAG84b]). His language is rich enough to model each of the three topics in Section 8.4.

Fernandez and colleagues describe a simulation IPG of a system with remote procedure calls in [FER84]. Lazowska et al. present models for remote data access from a diskless workstation in [LAZ84b]. Gostl and Greenberg use analytic techniques to determine the number of message buffers necessary in [GOS85]. Sevcik, Graham, and Zahorjan describe analytic system execution models that assist in configuration studies and capacity planning for distributed processing systems in [SEV80]. Smith and Loendorf present software models for an MIMD processor in [SMI82c]. A different type of model for evaluating the number of concurrent software threads is in [AGR82].

Models that represent precedence relations or synchronization of concurrent processes take several different perspectives. Bryant and Agre study the module allocation problem in [BRY81]. Thomasian combines Markov models with queueing network models to study the affect of task sequencing ([THO85]). Smith describes software models for FORK and JOIN, their mapping to queueing network models, and approximate analytic solutions in [SMI80b]. Heidelberger and Trivedi describe similar models with slightly different solution techniques in [HEI82] and [HEI83].

All these topics are active research areas. Consult recent information sources for the latest developments.

8.5 Using Advanced IPGs for SPE

Models are most useful when you embark on a large, complex system development project that uses emerging software development concepts or state-of-the-art computer environments. Yet, as the uncertainty about the software or environment increases, so does the difficulty in modeling its future behavior. Performance engineers commonly feel overwhelmed with uncertainty. The software or environment seems radically different from that of previous systems, and they are unsure how to approach the problem. In this situation, though, the *hardest task is getting started*. Once you delve into the system, you will learn more, gain more experience, and gain control of the modeling and analysis.

The purpose of this section is to introduce some of the software and environment challenges you may face, point out how to start using the SPE techniques in

Chapters 1 through 8, and mention some performance pitfalls that others have found. It is not meant to thoroughly explain the subjects. Consider the analogy to skiers who happen upon a steep slope covered with car-size moguls. Approach your project the same way expert skiers approach these slopes. First they learn the basic techniques (as in Chapters 1 through 8). Then they pause at the top to develop their strategy (or "line"). Then they apply the techniques to *make one turn at a time*. Problem situations, such as hidden rocks, often require course corrections. Skiers need new techniques to adapt to changing snow and slope conditions. Like skiers you need to learn and practice the basic techniques—*experience on other projects* (slopes), *persistence,* and *confidence are vital to success.* You may occasionally fall—you need sufficient skills and techniques to avoid serious accidents (verification and validation!)—from minor falls you gain experience that improves your future skills.

The following sections introduce software development topics and review computer environment challenges. They cover today's popular topics; new topics emerge each year. With experience, you will become more comfortable with new topics.

8.5.1 Software Development Topics

This section introduces the following software-related topics: (1) real-time systems, (2) Ada, (3) DB2 and other relational databases, (4) fourth-generation languages, (5) UNIX-based systems, (6) tiered architectures, (7) object-oriented systems, and (8) operating system and support software designs. Detailed coverage of all these topics is impossible—each could easily fill a book of its own. Instead the introduction to the topic provides a definition, the current motivation for using it on modern systems, and the reason why its performance is important. Then the discussion suggests similarities to analysis techniques described earlier and examines the differences and their effect on the models. When appropriate, you are alerted to performance pitfalls.

Real-Time Systems   Real-time systems receive data from periodic instrument or sensor readings, feedback from events, and operator commands and must react or respond by generating appropriate feedback displays or equipment control commands *within a specified time limit.* A flight-control system receives instrument readings, aircraft status data, supplemental pilot input, and other input and generates commands to control the aircraft flight. Similarly, process-control systems control equipment such as computerized manufacturing systems. They are characterized by their time limits for responses and by the complex system dynamics caused by the many data sources and the number of different ways to control the processes. There are many possible system states, and there are many subtle interactions between the software and hardware components.

Real-time systems were traditionally built by experts who understood both the systems they were controlling and the details of the software. Most of the code was assembly language. Because of the difficulty of maintaining assembly language code, the limited availability of experts, and the increased demand for real-time systems, the trend is to seek ways to improve productivity. The Ada programming language (discussed in the next subsection) and new software development methodologies are proposed productivity improvements. Real-time systems traditionally ran on a small computer. Today they are distributed throughout networks of mainframes, minis, and microcomputers. The raw computing power is greater, but process structure, process allocation, and communication are vital to its effective use. Because the number of experts is limited and response timeliness is vital, these new development technologies increase the risk of performance failures.

Early lifecycle SPE studies of real-time systems use the techniques discussed in Chapters 2 through 7. Start with software scenarios to drive the analysis, and use elementary system execution models to obtain metrics for checkpoint evaluations. Use all of Chapter 8's advanced IPG topics for more detailed study; pay close attention to the process structure and allocation.

Start with the previous modeling steps. The following additional faccts of real-time systems may be pertinent to your studies:

□ *Performance-availability-reliability, or PAR, are interrelated.* Availability is the percentage of time the system is operational; reliability is the likelihood that key components do not fail. Supplement performance models with availability and reliability assessments. Include workload scenarios of operation in the presence of failures, and operation under high-stress workload conditions.

□ *Worst-case performance and variance are vital to real-time system design.* Develop worst-case workload scenarios and supplement the mean-value checkpoint evaluations with variance assessments.

□ *Today's systems network together many autonomous computer systems.* Begin with the simple computer systems models for a checkpoint evaluation; then augment them early to capture: network performance to ensure timely transmission of control commands; and synchronization and coordination between computers to find possible timing problems.

□ *The control programs and the workload are closely coupled with the sensing and controlled equipment.* Make sure your models represent regular workload arrivals and short time intervals.

□ In addition to the end-to-end response time goals, *systems often have time constraints for intermediate steps.* This calls for phases in software models to enable phase time assessment and instrumentation probes in the system to enable measurement.

□ *The complexity of the environment increases the possibility that performance side effects may be overlooked* in the models. Instrument the software, make early measurements, and conduct early verification and validation studies.

Further descriptions of the characteristics of real-time process-control systems and references to the models and other work are in [LAW87]. Koptez has design principles to build in performance in [KOP86]. Both Trohoski ([TRO87]) and Fox ([FOX87]) describe key factors for successful SPE for real-time systems.

Ada   Ada is a programming language developed for the U.S. Department of Defense (DoD). It is the official language to be used for new DoD embedded computer systems. It is a structured language, similar to Pascal, that offers new language features for process structure *(packages)*, parallel processing *(tasks)*, communication and synchronization (entry-accept *rendezvous*), and others.

SPE is independent of the programming language choice; so all the SPE topics described so far apply to software written in Ada or any other programming language. Performance of Ada software is currently an important issue because:

- □ It is to be used for mission-critical real-time systems.
- □ It is new—few have completed large Ada systems, so Ada performance expertise is limited.
- □ Ada performance literature is also limited.
- □ The compiled code is less efficient that the earlier assembly language code.[7]
- □ It is difficult to effectively use the new language constructs for parallel and distributed processing.

The Ada rendezvous is a powerful language construct for intertask communication. Rather than make a system call to underlying communication routines (like the Network OS SYS_EXEC routine), Ada provides an **accept** construct for tasks to receive requests from other tasks. The requestor makes the request and then waits until the **accept** completes execution. This rendezvous facility makes software portable to different operating system environments and lets the Ada compiler check for errors. The following example shows how DRAWMOD and EDMS could use Ada rendezvous to communicate, and how to construct software execution and IPG models of the rendezvous.

EXAMPLE 8.25: Ada Rendezvous

DRAWMOD and EDMS are separate processes (tasks). DRAWMOD makes EDMS requests and then waits for the results. Focus on the FIND request. The following shows an Ada version of the EDMS processing when the request is FIND:

(continued)

---

[7]Early Ada compilers were notably inefficient—developers should have applied SPE! The compilation time and the efficiency of the compiled code are improving.

EXAMPLE 8.25 (*Continued*)

   EDMS Find routine:
   task body EDMS **is** ––Database control processing when
                          ––request is FIND (Figure 4.18)
    ––Declarations
    TABLE_NAME: TABLE;
    KEY_NEEDED: KEY;
    FOUND_LIST: RESULT;
   begin
    ––DB_MP Initiation:
    ALLOCATE_MEMORY;
    accept FIND (TABLE_NAME: **in** TABLE; KEY_NEEDED: **in** KEY;
               FOUND_LIST: **out** RESULT) **do**
    INTERPRET_REQUEST;
     ––rest of DBC processing
     ––DB_MP Termination
     FORMAT_REPLY;
    end FIND;
    FREE_MEMORY;
   end

The following shows how DRAWMOD might make the FIND request:

   DRAWMOD:
   task body DRAWMOD_DRIVER **is**
    ––Declarations
   begin
    ––Rendezvous with EDMS to DBOPEN, details omitted.
    FIND (Beams, Model_num, Result); ––Rendezvous with
                                ––EDMS process, proceed
                                ––after its **accept**
                                ––completes
    ––Rest of DRAWMOD
   end

The SPE models are in Figure 8.29. To rendezvous, DRAWMOD SENDs the FIND request, then RECEIVEs and waits for the reply. EDMS's **accept** turns into a RECEIVE, where it waits to be called, and a SEND upon **accept** completion.

   The IPG uses create nodes for SEND and allocate nodes for RECEIVE. Details of the computer system resources are omitted. Calculate IPG model parameters from the software execution models as before, and use Section 8.4.2's checkpoint evaluations to determine whether further study is advisable.

                                                                □

Note the similarity to the VIEW example in Section 8.4.2. The models use the same send-receive constructs, but the SYS_EXEC process is unnecessary. Even though the process is unnecessary, a substantial amount of overhead processing executes to conduct the rendezvous and pass data between tasks. Thus this example's resource requirements for SEND and RECEIVE would be higher than

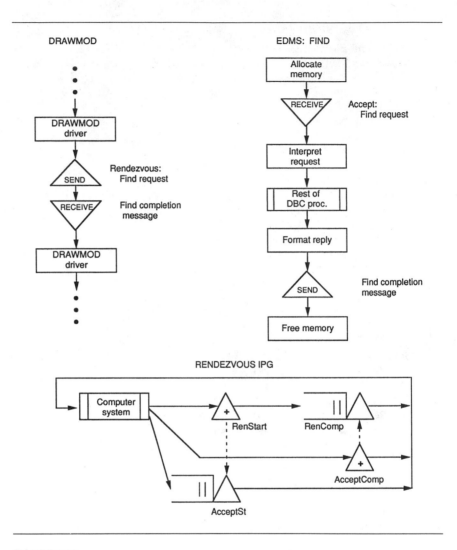

FIGURE 8.29
The Software Execution Models and Advanced IPG to Represent Ada Rendezvous.

the VIEW example's SEND and RECEIVE. Conduct measurement studies to determine resource requirements for the overhead processing in your environment (exclude the wait time—the models quantify synchronization delays).

Experts recommend careful use of dynamic process creation (**new** task types) and rendezvous (**entry** and **accept**) because of their large processing time overhead. Example 8.25 shows how to use software model SEND and RECEIVE and the advanced IPG techniques in Section 8.4.2 to analyze rendezvous. Similar extensions use the software model's FORK and advanced IPG's FORK or SPLIT to represent process creation.

Brender and Nassi give an overview of Ada in [BRE81]. Bray and Pokrass help programmers understand the language and give a thorough description of language features ([BRA85]). Buhr describes some important performance considerations in [BUH84].

DB2 and Other Relational Databases   DB2 is IBM's relational database product. SQL is a query language, used with relational databases, that is easy to learn and use. The popularity of relational products is primarily due to the simplified users' view of data as tables with columns and rows, and the user-friendly, easy-to-understand SQL commands for information access.

It is possible to achieve high performance from DB2 and other relational products with proper design of the database and the programs or transactions that access it. Nevertheless, there is an increased risk of performance problems when relational products are used for strategic systems. One reason is the relatively new technology— there are fewer development experts than for more mature products. Another reason is what Brooks calls the "second system effect": the tendency to overembellish new systems with features omitted in the earlier edition ([BRO75]). If you encounter redevelopment of a strategic system, read his delightful description of the second system effect, and watch for the performance and other pitfalls in your SPE studies. A third cause of increased risk is that a relational organization may be inappropriate for the typical access patterns. A relational organization is appropriate for data that naturally partitions into distinct tables that need to be joined infrequently. Network or hierarchical databases may be better for frequent navigation between related database nodes.

The DRAWMOD case study demonstrates SPE modeling and analysis for relational databases. The EDMS case study analyzed resource requirements for DRAWMOD's relational database calls. For DB2 and other relational database applications, you have at least three options for characterizing database-call resource requirements:

1. Measure the resource requirements for frequent representative SQL commands.
2. Use a modeling tool that has its own library of database-call resource requirements.
3. Ask your vendor representative—your IBM SE may obtain DB2 resource estimates for your software models using the ANDB2 tool ([IBM85]).

Some common performance problems associated with relational and other databases are:

□ *Fragmented database designs*—information should not be overly decomposed; fragmentation causes many SQL statements and thus many logical and physical I/Os to retrieve relatively small amounts of data.

□ *Insufficient data locality*—data items frequently needed together should be stored together to minimize physical I/Os.

□ *Database designs indifferent to high-volume transactions*—details of very-high-volume transactions should be defined early, and the database design should directly support them. Because they are usually trivial transactions, they are often designed long after the database, with a resulting mismatch that leads to excessive I/Os.

These and other data design problems are covered by the general principles in Chapter 2. (In fact, database design experiences led to many of the observations in Section 2.3.)

For recent experiences with DB2 performance, consult the Computer Measurement Group (CMG) Conference proceedings and the *CMG Transactions* ([*CMG*]). Its Spring 1987 special issue has several DB2 papers. Shane and Cook describe a particular performance problem that occurs with some DB2 programs run under CICS in [SHA87].

Fourth-Generation Languages   Fourth-generation languages (4GLs) are languages tailored to information retrieval and reporting applications. They were created to enable information system users to write their own applications. Database query languages were created for easy access to information stored in databases. The following illustrates the database query language SQL and some analogous 4GL statements for a simple retrieval:

```
SQL:   SELECT QTY-ORDERED     QTY-SHIPPED
          FROM INVENTORY
       WHERE REGION = 49
       ORDERED BY PRODUCT;


4GL:   TABLE FILE INVENTORY
       PRINT QTY-ORDERED     QTY-SHIPPED
          BY PRODUCT
       IF REGION EQ 49
       END
```

Fourth-generation and database query languages are similar, and the same SPE techniques apply to both.

Fourth-generation languages are a good productivity aid—they make the development of simple retrieval and reporting programs quick and easy. The productivity benefits usually increase the cost of executing the software due to increased computer resource requirements. The 4GLs may be interpreted at run time (as opposed to creating compiled code). The increased computer configuration cost may be offset by the productivity gains. The primary SPE considerations are to predict capacity requirements to ensure that the 4GL is cost-effective, and to ensure the achievement of responsiveness goals for the dominant workload functions. For responsiveness, developers may need to convert high-frequency 4GL transactions to a traditional, compiled programming language. Even then, an initial 4GL prototype may hasten development and testing of the subsequent programming language version.

As stated earlier, the SPE process is independent of the programming language choice; so all SPE techniques described thus far also apply to 4GLs. You will find it easier to specify resource requirements for software scenarios to be implemented in 4GLs if you first conduct a measurement study, collect CPU and other resource requirements for representative 4GL statements, and build a library of performance data (as mentioned in Chapter 7). If your organization has a standard 4GL, perhaps you can create a tool that uses the 4GL as input to an automatic software model generator.

See [WEI87b] for a discussion of 4GLs, query languages, and a survey of available products. Refer to the Spring 1988 issue of the *CMG Transactions* for two different views of 4GL performance.

UNIX Based Systems   UNIX is an operating system that is popular for software development because of its development "tool box" and particularly because it runs on many hardware platforms, including microcomputers, workstations, minicomputers, and mainframes. The wide variety of hardware support is advantageous because software is easily ported to other hardware platforms; and when multiple hardware platforms are networked together, users can easily use different machines, can move programs from one machine to another, and can log on and use multiple machines at the same time.

The operating system and hardware selected obviously affect software performance. Nevertheless, SPE techniques are independent of the hardware and operating system choices; so the SPE techniques described thus far also apply to software written for UNIX environments. Software models will be easier to parameterize if you measure the resource requirements for frequent UNIX calls on each type of hardware host and store them in a measurement library.

There are two common performance pitfalls in software written for a UNIX environment. First, it is easy to spawn concurrent processes and to use "pipes" to communicate between them. As in Ada, dynamic process creation is expensive and should be used sparingly, especially for dominant workload functions. Pipes may also be expensive—depending on your version of UNIX, pipes may require (physical) file I/O to send information and I/O to receive it. Thus two I/Os may be required to transmit one message. The second pitfall is overuse of dynamic memory allocation (malloc). The implications of dynamic memory allocation are discussed in Chapter 9.

Literature on UNIX performance is in various CMG conference proceedings, issues of the *CMG Transactions*, and at the Usenix (user group) conference.

Tiered Architectures   This is a concept introduced in the mid-1980s that suggests partitioning databases into a tree structure across multiple computers. The tiers are the root (central site) and successive levels in the tree. The central mainframe contains information pertinent to the overall organization, and successive levels encapsulate data unique to them (departments, sections, or individual users).

Tiered architectures are appropriate when partitions have high locality and it is seldom necessary to access other partitions. There are two common performance problems:

- In three-tiered architectures, the middle level often has insufficient locality of access. For example, while information can logically be associated with a department, because of the nature of the work requiring the data, it may only be accessed by end users and by mainframe batch programs. Both require remote data accesses when there are three tiers; with only two tiers, fewer remote accesses are required.
- Designers often have preconceived ideas about hardware size. They may assume that a minicomputer will suffice for the second tier. Typically, however, the second tier is only appropriate in very large organizations and it usually requires a large mainframe.

Analysis of software for a tiered architecture uses the early lifecycle, elementary IPG in Chapter 5. More detailed analyses in later lifecycle stages use the remote data access models in Section 8.3.1. The locality principle in Chapter 2 is vital for effective data partitioning.

Object-Oriented Systems   Object-oriented systems are based on a software engineering method that suggests (1) grouping information about entities or objects to combine the declarations for object type, attributes, internal representation, and instructions that access object information, and (2) hiding implementation details so that the internal representation and the instructions for accessing the object are unknown to the rest of the system. For example, an object may be a person with attributes such as name, address, and date of birth. In this example, details of how and where the birthdate is stored are hidden—the date could be calendar, julian, number of elapsed days (since predefined day 0), in character or integer format, and so forth. As long as the date is sent to the requestor in the defined (external) format, the overall system is indifferent to the internal representation. The advantage of object-oriented design is that it limits the effect of changes (the internal format of date affects only one object). The disadvantage is that with a straightforward implementation, performance may be degraded if every data reference requires a procedure call to the object.

The principles in Chapter 2 and the techniques in Section 2.3.3 address design issues for managing performance of object-oriented systems. For software performance analysis, the software models must represent frequent object accesses. For example, expand a high-level component such as "Get Social Security number" to define the hidden processing within the object definition that retrieves it. Include the overhead (for the object call), calculate the total resource requirements, and substitute the result everywhere the Social Security number is referenced. This includes resource requirements for object accesses into the software models. The other SPE techniques are the same.

Operating System and Support Software Designs   Designers of tomorrow's operating systems and support software are concerned about performance. Price and performance of a vendor's product are vital to its marketability. Systems are large and complex, and it is difficult to precisely model the complex interactions between components. Developers seldom build a completely new system; they tend to create evolutionary improvements to older systems with new features to capitalize on new hardware technology. Because of the magnitude of these projects, though, view them as new systems and apply the early lifecycle SPE techniques. Since they replace earlier systems, supplement models of new features with measurement data of unchanged parts to create early, accurate models.

SPE for OS development needs workload scenarios that represent end-user performance. People who evaluate new computer hardware usually base procurement decisions on measurements of their (end-user) software performance, not on OS service routine timings. Representative end-user scenarios are difficult but not impossible to create. Consult your marketing division or whoever knows the target audience for the new machine. It is true that an OS must satisfy the needs of all users, but it should excel at meeting the performance needs of the target audience. Some performance engineers on OS development projects collect measurement data at friendly installations and use it for trace-driven models. If these tactics for characterizing end-user workloads fail, look for users within your company. They can provide insights into how they use the machine. If you collect many user-workload profiles, they will identify the dominant workload functions. Because the key execution paths (such as sequential I/O paths and dispatching) are invoked by all users at all sites, they have a much larger performance impact than dominant workload functions in application systems. Performance improvements to them have a much larger overall effect.

After identifying representative workload scenarios, the SPE techniques described in Chapters 2 through 8 apply as usual. The Network Operating System case study illustrates the modeling process. During detailed design, more precise models of communication, synchronization, and memory use are essential. (Use the memory analysis techniques in Chapter 9.) Supplement the detailed software models with more precise models of the hardware environment as development proceeds.

There are many references to operating system performance, which was the first target for software performance engineering ([BER74], [CAM68], [LAS72]). Brice describes the selection process for new machines in [BRI82] and discusses the importance of end-user performance. SPE applications to operating system performance are in [FER84], [SAN77], and [SAN79].

Summary   This section covered topics that developers of today's software systems often face. It introduced each and discussed the pertinent performance considerations. To evaluate software systems that embody one or more of these concepts, start with SPE's early lifecycle techniques for gathering information and constructing software models. As detailed design progresses, use the advanced IPG models to study the complex interactions between software components or between the software and the hardware configuration. The advanced models are challenging, but not impossible. Seek additional modeling depth, in classes or published work, for the advanced models when you encounter extremely complex software systems.

8.5.2 Computer Environment Challenges

The models in Sections 8.3 and 8.4 cover the fundamental performance factors for detailed evaluation of today's software design alternatives. Topics in this section also affect performance, but primarily represent hardware performance rather than software design decisions. For example, I/O subsystems with cached controllers affect the elapsed time for I/O and thus software responsiveness, but (application) software designs are usually independent of I/O subsystem configurations. You must represent the environment in the system execution models in order to precisely predict software performance. The computer environment subjects discussed in this section are I/O subsystems, networks, and supercomputers. The purpose of this section is to introduce the concepts and provide sufficient information for you to begin SPE analysis of software that executes in these environments. We continue with the simplistic-to-realistic approach for hardware complexities.

I/O Subsystems   The models described thus far use a simplistic representation of an I/O subsystem. This is sufficient for early lifecycle analysis, but not for precise predictions of response time or throughput (nor for analysis of operating system or database management system I/O algorithms). There are numerous performance aspects of I/O subsystem *configuration* and *device characteristics* that are not represented in the simplistic models. Each is addressed below.

   I/O subsystem configurations include the I/O devices, controllers, and channels. During I/O execution there are instants when all are needed at the same time to conduct a transfer. The IPGs assume that a transaction category visits only one service node at a time. To minimize the time that one device may block others requiring use of the channel at the same time, configurations have alternate channel paths. Thus the routing through IPG nodes is load-dependent. I/O subsystems may be shared by multiple CPUs, increasing the potential for delays. The arbitration algorithms may delay one CPU's request to ensure data integrity even though a path is available.

I/O devices such as solid-state devices, mass store devices, and buffered tapes have **device characteristics** that affect device service times. Cached controllers retain data in the controller's memory to circumvent redundant device I/Os. Disk devices with rotational position-sensing hold channels only when needed for transfers, but may fail and retry their attempt to reconnect if the channel is busy.

All these facets of I/O subsystem performance are difficult to represent in analytic IPGs, but not impossible. There are many techniques for approximating their performance. Some modeling tools allow users to describe the I/O subsystem configuration and automatically approximate performance metrics.

For SPE, early lifecycle models ignore I/O subsystem details. Conduct best- and worst-case analyses to identify situations that warrant further study. Use measurement studies to determine approximate service times for simplistic IPG I/O subsystem representations (such as the ballpark 25 ms I/O time in the earlier models). For analysis techniques that more precisely predict performance, consult the literature on I/O subsystem models. The Fall 1986 special issue of the *CMG Transactions* covers I/O configuration management considerations ([BUZ86]). It contains a bibliography with additional references. Smith has another bibliography of related work in [SMIA81].

Networks   The term "computer network" traditionally referred only to the medium that connected terminals to mainframe computers. The interconnection devices are now sophisticated computers, the terminals are microcomputers and workstations, and the mainframes are collections of computers. Thus the term "computer network" now refers to a *collection of interconnected computers*. Section 8.4 did not crisply distinguish between parallel and distributed processing; the same ambiguity occurs in networks. They may be internal networks connecting tightly coupled multiprocessors, or external networks, such as local-area networks (LANs) and multipoint, wide-area telecommunication networks. The interconnection may be virtual: Computers may exchange information indirectly, but still be "interconnected." External and internal networks have similar performance issues—the primary distinction is speed or closeness of the connection. Internal multiprocessor connections require communication within nanoseconds, whereas external networks require communication within milliseconds. This section primarily addresses external networks, although many of the topics apply to both.

Performance analysts traditionally have separated computer performance from "network" performance. For example, a network performance specialist managed "network" performance and viewed the mainframe computer as a black box. For SPE, we must often consider the integrated view for the following reasons: End-user responsiveness goals are affected by both the interconnection and the computers; capacity planning for new systems requires both interconnection and host capacity; and the interconnection costs need to be considered in the new system's cost-benefit analysis. Otherwise, the software design may be over-constrained by interconnection limitations, or interconnection configurations may be overprescribed by a small percentage of the workload. The integrated view of networks incorporates both computers and their interconnection.

The reasons to analyze network performance are:

- □ To analyze its impact on new software performance
- □ To identify bottlenecks for performance tuning and capacity planning
- □ To apply SPE to network creation projects

The models differ in their level of detail depending on their purpose. SPE uses the simple-to-realistic analysis strategy to evaluate network performance. Initially, represent network subsystems as black box devices. Represent key components at a high level of detail, and use best, worst, and average analyses to identify situations that warrant further study. Incorporate additional details of key components as the system evolves and you need more precise data. Figure 8.30 illustrates a LAN configuration. The highest-level model is shown in Figure 8.31. The details of the Site computer are not shown—they would look much like the models in Section 8.4.1. The Net node represents the LAN, Net Interface, and the Bus Interface as a single IPG node. The next level of detail, in Figure 8.32, represents the interactions between the Site computers but still models the interconnection

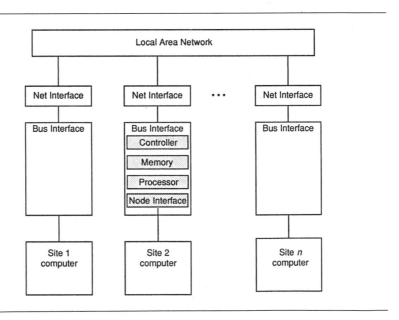

FIGURE 8.30
A Hypothetical Local-Area Network (LAN) Configuration.

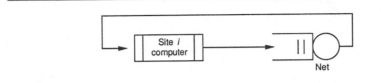

FIGURE 8.31
A high-level LAN model represents the entire network with a single node and focuses on one of the Site computers.

with one node (as in Section 8.4.2). Figure 8.33 represents the LAN and each Net Interface and Bus Interface with separate IPG nodes. Sucessive models expand the Bus and Net Interfaces and LAN nodes as appropriate. Far more processing occurs than is represented in these simple models. Construct software models or use measurements to characterize the key execution characteristics (such as for the seven layers of protocol overhead). Remember that the focus is on the software execution, not the network per se.

Facets of networks that are pertinent to performance in models include the topology of the network, switching and routing decisions, message scheduling, and protocols. The following paragraphs introduce the key performance implications of each of these facets and how they affect the advanced IPG representation.

Network topology for local-area networks defines the network structure. Networks may transport messages via bus or broadcast mode or may be connected in a ring, chordal ring, hypercube, or other structure. Similarly, wide-area networks may have a star topology or multipoint lines. The speed of the communica-

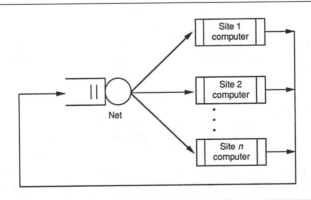

FIGURE 8.32
The next IPG representation depicts the interacting computers but keeps the high-level network node.

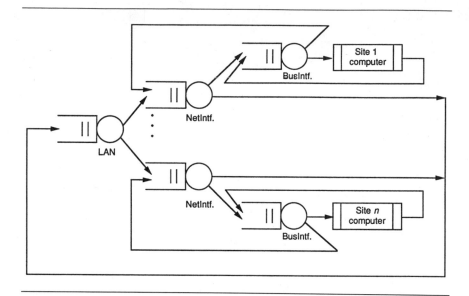

FIGURE 8.33
The next IPG progression adds nodes for the network and bus interface.

tion media between network sites may vary. Concentrators may collect or distribute data for low-speed links and provide higher-speed communication with a host. The network topology determines the advanced IPG nodes and their interconnection.

Switching or routing establishes a physical circuit for each virtual connection. Routing may be static—that is, the path is established when the network is configured—or dynamic. Dynamic connections may be established when a session begins (circuit or session switching) or may be established independently for each packet of information. Routing decisions may adapt to fluctuating congestion on paths. Packets contain either control information or data. Transfer of control packets has stricter performance constraints than for data packets. Switching strategies differ in their requirements for message buffers; a limited number of buffers may cause contention delays. Network designers seek to minimize fragmentation: the number of packets required for a single message and the number of unused bits in a packet. These switching considerations affect the number of visits per advanced IPG node and the service time of each. Define specific workload scenarios to fix as many of these dependencies as possible; then calculate visits and service times from their software models. Use passive resource tokens to represent message buffers.

Message or packet scheduling determines the order of transmission. Strategies may use priorities, may alternate among nodes, or may schedule first-come-first-served. LANs may transmit *frames* that are partitioned into *slots* to share transmission bandwidth among multiple senders. Data to be transmitted is broken into "chunks of bits" (or *packets*), and each is scheduled into a slot. Slots may be designated for voice or data when both share the transmission media. A *polling* scheduling strategy asks each site in turn if it has data for a slot. A *token-passing* strategy passes a permission token from one site to the next. A *carrier sense* strategy transmits information when it detects a free slot. Collisions may occur if several sites simultaneously detect a free slot and attempt to transmit. When a carrier is detected (busy slot) or a collision occurs, the sendee retries later. There are many different strategies for scheduling after collisions. All scheduling strategies introduce overhead processing. Scheduling seeks to minimize transmission delays by using slots effectively. Some strategies transmit (poll or token) messages across the network, thus reducing the capacity for data transmission. All require execution time on the interface units. Network scheduling is difficult to represent in analytic IPGs. Use approximate techniques to examine bounds for average behavior. Use advanced or simulation IPGs for better approximations and to characterize the standard deviation.

Protocols govern the exchange of data. The International Standards Organization specifies seven protocol layers: application, presentation, session, transport, link, packet, and hardware. Each provides communication functions such as transmission, error detection and correction, buffering for retries, acknowledgment of message receipt, and notification to receiving application program. Each requires processing and thus needs service from several network resources. For SPE, we need to estimate (or measure) the resource requirements to SEND and RECEIVE information, and include them in the software resource requirements as in Section 8.4.2. If you wish to apply SPE to a network creation project, your software execution models must explicitly represent each of the processing steps required to implement the protocol.

Precise network performance models are complex and relatively difficult to develop. This is an active research area, and many model improvements are being reported. For background information on modeling networks, consult Stuck and Arthurs ([STU85]) and Tanenbaum ([TAN81]). Kleinrock applies fundamental queueing theory to networks in [KLE76]. Reed and Grunwald evaluate multicomputer interconnections in [REE87]. Recent research is reported in the proceedings of the Symposium on the Simulation of Computer Networks and in the Sigmetrics conference proceedings ([*IEEE*], [*SIGM*]).

Supercomputers Supercomputers perform numerical computations at very high speeds. Their speed is commonly expressed in millions of floating-point operations per second (MFLOPS), rather than in MIPS, because one instruction may perform many floating-point operations (one Cyber 205 vector instruction may perform up to 130,000 floating-point operations ([BUC83]). It is not a perfect metric, however, because floating-point operations may use a much faster clock than scalar operations, so MFLOPS may not reflect overall performance. To achieve these high speeds the computer architectures have large word sizes, vector processors with large vector sizes, pipelined instruction execution, "wide" instructions, multiple processors, and other state-of-the-art technology.

Supercomputer performance strongly depends on the workload. Their advertised peak performance is seldom attained in practice. Performance is also heavily influenced by compilers—the extent that they optimize the code to capitalize on the high-speed vector operations. To achieve ultra high performance, programs often need to be hand tuned. Supercomputer workloads are typically long-running batch programs—a single program executes (alone) for 12 to 14 hours. Much of the published supercomputer performance analysis focuses only on computational speed—that is, instruction execution time plus memory access time—but for some workloads, I/O time is also important.

SPE addresses the supercomputer workload dependency with software scenarios. For the software resource requirements for each scenario component, specify both scalar instructions and floating-point operations. For vector operations, specify both startup and computation. Also specify the number of memory accesses. With these specifications you can *estimate* the computation time for each component and the time for the overall scenario. This analysis is useful early in the lifecycle to evaluate high-level designs, but it is likely to be optimistic because of the strong influence of the machine, its compiler, the software's memory reference patterns, and other factors. So run benchmarks and collect measurements as early in development as possible to more precisely predict performance.

Supercomputers may also use multiple parallel processors in addition to vector processors—that is, MIMD computers, each with vector-processing capability. To evaluate their software performance, extend the software models using the techniques in Section 8.4 to represent the process structure and allocation and resulting communication. By distinguishing the scalar, floating-point, vector startup and computation, and memory accesses of each software component, you can combine the analysis of vector and parallel computation.

Supercomputer software is similar to operating system software in that most development is an evolutionary change to previous codes rather than creation of revolutionary new software. This calls for measurements of existing software to drive the models of new systems. Current performance concerns focus on maximizing the benefits of the supercomputer architecture ([DON83], [SYD83]). Dramatic gains have been reported, though, when the software *design* is tailored to the machine architecture ([BOB83]). Bucher reports that converting the codes to exploit parallel MIMD processing offers good potential performance improvements; their studies of key workload elements show that the physical problems they simulate with (numerical) codes have strong locality ([BUC83]). Additional information on supercomputer performance is in [LUB85] and [HAC86]. This is an active research area; for recent results, consult the ACM Sigmetrics conference proceedings, the proceedings of the International Parallel Processing Conference, and supercomputer vendor-user group conferences.

Summary   This computer environment section covers some aspects of environments that affect software performance. All are compatible with SPE—they are covered by using system execution models to represent the salient performance aspects of the environment. Use the techniques in Sections 8.3 and 8.4 (and Chapter 9) to represent the basic elements of the environment. Supplement them with detailed processing characteristics of the environment as the software evolves. This section introduces three popular computer environment topics; there are far more, and new announcements are frequent. Adapt your SPE techniques to the rapid changes. Consult references that provide additional technical depth on factors that are important to the performance of your computer environment, and stay abreast of future trends through performance-related conferences.

8.6 Intricate Processing Models

SPE matches the modeling effort to the precision of the information about the new system. As the new system development progresses and you learn more about the software, you want the SPE models to evolve into a faithful representation of the key performance factors. Occasionally, you need results not readily available from analytic models, such as additional performance metrics (such as latency and throughput for pipelined processing) and performance of transient events (such as periodically locking and saving all key tables). SPE uses the simpler models to identify situations that warrant further study and to identify the key performance factors. Then we use additional modeling techniques—such as Timed Petri Nets and simulation IPGs— to incorporate the intricate or difficult-to-evaluate processing details into the models.

8.6.1 Timed Petri Nets

Petri nets explicitly represent concurrent events and synchronization of concurrent processes. They facilitate the study of event timings relative to one another, the probability of being in particular states, and other reliability and fault-tolerant properties such as operation in the presence of failures. They were first proposed by C. A. Petri to study concurrency and synchronization properties such as system liveness, deadlocks, and safeness of states ([PET65]). In 1974, Ramchandany added timed transitions ("Timed" Petri Nets) and thus made Petri nets useful for performance analysis ([RAM74]). They became very popular with the advent of parallel and distributed processing and are still an active research area. Recent results enrich their representational capabilities and propose methods for solving them efficiently.

Petri nets consist of **places** and **transitions** connected by **directed arcs.** Figure 8.34 illustrates four places (the large circles) and two transitions (the bars). The place named Request routed to EDMS is an *output place* of transition Route_Msg and an *input place* of transition EDMS: DB_MP Init receives request. In Timed Petri Nets, **execution times** are associated with each transition—the required time between its initiation and its termination. Zero or more **tokens** (the small dots) may reside in the places. A net's **marking** is the number of tokens in each place in the net. A transition is **enabled** when it has one or more tokens in each of its input places (the Route_Msg transition in the figure is enabled). An enabled transition initiates and removes one token from each input place; after its specified execution time, it terminates and deposits one token in each of its output places. This process is called **transition firing.** In the figure the enabled transition, Route_Msg, fires and after 0.139 time units deposits a token in Request routed to EDMS. This disables the Route_Msg transition and enables the EDMS: DB_MP Init receives request transition.

A more complex example is shown in Figure 8.35. It shows a Timed Petri Net model for the process structure and allocation software model from Figure 8.25.

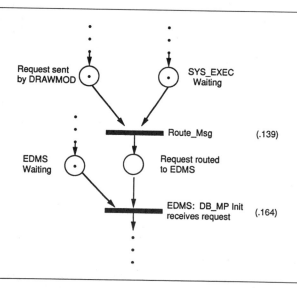

FIGURE 8.34
A simple Timed Petri Net model depicts the message passing between DRAW-MOD and EDMS.

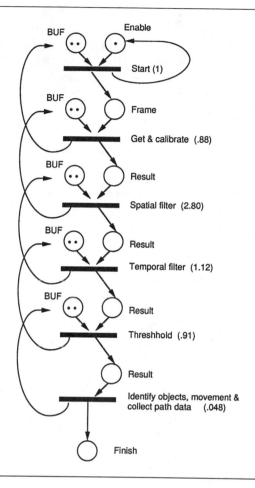

FIGURE 8.35
A Timed Petri Net model for the pipeline synchronization for the original signal-processing scenario process structure and allocation. Tokens represent the data buffers. The first transition (Start) generates a Frame of data every second. The rest of the processing is like the earlier scenario.

Note how the tokens explicitly represent output buffers and the arrival of input data. The net's initial marking shows that initially two output buffers are available for each processing stage. Note that when the Spatial filter transition is enabled, upon firing completion, the Spatial filter transition deposits a token in the Results place to signify filter completion and one in the BUF input place for the Get and calibrate transition. This signifies that the buffer has been used and is free for reuse. The Result places signify when a subsequent stage in the pipeline has the input data it needs to begin. Thus the model does not need "phases." Note the transition named Start. It represents the arrival of frames from the source (instrument). The interarrival time is the execution time of Start. With this model, Start is enabled whenever a buffer is available for the frame.

Figure 8.36 illustrates the Timed Petri Net model for the revised process structure and allocation from Figure 8.27. The SBUF places represent the smaller buffers that hold one quadrant of a frame. Note that there are four transitions for Spatial filters, one for each process on each processor, while there are only two

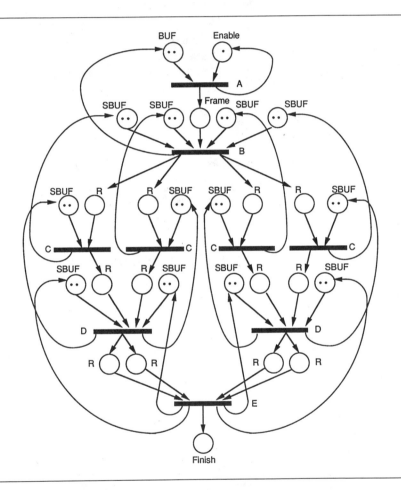

FIGURE 8.36
A Timed Petri Net model for the revised signal-processing scenario process structure and allocation. The Result places are labeled "R." The transitions are as follows: A is the Start (1) frame generation; B is Get and calibrate partition (.88); C is the Spatial filter (.70); D is the Temporal filter and Threshold (.62); and E is Identify objects, movement, and collect path data (.05).

transitions for Temporal filters and threshold. The execution times for the latter specify the time for two quadrants for each transition. Again, phases are unnecessary in this model.

These models can be solved analytically (to yield mean values) or solved by simulation. The analytic solution algorithms are in [SMI85a]. These models are computationally easy to solve because they are small and have no conflicts. A **conflict** is illustrated in Figure 8.37(a): two enabled transitions, Route_Msg and

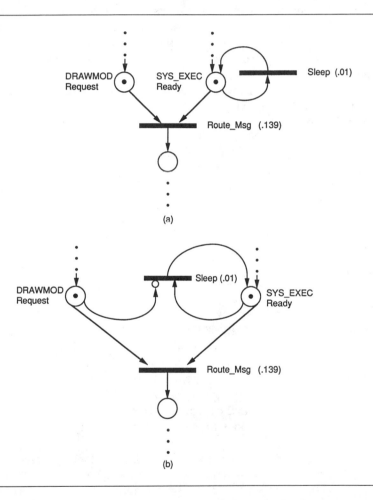

(a)

(b)

FIGURE 8.37
The Timed Petri Net in (a) has a conflict: The SYS_EXEC Ready is an input place into two transitions—if either one fires, it disables the other. The Timed Petri Net in (b) uses the inhibitor arc between DRAWMOD Request and Sleep to resolve the conflict. When SYS_EXEC Ready contains a token—if DRAWMOD Request contains a token—then only Route_Msg can fire; otherwise only Sleep can fire.

Sleep, share an input place—if either one fires, it disables the other. Research seeks to resolve conflicts and to reduce the state space to make analytic solutions feasible. Figure 8.37(b) shows one strategy for eliminating a conflict: The **inhibitor** arc between DRAWMOD Request and Sleep specifies that Sleep is enabled when *no token* is in the DRAWMOD Request input place (and one is in Sys_Exec Ready). Many other conflict resolution strategies have been proposed.

Stochastic Petri Nets introduce probabilistic behavior ([MOL80], [MOL82]). Distributions (such as exponential distributions) are used rather than deterministic firing times, and path probabilities are introduced. **Generalized Stochastic Petri Nets** (GSPNs) also have *immediate transitions,* represented by thin bars rather than the wide ones in the earlier figures ([MAR84]). They represent state changes due to logical events that require no execution time. Their use in computer system models greatly reduces the state space and thus the solution time.

Timed Petri Nets are convenient for representing concurrency and synchronization within a software system, but they have difficulty representing competition for computer system resources between software systems. For example, if the Route_Msg transition in Figure 8.37 executes on the same CPU server as other software, it may experience contention delays that make its elapsed time considerably longer than 139 ms. Researchers such as Balbo, Bruell, Ghanta and others seek ways of combining Petri nets and QNMs to represent such interactions ([BAL85a], [BAL85b]).

Good introductions to Petri nets are in [PET77] and [AGE79]. Recent research results are in the proceedings of the Timed Petri Net Conferences ([TPN85], [TPN87],) and in the ACM Sigmetrics Conference Proceedings ([*SIGM*]).

8.6.2 Simulation IPGs

Elementary IPGs provide features for a simplistic representation of a system execution model that can be solved analytically. Then advanced IPGs add features for a more precise representation; they are solved with analytic approximations, analytic checkpoint evaluations, or by simulation. For more detailed study, simulation IPGs add additional representational power. While it is possible to invent analytic checkpoint evaluations customized to the simulation model, there are no general approximation methods for simulation IPGs—they require simulation-based solutions.

Simulation IPG features are dependent on modeling tools. This section introduces simulation IPGs and describes features provided by the SES Workbench modeling tool ([*SES*]). Figure 8.38 shows the additional IPG nodes. The following paragraphs describe each node.

Memory allocation nodes manage memory elements (bytes, words, or pages, and so forth). Transaction categories request a specified number of contiguous memory elements. Memory allocation can be either first-fit or best-fit, so

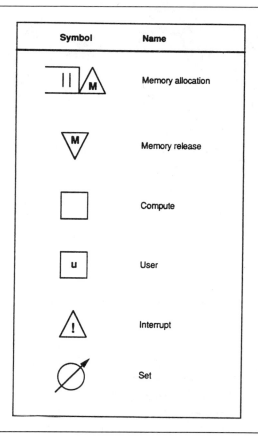

Symbol	Name
	Memory allocation
	Memory release
	Compute
	User
	Interrupt
	Set

FIGURE 8.38
The Simulation IPG Nodes in the SES Workbench Package.

the effect of memory fragmentation is explicitly modeled. **Memory release** nodes return specified memory elements to the memory allocation node that manages them.

Compute nodes interrogate values of user-defined variables or simulation state identifiers (such as time, queue length, token count, and phase number). Compute nodes may alter the user-defined variable values or a transaction's phase.[8] Figure 8.39 illustrates a compute node, CheckBuf, that checks token availability and routes transactions accordingly. It illustrates a modification to the message routing example in Figure 8.22 to dynamically create message buffers as needed. The CheckBuf node checks the number of mbuf tokens currently at the

[8]With SES Workbench, compute nodes may also control statistics collection and reporting.

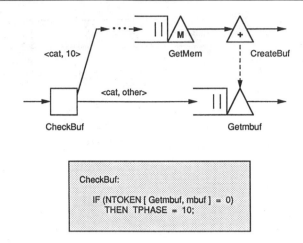

FIGURE 8.39
A Simulation IPG with a Compute Node That Checks Token Availability and Routes Jobs Accordingly.

Getmbuf allocate node (NTOKEN [Getmbuf, mbuf]). If no buffers are free, it changes the transaction's phase (to Phase 10) and routes it to the execution path, which requests more memory for the buffers at the memory allocation node, GetMem, and creates additional mbuf tokens at CreateBuf (for Getmbuf). The path may also include CPU and other resource usage. Eventually, the transaction's phase is restored and it goes to Getmbuf to complete its normal processing.

   User nodes invoke user-written subroutines. They may implement customized queue-scheduling disciplines, create additional output or reports, read input from a file to perform trace-driven simulation, or perform other tasks.

   Interrupt nodes cause one or more transactions to be "interrupted," given a new phase number, and removed from its queue. An alternative model for dynamic buffer creation uses an interrupt after the last buffer is allocated. It awakens a dormant operating system routine to create more buffers. With this alternative, buffer creation is anticipatory and concurrent with transaction processing.

   Set nodes adjust the service rate or power of service and resource allocation nodes. They may turn allocation nodes on or off and may assign variable service rates to active service nodes. For example, a set node may adjust a CPU service rate by a power of 4 when four processors are available, and reduce it to a power of 1 when at most one processor may be active.

   In addition to these IPG nodes, simulation IPGs allow more service time distributions, such as normal, uniform, constant, empirical, and others. They also allow more queue-scheduling disciplines, such as polling, round-robin-fixed-quantum, priority, and others.

For more information on simulation IPGs, check the simulation tool product descriptions. Examples of simulation models for a variety of system applications are in the proceedings of the winter and summer simulation conferences, *Simuletter,* in the newsletter of ACM's special interest group on Simulation (SIGSIM), and other performance publications.

8.7 Solution Tool Options

Requirements for solvers and solution options for elementary system execution models are in Section 5.5. The requirements for advanced system execution models are similar. An augmented list of the earlier requirements for SPE model solvers is below:

□ Solvers must be able to solve the elementary IPGs and accommodate the extensions for the advanced IPGs without significantly changing the model description.

□ They should provide abstraction—they should not require extremely detailed information for early analysis, but should allow selectively detailed submodels to increase the overall model fidelity.

□ For early analysis they should provide rapid solutions; later the solution time should match the intricacy of the analysis. We need rapid checkpoint evaluations (preferably automatic); for further study, longer simulations are acceptable.

□ It must be easy to grasp the key performance indicators without poring through pages of output. This becomes a vital requirement as model size and complexity grow.

□ It must be easy to evaluate alternatives. For advanced system execution models we need to quickly and easily perform checkpoint evaluations—one at a time.

Section 5.5 suggested three model solution options: implementing solvers with general-purpose tools; developing special-purpose programs; and using commercial products. It is possible to use the first two options for advanced IPGs, but those options are much less desirable. The tools are more labor-intensive to create and to maintain. It is preferable to rely on vendors to keep their products current with technology.

The earlier list of products is shown again in Table 8.33. As before, do not consider this list to be comprehensive or to contain the best tools for your needs, because new products appear at a very rapid rate. While the same tools are listed, you may find that none is ideally suited to both early lifecycle high-level analysis

TABLE 8.33
PRODUCTS FOR SOLVING SYSTEM
EXECUTION MODELS

Tool	Vendor/researcher
BEST/1	[*BGS*]
CADS	[*SES*]
COPE	[BEI84]
CRYSTAL	[*BGS*]
GPSM	[*SES*]
CA/ISS three	[*CA*]
MAP	[*QSP*]
MEDOC	[LeM82]
MODEL300	[*BOO*]
PANACEA	[RAM82]
PAW	[MEL85]
PAWS	[*SES*]
PET	[FAR86]
QNAP2	[VER84]
RESQ	[SAU82a, SAU82b]
SCERT II	[*PSI*]
SES Workbench	[*SES*]
VM PREDICTOR	[BAR78]

General-Purpose Simulation Tools:

GPSS	[GOR78, SCH74]
SIMSCRIPT II	[KIV69, RUS76, *CACI*]
SIMULA	[DAH66]
SLAM	[PRI79]

and to the later detailed analysis of performance factors that are key in your environment. Currently, there are few commercially available tools that provide selective abstraction and accurate and automatic detailed models. You may want to use different tools for different purposes. If so, you could create a central model library and implement an extractor that creates model input specifications in the format required by each tool.

A fourth solution option may be viable for advanced system execution models: Create a general-purpose simulation model. The second part of Table 8.33 shows some general-purpose simulation packages. They differ from the simulation packages listed in the first part of the table in that they do not assume an underlying "network of queues" model basis. They offer more generality in the models you can construct, but they may not offer model primitives that are inherent in the earlier tools, such as queue-scheduling disciplines and job flow through the queues.

There are currently few commercial products for solving Timed Petri Net models, though many such products will probably be introduced in the near future. So consult recent product literature in CMG, ACR, and other product reviews for more information ([*ACR*], [*CMG*]).

8.8 Summary

This chapter covers the advanced models used for detailed SPE evaluations. Section 8.1 defined the advanced Information Processing Graphs. Then Section 8.2 described some general analytic approximation methods. Sections 8.3 and 8.4 presented fundamental modeling techniques for complex systems, as well as analytic checkpoint evaluations to identify situations that warrant further study. Examples modeled serialization delays due to exclusive and shared resource use and covered three important aspects of parallel and distributed processing: remote data access, messages for interprocess communication, and process structure and allocation. Section 8.5 addressed software and computer environment factors that often arise in SPE studies and described how each fits into the SPE framework. Section 8.6 introduced models for representing intricate processing details: Timed Petri Nets and simulation IPGs. Finally, Section 8.7 reviewed the requirements for model solvers and some options for automated tool support.

The next chapter covers the last of the technical aspects of SPE: representing and assessing memory use.

Exercises

Review

8.1. Use Sevcik's shadow-server method in Algorithm 8.1 to study the effect on response times of using preemptive-priority scheduling for DEV1 in the IPG in Figure 5.8 and Table 5.6. First give Withdrawals the highest priority and solve the model; then change the model to give the highest priority to Get balance. Compare the performance metrics.

8.2. Construct a software execution model of the following scenario. Create an advanced IPG to study the effect of the lock on response time. Derive IPG model parameters from the software execution model. Perform a best-case lock evaluation (use both upper- and lower-bound resource requirements); then apply the aggregate-server method in Algorithm 8.2 to derive more realistic performance metrics. What would you recommend to the software developers?

Software scenario	Resource usage estimates		
Component	CPU (ms)	DB I/O	VSAM I/O
Identify & locate account-id	50–300	2–24	3
Fetch debits	50–100	3–15	2
Fetch credits	50–100	3–9	0
Fetch collection history	50–100	2–3	0
LOCK	100–200	0	1
Post activity	10–50	1	1
FREE	10–50	0	1
Format & send to screen	1–10	0	3

Scenario arrival rate: 4–10 transactions per second
DB I/O device service time: 20 ms
VSAM I/O device service time: 25 ms

8.3. Modify the software scenarios described in Example 8.5 as follows:

a. Add another I/O subsystem node (I/OSS-2) to the IPG.

b. Set the I/OSS service time for both devices to 0.05 sec.

c. Move the lock-share files to the new device (change the visits for all I/Os executed for lock, free, and share nodes to the new device).

d. Revise the model parameters calculated in Example 8.6 appropriately, and solve the model.

e. Create a table of results and compare to the results in Tables 8.16 and 8.17.

8.4. Revise the software model in Example 8.11 to use different resource requirements on the Remote computer as follows:

☐ $R_i = (100, 0, 2, 0)$ to Fetch account info
☐ $R_i = (200, 0, 4, 0)$ to Log the updates

Revise the IPG model parameters and solve the model. Compare the results to Table 8.23.

8.5. Replace the distribution of account requests for Example 8.14 (from Table 8.24) with the following:

	Account location		
Origin	Local	RemoteA	RemoteB
Local computer	.90	.04	.06
RemoteA	.30	.60	.10
RemoteB	.15	.05	.80

Revise the IPG model parameters and solve the model. Compare the results to Table 8.28.

8.6. Solve the revised model in Example 8.18 to evaluate the performance of larger message buffers combined with RETRIEVE BLOCKS. Compare the results for one and four EDMS threads.

8.7. Change the number of tracks in the parallel processing software model (Figure 8.23) from 50 to 500. Use the revised structure and allocation in Figure 8.27, update the model parameters in Example 8.24, and solve the model.

Further Study

8.8. Modify the software scenario in Example 8.4 to increase lock granularity as follows:

   a. Create 2 acct-lock tokens—one for each half of the account file.
   b. When a session requests an account lock, the two halves of the account file are equally likely to be chosen.
   c. Revise the IPG model parameters appropriately and solve the model.
   d. Create a table of results and compare to the results in Table 8.9.

8.9. Suppose you want to study the performance effect of "process migration" in Example 8.8. That is, if ATM transactions are for remote accounts, collect the transaction type, account, and amount for withdrawals; SEND a message to the Remote computer; execute the transaction there; RECEIVE the reply; dispense the receipt and money for withdrawals; then terminate. Revise the software and system execution models and solve. (Invent resource requirements proportional to those used in other steps for any new software components that you create.)

8.10. Review the Ada literature and find some representative resource requirement specifications for Ada rendezvous.

8.11. Review the Network literature and create a simple LAN model with representative service times. Substitute it for the Network node in Figure 8.17. Use your LAN model combined with the software execution model in Example 8.13 and the computer system submodels in Example 8.14. Solve the new model.

9

Memory Management Overhead

All processes require memory to execute. Memory use causes subtle and complex interactions between processes. These interactions make memory management overhead the most difficult aspect of performance to predict. Fortunately, with memory price decreases and configuration size increases, its effect on most systems is lessened. For some systems it remains a vital concern, particularly for a system with small real memory or no virtual memory. Even for machines with very large memory, the following are good reasons for assessing memory overhead early:

- New software must meet responsiveness goals, and memory use affects responsiveness.
- Software designs may lead to excessive memory demands or memory usage patterns that cause thrashing.
- If memory problems arise, they affect the software delivery schedule.
- There is always an upper bound on the amount of memory that can be added (for performance tuning), and new systems should preserve upward growth potential.
- Memory problems affect all software on the system, not just new systems under development.

Excessive memory requirements degrade performance in two ways: (1) by limiting the number of processes able to execute concurrently, and (2) by causing excessive CPU and I/O overhead for memory management. The net result of excessive memory use in each case is the same, thrashing, but the analyses are somewhat different.

There are two fundamental approaches to controlling memory use: system-level management of memory requirements, and memory design techniques for individual programs. **System-level management techniques** include controlling the maximum number of concurrent users, the amount of real memory allocated to each, the number of I/O buffers, fixing the high-use pages in memory, "fencing" programs to prevent page stealing, and properly placing page data sets in the memory hierarchy. **Memory design techniques for programs** reduce memory requirements, restructure virtual memory, and revise memory access patterns to improve locality. This section covers both management approaches.

The elementary IPGs used early in development ignore memory use. SPE calls for correcting any performance problems found in absence of memory overhead, before conducting more complex analyses. Later the advanced IPG models the software's execution environment. For computer systems with very large memories, one role of the advanced IPG is to quantify the effect of memory management on responsiveness and to provide checkpoint evaluations that identify potential memory problems. The advanced IPGs represent delays encountered by jobs that arrive while the maximum number of concurrent users are executing and represent the overhead for swapping, paging, or segmenting. In absence of major memory-related software design problems, developers manage memory use with the system-level techniques.

For a computer system with a relatively small memory, no virtual memory, a limit on real memory for each user (such as in VM/CMS), or for very large software systems, we apply memory design techniques. The **primary method** minimizes the subset of memory required by a program to execute without thrashing—that is, its *working set size*—and minimizes the number of *transitions* from one working set to another. The term *working set* is commonly associated with paged-memory systems, but the concepts also apply to non-paged systems. Large working sets mean fewer users can execute concurrently; small working sets, with few transitions to other working sets, minimize memory faults. This minimizes CPU overhead for scheduling memory locations and I/O overhead for memory fetches. Models for memory design issues use software models to compute memory demands for alternate design strategies and combine them with the advanced IPGs to quantify the resulting performance. Figure 9.1 highlights the memory topics covered in this chapter.

9.1 Memory Overhead Representation

Operating systems use three different strategies to manage memory:

- □ **Swapping:** An entire program is loaded into memory when needed and removed upon completion.

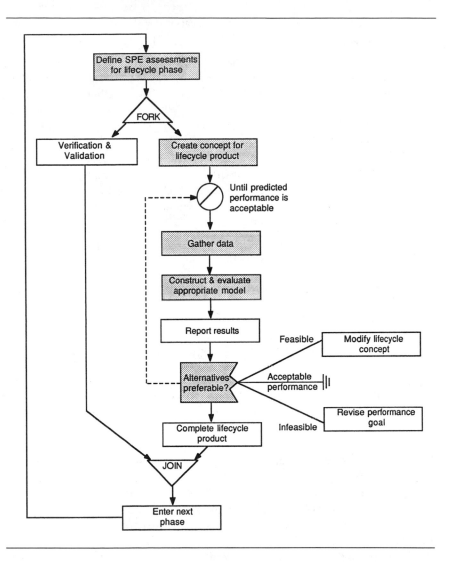

FIGURE 9.1
The SPE Methodology with the Focus of This Chapter Highlighted. The emphasis of all these topics is on memory management.

□ **Paging:** Each program's virtual memory is divided into fixed-size pages. Each virtual page is loaded into memory when it is needed. Another page may be removed first if free space is unavailable.

□ **Segmentation:** A program's virtual memory is divided into variable-size segments. Each segment is loaded into memory when it is needed. Segments

share designated (relative) memory locations and replace or overlay the
segment previously in that location.

All strategies have CPU and I/O overhead for identifying the real memory location
to be used; reading in the requested program, page, or segment; and (possibly)
writing out previous memory contents that changed after loading.

The first step in developing more realistic SPE models for memory use is to
represent the additional delays and memory management overhead in the advanced IPGs. The model solution then quantifies the effects of memory use on the
performance metrics. Checkpoint evaluations identify potential memory problems
for further study. This section describes procedures for representing constraints on
the maximum number of concurrent users, the overhead for swapping programs,
and the overhead for demand paging or segmenting.

9.1.1 Maximum Concurrent Users

System tuners control memory congestion by setting an upper bound on the maximum number of users that may actively execute on the system (also known as
maximum multiprogramming level or Max MPL). By choosing an appropriate
upper bound, active jobs have the memory they need to execute without thrashing,
and they have less processing for managing memory. Constraints introduce delays, however, for jobs that arrive while the maximum number is already in the
system.

Represent the possible delay to enter the system with an allocate node in
the advanced IPG. Specify an initial number of tokens for the maximum active
jobs or transactions allowed. Insert a release node that returns the tokens to the
allocate node before jobs depart the system.

As before, the allocate and release nodes prevent analytic solution. Note that
some model solvers automatically handle constraints on the number of concurrent
users with special model specifications. Without this feature, derive an analytic
approximation iteratively: Replace the allocate node with a delay server and the
release node with a branch point. First solve the model with no delay. Check the
maximum number of users. If there are more in the system than allowed, increase
the delay time and re-solve the model. Repeat the estimate-solve-check procedure
until you achieve the user limit. The following example illustrates the procedure.

EXAMPLE 9.1: Maximum Active Users

Figure 9.2 shows a simple closed model with two transaction categories, Batch and Develop. There is one Batch job in the system; when it completes, another one with similar
execution characteristics initiates (at EOJ). Job submission procedures ensure that only one
batch job executes. The Develop category is different. Fifty interactive USERS submit

(*continued*)

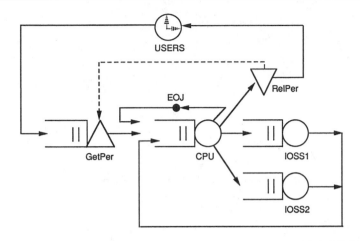

FIGURE 9.2
The Advanced IPG to Control the Maximum Number of Concurrent Users. Users must obtain a "permission to execute token" at node GetPer before entering the system.

EXAMPLE 9.1 (*Continued*)

requests to the system, the requests cycle through the CPU and the I/O subsystems, and then upon completion USERS receives the reply. After an average think time of 25 seconds, the user submits another request. We evaluate the performance of this system with a constraint of 10 active users.

Represent the potential delay to the other 40 users with the allocate node, GetPer. GetPer initially has 10 permission tokens. Develop users first visit GetPer and request one permission token. They wait if necessary to receive the token, then execute. Upon completion they visit the release node RelPer, where they return the permission token to GetPer. The model parameters are in Table 9.1.

For an analytic checkpoint evaluation, replace GetPer with a delay node and RelPer with a branch node. First solve the model with no delay. Table 9.2 shows the results. More than 10 users are within the system, so increase the delay time and iteratively solve the model until an average of 10 jobs are in the system. Table 9.2 also shows the results for an estimated delay of 600 ms. There are 9.53 + .5 = 10.03 active Develop transactions. This is a reasonable approximation for early SPE studies. To confirm your understanding, increase the delay time slightly and re-solve the model to further reduce the number of active transactions and see the effect on the performance metrics.

□

So far, all we see is the additional delay before entering the system, but not the resulting reduction in memory management overhead. We model the load-dependent memory congestion later. This simple model illustrates the procedures for modeling constraints on active users. This strategy works when there is one

TABLE 9.1
MAXIMUM ACTIVE USERS—PARAMETERS

Nodes	Batch		Develop	
	# visits	Request	# visits	Request
USERS	0		1	25 sec (think time)
CPU	200,001	.01 sec	11	.05 sec
IOSS1	100,000	.02 sec	10	.02 sec
IOSS2	100,000	.02 sec	0	
EOJ	1		0	
GetPer	0		1	(Permision, 1)
RelPer	0		1	(Permission, 1) to GetPer

1 Batch
50 Develop

Maximum 10 Develop "Active" → GetPer Initial = (Permission, 10) Tokens

TABLE 9.2
MAXIMUM ACTIVE USERS—RESULTS

Results with no delay

Node	Category	Utilization	Queue length	Residence time
USERS	Develop	39.28/50	39.28	25.00
CPU	Develop	.86	10.22	.59
	Batch	.07	.82	.11
IOSS1	Develop	.31	.50	.03
	Batch	.07	.11	.03
IOSS2	Batch	.07	.07	.02

Total in system:	Batch	1
	Develop	10.72
Total Response time:	Batch	27,990 seconds
	Develop	6.8 seconds

Results with 0.6 seconds delay

Node	Category	Utilization	Queue length	Residence time
USERS	Develop	39/50	39.00	25.00
CPU	Develop	.86	9.53	.56
	Batch	.08	.81	.11
IOSS1	Develop	.31	.50	.03
	Batch	.08	.12	.03
IOSS2	Batch	.08	.07	.02

Total in system:	Batch	1
	Develop	10.03
Total Response time:	Batch	26,560 seconds
	Develop	7.2 seconds

upper bound on active jobs irrespective of their category and when there is a separate upper bound for each category. It is easy to enhance this model to evaluate different constraints by transaction category. For example, a third transaction category could request its own permission token, and the allocate node could have an initial quantity corresponding to its maximum active users. The analytic approximation varies the estimated delay time by category.

Alternatively, you may want a model that regulates the number of jobs explicitly by the amount of memory available. You have two options. Rather than allocate permission tokens, allocate a specific number of memory tokens depending on jobs' memory requirements. If jobs need contiguous memory, use simulation IPGs with memory allocation nodes: Each transaction category requests the amount of memory it needs, and the node uses either a first-fit or best-fit allocation. Simulation IPGs were described in Section 8.6.

9.1.2 Swapping Overhead

Next we model the overhead for swapping that may occur for timesharing (program development) jobs. Timesharing jobs are usually short interactions that invoke small programs. So most timesharing systems load the entire program when the user makes a request. It is called "swapping" because the program usually replaces a previously active job while its user "thinks." The time to swap in the program, execute it, and return the response to the user is typically less than user think time. Occasionally, when programs change memory contents after they are loaded, the timesharing system must also swap out revised memory contents (write the changes to secondary storage). For most systems, swap-outs happen less than 10 percent of the time.[1]

To model swapping, add a service node to the IPG to represent the secondary storage device that contains the program to be loaded. Route the incoming jobs that require swap-in to the device. Estimate the device service time using the techniques described in Section 5.3.1. The I/O transfer time depends on the average program size, so estimate new program size—measure existing program size and/or average swap time.

A best-case model ignores swap-outs. To represent them for more realistic analysis, add a split node to the IPG and create an asynchronous swap-out transaction category. Set the probability of the swap-out to a reasonable value for your environment.[2] Route the swap-outs to the swap node (and to the CPU if the overhead processing to conduct the swap is significant) before they exit the sys-

---

[1]Check measurement data for your system to see the typical number of swap-outs per swap-in.

[2]Check measurement data for a good default value. If you are uncertain about future loads, conduct sensitivity studies on a reasonable range of values.

tem. Solve the model for performance metrics that include swap overhead. If your solver does not permit split jobs, use the analytic approximation from Section 8.4.1. The following example illustrates this procedure.

EXAMPLE 9.2: Swap Overhead

Figure 9.3 models swapping. To focus on swapping, we do not constrain the maximum number of active users. (We model the combination later in Section 9.1.) Figure 9.3 adds a SWAP node to represent the secondary storage device that contains the program to be loaded. Batch jobs do not swap, so they do not visit the SWAP device. Develop jobs visit SWAP once upon their arrival to the system; then they execute as usual. Note that in this model the SWAP device contains only programs (no data files); if the SWAP device also contains data files, route jobs to the SWAP device to access data by adjusting the device visits.

The model parameters are in Table 9.3. The service time for the SWAP device is 100 ms. It is larger than the 20 ms average disk service time for IOSS1 and IOSS2 because the program is larger than an average block of data, so the transfer time is correspondingly longer.

Jobs that alter memory and hence need to be written to the SWAP device cause additional congestion. They may increase the average residence time for swap-in jobs. To represent swap-outs in the advanced IPG, insert a split node for outgoing Develop jobs between the CPU and the USERS node. One of the split jobs goes to USERS; the other goes to the SWAP node and then exits the system. Figure 9.3 only shows the analytic approxima-

(continued)

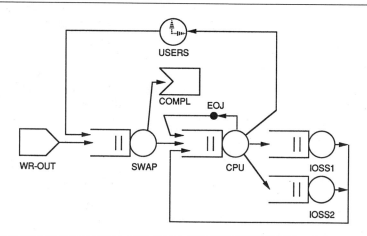

FIGURE 9.3
The System Execution Model to Represent Swapping. Users visit the SWAP node to represent loading the program code. The model approximates swap-out overhead by infusing swap-out jobs at node WR-OUT at the same rate they are generated by outgoing jobs.

TABLE 9.3
PROGRAM-SWAP PARAMETERS

Nodes	Batch # visits	Request	Develop # visits	Request	Swap-out # visits	Request
USERS	0		1	25 sec	0	
CPU	200,001	.01	11	.05	0	
IOSS1	100,000	.02	10	.02	0	
IOSS2	100,000	.02	0		0	
EOJ	1		0		0	
SWAP	0		1	.1	1	.1
WR-OUT	0		0		1	.1569/sec
COMPL	0		0		1	

1 Batch
50 Develop

TABLE 9.4
PROGRAM-SWAP RESULTS

Results with no swap-outs

Node	Category	Throughput	Utilization	Residence time
USERS	Develop	1.569	39.2/50	25
CPU	Develop	17.26	.86	.59
	Batch	7.36	.07	.11
IOSS1	Develop	1.57	.31	.03
	Batch	3.68	.07	.03
IOSS2	Batch	3.68	.07	.02
SWAP	Develop	1.57	.16	.12

Total Response time:	Batch	27,740 seconds
	Develop	6.9 seconds

Results with 10% swap-outs

Node	Category	Throughput	Utilization	Residence time
USERS	Develop	1.57	39.21/50	25
CPU	Develop	17.25	.86	.59
	Batch	7.36	.07	.11
IOSS1	Develop	1.57	.31	.03
	Batch	3.68	.07	.03
IOSS2	Batch	3.68	.07	.02
SWAP	Develop	1.57	.16	.12
	Swap-out	.157	.016	.12

Total Response time:	Batch	27,740 seconds
	Develop	6.9 seconds

EXAMPLE 9.2 (*Continued*)

tion for splits as described in Section 8.4.1. Approximate the swap-out congestion by creating jobs at the WR-OUT source node at the same rate that they are generated by outgoing jobs. Assume that 10 percent of the outgoing jobs require swap-outs; then the arrival rate for the Swap-out transaction category is 10 percent of the throughput of Develop jobs. Because throughput is a result of closed models, make an initial guess, solve the model, and iterate until Develop throughput matches swap-out arrivals.

Table 9.4 shows the model results with no swap-outs. Using its throughput to determine the Swap-out arrival rate—10 percent of the Develop throughput is:

$$.1 \times 1.569 = .1569$$

Table 9.4 also shows the results with 10 percent of the jobs causing swap-outs. The swap-outs have an insignificant effect in this model because there are relatively few of them and the swap device has low utilization.

□

Note that Example 9.2 assumes that once a job is swapped in, it remains in memory until its response is produced. In a heavily congested system it is possible for a job to be replaced in memory while it executes an I/O. This is a form of thrashing—it is preferable to minimize thrashing rather than develop more precise models to quantify its effects, especially when the secondary storage device has the same relative speed as the data I/O device. (Some systems use high-speed memory for these swaps so the effect is lessened.) To minimize thrashing, limit the maximum number of concurrent users to the number that fit in memory concurrently. The memory design techniques described in Sections 9.2 and 9.3 also reduce thrashing.

To model the effects of intermittent swap-ins, revise the model to have two paths after I/O completion—one returns to the CPU as usual, and the new path goes to SWAP to reload programs that have been replaced. Estimate the number of times the new path is taken, or perform a bounded analysis to determine the maximum number of reloads before response time degrades. If the replaced job must first be written out, adjust the rate of SWAP-OUTs to reflect the corresponding increase. Obtaining precise parameters for intermittent swaps is very difficult in early design. For SPE, use a simple bounded analysis to determine whether to study a more detailed model. Unless intermittent swaps seriously threaten the performance goal attainment, it is not fruitful to develop more precise models. If swap-outs have a significant performance impact, the memory design considerations described later are more important than more precise models.

9.1.3 Overhead for Paging or Segmenting

While timesharing systems usually swap entire programs for users, large transaction-oriented systems expect more requests for the same programs, so they typically use **demand paging** to satisfy memory references. Demand paging loads pages of a program into memory when they are referenced and tries to retain them as long as some user needs them. With this strategy, high-frequency transactions typically find their pages already present. (In fact, systems are tuned so that those pages are fixed in memory and cannot be replaced. This strategy is described in more detail in Section 9.2.) When a page must be loaded, it requires an I/O to the paging device and some CPU overhead for page location and placement.

Computer systems without demand paging use a similar strategy: They load **segments of programs** upon demand. The differences between segments and pages are their sizes and their compositions: Pages are fixed-size, whereas segments vary; and segments are logical software entities, usually related functions, whereas pages are contiguous pieces of the program that are arbitrarily divided at page boundaries irrespective of the relationship of the pieces that are broken. Segment loads also require an I/O to the secondary storage device and some CPU overhead for locating the segment. Most operating systems place segments in predetermined portions of memory. A specified segmentation plan seeks to use the same portion of memory for parts of programs that are unlikely to be needed at the same time (as discussed in Section 9.2).

The models that follow use a simplistic analysis to identify potential performance problems due to memory loads. If found, the memory design assessments in Section 9.2 provide more precise model parameters for performance prediction, and Section 9.3 discusses how to minimize memory management overhead. The analysis of pages and segments is similar. First we consider the analysis of pages, then the differences for segments. Note that computer systems with very large memories may allocate a portion of memory for staging pages (memory "above the line" of user-addressable memory). Page faults for medium-use pages are often found in the staging area and do not need the I/O to secondary storage. We assume that pages found in the staging area require negligible overhead, and thus we do not include them in the simple models. The paging in the following discussion is to secondary storage.

To represent the I/O for paging, add a paging node to the advanced IPG. Route jobs to the device for both page-reads and page-writes. Ideally, pages are stored on dedicated devices. When the paging devices also contain data files, adjust the models to reflect the additional data I/O visits. The best-case model assumes no paging, so the elementary IPG gives a lower bound for memory management overhead. For an **optimistic evaluation** that includes paging, assume that you can add new work to the system without increasing the system's current paging rate.[3] First measure the frequency of page-reads and page-writes. Then use Algorithm 4.7 to compute the total processing units for the software

---

[3]This assumes you add more work to an existing system. If the entire system is new, do some benchmark studies, or use various paging rates to determine a page-fault threshold for acceptable service.

scenario, T. Multiply this lower bound for scenario elapsed time by the system's current paging rate (page-reads and -writes) to get a lower bound for the number of visits to the paging device.[4] (For more realism, increase the scenario's CPU requirement by multiplying a CPU average per page times the number of pages.) Solve the model for an optimistic checkpoint evaluation. This procedure is explained with the following example.

EXAMPLE 9.3: Optimistic Paging Evaluation

Figure 9.4 represents a PAGEDEV and simplifies the model by ignoring swaps and constraints on active users. The software model specifies that the new transaction has 1 user interaction, 5 I/Os, and 120 ms total CPU time. There are 100 users who have an average think time of 25 seconds between requests. Data I/Os take an average of 20 ms. From system measurement data, we find that page I/Os take an average of 15 ms, and that the system has a (combined) paging rate of 5 pages per second. We need to compute the number of visits to PAGEDEV, which then gives the number of visits to the CPU and the average CPU service time.

Estimate (an optimistic) number of PAGEDEV visits from the system's average paging rate and the estimated duration of the new transaction. Using Algorithm 4.7 for computing the lower-bound elapsed time, T:

$$T = 120 \text{ ms CPU} + (5 \times .02) \text{ ms I/O} = 220 \text{ ms}$$

Then the expected number of pages is:

$$.22 \text{ secs} \times 5 \text{ pages/sec} = 1.1 \text{ pages}$$

So the optimistic lower bound is 1.1 visits to PAGEDEV. The number of visits to the CPU is 1 (USERS) + 5 (IOSS) + 1.1 (PAGEDEV) = 7.1, and its mean service time is 0.120/7.1 = 0.017 ms. Note that this excludes CPU overhead for paging. If you have measurement data that gives the average CPU time per page, you can multiply it by the number of pages and add it to the CPU requirement (120 ms) before computing the mean service time.   □

The solution to the model in Example 9.3 gives paging's effect on response time and on the device metrics. It is a very optimistic analysis, but if it shows that performance goals are not attained, problems must be solved before you proceed. You can also solve the optimistic model with various paging rates to determine a threshold for the maximum allowable rate.[5]

The optimistic paging model is likely to show acceptable performance. However, it assumes no increase in the system's paging rate, whereas adding work to an existing system is likely to increase memory congestion. High-use transactions

---

[4]It is optimistic because the lower-bound elapscd time, T, does not include queueing delays. You can get a better elapsed time estimate to use for the page computation from the elementary IPG, if you need to be more precise.

[5]You could also use a load driver to benchmark the system under heavier loading conditions to obtain estimates of future paging rates.

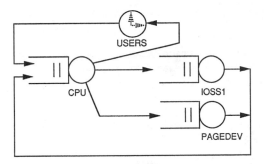

PARAMETERS

	NEWTRANS	
Nodes	# visits	Request (sec)
USERS	1	25 (think time)
CPU	7.1	.017
IOSS1	5	.02
PAGEDEV	1.1	.015

Number Users = 100
Response time = .41 sec

FIGURE 9.4
The Optimistic System Execution Model to Represent Demand Paging. Jobs visit PAGEDEV to read or write pages.

may still be resident, but lower-use transactions are likely to experience increased paging.

Another checkpoint evaluates the benchmark scenarios' performance when pages are not memory-resident and must be loaded. If performance goals are still met, further detailed study need not be undertaken early in the lifecycle. The number of page faults for the less optimistic model comes from the software model. Make an optimistic assumption that scenario pages only need to be loaded once. It holds for small transactions of short duration. (Large transactions and those with long execution times need the parameter calculation techniques discussed in Section 9.2.) Compute the total size of the transaction by adding the component sizes: Add the size of each component with execution frequency > 0; add components within loops once irrespective of the loop repetition factor. Divide the transaction's total size by the page size to get the total number of visits to PAGEDEV. This only models page-in requests. You can add an average number of page-outs based on the overall system average (such as the average ratio of pages written to pages read). Compute the remaining model parameters as before and solve the model. The following example illustrates the procedure.

EXAMPLE 9.4: Less Optimistic Paging Estimates from Software Execution Models

Figure 9.5 shows a software scenario in which each component has an estimated-size specification. To compute the total size of the transaction, we ignore the "other" component, and add components within the loop once to get:

12 + 15 + 1 + 16 + 8 + 8 + 4 = 64K Total

The page size is 4K, so the total pages is (64K/4K per page)= 16 pages. Compute the CPU and I/O requirements as usual:

CPU: .04 + 2(.01 + .003 + (.2)(.05) + (.3)(.02) + (.3)(.02) + .01 = 0.120 sec
I/O: 2 + 2(0 + 0 + (.2)(2) + (.3)(1) + (.3)(1) + (0)(2)) + 1 = 5

The IPG is like Figure 9.4. To calculate the number of visits to the PAGEDEV, assume that 10 percent of page-ins also require a page-out. So, the total PAGEDEV visits is:

16 page-ins + (16 × .1) page-outs = 17.6 visits

Compute as usual the rest of the model parameters, shown in Table 9.5. The results show that the predicted response time with 100 users is a marginal 3.54 seconds.

□

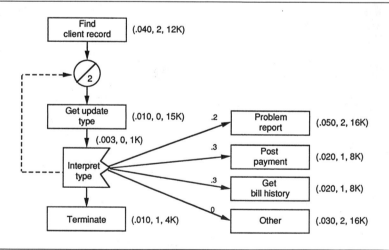

FIGURE 9.5
The software execution model specifications are augmented with memory-size estimates for each component. Analysis results provide device visits for the PAGEDEV in the system execution model.

TABLE 9.5
PESSIMISTIC PARAMETERS
FROM SOFTWARE MODEL

	NEWTRANS	
Nodes	# visits	Request (sec)
USERS	1	25 sec (think time)
CPU	23.6	.005
IOSS1	5	.02
PAGEDEV	17.6	.015

Number Users = 100
Response time = 3.54 seconds

Note that this evaluation assumes that each user encounters page faults upon executing the scenario. This is usually a valid assumption for medium- to low-use transactions. When the predicted performance of the less optimistic model is marginal (inadequate performance or very close to the goals), use the assessments described in Section 9.2 for more precise analysis, and the design techniques in 9.3 to avoid problems.

9.1.4 Adaptations for Segmentation

Models for segmentation are similar to paging models. For the optimistic model, the PAGEDEV device becomes SEGDEV and contains the program code to be loaded. Page sizes are fixed, but segment sizes differ. The optimistic model assumes that the average segment size of the new transactions is about the same as existing systems and that the rate of loads does not increase. So compute the number of visits to SEGDEV the same way as for the paging model, and use measurements to determine its service time.

The less optimistic model computes the number of loads from the total scenario size by dividing by an average segment size. If the average is 8K per segment, the number of loads for Figure 9.5 is (64K/8K per segment) = 8 loads. Include Segment writes by adding a percentage of the segment loads. Note that when you model the SEGDEV with an FCFS queue-scheduling discipline, the mean service time for each transaction category and phase must be the same. The actual service time may differ if segment sizes vary significantly. For a checkpoint evaluation either use the average service time with FCFS or change the queue-scheduling discipline to processor sharing (PS) and specify different service times by category and phase. Further study is needed if performance goals are not met with this simple analysis.

9.1.5 Summary

We modeled constraints on maximum active users with a permission-to-execute allocate node and a corresponding release-permission release node. We modeled swapping by adding a SWAP node and estimating its visits and service time. We modeled paging (or segmentation) by adding a PAGEDEV node and estimating its visits and service time with two different methods. We can combine the models—a hypothetical topology is in Figure 9.6. The figure does not show the parameters. The routing parameters would send only timesharing jobs to the SWAP device and only transaction jobs to PAGEDEV. Each would have its own threshold on maximum active users.

Note that these simple models omit many complexities found in memory management. The number of active users may depend on the size of each rather than on an absolute threshold. For example, the number of timesharing jobs allowed may depend on the number of already active transaction jobs. The models do not explicitly show the varying effect on the paging rate of the maximum number of active users. They do not explicitly consider shared pages, the effect of block sizes and number of buffers on the number of users, or the paging rate, or many other factors. Simulation IPGs can represent these complexities. The simple models indicate when you need more detailed memory assessments and when to use the memory design techniques, described later.

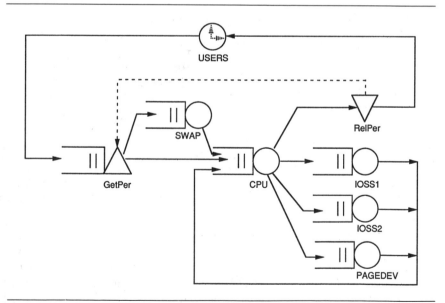

FIGURE 9.6
The advanced IPG represents the combination of swapping, paging, and maximum number of concurrent users.

9.2 Memory Design Assessment

Performance problems due to memory management overhead have traditionally been viewed as a computer system (environment) tuning problem. This is because memory problems generally occur because workloads grow or new software increases memory congestion, and because memory problems are typically corrected with larger memories. Nevertheless, excessive memory requirements are often due to an inappropriate software implementation strategy. If the software system has memory references that are spread uniformly throughout its entire address space, it requires the entire address space to execute efficiently, or it incurs substantial memory management overhead to load needed portions. If, on the other hand, the software has locality—memory references that are concentrated in small areas of the address space for substantial portions of its execution time— then memory management overhead is minimized. There are thus two facets to effective memory management for new systems: designing systems with strong locality and predicting the memory management overhead of proposed designs. Techniques for memory locality design are described in Section 9.3. The assessments are described here.

9.2.1 Lifecycle Questions and Evaluations

Memory assessments differ with the lifecycle stage. For early analyses of memory requirements, we use simple, optimistic calculations to quickly distinguish designs with clearly unacceptable performance from those that are suitable. A design with borderline performance is identified for close scrutiny throughout development. Memory analysis thus uses SPE's adaptive-analysis approach: The assessments increase in precision when early results call for further study and data becomes available. This section covers the memory design questions that you should ask, when they are revelant, and why they are important. The algorithms for obtaining answers for both paged and non-paged environments follow (in Section 9.2.2).

Assessment 1: Does this design have critical memory requirements?
Ask this question as soon as designers formulate a high-level design plan. Gather specifications for the amount of memory available for the new software and the estimated and upper-bound size of the software components. If the total upper-bound size is less than the memory available to the software, the memory requirements are not likely to be critical. If the proposed software is larger than the available memory, check whether it is possible to partition the software, and estimate a threshold for the allowable number of memory faults. If partitioning is impossible, the design is unacceptable; otherwise, continue to monitor memory requirements as the software evolves.

Assessment 2: What are the software localities? Do they fit in the available memory without thrashing?   Ask this question when the software size is greater than the available memory. Repeat the analysis when changes may either increase the software size or decrease the amount of memory available. This analysis identifies the localities of the software and estimates the number of memory faults. Then you can quickly compare the estimate to Assessment 1's threshold or use the result in Assessment 3's advanced IPG. The results also guide the detailed design— design choices should preserve these localities to avoid excessive thrashing.

Assessment 3: Should additional memory be acquired and, if so, how much?   Ask this question after you have results for Assessment 2. The localities, combined with the software models, provide more realistic page-fault parameters for Section 9.1's advanced IPG. When you detect memory problems, use a more realistic system execution model to provide quantitative (performance) data for design improvement versus host configuration upgrade alternatives.

Assessment 4: Which component sizes are critical?   Ask this question for systems under close scrutiny each time design changes may affect locality size or composition. Identify critical components and implement them first, using measurement data (rather than estimates) for the memory assessments. Concentrate optimization efforts on critical components for the greatest leverage.

Assessment 5: Should we impose size constraints on components? This question applies to non-paged systems or paged systems with small real memory. Early studies produce size guidelines. Impose constraints during implementation when components must fit within size limits for the system to meet performance goals.

Assessment 6: How should memory be organized?   This question primarily applies to large software systems in non-paged environments. Previously, segmentation plans were derived manually, by trial and error, and as a result many attempts were needed to eliminate thrashing. Finding a feasible partitioning, much less an optimal one, was difficult and time-consuming. In paged memory environments, memory organization is a less critical problem because compilers and loaders determine initial pagination, and optimizers can restructure pages if necessary. Some memory organization strategies, such as locking highly used pages in memory, further improve performance in systems that are sensitive to memory management overhead.

Apply this analysis once the component sizes are "known" (usually during implementation after unit testing and before integration testing) to determine memory organizations for both the test system and the final product. Code added for debugging may increase the test-version size such that the test and production organizations differ significantly. Performance is as critical during the testing phase as it is in the production phase—poor responsiveness then often leads to late delivery of software. Because testing is in progress, sizes may change, so update the specifications and repeat the analysis to determine production organizations.

9.2.2 Analysis to Obtain Answers

The analysis to answer the assessment questions uses the standard SPE strategy: Start with simple calculations and use more realistic analyses as better data becomes available. This is particularly important for memory design assessments because not only are overly complex analyses unnecessary for problem identification—they may obscure the problem. The calculations that follow are simple, intuitively obvious heuristics. With practice you can tailor these or develop new ones for your environment. Automate them with a spreadsheet or statistical analysis package so you can adapt the heuristics and quickly solve them with varying parameters. For example, one calculation assumes that 80 percent of the memory accesses are in a small number of components. Vary the percentage to examine the sensitivity of the results in your environment. In another calculation you should vary the amount of memory available, to study its effects.

The calculations implicitly assume that high-use components are fixed in memory and thus are ineligible for replacement. Low-use components are ignored, and the algorithms focus on estimating overhead for medium-use components. This is consistent with system tuning practices. If your installation uses a different tuning strategy, adapt the algorithms accordingly.

9.2.3 Data Requirements

Memory analysis requires the following **software and environment specifications:**

τ Response time goal

M Amount of memory available

sz_i Size of component i

t Average processing time per memory load (the sum of the CPU processing to initiate it and average seek, latency, and transfer time to fetch it)

sz_l Average size of a load (page size or average segment size)

The amount of memory, M, is the maximum real memory to be allocated to the new system. It excludes the operating system and other software systems. For paged-memory systems, this is a target rather than an absolute threshold. The size of each component, sz_i, includes code, data, I/O buffers, and so forth (thus the size of the virtual address space). The average processing time per load, t, excludes queueing delays. In this discussion, a **load,** is a generic term for locating, fetching, and placing either a page or a segment in real memory. The time for a load, of course, depends on whether you have paged or segmented memory management.

The analysis also uses the following **data derived from the software or system execution models:**

N Number of (unique) components in the software

SZ Total size of the software $\sum\limits_{i=1}^{N} sz_i$

RT Total scenario response time (excluding memory overhead)

f_i Expected execution frequency of component i—the sum of the number of calls and returns to i

n_{ij} Number of times component i references (calls, invokes, transfers to, and so forth) component j

It is not necessary to count the number of components, N—it is only used to precisely state the mathematical expressions (such as that for SZ, above). *Unique components* means that components in repetition loops or that are called multiple times are only included once in the SZ size calculations. For the response time, RT, in early memory analyses use the "total processing units," T, derived from the software models (Algorithm 4.7). Later use the scenario response time, RT, from the elementary IPG. To calculate component execution frequency, f_i, first multiply applicable loop repetitions and conditional execution probabilities to determine the average number of times each component executes within each scenario. Next multiply each by the number of scenario executions expected in the time interval of interest, say a peak hour (because these memory analyses focus on overall system performance rather than on individual scenarios). Finally, sum the frequencies for components that appear in multiple scenarios. The following example demonstrates the calculation.

EXAMPLE 9.5: Component Execution Frequency Calculation

We will calculate component execution frequencies for the Withdrawal scenario in Figures 8.10 and 8.11 and the Get balance scenario in Figure 8.11.

To compute average number of executions within a scenario, multiply each component by all applicable loop repetition factors and execution frequencies. The results are in the "Within scenario" columns in Table 9.6.

Next multiply by the number of scenario arrivals expected in the time interval of interest. For this demonstration we assume a peak arrival rate of 25 Withdrawal sessions and 2 Get balance sessions per second. The results are in the "Weighted by arrivals" columns.

Finally, sum the execution frequency for components that execute in multiple scenarios. The results are in the "Total" column.

□

TABLE 9.6
COMPONENT EXECUTION FREQUENCIES

Component	Frequency				
	Withdrawal		Get balance		
	Within scenario	Weighted by arrivals (peak = 25/sec)	Within scenario	Weighted by arrivals (peak = 2/sec)	Total
Initiate session	1	25	1	2	27
Get request	2	50	1	2	52
Process request: Withdrawal					
Get info	2	50			50
Lock	2	50			50
Process withdrawal	2	50			50
Update balance	2	50			50
Process request: Get balance					
Build key			1	2	2
Share			1	2	2
Read record			1	2	2
Extract balance			1	2	2
Free	2	50	1	2	52
Terminate	1	25	1	2	27

Early calculations use the execution frequency of each component, f_i. Later analyses yield more precise results by using component connectivity, n_{ij}, rather than execution frequency. Weight the scenarios by the number of executions expected in the time interval, and use the loop repetitions and conditional execution probability as before. Replace the computation of the number of times component i executes with a calculation of the number of times component i references (calls, invokes, or transfers to) component j. Note that the execution frequency, f_i, and the number of component references, n_{ij}, use the control flow (arc) information in the software models. Earlier (in Section 4.1.3) we discussed the value of specifying control flow in the software models. It is necessary for memory analyses, and it is easier to gather this information as the software evolves than to wait until problems surface. So if you have a non-paged or small-memory system, track the control flow as carefully as the other execution characteristics.

The **memory analysis computes and uses the following data:**

C_R The set of components to be fixed or resident in memory

C_M The set of components with medium frequency, f_i

C_O The set of components with low frequency, f_i

M_R Amount of memory for resident set

M_L Amount of memory available for loads

M_c Amount of memory in a cluster

T_L Expected total execution time for memory loads

L Maximum number of loads acceptable

L_M Estimated number of loads for C_M

l_x Number of loads for cluster c_x

These terms are explained as they are used in the following assessments. For convenient reference, the terminology is summarized in the inset. In the discussion that follows, the earlier questions are repeated, along with the analysis that gives the answers. The following example illustrates the computations.

EXAMPLE 9.6: Data to Illustrate Memory Analysis

This example is based on measurement data from a system similar to the case studies. It illustrates computations for both segmented and paged memories and for two different memory sizes—1 megabyte and 256K. We gather the following specifications in a performance walkthrough:

- ☐ Response time goal, τ = 6 seconds
- ☐ Memory available, M = 1MB or 256K
- ☐ Average processing time per load:
  —paged memory system, 4K pages, t_p = .015 seconds
  —segmented memory system, 20K segments, t_s = .02 seconds

The elementary IPG gives the scenario response time, RT = 5 seconds.

Table 9.7 shows component numbers and sizes (for code and data) in columns 1 and 2. The execution frequency, f_i, is in the third column. The fourth and fifth columns are cumulative values for the data in columns 2 and 3, respectively. (We calculate the values in column 6 later.) This data is from measurements. For early development evaluations, gather specifications for columns 1 and 2; calculate column 3 from the software models, and then compute the values in other columns from these.   ☐

9.2.4 Assessment 1: Does This Design Have Critical Memory Requirements?

If the total size of all scenarios in a system, SZ, is less than the amount of memory available to the new system, memory management is not a critical early design issue. Example 9.6's memory data shows that the total size for the scenarios is 346K. With 1 megabyte of memory available, memory is not a critical problem.

TABLE 9.7
SOFTWARE MODEL DATA

Component	Size	Frequency	Cum. size	Cum. freq.	Cum. % freq.
1	1064	1597	1064	1597	0.08611
2	432	1558	1496	3155	0.17011
3	56	1531	1552	4686	0.25266
4	1720	883	3272	5569	0.30026
5	512	855	3784	6424	0.34636
6	1640	643	5424	7067	0.38103
7	592	643	6016	7710	0.41570
8	816	643	6832	8353	0.45037
9	488	640	7320	8993	0.48488
10	840	640	8160	9633	0.51938
11	840	464	9000	10097	0.54440
12	936	463	9936	10560	0.56936
13	320	463	10256	11023	0.59433
14	352	463	10608	11486	0.61929
15	416	463	11024	11949	0.64426
16	1216	463	12240	12412	0.66922
17	800	460	13040	12872	0.69402
18	512	430	13552	13302	0.71720
19	336	426	13888	13728	0.74017
20	5400	426	19288	14154	0.76314
21	176	423	19464	14577	0.78595
22	1008	420	20472	14997	0.80859
23	368	418	20840	15415	0.83113
24	1680	408	22520	15823	0.85313
25	1688	232	24208	16055	0.86564
26	2672	231	26880	16286	0.87809
27	344	212	27224	16498	0.88952
28	1784	206	29008	16704	0.90063
29	2456	184	31464	16888	0.91055
30	1392	184	32856	17072	0.92047
31	3792	183	36648	17255	0.93034
32	1232	122	37880	17377	0.93692
33	11560	122	49440	17499	0.94349
35	1232	92	50672	17591	0.94846
36	8040	80	58712	17671	0.95277
38	1976	64	60688	17735	0.95622
39	2000	53	62688	17788	0.95908
40	440	39	63128	17827	0.96118
41	808	37	63936	17864	0.96317
42	288	37	64224	17901	0.96517
43	424	34	64648	17935	0.96700
44	2088	34	66736	17969	0.96884
45	4840	32	71576	18001	0.97056
48	2416	27	73992	18028	0.97202
49	448	26	74440	18054	0.97342

(*continued*)

TABLE 9.7
(*Continued*)

Component	Size	Frequency	Cum. size	Cum. freq.	Cum. % freq.
50	160	26	74600	18080	0.97482
51	1688	25	76288	18105	0.97617
46	432	15	76720	18120	0.97698
47	112	15	76832	18135	0.97779
53	1960	15	78792	18150	0.97859
54	1960	15	80752	18165	0.97940
55	320	15	81072	18180	0.98021
56	512	15	81584	18195	0.98102
57	1704	14	83288	18209	0.98178
59	536	12	83824	18221	0.98242
61	848	11	84672	18232	0.98302
62	4088	11	88760	18243	0.98361
63	376	9	89136	18252	0.98409
64	1656	9	90792	18261	0.98458
65	208	9	91000	18270	0.98506
66	1800	8	92800	18278	0.98550
67	1144	8	93944	18286	0.98593
68	2000	8	95944	18294	0.98636
70	1960	8	97904	18302	0.98679
71	1960	8	99864	18310	0.98722
72	1336	7	101200	18317	0.98760
73	616	7	101816	18324	0.98798
75	920	6	102736	18330	0.98830
77	1256	5	103992	18335	0.98857
79	1792	5	105784	18340	0.98884
78	2088	4	107872	18344	0.98905
80	808	4	108680	18348	0.98927
81	904	4	109584	18352	0.98949
82	936	4	110520	18356	0.98970
83	200	4	110720	18360	0.98992
84	3304	4	114024	18364	0.99013
85	4336	4	118360	18368	0.99035
86	184	4	118544	18372	0.99056
87	840	4	119384	18376	0.99078
88	576	4	119960	18380	0.99100
89	400	4	120360	18384	0.99121
90	2600	4	122960	18388	0.99143
96	1960	4	124920	18392	0.99164
91	1960	3	126880	18395	0.99180
92	1960	3	128840	18398	0.99197
93	1960	3	130800	18401	0.99213
94	1960	3	132760	18404	0.99229
97	3216	3	135976	18407	0.99245
98	2688	3	138664	18410	0.99261
99	1320	3	139984	18413	0.99278

(*continued*)

TABLE 9.7
(*Continued*)

Component	Size	Frequency	Cum. size	Cum. freq.	Cum. % freq.
100	1688	3	141672	18416	0.99294
101	1960	3	143632	18419	0.99310
102	2168	3	145800	18422	0.99326
103	1136	3	146936	18425	0.99342
104	5816	3	152752	.18428	0.99358
105	2176	3	154928	18431	0.99375
106	2568	3	157496	18434	0.99391
107	1128	3	158624	18437	0.99407
108	400	3	159024	18440	0.99423
109	2808	3	161832	18443	0.99439
110	2496	3	164328	18446	0.99455
111	2176	3	166504	18449	0.99472
112	4032	3	170536	18452	0.99488
113	416	3	170952	18455	0.99504
114	1256	3	172208	18458	0.99520
115	2576	3	174784	18461	0.99536
116	1960	3	176744	18464	0.99552
117	1960	3	178704	18467	0.99569
118	1960	3	180664	18470	0.99585
119	2720	3	183384	18473	0.99601
120	40	2	183424	18475	0.99612
121	1296	2	184720	18477	0.99623
122	3312	2	188032	18479	0.99633
123	376	2	188408	18481	0.99644
125	1960	2	190368	18483	0.99655
126	1280	2	191648	18485	0.99666
127	1960	2	193608	18487	0.99676
128	1224	2	194832	18489	0.99687
130	1960	2	196792	18491	0.99698
131	2200	2	198992	18493	0.99709
132	416	1	199408	18494	0.99714
133	2752	1	202160	18495	0.99720
134	176	1	202336	18496	0.99725
135	2680	1	205016	18497	0.99730
136	2160	1	207176	18498	0.99736
137	2008	1	209184	18499	0.99741
138	2056	1	211240	18500	0.99747
139	368	1	211608	18501	0.99752
140	432	1	212040	18502	0.99757
141	4504	1	216544	18503	0.99763
142	2896	1	219440	18504	0.99768
143	992	1	220432	18505	0.99774
144	480	1	220912	18506	0.99779
145	2512	1	223424	18507	0.99784
146	416	1	223840	18508	0.99790

(*continued*)

TABLE 9.7
(Continued)

Component	Size	Frequency	Cum. size	Cum. freq.	Cum. % freq.
147	408	1	224248	18509	0.99795
148	1064	1	225312	18510	0.99801
149	80	1	225392	18511	0.99806
150	2560	1	227952	18512	0.99811
151	1600	1	229552	18513	0.99817
152	1392	1	230944	18514	0.99822
153	8536	1	239480	18515	0.99827
154	12216	1	251696	18516	0.99833
155	11696	1	263392	18517	0.99838
156	584	1	263976	18518	0.99844
157	288	1	264264	18519	0.99849
158	280	1	264544	18520	0.99854
159	1064	1	265608	18521	0.99860
160	13416	1	279024	18522	0.99865
161	440	1	279464	18523	0.99871
162	928	1	280392	18524	0.99876
163	5944	1	286336	18525	0.99881
164	6000	1	292336	18526	0.99887
165	4056	1	296392	18527	0.99892
166	2488	1	298880	18528	0.99898
167	1848	1	300728	18529	0.99903
168	3456	1	304184	18530	0.99908
169	4416	1	308600	18531	0.99914
170	168	1	308768	18532	0.99919
171	1960	1	310728	18533	0.99925
172	1328	1	312056	18534	0.99930
173	568	1	312624	18535	0.99935
174	1312	1	313936	18536	0.99941
175	11552	1	325488	18537	0.99946
176	456	1	325944	18538	0.99951
177	5296	1	331240	18539	0.99957
178	1384	1	332624	18540	0.99962
179	1016	1	333640	18541	0.99968
180	1960	1	335600	18542	0.99973
181	1960	1	337560	18543	0.99978
182	1960	1	339520	18544	0.99984
183	1960	1	341480	18545	0.99989
184	1960	1	343440	18546	0.99995
185	2600	1	346040	18547	1.00000

For 256K available memory, requirements may be critical, so we apply the following assessments.

When the total size, SZ, is larger than M, loads are likely. We first compute L, the threshold for the maximum number of loads that can be executed without

Memory Analysis Terminology

C_M The set of components with medium f_i

C_O The set of components with low f_i

C_R The set of components to be fixed or *resident* in memory

f_i Expected execution frequency of component i—the sum of the number of calls and returns to i

L Maximum number of loads acceptable

L_M Estimated number of loads for C_M

l_x Number of loads for cluster c_x

M Amount of memory available

M_c Amount of memory in a cluster

M_L Amount of memory available for loads

M_R Amount of memory for resident set

N Number of (unique) components in the scenario

n_{ij} Number of times component i references (calls, invokes, transfers to, etcetera) component j

RT Total scenario response time (excluding memory overhead)

sz_i Size of component i

sz_l Average size loaded (page size or average segment size)

SZ Total size of the scenario:

$$\sum_{i=1}^{N} sz_i$$

τ Response time goal

T Total processing units

T_L Expected total execution time for memory loads

t Average processing time per memory load (the sum of the CPU processing to initiate it and average seek, latency, and transfer time to fetch it)

---

exceeding response time goals. Then we partition the software components into high-, medium-, and low-use sets. We assume the high-use set is memory-resident, ignore the low-use sets, estimate the expected number of loads for the medium-use set, and look for problems. We use simple heuristic calculations for these estimates. Heuristics differ from algorithms: Heuristics are simple calculations that yield "good" results most of the time. The goodness of the results depends on the system characteristics, so examine the sensitivity of your results to different values in the formulas.

HEURISTIC 9.1: Maximum Number of Loads, L

First compute the slack time for the scenario of interest. It is the difference between the (current) expected execution time of the scenario RT, and its response time goal, τ:

$$\tau - RT$$

The elapsed execution time for all loads T_L, including queueing delays, must be less than the slack time:

$$T_L < \tau - RT$$

Similarly, the average processing time per load t times the threshold L must be less than the elapsed time for loads T_L (because T_L includes queueing delays, but $L \times t$ does not). So:

$$(L)(t) < T_L < \tau - RT$$

So, **an absolute upper bound for L is:**

$$L < \frac{\tau - RT}{t}$$

This threshold for L is absolute because it allows no queueing delays for loads (and it uses an optimistic value for RT).

A **better bound** sets an upper bound on the utilization of the page (or segment) device. From the open QNM computations in Algorithm 5.1, the residence time at a device, i, including queueing delay, is:

$$RT_i = \frac{S_i}{1 - U_i}$$

Choose a reasonable upper bound for the device utilization for your environment; this illustration uses 35 percent. With service time $= t$ (average time for a load), the average residence time for 35 percent utilization is:

$$\frac{t}{1 - .35} = 1.54t$$

so, a **more realistic upper bound** for L is:

$$L < \frac{\tau - RT}{1.54t}$$

□

RT is an optimistic value in early design stages, so the threshold for L from this analysis is still high. Memory problems are already indicated if we analyze the software model and find that its estimated loads exceed the threshold.

EXAMPLE 9.7: Maximum Number of Loads

From the specifications in Example 9.6, the slack time is $6 - 5 = 1$ second. Combine this with the data in Table 9.7 to get the following absolute upper bound for L:

$$L < \frac{6 - 5}{(.015)} = 67 \text{ for paged systems}$$

$$L < \frac{6 - 5}{(.02)} = 50 \text{ for segmented systems}$$

With a load-device utilization less than 35 percent, the threshold is:

$$L < \frac{6 - 5}{(1.54)(.015)} = 43 \text{ for paged systems}$$

$$L < \frac{6 - 5}{(1.54)(.02)} = 32 \text{ for segmented systems}$$

□

Next we partition the software components into high-, medium-, and low-use sets. First identify the resident set, C_R, and compute its size, M_R. The resident set is the small subset of the components that accounts for the majority of the executions. Two heuristic calculations follow for selecting C_R. The quality of their results depends on the actual distribution of component frequencies and sizes. Check your system's sensitivity.

To use the first heuristic, sort components by execution frequency such that $f_1 \geq f_2 \geq \ldots \geq f_N$. Start with the component with the highest frequency, f_1, and assign it to the set, C_R. Then repeat the process—check the next highest frequency, f_{j+1} ($j = 1$, initially), and assign the component to C_R if its execution frequency accounts for the majority of executions. To illustrate, we assign components to C_R if they account for part of 90 percent of the executions. The procedure below expresses the heuristic formally:

HEURISTIC 9.2: Frequency-Based C_R Selection

1. Sort components by execution frequency such that $f_1 \geq f_2 \geq \ldots \geq f_N$
2. Assign component $j = 1$ to C_R
3. Set $j := j + 1$ and repeat Step 4 until you find a j that is not assigned.
4. Assign component j to C_R if:

$$\sum_{i=1}^{j} f_i \leq .9 \sum_{i=1}^{N} f_i$$

The formula in Step 4 sums the frequencies of components tentatively assigned to C_R (on the left of the equation). If the sum is less than or equal to 90 percent of the total executions (expressed on the right of the equation), component j is also assigned to C_R.

□

A slight variation of the frequency-based heuristic designates a percentage of available memory to contain C_R. For illustration, designate 20 percent of M to contain C_R. The sized-based heuristic procedure is:

HEURISTIC 9.3: Size-Based C_R Selection

1. Sort components by execution frequency such that $f_1 \geq f_2 \geq \ldots \geq f_N$
2. Assign component $j = 1$ to C_R
3. Set $j := j + 1$ and repeat Step 4 until you find a j that is not assigned.
4. Assign component j to C_R if:

$$\sum_{i=1}^{j} sz_i \leq .2M$$

□

The following example demonstrates both the frequency- and the size-based heuristics. Note that the analysis is much easier than the mathematical formulas imply.

EXAMPLE 9.8: Heuristic Assignment to C_R

Frequency-based heuristic

Column 5 in Table 9.7 shows the cumulative executive frequency of components (the left side of the frequency heuristic's Equation 4). Column 6 is the cumulative percentage of execution frequencies. To calculate a value in column 6, divide the corresponding value in column 5 by the total executions reported in column 3 (which is also the last value in column 5: 18,547). With this heuristic, we assign components 1 through 27 to C_R.

Sized-based heuristic

Column 4 in Table 9.7 has the cumulative size of components. If we allocate 20 percent of M to C_R,

$(.2)(256) = 51.2K$

is the value in the right side of the size heuristic's Equation 4. So we assign components 1 through 35 to C_R.

Results

Note that C_R accounts for almost 95 percent of the executions if 20 percent of memory is allocated to C_R. This appears to be a reasonable assignment, so we use this definition for C_R (components 1 through 35) in the following analyses. To check your understanding, try the frequency heuristic for 85 percent of the executions and the size heuristic for 25 percent of M.

□

We assign the remaining software components to either C_M or C_O, the set of medium-use or low-use components, respectively. The low-use components are "unlikely" to be executed. As before, the definition of "unlikely" is arbitrary. Early in design when you do not have measurements, use a heuristic to compose C_O: Select an arbitrary percentage of components, such as 20 percent; and assign components to C_O that account for less than 20 percent of the executions (using an appropriately modified version of the frequency heuristic). Try several percentages and examine the results. Twenty percent is a conservative value for many systems. The data in Table 9.7 represents only 24 percent of all components in the system, so C_O is 76 percent of all components. (Even though only 24 percent of all components are executed in the test, the scenario is representative of the behavior of the overall system.)

After excluding components unlikely to be executed, assign all remaining components to C_M. After partitioning the software, compute the memory C_R and C_M require:

$$M_R = \sum_{j \in C_R} sz_j$$

The size of C_M is:

$$\sum_{j \in C_M} sz_j$$

For the frequency heuristic, if $M_R \geq M$, the system is likely to have memory problems. For the size heuristic, we must estimate the number of loads to identify problems.

An **optimistic assessment** assumes that one load per page or segment in C_M suffices; that is, C_R is resident, and it is never necessary to reload the same portion of virtual memory in C_M into real memory. It also ignores loads for C_O and assumes that no page or segment writes are needed. If the resulting number of loads still exceeds (the pessimistic) L, problems are clearly indicated. Correct problems before proceeding with the more realistic analyses.

Estimate the number of loads, divide the (virtual) memory size of C_M by the average size of a load, sz_l (the page size or average segment size), and compare the result to L:

$$\frac{\sum_{j \in C_M} sz_j}{sz_l} \overset{?}{>} L$$

EXAMPLE 9.9: Simple Estimate of Number of Loads

The memory data in Table 9.7 comes from measurements, so for this example we assume that "unlikely" components are already excluded from the data. We assign components that

(continued)

EXAMPLE 9.9 (*Continued*)

were not executed in the test to the set of low-use components C_O (they are not in the table). So we assign the remaining components in the table to C_M. The size of C_M for Table 9.7's memory data is 295K. The (optimistic) estimated number of loads for the example memory data is:

$$\frac{295}{20} = 15 \text{ segment loads}$$

$$\frac{295}{4} = 74 \text{ page loads}$$

The segment loads are within the threshold, L, but the page loads are not. This calls for further study of potential memory contention problems.

□

Note that your computer configuration may soften the blow of page-load problems. If you store pages on a disk device connected to a controller with a memory cache, the operating system may find many pages in the cache. Alternatively, your operating system may pre-fetch contiguous pages and retain them in a buffer. You can achieve a 5:1 ratio of page loads to physical I/Os for page fetches when contiguous pages on the disk device match the localities needed. (The ratio comes from the maximum number of pages that can be read with one physical I/O [a track].) Modify this ratio to fit your device or operating system characteristics. Calculate a more realistic threshold L for page loads by modifying the average time per load to match the 5:1 assumption (or your customized ratio). For example, if 1 load requires 15 ms, and the next 4 loads complete in 2 ms (by avoiding the physical I/O),

$$t_p = \frac{.015 + (4)(.002)}{5} = .0046 \text{ seconds average}$$

The revised threshold L for Example 9.5 is 141, so the threat of memory problems is lessened if the software has sufficient locality and the computer configuration exploits contiguous pages. That is the good news; the bad news is that this estimate of loads is very optimistic. If you find problems, they are likely to be even worse than these calculations show. To obtain a more realistic estimate of loads, the next assessment examines the software locality and uses localities to project load estimates.

9.2.5 Assessment 2: What Are the Software Localities, and Do They Fit in the Available Memory Without Thrashing?

We start by selecting a target locality size, group software components into clusters according to their usage patterns, assume that the clusters correspond to localities, and then estimate the resulting number of loads.

We begin by **clustering the software components in** C_M. The first clustering heuristic uses execution frequencies and sizes. The results are close to those produced by the more realistic analyses described later and match the data that is easily obtained in early lifecycle stages. It works best when component sizes are smaller than cluster sizes, so decompose large components or increase cluster sizes appropriately. The heuristic is formulated as a "knapsack problem" of mathematical programming. The problem's analogy is a knapsack with limited capacity. We have many items we wish to place in it, each having a different size and a different "desirability." We wish to maximize the desirability of the items in the knapsack subject to the capacity constraint. For the memory analysis, the knapsack's capacity is the cluster size, and the desirability is the execution frequency. The problem is first stated formally, and then a technique for easily solving it follows.

HEURISTIC 9.4: Knapsack Assignment of C_M Components to Clusters

Let x_i be a variable that has value 1 if component i is assigned to the cluster and has a value 0 otherwise. A solution to the following problem identifies clusters of size M_c.

Maximize

$$\sum_{i \in \hat{C}_M} f_i x_i$$

Subject to

$$\sum_{i \in \hat{C}_M} sz_i x_i \leq M_c$$

and

$x_i = 0$ or 1
where $\hat{C}_M$ contains the components of C_M not yet assigned to clusters

The execution frequency, f_i, is the desirability of including component i, so the first line maximizes the desirability of the i's assigned. The second line adds the condition that their sizes be less than or equal to the cluster size. Solve the problem, remove selected components ($x_i = 1$) from $\hat{C}_M$, and repeat the process.

The problem is unfortunately NP-complete. For a heuristic solution:

1. Sort the components of $\hat{C}_M$ such that

$$\frac{f_1}{sz_1} \geq \frac{f_2}{sz_2} \geq \ldots \geq \frac{f_n}{sz_n}$$

2. Assign $x_1 = 1, x_2 = 1, \ldots$, until $x_k = 1$ would violate the size constraint.

You may wish to fine-tune the heuristic's solution. For example, a large component, k, may violate the size constraint, but the next component, $k + 1$, may execute frequently and be small enough to fit. Occasionally you may wish to skip a large component k because many smaller ones with high execution frequencies may fit instead. Study alternative solutions by varying cluster sizes, component decompositions, and borderline assignments.

□

TABLE 9.8
FREQUENCY-SIZE HEURISTIC DATA

Component	Size	Frequency	Cum. size	Freq/Size
50	160	26	160	0.16250
47	112	15	272	0.13393
42	288	37	560	0.12847
40	440	39	1000	0.08864
43	424	34	1424	0.08019
49	448	26	1872	0.05804
120	40	2	1912	0.05000
55	320	15	2232	0.04688
41	808	37	3040	0.04579
65	208	9	3248	0.04327
46	432	15	3680	0.03472
38	1976	64	5656	0.03239
56	512	15	6168	0.02930
39	2000	53	8168	0.02650
63	376	9	8544	0.02394
59	536	12	9080	0.02239
86	184	4	9264	0.02174
83	200	4	9464	0.02000
44	2088	34	11552	0.01628
51	1688	25	13240	0.01481
61	848	11	14088	0.01297
149	80	1	14168	0.01250
73	616	7	14784	0.01136
48	2416	27	17200	0.01118
89	400	4	17600	0.01000
36	8040	80	25640	0.00995
57	1704	14	27344	0.00822
53	1960	15	29304	0.00765
54	1960	15	31264	0.00765
108	400	3	31664	0.00750
113	416	3	32080	0.00721
67	1144	8	33224	0.00699
88	576	4	33800	0.00694
45	4840	32	38640	0.00661
75	920	6	39560	0.00652
170	168	1	39728	0.00595
134	176	1	39904	0.00568
64	1656	9	41560	0.00543
123	376	2	41936	0.00532
72	1336	7	43272	0.00524
80	808	4	44080	0.00495
87	840	4	44920	0.00476
66	1800	8	46720	0.00444
81	904	4	47624	0.00442
82	936	4	48560	0.00427
71	1960	8	50520	0.00408

It is much easier to solve the assignment problem than to state it formally. The following example demonstrates.

EXAMPLE 9.10: Knapsack Assignment of C_M Components to Partitions

Table 9.8 shows a subset of the memory data from Table 9.7. It excludes components 1 through 35 that were assigned to the resident set, and sorts the data into decreasing sequence by column 5, which contains the f_i / sz_i ratio for each component. Table 9.8 shows the 40 of the C_M components with the highest frequency-size ratio. For convenience, the assignment is illustrated with a cluster size of 20K (because the same computation then works for 20K segments and for 4K pages cached 5:1 as above). Select an appropriate size for your environment.

With the knapsack heuristic, the first cluster breaks between components 89 and 36, and the next cluster breaks between components 88 and 45. Fine-tuning improves these clusters. Component 36 is not assigned to partition 1 because 17.6K of the 20K is already allocated and component 36 is 8.04K. However, component 57 fits in the remaining space in cluster 1. By assigning it to cluster 1, more room is available in cluster 2, and so on.   □

More information on using the knapsack problem for similar memory analyses is in [BAS70].

As the design evolves, use more realistic analyses to determine clusters and estimate loads. Ferrari describes several heuristics for identifying localities in [FER78]. Actually, he addresses the problem of assigning blocks of programs to pages, but the concepts and the heuristics are the same as for this application. Ferrari uses n_{ij}—the number of references from component i to component j—and clusters components to "maximize" the number of references falling within the same partition.

He also describes more sophisticated analysis techniques that use memory reference patterns. They consider the *order* of the component references and the placement algorithms in the operating system, to minimize the number of references to pages (or segments) that require loads. Each of the heuristics yields better results than the previous one, but at a higher cost. The frequency-size knapsack heuristic yields results sufficient for early studies.

Having identified segments or clusters of size M_c, the next step is to **estimate the number of loads** for the medium-use components, C_M, given the cluster assignments. We assume that the clusters correspond to the software localities.

HEURISTIC 9.5: Estimate Number of Loads for C_M

Let $c_1, c_2, \ldots, c_n$ be the localities of C_M found with one of the cluster heuristics.

1. For an early estimate of the number of loads, use the knapsack assignment and the best-case estimate of one load per cluster (n loads).

(continued)

HEURISTIC 9.5 (*Continued*)

2. For a pessimistic estimate of the number of loads, use n_{ij}, the number of times component i references component j—the maximum number of loads for each locality k, l_k, is:

$$max \; l_k \; = \; \sum_{\substack{j \in c_k \\ i \notin c_k}} n_{ij}$$

That is the number of calls to k made by components in other clusters.

3. A more optimistic estimate assumes that references between components of the resident set, C_R, and the cluster, c_k, do not require loads. It also ignores references to low-use components, C_O, and computes the number of references between clusters within C_M. With these assumptions, the estimate for l_k is:

$$l_k \; = \; \sum_{\substack{j \in c_k \\ i \in C_M - c_k}} n_{ij}$$

4. Use the estimate of the loads for each locality, k (from either Step 2 or Step 3) to compute the total loads for C_M:

$$L_M \; = \; \sum_{k=1}^{n} l_k$$

Compare your estimate of the number of loads, L_M, to the threshold L to check for problems. The following example demonstrates the load estimation.

EXAMPLE 9.11: More Realistic Estimate of Number of Loads

For Table 9.8's data, the best case is 15 loads. More realistic analysis uses the number of calls from component i to component j, n_{ij}. Table 9.9 shows part of the n_{ij} data corresponding to the memory data in Tables 9.7 and 9.8. Column 1 is the component making the reference, column 2 is the referenced component, and column 3 is the number of references. Columns 4 and 5 have the locality number that contains the referencing and referenced components, respectively. (The localities were composed with the frequency-size knapsack heuristic.) Locality 0 is the resident set C_R. Column 6 has the cumulative number of references between localities. The table is sorted by the locality number that contains the destination component j.

The table shows that the number of calls from locality 1 to 0 is 259 and from 0 to 1 is 258, for a total of 517 calls. Ninety-eight calls are made from localities 2–15 to locality 1. The maximum loads for locality 1, $max \; l_1 \; = \; 615$. Excluding calls from locality 0 (the resident set) gives $l_1 \; = \; 98$. The total loads for all the medium-use components, excluding those from locality 0, is $L_M \; = \; 373$. This is higher than the maximum number of loads, L, so further study is advised.   □

TABLE 9.9
NUMBER OF LOADS

From	To	# calls	From Loc	To Loc	Cum. calls per group	Max. loads	Est. loads
56	14	15	1	0	15	15	0
63	29	9	1	0	24	9	0
38	6	11	1	0	35	11	0
40	17	25	1	0	60	25	0
43	35	34	1	0	94	34	0
38	3	27	1	0	121	27	0
89	24	4	1	0	125	4	0
41	2	37	1	0	162	37	0
40	8	3	1	0	165	3	0
48	1	27	1	0	192	27	0
50	1	26	1	0	218	26	0
65	4	9	1	0	227	9	0
51	4	25	1	0	252	25	0
73	18	7	1	0	259	7	0
1	42	7	0	1	7	7	0
1	51	4	0	1	11	4	0
2	65	1	0	1	12	1	0
1	89	4	0	1	16	4	0
9	42	3	0	1	19	3	0
2	149	1	0	1	20	1	0
2	42	6	0	1	26	6	0
18	51	1	0	1	27	1	0
18	73	7	0	1	34	7	0
27	65	1	0	1	35	1	0
12	50	11	0	1	46	11	0
1	61	11	0	1	57	11	0
2	59	9	0	1	66	9	0
12	59	3	0	1	69	3	0
18	63	9	0	1	78	9	0
4	40	25	0	1	103	25	0
32	44	32	0	1	135	32	0
1	49	26	0	1	161	26	0
2	41	28	0	1	189	28	0
1	39	27	0	1	216	27	0
12	46	15	0	1	231	15	0
2	51	8	0	1	239	8	0
35	42	2	0	1	241	2	0
1	48	8	0	1	249	8	0
2	38	9	0	1	258	9	0
86	42	1	1	1	1	0	0
44	43	34	1	1	35	0	0
46	47	15	1	1	50	0	0
59	40	12	1	1	62	0	0

(continued)

TABLE 9.9
(Continued)

From	To	# calls	From Loc	To Loc	Cum. calls per group	Max. loads	Est. loads
49	39	26	1	1	88	0	0
47	55	15	1	1	103	0	0
38	40	2	1	1	105	0	0
40	41	9	1	1	114	0	0
39	38	53	1	1	167	0	0
40	38	2	1	1	169	0	0
36	48	1	2	1	1	1	1
113	48	1	2	1	2	1	1
36	65	4	2	1	6	4	4
36	42	8	2	1	14	8	8
113	51	2	2	1	16	2	2
36	50	15	2	1	31	15	15
36	51	6	2	1	37	6	6
57	56	14	2	1	51	14	14
134	48	1	3	1	1	1	1
170	65	1	3	1	2	1	1
158	51	1	4	1	1	1	1
77	65	1	4	1	2	1	1
92	42	3	5	1	3	3	3
78	86	4	5	1	7	4	4
90	48	4	5	1	11	4	4
118	48	2	5	1	13	2	2
126	48	2	5	1	15	2	2
116	44	1	5	1	16	1	1
121	120	2	5	1	18	2	2
93	42	2	6	1	2	2	2
84	83	4	6	1	6	4	4
94	42	2	6	1	8	2	2
101	48	3	6	1	11	3	3
162	42	1	7	1	1	1	1
109	48	3	7	1	4	3	3
97	51	3	8	1	3	3	3
172	44	1	8	1	4	1	1
135	56	1	11	1	1	1	1
142	65	1	11	1	2	1	1
165	48	1	12	1	1	1	1
153	42	1	13	1	1	1	1
163	48	1	13	1	2	1	1
160	42	1	15	1	1	1	1
38	36	9	1	2	9	9	9
42	36	37	1	2	46	37	37
55	54	15	1	2	61	15	15
				Total:		676	159

The frequency-size knapsack heuristic gives a pessimistic number of loads because it does not consider which components reference one another. It works well for small components with many references, but it seldom clusters components with few references with the components they reference. Clustering algorithms, such as those in [FER78] and [FER81], work better for the low-frequency components because they use the n_{ij} call relationships to form the clusters. For example, a version of Ferrari's n_{ij}-based clustering algorithm (modified to create fixed-size clusters of 20K) gives a total $L_M = 165$.

The localities and the number of loads in these examples are sensitive to the value chosen for M_c. Individual scenarios minimize their loads if M_c is the maximum memory available $(M - M_R)$. However, this reduces the number of concurrent users and thus has a negative overall impact on performance. To increase concurrency, each active user needs its locality resident. We also want to avoid having low-use components (in C_O) replace higher-use localities. Therefore, we allocate a small amount of memory for low-use components, M_O. Fine-tune this amount for your environment by studying average component sizes in C_O, and by examining the sensitivity of the number of loads to the amount allocated. For this example, we use $M_O = 4K$. Since $M_R = 52K$, this leaves $256 - 56 = 200K$ for M_L. If we want 10 active users, each gets 20K of the 200K; for 5 active users each gets 40K. With 40K, each user could have 2 clusters resident at a time. This reduces l_k accordingly. Analyze the effect by eliminating loads for pairs of c_k with the highest number of references between them (for the best case). For Table 9.9, 112 loads between c_1 and c_2 could be eliminated. Examining all pairs is time-consuming, so use simpler best- and worst-case estimates. Alternatively, use $M_L = 40K$ and repeat the cluster assignment heuristic. In this example, the n_{ij} clustering heuristic reduces the loads from 165 with 20K segments to 136 with 40K segments.

An optimistic analysis assumes that components are reentrant and can be shared by all active users. With ideal cooperation, all users execute within the same locality at the same time. In the memory example, this corresponds to the analysis results for $M_c = 200K$.

9.2.6 Assessment 3: Should Additional Memory Be Acquired and, If So, How Much?

Answer the question of need for additional memory by combining the results for the estimated number of concurrent users and the number of loads with the models for memory overhead representation in Section 9.1. Figure 9.7 shows the advanced IPG topology for the memory example. The ReqPer node limits the number of active users in the system. With 5 active users, the estimated number of loads is 136. With 10 active users, the estimated number of loads is 165. These parameters are in Table 9.10, along with the other usual parameters. Note that the

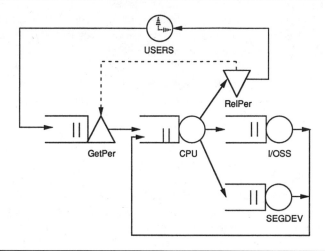

FIGURE 9.7
The Advanced IPG Used to Predict the Interaction Between the Maximum Number of Concurrent Users and the Segment (or Page) Loads. The parameters come from software execution models and the algorithms in Section 9.2.

parameters specify a very fast SEGDEV. Either a solid-state device or a cache controller is necessary to support the high number of loads. Table 9.11 shows the approximate analytic results for 10 users. The average response time is 10.83 seconds, of which jobs spend 1.48 seconds at GetPer waiting to enter active execution. The approximate analytic results for 5 users are also in the table. The average response time is 15.75 seconds, of which 10.70 seconds are at GetPer. Therefore, in this example it is undesirable to give users more memory at the expense of reducing the number of active users. Because of the very fast SEGDEV

TABLE 9.10
MEMORY SIZING

Nodes	10 Active users		5 Active users	
	# visits	Request	# visits	Request
USERS	1	60 sec think time	1	60 sec think time
GetPer	1	(Permission, 1)	1	(Permission, 1)
CPU	200	.0025	171	.0029
I/OSS	34	.02	34	.02
SEGDEV	165	.005	136	.005
RelPer	1	(Permission, 1) to GetPer	1	(Permission, 1) to GetPer

Total number of users = 75

TABLE 9.11
MODEL RESULTS

Model results—10 active users

Node	Utilization	Queue length	Residence time
USERS		63.53	60
GetPer		1.48	1.4
CPU	.53	1.11	.005
I/OSS	.72	2.50	.007
SEGDEV	.87	6.37	.004

Response Time: 10.83 seconds

Model results—5 active users

Node	Utilization	Queue length	Residence time
USERS		59.40	60
GetPer		10.59	10.7
CPU	.50	.97	.006
I/OSS	.67	2.02	.006
SEGDEV	.67	2.02	.001

Response Time: 15.75 seconds

and the relatively small reduction in the number of loads, the reduced execution time does not offset the additional delay at GetPer. Note that even though a user spends an average of 10.70 seconds at GetPer, the net response time only increases by 4.92 seconds. This is because of the reduced processing requirements and the reduced device contention with fewer active users.

To analyze the effect of more memory, increase the resident set size appropriately and repeat the locality analysis with larger memory for loads M_c. The revised estimates give new SEGDEV visit parameters for the advanced IPG.

9.2.7 Assessment 4: Which Component Sizes Are Critical?

The size of all components assigned to the resident set, C_R, is critical. It affects the number of components assigned to C_R, the memory available for loads, and thus the number of loads. Large components in C_M are also critical. According to Ferrari ([FER78]), the locality identification heuristics work well when component sizes are between 1/10 and 1/3 of M_c. So component size is critical if it is estimated to be equal or greater than $1/3M_c$. Implement these critical components first, and use their measured size in the early analyses to produce more realistic results.

9.2.8 Assessment 5: Should We Impose Size Constraints on Components?

For computer systems with performance that is sensitive to memory management overhead, the early analyses find thresholds for acceptable performance. The threshold depends on values for M_R and M_c. These introduce guidelines for sizes of critical components. As they are implemented, compare the actual size to the guideline. Impose constraints for unimplemented components so they will fit into the remaining memory allocated for M_R and M_c. Some installations use the size estimates given for early models as constraints. They build the system to match the model (rather than vice versa). This strategy is successful in constrained memory environments.

9.2.9 Assessment 6: How Should Memory Be Organized?

For non-paged systems, you need to create a segmentation plan that specifies which components are to be resident, identifies components assigned to segments, and specifies which segments share the same memory regions. Use the earlier locality identification heuristics with measurements of memory reference strings to determine an appropriate segmentation plan. Analyze the reference string with different assignments of components to clusters to estimate the number of loads for each proposed segmentation plan. For paged systems, you need to specify the components to be resident.

Tools are available that improve locality of existing systems. They measure memory references and restructure programs to minimize the number of page faults. When systems are designed for locality, they seldom need additional manual tuning to reduce memory management overhead.

9.3 Memory Design Issues

Memory management overhead has two effects on performance: *internal effects,* the time required for memory accesses; and *external effects,* the competitive effects between concurrent users for the use of main memory. Memory management problems are usually solved by tuning operating system routines. However, careful attention and consideration of memory effects at design time can improve the performance of the new software as well as the execution environment performance.

The memory locality-design principle in Chapter 2 says:

Design systems to have good spatial and temporal locality.

Systems with good locality minimize both the internal and external effects of memory management. This section explains how to apply locality design and other performance principles to minimize both the internal and the external memory effects that system and program design can reduce.

The locality-design principle seeks good spatial and temporal locality, which is *not the same as minimizing space*. One large software system developed for a constrained memory environment sought tight control over program memory. No space was held by programs—"allocate" routines were called every time space was needed, and "free" routines released it as soon as possible. As a result, the code to manage the free space offset the space savings for the dominant workload, and the long execution path lengths for "allocate" and "free" and the frequent calls to them increased processing time to the extent that response-time goals were not met. Thus, over-concern with memory can be detrimental. The problems occurred because designers focused on minimizing space rather than seeking good spatial and temporal locality. Effective application of the locality-design principle controls memory overhead. Effective use dictates that it be applied early to identify an appropriate design. Even with an appropriate design, memory thrashing problems may be introduced during detailed design and implementation. Early locality design is described first, followed by middle lifecycle locality design.

9.3.1 Early Lifecycle Locality Design

Early in the lifecycle, apply memory locality design to the overall design and to find a system structure that concentrates memory references in a small number of components. Avoid "long" loops and recursive calls with "long" processing for each, because they may cause thrashing. "Long" means a large space requirement and a long time interval between references to portions of the space. The following example demonstrates a long loop improvement.

EXAMPLE 9.12: Avoid "Long" Loops

The example in Figure 9.8(a) shows an excerpt from the DRAWMOD scenario containing a long loop. The components are large and the processing time between one beam-row retrieval, the completion of the outer loop, and the next beam-row retrieval is extensive. Thrashing is not certain, but it is a possibility. The revised structure in Figure 9.8(b) replaces the long loop with two tighter loops. The first RETRIEVEs all the beams for the

(continued)

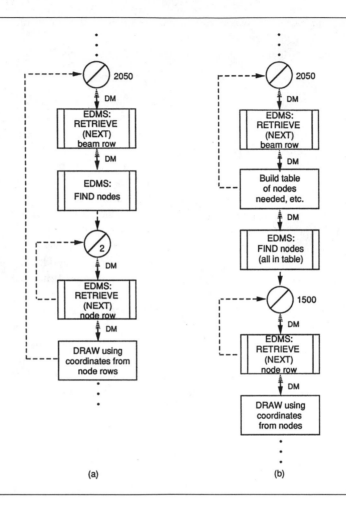

(a)

(b)

FIGURE 9.8
The software execution model in (a) is an excerpt from the original DRAWMOD scenario. The modification in (b) improves memory locality by replacing the "long" outer loop for each beam row with two loops with "shorter" execution times.

EXAMPLE 9.12 (*Continued*)

model and builds a table or list of the nodes that DRAWMOD needs.[6] Then one FIND locates all the nodes, and DRAWMOD retrieves them and draws the picture when all information is available.

Not only does the tighter loop strategy improve memory locality, but (in this example) it also reduces processing time. Because of the finite element model structure described in Chapter 6, two adjacent beam elements share a common node. With the revised processing

(*continued*)

---

[6]The table contains only node numbers so it easily fits within one memory page.

EXAMPLE 9.12 (*Continued*)

structure, DRAWMOD retrieves the nodes only once, so the node loop repetition factor becomes the number of nodes in the model, 1500. This reduces the number of calls to RETRIEVE (NEXT) node from (2 × 2050) = 4100 to 1500. If the EDMS database provides a RETRIEVE (ALL), DRAWMOD would only need one call. Note that the DRAW routine in Figure 9.8(b) changes—it draws the entire picture with one call.

The locality improvement is also an instance of the processing versus frequency tradeoff principle. The beam retrieval executes more processing when it builds the node table, but it reduces the node retrieval frequency.

☐

Similar techniques improve locality for recursive calls. If the processing time and space between one reference to the routine and the next is long (between one entry until the next recursive call, or between a recursive call and the return), the routine may no longer be in memory and will require reloading. Examine whether recursive calls are an appropriate design strategy, and, if so, shorten the space and time between references that frequently occur in the dominant workload.

9.3.2 Middle Lifecycle Locality Design

If you select an appropriate software structure early in the lifecycle, you can usually correct memory problems that occur in mid-lifecycle or later by tuning; however, it is easier to prevent mid-lifecycle memory usage flaws and the side effects of corrective action. Preventing them means you expedite testing, use personnel to make further progress rather than fix problems, and avoid code entropy due to tuning changes. The middle lifecycle strategy is to *create software that matches the memory organization policy* (fixing high-use components in memory, and so on), and to *match the size of components to their frequency of use*. That is, tailor the software so that the heuristics in Section 9.2 work well, and the resulting performance will be good. Subsequent subsections describe two ways to accomplish this strategy: (1) Reduce the number of loads for C_M by localizing memory reference patterns and (2) control dynamic storage requests.

Localize Memory References   The **memory reference pattern** of a software system is the sequence of virtual addresses that the software references over a time interval. Section 9.2 proposed the following memory management strategy: Lock high-use components into memory so they will not be replaced, minimize the loads for medium-use components, and isolate low-use components to minimize interference with higher-use components. The effectiveness of this strategy depends on memory reference patterns, which can be controlled in detailed design. The memory locality-design principle yields the following design maxims:

- ☐ **Make frequently used components as small as possible.**
- ☐ **Do not mix infrequent functions with higher-use functions.**
- ☐ **Minimize the software's space-time product.**

When these properties hold, the software is well suited for Section 9.2's memory management strategy.

EXAMPLE 9.13: Size and Structure of ATM Components

In the ATM example, the high-use components include those that provide the abstract machine functions, such as transferring data between the ATM site and the central computer. The low-use components are those that handle unusual error conditions that are highly unlikely to occur in normal operations. Other low-use components perform infrequent ATM functions, such as transferring money from a money-market account to a savings account. The routine that prints the customer receipt is a medium-use component because it executes once for each transaction.

Design the ATM system to make the service routines for the ATM's abstract machine functions independent of one another and make the typical routines quite small. Exclude handling of unlikely events within the medium-use print receipt component, such as canceling a transaction after the receipt is half-printed.

□

Minimizing the size of frequently used components lessens the memory requirement for the resident set, M_R, and either makes room for additional components in the set, C_R, or makes more room for loading medium-use components, C_M. Removing an infrequent function j from a component i in C_M and placing j with low-use components in C_O makes room for additional components in i's cluster. The net effect of both maxims is to reduce the number of loads for C_M.

The **space-time product** is the amount of virtual address space a process needs to execute and the elapsed execution time it is held. When much memory is needed for a long time, either few users execute concurrently or thrashing occurs. Operating system memory management policies seek to reduce thrashing by limiting the number of active users as their memory demands grow. We seek to minimize the space-time product to maximize the users that can execute concurrently without thrashing. Its primary performance effect is to increase the likelihood that segments or pages remain in memory while needed, thus validating the optimistic assumption that reloads are unnecessary. In a paged memory environment, it also reduces the number of loads because only the referenced (contiguous) portions of a component need be loaded. Even though the memory management strategies on paged and non-paged systems differ, system performance improves with a minimal space-time product.

Reduce space by structuring modules to place typically used code in contiguous locations. Time reductions use Chapter 2's general principles to minimize processing, eliminate I/Os, and so on. Figure 9.9 illustrates a structuring technique that improves the space-time product. The shaded components in part (a) show the most frequent execution path. The structure in part (b) reduces the working-set size. If the typical path executes very frequently, evaluate the performance of moving the CALC_FICA code inline within the *if* statement. You may

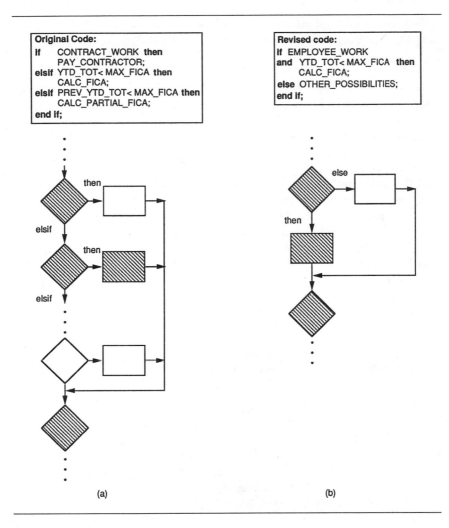

```
Original Code:
If    CONTRACT_WORK then
      PAY_CONTRACTOR;
elsif YTD_TOT< MAX_FICA then
      CALC_FICA;
elsif PREV_YTD_TOT< MAX_FICA then
      CALC_PARTIAL_FICA;
end if;
```

```
Revised code:
If EMPLOYEE_WORK
and  YTD_TOT< MAX_FICA  then
      CALC_FICA;
else OTHER_POSSIBILITIES;
end if;
```

(a)   (b)

FIGURE 9.9
The flowchart in (a) highlights the most frequent execution paths in the original code. The revision in (b) improves memory locality by clustering the frequently executed code together and by moving unlikely choices elsewhere.

further improve the structure if the code can check for OTHER_POSSIBILITIES later, thus eliminating the *else* in this high-frequency code.

Program algorithms and data structures affect working-set sizes, so evaluate their memory requirements along with processing times to identify the appropriate algorithm and data structure combination. For example, a binary search of a large ordered table may have a lower CPU requirement than other search strategies. But if the table is very large, many probes into the table may cause page faults, so the net performance may not be as good as another search algorithm and data structure.

Control Dynamic Storage Requests   Dynamic storage requests are requests for temporary storage made at execution time. Dynamic storage requests are made in Ada when **access** type variables are used with the allocator **new,** and in Pascal programs when pointer variables are used in a call to the NEW procedure. In other languages they require a system call (IBM's "GETMAIN" and UNIX's "malloc"). Dynamic storage requests satisfy many needs. For example, if multiple ATM inquiry transactions are simultaneously active, you could use two strategies: One uses a separate copy of the balance inquiry program for each active user (ATM); the other shares one copy of the program code among all users, but uses a separate copy of the data areas for each user. The savings using the latter strategy are significant if there are many users active and if the program code is large. Dynamic storage requests establish the data areas for each user.

The overhead for dynamic storage requests is considerable—the path length ranges from several hundred instructions to many thousand instructions. The centering and the processing versus frequency tradeoff principles lead to the following maxim:

> **Combine calls for dynamic storage requests; allocate enough space for the dominant workload functions with one request.**

The performance effect of combining dynamic storage requests is to reduce processing time and memory management overhead with a slight space increase.

In the ATM example, the exact storage requirements are unknown when a session begins. They depend on the number of transactions, functions requested, and so on. One strategy is to request the dynamic storage after specific requirements are known. The maxim suggests an alternative: Allocate the amount of storage likely to be needed for dominant workload functions with one request, and later make additional requests when necessary (for larger, less frequent functions).

9.4 Summary and Further Reading

This chapter described a lifecycle approach to evaluating and controlling the performance effects of memory use. Section 9.1 described advanced IPGs for assessing constraints on the maximum number of concurrent users, the overhead for swapping programs, and the overhead for demand paging or segmenting. Then Section 9.2 suggested that memory thrashing may be due to inadequate locality in software designs. It described six assessments appropriate during different stages of the lifecycle to detect memory use problems. Finally, Section 9.3 described techniques for designing software to enhance memory locality.

There have been many papers describing system execution models that represent aspects of memory management overhead. A. J. Smith has authored many of them; he provides a comprehensive bibliography of his and other works in [SMIA78]. Ramamoorthy presents a graph-based technique for segmenting programs too large to fit into executable memory ([RAM66]). Graph-based algorithms that use boolean connectivity to determine optimal segmentation are by Baer ([BAE72], [BAE78]), Kernigan ([KER71]), Lowe ([LOW70]), and Ver Hoef ([VerH71]). Lew discusses the problem of simultaneously optimizing page replacement, allotment, and pagination strategies in [LEW73]. Some techniques for automatically restructuring software after implementation are in [FER73], [LOW70], and [VerH71]. Several authors describe software design techniques to improve locality ([BAR79], [FER78], [FER81], [MAS79], [ROG75]).

This concludes the discussion of the technical aspects of SPE. Next we examine its integration into software development environments.

Exercises

Review

9.1. Make the following changes to the model in Example 9.1 and solve:
- ☐ Change CPU service of Develop to 0.04 sec.
- ☐ Increase number of Batch to 2.
- ☐ Decrease maximum number of Develop to 9.

9.2. Revise the model in Example 9.2 to represent intermittent swap-ins as follows:
- ☐ Assume that 90 percent of I/O completions proceed to the CPU as before, but 10 percent must visit the SWAP node to reload their program.
- ☐ Solve the model.
- ☐ If the average Develop response time must be less than 10 sec, what is the threshold for intermittent swap-ins?

9.3. Create an advanced IPG like the combined model in Figure 9.6. Use the following model parameters:
- ☐ Batch category: Use the parameters in Table 9.1.
- ☐ Develop category: Use the parameters in Table 9.1, but lower the CPU service request to 0.03 sec.
- ☐ Newtrans category: Use the parameters in Table 9.5.

Solve the model.

9.4. Create and solve the two models in Table 9.10. Compare your results to Table 9.11.

Further Study

9.5. a. Collect memory data for your case study and perform the assessments in Section 9.2.

b. Alternatively create a spreadsheet containing data like that in Tables 9.7 and 9.8. Use a random number generator to produce sz_i and n_{ij} values. (Calculate f_i from the n_{ij}.) Perform the assessments. Study the sensitivity of the results to the distribution of random variables that you use for sz_i and n_{ij}.

9.6. Review Ferrari's heuristics for identifying localities in [FER78]. Select one and apply it to the data in Question 9.5. Compare the resulting number of loads.

10

SPE Environment

We have completed the definition of software performance engineering. This chapter concludes with some advice to increase the likelihood that you will be successful in your initial SPE ventures. It reviews what we have covered and why, addresses SPE's integration into the software development process, examines the general process of transferring new technology into work environments (with specific suggestions for SPE adoption), reviews some critical success factors for effective SPE projects, and finally, speculates on the future of SPE.

10.1 SPE Review

We began with the motivation and goals for SPE and an overview of the methodology in Chapter 1. It answered questions about what SPE is and why it is important.

Chapter 2 defined the general principles for performance-oriented design and offered examples of their application to system requirements definition and design. It identified the "expert knowledge" that experienced performance specialists apply to engineer performance, established a formal basis for creating high-performance systems, and provided the rationale for alternatives that improve performance.

Chapter 3 covered the SPE data requirements. It told us what we need and how to get it and offered pragmatic hints to avoid data collection pitfalls.

The software models were in Chapter 4. It described how we characterize workloads for new systems under development, how to represent them with software models, and how to analyze them. The analysis gives an early checkpoint evaluation against performance goals and gives data for later models.

The system execution models in Chapter 5 represent contention for computer system resources. The model provides more realistic performance predictions and a basis for capacity plans that project computer configuration requirements of new software systems.

Chapter 6 described the engineering process that iteratively represents, assesses, and reports results for various circumstances. The process evaluates predictions against performance goals, substantiates results, and influences the selection of alternatives.

Chapter 7 focused on performance measurement for SPE. It reviewed the measurements of interest and their SPE uses, then described the measurement options. It suggested archiving SPE data in libraries and SPE databases for easy reference.

The advanced system execution models in Chapter 8 represent the more detailed execution behavior of serialization delays and parallel processing. They offer more realistic performance predictions that match modeling effort to the knowledge of the software as it evolves.

Chapter 9 covered the representation and assessment of memory management overhead. Its models produce more precise performance predictions, its lifecycle assessments provide checkpoint evaluations to identify trouble during implementation, and its memory design advice controls the overhead processing.

Next, Chapter 10 completes the SPE discussions with its integration with other software engineering methods, its adoption, and its effective use. It suggests how to get started and how to be successful on your initial projects.

10.2 SPE Integration

First we consider whether SPE is compatible with current software engineering practices such as software development tools, development methods, project management, and software quality assurance techniques. Then we consider when SPE is appropriate, its costs, benefits, and risks. Finally, we examine some SPE project organization alternatives.

10.2.1 SPE Compatibility

Is SPE compatible with software development tools? Three types of tools play a significant role in software development:

□ *Computer-aided software engineering (CASE)* tools provide automated support for early lifecycle activities (such as creating data flow diagrams, and maintaining data dictionaries).

□ *High-level languages* allow users to create their own programs for information retrieval and analysis.

□ *Automatic program generators* produce executable code from high-level specifications.

We can expect future **CASE** tools to incorporate performance prediction and assessment features. In the meantime, they are compatible with SPE, but they offer little support. Some tools capture much information needed for software models, such as execution frequencies, and store the information in a database. It may be possible to create your own data extraction programs to automate some of the software model-building steps.

High-level languages and **automatic program generators** usually produce code that is less efficient than handcrafted programs, but this does not mean they are incompatible with SPE. The centering principle suggests that these tools are inappropriate for dominant workload functions. They are fine, however, for prototype versions of the dominant workload functions and for low-frequency functions. Thus SPE guides the effective use of these productivity aids and quantifies their machine resource costs early. Managers can then make educated decisions about the tools' applicability.

Is SPE compatible with software development methods? Three types of methods aid the development of large software systems:

□ *Information engineering* first defines an enterprise's data architecture and information flow, then later defines its software processes ([*MAR*]).

□ *Requirements and design methods* provide a framework and a language for developing requirements and design specifications from business needs. Some examples are Data Structured Systems Development ([*ORR*]), Dynamic Analysis & Specification ([*SDC*]), Software Cost Reduction ([CLE85], [HEN80]), Jackson System Development ([*JAC*]), and others.

□ *Rapid prototyping* creates a scaled-down replica of new software to demonstrate feasibility and refine requirements and specifications.

It is easy to develop software execution models from **Information Engineering's** process action diagrams. It is also possible to develop preliminary models earlier, from the architecture definition, using performance walkthrough techniques. Thus Information Engineering is compatible with SPE.

Some of the **requirements** and **design methods** advocate the archaic "fix-it-later" approach. "Fix it later" is incompatible with the SPE philosophy. On the other hand, there is nothing in the requirements and design methods' framework or languages that precludes using SPE with them. For example, one can describe a system with data flow diagrams, then construct a corresponding software execution model, using the data flow information, to assess performance—even though the design method does not prescribe the performance assessment at that stage.

Traditionally, developers of **rapid prototypes** seldom worried about performance; establishing feasibility and requirements were their primary concerns. SPE techniques may make prototypes more effective:

◻ Performance of one particular prototype was so poor that the entire system concept was prematurely deemed infeasible.

◻ Prototypes must represent dominant workload functions if realistic execution behavior is to be evaluated.

◻ Prototypes can provide measurement data for critical software components.

Thus, SPE and rapid prototypes are compatible, and each benefits from the other.

Is SPE compatible with project management practices? Project management practices we address here are costs and schedules, manpower, and project organization. This section later addresses the specific time, effort, and staffing requirements of SPE, and discusses pertinent critical success factors. Here we consider SPE's compatibility with current project management aspects of these topics.

Many projects use automated tools to produce planned **costs and schedules.** Some, such as Boehm's Cocomo ([BOE81]), inflate project cost and time when software's efficiency is of primary concern. The inflation factor comes from historical data, when SPE tools were limited and labor-intensive methods were required to achieve high performance. We can expect future adjustments to more accurately reflect time and costs with the more modern SPE methods. Note that the cost tools also inflate time and cost when computer resources for development and testing are constrained. Thus, without SPE, software tests may require excessive computer resources—cost tools quantify the resulting additional development time and cost. Schedules must include time for SPE studies and reaction to their results. If scheduling tools do not automatically factor it in, manual adjustments are needed. Thus SPE is compatible with current practices for developing costs and schedules, but they may require fine-tuning until the tools explicitly account for SPE.

Manpower problems have always plagued software development projects. Brooks cites the Mythical Man Month problem, "Adding more people to a late project makes it later," in [BRO75]. He offers other project management methods for timely delivery of software and effective use of manpower, such as sharp milestones, critical-path schedules, hustle, prototyping, configuration management, and others. Not only are software delivery and software quality threatened by the late addition of manpower; software performance also suffers. Brooks's solutions to the productivity and quality problems are compatible with SPE, but he does not specifically advocate SPE. In [BRO86] he advocates strategies such as growing software rather than building it and developing expert designers. SPE, as described here, is based on the "building software" paradigm. It is compatible with Brooks's "growing software" paradigm, but the methods require some adaptation. His "expert designers" need the performance intuition provided by Chapter 2's performance-oriented design principles.

Project organizations generally have team structures. One type is the "chief programmer team," in which the chief is an expert who performs the primary creative work. Other team members perform support functions, such as documentation or researching language questions. The more popular team structure shares creative work among team members by logically partitioning tasks. With chief programmer teams, a software performance engineer supports the chief by conducting measurement studies, solving models, etcetera, upon request. With the "standard team" approach, the software performance engineer combines pertinent information from team members and presents the global performance view. SPE is compatible with both approaches.

Is SPE compatible with software quality? The three aspects of software quality considered here are ergonomics (or user friendliness), software metrics (quantitative measures of quality), and correctness (software correctly and completely specified and conforming to specifications). We saw several examples in Chapter 2 in which responsiveness improved as a result of streamlining user interfaces. Often performance and **usability** are mutually compatible. Occasionally you may find conflicts, but SPE and ergonomics are fundamentally compatible.

Software metrics are maturing in their ability to quantify software quality. One particularly promising approach is the Quality Assurance Framework advocated by the Rome Air Development Center ([CAV78], [McC77], [McC81], [WAL79]). Unfortunately, their original framework views efficiency as conflicting with most other quality factors. This is due to the historical view of efficiency and previous methods used to achieve it. SPE advocates responsiveness rather than efficiency. With the SPE methods, responsiveness is usually attainable without "tricky code" and other historical techniques that were detrimental to quality. SPE is thus compatible with software quality. Moreover, once the software metrics mature and predictive models are developed, it should be possible to apply techniques similar to SPE's to achieve quantitative goals for software quality factors (for example, to construct software with ≥ 0.9 maintainability and ≥ 0.85 availability).

Performance was historically sacrificed in favor of **correctness,** but the two are not mutually exclusive. SPE practitioners have found and corrected many serious design errors during performance walkthroughs that would have been difficult to isolate and correct after code was implemented. In some cases, response within a specified time interval is a correctness requirement. New techniques (and CASE tools) seek executable specifications for early confirmation of correctness. SPE can provide operational scenarios to drive the tests. It can also use measurements derived from such tests (such as number of path executions). Thus correctness and current approaches for achieving it are compatible with SPE.

10.2.2 Effectiveness Is Overriding

Boehm gives an example of a software system with a fundamental problem ([BOE76]). Consider the following description of his example and its implications for performance engineering.

EXAMPLE 10.1: Alternatives for System Modernization

A new system is to replace a problematic older system for subscription processing: When new orders, renewals, gifts, etcetera, are received, it performs appropriate edits and updates and prints bills, notices, mailing labels, etcetera. The older system executes on very old hardware technology, is slow, cannot handle peak loads, and is labor-intensive and error-prone, and the company has many customer complaints. The new system is to remedy these problems.

The first replacement, or "programming solution," upgraded the technology: It used the fastest hardware available, created a more comprehensive customer database, and introduced more transaction edits to ensure database correctness and integrity. Upon implementation it was found to have much higher costs and more data errors and to require more clerical staff to correct errors than the older system. It resulted in serious employee morale problems and high turnover.

The "programming solution" overlooked some key factors in the older system and the overall subscription-handling process: Labor-intensive mail handling was not addressed; the primary source of errors and error correction methods were external to the computer processing; the new system detected more data errors that were incorrectly treated as fatal errors; and the automated processing was only a "minor" part of the overall system (trivial reporting and file updates), not the real problem. Thus the cost of the new software, hardware, and its operation exceeded its value.

The "economic solution" replaced the expensive hardware with less expensive microprocessors. It solved mail-handling problems at the post office with different addresses that specified the handling required and used local intelligent microprocessors to edit for key data errors and allow corrections as entered. The data was collected and sent to a service bureau for the high-volume printing and customer database updates.

☐

Example 10.1 illustrates a potential problem for SPE studies: It is conceivable that a performance engineer could conduct walkthroughs, construct models, and predict hardware capacity requirements and processing time for the "programming solution" with the conclusion that the software would execute within its batch window. That is, if performance engineers are not aware of the overall process and its performance goal, they cannot detect problems with system effectiveness.

The problem is clear: The first and most important goal for new systems is to build the right system; the secondary goal is to build the system "right." Boehm's book suggests methods for the former ([BOE81]). SPE primarily addresses the latter, but occasionally also needs to confirm that it is the "right system." Because the workload must be characterized, SPE studies often reveal inappropriate solutions to business needs in addition to inappropriate implementations of the solutions.

10.2.3 When Is SPE Appropriate?

Building performance into software systems requires some time up-front to collect data, model, and present and act upon results. If SPE detects and corrects severe performance problems, the result is a net time savings; if not, you have spent some extra time, but you have gained assurance that performance will be satisfactory. Thus SPE is analogous to insurance premiums. Like insurance, it is sometimes vital, and sometimes the risk is low enough that it is not warranted.

SPE is vital in the following situations:

- ☐ Systems with strict performance requirements
- ☐ Life-critical applications
- ☐ Strategic systems that are vital to the success of the business
- ☐ Systems with wide distribution (and thus a very high cost to correct problems)

Other situations with a high risk of performance problems include:

- ☐ *Very large systems*—because they require a large development team, the risk of communication failures is high, resulting in locally acceptable pieces that fail due to global mismatches.
- ☐ *New technology*—new hardware, software, or support technology implies that few have experience with actual performance characteristics (as opposed to advertised performance). Developers tend to try many new features that may or may not perform as expected.
- ☐ *Inexperienced personnel* lack the performance intuition to recognize the implications of the various alternatives they consider, thus increasing the likelihood of problems.

Even with the powerful computer systems currently available, the demand-response-time curve (Figure 10.1) often puts new systems in jeopardy when their

FIGURE 10.1
The Demand–Response-Time Curve. Apply SPE to systems with high demand because the risk of performance failure is much greater than the risk for systems with low demands.

resource requirements are high. The region with the arrow shows that when demand is high, as with the use of resource-intensive support tools (such as powerful database management systems, fourth-generation languages, and code generators), a slight demand increase can have a significant response time impact.

Conversely, full-scale SPE is probably not warranted for a small system, built by a small team who are experts in the applications area and with the technology. In general, when one (performance) expert understands the overall system and controls the design and implementation of the parts that fit together, performance is seldom problematic. Even then, the best- and worst-case models and simple checkpoint evaluations are easy to formulate. They confirm that performance is acceptable, provide quantitative data on subtle interactions (such as serialization delays), and increase the performance expertise of team members.

10.2.4 Costs, Benefits, and Risks

It is difficult to quantify the costs of SPE because costs depend on the size and complexity of the system and numerous other factors. Thus it is difficult to relate data from one project to other unrelated projects. Nevertheless, experience indicates that the costs for SPE are very low relative to the total project cost (most are less than 1 percent).

The relevant costs are time, effort, and money. You can minimize the critical path time if a performance specialist supports developers by constructing and evaluating the models, studying possible alternatives, and reporting the results. Most of the SPE work can then be done in parallel with the software development. The design team and the user representatives must devote **time** to gather data and review results. Approximately one-half to one day per month should be sufficient once performance engineers are proficient, developers become familiar with the SPE process, and you begin SPE in the requirements definition lifecycle phase (as opposed to trying to later catch up with the design). An experienced performance analyst with automated tools should be able to produce model results within a few days of each walkthrough. Performance analysis effort varies over the lifecycle; analysis requires more time in later stages because more data must be analyzed and models are more sophisticated.

If software modifications are necessary to meet performance goals, the design team must make changes—the amount of time depends on the extent of the modifications. However, if performance modifications are necessary, they will require much less total time early—prior to implementation—than if they are deferred as in "fix it later" (ratios of 1:100 and even higher have been reported). The scope of effect is much greater when code must be modified and retested.

The **effort and skills** required are similar to conventional capacity planning skills—the SPE data gathering and the translation into model parameters differ slightly from capacity planning. The dollar **cost** is essentially funding for a performance specialist. One person for a 50- to 100-person project is reasonable.

As stated earlier, the costs for SPE are analogous to insurance; the premiums add a small initial cost, but the savings can be quite large. If one elects not to pay the premium and a (performance) disaster occurs, the costs to correct the problem are much greater.

There are numerous **benefits.** Performance goals can be met with little or no additional development time or cost without sacrificing understandability and maintainability. The performance can be orders of magnitude better when optimization is performed early, at high levels, rather than later at the code-tuning level. And SPE improves user relations by avoiding long interim periods of poor responsiveness while new systems undergo crisis performance-tuning.

There are other beneficial effects:

- ☐ SPE involves user representatives in the software performance management. This results in better workload specifications and thus a product that is customized to fit its most frequent uses.

- ☐ The analysis procedure integrates software component specifications. It detects and corrects design inconsistencies before coding begins, thus averting later integration problems.

- ☐ The testing and integration phases are expedited because better performance implies better turnaround for test cases. Thus the productivity of developers is improved.

- ☐ The early identification of performance-critical components enables more effective project management.

There are several **risks** in applying SPE. First, the time or cost to conduct SPE may exceed the SPE budget. This is a problem with software development projects in general, and it is controlled by improved project management. Another risk is of inaccurate model predictions due to potential model or specification errors. This is a dangerous risk; however, it also can be controlled. When the impact of the predictions is substantial, as, for example, when models call for extensive modifications, expend the effort to verify performance specifications with experimental benchmarks, and validate results with measurement studies or additional models (such as simulation models to compare against analytic models).

These risks are minor compared to the risks of developing critical new systems without SPE. The risk of making a large expenditure for a strategic software project and failing to develop an acceptable product is of much consequence. Chapter 1 cited many examples that demonstrate the increasing likelihood of this threat.

The final risk is that SPE is ineffective—that is, conducting the SPE activities, but (for any number of reasons) failing to act on the results of the evaluation. This risk is controlled with the critical success factors outlined in Section 10.4.

10.2.5 How Should SPE Be Organized?

Should SPE be a centralized group from which performance engineers work with development projects on request? Should performance engineers be a part of the design team? There is no one answer applicable to all organizations. We first consider the advantages and disadvantages of each approach, then consider alternatives for organizational placement.

Centralized SPE groups have the following advantages:

- Better opportunities to develop modeling expertise through broad experience and concentrated training
- Leveraged efforts because spare time can be used to develop tools useful for multiple projects
- Better objectivity—analysts who become deeply involved in design decisions may lose the big picture, or overlook other performance implications

The primary disadvantage is that the external group may have responsibility for SPE studies without authority to act upon results. It can be extremely frustrating to watch disasters building and be unable to remedy them.

The following advantages accrue when performance engineers are **part of the design team:**

- Their performance intuition influences early design decisions and offers viable alternatives when problems occur.
- Their firsthand knowledge of the system expedites data collection.
- They are an integral part of the team rather than providers of an external activity that is easily expendable under time crunches.

The primary disadvantage is the loss of impartiality and objectivity, as mentioned earlier.

Some organizations have successfully combined the two approaches: A performance engineer participates on the design team, and periodically an outside team conducts a performance review as added confirmation that nothing important has been overlooked. The central group develops tools, builds modeling expertise, and assists the project team's performance engineer with complex models. The central group uses the performance models developed by all development teams for a central capacity planning model. This combines the advantages of the two approaches without the previous disadvantages, but it is more costly.

Central groups may report to the capacity planning manager, the performance manager, a quality assurance director, or at a higher level such as the data processing manager. The team's performance engineer may report to the chief architect or designer or to the project manager. The proper choice depends on your organizational dynamics, and none is best in all cases.

10.2.6 Summary

These are the primary SPE integration issues: SPE's compatibility with current software engineering practices; its appropriateness in your environment; its costs, benefits, and risks; and how it should be organized. Next we consider the process of transferring new technology, such as SPE, into an organization.

10.3 SPE Adoption

This section is for readers who face difficulties persuading others to use SPE, have recently adopted SPE and want to ensure its initial success, or are interested in the process of transferring new technology into work environments.

SPE use has obvious benefits, and without it there is serious risk of performance failures that may result in business failures. The inability to operate on a peak business day, to respond to customer inquiries, or to generate bills or process payments can have serious consequences. Excessive operational costs lower profit margins. SPE has the potential to reduce the risk of performance failures. So why do some organizations continue to develop systems without it? Why do other organizations readily adopt it?

Researchers in the field of **technology transfer** study the process that occurs between the formation of new technology and its widespread use. They study many different types of technology—including hybrid corn, engineering advances, and computer technology—and publish results in technology transfer journals, conferences, and other media. Their research suggests that, in general, it takes 15 to 20 years from the time that new technology emerges until its widespread use in industry. The range holds for most new technologies, whether they are computer-related, such as structured programming or UNIX, or in other domains such as hybrid corn. Research seeks ways to identify promising technology early and hasten its adoption. Ideas come from studying differences in organizations that readily adopt and those that lag behind, from studying differences in situations that hasten transfer, and from other techniques.

It is difficult to define exactly when SPE emerged. Papers published in the late 1970s advocated its use; by 1980 modeling support tools were available and the software modeling techniques were documented; and by 1981 the SPE methodology was documented. Thus it is still fairly early in the transfer process, so it is not surprising that some organizations have not yet adopted it. The sequence of events in its evolution so far indicates that it is likely to become commonplace (some technologies are never transferred). Can we hasten the process? According to technology transfer research, you can help.

Researchers have indentified **key factors to successful technology transfer.** For transfer to be successful, organizations must try new technology, and it must work. Both are more likely to occur in organizations that have a **strong advocate** who:

□ Persisently encourages and follows up on its use

□ Helps resolve problems that arise

□ Serves as a two-way communications channel between technology users and technology developers

The latter is for new technologies that are not thoroughly documented. It is analogous to telephone consulting services offered for new software products. Customers frequently call when they first use a product to seek clarification on usage details. Vendors often learn of new modes of use and modify products accordingly. Similarly, when an organization tries a new technology, it is more likely to be successful when **an expert participates on the project and contributes to its success.**

Technologies are more readily adopted when they:

□ Have a clear benefit

□ Are compatible with existing methods, experiences, and needs

□ Are easy to understand and try

□ Produce a measurable result

That is, organizations must have a clear need for the technology, and it must clearly have the potential to resolve problems. Technology transfer during wars, for example, has traditionally been faster than the 15-to-20-year average because needs were apparent. Compatibility was addressed in the previous section. Note that measurable results are key—the organization must recognize that the technology resolves problems. This is a "Catch-22" problem: Successful SPE results in the absence of performance problems and is thus invisible, whereas performance failures are visible. Suggestions for resolving this dilemma are offered in Section 10.4.

If you face resistance in SPE adoption, these technology transfer results suggest **actions you can take.** The most important steps are to **make others aware of SPE**—what it is, its potential for risk management, when it is appropriate, others who use it successfully, and so on—and to **find or become an SPE advocate.** Specifically, you can:

□ Identify specific needs in your organization: specific threats or high-risk situations (identified in Section 10.2), or quantify failures that occurred without SPE.

□ Find individuals who are accountable for failures and explain the needs and describe SPE and its potential for resolving the problems (quantify the benefits when possible).

□ Document SPE's compatibility in your environment.

□ Substantiate SPE's potential by writing a position paper, or copying and distributing general articles that report successful use or failures without it ([BEL87], [SMI88], [LEV87], [SMI87a], [SMI87b]).

□ Apply SPE to a pilot project—perhaps a system that already exists and can be measured. Explain the project, the models, and results to others to demonstrate the potential.

Other suggestions were offered by the panelists on Successful Software Performance Engineering ([CMG87]). They point out the need for more tools and for performance accountability of systems developers, and make other excellent suggestions.

The above suggestions help persuade organizations to try SPE. The next section reviews strategies and techniques that lead to SPE successes, and warn of pitfalls and ways to avoid them. Initial efforts must be successful if SPE is to be adopted and used.

10.4 Successful SPE

Commitment of managers and developers is vital to the success of SPE. They face many conflicting goals and must constantly weigh schedule and cost impacts against quality benefits. Performance goals must be quantified and reasonable efforts devoted to achieving them. Without commitment, developers may expend minimal effort and be unwilling to cooperate when changes are required.

Schedule SPE tasks into the initial project schedule to ensure that ample time is available for SPE studies and for performance remedies should they be necessary. Many projects fall behind schedule during detailed design. Because performance problems are not yet apparent, developers may be tempted to omit SPE studies that are not in the project schedule in favor of meeting explicit milestones. If scheduled SPE milestones must be met, it is difficult to avoid them.

Establish performance goals and **hold developers accountable** for meeting them. Unless the objectives and expectations are clearly defined, it is unlikely they will be met. When developers are accountable for their system's performance, they are more likely to react to significant results.

Studies must produce **credible results.** Thus, performance analysts need the necessary modeling skills, and the project team must have confidence in both the analysts' and the models' predictive ability. Without these, it is easier to attribute performance problems to model errors rather than to problems with the design.

Representative workloads must be modeled. It is easy for developers to rationalize that poor performance is unlikely if they do not agree that the workloads in the models are representative and frequently occur.

Critical resource requirements must be **measured early.** This substantiates model predictions and confirms that key performance factors are not overlooked. Software execution characteristics are occasionally omitted from models because their effect is perceived to be minimal, but later they are discovered to have serious consequences. The following example cites a "minor detail" omitted from early models.

EXAMPLE 10.2: Software Details That Influence Performance Predictions

An early lifecycle model specified a transaction with 5 database "Selects." During detailed design, "Order by" clauses were added to 3 of the "Selects." The developers viewed the additional clause as "insignificant" because only 1–5 records would be sorted for each "Select." Upon investigation, however, the performance analyst discovered that over 50,000 instructions were executed for each sort!

□

Examples abound of seemingly inconsequential details that have serious performance consequences. They must be detected either through the analyst's experience or with early measurements to make precise performance predictions.

Best- and worst-case results are required, especially when serious performance problems occur. When performance goals can never be met, they focus attention on potential design problems rather than on model assumptions. They also provide sensitivity analysis and reference points to assess the severity of problems and the likelihood that they will occur.

Timely presentation of results and recommendations is vital when corrective action is required. If significant decisions are made before the SPE results are available, the results are too late. It becomes more difficult to institute changes, and if additional development activities intervene, the corrections may become infeasible.

Quantitative data on the anticipated effect of changes is necessary to make intelligent cost-benefit analyses. This point is made throughout the book, particularly in Chapter 3's discussion of walkthroughs and Chapter 6's presentations. It is further substantiated by the technology transfer requirement for measurable results. That is, the quantitative data is needed not only for evaluation of alternatives, but also for visible results for SPE.

Verify and validate models and their predictions. It is not easy to demonstrate that early SPE models predict later behavior, because they are optimistic models that omit many processing details and because many software changes occur between the initial design and the final implementation. As mentioned earlier, however, it is essential if SPE is to be adopted rather than abandoned.

Acquire or develop **tools and expertise.** Measurement tools are vital to obtain resource consumption data, to evaluate performance against objectives, and to verify and validate results. Modeling tools expedite SPE studies and limit the mathematical background required to construct models. Expertise helps to detect problems early, conduct studies rapidly, and instill confidence in their results.

Secure cooperation and work to **achieve performance goals.** User representatives, managers, designers, and performance analysts should form a cooperative team working toward the common goal of developing a good product. The purpose of SPE is not to solve models, to point out flaws in either designs or models, or to make predictions—it is to **make sure that performance requirements are correctly specified and are achieved in the final product.**

10.5 The Future of SPE

Since computers were invented, we have heard promises that the next hardware generation will offer significant cost-performance enhancements, so it will no longer be necessary to worry about performance. Will tomorrow's hardware solve all performance problems and make SPE obsolete? It has not happened yet. Hardware advances merely make new software solutions feasible, so software size and sophistication offset hardware improvements. There is nothing wrong with using more powerful hardware to meet performance objectives, but SPE suggests evaluating all options early and selecting the most effective one. Thus hardware may be the solution, but it should be explicitly chosen—early enough to enable orderly procurement. SPE still plays a role.

There was a time, in the early 1970s, when computing power exceeded demand in most environments. The cost of achieving performance goals, with the tools and methods of the era, made SPE uneconomical for many batch systems—its cost exceeded its savings. The challenge for the future is to automate the sometimes cumbersome SPE activities and to evolve SPE to make it easy and economical for future environments.

The three primary elements in SPE's evolution are the *models* for performance prediction, the *tools* that facilitate the studies, and the *methods* for applying them to systems under development. With these the *use* of SPE increases, and new design *concepts* develop that lead to high-performance systems. Future evolution in these areas will change the nature of SPE, but not its underlying philosophy to build performance into systems. The following paragraphs speculate on future developments in each of these areas.

Both research and development will produce the **tools** of the future. We seek better integration of the models and their analysis with software engineering tools such as fourth-generation languages (4GLs), automatic program generators, and CASE tools. Then software changes automatically update prediction models. Simple models can be transparent to designers—designers could press a function key while formulating designs and view automatically generated predictions.

Expert systems could automatically suggest alternatives. Visual user interfaces could make analysis and reporting more effective. Software measurement tools could automatically capture, reduce, interpret, and report data at a level of detail appropriate for designers. They could automatically generate performance tests, then automate the verification and validation process by comparing specifications to measurements and predictions to actual performance, and reporting discrepancies. Each of these tools could interface with an SPE database to store evolutionary design and model data and support queries against it.

While simple versions of each of these tools are feasible with today's technology, research must establish the framework for fully functional versions. For example, if a CASE tool supports data flow diagrams and structure charts, how do you automatically convert them to software models? How should you integrate performance models with 4GLs or automatic program generators—should you begin with models and generate code from them, or should you write the code and let underlying models select efficient implementations, or some other combination? How can expert systems detect problems? Can you automatically determine from software models where instrumentation probes should be inserted? Can you automatically reduce data to appropriate levels of detail? Can you automatically generate performance tests? Each of these topics represents extensive research projects.

Performance models currently have limits in their ability to analytically solve models of tomorrow's complex environments. Models of extensive parallel or distributed environments must be hand-crafted, with many analytic checkpoints tailored to the problem. More automatic solutions are desired. Secondly, the analytic queueing network models yield only mean value results. We desire analytic models of transient behavior to study periodic behavior or unusual execution characteristics. For example, averaged over a 10-hour period, locking effects may be insignificant, but there may be short 1-minute intervals in which locks cause all other active jobs to "log jam," and it may take 30 minutes for the log jam to clear. Mean value results do not reflect these after-effects; transient behavior models would. Petri nets and simulation offer the desired capabilities. Finally, as computer environments evolve, model technology must also develop. Thus, research opportunities are rich in software and computer environment models.

Technology transfer suggests that the **use of SPE** is likely to spread. More literature documenting SPE experiences is likely to appear. As it is applied to new, state-of-the-art software systems, new problems will be discovered that require research solutions. Future SPE applications will require skills in multiple domains and offer many new learning opportunities.

The **concepts for building high-performance systems** will evolve as SPE use spreads. As we gain experience and develop many cases to illustrate the difference between high- and low-performance software, we can use them to train new software engineers. As SPE matures, we should be able to apply its techniques to build in other quality attributes, such as reliability, availability, testa-

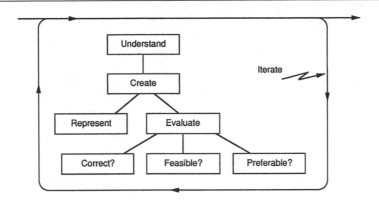

FIGURE 10.2
The engineering design process shows the following steps: Understand the problem, create the solution alternatives, represent each solution (initially with general ideas, later with formal specifications), and evaluate the correctness, feasibility, and preferabllity of each alternative. It is an iterative process; each iteration refines the design.

bility, and maintainability. Research in these areas is challenging. For example: Do existing software metrics accurately represent quality factors? Can you develop predictive models? What data do you need to drive the models? What design concepts lead to improved quality?

SPE methods should undergo significant change as SPE's usage increases. The methods should be better integrated into design, to make software design more like the engineering design process shown (again) in Figure 10.2, rather than an add-on activity. SPE should be better integrated into capacity planning as well. As they become integrated, many of the pragmatic techniques in earlier chapters should be unnecessary (how to convince designers there is a serious problem, how to get data, and so on). The nature of SPE should then change. Performance walkthroughs will not be necessary for data gathering; they may only review performance during the course of regular design walkthroughs. The emphasis will change from finding and correcting design flaws to verification and validation that the system performs as expected. Additional research into automatic techniques for measuring software designs is needed, for calibrating models and for reporting discrepancies.

With these improvements in tools, models, concepts, and methods, software performance engineering of most systems will become automatic. Then we can either study the challenges of SPE for revolutionary new system concepts or move to new horizons. Meanwhile, there are many systems that require today's SPE methods to achieve their performance goals, and with the understanding you have gained, you are well on your way toward success in dealing with them.

Bibliography[1]

[ACM82] *Proceedings of the Second Software Engineering Symposium: Workshop on Rapid Prototyping,* ACM SIGSOFT, Apr. 1981.

[ADA82a] L. Adams, "A Multicolor Algorithm for Parallel Computation on a Array Computer," University of Virginia Tech. Rpt., May 1982.

[ADA82b] L. Adams, "Iterative Algorithms for Large Sparse Linear Systems on Parallel Computers," Ph.D. Dissertation, U. of Virginia, in Contractor Report 166027, Nov. 1982.

[ADE84] B. Adelson, D. Littman, K. Ehrlich, J. Black, and E. Soloway, "Novice-Expert Differences in Software Design," *Conference on Human-Computer Interaction*, London, 1984.

[AGE79] T. Agerwala, "Putting Petri Nets to Work," *IEEE Computer*, 12, 12, Dec. 1979, 85–95.

[AGR82] Jon R. Agre and Satish K. Tripathi, "Modeling Reentrant and Non-Reentrant Software," *Proc. Conference on Measurement and Modeling of Computer Systems*, Seattle, Aug. 1982, 163–178. (MDLG)

[AGR83a] S. C. Agrawal and J. P. Buzen, "The Aggregate Server Method for Analyzing Serialization Delays in Computer Systems," *ACM TOCS* 1, 2, May 1983, 116–143.

[AGR83b] S. C. Agrawal, "Metamodeling: A Study of Approximations in Queueing Models," Ph.D. Thesis, Purdue University, W. Lafayette, IN, 1983.

---

[1]Keywords following citations have the following meaning: EXPR reports experience with SPE; HIST reports experience prior to 1975; METH describes aspects of the SPE methodology; MDLG–techniques for modeling software performance; MEAS–techniques for measuring software; PGMS–techniques for improving program performance; PRIN–design guidelines or principles for constructing high-performance software; and TOOL–tools for performance modeling.

[ALE82] William Alexander and Richard Brice, "Performance Modeling in the Design Process," *Proc. National Computer Conference*, Houston, June 1982. (EXPR)

[ALE86] C. T. Alexander, "Performance Engineering: Various Techniques and Tools," *Proc. CMG 86*, Dec. 1986, pp. 264–267. (METH)

[ALL79] F. W. Allen, "A Predictive Performance Evaluation Technique for Information Systems," *Proc. Fourth International Symposium on Modeling and Performance Evaluation of Computer Systems*, Vienna, February 1979. (MDLG)

[ALL82] Leilani E. Allen, "How to Obtain Accurate Workload Forecasts from Users," *Proc. Computer Measurement Group Conference XIII*, San Diego, Dec. 1982, 109–118. (METH)

[ALL83] Karl S. Allen and Allan I. Levy, "A Case Study in Software Performance Engineering," *Proc. International Conference on Computer Capacity Management*, April 1983, 255–266. (EXPR)

[ALL85] A. O. Allen, "Introduction to Information System Modeling," *Proc. International Conference on Information Management*, April 1985, pp. 152–158. (METH)

[ALM79] Guy T. Almes and Edward D. Lazowska, "The Behavior of Ethernet-Like Computer Communications Networks," *Proc. 7th ACM Symposium on Operating Systems Principles*, December 1979. (MDLG)

[AMM83] Reda Ammar, "Software Optimization Using User Models," University of Connecticut Technical Report CS-83-12, 1983. (METH)

[AND84] Gordon E. Anderson, "The Coordinated Use of Five Performance Evaluation Methodologies," *CACM*, 27, 2, Feb. 1984, 119–125. (EXPR)

[ARMY84] U.S. Army Computer Systems Command, Quality Assurance Directorate, *Software Performance Engineering Handbook*, Fort Belvoir, VA, 1984.

[BAE72] J. L. Baer and R. Caughey, "Segmentation and Optimization of Programs from Cyclic Structure Analysis," *Proc. AFIPS* (SJCC) 40.

[BAE78] J. L. Baer,"Graph Models in Programming Systems," in K. M. Chandy and R. T. Yeh, eds., *Current Trends in Programming Methodology*, Prentice-Hall, Englewood Cliffs, NJ, 1978, 168–230.

[BAG84a] R. Bagrodia, K. M. Chandy, and J. Misra, "May: A Message-Based Simulation Language for Small Computers," *Proc. of COMPCON*, Fall 1984, Washington, D.C., Sept. 1984. (MDLG)

[BAG84b] R. Bagrodia, "Performance Analysis of Distributed Software Using Message-Based Simulation," *Proc. CMG XV*, San Francisco, December 1984. (MDLG)

[BAL85a] G. Balbo, S. C. Bruell, and S. Ghanta, "Combining Queueing Network and Generalized Stochastic Petri Net Models for the Analysis of a Software Blocking Phenomenon," *Proc. International Workshop on Timed Petri Nets*, Torino, Italy, July 1985, 208–225.

[BAL85b] G. Balbo, S. C. Bruell, and S. Ghanta, "Modeling Priority Schemes," *Proc. ACM Sigmetrics Conference on Measurement and Modeling of Computer Systems*, Austin, TX, Aug. 1985, 15–26.

[BAR78] Y. Bard, "An Analytical Model of the VM/370 System," *IBM Journal of Research and Development 22*, Sept. 78, 333–342.

[BAR79] A. L. Barrese and S. D. Shapiro, "Structuring Programs for Efficient Operation in Virtual Memory Systems," *IEEE TSE*, SE–5, 6, Nov. 79, 643–652.

[BAS70] F. Baskett, J. C. Browne and W. M. Raike, "The Management of a Multi-Level Non-Paged Memory System," *Proc. AFIPS* (SJCC) 36.

[BAT76] D. Bates (ed)., "Program Optimization," Infotech State of the Art Report 30, Infotech International, Maidenhead 1976. (PGMS)

[BEI84] H. Beilner and J. Mater, "COPE: Past, Presence and Future," *Proc. of the International Conference on Modelling Techniques and Tools for Performance Analysis*, Paris, May 1984.

[BEI78] Boris Beizer, *Micro-Analysis of Computer System Performance*, Von Nostrand Reinhold, New York, 1978. (MDLG)

[BEI84] Boris Beizer, "Software Performance," in C. R. Vick and C. V. Ramamoorthy, eds., *Handbook of Software Engineering*, Von Nostrand Reinhold, New York, 1984, pp.413–436. (MDLG)

[BEK85] G. A. Becker, "Capacity Planning for Applications Still Under Development," *Proc. CMG 85*, Dallas, Dec. 1985, 700–703. (METH)

[BEL80] L. A. Belady, "Modifiability of Large Software Systems," IBM Report RC8525, Yorktown, NY, Sept. 1980.

[BEL77] T. E. Bell, D. C. Bixler, amd M. E. Dyer, "An Extendable Approach to Computer-Aided Software Requirements Engineering," *IEEE Trans. Software Engineering*, SE-3,1, January 1977, 49–59. (TOOL)

[BEL87] T. E. Bell and A. M. Falk, "Performance Engineering: Some Lessons from the Trenches," *Proc. CMG 87*, Orlando, FL, Dec. 1987, 549–552. (EXPR)

[BEL87] T. E. Bell and A. M. Falk, "Performance Engineering: Some Lessons from the Trenchcs," *Proc. CMG 87*, Orlando, FL, Dec. 1987, 549–552. (EXPR)

[BEL88] T. E. Bell (guest ed.), "Special Issue on Software Performance Engineering," *CMG Trans.*, Spring 1988.

[BEN82] Jon L. Bentley, *Writing Efficient Programs*, Prentice-Hall, Englewood Cliffs, NJ, 1982. (PGMS)

[BER58] C. Berge, *Theorie des Graphes et Ses Applications*, Paris, Dunod, 1958.

[BER74] T. Beretvas, "A Simulation Model Representing the OS/VS2 Release 2 Control Program," Lecture notes in Computer Science 16, Springer Verlag, 1974, 15–29. (HIST)

[BER84] Margaret E. Berry, "The Best of Both Worlds: An Integrated Approach to Capacity Planning and Software Performance Engineering," *Proc. Computer Measurement Group Conference XV*, San Francisco, Dec. 1984, 462–466. (EXPR)

[BOB83] F. W. Bobrowicz, J. E. Lynch, K. J. Fisher, and J. E. Tabor, "Vectorized Monte Carlo PhotonTransport," Los Alamos National Lab, Technical Report LA–9752-MS, Los Alamos, NM, May 1983.

[BOE76] B. W. Boehm, "Software Engineering," *IEEE Trans. on Computers*, Vol. C-25, No. 12, Dec. 1976.

[BOE81] Barry W. Boehm, *Software Engineering Economics*, Prentice-Hall, Englewood Cliffs, NJ, 1981.

[BOO83] G. Booch, *Software Engineering with Ada*, Benjamin/Cummings, Menlo Park, CA, 1983.

[BOO79a] T. L. Booth, "Use of Computation Structure Models to Measure Computation Performance," *Proc. Conference on Simulation, Measurement and Modeling of Computer Systems*, Boulder, CO, Aug. 1979. (MDLG)

[BOO79b] T. L. Booth, "Performance Optimization of Software Systems Processing Information Sequences Modeled by Probabilistic Languages," *IEEE Trans. on Software Engineering*, Vol. SE-5, 1, Jan. 1979, 31–44. (MDLG)

[BOO80] Taylor L. Booth and Cheryl A. Wiecek, "Performance Abstract Data Types as a Tool in Software Performance Analysis and Design," *IEEE Trans. Software Engineering*, SE-6, 2, Mar. 1980, 138–151. (MDLG)

[BOO81] T. L. Booth, R. Ammar, and R. Lenk, "An Instrumentation System to Measure User Performance in Interactive Systems," *Journal of Systems and Software*, 2, 1981, 139–146. (MEAS)

[BOO86] T. Booth, R. Hart, and B. Qin, "High Performance Software," *Proc. Hawaii International Conference Systems Sciences*, Jan. 1986, 41–52. (EXPR)

[BOU85] J. P. Bouhana, "Software Systems Instrumentation: An End-to-End View," *Proc. Hawaii International Conference on System Science*, 1, Jan. 1985. (MEAS)

[BRA85] Gary Bray and David Pokrass, *Understanding Ada*, Wiley, New York, 1985.

[BRE81] R. F. Brender and I. R. Nassi, "What Is Ada?" *Computer*, 14, 6, June 1981, 17–24.

[BRI80] Richard S. Brice and J. Wayne Anderson, "Performance Evolution in a Large Scale System," *Proc. Computer Performance Evaluation Users Group 16*, Orlando, FL, Oct. 1980, 319–330. (EXPR)

[BRI82] R. S. Brice, "Benchmarking Your Benchmarks: A User's Perspective," *Proc. CMG 82*, San Diego, CA, Dec. 1982, 51–55.

[BRO75] F. P. Brooks, *The Mythical Man Month*, Addison-Wesley, Reading, MA, 1975.

[BRO86] F. P. Brooks, Jr., "No Silver Bullet—Essence and Accidents of Software Engineering," *Information Processing 86*, Elsevier Science Publishers B.V., New York, 1986, pp. 1069–1976.

[BRO77] R. M. Brown, J. C. Browne, and K. M. Chandy, "Memory Management and Response Time," *CACM*, 20, 3, Mar. 77, 153–165.

[BRO85] J. C. Browne, D. M. Neuse, Jim Dutton, and Keh-Chiang Yu, "Graphical Programming for Simulation Models of Computer Systems," *Proc. 18th Annual Simulation Symposium*, Tampa, FL, March, 1985. (TOOL)

[BRY81] R. M. Bryant and J. R. Agre, "A Queueing Network Approach to the Module Allocation Problem in Distributed Systems, " *Proc. 1981 SIGMETRICS Conference on Measurement and Modeling of Computer Systems*, ACM, Las Vegas, NV, May 1981, 191–204.

[BRY83] R. M. Bryant and A. E. Krzesinski, "The MVA Pre-empt Resume Priority Approximation," pre-RC, IBM, T. J. Watson Research Center, Yorktown Heights, NY, 1983.

[BUC83] Ingrid Y. Bucher, "The Computational Speed of Supercomputers," *Proc. ACM SIGMETRICS Conference on Measurement and Modeling of Computer Systems*, Minneapolis, MN, Aug. 1983, 151–165.

[BUH84] R. J. A. Buhr, *System Design with Ada*, Prentice-Hall, Englewood Cliffs, NJ, 1984.

[BUZ81] Jeffrey P. Buzen, A. I. Levy, et al., "Predicting Software Performance with CRYSTAL," *Proc. International Conference on Computer Capacity Management*, Chicago, 1981, 275–284. (METH)

[BUZ86] J. P. Buzen (guest ed.), "Special Issue I/O Configuration Management," *CMG Trans.*, 54, Fall 1986, 16–127.

[CAB81a] L. F. Cabrera, "Syntax Oriented Analysis of the Run Time Performance of Programs," Ph.D. Thesis, University of Calif., Berkeley, Electronics Research Laboratory Memorandum No. UCB/ERLM81/30, 1–187, May 1981. (MEAS)

[CAB81b] L. F. Cabrera, "On the Efficient Generation of Dynamic Program Profiles," *Proc. COMPSAC 81*, Chicago, IL, Oct. 1981, 219–224. (MEAS)

[CAB84] L. F. Cabrera and G. Rodriguez-Galant, "Predicting Performance in UNIX Systems from Portable Workload Estimators Based on the Terminal Probe Method," Report No. UCB/CSD 84/194, University of California, Berkeley, Aug. 1984. (MEAS)

[CAM68] D. J. Campbell and W. J. Heffner, "Measurement and Analysis of Large Operating Systems During System Development," *Proc. 1968 Fall Joint Computer Conference AFIPS*, Vol. 37, AFIPS Press, 1968, 903–914. (HIST)

[CAV78] J. P. Cavano and J. A. McCall, "A Framework for the Measurement of Software Quality," *Proc. Quality Assurance Workshop*, San Diego, CA, Nov. 78.

[CHA82a] K. M. Chandy, J. Misra, R. Berry, and D. Neuse, "The Use of Performance Models in Systematic Design," *Proc. National Computer Conference*, Houston, TX, June 1982, 251–256. (METH)

[CHA82b] K. M. Chandy, "Planning Information Systems," *Journal of Capacity Management*, 1, 1, 1982, 9–21. (METH)

[CHA83] K. M. Chandy and M. S. Laksmi, "An Approximation Technique for Queueing Networks with Preemptive Priority Queues," Tech. Report, Dept. of Comp. Sci., University of Texas at Austin, Austin, TX, 1983.

[CHU85] L. W. Chung, "A Large UNIX Application Sizing Methodology," *Proc. CMG 85*, Dallas, TX, Dec. 1985, 80–84. (EXPR)

[CLE85] P. Clements, "Software Cost Reduction Through Disciplined Design," Naval Research Laboratory, Washington, D.C., Feb. 1985.

[CMG87] Successful Software Performance Engineering Panel, *Proc. CMG 87*, Orlando, FL, Dec. 1987, 991–993.

[COH74] J. Cohen and C. Zuckerman, "Two Languages for Estimating Program Efficiency," *Communications of the ACM*, No. 6, Vol. 17, June 1974, 301–308. (PGMS)

[COH77] J. Cohen and N. Carpenter, "A Language for Inquiring About the Run-Time Behavior of Programs," *Software—Practice and Experience*, Vol. 7, Sept. 1977, 261–271. (MEAS)

[COM79] Douglas Comer, "The Ubiquitous B-Tree," *ACM Computing Surveys*, 11, 2, June 1979, 121–137.

[DAH66] O. Dahl and K. Nygaard, "SIMULA: An ALGOL-Based Simulation Language," *Communications of the ACM*, 9, 9, Sept. 1966, 671–678.

[DEN78] P. J. Denning and J. P. Buzen, "The Operational Analysis of Queueing Network Models," *ACM Computing Surveys*, 10, 3, Sept. 1978, 225–261.

[DIX79] W. J. Dixon, ed., *BMDP-Biomedical Computer Programs*, University of California Press, Berkeley, CA, 1979.

[DON83] J. J. Dongarra and S. C. Eisenstat, "Squeezing the Most Out of an Algorithm in Cray Fortran," ANL Technical Memo ANL/MCS-TM–9, Argonne, IL, May 1983.

[EIN87] P. Ein-Dor and J. Feldmesser, "Attributes of the Performance of Central Processing Units: A Relative Performance Prediction Model," *Communications of the ACM*, 30, 4, Apr. 1987, 308–317.

[ERW88] Harry R. Erwin, "Performance Engineering Techniques for Complex Dynamic Systems," *Proc. CMG 88,* Dallas, TX, Dec. 1988, 1–4. (MDLG)

[FAL86] Anne M. Falk, "Minicomputer Performance Engineering: A Case Study," *CMG Transactions*, Summer 1986, 14–21. (EXPR)

[FAR86] B. L. Farrell and G. Ramamurthy, "A Prototype Performance Engineering/Management Tool for UNIX Based Systems," *Proc. CMG 86*, Las Vegas, NV, Dec. 1986, 345–352. (TOOL)

[FER84] V. Fernandes, J. C. Browne, D. M. Neuse, and R. Velpuri, "Some Performance Models of Distributed Systems," *Proc. Computer Measurement Group XV*, San Francisco, Dec. 1984, 30–37. (MDLG)

[FER73] Domenico Ferrari, "A Tool for Program Restructuring," *Proc. ACM 73*, Atlanta, GA, Aug. 1973.

[FER78] Domenico Ferrari, *Computer Systems Performance Evaluation*, Prentice-Hall, Englewood Cliffs, NJ, 1978. (METH)

[FER81] Domenico Ferrari, "A Generative Model of Working Set Dynamics," *Proc. ACM Sigmetrics Performance Evaluation Review*, 10, 3, Fall 1981, 52–57.

[FER83a] Domenico Ferrari, "Software Monitors," in A. Ralston, ed., *Encyclopedia of Computer Science and Engineering*, 2nd edition, Van Nostrand Reinhold, Florence, KY, 1983, 1362–1364. (MEAS)

[FER83b] D. Ferrari, G. Serazzi, and A. Zeigner, *Measurement and Tuning of Computer Systems*, Prentice-Hall, Englewood Cliffs, NJ, 1983. (METH)

[FOU85] R. A. Fournet, "Establishing Information Engineering," *Proc. International Conference on Information Management*, Apr. 1985, 48–65. (METH)

[FOX87] G. Fox, "Take Practical Performance Engineering Steps Early," Panel Discussion, *Proc. CMG 87*, Orlando, FL, Dec. 1987, 992–993. (EXPR)

[FOX89] G. Fox, "Performance Engineering as a Part of the Development Life Cycle for Large-Scale Software Systems," *Proc. 11th International Conference on Software Engineering*, Pittsburgh, PA, May 1989, 85–94. (METH, EXPR)

[FRA85] G. A. Frank, C. U. Smith, and J. L. Cuadrado, "Software/Hardware Codesign with an Architecture Design and Assessment System," *Proc. Design Automation Conference*, Las Vegas, NV, 1985. (TOOL)

[FRA85b] J. L. Franklin, P. Hwang, A. Wrenn, and T. Park, "Software Analysis Tools: A Method for Developing Performance Model Inputs," *Proc. CMG 85*, Dallas, TX, Dec. 1985, 400–410. (TOOL)

[FRI85] L. Jeanne Friedman, "Integrating Performance and Capacity Planning into the Application Design Review Process," *CMG Trans.*, 47, Mar. 1985, 28–29. (METH)

[FUT81] Y. Futamura, T. Kawai, H. Horikoshi, and M. Tsutsumi, "Development of Computer Programs by Problem Analysis Diagram (PAD)," *Proc. 5th International Conference on Software Engineering*, San Diego, CA, Mar. 1981, 325–332.

[GAF85] J. E. Gaffney, "Some Metrics for Assessing the Degree of 'Fit' of Software to Its Host Computer," *Proc. CMG 85*, Dallas, TX, Dec. 1985, 434–437. (MDLG)

[GIA88] Glynn B. Giaconne, "DB2 Performance Engineering and Capacity Planning," *Proc. CMG 88*, Dallas, TX, Dec. 1988, 387–400. (EXPR)

[GIF85] David Gifford and Alfred Spector, "The Cirrus Banking Network," *Communications of the ACM*, 28, 8, Aug. 1985, 797–807.

[GIR83] P. P. V. Giri, "Functional Design of On-Line Applications for Performance," *Proc. International Conference on Computer Capacity Management*, New Orleans, LA, 1983, 147–163. (EXPR)

[GOD85] W. Godwin and W. Suhler, "A Timing Estimation Method for Large System Software Development," *Proc. CMG 85*, Dallas, TX, Dec. 1985, 438–444. (TOOL)

[GOL78] R. P. Goldberg, A. I. Levy, and H. S. Schwenk, "Analysis of an Automated Bibliographic Retrieval System," *Proc. Computer Performance Evaluation User's Group*, Boston, MA, Oct. 1978. (EXPR)

[GOR78] G. Gordon, *System Simulation,* 2nd edition, Prentice-Hall, Englewood Cliffs, NJ, 1978.

[GOS85] J. Gostl and I. Greenberg, "An Application of Queueing Theory to the Design of a Message-Switching Computer System," *Communications of the ACM*, 28,5, May 1985, 500–505. (EXPR)

[GRA73] R. M. Graham, G. J. Clancy, and D. B. DeVaney, "A Software Design and Evaluation System," *Communications of the ACM,* 16,2, Feb. 1973. (HIST)

[GRA82] G. S. Graham, E. D. Lazowska, and K. C. Sevcik, "Components of Software Packages for the Solution of Queueing Network Models," *Proc. CPEUG Conference*, Oct. 1982. (TOOL)

[HAC86] James J. Hack, "Peak vs. Sustained Performance in Highly Concurrent Vector Machines," *IEEE Computer*, 19, 9, Sept. 1986, 11–19.

[HAM82] Richard Hamlet, *Proc. Hawaii International Conference on System Sciences,* 15, Jan. 1982.

[HAR84] G. Haring and W. Konvicka, "Capacity Planning for an Electronic Mail System," *Proc. European Computer Measurement Association—12*, Munich, Oct. 1984, 119–125. (EXPR)

[HEI82] P. Heidelberger and K. S. Trivedi, "Queueing Network Models for Parallel Processing with Asynchronous Tasks," *IEEE Trans. Computers*, C-31, 11, Nov. 1982, 1099–1108.

[HEI83] P. Heidelberger and K. S. Trivedi, "Analytic Queueing Models for Programs with Internal Concurrency," *IEEE Trans. Computers,* 32, 1, Jan. 83, 73–82.

[HEN80] K. Heninger, "Specifying Software Requirements for Complex Systems: New Techniques and Their Application," *IEEE Trans. Software Engineering*, Vol. SE-6, 1, Jan. 1980.

[IBM85] International Business Machines, Inc., *ANDB2 Usage Guide*, Santa Teresa, CA, June 1985. (TOOL)

[ING82] Frank T. Ingrassia, "The Role of Capacity Planning in Software Development," *Proc. Computer Measurement Group XIII*, San Diego, CA, Dec. 1982, 226–235. (EXPR)

[ING85] Frank T. Ingrassia, "Modeling the Performance of New Online Systems," *Proc. CMG 85*, Dallas, TX, Dec. 1985, 346–357. (METH)

[JAC83] Patricia A. Jacobson and Edward D. Lazowska, "A Reduction Technique for Evaluating Queueing Networks with Serialization Delays," *Proc. International Federation Information Processing Working Group 7.3, International Symposium on Computer Performance Modeling, Measurement, and Evaluation*, 1983, 45–59.

[JAL77] P. J. Jalics, "Improving Performance the Easy Way," *Datamation*, 23,4, Apr. 1977, 135 148. (PGMS)

[JEN82] S. F. Jennings and A. E. Oldehoeft, "An Analysis of Program Execution on a Recursive Stream-Oriented Data Flow Architecture," *Proc. Hawaii International Conference on System Sciences*, Jan. 1982, 178–187. (MDLG)

[JEN87] Thad Jennings and Connie Smith, "GQUE: Using Workstation Power for Software Design Assessment," L&S Computer Technology, Inc., Tech. Report, MS120, PO Box 9802, Austin, TX 78766, 1987.

[JOU83] W. Jouris, "Introduction to Tuning Batch Applications," *Proc. Computer Measurement Group Conference XIV*, Washington, D.C., Dec. 1983, 371–373. (PGMS)

[KEL74] J. C. Kelly, "The Theory of Repetition Networks with Application to Computer Programs," Ph.D. Dissertation, Purdue University, Dec. 1974. (MDLG)

[KER71] B. W. Kernigan, "Optimal Sequential Partitioning of Graphs," *Journal of the ACM*, 18, 1971.

[KIV69] P. J. Kiviat, R. Villanueva, and H. Markowitz, *The SIMSCRIPT II Programming Language*, Prentice-Hall, Englewood Cliffs, NJ, 1969.

[KLE76] Leonard Kleinrock, *Queueing Systems Volume II: Computer Applications*, Wiley, NY, 1976.

[KNU68] D. E. Knuth, *The Art of Computer Programming*, Vol. 1: *Fundamental Algorithms*, Addison-Wesley, Reading, MA, 1968.

[KNU71] Donald E. Knuth, "An Empirical Study of FORTRAN Programs," *Software-Practice and Experience*, Vol. 1, 1971, 105–133. (PGMS)

[KOB78] H. Kobayashi, *Modeling and Analysis—An Introduction to System Performance Evaluation Methodology*, Addison-Wesley, Reading, MA, 1978. (METH)

[KOP86] H. Kopetz, "Design Principles for Fault Tolerant Real Time Systems," *Proc. Hawaii International Conference System Sciences*, Jan. 1986, 53–62. (PRIN)

[LAK86] S. Lakshmi, S. Calo, and P. Gupta, "Frame Caching in Menu-Driven Videotex Systems," *Proc. Fall Joint Computer Conference*, Nov. 1986, pp.655–664. (EXPR)

[LAK87] M. Seetha Lakshmi, "Performance Engineering of a Videotex System," *Proc. Hawaii International Conference System Sciences*, Jan. 1987. (EXPR)

[LAM84] B. W. Lampson, "Hints for Computer System Design," *IEEE Software*, Feb. 1984, 11–28. (PRIN)

[LAS72] E. R. Lassettre and A. L. Scherr, "Modeling the Performance of the OS/360 Time Sharing Option (TSO)," in W. Freiberger (ed.), *Statistical Computer Performance Evaluation*, Academic Press, New York, 1972, 57–72. (HIST)

[LAW87] J. Dennis Lawrence, "Conceptual Issues in Measuring the Behavior of a Distributed Real-Time Process-Control Computer System," *Proc. CMG 87*, Orlando, FL, Dec. 87, 474–481.

[LAZ80] Edward D. Lazowska, "The Use of Analytic Modeling in System Selection," *Proc. CMG International Conference*, Dec. 1980. (METH)

[LAZ84a] E. D. Lazowska, J. Zahorjan, G. S. Graham, and K. C. Sevcik, *Quantitative System Performance: Computer System Analysis Using Queueing Network Models*, Prentice-Hall, Englewood Cliffs, NJ, 1984. (MDLG)

[LAZ84b] Edward D. Lazowska, John Zahorjan, David R. Cheriton, and Willy Zwaenepoel, "File Access Performance of Diskless Workstations," *ACM Trans. Computer Systems*, 4, 3, Aug. 1986, 238–268. (MDLG)

[LeM82] Eric LeMer, "MEDOC: A Methodology for Designing and Evaluating Large-Scale Real-Time Systems," *Proc. National Computer Conference*, Houston, TX, June 1982, 263–272. (METH)

[LEV80] A. I. Levy, "Practical Operational Analysis: An MVS Perspective," *Proc. CMG 80*, Boston, Dec. 1980. (MDLG)

[LEV85] A. I. Levy and K. S. Allen, "The Role of Performance Engineering in Applications Development," *Proc. International Conference on Information Management*, Apr. 1985, 9–19. Also in *Journal of Capacity Management*, Vol. 3, No. 1, Fall 1985. (METH)

[LEV86] A. I. Levy and V. C. Soder, "Performance Analysis During Application Design: A Case Study," *Proc. CMG 86*, Dec. 1986, 167–172. (EXPR)

[LEV87] A. I. Levy and V. C. Soder, "Performance Analysis During Application Design: An IMS Case Study," *CMG Trans.*, 58, Fall 1987, 101–106. (EXPR)

[LEW73] A. Lew, "Memory Allocation in Paging Systems," *Proc. ACM 73*, Atlanta, GA, Aug. 1973.

[LIN76] T. A. Linden, "The Use of Abstract Data Types to Simplify Program Modifications," *ACM SIGPLAN Notices* (Special Issue), Vol. II, 1976.

[LIN86] David S. Lindsey, "Do Fortran Compilers Really Optimize?" *CMG Trans.*, Spring 1986, 23–27.(PGMS)

[LIT 61] J. D. C. Little, "A Proof of the Queuing Formula $L = \lambda W$," *Operations Research*, 9, 1961.

[LOE83] D. Loendorf, "Advanced Computer Architecture for Engineering Analysis and Design," Ph.D. Dissertation, University of Michigan, 1983.

[LON87] A. Long and S. W. Suhler, "A Flexible Approach to Performance Prediction for Large System Software Development," *Proc. CMG 87*, Orlando, FL, Dec. 1987, 167–171. (METH)

[LOW70] T. C. Lowe, "Automatic Segmentation of Cyclic Program Structure Based on Connectivity and Processor Timing," *Communications of the ACM*, 13, 1, Jan. 1970.

[LUB85] O. Lubeck, J. Moore, and R. Mendez, "A Benchmark Comparison of Three Supercomputers: Fujitsu VP-200, Hitachi S810, and Cray XMP/2," *IEEE Computer*, 18, 12, Dec. 1985, 10–24.

[MAC85] Edward A. MacNair and Charles H. Sauer, *Elements of Practical Performance Modeling*, Prentice-Hall, Englewood Cliffs, NJ, 1985.

[MAR84] M. A. Marsan, G. Conti, and G. Balbo, "A Class of Generalized Stochastic Petri Nets for the Performance Evaluation of Multiprocessor Systems," *ACM Trans. Computer Systems*, 2, 2, May 1984, 93–122. (MDLG)

[MAS79] T. Masuda, "Methods for the Measurement of Memory Utilization and the Improvement of Program Locality," *IEEE Trans. Software Engineering*, SE-5, 6, Nov. 1979, 618–631.

[McB87] Doug McBride, "The System Performance Cycle: A Methodology for Architecting Product Performance," *Proc. CMG 87,* Orlando, FL, Dec. 1987, 145–150. (METH)

[McB88a] Doug McBride, "The Performance Tracking Document: A Vehicle for Managing the Software Performance Engineering Process," *Proc. CMG 88,* Dallas, TX, Dec. 1988, 5–7. (METH)

[McB88b] Doug McBride (moderator), "System Performance Engineering: Pay Me Now or Pay Me More Later (panel)," *Proc. CMG 88,* Dallas, TX, Dec. 1988, 1099–1101. (EXPR)

[McC77] J. A. McCall, P. K. Richards, and G. F. Walters, *Factors in Software Quality: Concept and Definitions of Software Quality* (3 vols.), Rome Air Development Center TR-77-369, Griffiss AFB, NY, Nov. 1977.

[McC81] J. A. McCall, D. Markham, M. Stosick, and R. McGindly, "The Automated Measurement of Software Quality," *Proc. IEEE Compsac,* Chicago, Nov. 81, 52–58.

[McN80] M. McNeil and W. Tracy, "PL/I Program Efficiency," *SIGPLAN Notices* 15, 6, June, 1980, 46–80. (PGMS)

[MEL85] B. Melamed and R. J. T. Morris, "Visual Simulation: The Performance Analysis Workstation," *IEEE Computer,* 18, 8, Aug. 1985, 87–94. (TOOL)

[MER85] Barry Merrill, *Merrill's Expanded Guide to Computer Performance Evaluation,* SAS Institute, Inc., Research Triangle Park, NC, 1985.

[MEY88] Bertrand Meyer, *Object-Oriented Software Construction,* Prentice-Hall, New York, 1988.

[MOL80] M. K. Molloy, "On the Integration of Delay and Throughput Measures in Distributed Processing Models," Ph.D. Dissertation, UCLA, 1980. (MDLG)

[MOL82] M. K. Molloy, "Performance Analysis Using Stochastic Petri Nets," *IEEE Trans. Computers,* C-31, 9, Sept. 1982, 913–917. (MDLG)

[MOR86] G. A. Morrison, "Performance for a Large, Complex Application," *Proc. CMG 86,* Dec. 1986, 316–320. (METH)

[NIE75] N. H. Nie et al., *SPSS-Statistical Package for the Social Sciences,* McGraw-Hill, New York, 1975.

[NEU83] D. M. Neuse and J. C. Browne, "Graphical Tools for Software System Performance Engineering," *Proc. Computer Measurement Group Conference XIV,* Washington, D.C., Dec. 1983, 353–355. (TOOL)

[NUT75] Gary Nutt, "Computer System Monitors," *IEEE Computer,* 8, 11, Nov. 1975, 51–61.

[PAA84] Ronald Paans, "Effect of Response Times on Project Costs in MVS Centres," *Proc. European Computer Measurement Association—12,* Munich, Oct. 1984, 329–338. (METH)

[PAR72] D. L. Parnas, "On the Criteria to Be Used in Decomposing Systems into Modules," *Communications of the ACM,* 15, 12, Dec. 1972, p. 1053–1058.

[PAR79] D. L. Parnas, "Designing Software for Ease of Extension and Contraction," *IEEE Trans. Software Engineering,* SE-5, 2, Mar. 1979, 128–137.

[PET65] C. A. Petri, "Kommunikation mit Automaten," Ph.D. Disseration, translation in Tech. Rep. RADC-TR-65-337, Vol. I, Rome Air Development Center, Griffiss AFB, NY, 1965.

[PET77] J. L. Peterson, "Petri Nets," *ACM Computing Surveys*, 9, 3, Sept. 77, 223–252.

[PET81] Lawrence J. Peters, *Software Design: Methods and Techniques,* Yourdan Press, New York, 1981, 44–48.

[PRI79] A. A. B. Pritsker and C. D. Pegden, *Introduction to Simulation and SLAM*, Systems Publishing, West Lafayette, IN, 1979.

[RAM82] K. G. Ramakrishnan and D. Mitra, "An Overview of PANACEA: A Software Package for Analyzing Markovian Queueing Networks," *Bell System Technical Journal*, 61, 10, 1982, 2849–2872.

[RAM66] C. V. Ramamoorthy, "The Analytical Design of a Dynamic Lookahead and Program Segmenting Scheme for Multiprogrammed Computers," *Proc. ACM*, 23, 1966.

[RAM74] C. Ramchandani, "Analysis of Asynchronous Concurrent Systems by Timed Petri Nets," Ph.D. Thesis, MIT 1974, Project Mac Report #MAC-TR–120. (MDLG)

[REE87] D. A. Reed and D. C. Grunwald, "The Performance of Multicomputer Interconnection Networks," *IEEE Computer*, 20, 6, June 1987, 63–73.

[REI85] J. Reilly, "A Performance Engineering Case Study and Analysis," *Journal of Capacity Management*, Vol. 2, No. 4, 322–339. (EXPR)

[RID78] W. E. Riddle, J. C. Wileden, J. H. Sayler, A. R. Segal, and A. M. Stavely, "Behavior Modeling During Software Design," *IEEE Trans. Software Engineering*, 4, 1978. (METH)

[RIV81] Elizabeth A. Rivet, "Performance Evaluation During System Selection," *Proc. Computer Measurement Group Conference XII*, Dec. 1981, 1–4. (EXPR)

[ROG75] J. G. Rogers, "Structured Programming for Virtual Storage Systems," *IBM Systems Journal*, 14, 4, 1975, 385–406.

[ROL88] Jerome A. Rolia, "Performance Estimate for Systems with Software Servers: The Lazy Boss Method," *Proc. VIII SCCC International Conference on Computer Science*, Santiago, Chile, July 1988. (MDLG)

[RUB84] Richard Rubinstein and Harry Hersh, *The Human Factor: Designing Computer Systems for People,* Digital Press, Burlington, MA, 1984.

[RUS76] E. C. Russell, *Simulation and SIMSCRIPT II.5*, CACI, Inc., Los Angeles, CA, 1976.

[RZE86] W. E. Rzepka and P. C. Daley, "A Prototyping Tool to Assist in Requirements Engineering," *Proc. Hawaii International Conference System Sciences*, Jan. 1986, 608–618.

[SAH85a] Robin A. Sahner and Kishor S. Trivedi, "SPADE: A Tool for Performance and Reliability Evaluation," *Proc. International Conference Modelling Techniques and Tools for Performance Analysis*, Sophia Antipolis, France, June 1985, 153–169. (TOOL)

[SAH85b] Robin A. Sahner, "A Hybrid, Combinatorial-Markov Method of Solving Performance and Reliability Models," Ph.D. Dissertation, Duke University, Dec. 1985.

[SAL88] Michael A. Salsburg, "The Performance Evaluation of a Transaction Processing Application," *Proc. CMG 88,* Dallas, TX, Dec. 1988, 444–449. (EXPR)

[SAN77] J. W. Sanguinetti, "Performance Prediction in an Operating System Design Methodology," Ph.D. Dissertation, RSSM/32, University of Michigan, May 1977. (MDLG)

[SAN78] J. W. Sanguinetti, "A Formal Technique for Analyzing the Performance of Complex Systems," *Proc. Computer Performance Evaluation Users Group 14*, Boston, Oct. 1978. (MDLG)

[SAN79] J. W. Sanguinetti, "A Technique for Integrating Simulation and System Design," *Proc. Conference on Simulation Measurement and Modeling of Computer Systems*, Boulder, CO, Aug. 1979. (MDLG)

[SAN84] J. Sanguinetti, "Program Optimization for a Pipelined Machine: A Case Study," *Proc. SIGMETRICS Conference on Measurement and Modeling of Computer Systems*, Cambridge, MA, Aug. 1984, 88–95. (PGMS)

[SAU81] C. H. Sauer and K. M. Chandy, *Computer Systems Performance Modeling*, Prentice-Hall, Englewood Cliffs, NJ, 1981.

[SAU82a] Charles H. Sauer, Edward A. MacNair, and James F. Kurose, "The Research Queueing Package: Past, Present, and Future," *Proc. National Computer Conference*, Houston, TX, June 1982, 273–280. (TOOL)

[SAU82b] C. H. Sauer, E. A. MacNair, and J. F. Kurose, "The Research Queueing Package, Version 2: Introduction and Examples," Report RA128, IBM T.J. Watson Research Center, Yorktown Heights, NY, Apr. 1982. (TOOL)

[SCH74] T. J. Schriber, *Simulation Using GPSS*, Wiley, New York, 1974.

[SCH82] Herb Schwetman, "Implementing the Mean Value Algorithm for the Solution of Queueing Network Models," Purdue University Report CSD-TR-355, Feb. 1982. (TOOL)

[SCH84] Paul A. Scheffer and William E. Rzepka, "A Large System Evaluation of SREM," *Proc. International Conference Software Engineering*, 7, IEEE Catalog No. 84C+12011-5, Orlando, FL, Mar. 1984, 172–180. (EXPR)

[SCO78] L. R. Scott, "An Engineering Methodology for Presenting Software Functional Architecture," *Proc. Third International Conference Software Engineering*, IEEE Computer Society, 1978, 222–229.

[SEE82] Deborah J. Seeliger, "Application of PAWS in the Sperry Univac Environment: Phase 1," *Proc. Computer Measurement Group XIII*, San Diego, CA, Dec. 1982, 200–219. (EXPR)

[SEV77] K. C. Sevcik, "Priority Scheduling Disciplines in Queueing Network Models of Computer Systems," *Proc. IFIP Congress 77*, North-Holland Publishing Co., Amsterdam, 1977, 565–570.

[SEV79] K. C. Sevcik and I. Mitrani, "The Distribution of Queueing Network States at Input and Output Instants," in *Performance of Computer Systems*, Arato et al., eds., North-Holland, New York, 1979, 319–335.

[SEV80] K. C. Sevcik, G. S. Graham, and T. Zahorjan, "Configuration and Capacity Planning in a Distributed Processing System," *Proc. 16th Computer Performance Evaluation Users Group*, Orlando, FL, 1980, 165–171.

[SEV81] K. C. Sevcik and E. Lazowska, "Generating Queueing Network Models from High-Level System Specifications," *Proc. Computer Measurement Group Conference XV*, San Francisco, Dec. 1984, 103–197.

[SEV83] K. C. Sevcik, "Comparison of Concurrency Control Algorithms Using Analytical Models," *Proc. IFIP Congress*, 1983.

[SHA87] J. G. Shane and J. R. Cook, "CICS and DB2: A Marriage Made in Heaven?" *Proc. CMG 87*, Orlando, FL, Dec. 87, 822–827.

[SHA79] M. Shaw, "A Formal System for Specifying and Verifying Program Performance," Report CMU-CS-79-129, Carnegie-Mellon University, Pittsburgh, PA, June 1979. (METH)

[SHO75] H. A. Sholl and T. L. Booth, "Software Performance Modeling Using Computation Structures," *IEEE Trans. Software Engineering*, 1, 4, Dec. 1975. (MDLG)

[SHO86] H. Sholl and S. Kim, "An Approach to Performance Modelling as an Aid in Structuring Real-Time, Distributed System Software," *Proc. Hawaii International Conference Systems Sciences*, Jan. 1986, 5–16. (MDLG)

[SIL82] H. Fred Silver, "A Pragmatic Approach to the Management of Software Development Life Cycles," *Proc. Computer Measurement Group Conference XIII*, San Diego, CA, Dec. 1982, 142–155. (METH)

[SIN86] J. B. Sinclair and S. Madala, "A Graphical Interface for Specification of Extended Queueing Network Models," *Proc. Fall Joint Computer Conference*, Dallas, TX, Nov. 1986, 709–718.

[SMIA78] A. J. Smith, "Bibliography on Paging and Related Topics," *Operating Systems Review*, Vol. 12, No. 4, Oct. 1978, 36–56.

[SMIA81] Alan J. Smith, "Bibliography on File System and Input/Output Optimization and Related Topics," *Operating Systems Review*, 15, 4, Oct. 1981, 39–54.

[SMI79a] Connie U. Smith and J. C. Browne, "Performance Specifications and Analysis of Software Designs," *Proc. Conference on Simulation Measurement and Modeling of Computer Systems*, Boulder, CO, Aug. 1979. (MDLG)

[SMI79b] Connie U. Smith and J. C. Browne, "Modeling Software Systems for Performance Predictions," *Proc. Computer Measurement Group X*, Dallas, TX, Dec. 1979. (MDLG)

[SMI80a] Connie U. Smith and J. C. Browne, "Aspects of Software Design Analysis: Concurrency and Blocking," *Proc. Performance 80*. Also in *ACM Performance Evaluation Review*, 9, 2, Summer 1980. (MDLG)

[SMI80b] Connie U. Smith, "The Prediction and Evaluation of the Performance of Software from Extended Design Specifications," Ph.D. Dissertation, University of Texas at Austin, University Microfilms Pub. No. KRA81-00963, Aug. 1980. (MDLG)

[SMI80c] Connie Smith, "Consider the Performance of Large Software Systems Before Implementation," *Proc. Computer Measurement Group Conference XI*, Dec. 1980, 138–144. (METH)

[SMI81] Connie U. Smith, "Software Performance Engineering," *Proc. Computer Measurement Group Conference XII*, Dec. 1981, 5–14. (METH)

[SMI82a] Connie U. Smith, "A Methodology for Predicting the Memory Management Overhead of New Software Systems," *Proc. Hawaii International Conference on System Sciences*, 15, Jan. 1982, 200–209. (MDLG)

[SMI82b] Connie U. Smith and J. C. Browne, "Performance Engineering of Software Systems: A Case Study," *Proc. National Computer Conference*, Vol. 15, Houston, TX, June 1982, 217–224. (EXPR)

[SMI82c] Connie U. Smith and David D. Loendorf, "Performance Analysis of Software for an MIMD Computer," *Proc. 1982 Conference on Measurement and Modeling of Computer Systems*, Aug. 1982, 151–162. (MDLG)

[SMI84] Connie U. Smith, "Effective Implementation of Software Performance Engineering," *Proc. European Computer Measurement Association 12*, Munich, Oct. 1984, 241–245. Also in *Journal of Capacity Management*, Vol. 3, No. 1, 1985. (METH)

[SMI85a] Connie U. Smith, "Robust Models for the Performance Evaluation of Software/Hardware Designs," *Proc. International Conference Timed Petri Nets*, Torino, Italy, July 1985, 172–180. (MDLG)

[SMI85b] Connie U. Smith, "Experience with Tools for Software Performance Engineering," *Proc. CMG 85*, Dallas, TX, Dec. 1985, 411–417. (TOOL)

[SMI86a] Connie U. Smith, "Independent General Principles for Constructing Responsive Software Systems," *ACM Trans. Computer Systems*, 4,1, Feb. 1986, 1–31. (PRIN)

[SMI86b] Connie U. Smith, "Evolution of Software Performance Engineering: A Survey," *Proc. FJCC*, Dallas, TX, Nov. 1986, 778–783. (METH)

[SMI87a] Connie U. Smith, "Better Performance Through Engineering," *ComputerWorld*, Oct. 19, 1987, p. S15.

[SMI87b] Connie U. Smith, "Software Fire Prevention," *Software News*, Nov. 1987, 69–82.

[SMI87c] Connie U. Smith, "General Principles for Performance-Oriented Design," *Proc. CMG 87*, Orlando, FL, Dec. 1987, 138–144. (PRIN)

[SMI88a] Connie U. Smith, "Who Uses SPE?" *CMG Trans.*, Spring, 1988, 69–75.

[SMI88b] Connie U. Smith, "Applying Synthesis Principles to Create Responsive Software Systems," *IEEE Trans. Software Engineering*, Oct. 1988, 1394–1408. (PRIN)

[SMI88c] Connie U. Smith, "How to Obtain Data for Software Performance Engineering Studies," *Proc. CMG 88*, Dallas, TX, Dec. 1988, 321–329.

[SOL84] E. Soloway and K. Ehrlich, "Empirical Studies of Programming Knowledge," *IEEE Trans. Software Engineering*, SE 10, 5, Sept. 1984, 595–609.

[SQI86] D. J. Squillance and W. F. Hartman, "Applications Tuning in the IBM MVS Environment: Techniques, Tools, and Politics," *Proc. CMG 86*, Las Vegas, NV, Dec. 1986, 716–718. (PGMS)

[STU85] B. W. Stuck and E. Arthurs, *A Computer and Communications Network Performance Analysis Primer*, Prentice-Hall, Englewood Cliffs, NJ, 1985.

[SVO77] L. Svobodova, *Computer Performance Measurement and Evaluation Methods: Analysis and Applications*, Elsevier, New York, 1977.

[SYD83] P. J. Sydow, "Cray Computer Systems Optimization Guide," Cray Research, Inc. Technical Publication SN-0220, Mendota Heights, MN, Dec. 1983.

[TAN81] Andrew S. Tanenbaum, *Computer Networks*, Prentice-Hall, Englewood Cliffs, NJ, 1981.

[TAY84] Y. C. Tay, N. Goodman, and R. Suri, "Performance Evaluation of Locking in Database," TR-17-84, Harvard University, 1984.

[TER84] Ralph Terkowitz, "Performance Management During Application Development," *Proc. Computer Measurement Group Conference XV*, San Francisco, Dec. 1984, 467–470. (EXPR)

[THO83] A. Thomasian, "Queueing Network Models to Estimate Serialization Delays in Multiprogrammed Computer Systems," in *Performance '83*, A. K. Agrawal and S. K. Tripathi, eds., Elsevier Science, Amsterdam, 1983, 61–81.

[THO85] A. Thomasian and P. Bay, "Performance Analysis of Task Systems Using a

Queueing Network Model," *Proc. International Conference Timed Petri Nets*, Torino, Italy, July 1985, 234–242.

[TPN85] *Proc. International Workshop on Timed Petri Nets*, IEEE Computer Society, Order Number 674, Torino, Italy, July 1985.

[TPN87] *Proc. International Workshop on Timed Petri Nets*, IEEE Computer Society, Order Number 796, Madison, WI, Aug. 1987.

[TRO87] N. Trohoski, "Acceptance Is the Key Aspect of Effective Performance Engineering," Panel Discussion, *Proc. CMG 87*, Orlando, FL, Dec. 1987, 993. (EXPR)

[VAN78] D. Van Tassel, *Program Style, Design, Efficiency, Debugging and Testing*, Prentice-Hall, Englewood Cliffs, NJ, 1978. (PGMS)

[VER84] M. Veran and D. Potier, "QNAP2: A Portable Environment for Queueing Systems Modelling," *Proc. of the International Conference on Modelling Techniques and Tools for Performance Analysis*, Paris, May 1984.

[VerH71] E. W. Ver Hoef, "Automatic Segmentation Based on Boolean Connectivity," *Proc. AFIPS Spring Joint Computer Conference*, 38, 1971.

[VIA81] Duc J. Vianney, "Predicting Software Efficiency During the Design Process Using Software and Performance Metrics," *Proc. Computer Measurement Group Conference XII*, Dec. 1981, 15–19. (MDLG)

[VOL82] Elaine Volansky, "Performance Measurement of the Tracking and Data Relay Satellite," *Proc. Computer Measurement Group Conference XIII*, San Diego, CA, Dec. 1982, 121–129. (EXPR)

[WAL79] Barbara Walter, "Programmer Productivity in Cobol Application Tuning," *Proc. Computer Measurement Group Conference X*, Dallas, TX, Dec. 1979, 477–516. (PGMS)

[WAL79] G. F. Walters, and J. A. McCall, "Software Quality Metrics for Life Cycle Cost Reduction," *IEEE Trans. Reliability*, Vol. R-28, 3, Aug. 1979, 212–220.

[WEI87a] Doyle J. Weishar, "Incorporating Expert Systems Technology into Software Performance Engineering," *Proc. CMG 87*, Orlando, FL, Dec. 1987, 720–722. (EXPR)

[WEI87b] Lori Weitz and Johanna Ambrosio, "Fourth Generation Languages: On a Converging Path," *Software News*, 7, 14, Dec. 87, 38–49.

[WET83] T. T. Wetmore, "Performance Analysis and Prediction from Computer Source Program Code," Ph.D. Dissertation, University of Connecticut, TR#CS-83-6, 1983. (MDLG)

[WIL78] R. R. Willis, "DAS: An Automated System to Support Design Analysis," *Proc. 12 Asilomar Conference on Circuits, Systems, and Computers*, Asilomar, CA, Nov. 1978.

[WON83] Kin L. Wong, "Design—A Tool for Software Performance Engineering" *CMG Trans.*, 41, Sept. 1983. (TOOL)

[YAN84] Bonnie Yantis, "Software Evolution Through Prototyping and Performance Prediction," M.S. Thesis, University of Nevada, Las Vegas, 1984. (TOOL)

[YAU81] S. S. Yau, C. C. Yang, and S. M. Shatz, "An Approach to Distributed System Software Design," *IEEE Trans. Software Engineering*, SE 7, 4, July 1981. (MDLG)

[ZAH88] William Z. Zahavi and James P. Bouhana, "Business-Level Description of Transaction Processing Applications," *Proc. CMG 88*, Dallas, TX, Dec. 1988, 720–726.

Vendor References

[*ACR*] Applied Computer Research, P.O. Box 9280, Phoenix, AZ, (800) 234–2227.

[*BOO*] Boole & Babbage, Inc., 510 Oakmead Parkway, Sunnyvale, CA 94086, (408) 735–9550.

[*BGS*] BGS Systems, Inc., 128 Technology Center, Waltham, MA 02254, (617) 891–0000.

[*CA*] Computer Associates, 711 Stewart Ave., Garden City, NY 11530, (516) 227–3300.

[*CACI*] CACI, 3344 N. Torrey Pines, La Jolla, CA 92037.

[*CAN*] Candle Corp., 1999 Bundy Dr., Los Angeles, CA 90025, (213) 207–1400.

[*CMG*] Computer Measurement Group Headquarters, 111 E. Wacker Dr., Chicago, IL 60601, (312) 938–1228.

[*IEEE*] *Proc. Symposium on the Simulation of Computer Networks*, Computer Society of the IEEE, PO Box 04699, Los Angeles, CA 90051.

[*INRIA*] INRIA, Domaine de Voluceau, Rocquencourt BP105, 78153 Le Chesnay, Cedex, France.

[*JAC*] Michael Jackson Systems, Ltd., 22 Little Portland St., London WIN 5AF, England.

[*LEG*] Legent Corp., Two Allegheny Center, Pittsburgh, PA 15212, (412) 323–2600.

[*MAR*] Information Engineering Methodology, James Martin Associates, Inc., 11718 Bowman Green Dr., Reston, VA 22090.

[*MER*] Merrill Consultants, 10717 Cromwell Dr., Dallas, TX 75229, (214) 351–1966.

[*ORR*] Ken Orr & Associates, Inc., 1725 Gage, Topeka, KS 66604, (800) 255–2458.

[*PES*] Performance Engineering Services, 1114 Buckman Rd., Santa Fe, NM 87501, (505) 988–3811.

[*PRO*] Programart, 1280 Massachusetts Ave., Cambridge, MA 02138, (617) 661–3020.

[*PSI*] Performance Systems, Inc., 30 Courthouse Square, Rockville, MD 20850, (301) 762–0300.

[*QSP*] Quantitative System Performance, 3562 N.W. 68, Seattle, WA 98117.

[*RTI*] RIM Technology, Inc., 1775 12th Ave. Suite 115, Issaquah, WA 98027, (206) 392–4776.

[*SAS*] SAS Institute, Inc., SAS Circle, Box 8000, Cary, NC 27511–8000, (919) 467–8000.

[*SDC*] Software Development Concepts, 424 West End Ave., Apt. 11E, New York, NY 10024, (212) 362–1391.

[*SES*] Scientific and Engineering Software, 1301 W. 25th, Suite 300, Austin, TX 78705, (512) 474–4526.

[*SIGM*] *Proc. ACM SIGMETRICS Conference on Measurement and Modeling of Computer Systems*, ACM, 11 West 42nd St., New York, NY 10036.

INDEX